AMERICAN BUSINESS

AN INTRODUCTION
SIXTH EDITION

Cover photo © S. Simpson, 1985

Copyright © 1986, 1982, 1978, 1974, 1970 by Harcourt Brace Jovanovich, Inc.

All rights reserved. No part of this publication may be reproduced or transmitted in any form or by any means, electronic or mechanical, including photocopy, recording, or any information storage and retrieval system, without permission in writing from the publisher.

Requests for permission to make copies of any part of the work should be mailed to: Permissions, Harcourt Brace Jovanovich, Publishers, Orlando, Florida 32887.

ISBN: 0-15-502315-2

Library of Congress Catalog Card Number: 85-60873

Printed in the United States of America

Credits begin on page 714, which constitutes a continuation of the copyright page.

AMERICAN BUSINESS

Ferdinand F. Mauser

David J. Schwartz
GEORGIA STATE UNIVERSITY

AN INTRODUCTION
SIXTH EDITION

The Dryden Press
Harcourt Brace Jovanovich College Publishers
Fort Worth   Philadelphia   San Diego
New York   Orlando   Austin   San Antonio
Toronto   Montreal   London   Sydney   Tokyo

PREFACE

AMERICAN BUSINESS: AN INTRODUCTION, Sixth Edition, focuses on the needs of students taking their first course in business. The text provides an overview of the American private enterprise system and gives students a broad perspective of the business world.

The text stresses creativity, entrepreneurship, and private enterprise. Students learn about the opportunities and challenges of careers in American business and receive a background in the various business disciplines. From this fundamental course, students can select the area or areas they wish to pursue in future study. This text provides exposure to economics, finance, marketing and distribution, management, accounting, business information and research, computers, business law, international business, and nonprofit organizations.

This edition of *American Business: An Introduction* has been reorganized and expanded, as well as updated. Beginning with a discussion of the American economic system, the text parallels the organization and development of an individual business. This step-by-step approach to business provides students with a clear and orderly course. Each chapter is a building block for the next, and the special feature "Evolution of a Business" provides a practical application of the text material for students to use. The content of every chapter has been improved, enriched, and updated; vivid new artwork and graphic examples illustrate points throughout the text; and many current topics, some of them controversial, challenge students to think critically, to evaluate, and to seek answers and implement improvements in American business.

ORGANIZATION OF THE TEXT

American Business: An Introduction, Sixth Edition, has twenty-two chapters, written in clear and practical language and illustrated with many graphic examples. Students should have no difficulty following the principles and theories presented in the six parts.

Part I provides an introduction to the American business system. These first four chapters introduce students to private enterprise and its main competitors, socialism and communism; define the basic types of businesses, proprietorships, partnerships, and corporations; show the role of entrepreneurs and small businesses; and discuss the interrelationship among business, government, and society.

Part II, Chapters 5–8, deals with financial matters. Explained in these chapters are long- and short-term financing methods, leasing, financial institutions, the Federal Reserve System, supercompany financial institutions, business and consumer credit, security markets, business news media, risk management, and insurance.

Part III, Chapters 9–13, explores the marketing function. These chapters provide an explanation of the importance of marketing to society and business, the marketing mix, the marketing concept, distribution channels, types of retail establishments, wholesaling, and the difference between marketing services and tangible products. Consumer behavior is also explored. Chapter 10 deals with demographics, income, and consumer motivation. This chapter also includes a discussion of psychographics. Products, packaging, and pricing are discussed in detail in Chapter 11. Chapter 12 concerns marketing communications: selling, advertising, promotion, and public relations. The physical elements of business—such as location, purchasing, mechanization, inventory, and transportation—are the subjects of Chapter 13.

The discipline of management is the focus of Chapters 14–16 in Part IV. Among the management topics discussed are a definition of management, the universal need for management, the power vested in managers, planning, organizing, delegation, organization charts, the informal organization, control, and the future of management. Chapter 15 covers human resource management: staffing and directing, including selection, training, compensation, and evaluation as well as employee motivation, leadership, and communication. Chapter 16 deals with the highly volatile area of management and labor relations, along with a summary of labor unions' history and tactics, the changing makeup of the labor force, collective bargaining, and several newer concepts (such as QWL and co-determination) that have contributed to the decline in the importance of labor unions.

Chapters 17–19, Part V, deal with specific functions and tools that business uses in controlling operations and planning for the future. Chapter 17 explains the role of accounting and financial statements in operating a business. Chapter 18 defines and explains the importance of business information and research, including steps in the research procedure, methods for collecting data, sources of business information, the use of statistics, and basic principles of report writing. Students learn how to make a report effective and efficient.

Computers are the topic of Chapter 19. Highlights of this chapter are a history of data processing, the advantages of computerization, common business applications of the computer, the use of basic computer hardware and software, the roles of systems analysts and computer programmers, and the latest in electronic technology for business.

The final three chapters, Part VI, each present an overview of their subject. Chapter 20 explains business law and legal services, including contracts, agency, negotiation, bankruptcy, intangible business assets (trademarks, patents, and copyrights), and the disturbing area of crime and its effect on business. Chapter 21 defines international business and trade, explaining its importance, the various obstacles encountered, exporting and importing channels, free trade zones, multinationals and cartels, and trends in international trade. Chapter 22 discusses nonprofit organizations and their role in American society. A widely expanded section on government is included in this chapter.

An Appendix—presenting practical information on careers—and a Glossary—providing clear and concise definitions of up-to-date business terms—appear at the end of the book.

FEATURES

Special features in each chapter facilitate learning, maintain interest, and illustrate the practical application of principles and theories presented.

- *Instructional Goals* At the beginning of each chapter, learning objectives help students understand what they should know after they have studied the material.

- *People Who Make Things Happen* A profile of a business practitioner or theorist appears in several chapters. Among those profiled are the Gucci family and Charles Dow and Edward Jones.

- *Contemporary Issues* Up-to-date sources provide readings on topics of current interest, such as "IRS Roulette Helps Cause Deficit," "Mazda's Bold Embrace of the United Auto Workers," and "How Will Business Information Be Managed?"

- *Issues for Debate* Discussions of controversial, contemporary issues help students understand the complexities involved in making decisions and show them that decision making is not easy or clear-cut. Each feature explains the issue briefly and follows with arguments for and against the proposition. Questions designed to stimulate further thought and debate follow each Issue.

   Some of the topics included in the Issue for Debate segments are: "Should the U.S. Trade with Nations That Practice

Discrimination?" "Are Adjustable Rate Mortgages (ARMs) a Good Idea?" "Is Social Security a Fair System for Providing Financial Security?" "All Promotion of Cigarettes Should be Banned," and "Should Doctors and Lawyers Be Considered Businesses and Market Their Services like Other Commercial Enterprises?"

- *Application to Personal Affairs* Throughout the text, helpful exercises apply chapter material to students' personal experience and daily life. Topics for these sections include: "Can I Succeed in a Business of My Own?" "How to Evaluate a Franchising Opportunity," "Uncle Sam's Agencies and Offices That Stand Ready to Help," "Guidelines for the Beginning Investor," and "Tips for Shopping by Mail."

- *America's Reemerging Creativity* Emphasizing the spirit of entrepreneurship and the freedom of the American private enterprise system, these exercises allow students to think and expand their own creative abilities. Titles include: "The Space Shuttle," "Teaching Entrepreneurship," "Electronic Funds Transfer Systems," "Health Maintenance Organizations," and "Using Cash Rebates and Coupons to Stimulate Buying."

- *Summary* A concise review of key points and concepts appears at the end of each chapter. These summaries help reinforce learning.

- *Key Terms You Should Know* Business has its own specialized vocabulary. The text, therefore, defines terms used in business. At the end of each chapter, a list of new terms reminds students what new language they need to understand and remember.

- *Questions for Review/Questions for Discussion* Each chapter also contains a group of review questions, which require fairly specific answers students can find in the text, and discussion questions designed to stimulate students to think and check their assimilation of information and ideas.

- *Case Studies* At the end of each chapter are case studies, in dialogue form. Each case presents a business problem that students are asked to solve, using the information presented in the chapter. The cases deal with timely, practical situations, such as "How to Plan for the Robots" and "Should J. T. Borders Sell Land to Foreigners?"

- *Evolution of a Business* Throughout the text students follow the development of a business—a travel agency—from the initial idea stage through financing, marketing, management problems and decisions, expansion, and legal questions. Each chapter builds on the previous ones to show students how every business decision evolves and affects the future success and/or problems. This practical and clear-cut feature helps students to relate the principles and ideas in each chapter to the real business world. It is a dynamic teaching tool that holds student interest and promotes lively classroom participation.

SUPPLEMENTS

The supplementary aids for the Sixth Edition of *American Business: An Introduction* have been completely revised. A comprehensive Study Guide for students, which includes a programmed learning section designed as both a preview and a review of each chapter's content, is now available. In addition, the Study Guide reinforces the learning objectives of the chapter and provides two self-teaching exercises, one multiple choice and one true-false. Key terms from each chapter are also defined in the Study Guide. The revised Study Guide should prove useful to students in reinforcing the text material and preparing for examinations.

An Instructor's Manual—essentially a resource book—includes specific learning objectives of each chapter; answers to all questions raised in the special features and at the end of each chapter; additional case studies for each chapter; an up-to-date list of suggested readings to supplement the general ideas presented in each chapter; and professional and trade information for supplementing classroom materials. A Test Book, featuring two different sets of questions (each a combination of multiple choice and true-false) for each chapter is available in both book and computerized format. Transparencies suitable for projection are also available for instructors who wish to expand graphic presentations in class.

Ferdinand F. Mauser, co-author of the first five editions of *American Business: An Introduction,* did not participate in the revision of the Sixth Edition.

CONTENTS

PREFACE   *v*

HOW OUR PRIVATE ENTERPRISE SYSTEM WORKS   1

1 THE AMERICAN PRIVATE ENTERPRISE SYSTEM   5

Is Business Satisfying the Needs of Americans?	6
Individual Rights under the Private Enterprise System	11
APPLICATION TO PERSONAL AFFAIRS: Can I Succeed in a Business of My Own?	14
Other Characteristics of the Private Enterprise System	16
How Does Our System Compare with Others?	19
PEOPLE WHO MAKE THINGS HAPPEN: A Profile of Adam Smith	20
Can Capitalism Work in Planned Economies?	26
Will Capitalism Survive?	27
AMERICA'S REEMERGING CREATIVITY: The Revitalization of the United States	28
CASE STUDY: How a Foreigner Views Contemporary America	33
EVOLUTION OF A BUSINESS: Birth of a New Business Idea	34

2 PROPRIETORSHIPS, PARTNERSHIPS, AND CORPORATIONS — 37

Running a Business Alone: The Sole Proprietorship — 40
AMERICA'S REEMERGING CREATIVITY:
  Fueling the Creative Spirit — 42
Running a Business with Others: The General and the Limited Partnership — 44
APPLICATION TO PERSONAL AFFAIRS:
  Compatibility: A Necessary Ingredient for a Business Partnership — 47
Running A Business under a Charter: The Corporation — 47
ISSUE FOR DEBATE:
  Should Double Taxation of Corporate Profits Be Ended? — 51
Other Forms of Ownership — 59
CASE STUDY:
  Jerry and Fritz: Should They Start a Business of Their Own or Become Corporate Management Trainees? — 62
EVOLUTION OF A BUSINESS:
  Partnership or Sole Proprietorship? — 63

3 ENTREPRENEURSHIP: SMALL BUSINESS AND FRANCHISING — 65

Small Business: What It Is and Does — 67
Franchising — 79
CONTEMPORARY ISSUE:
  Is This the Decade of the Woman Entrepreneur? — 80
PEOPLE WHO MAKE THINGS HAPPEN:
  A Profile of Ray Kroc — 82
APPLICATION TO PERSONAL AFFAIRS:
  How to Evaluate a Franchising Opportunity — 84
Big Business Rediscovers Entrepreneurship — 85
AMERICA'S REEMERGING CREATIVITY:
  Teaching Entrepreneurship — 87
CASE STUDY:
  Positive Thinking and Working on the Side — 90
EVOLUTION OF A BUSINESS:
  Acquire a Franchise? Start from Scratch? Or What? — 91

4 BUSINESS, GOVERNMENT, AND SOCIETY 93

What Is Social Responsibility? 94
Major Social Movements Affecting Business 95
What Role Does Government Play? 102
APPLICATION TO PERSONAL AFFAIRS:
  Uncle Sam's Agencies and Offices That Stand Ready to Help 104
Taxation 109
CONTEMPORARY ISSUE:
  How Life and Health Insurance Companies Help Meet Social Needs 116
CASE STUDY:
  Should Pressure Be Put on Employees to Contribute to the We Help People Campaign? 119
EVOLUTION OF A BUSINESS:
  What Is and Is Not Ethical 120

II USING MONEY IN BUSINESS

5 LONG- AND SHORT-TERM FINANCING 125

Long-term Financing for Small Businesses 126
Long-term Financing for Large Businesses 127
PEOPLE WHO MAKE THINGS HAPPEN:
  A Profile of Frederick W. Smith 135
Short-term Financing by Business 139
CONTEMPORARY ISSUE:
  Converting Short-term into Long-term Debt 140
ISSUE FOR DEBATE:
  Should Commercial Banks Be Allowed to Engage in Interstate Banking? 143
Financial Management 145

xiv CONTENTS

Putting Idle Money to Productive Use	146
CASE STUDY:	
How to Finance the Purchase of a Laboratory	150
EVOLUTION OF A BUSINESS:	
The Ins and Outs of Raising Capital	151

6 FINANCIAL INSTITUTIONS 153

The Financial Services Industry Is Competitive	154
The Financial Services Industry Is Dynamic	155
Major Financial Institutions	156
AMERICA'S REEMERGING CREATIVITY:	
Electronic Funds Transfer Systems	158
The Federal Reserve System	161
The Federal Deposit Insurance Corporation	162
Major Sources of Consumer Credit	163
ISSUE FOR DEBATE:	
Should Credit Card Customers Pay More than People Who Pay Cash?	166
Supercompany Financial Institutions Emerge	168
Credit Management	172
CASE STUDY:	
Is an Economic Doomsday Inevitable?	178
EVOLUTION OF A BUSINESS:	
Owning Real Estate—Pros and Cons	179

7 SECURITY MARKETS AND BUSINESS NEWS 181

What Are Security Exchanges?	182
Investing in the Mutual Funds Market	190
APPLICATION TO PERSONAL AFFAIRS:	
Guidelines for the Beginning Investor	191
Regulation of Securities Trading	192
How to Interpret Business News	194
PEOPLE WHO MAKE THINGS HAPPEN:	
A Profile of Charles Dow and Edward Jones	196

CONTENTS　xv

ISSUE FOR DEBATE:
　Are Adjustable Rate Mortgages (ARMs) a Good Idea?　**204**
CASE STUDY:
　What Should Ted Do with a $50,000 Inheritance?　**208**
EVOLUTION OF A BUSINESS:
　Sizing Up the Travel Market　**209**

8 RISK MANAGEMENT AND INSURANCE　**211**

Methods of Meeting Risk　**212**
Types of Insurance Companies　**216**
Property and Other Related Insurance　**218**
Life Insurance　**226**
Private Health Insurance　**231**
AMERICA'S REEMERGING CREATIVITY:
　Health Maintenance Organizations　**236**
Public or Social Insurance: Social Security　**237**
ISSUE FOR DEBATE:
　Is Social Security a Fair System for Providing Financial Security?　**240**
Other Forms of Social or Government Insurance　**241**
What's New in the Insurance Field?　**242**
CASE STUDY:
　Is Self-Insurance a Good Idea?　**246**
EVOLUTION OF A BUSINESS:
　Reducing Risk, the Eternal Worry　**247**

III GETTING PRODUCTS TO CONSUMERS

9 AN OVERVIEW OF MARKETING　**251**

What Is Marketing?　**252**
Why Is Marketing Important?　**253**
The Four Ps Make Up the Marketing Mix　**255**

xvi CONTENTS

What Is the Marketing Concept?	255
CONTEMPORARY ISSUE:	
The Four Ps in Practice: Pollo	256
ISSUE FOR DEBATE:	
All Promotion of Cigarettes Should Be Banned	257
How Are Industrial Goods Marketed?	263
What Are Distribution Channels?	263
Retailers	265
AMERICA'S REEMERGING CREATIVITY:	
The Spread of the Self-Service Concept	268
How Retailers Combine or Unite	269
What Is Non-Store Retailing?	270
APPLICATION TO PERSONAL AFFAIRS:	
Tips for Shopping by Mail	271
Wholesalers	271
What Are Agent Wholesale Intermediaries?	273
How Marketing Services and Tangible Products Differ	275
PEOPLE WHO MAKE THINGS HAPPEN:	
A Profile of Fred Bureau	276
Future of Service Marketing Is Excellent	277
CASE STUDY:	
Is Valerie's Idea for an Apparel Firm Feasible?	280
EVOLUTION OF A BUSINESS:	
The Travel Industry's Wholesale Practices	281

10 THE CONSUMER: DEMOGRAPHICS, INCOME, AND MOTIVATION — 283

Population and Consumption	284
Income and Consumption	296
Consumer Motivation: Why People Buy What They Do	301
Why People Buy Where They Do	306
Psychographics, Lifestyle Changes, and Consumption	307
PEOPLE WHO MAKE THINGS HAPPEN:	
A Profile of The Gucci Family	308

CASE STUDY:
  Making Practical Use of the Marketing Formula 312
EVOLUTION OF A BUSINESS:
  Targeting a Market Segment 313

11 PRODUCTS, PACKAGING, AND PRICING 315

What Are Products? 316
ISSUE FOR DEBATE:
  Should Doctors and Lawyers Be Considered Businesses and Market Their Services like Other Commercial Enterprises? 320
Packaging, Labeling, and Branding 324
AMERICA'S REEMERGING CREATIVITY:
  The Universal Product Code (UPC) 326
Pricing 329
CASE STUDY:
  Should the College Cafeteria Buy No-Name Brands? 342
EVOLUTION OF A BUSINESS:
  Solving Operational Problems with Pricing 343

12 MARKETING COMMUNICATIONS: SELLING, ADVERTISING, PROMOTION, AND PUBLIC RELATIONS 345

What Goes into the Promotional Mix? 346
Promotion Tool #1: Personal Selling 347
Promotion Tool #2: Advertising 351
Promotion Tool #3: Sales Promotion 360
AMERICA'S REEMERGING CREATIVITY:
  Using Cash Rebates and Coupons to Stimulate Buying 362
Promotion Tool #4: Public Relations 362
Evaluating the Productivity of Marketing Efforts 366
CASE STUDY:
  How Can "Great Chicken" Stimulate Demand? 368
EVOLUTION OF A BUSINESS:
  Is Ignorance Bliss? 369

13 PHYSICAL ELEMENTS OF BUSINESS — 371

Physical Element #1: Choosing an Industrial Location	372
Physical Element #2: Purchasing	376
APPLICATION TO PERSONAL AFFAIRS: How to Evaluate a Community Before You Move	377
PEOPLE WHO MAKE THINGS HAPPEN: A Profile of Bill Hewlett and Dave Packard	378
Physical Element #3: Production Management	381
AMERICA'S REEMERGING CREATIVITY: The Industrial Robot Expansion in Perspective	384
Physical Element #4: Inventory Management and Storage	386
Physical Element #5: Transportation	387
The Physical Aspects of Business in Perspective	392
CASE STUDY: How to Plan for the Robots	394
EVOLUTION OF A BUSINESS: Overcoming Logistical Problems to Build Goodwill	395

IV MANAGING: MAKING THE BUSINESS WORK

14 PLANNING, ORGANIZING, AND CONTROLLING THE ENTERPRISE — 399

What Is Management?	400
What Is Planning?	402
APPLICATION TO PERSONAL AFFAIRS: Do You Want to Be a Manager?	403
What Is Organizing?	409
PEOPLE WHO MAKE THINGS HAPPEN: A Profile of Peter Drucker	410
AMERICA'S REEMERGING CREATIVITY: Growing Use of Employee Suggestion Systems	420
What Is Controlling?	421

CONTENTS xix

Where Is Management Headed? 424
CASE STUDY:
  Should the "Great Sounds" Record Store Develop Formalized Plans? 426
EVOLUTION OF A BUSINESS:
  How Systemized Should a Small Office Be? 427

15 HUMAN RESOURCE MANAGEMENT: STAFFING AND DIRECTING 429

What Is Staffing? 430
APPLICATION TO PERSONAL AFFAIRS:
  Do's and Don'ts in Job Interviews 438
AMERICA'S REEMERGING CREATIVITY:
  The Dramatic Increase in Business School Enrollments 440
CONTEMPORARY ISSUE:
  Should There Be a Minimum Wage Differential for Youth? 446
What Is Directing? 451
PEOPLE WHO MAKE THINGS HAPPEN:
  A Profile of John J. Allen 452
CASE STUDY:
  Should Ace Electronics Pay Tuition for Employees? 462
EVOLUTION OF A BUSINESS:
  Who's Boss? And What About Incentives? 463

16 MANAGEMENT AND LABOR RELATIONS 465

What Is Labor? 466
ISSUE FOR DEBATE:
  Is Domestic Content Legislation in the Best Interests of Business and Labor? 469
CONTEMPORARY ISSUE:
  Mazda's Bold Embrace of the United Auto Workers 472
How Labor Unions Relate to Business 476
AMERICA'S REEMERGING CREATIVITY:
  Focusing on Long-run Results 477
How Labor Attempts to Further Its Interests 483
How Management Attempts to Restrain Labor 484
How Collective Bargaining Works 486
Organized Labor Today 488

xx CONTENTS

CASE STUDY:
What Prompts Workers to Unionize? — 494
EVOLUTION OF A BUSINESS:
The Labor Movement and Employee Morale — 495

USING INFORMATION IN BUSINESS V

17 ACCOUNTING AND FINANCIAL STATEMENTS — 499

What Is Accounting? — 500
CONTEMPORARY ISSUE:
"IRS Roulette" Helps Cause Deficit — 503
Accounting as a Professional Field — 504
AMERICA'S REEMERGING CREATIVITY:
The Accounting Profession's Challenge: Reduce Paperwork and Manipulation — 505
The Accounting Process — 508
Accounting Statements — 509
What Is Ratio Analysis? — 513
Cost Accounting and Standard Costs — 514
Auditing — 514
The Annual Report — 515
AMERICA'S REEMERGING CREATIVITY:
How the Nation's Largest Auditing Agency Operates — 517
What Is Budgeting? — 518
ISSUE FOR DEBATE:
Is a Balanced Federal Budget Amendment Needed? — 520
CASE STUDY:
How to Increase Your Net Worth — 524
EVOLUTION OF A BUSINESS:
Analyzing Figures to Produce Efficiencies — 525

18 BUSINESS INFORMATION AND RESEARCH — 527

What Is Business Research? — 528
AMERICA'S REEMERGING CREATIVITY:
Using Information Technology for Better Business — 531

The Three Steps in Researching	533
Sources of Business Information	536
Experience Is a Good Teacher, but...	540
Statistics: The Basic Tool of Research	541
Research Includes Forecasting Events	546
PEOPLE WHO MAKE THINGS HAPPEN: A Profile of Wolfberg, Alvarez, Taracido & Associates	547
How to Present Statistical Data	548
The Business Report	550
APPLICATION TO PERSONAL AFFAIRS: The Importance of Time Management	553
CONTEMPORARY ISSUE: How Will Business Information Be Managed?	555
CASE STUDY: Predicting the Birth Rate for the Next 20 Years	558
EVOLUTION OF A BUSINESS: Whither Changing Lifestyles?	559

19 COMPUTERS: THE ELECTRONIC SIDE OF BUSINESS — 561

What Is a Computer?	562
ISSUE FOR DEBATE: Will the New Technology Create Massive Unemployment?	564
How Old Is Data Processing?	565
What Are the Basic Advantages of Computers?	568
How Are Computers Used?	570
What Is Computer Hardware?	577
What Is Computer Software?	580
What Do Systems Analysts and Computer Programmers Do?	581
Where Is the Computer Industry Headed?	584
AMERICA'S REEMERGING CREATIVITY: The Space Shuttle	586
CASE STUDY: Can a Computerize-the-Phone-Book Venture Succeed?	588
EVOLUTION OF A BUSINESS: Using Computer Output in the Marketing Effort	589

SPECIAL BUSINESS SITUATIONS VI

20 BUSINESS LAW AND LEGAL SERVICES — 593

Why Demand for Lawyers Continues to Grow	594
How Are Legal Disputes Resolved?	596
What Is Business Law?	597
Why Be Familiar with Business Law?	597
Contracts	598
APPLICATION TO PERSONAL AFFAIRS:	
Nine Tips for Selecting and Working with a Lawyer	600
Law of Agency	602
Law of Employer-Employee	603
Sale of Personal Property	604
Negotiable Instruments Help Transfer Property	605
Negotiating: An Art Whose Time Has Come	607
Bankruptcy Is a Popular Legal Remedy for Debt	608
ISSUE FOR DEBATE:	
Who Is Primarily Responsible for Bankruptcies: Business or Consumers?	610
Trademarks, Patents, and Copyrights	611
How Crime Affects Business	614
CASE STUDY:	
Should Williams Printing Company Employ a Staff Lawyer?	620
EVOLUTION OF A BUSINESS:	
Establishing Credibility and Trust	621

21 INTERNATIONAL BUSINESS — 623

International Business: Products, Investments, and Ideas	624
International Trade and American Business	626
What Is International Trade?	626
World Trade and the U.S. Economy	629
What Obstacles Restrict International Trade?	633

AMERICA'S REEMERGING CREATIVITY: How U.S. and Global Revitalization Relate	634
ISSUE FOR DEBATE: Should the U.S. Trade with Nations That Practice Discrimination?	636
How to Organize for Exporting	639
How to Organize for Importing	641
What Are Multinationals?	645
World Economic Organizations	646
APPLICATION TO PERSONAL AFFAIRS: Should You Seek Employment Overseas?	648
Where Is International Trade Headed?	649
CASE STUDY: Should J. T. Borders Sell Land to Foreigners?	652
EVOLUTION OF A BUSINESS: The International Side of the Travel Business	653

22 NONPROFIT ORGANIZATIONS 655

Governments Are the Most Important Nonprofits	657
How Governments Differ from Other Nonprofits	659
How Nonprofits Operate	660
How Nonprofits Market Their Services	661
Effective Public Relations Is a Must for Nonprofits	661
PEOPLE WHO MAKE THINGS HAPPEN: A Profile of Nathaniel R. Woods	667
Management of Nonprofit Organizations: A Viable Career Alternative	669
Activity Areas for Nonprofit Organizations	670
AMERICA'S REEMERGING CREATIVITY: Growth in Continuing Education for Business	671
American Cancer Society: An Example of a Leading Nonprofit Organization at Work	674
CASE STUDY: Developing a Plan for Financing a Trade Association	678
APPENDIX: Tips on Selecting a Career and Finding a Job	679
Glossary	691
Index	716

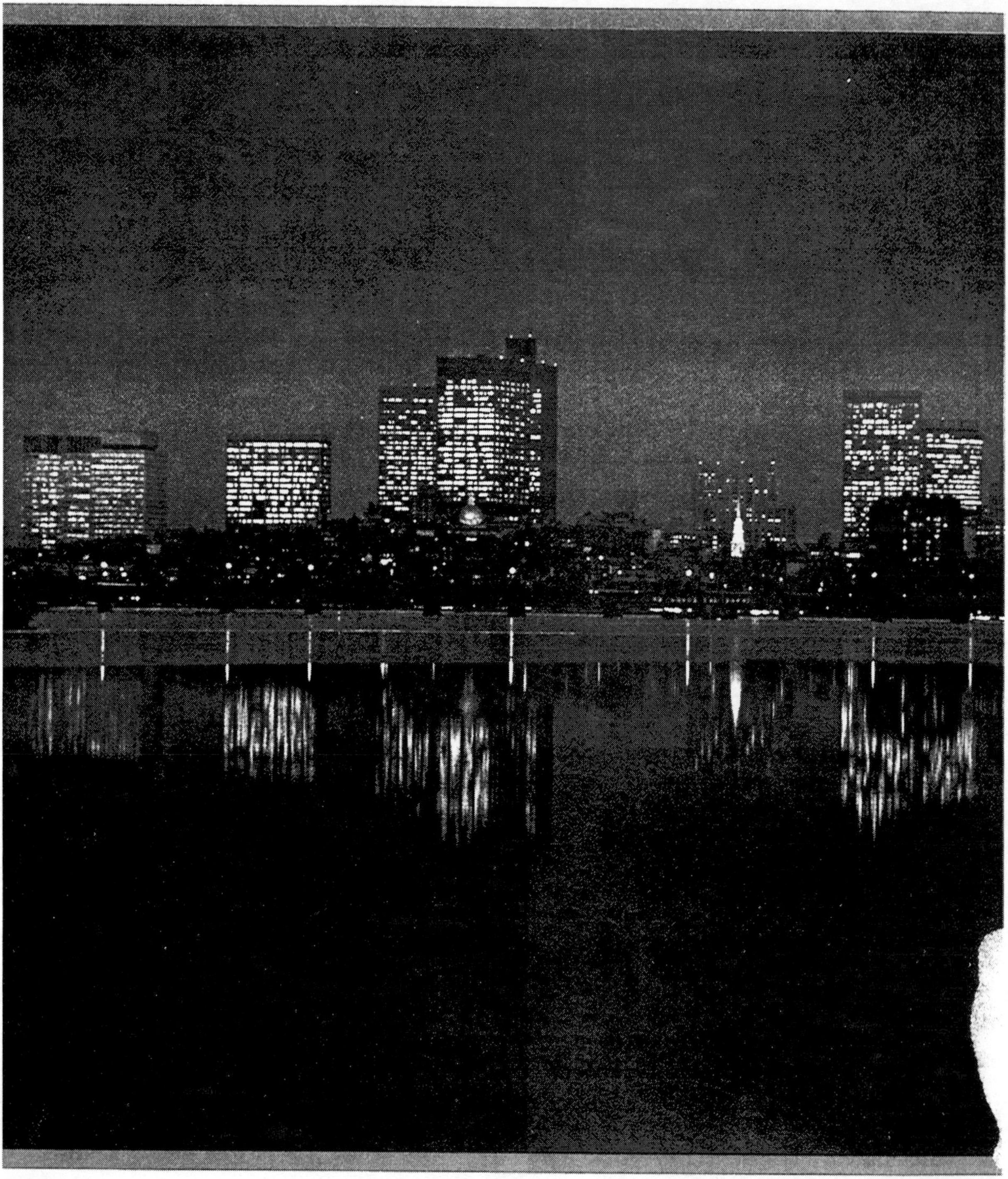

HOW OUR PRIVATE ENTERPRISE SYSTEM WORKS

1 THE AMERICAN PRIVATE ENTERPRISE SYSTEM

2 PROPRIETORSHIPS, PARTNERSHIPS, AND CORPORATIONS

3 ENTREPRENEURSHIP: SMALL BUSINESS AND FRANCHISING

4 BUSINESS, GOVERNMENT, AND SOCIETY

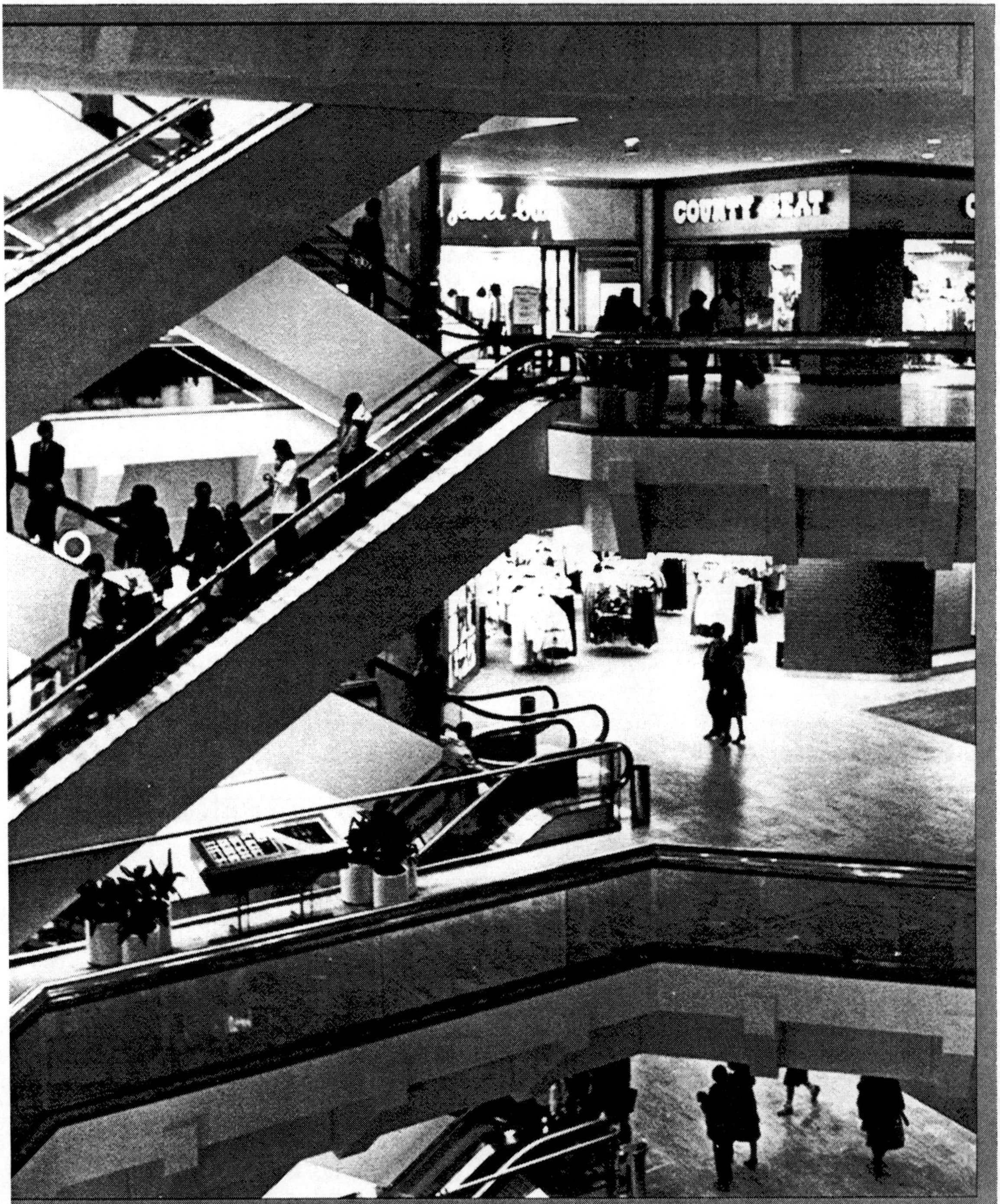
COUNTY SEAT

THE AMERICAN PRIVATE ENTERPRISE SYSTEM
The Roots of Business

READ THIS CHAPTER SO YOU CAN:

Define "business," and discuss the question "Is business satisfying the needs of Americans?"

Define "quantitative standard of living" and "qualitative standard of living."

Explain the basic rights guaranteed by the private enterprise system.

Examine the roles of profit, government, and individual risk in the private enterprise system.

Compare capitalism with its main competitors: socialism and communism.

Discuss the future of capitalism.

Evaluate the potential of private enterprise in non-capitalistic countries.

Business is the heart of the American economic system and is our most discussed and observed institution. A large part of our vocabulary relates directly or indirectly to business. Words like "inflation," "deficits," "strikes," "prices," "profits," "employment," and "recession" clearly reflect our commercial life.

The word **business** generally has two meanings. First, it designates *any establishment that serves the public through the production or distribution of goods or through the provision of services*. In this sense, there are three kinds of businesses. A **production business,** such as IBM or a local bakery, is *a firm that manufactures and markets products*. A **distribution business,** such as the J. C. Penney Company or a car dealership is *an enterprise that sells products made by other firms*. A **service business,** such as the Hertz Corporation or a dry cleaner, is *an organization that provides assistance but does not produce or distribute a tangible good*.

Second, the word **business** refers to *the commercial life of a nation*. In this sense, business includes all economic activity—banking, production, distribution, transportation, and so on. When President Calvin Coolidge said, "The business of America is business," he had the second meaning in mind.

IS BUSINESS SATISFYING THE NEEDS OF AMERICANS?

Basically, the objective of any human activity is to fulfill physical wants and/or to provide psychological satisfactions. Thus, before we examine American business activities in detail, we should consider whether these activities satisfy human needs. To do this, we must consider quantitative as well as qualitative factors.

What Is a Quantitative Standard of Living?

A **quantitative standard of living** is *a measure of how many products and services are consumed, and of* **per capita income** *(income per person)*. As Table 1–1 suggests, the United States has one of the highest standards of living in the world in terms of basic consumer products and services. Americans also have a high per capita income, and the work time required to buy everyday items is in most cases less here than in other nations.

What Is Happening to Our GNP?

In comparing standards of living, we refer to a nation's **Gross National Product (GNP),** which is *the total output of goods and services valued at market prices*. As Table 1–2 shows, our GNP increased 4.7 times in current dollars. However, these figures ignore the effects of inflation. When these amounts are expressed in *real terms*

TABLE 1-1 Cars, Telephones, and Television Sets per 1,000 People (Selected Nations)

	CARS	TELEPHONES	TVs
USA	500	789	624
Australia	417	489	378
Brazil	70	63	122
Canada	435	694	471
France	370	498	354
India	1	4	2
Japan	217	502	539
China	0.5	8	5
Sweden	357	828	381
USSR	36	89	303
Britain	286	507	404
West Germany	385	488	337

SOURCE: "NIRVANA, by the Numbers," *The Economist* (December 24, 1983), 53, 55.

TABLE 1-2 U.S. GNP per capita in 1960 and 1983

	1960	1983
Current dollars	$2,802	$13,239
Constant dollars (1972 = 100)	$3,790	$ 8,693

SOURCE: *Statistical Abstract of the United States, 1984*, Table 739, 451.

(that is, adjusted for inflation using the value of the dollar in 1972 as 100), the increase is only about 1.7 times.

What about Family Income Distribution?

As suggested in Figure 1-1, income is far from equally divided in our economy. The richest fifth of the population holds far more total income (42.7 percent) than the bottom three-fifths, who together represent only 33 percent. Moreover, one-twentieth of the population received more income (16 percent) than the bottom two-fifths combined (15.9 percent).

Inequality of income is often discussed as a social problem. But three observations are in order: First, no lid or ceiling is placed on how much an individual or family may earn. Second, the income figures do not consider taxes. (Higher income families pay more taxes

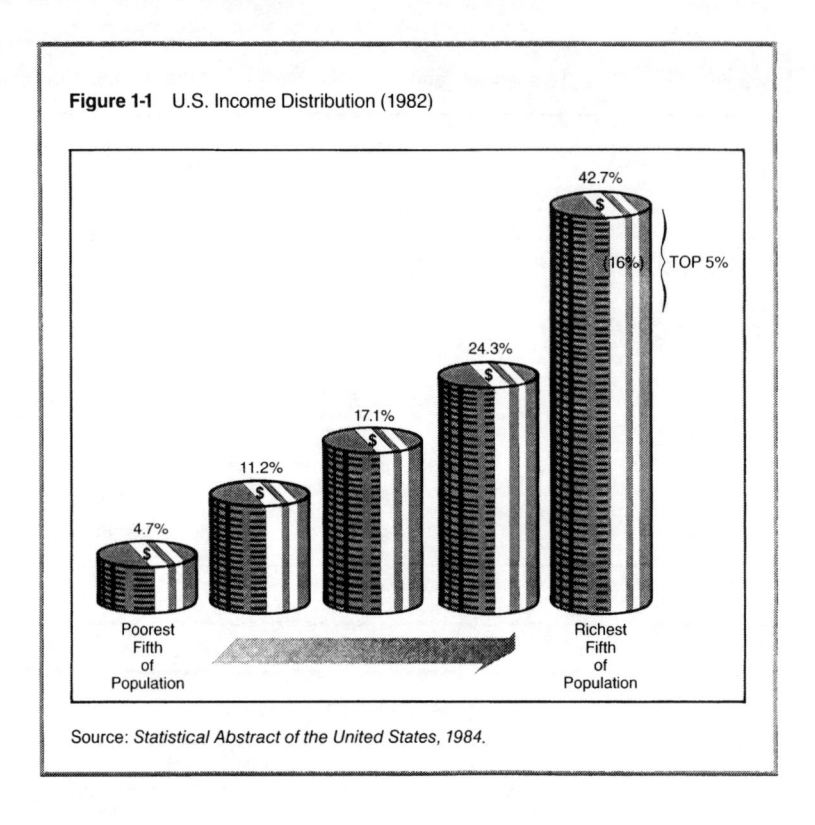

Figure 1-1 U.S. Income Distribution (1982)

Poorest Fifth of Population: 4.7%
11.2%
17.1%
24.3%
Richest Fifth of Population: 42.7% (16%) TOP 5%

Source: *Statistical Abstract of the United States, 1984.*

than lower income families.) Third, in many nations, income distribution is even more unbalanced.

What Is a Qualitative Standard of Living?

Despite our obvious high standard of living in material terms, in recent years thoughtful people have been asking, "Is more always better? Should more emphasis be placed on quality and less on quantity?"

A **qualitative standard of living** is *a measure of how "good" life is in terms of crime, education, the environment, and so on.* It is difficult to measure—the richest communities do not necessarily have the fewest problems. Statistics may tell us that there are X number of library books, parks, and street cleaners per 1,000 citizens in a community. But if that community has a high delinquency rate, if it is polluted and crime-ridden, can we say that its qualitative standard of living is high? The United States, for instance, despite its high quantitative standard of living, falls short of world leadership in several basic aspects of a qualitative standard of living (see Table 1–3).

TABLE 1-3 Qualitative Standard of Living (Selected Nations)

COUNTRY	LIFE EXPECTANCY AT BIRTH	NUMBER OF DOCTORS PER 100,000	HOMICIDE AND SERIOUS ASSAULT PER 100,000	SUICIDES PER 100,000	PERCENT OF MARRIAGES ENDING IN DIVORCE	PINTS OF PURE ALCOHOL CONSUMED PER PERSON
USA	75	192	9	12	50	14.6
Japan	77	128	1	18	18	9.9
West Germany	73	222	1	21	9	22.0
France	76	172	1	17	22	24.1
Britain	74	154	1	9	36	12.5
Canada	75	182	2	15	32	16.0
Australia	74	179	2	11	44	17.6
Sweden	77	204	1	19	53	9.5
Spain	74	217	1	4	*	22.9
Switzerland	76	244	1	25	31	19.4
Saudi Arabia	55	61	2	2	*	0.0
Israel	73	270	2	6	14	12.0
USSR	72	357	3	45	33	10.9
Mexico	66	79	16	2	5	4.2
Brazil	64	59	16	2	*	15.0
India	52	27	5	3	1	5.0
China	67	52	1	3	*	5.0

SOURCE: *Statistical Abstract of the United States, 1984;* Comparative International Statistics Section 33, 853–82.

*No provision for divorce.

Life quality means different things to different people. For example, although some people feel the development of more nuclear power plants is an important goal for the United States, others would object to the possible environmental damage of that action.

Moreover, the differing views of life quality can be illustrated by some current contradictory trends in America. For example, how does one explain the following?

- Even though the crime rate is high, more books are published each year.
- Even though alcoholism and drug addiction increase, jogging, tennis, and skiing soar in popularity.
- Even though pollution, acid rain, and hazardous waste disposal create greater problems, national parks expand.

- Even though the rate of high-school dropouts continues to rise, adult education programs explode in popularity.

Business is often accused of selling a self-indulgent philosophy of "Buy more—enjoy life more." Actually business merely provides each of us with a wide range of options. It can't *make* us buy anything. We make the choices. We decide whether to buy a tennis racket, several lottery tickets, or a rack of lamb. It is we the people—not business—who determine life quality.

What Makes Our Standard of Living High?

Although the United States may not match or surpass other nations in some qualitative terms, it still has the largest GNP and is the leading trading nation in the world. The success of American business enables us to enjoy a quantitative standard of living that most people of the world envy. Why? What aspects of American business make it so vigorous?

- *A technological economy.* U.S. business has developed many technical devices and processes that help maximize human effort. Our traditional success in mass production, standardization, automation, and computerization illustrates this.
- *A marketing system devoted to selling more goods at a smaller profit per unit rather than fewer goods at a larger profit per unit.* This system provides more goods for more people.
- *A competitively oriented business system under which weak and inefficient businesses must give way to strong ones.* Thus, the emphasis is on efficiency.
- *An economic philosophy that encourages thousands of centers of initiative.* As will be discussed shortly, the American economic system provides strong motivation for individuals to strive for success and to innovate.
- *Relatively little government control over business activities.* Competition is encouraged.

As this list indicates, the vigor of American business is largely a result of an economic environment called the **private** (or **free**) **enterprise system, capitalism** or, sometimes, the **profit system.** Private enterprise is *an economic system under which individuals have certain basic rights and one of whose major objectives is profit making.*

Although most people acknowledge the attainments of our system, some nations with different economic systems and some of our own citizens as well criticize it. Ironically, the most outspoken critics of private enterprise—those who would replace it with something substantially different—are often those who least understand how it works.

INDIVIDUAL RIGHTS UNDER THE PRIVATE ENTERPRISE SYSTEM

Because the United States operates under the private enterprise system, we are guaranteed certain basic economic rights: to own property, to compete freely, to sell goods and services in a free market, to become an entrepreneur, and to choose an occupation.

The Right to Own Property

Often taken for granted, the right to private ownership of property carries with it the right to use that property in any way that is not detrimental to the public welfare. The owner may sell it, alter it, bequeath it to heirs, or give it away. Most property in the United States—oil wells, factories, mines, office buildings, stores, farms, homes—is owned by individuals, singly or in groups (corporations and partnerships), rather than by the government. (However, federal, state, and local governments own over one-third of all *land* in the United States.)

Private ownership of property affects the economy in several ways. First, the wealth of the nation generally receives better, more conscientious care under private ownership than it does under public ownership. For example, owner-occupied homes are usually better maintained than housing rented from the government.

Second, the right to private ownership of property is a strong motivating factor for people and businesses. People work harder and are more ambitious when they know that their income can be used to invest in property that they and their families can enjoy, take pride in owning, use to provide further income, and pass on to their heirs as they choose. Businesses, in the same context, have an incentive to expand operations and make larger profits. Thus, the right to accumulate property leads to greater production for a society as a whole.

Third, privately owned property provides a base for taxation. However, the merits of the property tax are controversial. Those who favor the tax argue that as property is improved, a larger tax base is developed for local and state governments to use in providing public services. Those opposed to the tax argue that it penalizes people who improve property (rather than rewarding them) and therefore contributes to the chronic problem of urban decay, which in the long run erodes the tax base.

The right to private ownership of property, like any right, can be abused. To prevent excesses on the part of a few and to protect the welfare of society as a whole, such restrictive measures as inheritance

> *"Any entrepreneur who feels he is entitled to praise should not really try to be one."*
>
> DEREK F. DU TOIT

This stylist runs her own hair salon. By providing the best possible service, she retains faithful customers and attracts new ones from competitors.

taxes, conservation and zoning laws, and building codes have been established.

The Right to Compete Freely

One of the most outstanding characteristics of private enterprise is **competition**—*the independent effort of two or more businesses to secure the patronage of the same customers.* Competition thrives under private enterprise because each business knows that, in general, the more successfully it competes with other firms, the larger its profit will be.

Not all businesses have equal opportunities to compete successfully. Some have greater capital resources, an established reputation, or more experience. New firms, as might be expected, often encounter severe competition from established firms. However, the beginning firm can overcome these inequalities if it is well managed and if its products serve real needs.

LOWER PRICES TO CONSUMERS

Other things being equal, consumers generally buy from the seller who offers a product or a service at the lowest price and biggest savings. Consequently, all businesses are encouraged to eliminate waste and inefficiency in production and marketing so that their products can be offered to the public at a competitive price.

BETTER SERVICE

Competition encourages better service to attract consumers. A department store, for example, will provide credit, attractive interiors, free delivery, and numerous other services for the comfort or convenience of shoppers. Were it not for the competitive urge to earn larger profits, there would be little incentive to provide desirable services.

NEW AND BETTER PRODUCTS

Firms try to attract customers by making superior products and offering desired services. As a result of competition, practically all products—tires, computers, aircraft, vacation packages, and thousands more—are now markedly better than when they were first developed. One observer has pointed out a not widely recognized aspect of why this happens: "The instinct of the American mind to look into, examine, and experiment—this led to, among other things, a willingness to 'scrap' not only old machinery but old formulas, old ideas; and brought about, among other results, the condition expressed in the saying that 'American mechanical progress could be measured by the size of its scrap heaps.'"[1]

---

[1]Mark Sullivan, *Our Times,* vol. 1 (1926); quoted in *The History of American Business and Industry* (New York: American Heritage, 1972), 71.

BETTER RESOURCE ALLOCATION

Under private enterprise, well-managed businesses that provide what the customer wants are likely to succeed. Providing "what the customer wants" does not necessarily mean satisfying every potential customer. For example, fast-food chains like McDonald's and Kentucky Fried Chicken offer limited menus and simple surroundings. However, their success indicates that they meet a real need by offering satisfactory products at a low price.

A business that cannot compete successfully must either improve its methods of operation or forfeit its right to be in business. This weeding-out process, sometimes called the "right to fail," may seem harsh. However, it often improves the allocation of **national resources,** or *the tangible and intangible wealth of a nation.* The private enterprise system is a self-regulating, unbureaucratic method for shifting material and human resources to where consumers want them.

The Right to Sell Goods and Services in a Free Market

A free market for goods and services is a third characteristic of private enterprise. Basically, in a **free market** *economic system, owners of products seek to sell them at the highest possible price, and consumers of products seek to buy them at the lowest possible price.* Before a sale can be made, buyer and seller must agree, often on a compromise price. According to the **law of supply and demand,** *if supply is greater than demand, the buyer has the advantage and a lower price will result; if supply is less than demand, the seller has the advantage and a higher price will be set.*

The law of supply and demand is fundamental to our private enterprise economy. Until recently, the government has attempted to stimulate the economy by increasing demand. Since the days of the New Deal (1930s), government policy has been one of **demand-side economics**—that is, *pouring government funds into the economy to expand demand.* Beginning in 1981, policy has favored **supply-side economics,** or *stimulating the elements of the productive process: capital investment, savings, productivity, work effort, and initiative.* Both supply-side and demand-side economics are controversial; neither is applied in its purest form.

Prices determined in a free market influence future production plans. If the price of a product covers more than costs and results in a profit, producers are encouraged to produce more. But if they think the price is not good, they curtail production. In this way, the free market directs resources into the production of wanted items and away from unwanted products.

When prices are controlled by government, the law of supply and demand does not function. In the end, the price of the finished

This businessman either didn't provide superior service, didn't stock popular styles, or didn't manage his business well.

APPLICATION TO PERSONAL AFFAIRS

Can I Succeed in a Business of My Own?

Success in one's own business relates closely to one's personal traits. The Department of Commerce developed the following self-analysis test to help individuals determine whether they have the psychological makeup to become successful entrepreneurs. Under each question, check the answer that says what you feel or comes closest to it. Be honest with yourself.

Are you a self-starter?
- ☐ I do things on my own. Nobody has to tell me to get going.
- ☐ If someone gets me started, I keep going all right.
- ☐ Easy does it. I don't put myself out until I have to.

How do you feel about other people?
- ☐ I like people. I can get along with just about anybody.
- ☐ I have plenty of friends—I don't need anyone else.
- ☐ Most people irritate me.

Can you lead others?
- ☐ I can get most people to go along when I start something.
- ☐ I can give the orders if someone tells me what we should do.
- ☐ I let someone else get things moving. Then I go along if I feel like it.

Can you take responsibility?
- ☐ I like to take charge of things and see them through.
- ☐ I'll take over if I have to, but I'd rather let someone else be responsible.
- ☐ There's always some eager beaver around wanting to show how smart he is. I say let him.

How good an organizer are you?
- ☐ I like to have a plan before I start. I'm usually the one to get things lined up when the group wants to do something.
- ☐ I do all right unless things get too confused. Then I quit.
- ☐ You get all set and then something comes along and presents too many problems. So I just take things as they come.

How good a worker are you?
- ☐ I can keep going as long as I need to. I don't mind working hard for something I want.
- ☐ I'll work hard for a while, but when I've had enough, that's it.
- ☐ I can't see that hard work gets you anywhere.

Can you make decisions?
- ☐ I can make up my mind in a hurry if I have to. It usually turns out O.K., too.
- ☐ I can if I have plenty of time. If I have to make up my mind fast, I think later I should have decided the other way.
- ☐ I don't like to be the one who has to decide things.

Can people trust what you say?
- ☐ You bet they can. I don't say things I don't mean.
- ☐ I try to be on the level most of the time, but sometimes I just say what's easiest.
- ☐ Why bother if the other fellow doesn't know the difference?

Can you stick with it?
- ☐ If I make up my mind to do something, I don't let *anything* stop me.
- ☐ I usually finish what I start—if it goes well.
- ☐ If it doesn't work right away, I quit. Why beat your brains out?

How good is your health?
- ☐ I *never* run down!
- ☐ I have enough energy for most things I want to do.
- ☐ I run out of energy sooner than most of my friends seem to.

> If most of your checks are beside the first answers, you probably have what it takes to run a business. If not, you're likely to have more trouble than you can handle by yourself. Better find a partner who is strong on the points you're weak on. If many checks are beside the third answer, not even a good partner will be able to shore you up.
>
> Source: Adapted from U.S. Small Business Administration, Checklist for Going Into Business, *Management Aids 2.016* (Washington, D.C. 1984), 2–3.

product is usually artificially high or low, and there is overproduction or underproduction of goods. In other words, supply does not match demand, and resources are poorly allocated.

The Right to Become an Entrepreneur

Another important feature of private enterprise is the right to start one's own business. *An individual who starts a business* is called an **entrepreneur.** Although licenses may be required for certain businesses, relatively few obstacles impede a prospective entrepreneur.

Entrepreneurship gives our system vitality. Each year thousands of individuals start businesses, hoping to fill a perceived gap in what people require. These new initiatives provide consumers with a richer variety of choices and, by increasing the competition, keep existing companies from stagnating.

The right to become an entrepreneur does not guarantee success. People's aptitudes, training, and experience differ greatly—and in many cases even a good idea may fail for unanticipated reasons. However, most Americans believe it is better to have some failures of this nature than to have the government specify who may and who may not enter business.

The Right to Choose an Occupation

Because of specialization, mass production, and the growth of large-scale industry, most people do not enter business for themselves but become employees. The same principle of private enterprise that permits entrepreneurship also guarantees people the privilege of selling their services to whomever they choose.

People who are free to choose their work have the incentive to prepare themselves, through education and training, for more responsible positions. The computer programmer, for example, who realizes that he or she can receive more money and more job satisfaction by becoming a manager is motivated to prepare in various ways for more responsibility. Similarly, people who are free to change from one occupation to another may become more successful and productive in the new field. By making the greatest use of their talents, people maximize their contributions to the national welfare; by realizing their goals, they become more productive.

> When Roger E. Birk became chief executive of Merrill Lynch in 1981 at the relatively young age of 50, he told the *New York Times:* "If you're looking for praise on everything you do, you'll never accomplish much. You just go about your business with the satisfaction of doing a good job."
>
> The following maxim is framed on his office wall: "It's amazing what people can accomplish if they have no concern about who receives credit." The remarks made about Birk when he assumed the top job are also revealing: "He was not driven to be stage center"; "Good listener"; "A guy who knows how to motivate people in a quiet way"; "Doesn't use [the] personal pronoun."

OTHER CHARACTERISTICS OF THE PRIVATE ENTERPRISE SYSTEM

In addition to the basic rights just discussed, the private enterprise system also has the following characteristics: Profits are a key goal of most businesses; government direction is minimized; and risks are incurred by individuals rather than the government.

Profits Are a Key Goal

In the private enterprise system, a major objective of business is to make a **profit,** or *income in excess of expenditures,* over a period of time. This is true whether the business is a small boutique or a huge organization such as General Motors.

All organizations must recognize the importance of the **profit principle** if they are to survive and expand. *No business can operate at a loss indefinitely.* If income does not exceed expenditures, a business must make up the difference with donations or subsidies, higher prices, or reduction of services; otherwise it will fail. Even "antiestablishment" enterprises understand the need for profit when it concerns their own activities. For example, before they went out of business, New York underground newspapers *East Village Other* and *The Rat* hired Dun & Bradstreet's collection division to hound their delinquent subscribers!

Two major myths surround the idea of profit. First, many people believe that American business profits are outrageously high. Second, some people believe that business profits can have a detrimental effect on our economy.

ARE PROFITS SKY HIGH?

Many people grossly exaggerate the amount of profit earned by businesses. Certainly some companies take unfair advantage of shortages and other market conditions to reap windfall profits from time to time. However, on the whole, business profits are not as high as most people think (see Table 1–4). Taxes take a particularly large bite out of corporate profits. In 1984, for example, American businesses had gross profits of $203.2 billion, out of which they paid $75.8 billion in federal and state taxes.

HOW DO BUSINESS PROFITS BENEFIT OUR ECONOMY?

The role of profit in our economy is often not well understood. Some people feel that if profits were eliminated, lower prices and a higher standard of living would result. Others believe that profits prevent our economy from stagnating or declining.

First, *profits provide the incentive for investment.* People normally invest money in a business only if they believe that the com-

TABLE 1-4 Profits per Sales Dollar (Selected Industries, 1975, 1980, and 1984)

	(IN CENTS)		
	1975	1980	1984
Iron and steel	5.0	2.9	−4.0
Motor vehicles and equipment	2.2	−3.4	5.0
Food and kindred products	3.2	3.4	3.3
Tobacco manufacturers	9.2	11.7	12.1
Paper and allied products	5.6	6.1	3.6
Printing and publishing	4.6	5.5	5.8
Petroleum and coal products	7.6	7.7	6.2
Rubber and miscellaneous plastic products	3.0	2.0	3.5

SOURCE: *Statistical Abstract of the United States, 1985,* 533.

pany will earn profits. The investments they make may enable a business to invest in new equipment or in research and development. New technology is one of the key factors in improving a country's standard of living.

Second, *profits encourage efficiency.* Businesses know their profits depend not only on the amount of goods and services they sell but on their ability to keep costs down. Consequently, the profit incentive encourages businesses to reduce waste and inefficiency.

Third, *profits account for a large part of tax revenue.* Roughly 40 percent of profits earned by American business are paid as taxes to local, state, and national governments. As tax revenue, profits fund a considerable share of our social programs and national defense.

Government Direction Minimized

In a private enterprise system, businesses may produce what they want, in whatever amounts they want, through whatever means they choose so long as the public welfare is not jeopardized. This **laissez faire** ("let alone") arrangement is *an economic system in which business is conducted with relatively little interference or direction from the government.* In contrast, as will be seen later, some countries have economic systems that are centrally planned by the government.

One of the most significant trends in recent decades has been the growing influence of the government. Some economists, in fact, refer to our current system as a "modified" or "mixed" system rather than as a private enterprise, or capitalistic, system. Table 1–5 explains the role that government plays in business decisions. A man-

TABLE 1-5 Government Influences on Decision Making

TYPE OF DECISION	EXAMPLES OF QUESTIONS THAT MANAGERS MUST ASK
Product decision	Will the product meet government safety standards?
Employment decision	Are we meeting EEOC requirements concerning the employment of women and minorities?
Personnel termination decision	If a government agency were to consider this case, would it feel the employee was terminated for "just cause"?
Advertising plan	Can we point out directly in our advertising the weaknesses of our competitor's product?
Sale of stock in the company	What must we do to conform to Securities and Exchange Commission regulations?
Labeling decision	Does our label say everything it is required to say?
Location decision	Will local authorities rezone the property for our purposes?
Worker safety decision	Do our production facilities meet federal standards?
Accounting decision	Will our accounting system be acceptable if the IRS audits us?
Merger decision	What requirements must we meet to get our planned merger approved?

ager who is about to make a decision must ask, "Would the proposed decision violate some government rule, guideline, or law?"

THE RATIONALE FOR GOVERNMENT REGULATION

The philosophy underlying the private enterprise system is this: Each individual or business may advance its own interests—but only so long as what is done also advances the welfare of the whole society. In other words, a business is granted the privilege of working for its own ends, but only if it acts responsibly. To further the general welfare of the nation, the government, elected by the citizens, is empowered to intervene in business when intervention is believed essential for the good of all. For example, the government protects American business from foreign competition by imposing tariffs on certain imports and aids product distribution by maintaining harbors, roads, and airports. The government also seeks to prevent companies from taking unfair advantage of their employees, competitors, or consumers.

THE GROWING DEBATE

The issue of government regulation is controversial. At one extreme, some people say government regulation of business should be curtailed because self-regulation is adequate and because the need to adhere to government regulations is burying American businesses in mountains of paperwork. At the other extreme, some people advocate increased government intervention in business. They point out that capital and opportunity are not divided equitably and that consequently many people are poorly clothed, sheltered, and fed; that resources are being wasted; that numerous public improvements are needed; and that many unfair business practices exist. In particular, critics point to poverty, pollution, and social unrest as proof of the need for increased government involvement.

The issue is not simple to resolve. Most businesspeople take a position between the two extremes, feeling that some regulation is essential but that in the long run too much regulation would lead to an inefficient economic system.

Risks Incurred by Individuals

Practically every business situation involves some element of risk. The very act of going into business carries with it a risk of failure. A corporation may expand without assurance that the enlargement will pay off. A business may risk thousands of dollars on a new product, never certain whether the public will accept or reject it. For example, Du Pont lost $100 million on Corfam, a synthetic leather. According to Crawford H. Greenewalt, former chairman of Du Pont, "The only power corporations have, whether large or small, is the right to stand in the marketplace and cry out their wares."

In a private enterprise system, risks are incurred largely by individuals rather than the government. Many people believe that the riskiness of business works to the benefit of the economic system. They argue that under the current system, managers exercise greater care in making business decisions, and organizations tend to precede each important business venture with extensive research. As a result, errors in judgment, inefficiency, and waste of our national resources are reduced.

HOW DOES OUR SYSTEM COMPARE WITH OTHERS?

There are a wide variety of economic systems in existence. Some systems, like that of West Germany, are close cousins of our own; others, like the system prevailing in the U.S.S.R., are strikingly different.

Economic systems are generally divided into three basic categories: *capitalism, socialism,* and *communism.* Critics of American capitalism tend to propose varying degrees of socialism or communism as an alternative. It is necessary to understand the economic strengths and weaknesses of these different systems in order to evaluate their arguments.

Even in a Communist country, American products are popular. Here Chinese citizens buy Coca-Cola from a newly opened plant in Peking. (The four characters written on the banner near center mean "tasty and pleasant," the name for Coca-Cola in Chinese.)

PEOPLE WHO MAKE THINGS HAPPEN

A PROFILE OF ADAM SMITH

Unlike the other people profiled in this book, Adam Smith was not a businessperson but an economist and scholar. He was born in Kirkaldy, Scotland, in 1723. He attended Glasgow College, taught logic and moral philosophy at Glasgow for some 13 years, and then lived in France for two years while serving as a tutor.

Through most of these years Smith was absorbed in the study of economics, which he called "political economy." His curiosity about the subject led him to interview businessmen, visit workplaces, and read everything he could find that pertained to money and trade.

In 1776, Smith published *An Inquiry into the Nature and Causes of the Wealth of Nations*, which brought him instant fame and challenged the prevailing ideas with regard to money and trade. Under the then current doctrine of mercantilism, gold and silver were regarded as the most desirable forms of wealth, and it was felt that a strong central government was needed to regulate business. Smith, in contrast, said that the goods produced annually by a society were the most important form of wealth. His most revolutionary concept was the idea that free competition was beneficial. According to Smith, when many people act to promote their own interests, an "invisible hand," which automatically promotes the well-being of society, is set in motion.

Smith felt governments were corrupt and inefficient, and favored laissez faire—nonintervention by government in business. Although he seldom had anything good to say about government, he did single out the English government as the least harmful: "England's capital has been silently and gradually accumulated by the private frugality and good conduct of individuals, by their universal, continual, and uninterrupted effort to better their own condition. It is this effort, protected by law and allowed by liberty to exert itself in the manner that is most advantageous, which has maintained the progress of England...."

In later centuries, Smith's doctrine of the invisible hand was often used to justify ruthless behavior on the part of capitalists who argued, "when I accumulate wealth, society benefits." Smith himself would probably not have condoned such an attitude. Although he recognized the strength of material wealth as a motivator, he himself had little interest in money and spent most of his life living quietly. It is believed that he secretly donated a large proportion of his royalties to charities. Here are some of Smith's ideas from *The Wealth of Nations*:

On human equality. "The difference of natural talents of different men is, in reality, much less than we are aware of.... The difference between the most dissimilar characters, between a philosopher and a common street porter, for example, seems to arise not so much from nature, as from habit, custom, and education."

On college rules. "The discipline of colleges and universities is ... contrived, not for the benefit of the students, but for the interest, or more properly speaking, for the ease of the masters."

On distribution of wealth. "No society can surely be flourishing and happy, of which the far greater part of the members are poor and miserable. It is but equity, besides, that they who feed, clothe, and lodge the whole body of the people, should have such a share of the produce of their own labor as to be themselves tolerably well fed, clothed, and lodged."

Capitalism vs. Socialism and Communism

Economists differentiate among capitalism, socialism, and communism in terms of the ownership of **capital**, or *wealth used to produce more wealth*. Clothes, homes, furniture, and cars are wealth but not capital, because they do not produce more wealth. On the other hand, machines, tools, equipment, and supplies are both wealth *and* capital, because such goods are used to produce additional wealth. Money can also be capital if it is used to produce more wealth (for example, savings accounts that earn interest).

Capital is essential to the economic development of every nation, whether its economic system is capitalism, communism, or socialism. The significant economic distinction is: Who owns the capital—individuals or the government?

Under communism, capital is owned by the state. Under socialism, the state owns major industries, such as utilities and transportation. Under capitalism, capital is privately owned—either by entrepreneurs or by investors. Entrepreneurs, such as farmers and owners of businesses, are the most familiar types of "capitalists." However, investors are also properly considered capitalists, because they own wealth that is used to produce more wealth. In the mid-1980s there were more than 42 million shareholders in the United States, which means that approximately one out of four Americans now owns stock (see Table 1–6). Millions more have other forms of wealth, such as savings accounts, pension plans, and life insurance policies.

TABLE 1–6   Who Owns Stock in American Business?

	1970	1983
Number of individual shareowners	30,850,000	42,360,000
Number owning shares listed on New York Stock Exchange	18,290,000	26,029,000
Adult shareholders in total population	1 in 4	1 in 4
Median household income	$13,500	$33,200
Number of adult female shareowners	14,290,000	20,385,000
Number of adult male shareowners	14,340,000	19,226,000

SOURCE: *1984 Fact Book*, New York Stock Exchange, 54.

SOCIALISM

Socialism is generally held to be *an economic system in which the country's major resources and industries are owned by the government*. These include minerals (coal, oil), communications (radio, telephone, television), transportation (railroads, airlines, shipping), utilities (gas, electricity), and major manufacturing establishments (steel, automobiles). Whereas under capitalism the government intervenes in business primarily to further competition (on the theory that competition enhances efficiency and stimulates progress), under socialism the government tries to eliminate most forms of competition (on the theory that competition is ruthless and wasteful).

Under socialism, individuals are permitted to own personal property, small businesses, and land, and they are free to choose their own occupations. However, because the major parts of the socialist economy are controlled by the state, government leaders have much greater power over industries than do government leaders in capitalistic countries.

WHAT ARE SOCIALISM'S ADVANTAGES?

Its advocates claim that socialism has four major advantages over capitalism. First, they believe socialism results in more stable employment. According to socialist theory, the government can control the number and types of jobs available, because it is free to regulate the kind and amount of goods and services provided.

Second, socialists argue that their system eliminates the wastes of competition. Socialists believe that capitalism encourages too many competing stores, factories, airlines, and other forms of business. They ask why there should be four competing stores in one shopping center when one would be sufficient. They contend that socialism is more efficient because it eliminates duplication of effort.

Third, advocates of socialism maintain that the system results in a more equitable distribution of wealth by maintaining large inheritance taxes, maximum wage ceilings, limitations on profits, and various other measures.

Fourth, proponents contend that socialism is better able to provide for the welfare of all the people. For example, they feel that it is the obligation of the state to provide hospital and medical care, housing, and transportation systems.

WHAT ARE SOCIALISM'S WEAKNESSES?

Critics of socialism say that it has three major weaknesses. First, government managers tend to be less efficient than managers in privately owned businesses, since many are appointed for political rather than business skills. Under capitalism, leaders are selected by the competitive process. Employees compete with employees until the best-qualified eventually direct the enterprise.

Second, even if government managers are competent, a sizable bureaucracy is needed to make, control, and administer the plans of the state. Such a bureaucracy tends to favor the status quo and is expensive to maintain—factors that may substantially reduce the efficiency of the system.

Third, socialism is less effective than capitalism in stimulating individual incentive. People generally work harder and produce more if they know they will reap the full rewards of their efforts. Thus, capitalism stimulates people to develop their skills and abilities. Under socialism, an "I don't care" attitude can develop because individual effort is not related directly to reward. This tends to result in laxness, a lessening of self-reliance, and less stress on innovation.

When socialism's weaknesses are pointed out to socialist supporters, they are inclined to reply that private enterprise pays too great a price for its superior productivity and efficiency. To make his point, a socialist from a Scandinavian country that is largely socialistic said, "If forced to choose, traditional [private] enterprise Americans would prefer property rights over human rights, competition over cooperation, secrecy over openness, technology requirements over human needs, and puritanism over hedonism. The ideal of socialism is to reverse these choices."

COMMUNISM

Under the *economic system* of **communism,** *all property and resources are owned by the government, and individuals have little economic freedom.* To an even greater degree than socialism, communism relies on a planned and controlled economic order. The U.S.S.R. and China, the leading communist nations, permit virtually no private ownership of property. The state dictates not only what will be produced but who will produce it and when.

WHAT ARE COMMUNISM'S ADVANTAGES?

Advocates of communism claim it results in equitable distribution of a nation's wealth, that there is even less wasted effort and inefficiency than under socialism, and that the system enables a nation to grow more rapidly because the government can ensure that wealth is invested in technology rather than spent on consumer products.

WHAT ARE COMMUNISM'S WEAKNESSES?

The chief weakness of communism is the severe limitation it places on individual freedom. The state allows little opportunity to remove those in power from office. Individuals must conform to what the state prescribes. Whereas capitalism makes each person a center of initiative, communism makes the individual a part in a vast plan. Under capitalism, consumers dictate to business what is to be provided in the marketplace; under communism, state planners dictate the nature of all economic activity.

Other weaknesses of communism include all those inherent in a planned state. Personal service is often poor because there is no incentive to urge customers to patronize a business. Government man-

TABLE 1–7 Comparison of Capitalism, Socialism, and Communism

ECONOMIC FACTORS	CAPITALISM	SOCIALISM	COMMUNISM
Ownership of production capacity	Private ownership under constitutional guarantee of certain inalienable human rights.	Basic industries, such as utilities, transportation, automobile production, and steel, are state-owned.	State owns all productive capacity.
Funds to finance capital investment	Dependent on citizen investments, business profits, and credit reliability of business.	Come from citizen investment in state bonds and from prices paid for goods.	Come from state-levied turnover taxes on all goods sold. Some limited interest bonds.
Incentives	Wages and profits in direct relationship to one's ability to compete in a free market.	Wages according to the principle, "From each according to his ability, to each according to his need." Some modest wage incentives.	Work norms plus bonuses for exceeding norms; appeals to produce effectively for glory of state; fear of legal action; public acclaim; medals.
Competition	Competition an inherent right established by custom and upheld by law. Determines efficiency, prices.	Basic production according to national economic plan. Privately owned industries sometimes pressured to comply with state plans.	Prohibited. State cooperation and state planning enforced by law. Legal action against competition.

agers are often ineffective, as they are under socialism. Furthermore, government agencies frequently fail to anticipate the amounts and types of products that will be needed. As a result, oversupplies of some goods and severe shortages of others often occur. Although this may also occur in a capitalistic economy, the private enterprise system seems to result in fewer gross errors in resource allocation.

Table 1–7 summarizes the differences among capitalism, socialism, and communism. These characteristics are generalizations and do not necessarily describe any particular economic system that exists in the world today. Every economic system is mixed to some degree; elements of capitalism are found in even the most communistic society, and vice versa.

U.S.A. Capitalism vs. Capitalism in Other Countries

Capitalism takes on different forms in different nations. The Canadian system is similar to our own. There, as here, the government operates essential services, such as defense, education, and the postal system. Business is given maximum freedom as long as it operates within the laws.

TABLE 1-7 (continued)

ECONOMIC FACTORS	CAPITALISM	SOCIALISM	COMMUNISM
Risks and losses	Assumed by private investors.	Assumed by the people of the entire state for state-owned industries. Losses are made up by taxes or higher prices.	Assumed without choice by the people of the entire state. Losses curtail standard of living.
Labor	Complete freedom in choosing place and kind of work.	Through planning, state attempts to encourage people to enter certain vocations and discourage them from entering others. People allowed free choice of kind of work.	Amount and kind of work ordinarily prescribed and provided by state. State the only employer. Legal action against individuals attempting to employ labor.
Management	Management selected largely on basis of ability. Must perform well and be accepted by employees to survive.	Stress put on nonmonetary incentives, prestige, privileges. Dangers of political bureaucracy inherent in management.	Party membership required of key managers. Political considerations cause management deficiencies. Authority backed by legal action. Highly bureaucratic.
Relation of government to business	Government's broad function is to foster individual initiative. Purpose of regulation is to promote competition.	State develops a master plan to which most economic activity is geared.	Government owns and operates all economic units according to plans.

The economy of Japan can be described as capitalism mixed with government paternalism. Almost all industry is privately owned, and the government provides "official guidance" to business and encourages it through beneficial tax policies, easy credit, and other assistance.

In Great Britain, France, and Italy, most means of production are privately owned and operated, but the government owns some key industries. In France, for example, the government develops national economic plans, which it tries to "sell" to private industry. In Great Britain, most steel and coal companies are owned by the government.

The economic system in Sweden could be called either welfare capitalism or private enterprise socialism. Private companies carry on an estimated 95 percent of the production, but income taxes are very high in order to support a great variety of social services.

American farmers using the private enterprise system and agricultural technology can amass land holdings while they feed vast numbers of people. In Communist communes many people live and work on publicly owned land to raise crops. Top: a farm in rural Wisconsin. Bottom: a commune in the Russian Ukraine.

CAN CAPITALISM WORK IN PLANNED ECONOMIES?

Private enterprise, a key distinguishing feature of capitalism, appears to work when practiced in planned or communist societies.[2] Hungary, a communist nation for decades, has adopted certain capitalistic

---

[2] See Frank Lipsiur's "Capitalism in the Soviet's Front Yard," *Business and Society Review,* Summer 1983, vol. 46, 57–61.

practices in recent years such as, (a) joining the International Monetary Fund (an international bank owned by participating nations which makes loans to developing countries); (b) engaging in a joint venture with Levi-Strauss to produce and market jeans; (c) licensing over 12,000 privately owned companies; (d) encouraging trade with capitalistic nations; and (e) permitting its farmers to engage in private enterprise at least in part. It is probably not coincidental that Hungary has the most successful communist economy.

Private enterprise is also being tried in the People's Republic of China. According to one report, "In the eight years since the death of Mao, Deng (the leader of China) has installed the revolutionary notion that people produce more if offered incentives. Without upheaval or fanfare, without blatant feuds at the top or bloody purges at the grass roots, Deng and his pragmatic colleagues have brought about the most sweeping reforms ever attempted under the banner of Marxism. They have transformed the nation's agricultural system, awakened its cultural life, and quintupled the income of millions of peasants. Their ambitions, moreover, seem almost limitless: They aim to quadruple the gross national product, double the nation's output of energy, and raise per capita annual income from the present $300 to $800 by the year 2000."

Not only have Chinese farmworkers been liberated from the cruel and often capricious authority of the "team leaders" who had previously supervised the communes; they have been given tangible inducements to work hard, earn more, and live well. In 1979, Deng introduced an "agricultural responsibility system," whereby China's 800 million peasants could contract with the state to sell a fixed amount of produce at a set price each year. After that level was reached, the workers could sell any surplus to the state at a markup of 50 percent—or, on the open market, at whatever price they could get. To swell production further, Deng hiked the price the government would pay for grain by 23 percent, while urging farmers to supplement their incomes by raising vegetables, poultry, or pigs on the side. Almost immediately, the incentive system began to pay off. Between 1978 and 1982, according to official reports, agricultural production grew at a steady annual rate of 7.5 percent.[3]

> **The American journey has not ended. America is never accomplished; America is always still to build.**
>
> ARCHIBALD MACLEISH

WILL CAPITALISM SURVIVE?

America's chief economic goal is to provide its citizens with economic opportunity and the highest standard of living possible. Historically, America has succeeded admirably in doing this. The ancestors of most Americans came to its shores because it was the Land of Golden Opportunity. In the past, the United States always led in productiv-

---

[3] Lyer, Pico. "Capitalism in the Making," *Time*, April 30, 1984, 26–28. Reported by David Aikman and Jaine A. Flor Cruz.

AMERICA'S REEMERGING CREATIVITY

The Revitalization of the United States

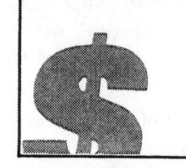

Have you ever wondered what happened to those men who signed the Declaration of Independence? Five were captured by the British as traitors. At least a dozen had their homes ransacked and burned. Two lost their sons in the Continental Army. Another had two sons captured. Several took part in various battles of the American Revolution, and many suffered wounds or other physical hardships.

What kind of men were they? Twenty-five were lawyers or jurists. Eleven were merchants. Nine were farmers or large plantation owners. These were men of means and education. Yet they signed the Declaration ... knowing full well that the penalty could be death if they were captured.... They pledged their lives, their fortunes, and their sacred honor to the cause of freedom and independence.

Richard Stockton returned to New Jersey in the fall of 1776 to find the state overrun by the enemy. He removed his wife to safety but was himself captured. His home, his fine library, his writings—all were destroyed. Stockton was so badly treated in prison that his health was ruined, and he died before the war's end.

Carter Braxton was a wealthy planter and trader. One by one his ships were captured by the British Navy. He loaned a large sum of money to the American cause; it was never paid back. He was forced to sell his plantations and mortgage his other properties to pay his debts.

Thomas McKean was so hounded by the British that he had to move his family almost constantly. He served in the Continental Congress without pay, and kept his family in hiding.

Vandals or soldiers or both looted the properties of Ellery, Clymer, Hall, Heyward, Middleton, Harrison, Hopkinson and Livingston.

At the Battle of Yorktown, [the American patriot] Thomas Nelson, Jr., noted that the British General Cornwallis had taken over the family home for his headquarters. Nelson urged General George Washington to open fire on his own home. This was done, and the home was destroyed. Nelson later died bankrupt.

Francis Lewis also had his home and properties destroyed. The enemy jailed his wife for two months, and that and other hardships from the war so affected her health she died only two years later.

'Honest John' Hart was driven from his wife's bedside when she was near death. Their thirteen children fled for their lives. Hart's fields and his grist mill were laid waste. While eluding capture, ... he often slept in forests and caves. When he returned home, he found that his wife had died, and his children were gone.

Such are the stories and sacrifices typical of those who risked everything to sign the Declaration of Independence. These men were not wild-eyed, rabble-rousing ruffians. They were soft-spoken men of means and education. They had security, but they valued liberty more.*

The signers of the Declaration and others like them sacrificed much to give us an independent America. Sometimes, though, particularly in the areas of the economy and business, our creativity and foresight have not matched theirs. For instance, we have allowed our productivity to lag, our supply of energy to depend on others, our sense of teamwork to diminish, our national economic goals to become confused.

However, a renaissance spirit is now sweeping the land. The country is becoming infused with enthusiasm for **revitalization,** *or turning the country around economically*. This feature of the book will present key concepts and technologies that will help us achieve that goal.

"What's ailing U.S. industry?" is a common question these days. Thoughtful answers focus on America's "thrust to innovate" and the "dampening of America's entrepreneurial spirit." *Business Week* points out that "the flood of new products is dwindling and there is a fear that the U.S. may be reaching the bottom of its technological cornucopia." It quotes Allan H. Skaggs, director of the research center of the Aerospace Industry Association of America: "It is abundantly evident that U.S. technological innovation and productivity are on the decline." Thus the crux of the nation's revitalization lies in restoring creativity and the traditional entrepreneurial spirit.

Questions for Discussion

1. What is the entrepreneurial spirit? How can you foster it in yourself and others?
2. Is creativity a special gift that only certain people have, or can it be fostered in everyone?
3. What is especially significant in the remarks quoted?
4. Describe the kind of environment in which you believe creativity and the entrepreneurial spirit flourish best.
5. How is entrepreneurship related to personal happiness? Explain.

*Adapted from The Price They Paid (San Mateo, Calif.: National Federation of Independent Business Research and Education Foundation).

---

ity, thereby delivering a higher standard of living to more people than any other nation. **Productivity** is a nation's *output per hour of work*. It is a measure of an economy's efficiency and its ability to compete with other nations.

In the 1980s, the United States is still outproducing and outconsuming all other economies. However, in the 1970s, the country's annual rate of productivity growth started to lag. It slipped from being number one in the world to number seven, and the value of the dollar plunged in world markets. Because it took more dollars to buy the

The signers of the Declaration of Independence, although educated men of means with social and financial security, were willing to take great personal risks to attain the liberty they valued above all else.

TABLE 1-8 Private Enterprise: It Makes a Difference

COMMODITY	APPROXIMATE WORK TIME REQUIRED TO BUY*		
	WASHINGTON	LONDON	MOSCOW
Milk (1 liter)	7 minutes	9 minutes	18 minutes
Hamburger meat, beef (1 kg)	43 minutes	57 minutes	128 minutes
Sausages, pork (1 kg)	31 minutes	43 minutes	145 minutes
Potatoes (1 kg)	2 minutes	4 minutes	7 minutes
Apples, eating (1 kg)	11 minutes	15 minutes	40 minutes
Sugar (1 kg)	5 minutes	11 minutes	59 minutes
White bread (1 KG)	8 minutes	12 minutes	18 minutes
Eggs (10)	10 minutes	20 minutes	99 minutes
Vodka (0.5 liter)	52 minutes	161 minutes	380 minutes
Cigarettes (20)	9 minutes	22 minutes	23 minutes
Weekly food basket for four people	12.5 hours	21.4 hours	42.3 hours
Soap, toilet (150 grams)	5 minutes	6 minutes	23 minutes
Lipstick	26 minutes	50 minutes	72 minutes[†]
Panty hose	22 minutes	11 minutes	427 minutes[†]
Men's leather shoes	8 hours	11 hours	33 hours
Man's business suit	20 hours	25 hours	68 hours
Refrigerator, small (120 liters)	43 hours	35 hours	208 hours
Color TV set, large (59 cm screen)	86 hours	177 hours	713 hours
Automobile (Ford Fairline/Granada/Volga GAZ-24)	4.1 months	8.5 months	35 months

SOURCE: "What's the Difference?" (San Mateo, California: National Federation of Independent Business, Research and Education Foundation, 1979).

*Based on prices in retail stores in Washington, D.C., and London, and on state-fixed prices in Moscow during March 1979. Work time is based on average take-home pay of male and female manufacturing workers. Income taxes, Social Security taxes (U.S. and U.K.), health insurance premiums (U.S. and U.K.), and unemployment insurance (U.K. only) have been deducted from wages; family allowances (U.K. and U.S.S.R.) have been added for a family of four. In dollars, hourly take-home pay in January 1979 was $4.61 for American workers, $3.25 for British workers, and $1.38 for Russian workers.

[†] Some items, such as lipstick and panty hose, could not be found by any surveyor in Moscow in any state retail store at the time of the survey. The price given is that seen in the past.

currencies of most other economically strong countries, the dollar bought less in those countries. This poses an intriguing question: Which economic systems threaten to surpass that of the United States, and why?

Communism, the economic system embraced by many countries starting with the Russian Revolution in 1917, has never proved itself capable of releasing people's creative energies and of effectively using human, capital, and material resources to match or even approach the economic achievements of private enterprise societies.

The productivity records of labor governments, which lean heavily toward socialism, as in Scandinavia, Italy, and Great Britain, are also less than impressive.

Significantly, countries that have surpassed the United States in annual productivity increases, such as Japan and West Germany, are those with strong governments that facilitate labor and management working together, curb business excesses, and provide economic leadership while encouraging private enterprise.

Table 1-8 shows how much more effective our capitalistic private enterprise system is in delivering a standard of living than are the British system (heavily influenced by socialism) and the Russian system (essentially pure communism). In the United States, it takes less work time to buy all the items shown except for small refrigerators and panty hose!

Most business leaders firmly believe that America's lag in productivity and loss of position on the international scene is only temporary. The U.S. economic system has produced miracles in the past, and it will do so again. It is reassuring that young people in America are again fired up with an interest in entrepreneurship. A major thrust throughout this book will be to focus on the entrepreneur and creativity, America's hope for the future.

SUMMARY

- A "business" is any commercial establishment that provides goods or services. The term "business" also refers to the commercial life of the nation.

- Key factors that contribute to our high standard of living are technology, effective marketing, competition, and our economic philosophy.

- Under private enterprise, individuals have the rights to own property, compete freely, sell goods and services in a free market, be an entrepreneur, and choose an occupation.

- Private enterprise is also characterized by an emphasis on profits, minimum government direction, and assumption of risk by individuals.

- Economic systems can be divided into three categories: capitalism, socialism, and communism. Under capitalism, most of the capital is owned by private individuals. Under socialism, most major resources and industries are owned by the state. Under communism, nearly all resources and industries are owned by the state.

- Capitalism continues to have a bright future because it encourages entrepreneurship; competing systems have not been particularly successful.

- Entrepreneurs are crucial to the American economy. Although possessing diverse personalities, they have two things in common: initiative and inspiration.

KEY TERMS YOU SHOULD KNOW

business
capital
communism
competition
demand-side economics
distribution business
entrepreneur
free market
gross national product (GNP)

laissez faire
law of supply and demand
national resources
per capita income
private enterprise system
   (capitalism)
production business
productivity
profit

profit principle
qualitative standard
   of living
quantitative standard
   of living
revitalization
service business
socialism
supply-side economics

QUESTIONS FOR REVIEW

1. What is the difference between a *quantitative* standard of living and a *qualitative* standard of living?
2. What factors contribute to the high quantitative standard of living enjoyed in the United States?
3. Mention and explain each of the five basic rights guaranteed under our private enterprise system.
4. In addition to the five basic rights of private enterprise, what are the other characteristics of our system?
5. What are the advantages and disadvantages of socialism, communism, and capitalism?
6. Compare capitalism, socialism, and communism in terms of (a) ownership of production capacity, (b) funds to finance capital investment, (c) incentives, (d) competition, (e) risks and losses, (f) labor, (g) management, and (h) the relation of government to business.
7. Describe how private enterprise has been used successfully in Hungary and the People's Republic of China.

QUESTIONS FOR DISCUSSION

1. Given a choice between a high quantitative standard of living and a high qualitative standard of living, which would you choose? Why?
2. What specifically do you feel the United States should do to improve its qualitative standard of living?
3. Despite its economic superiority in many respects, the United States does not lead the world in life expectancy and number of people per physician (see Table 1–3). Why, do you think, is this so?
4. Which is a fairer and more efficient way to spend the GNP: to let individuals spend it the way they wish or to let the government spend it on programs such as Medicare, food stamps, public housing, and so on? How does this relate to supply- and demand-side economics?
5. Do you think that any one of the five basic individual rights on which the private enterprise system is based is more important than the others? Why or why not?
6. A recent development at universities is the establishment of chairs or institutes devoted to the study of private enterprise and financed by corporations. Consider the pros and cons of this idea, and explain why you are for or against it.
7. Some automobiles, such as the Volvo (Sweden) and the Renault (France), are made by automobile companies that are owned by the government. How can these products made in socialist countries compete favorably with American-made cars?

CASE STUDY

How a Foreigner Views Contemporary America

Lars Jensson, a native of Sweden, has been studying business at an American college for two years. He is about to go home. The following discussion takes place between Lars and Alfred Miller, his closest American friend.

Alfred: Now that you've been here two years, what are your impressions of America?
Lars: It's a great country. I was impressed with how well middle- and upper-middle-income families live. Some suburban areas I visited were unbelievably nice and well cared for. And some of the resorts I visited in Florida and California equal the Riviera.
A: You must have some negative impressions of the States. What are they?
L: Well, I feel Americans are too occupied with making money. People are judged not by what they do but by the size of their homes, the kinds of cars they own, and where they eat out. Preoccupation with money is so bad in the United States that people don't seem to enjoy life.
A: You mean an American is a somebody if he drives a Volvo and a nobody if he drives a Ford?
L: *(laughing)* Oh, we're glad to sell you Volvos! But I just think Americans go to extremes in seeking a high standard of living.
A: I know you're aware that the United States has a lot of unemployment. What are your views on that?
L: It surprises me that you have any. Every daily newspaper I read while I was here had jobs, jobs, and more jobs advertised. I think your welfare system is too liberal.
A: I'm surprised to hear you say that. After all, you come from a socialist country.
L: Yes, but in Sweden able-bodied workers work. In the States there are so many loopholes that people who don't want to work can still collect benefits.
A: A moment ago, you said Americans are too occupied with making money. Now you're telling me that some Americans are content to live off welfare.
L: What I meant to say was that many Americans—the achievers—put too much emphasis on making money. Some of them have two jobs—that really surprised me.
A: I know you worked full-time two summers and part-time while you were taking classes. What were your impressions of American workers?
L: Well, the work I did was unskilled, so I didn't have an opportunity to observe skilled workers and managers firsthand. But what I saw on the assembly line disappointed me. Nobody did any more than was required. The American workers I saw lacked pride in their work. And absenteeism was very high. I believe you Americans need to improve the work ethic.

Questions

1. What are your reactions to Lars's believing that Americans are too occupied with making money?
2. Lars thinks that a liberal welfare system is a cause of unemployment. Do you agree with him? Explain.
3. Do you agree with Lars that we need to improve the work ethic?
4. On the overall, how would you differ from Lars in sizing up the pros and cons of America?

EVOLUTION OF A BUSINESS

Birth of a New Business Idea

Sara Emden and Ray Laski met on a flight back from a trip to South America. They happened to sit next to each other and found that they both lived in the same Ohio city. Sara, who was 27, had majored in accounting in college and had been working as an auditor for the Internal Revenue Service for the last five years. Ray, 32 years old, had majored in history and had worked as a reporter for a large newspaper for several years. He now was working in public relations, as a media contact executive for one of the country's largest automobile manufacturers.

Sara and Ray soon discovered that they had more in common than living in the same city. They were both restless in their present jobs. Sara found working for the government stifling; she disliked the fixed procedures and repetitive nature of the work. Ray had a somewhat similar complaint. "I'm just not an 'organization man,'" he said. "Everything has to be done the company's way, and I'm not happy unless I'm doing things my own way."

They also shared a dissatisfaction with the travel agencies they had used for the South America trip. The two exchanged "horror stories" for a while—misleading advertisements, bad accommodations, extra charges tacked on unexpectedly—and then had the following conversation.

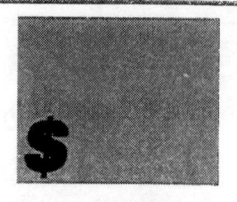

Note: A special feature titled "Evolution of a Business" appears at the end of each chapter. It is the continuing story of an imaginary business and how it evolves. Each installment portrays a business situation that relates to some degree to the subject matter in the chapter. The questions that follow the feature introduce you to the decision-making process and realistically involve you in the problems that business people face.

Ray: Every travel agency I've dealt with in our hometown appears to be badly run. It seems like somebody could make a lot of money if they just ran an agency that was halfway competent.

Sara: You're right. I think even you and I could do better, and we don't know anything about the business.

Ray: It's an interesting idea. You know, as dissatisfied as I've been with my work lately, I've never thought of starting my own company. I know that's how the country works—even the huge company I work for now started small—but it never seemed like a realistic option.

The two got caught up in the idea and spent the remaining four hours of the flight talking about how they would run "their" travel agency if they did begin one.

Questions

1. Are the backgrounds of Sara and Ray generally suitable for going into business? What questions should they be asking themselves? (See Application to Personal Affairs, page 14.)
2. How can they determine whether the travel agency business in particular is a good one to enter?
3. What are Sara's limitations and strengths, in that she has worked only for the government?
4. What are Ray's limitations and strengths, in that he has worked only for large corporations?

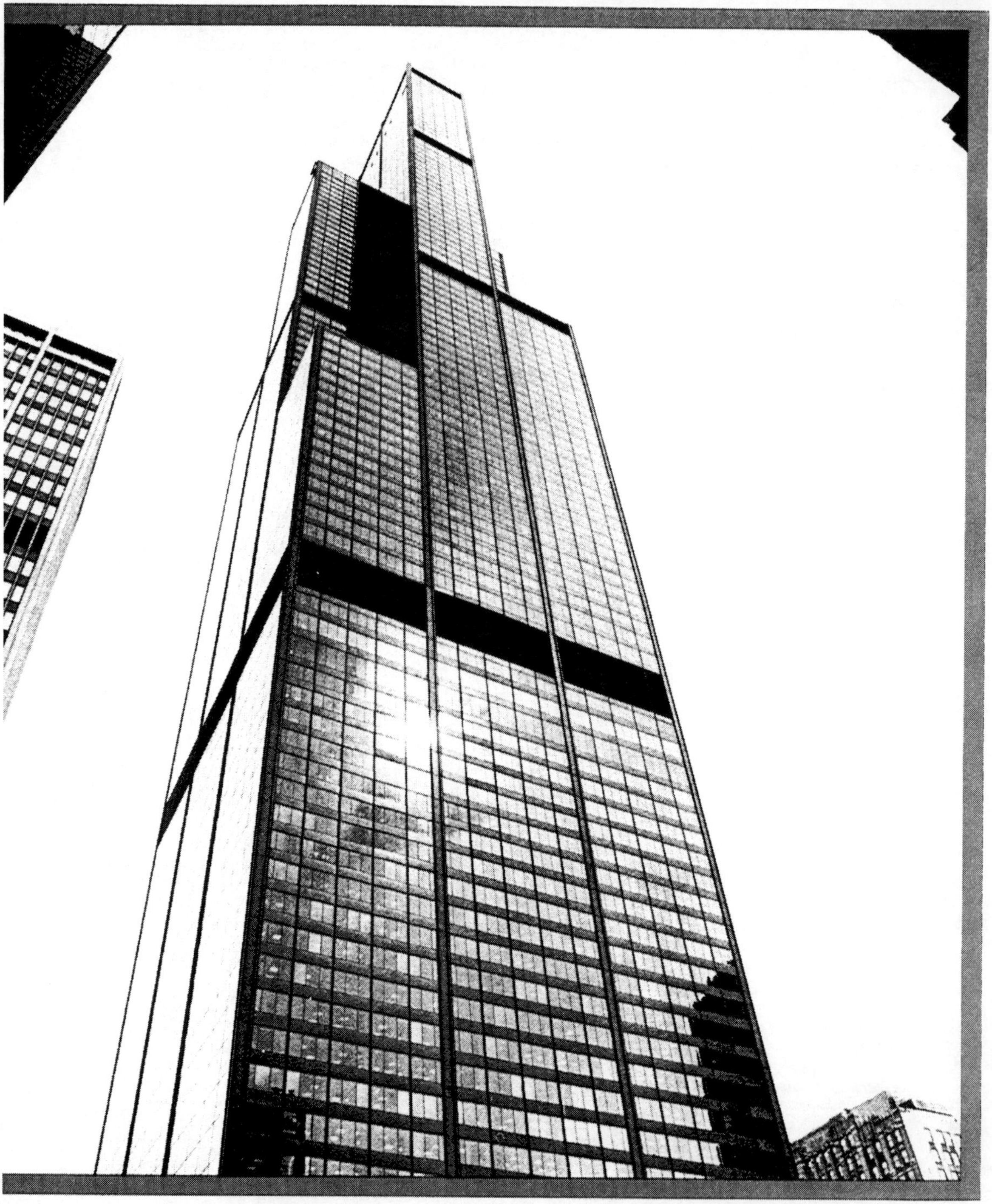

2

PROPRIETORSHIPS, PARTNERSHIPS, AND CORPORATIONS

Ownership Choices: You Decide

READ THIS CHAPTER SO YOU CAN:

Discuss the advantages and disadvantages of the sole proprietorship.

Discuss what matters should be covered in the partnership agreement, and explain the pros and cons of the general partnership.

Define "limited partnership," and discuss how it is used in business.

Describe the various types of corporations and the advantages and disadvantages of the corporate form of ownership.

List and explain what must be taken into account in forming a corporation.

Discuss the role of stockholders in a corporation.

Define and describe cooperatives.

A person who is thinking of starting a business must answer one key question: "What should the form of ownership be?" That is, should the business be organized as a sole proprietorship, a partnership, or a corporation?

There is no one ideal form of business ownership. Each has advantages and drawbacks, and the best choice depends on the particular circumstances. If you were considering setting up a business, you would need answers to questions such as:

- Which form of ownership is the simplest and involves the least red tape?
- What would the initial legal fees be for each form?
- What about legal liability? Would my creditors be able to take my car, house, or savings if the business fails?
- Which type of ownership would be best if I need to raise additional capital?
- Which form is best if I want to expand my business someday?
- What would happen to the ownership of the business if I die or divorce?
- Which form makes it easiest to sell the business later on?
- What are the tax advantages and disadvantages of each form?

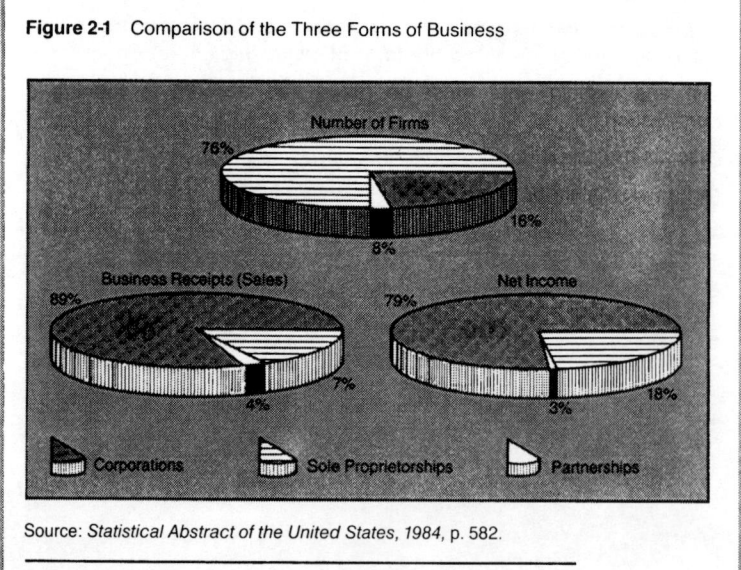

Figure 2-1 Comparison of the Three Forms of Business

Number of Firms: 76% Sole Proprietorships, 16% Corporations, 8% Partnerships

Business Receipts (Sales): 89% Corporations, 7% Sole Proprietorships, 4% Partnerships

Net Income: 79% Corporations, 18% Partnerships, 3% Sole Proprietorships

Source: *Statistical Abstract of the United States, 1984*, p. 582.

Note: Data based on tax returns filed by 16,793,000 businesses.

The three most common forms of ownership are the *sole proprietorship,* the *partnership,* and the *corporation.* Before we discuss their features, we'll consider how each one fits into the American economy. As Figure 2–1 shows, sole proprietorships are most numerous (76 percent). However, corporations account for most business receipts (89 percent) and net income (79 percent), and have by far the highest net income per firm.

In addition, we find that most businesses are small (Table 2–1).

TABLE 2–1 Classification of 16,793,000 Business Firms by Receipts, 1984

RECEIPTS	NUMBER OF FIRMS	PERCENT OF FIRMS	PERCENT OF RECEIPTS
Under $25,000	8,028,000	57.9	.67
$25,000–49,000	1,474,000	10.6	.73
$50,000–99,999	1,352,000	9.8	1.3
$100,000–499,999	2,068,000	14.9	6.3
$500,000–999,999	423,000	3.1	4.1
$1,000,000 or more	512,000	3.7	86.9

SOURCE: *Statistical Abstract of the United States, 1985,* 516.

Many entrepreneurs and sole proprietors have offices and light manufacturing plants in industrial parks. Such parks provide reasonably priced centralized space for diversified industry on relatively low-cost land in areas surrounding major cities.

In 1984, 57 percent had receipts of under $25,000, and more than 78 percent had less than $100,000 receipts. In 1984, businesses with receipts of $1,000,000 or more accounted for only 3.7 percent of all firms and 86.9 percent of all receipts. Of the more than 16 million enterprises that make up our business population, a large share are part-time or sideline ventures. The owners of such businesses usually hold another job, and take care of their own business in their spare time.

RUNNING A BUSINESS ALONE: THE SOLE PROPRIETORSHIP

A **sole proprietorship**—also called **single proprietorship, individual proprietorship**, or, simply, **proprietorship**—is *a business owned by a single person who receives all profits and assumes all risks*. Sole proprietors are often referred to as "self-employed." Usually they are also active managers.

Sole proprietorship is the oldest form of business organization. It is also the easiest type of business to start, operate, and dissolve—which accounts for its being the most common form of ownership. It is especially common in retailing, personal services, and agricultural industries.

What Are the Pros of Sole Proprietorship?

SIMPLICITY OF ORGANIZATION

To illustrate the simplicity of establishing a sole proprietorship, let us suppose you decide that your community needs an outdoor fruit market. You rent a vacant stand and purchase a supply of fruit; you are now in business as a sole proprietor. No state charter, legal agreement, or other "red tape" is involved. A state or city license may be required. The only other requirement for starting a sole proprietorship is that the activity be legal.

FREEDOM AND FLEXIBILITY

The sole proprietor has maximum freedom in making business decisions. The sole proprietor of an apparel store, for example, can make decisions about quantity, quality, and prices without consulting anyone else. Because no other people are legally involved, the sole proprietor can also take action more promptly than partners and corporate executives normally can. The owner can quickly change his or her method of doing business to meet changes in competition, consumer buying habits, and economic conditions.

For example, Don Palmer, the sole proprietor of Don's Fruit Market, can act quickly because he has no absentee owner or partner to consult. He switched produce shipments coming from a nearby city to a neighbor's truck almost immediately when he heard that his neighbor returned from the city with it empty each day and would be willing to carry a return load of fruit at half the regular rate. The chain store competing with Don's Fruit Market would not have such flexibility.

MAXIMUM INCENTIVE

Sole proprietors are very aware that the business is *their* business. Since all profits go to them, they are encouraged to work hard, exercise close supervision over their businesses, make decisions carefully, and expand operations.

Sole proprietors often work 60 to 70 hours a week and enjoy doing so. These may be the same people who complained about work-

This sole proprietor can call his own shots on how, where, and what he markets. He can set prices to beat his competition and offer unique services.

AMERICA'S REEMERGING CREATIVITY

Fueling the Creative Spirit

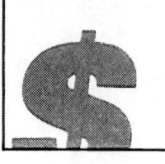

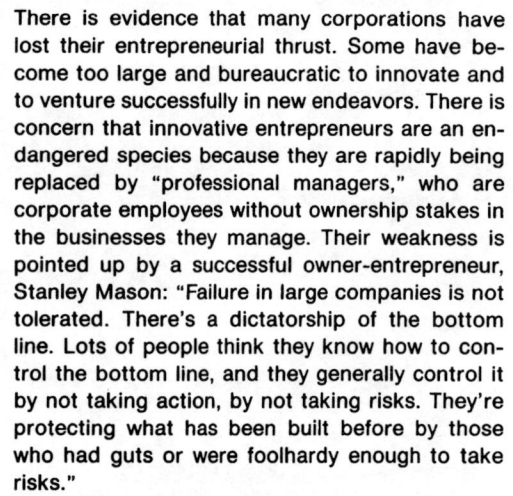

There is evidence that many corporations have lost their entrepreneurial thrust. Some have become too large and bureaucratic to innovate and to venture successfully in new endeavors. There is concern that innovative entrepreneurs are an endangered species because they are rapidly being replaced by "professional managers," who are corporate employees without ownership stakes in the businesses they manage. Their weakness is pointed up by a successful owner-entrepreneur, Stanley Mason: "Failure in large companies is not tolerated. There's a dictatorship of the bottom line. Lots of people think they know how to control the bottom line, and they generally control it by not taking action, by not taking risks. They're protecting what has been built before by those who had guts or were foolhardy enough to take risks."

Fortunately, since 1980 there is evidence of a renewed dedication to innovation through research and development. The following 15 firms together spent more than $15 billion in 1982 on exploring ways to increase productivity, improve products, and experiment with new ideas:*

General Motors	$2,175,000,000
ATT	2,126,000,000
IBM	2,053,000,000
Ford Motor	1,764,000,000
Du Pont	879,000,000
United Technologies	834,000,000
General Electric	781,000,000
Eastman Kodak	710,000,000
Exxon	707,000,000
Boeing	691,000,000
Xerox	565,000,000
ITT	519,000,000
Dow Chemical	460,000,000
Hewlett-Packard	424,000,000
Sperry	398,000,000

In a very real sense, the destiny of American business—and our standard of living—relates directly to how much money is committed to research and development (R & D). Money spent on R & D is an investment in everyone's future.

Questions for Discussion

1. Is America's new interest in R & D based on economic considerations, a new confidence, or on other factors?
2. What motivates a business to spend money on R & D since the pay-off—if there is any—may be years away?
3. Are investors who want profits paid out as dividends shortchanged by firms that invest in R & D?

*Business Week, June 20, 1983, 63.

---

ing 40 hours a week before they became self-employed. In this sense, the sole proprietorship functions as the ideal private enterprise system.

LOW ORGANIZATIONAL COSTS

Organizational costs of a sole proprietorship are low, frequently amounting to almost nothing. Corporations must purchase legal services to get established and pay fees for securing a charter from the state; partnerships may bear the expense of legal agreements. Sole proprietorships incur neither expense.

What Are the Cons of Sole Proprietorship?

DIFFICULTY IN RAISING CAPITAL

A serious disadvantage of the sole proprietorship is the difficulty involved in raising capital to start and expand business operations. Capital comes from the proprietor's own investment plus what can be borrowed from banks, friends, relatives, and other sources. While the sole proprietor may have a favorable credit standing, banks often will not lend more to an individual than the value of his or her personal assets. The sole proprietor cannot attract investors by sharing the ownership of the business, as a partnership or corporation can. Also, because the sole proprietor's credit rating is usually not as high as that of a larger firm, he or she must pay a higher interest rate on borrowed money.

Once the sole proprietorship is in operation, it may be expanded through reinvestment of part or all of its profits. But even when the business is quite successful, profits alone are usually insufficient to fund rapid expansion. Thus, a sole proprietor who wishes to expand operations significantly will usually change to some other form of business ownership, and obtain investment capital from his or her new partners.

LIMITED LIFE

Sole proprietorships are legally terminated in the event of death, bankruptcy, imprisonment, or insanity of the owner. Many are ended each year because of the proprietor's disability or advanced age. The sole proprietorship is often so much a one-person business that it is profitable only so long as the owner is active. Because of the uncertain life of the sole proprietorship, banks or other businesses are generally unwilling to make long-term financial commitments with the sole proprietor.

UNLIMITED LIABILITY OF OWNER

Some firms are more willing to lend money to an individual whose personal property can be attached in the event of business failure. This type of agreement, called **unlimited liability,** often enables a sole proprietor to gain credit more easily. However, unlimited liability is a major disadvantage if the business fails, since the owner risks losing most of his or her personal savings and possessions. This risk discourages many people from going into business for themselves and often prompts those who do establish a sole proprietorship to seek another type of ownership.

LACK OF SPECIALIZED MANAGEMENT

Typically, the sole proprietor performs all the managerial functions in the business. More often than not, the owner serves simultaneously as general manager, sales manager, advertising manager, accountant, personnel manager, and purchasing agent. Few people are qualified by training, personality, intelligence, and inclination to perform all these tasks effectively. As a result, one or more phases of the business suffer or are neglected. Managerial assistance from employees is usually limited, because employees with specialized skills or those with managerial talents tend not to take jobs in businesses that have limited opportunities for advancement.

OPERATIONAL PROBLEMS

Because of the difficulty of acquiring enough capital, certain operational problems may be more acute in sole proprietorships than in other forms of business ownership. Some of these are poor location; inadequate buildings and equipment; inability to pay wages that attract the most productive, ambitious employees; and inability to purchase merchandise in large enough volume to secure quantity discounts.

> "Ambition is the fuel of achievement."
>
> JOSEPH EPSTEIN

RUNNING A BUSINESS WITH OTHERS: THE GENERAL AND THE LIMITED PARTNERSHIP

A **general partnership** is *a legal relationship between two or more persons who co-own a business for profit and who have unlimited liability for the business' debts.* Most general partnerships have only two or three members, although there is no limit to the number of individuals who can form one. While the members of a general partnership may agree to divide profits and losses in any manner they like, in the absence of a specific agreement they are presumed to share them equally. Nor is it essential that each partner contribute an equal amount of capital. In some instances, a partner contributes no capital but is brought into the organization because of his or her skill or specialized knowledge. Partnerships, like sole proprietorships, are found primarily in retailing, agriculture, and services such as law, accounting, and medicine. The partnership is not well suited to large businesses.

The Partnership Agreement

Fundamental to all partnerships is an agreement among the members. A **partnership agreement** is *an oral, written, or implied (by actions of the parties) agreement among partners as to the specifics of the business.* The agreement should be written to avoid later misunderstandings, but an oral or implied agreement can be binding. The partnership agreement should specify the name of the partnership, the names of each partner, the kind of business to be conducted, the location of the business, the authority of each partner, the duration of the agreement, the amount invested by each person, the way in which profits and losses will be shared and how partners will be compensated, the limitations on the amount of capital that can be withdrawn by a partner, the accounting procedures to be used, the method of resolving disagreements, and the procedures for dissolving the partnership.

What Are the Pros of General Partnership?

FINANCIAL STRENGTH

Compared with the sole proprietorship, the general partnership is normally stronger financially because (1) two or more persons are usually able to invest more money in a business than one person is, and (2) the personal property and other wealth of every partner is subject to attachment should the partnership be unable to meet its obligations.

MORE MANAGEMENT KNOW-HOW

Unlike the sole proprietor, partners can share managerial functions. Often partnerships pool the talents of people with contrasting skills and abilities. For example, one partner may be an expert accountant and purchasing manager, while the other may be well qualified in marketing. Division of duties in accordance with the special qualifications of each partner helps to build a more efficient organization.

SIMPLICITY OF ORGANIZATION

Partnerships are only slightly more difficult to organize than sole proprietorships. Essentially, all that is needed is an agreement between the partners. While legal assistance is desirable in preparing the agreement, it is not mandatory. State approval is not required, and usually no taxes are levied specifically against partnerships. Dissolving a partnership is also simple.

MAXIMUM INCENTIVE

The partnership also retains much of the individual incentive found in the sole proprietorship—what is beneficial to the partnership is also beneficial to each partner.

What Are the Cons of General Partnership?

UNLIMITED LIABILITY FOR INDEBTEDNESS

The main disadvantage of a general partnership is the unlimited liability of each partner. If one partner is unable to assume his or her full share of a loss, the other partners may be required to make good the deficit.

DIVIDED AUTHORITY

The fact that each partner has a voice in the management of the business has disadvantages. The possibility of disagreements means that decisions are often more difficult to reach. Employees sometimes become confused when they receive conflicting instructions from the partners. Also, because one partner can act on behalf of the business, there is a danger that private commitments will be made by one partner without the sanction of the others.

POSSIBILITY OF MUTUAL DISTRUST

A very high degree of mutual respect among partners is necessary for a partnership to function smoothly. A major mistake by any one partner can destroy the personal fortunes of the others. Unless all persons involved have full confidence in one another's honesty and business ability, a feeling of uneasiness may result. (*See* Compatibility: A Necessary Ingredient for a Business Partnership.)

LACK OF PERMANENCE

The partnership is the least permanent form of business. The death or withdrawal of a partner terminates the partnership; the remaining partners may reorganize and form a new partnership, sole proprietorship, or corporation, but in practice this is not usually done. In some cases, the remaining partner or partners lack the financial resources to buy the deceased or withdrawing partner's interest. Because of this uncertainty, other businesses may be reluctant to make long-term commitments with the partnership.

Is a Limited Partnership Better?

A **limited partnership** is *an agreement between one or more general partners, whose liability is unlimited, and one or more special, or limited, partners, whose liability is limited to the amount of capital they have contributed to the firm unless otherwise stated in the agreement.* Thus, the limited partnership is not handicapped by the unlimited liability of all the partners.

A formal agreement is always required in the formation of a limited partnership. This agreement must be filed with an appropriate public official—usually the county clerk—and must name the general partners and the limited partners. It is impossible to form a limited partnership without at least one general partner.

Limited partners cannot perform any managerial functions. If they do, the courts recognize them as general partners, and their liability becomes unlimited. Further, a limited partnership may vary from one state to another. If a limited partnership wishes to do business in another state, it must comply with the statutes of that state or the limited partners will be considered general partners there.

> ### APPLICATION TO PERSONAL AFFAIRS
>
> Compatibility: A Necessary Ingredient for a Business Partnership
>
> Incompatibility between marriage partners is highly visible since 50 percent of all marriages end in divorce. What is less visible is the quarreling, feuding, and bickering that damages many business relationships, especially partnerships. Business partners have been known to engage in physical fights or go without speaking for months—even years.
>
> Partners may quarrel over such things as what products the firm should sell, division of authority, selection of personnel, whether to bring family members into the business, and whether to expand. A very common area for disagreement is who is contributing most to the success (or failure) of the enterprise.
>
> Quarrels between business associates have become so common that a new form of therapy has evolved, called "business dispute therapy." Psychologists, working with lawyers, function much the same as marriage counselors, and encourage partners to either reconcile their differences or terminate their business relationship in a mutually satisfactory way. Two suggestions business therapists offer to potential business partners are: (1) choose a partner whose interests, personality, and abilities are different from yours, and (2) at the beginning of the relationship, develop a fair method whereby each partner can buy out the interests of the other partner.*
>
> ---
> *For an informative discussion of dealing with partnership conflicts, see Robert A. Mamis, Sparring Partners, *INC*, March 1984, 43–50.

The major advantage of the limited partnership is that it tends to attract people who can contribute capital to the partnership. As limited partners, they risk only their original investment. Many oil exploration companies and real estate development firms, which involve considerable risk, sell limited partnerships, perhaps in units of $5,000. In this way, the general partners can raise needed capital, and investors can become limited partners in speculative activities with a fixed potential loss.

RUNNING A BUSINESS UNDER A CHARTER: THE CORPORATION

The most widely accepted definition of a **corporation** is that given by Chief Justice John Marshall in 1819, "A corporation is *an artificial being, invisible, intangible, and existing only in the contemplation of law. Being the mere creature of law, it possesses only those properties which the charter of its creation confers upon it, either expressly or as incidental to its existence.*"[1] That is, it is *a legal entity that has certain characteristics, rights, and obligations as set forth in the charter that created it.*

---
[1]*Dartmouth College* v. *Woodward,* 4 Wheaton 518 (1819).

The corporation is granted many of the same rights as individuals. These include the rights to own, mortgage, and dispose of property; to manage its own affairs; and to sue. Like an individual, the corporation may also be sued.

People desiring to form a corporation apply for a **corporation charter,** *a document granted by the state that explains in some detail the rights and privileges of the corporation.* The corporation has continuous life for the period specified in its charter (usually 35 years) or, if no limit is indicated, for perpetuity.

Types of Corporations

PUBLIC AND PRIVATE CORPORATIONS

A corporation whose stock is offered for sale to the general public is known as a **public corporation.** *A corporation whose stock is not offered for sale to the public is called a* **private,** *or* **nonpublic, corporation.**[2] Some businesses begin as private corporations with only a few stockholders, each of whom is active in the management of the business. Then, as the business shows promise of success and additional capital is needed, the corporation may decide to become public by selling shares to other investors.

Most corporations are private. However, practically all large corporations are public—it is generally advantageous to a corporation for its stock, or shares, to be widely owned.

NONPROFIT CORPORATIONS

Not all corporations are organized for the purpose of making a profit. A corporation can be formed for any legal purpose; its rationale need not be economic. *A corporation that facilitates the operation of a nonprofit organization* is called a **nonprofit corporation.** There are tens of thousands of nonprofit corporations—including municipalities, churches, fraternities, cooperatives, trade associations, foundations, societies, and political parties (see Chapter 22). The principal reasons nonprofit organizations incorporate are to (1) provide legal protection for their members, (2) qualify for nontaxable status, and (3) better organize and direct its operations.

CONGLOMERATES

A **conglomerate** is simply *a corporation made up of a number of previously independent companies* called *subsidiaries.* An example would be Heublein, a company that is mainly involved in wines and liquors, which has Kentucky Fried Chicken as a subsidiary. Another

---

[2]The New York Stock Exchange prefers the use of the terms "public" and "private" as opposed to the former "open" and "closed," respectively.

example is the New York Mets, a subsidiary of Doubleday since 1980. Typically, conglomerate headquarters provides general guidance for the operation of the subsidiary units, while top executives in the individual companies provide specific management direction.

What Are the Pros of Corporations?

LIMITED LIABILITY OF OWNERS

A very serious weakness of the sole proprietorship and the general partnership is the problem of unlimited liability. This disadvantage is eliminated under the corporate form of organization. *Owners of a corporation,* called **stockholders** or **shareholders,** can, in most cases, lose no more than the value of their investment. Thus, if a person purchases a $100 share in a corporation that subsequently fails, the most that he or she can lose is $100. Creditors of the corporation can acquire the assets of the corporation but cannot claim the assets of the stockholders.

EASE OF OWNERSHIP TRANSFER

In a public corporation, an important advantage is the ease with which ownership can be transferred. *Organized markets for corporate securities,* called **stock exchanges** (such as the New York Stock Exchange and the American Stock Exchange), enable stockholders to sell their shares or buy additional shares quickly and simply. In cases of stocks listed on exchanges, it is necessary merely to place an order with a stockbroker, who completes the buying or selling transaction in a matter of minutes. For a sell order, the price lowers until a buyer is found. For a buy order, the price rises until an owner is willing to sell.

In addition, there are **over-the-counter markets** *that deal in unlisted securities outside the organized stock exchanges* (see Chapter 7). They deal in shares of thousands of relatively small, publicly owned corporations.

This ease of ownership transfer contrasts sharply with the difficulty often experienced by sole proprietors or general partners who wish to dispose of their interests. It should be noted, however, that many private corporations do not have sufficiently widespread ownership to make an active market in their shares. In such cases, disposal of stock is not always easy.

CONTINUOUS LIFE

Corporations can be dissolved in only four ways: (1) by court order—for example, when the business goes bankrupt or engages in illegal activity; (2) by the approval of the owners of a majority of the shares; (3) by the expiration of the corporate charter; or (4) by order of the state.

For practical purposes, corporations have perpetual life. Generally, courts are reluctant to revoke a charter unless it can be proved beyond question that the public interest is adversely affected by the corporation's activities. Corporations are seldom dissolved by their shareholders, and renewal of the charter is only a legal formality in most cases. Finally, the state may revoke the charter only for nonuse or misuse of its franchises and powers.

The death of a stockholder in no way affects the life of a corporation as it does a sole proprietorship or a partnership. When stockholders die, their stock passes on to their heirs in the same manner as other assets that make up their estates.

ABILITY TO ACQUIRE CAPITAL

The corporation usually can acquire capital more readily than any other form of business ownership. Several reasons for this have already been noted, including limited liability of owners, ease of transferring ownership, and permanent life of the corporation. Two additional factors help simplify capital acquisition. First, shares of ownership generally have a relatively small dollar value. Most stocks, when first issued, sell for less than $20. This feature attracts many people of average and even below-average income who want to invest in a business but find it difficult to raise the larger amounts of money usually required for a sole proprietorship or a general partnership. Second, corporations can issue different types of stock (preferred and common stock, discussed in Chapter 5) that appeal to different types of investors.

SPECIALIZED MANAGEMENT

Because corporations are generally larger than sole proprietorships or partnerships, they can afford to hire specialists to a much greater extent. In a sole proprietorship or partnership, one or a few individuals must perform all managerial functions. In a corporation, experts in production, marketing, finance, accounting, and research perform these functions.

What Are the Cons of Corporations?

COST AND DIFFICULTY OF ORGANIZATION

A corporation is more difficult to organize than either a sole proprietorship or a partnership. Legal assistance is usually necessary to form a corporation, and while legal fees may be low for setting up a simple type of corporation, they may run to thousands of dollars if the corporation is large. State fees or taxes must be paid at the time of incorporation. Months may pass before the corporation is formally approved. The costly legal procedures and the time involved undoubtedly deter businesses from incorporating.

ISSUE FOR DEBATE

Should Double Taxation of Corporate Profits Be Ended?

A corporation now pays 27 cents in federal income tax on each dollar of profit. The stockholder is then taxed on the dividend, which comes from the remaining 73 cents.

IS THIS TAX POLICY RIGHT OR WRONG?

PROS	CONS
Double taxation is wrong.	Double taxation is necessary.
Owners of sole proprietorships and partnerships are taxed only once on profits they make. Therefore, double tax on corporate owners is unfair.	Many shareholders have above average incomes. They can afford to pay the double tax.
	As long as there are deficits in government, we need to tax corporate profits *and* dividends paid from these profits. Without a double tax on corporate profits the budget deficit would be even larger.
Elimination of the double tax would encourage more people to invest in stocks, thereby supplying corporations with more money for business expansion.	The double tax on corporate profits encourages businesses to invest their surplus in research and development and business expansion, both of which may be tax deductible. These investments also benefit the corporation.
The double tax simply gives politicians control over more money and encourages wasteful spending.	The income tax law already grants as tax-free the first $200 of dividends received by a shareholder. "Where's the beef?"

Questions

1. What would be the effect of eliminating the double tax? If it were eliminated, which party should get the relief—the corporation or the shareholder?
2. What additional arguments, both pro and con, can you think of on this issue?

MANY LEGAL RESTRICTIONS
A corporation can engage in only those activities stated or implied in its charter. If a business incorporated to sell paint and related products should later decide to manufacture these products as well, it will have to amend the corporation charter. While amending a corporate charter is usually simple, it requires state approval and legal assist-

ance. For this reason, corporations usually define their purposes as broadly as possible in the original charter.

DOUBLE PAYMENT OF TAXES

The most important disadvantage of the corporation is that it must pay a federal income tax, in much the same manner as an individual. This results in "double taxation" of corporate income. First, the net profits are taxed, and second, that portion of the profits distributed to shareholders is subject to the individual income tax. Both the sole proprietorship and the partnership are exempt from federal taxes as business entities. Many people who receive dividends consider the double taxation of corporate income unfair. (See *Issue for Debate* on page 51.)

LACK OF OWNER INTEREST

Large corporations have thousands of owners, most of whom own a very small part of the business. These shareholders tend to have little interest in the management of the company; many do not even know the name of the president! Their interest is confined to three questions: Will the company pay dividends, how much will they be, and will the stock increase in value?

Lack of owner interest often leaves corporations under the control of self-perpetuating, hired managers who own only a small part of the business. The impersonal character of the corporation may also cause employees to feel less responsible and less loyal to their company than they would in a proprietorship or partnership.

OTHER DISADVANTAGES

In addition to the disadvantages already discussed, corporations have several other drawbacks:

- They are required to submit various reports to state and federal authorities.

- They often need legal approval to establish a new branch in another state.

- They are required to keep records and make business disclosures public in order to sell stock.

- They are difficult and costly to dissolve.

Table 2–2 summarizes the key considerations in choosing a form of business ownership.

TABLE 2-2 Key Considerations in Selecting a Form of Business Ownership

CONSIDERATION	SOLE PROPRIETORSHIP	PARTNERSHIP	CORPORATION
Raising initial capital	Difficult	Moderately difficult	Somewhat easier
Organizational expense	Very low	Low	Usually considerable
Simplicity of organization	Very simple	Simple	Relatively complex
Legal restrictions	Minimal	Minimal	Many
Personal liability	Considerable	Considerable	Minimal
Government regulation	Comparatively moderate	Comparatively moderate	A great deal
Raising capital for expansion	Generally difficult	Often difficult	Easy if the company is successful
Confidentiality of operations	Maximum	Considerable	Often difficult to maintain
Specialized management	None	Some	Considerable
Incentive to owners	Great	Great	Moderate
Flexibility of operations	Very flexible	Flexible	Relatively flexible
Life	Limited	Limited	In theory, unlimited
Transfer of ownership	Easy if successful	Moderately easy	Easy if publicly held

What to Consider in Forming a Corporation

CHOICE OF STATE

If a corporation is small and expects to operate primarily in one state, it is obviously convenient and advantageous to incorporate in that state. But if the undertaking is large and business is to be transacted nationwide, it is wise to compare the relative advantages and disadvantages of incorporating in various states. State laws differ widely as to taxes, types of stock that can be issued, restrictions on corporate debt, restrictions on the kinds of business that can be transacted, and the breadth of power granted to corporations.

Historically, the state of Delaware has had the country's most favorable general corporate laws. Thus 119,000 companies, including many of the largest, are registered there. For example, in 1954, the remarkable entrepreneur Ray Kroc incorporated McDonald's in Illinois, where his company is headquartered. Just two years later, McDonald's became a Delaware corporation. Now, many other states anxious to attract industry have laws that are equally favorable.

54 CHAPTER 2/PROPRIETORSHIPS, PARTNERSHIPS, AND CORPORATIONS

Figure 2–2 Corporate Art Quiz – Can you identify these logos?

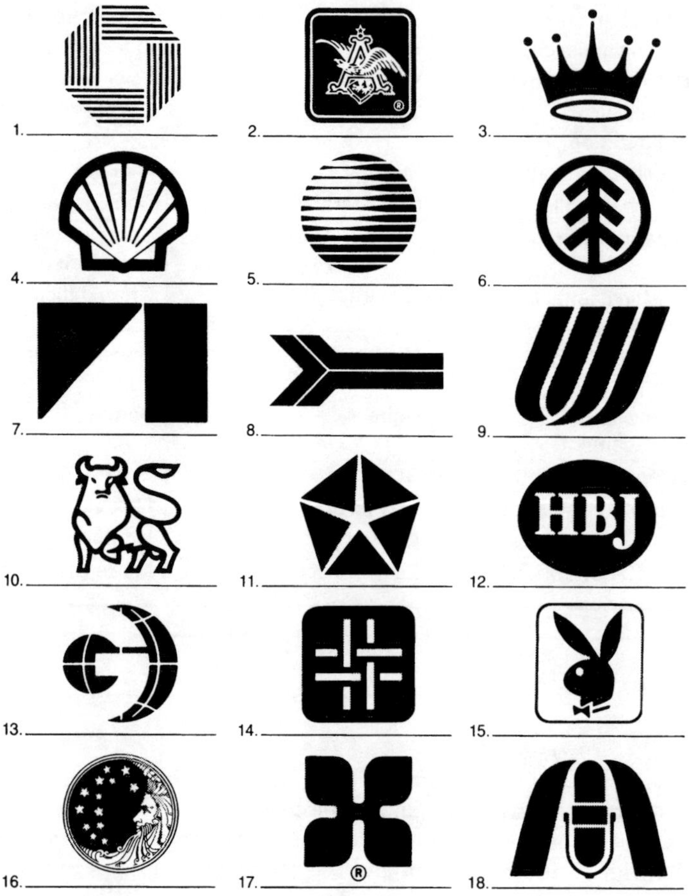

(1) Chase Manhattan Bank; (2) Anheuser-Busch; (3) Hallmark; (4) Shell Oil; (5) American Telephone & Telegraph—AT&T; (6) Boise Cascade; (7) American Motors; (8) Amtrak; (9) United Airlines; (10) Merrill Lynch; (11) Chrysler; (12) Harcourt Brace Jovanovich; (13) Gannett; (14) Burlington Industries; (15) Playboy; (16) Procter and Gamble; (17) Hershey's; (18) Mutual Broadcasting

Adapted from: *Business and Society Review*, Summer 1983, Number 46, p. 51.

CORPORATION CHARTER

To obtain a charter, the incorporators must submit a written application to the appropriate state official, usually the secretary of state. When approved, the application is recorded and filed; it then serves as the corporation charter, or certificate of incorporation. The charter is a three-way contract: between the state and the stockholders, between the stockholder and the corporation, and between the incorporators and the state. The charter contains the following information:

- Name and address of the proposed corporation
- Names and addresses of the incorporators and directors
- Purposes for which the corporation is being formed
- Amount and kind of capital stock to be authorized
- Privileges and voting powers of each type of stockholder
- Duration of the life of the corporation

NAMING THE CORPORATION

It is important to choose a name for a corporation carefully, because changing a name can be costly as well as confusing. Yet numerous corporations change names each year. The most costly name change in history came to about $100 million, when Esso (derived from the initials "S" and "O" for Standard Oil) changed its name to Exxon. The name change took place between 1972 and 1973, and included the cost of 25,000 signs for service stations, plaques for 22,000 oil wells and 18,000 building and storage tanks, 55,000 signs warning about underground pipelines, 300 million sales slips, and 11 million credit cards!

Most states require that a name not be too similar to one already chartered by someone else in the state. This often poses a problem for a company doing business in other states. One incorporator, after a long search for a suitable and acceptable name, was granted a charter as Red Robin Estates. A shoe store, Red Robin Shoes, challenged the name, and the state asked that another name be submitted. The state had made an error, a "boo boo," in allowing the name. The frustrated entrepreneur proposed the name Bu Bu Estates, under which the corporation is still prospering.

Sometimes, even an acceptable pronunciation can be a problem. Take, for example, the $25 million lawsuit filed by Vidal Sassoon Inc., maker of hair and beauty care products, against jean manufacturer Sasson Inc. The 25-year-old company objected to television advertisements in which Sasson pronounced the last syllable of its name as "soon." Sasson Inc. filed a countersuit, however, when it learned that Vidal Sassoon was planning his own line of "celebrity" jeans. Under the settlement, Sasson Inc. agreed to change the pronunciation of its name, and Vidal Sassoon agreed to use its full name on the company's new line of jeans.

BOARD OF DIRECTORS

The governing body of a corporation, elected by the stockholders, is the **board of directors.** Most corporations require a minimum of three directors. Some states require that each director own stock in the corporation, but ownership of a single share usually satisfies this requirement. In small corporations, the board of directors is usually composed of the chief stockholders.

Directors are in a position of trust and may be held personally liable to the stockholders for fraud, gross negligence, or use of the corporation for personal gain to the detriment of the firm. They cannot be held liable for honest mistakes in judgment.

The current directors of a corporation propose new directors, not necessarily for their knowledge of the details of the business but for their specialized business experience, integrity, vision, and philosophy. They are often successful people of widely different backgrounds in fields such as law, finance, and accounting. It would not be unusual, for example, for a major retailing executive to be asked to serve on the board of directors of a carpet manufacturing company. The amount of prestige that directors lend to the corporation also enters into their selection.

Major responsibilities of the board of directors are:

- *To appoint corporate officers*—Directors of the corporation appoint a president, a secretary, a treasurer, and other executive officers who will handle the actual management. The president and other high-ranking officers are often elected board members.

- *To make major policy decisions*—The board of directors decides such fundamental questions as: Should the business be expanded? Should another plant be purchased? Should the product line be changed? Seeing that major policy decisions are carried out, however, is a function of the corporate officers, not the board.

- *To declare dividends*—The board of directors has sole responsibility for the declaration of dividends. The board must decide what percentage of the year's earnings should be retained for company use and, if dividends are to be declared, whether they should be paid in cash or in stock.

Additional duties of the board of directors are financial plan-

In the past few years, Lee Iacocca's business expertise has helped bring Chrysler Corporation back from the edge of bankruptcy. He engineered a $1.5 billion federal government aid package that gave the company a new lease on life.

ning, authorizing unusual business expenditures or transactions, and calling special meetings of stockholders.

OFFICERS

An **officer** of a corporation is *an executive appointed by the board of directors who is responsible for carrying out business policies.* The essential corporate officers and their duties are usually defined by law. Most states require that every corporation have a president (chief executive officer), a secretary (recording officer), and a treasurer (chief financial officer). In addition, the board of directors may appoint an executive vice-president and other vice-presidents who are responsible for various divisions of the business.

What Role Do Stockholders Play?

Stockholders usually exercise only indirect control over the actual management of a corporation. However, in a very small corporation or in a large corporation owned by a single family, the owners do exercise close control. In such cases, the principal stockholders usually elect themselves to the board of directors and then appoint themselves to key executive positions.

THE STOCKHOLDERS' MEETING

Corporation stockholders meet annually to elect directors and to vote on such major issues as stock splits and compensation plans for top management. In elections, stockholders usually have the right to cast one vote for each share of stock they own. To give minority stockholders some power, individual stockholders are sometimes allowed to cast all their votes for one director.

In practice, individual stockholders have very little voice in how the corporation is run. This is true for two reasons. First, most stockholders in a large corporation own only a small amount of stock, and their vote is therefore too small to be significant. Second, many stockholders are indifferent toward the corporation's entrenched management and give rubber-stamp approval to its recommendations because they feel it knows more than they do about the business. When they believe the corporation is slowing down or losing money, their first inclination is to sell their stock rather than to try to influence management. Former Securities and Exchange Commission (SEC) Commissioner Robert S. Karmel explained it this way: "People don't buy stocks to exercise their political franchise."[3]

When stockholders are notified of a forthcoming meeting, they are given a **proxy,** *a legal statement by which stockholders can transfer the right to cast their votes to someone else.* When signed

> *"If you think you're tops, you won't do much climbing."*
>
> ARNOLD GLASOW

---
[3]*Business Week* (November 5, 1979).

Individuals can participate in large corporations by buying stock shares in these companies. Here buy–sell transactions take place on the New York Stock Exchange.

and returned, the proxy authorizes the existing management to, in effect, vote for itself. Proxies are used because it is impractical to expect more than a handful of stockholders to attend stockholders' meetings.

Sometimes a larger group of stockholders becomes dissatisfied with the existing management and attempts to gain control by asking fellow stockholders for their proxies. Business history contains interesting stories of bitter "proxy wars" that have been fought for control of corporations.

ADDITIONAL RIGHTS OF STOCKHOLDERS

In addition to electing directors and voting on major issues, stockholders have the right to receive dividends when declared, to inspect corporate records, to vote on amendments to the corporation's bylaws or charter, and to share in the assets of the corporation in its dissolution.

Special Kinds of Corporations

S CORPORATIONS

In an **S Corporation** form of ownership (from Subchapter S of the Internal Revenue Code), the corporation pays no income tax. Its net taxable income passes directly to its individual shareholders who in turn must report any income received on their income tax returns. If income tax rates on corporate profits are higher than personal income tax rates, S corporation shareholders save tax dollars.

PROFESSIONAL CORPORATIONS

Traditionally, licensed professionals such as accountants, architects, attorneys, chiropractors, dentists, physicians, and optometrists were not permitted to incorporate. However, new laws now permit these professionals to incorporate their practices. The initials P.C. after a physician's name means his or her practice is incorporated.

As a corporation, licensed professionals may take advantage of legislation that enables them to enjoy tax-free and tax-deferred fringe benefits. A professional organized as a **professional corporation** is not relieved of responsibility for negligent acts.

OTHER FORMS OF OWNERSHIP

Cooperatives

A **cooperative** is *a nonprofit enterprise owned and operated by those using its services.* The primary aim of a cooperative is to render a service to its members. Farmers' cooperatives are the most common. For example, Land O' Lakes Creameries is owned by 175,000 farmers in six states, including Nebraska, Minnesota, Iowa, Wisconsin, and the Dakotas.

Some states require a special charter in forming a cooperative. Capital is raised by selling shares to people who become members of the cooperative and use its services. Interest is paid on money invested in shares. Earnings, if any, are reinvested in the business or returned to the members as a rebate on their purchases. Each member of the cooperative has one vote, regardless of how many ownership shares he or she may have purchased.

There are basically three types of cooperatives. **Producer cooperatives** are *organized to enable producers* (usually farmers) *to obtain better prices for their products than they would if they bargained individually.* **Buying cooperatives** are *formed to buy supplies* (for example, fertilizers, seeds, and other farm materials in the case of agricultural cooperatives) *to sell to their members at good prices.* **Consumer cooperatives** are *organized for the benefit of consumers.* The most important type is the credit union, which offers loans to members at relatively low interest rates.

Cooperatives have not been notably successful in this country, chiefly because of their inability to compete with efficiently operated profit-making organizations. Some exceptions to this generalization are Sunkist Growers and Land O' Lakes Creameries. Cooperatives have experienced most success in rural and agricultural areas.

Mutuals

A **mutual** is *a nonprofit corporation similar to a cooperative but without stockholders, whose members are the owners.* In practice, the word "mutual" has come to be associated with savings banks, insurance companies, and loan associations. In mutuals, profits may be either reinvested or returned to the members as a rebate or a dividend.

Joint Ventures

A **joint venture** (sometimes called a **syndicate**) is *a group of people or businesses who combine under an agreement to carry out a particular transaction or project.* It resembles a partnership except that the "partners" may be corporations or sole proprietorships. Joint ventures are most commonly formed in connection with real estate development or international dealings involving a foreign company and an American firm.

SUMMARY

- The three most common forms of business ownership are proprietorships, partnerships, and corporations. Proprietorships are the most numerous, but corporations account for the most sales.
- The main advantages of sole proprietorship are simplicity of organization, freedom and flexibility, maximum incentive, and low organizational costs. Main limitations are difficulty in raising capital, limited life, unlimited liability of owner, lack of specialized management, and operational problems.
- Key advantages of the general partnership are greater financial strength than a proprietorship and more management know-how. The general partnership is also simple to organize, and there is considerable personal incentive. Main limitations are unlimited liability for indebtedness, divided authority, possibility of mutual distrust, and lack of permanence.
- In a limited partnership, one or more partners have limited liability and are not permitted to exercise any managerial functions.
- Most corporations are either public, private, nonprofit, or conglomerates.
- Advantages of the corporate form of organization are limited liability of owners, ease of ownership transfer, continuous life, ability to acquire capital, and specialized management. Main disadvantages are cost and difficulty of organization, legal restrictions on business activities, double taxes, and lack of owner interest.
- In forming a corporation, the following considerations should be taken into account: state, corporation charter, name, board of directors, officers.
- Stockholders, the owners of a corporation, are responsible for electing a board of directors and voting on major issues.
- Some other forms of ownership are cooperatives, mutuals, and joint ventures.

KEY TERMS YOU SHOULD KNOW

board of directors	limited liability	professional corporation
buying cooperative	limited partnership	proxy
conglomerate	mutual	public corporation
consumer cooperative	nonprofit corporation	S corporation
cooperative	officer	sole proprietorship
corporation	over-the-counter market	stock exchange
corporation charter	partnership agreement	stockholder
general partnership	private corporation	unlimited liability
joint venture	producer cooperative	

QUESTIONS FOR REVIEW

1. What are the three common forms of business ownership? Which one is most important in terms of numbers? Which one is most important in terms of receipts?

2. What is a sole proprietorship? What are the advantages of this form of ownership? The disadvantages?

3. What is a general partnership?

4. What is a partnership agreement? What should it cover?

5. What are the advantages of a general partnership? The disadvantages?

6. What is a corporation? What is the difference between a public and a private corporation?

7. Explain "nonprofit corporation" and give three examples.

8. What are the pros and cons of the corporate form of ownership?

9. Explain why choice of state, the corporate charter, the name of the corporation, the board of directors, and the appointment of corporate officers are all important.

10. What role do stockholders play in a corporation?

11. Define cooperatives, mutuals, and joint ventures.

QUESTIONS FOR DISCUSSION

1. Assume that you want to go into business as a sole proprietor. However, you feel that from a practical standpoint it would be wiser to form a partnership with one other person. Make a list of the personal, professional, and psychological qualities you would want the person to have. Will you be able to find all of these qualities in one individual? Explain.

2. Why are most small businesses sole proprietorships?

3. List three sideline businesses that interest you. Explain why each interests you.

4. Evaluate this statement. "People grossly exaggerate the amount of money required to start one's own business."

5. No law requires you to use an attorney to incorporate. Does it make sense then to retain legal counsel to set up a corporation? Why or why not?

6. Why are cooperatives not a widely used form of business ownership?

7. Think of a small business venture you are familiar with that failed. Then explain why, in your opinion, the enterprise didn't make it.

CASE STUDY

Jerry and Fritz: Should They Start a Business of Their Own or Become Corporate Management Trainees?

For the past three summers, Jerry Mailer and Fritz Johnson have worked for Lawn Care. Basically, what Jerry and Fritz did was to cut grass and trim shrubbery. It's now February, and Fritz and Jerry, about to graduate in June, are being interviewed for jobs by employers who visit their campus. The following conversation takes place one day in the student center.

Jerry: Fritz, I'm a little discouraged. I've been offered three jobs, but I don't want any of them.

Fritz: I've had some offers, too, and like you, I've said no. The starting pay is OK. But I ask myself, where will I be in five or ten years?

J: I've got an idea for the two of us, but I'm almost too embarrassed to propose it.

F: Look, we've been buddies for years. Go ahead. If your idea will make money, I want to hear it.

J: Well, we worked for Lawn Care three summers, and we both know that the owner was a lousy manager. He didn't sell the service—people called him instead. My idea is that you and I form a company and compete with Lawn Care.

You're a management major—you could hire and supervise the crews. Since I studied marketing, I'll sell the service.

F: But, Jerry, doesn't that mean we would have wasted four years of college? After all, anybody can cut grass. And you don't need a degree to trim shrubs. Besides, what would our friends who go to work for big-name companies think of us?

J: We could use everything we've studied in college—accounting, finance, management, everything. It's obvious to me, as I think of Lawn Care, that the owner made many mistakes because he had not studied business. His employees (including us) looked like bums, he had no incentive-pay plan, his record keeping was awful—that's what got him into trouble with the IRS—and he didn't know how to market the service.

Now, what our friends think is up to them. If they laugh at us, then they aren't really our friends. Besides, when we trade in our old cars for BMW's, they'll be so jealous they won't be able to stand it. And we could start the business with very little capital.

F: What you say sounds good. But you're overlooking one single point.

J: What's that?

F: Lawn Care is a seasonal business. We'd have nothing to do for six months out of the year.

J: I figured you'd say that. What I also propose is that we get into the plant-care business. All the good hotels, restaurants, and office buildings now have expensive plants. We could have a division that provides a regular service to lease plants or keep those that they have healthy.

F: OK. But where will we be in five or ten years? I confess—I'm hungry.

J: I'm hungry, too. Fritz, you've got to think big. One day I see us owning a chain of nurseries and lawn-care centers all over the region—maybe the nation. Or maybe we can expand faster by developing a franchise system.

F: Jerry, you make it sound really good. Give me a few days to think it over.

Questions

1. Is the demand for lawn-care service likely to expand in the future? Why or why not?
2. Plant-care requires some knowledge of horticulture. How could Jerry and Fritz overcome their lack of knowledge in this field?
3. How might Jerry and Fritz market their lawn-care service? Their plant-care and leasing service?
4. What problems that haven't been mentioned would this business face?
5. If you were Fritz, would you go for Jerry's proposal? Why or why not?

EVOLUTION OF A BUSINESS

Partnership or Sole Proprietorship?

Months after their return from South America, Sara and Ray are still friends and meet frequently for lunch or coffee. The talk regularly turns to their hypothetical travel agency—in fact, one or the other of them generally brings along a recent magazine article, newspaper clipping, or book on the subject. Ray has even done some marketing research on the field and thinks prospects look good. One day the conversation gets down to specifics.

Ray: I don't think you and I would have the usual squabbles as partners in a business, since our areas of expertise are so clear-cut. You'd be mainly the financial person and I'd be mainly the advertising and marketing person.

Sara: I agree with you there, but I'm not so sure we should organize as a partnership.

Ray: Isn't that what we've been assuming all along?

Sara: Yes, but I've been having some doubts about quitting my job with the IRS since this is such a chancy thing. How about if you started the business alone, as a sole proprietor, and I helped with the financial end in my spare time until the business really got going? Or maybe I could be a limited partner—invest a certain amount and then serve as an adviser.

Ray: Sara, do I get the feeling you're trying to avoid taking any risks? I don't know about you accountants . . .

Sara: Watch it, Ray. I'm sure I could come up with some cracks about public relations people!

Ray: So this is why they say friends shouldn't go into business together. Well, anyway, Sara, I'm not sure what you propose would work. I'm afraid that as a sole proprietor I wouldn't be able to raise enough initial capital and would have trouble getting credit once I was in business. Plus it seems to me that during the first year, the financial planning and management would be a full-time job.

Questions

1. What do you think of Sara's ideas?
2. What are the advantages and disadvantages of Ray's proposed approach?
3. What additional questions should Sara and Ray be concerned about in determining which form of organization to use?
4. Do you think Sara and Ray's basic differences in character will benefit or harm the business in the long run?

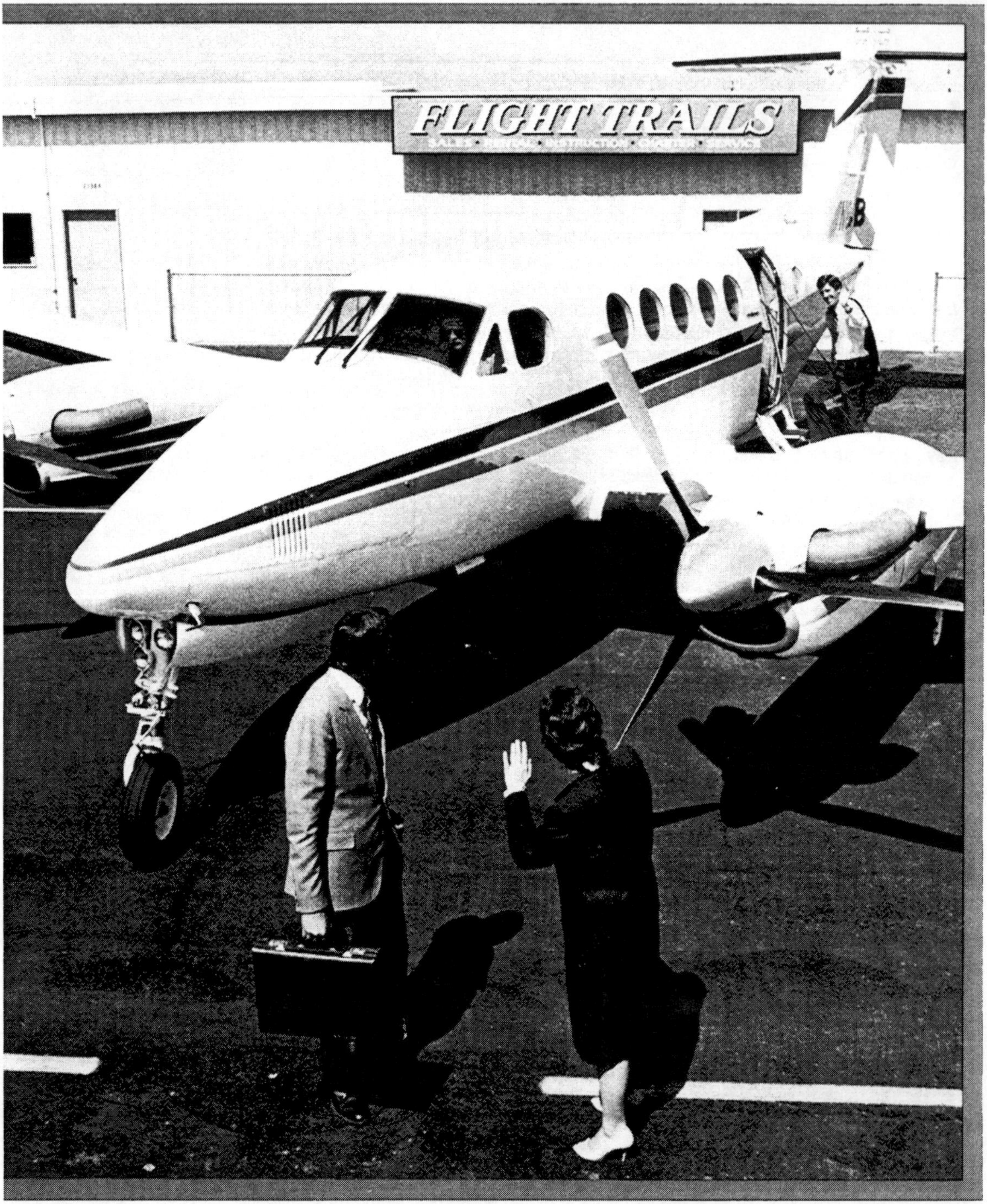
FLIGHT TRAILS

ENTREPRENEURSHIP: SMALL BUSINESS AND FRANCHISING
The Magic Spark

READ THIS CHAPTER SO YOU CAN:

Define the term "small business," and examine the role of small business in our economy.

Discuss the advantages and disadvantages of operating a small business.

Describe the role the Small Business Administration plays.

Explain franchising and the typical contractual relationships between the franchisor and the franchisee.

Discuss how big business has rediscovered entrepreneurship.

All giant enterprises once were small: This is a truism of American business. Apple Computer began in a garage; so did Ford Motor Company. Delta Air Lines began as a small crop-dusting company. McDonald's and Kentucky Fried Chicken were once shoestring businesses, as were IBM, Federated Department Stores, Sears Roebuck, Nationwide Insurance, Merrill Lynch, Holiday Inns, and hundreds of other now famous firms. Entrepreneurship is the magic spark that makes such growth possible. In this chapter we will see how this spark powers small business and franchising. We will also look briefly at several entrepreneurial trends in big business.

Entrepreneurship is *the willingness to exercise initiative and take considerable risk to operate one's own business.* Our giant industrial and commercial base was founded by tough-minded, rugged individuals who had the initiative and courage to convert ideas into businesses designed to meet people's needs. Today thousands of entrepreneurs are creating the commercial structure of the decades ahead. Those who succeed will acquire fortunes; in the process, they will serve the ever-increasing and divergent needs of society.

Entrepreneurship is important for other reasons. Small business offers more chances to people who might otherwise face barriers in big business for reasons of race, gender, or age. Consider three national success stories: First, Wally (Famous) Amos is perhaps the country's best-known maker of chocolate chip cookies. He is also a minority business person par excellence. His privately owned company, begun on a shoestring in 1975, now has annual sales of over $7 million. That figure will climb when The Famous Amos Chocolate Chip Cookie Corporation opens recently announced retail franchises. Second, even if you do not know Bette Nesmith Graham's name, you will know her invention. In 1951, while employed as a secretary, Graham created a typewriter correction fluid. With a $500 loan she began a company that later became Liquid Paper Corporation. When the company was sold to Gillette Company in 1980 for $47.5 million, Graham—who held nearly half the shares of stock—profited handsomely. Finally, Ray Kroc was in his fifties and with several careers behind him when he started what became his McDonald's empire of fast-food restaurants. (We discuss Kroc's success later in this chapter.) These entrepreneurs created their own businesses—and their own opportunities.

Another reason why small business is so important in the 1980s is that young people entering the business arena now look for careers that will serve their personal as well as financial goals. One observer notes:

Many college and business school graduates are reflecting the social trend to independence in the 1980s by disclaiming employee status—

"who wants to work for someone else?"—for some form of being on their own. Even when they choose to work for a large corporation, they prefer sales jobs where they are not tied to an office all day or some of the newer free form positions that permit a great deal of personal initiative and inventiveness as long as there are results. Foremost among these newer corporate roles is the entrepreneur.[1]

Later in this chapter we will look at this new breed, the corporate entrepreneur.

Does this desire to be independent still prevail? Dean Victor Lindquist, head of placement at Northwestern University, says that personal development is still a prime concern of graduating students, who tend to "look for jobs in companies with good growth potential." This suggests that personal growth opportunities might be most readily available in smaller, "comer" companies. We see the same desire for independence on campus in the tremendous increase in courses designed to teach entrepreneurship (see page 87).

SMALL BUSINESS: WHAT IT IS AND DOES

Most people use the term "small business" to describe small drugstores, beauty shops, laundries, restaurants, insurance agencies, and other small enterprises. The term can also describe a manufacturer of silicon microprocessing chips, a management consultant, or a research firm attempting to engineer the genetics of feed grain. Small business is difficult to define precisely. The Small Business Act of 1953 establishes limits—admittedly arbitrary—that distinguish small from large businesses. It states that a **small business** is one *"which is independently owned and operated and which is not dominant in its field of operation."*

For loan and other special assistance programs, the Small Business Administration sets size guidelines by specific fields, as shown in Figure 3–1. Some manufacturers, for example, could employ up to 1,500 employees and still be considered a small business; in agriculture, a firm's annual receipts could range up to $3.5 million and still be considered small.

Many Small Businesses Are Part-time or One-Person Operations

Thirty-eight percent of all small businesses, as shown in Figure 3–2, are part-time nonfarm enterprises with no paid employees. Another 12 percent of small firms are full-time operations but are also without

---

[1] Mack Hanan, "The Corporate Entrepreneur," *Guide to Careers in Business*, Fall/Winter 1983, 75.

Figure 3-1 How Big Is Small?

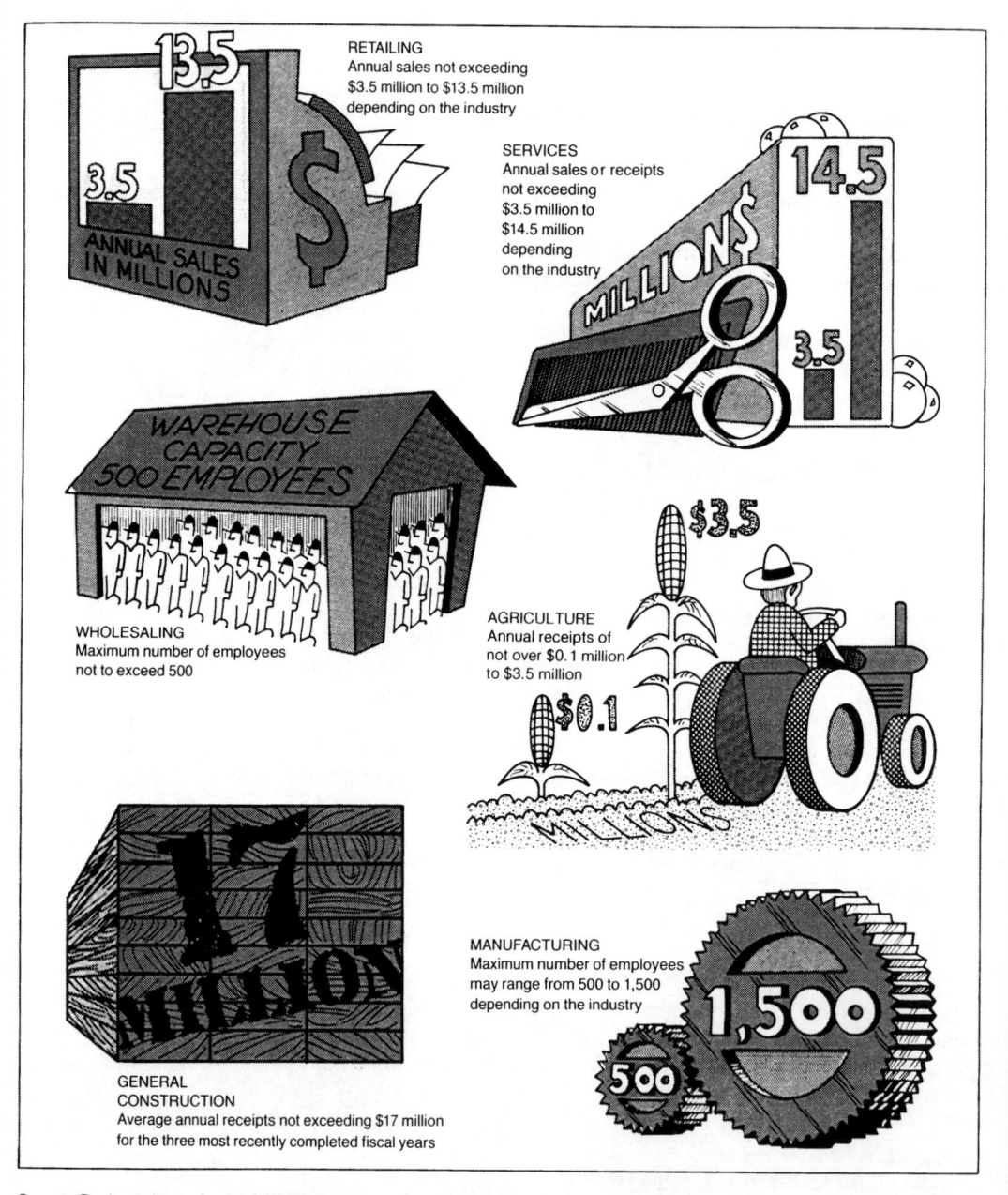

RETAILING
Annual sales not exceeding $3.5 million to $13.5 million depending on the industry

SERVICES
Annual sales or receipts not exceeding $3.5 million to $14.5 million depending on the industry

WHOLESALING
Maximum number of employees not to exceed 500

AGRICULTURE
Annual receipts of not over $0.1 million to $3.5 million

GENERAL CONSTRUCTION
Average annual receipts not exceeding $17 million for the three most recently completed fiscal years

MANUFACTURING
Maximum number of employees may range from 500 to 1,500 depending on the industry

Source: *Business Loans for the SBA,* Washington, D.C.: Small Business Administration, 1981.

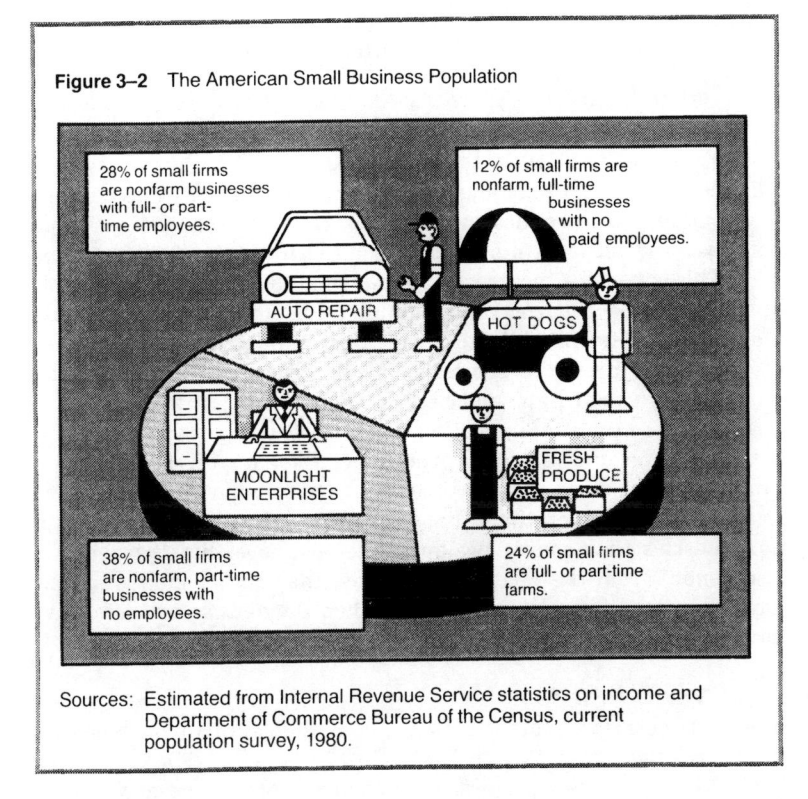

Figure 3–2 The American Small Business Population

- 28% of small firms are nonfarm businesses with full- or part-time employees.
- 12% of small firms are nonfarm, full-time businesses with no paid employees.
- 38% of small firms are nonfarm, part-time businesses with no employees.
- 24% of small firms are full- or part-time farms.

Sources: Estimated from Internal Revenue Service statistics on income and Department of Commerce Bureau of the Census, current population survey, 1980.

paid employees. Only 28 percent of all nonfarm small businesses have paid employees.[2]

Other Features of Small Business

Apart from size, three characteristics usually distinguish small business:

- *Capital is supplied by one person or a small number of persons*—Absentee ownership is rare.
- *Management is independent, reporting only to itself and not to a board of directors or a distant home office*—Most small businesses are sole proprietorships, partnerships, or family-owned corporations. In most instances, the manager or managers are also the owners.
- *The business is basically a local one*—The employees and employer usually live in the community in which the business is located. The market for the business is usually local as well,

---

[2]*The American Small Business Population,* Estimated from Internal Revenue Service Statistics on Income and Department of Commerce Bureau of the Census, Current Population Survey, Washington, 1980.

although it need not be. Mail-order houses, for example, may be small businesses but sell to scattered markets.

What Role Does Small Business Play?

MAKING BIG BUSINESS POSSIBLE

The economic strength enjoyed by the United States is often credited to our large, mass-production industries. However, big business could not exist without large numbers of small businesses.

This is true for two reasons. First, small businesses help link big businesses with the consuming public. The industrial giants that manufacture tires, refrigerators, electrical appliances, and hundreds of other mass–produced consumer goods rely on thousands of small businesses to distribute and service their products. Second, small businesses are the suppliers of big businesses. It is generally impossible (and often uneconomical even if possible) for big businesses to produce all the parts, supplies, services, and raw materials they need to carry on their operations. Thus, small businesses provide the support muscles that enable big businesses to move. Small businesses also benefit from the relationship. When they act as suppliers, they have large businesses as customers. When they act as retailers, they have well-known products to sell.

GENERATING JOBS

Small business does more for our economy than *support* big business; in at least two areas its role is *equal to or greater than* that of big business. First, small business now creates more of the new jobs in our economy. This is true in part because our economy is moving gradually from an industrial base to a service base—and small business is especially strong in service. A recent presidential report notes that small businesses furnish two out of three workers with their first jobs, many of which are in the service sector; and that service industries now employ about 20 million people workers, the same number of workers as work in the manufacturing sector. The report also notes that in virtually every industry between 1980 and 1982, overall employment grew in small firms and declined in large firms; in fact, small enterprises with under 20 employees generated all of the net new jobs in the economy for that period.[3] These trends are likely to continue.

Second, small business now matches big business worker for worker. "Independent small businesses now employ one-half of the private sector labor force."[4] Without small business, half of the private sector would be out of work.

> *"A good idea is the enemy of a better one. You stop looking for alternatives."*
>
> DR. TUDOR RICKARDS

---

[3]*The State of Small Business: A Report of the President* (Washington, D.C.: Government Printing Office, 1984), *xvi*, 25.

[4]*The State of Small Business, xvi.*

When Small Business Has the Edge

Big business clearly has the advantage in situations in which **markets** (*numbers of potential customers*) are very large, products are highly standardized and can be mass produced, large sums of capital are essential, extensive division of labor is possible, a large labor force is needed, and demand is steady. Small business is seldom able to compete directly with big business. A small soap manufacturer that tries to imitate an operation like Procter & Gamble's is doomed to fail. However, under the conditions listed below, a small business has definite advantages.

- *When the market is limited*—Small stores are best for the thousands of communities that cannot support a large business—a department store, for example—because the market is too small.
- *When craftsmanship is important*—Small businesses are particularly well suited to provide custom-made goods. Examples of such businesses are tailor shops, custom furniture manufacturers, interior decorators, and TV repair shops.
- *When service is personal*—Beauty salons and landscapers, for example, provide highly personal services, which small businesses have a clear advantage in doing.
- *When convenience is important*—The small store around the corner that stays open late has a convenience feature that lets the owner compete with larger stores.
- *When demand is irregular*—Seasonal businesses often don't lend themselves to large-scale organization. Examples include boat concessions in a park, winter and summer resort facilities, and roadside produce markets.

American business is blessed with a remarkable small business support system. Standing ready to serve big business and the ultimate consumer are thousands of independent centers of initiative ready to spring to life whenever a need is not being met or an opportunity beckons.

What Are the Strengths of Small Business?

FREEDOM TO ACT QUICKLY

The typical small business acts quickly and operates more flexibly because decisions don't pass through several levels of management. Suppose that an independent shoe retailer learns of a new design for shoe-store fronts that will attract customers and increase store traffic. He or she can call in a builder and complete the conversion in days. When the independent's chain-store competitor, which operates hundreds of stores, learns of the design, it could take months to

This stained glass craftsman provides his customers with unique handmade products they could not obtain from assembly-line producers.

reach a policy decision to make the changeover—and more months to remodel several hundred stores.

ABILITY TO ADAPT TO LOCAL NEEDS

The owner of a small business can study the desires, preferences, customs, spending habits, and other characteristics of the local market in depth. Thus, the owner can adapt business methods to local peculiarities. By contrast, regional or national market characteristics generally govern the methods of large businesses. Local retailers can appeal directly to customers and virtually shut out successful national companies from certain markets.

PUBLIC FAVOR

Public attitudes in the United States favor protecting and furthering the interests of small business. Americans tend to "stick up for the little guy," and much government legislation is designed to aid small business. For example, often small business is subject to lower taxes than big business is. Large corporations are often the targets of legislation that tends to restrict growth.

LOWER OPERATING COSTS

Typically, the small business' operating costs are proportionately lower than those of the large business. Why? Wages, rent, investment in plant and equipment, administrative costs, and employee benefit costs are comparatively lower. Often the owner's family contributes much labor for which no direct charge is made.

What Are the Weaknesses of Small Business?

DIFFICULTY IN ATTRACTING THE BEST EMPLOYEES
Small business generally is at a competitive disadvantage with big business in securing good employees. Researchers for the Institute for the Advancement of Small Business surveyed 1,009 small businesses and found that getting competent help was their major worry, while motivating employees was second.[5] Sole proprietorships, for example, typically pay relatively low wages, provide less secure employment, give no formal training, and offer few fringe benefits like paid vacations and pension programs. Because sole proprietorships are small, chances for promotion are limited. Also, many people prefer the prestige of working for a large firm. For these reasons, well-qualified people as a rule do not work permanently as employees in small businesses.

However, one of these drawbacks—the lack of pension programs—may be overcome by the government provision that now permits individual pension arrangements. Under the **Individual Retirement Account (IRA)**, *workers may take a tax deduction of up to $2,000 a year and place the funds in an IRA account at an approved bank, mutual fund, or other approved investment vehicle.* There the money accumulates tax-free until the worker retires.

Another arrangement—the **Keogh Plan**—provides *a pension plan mechanism for the self-employed. It is similar in many respects to the IRA except that the maximum is $15,000 annually or 15 percent of earnings, whichever is less.* Keogh-plan participants may also have an IRA.

LACK OF SPECIALIZED MANAGEMENT
Many small businesses are at a disadvantage because one person is responsible for all major business functions, like policy setting, selling, buying, personnel management, advertising, and accounting. The large business can employ people with specialized training and experience for each important business function. In addition, research—which is considered essential for maximum success in many fields—is too expensive for most small firms.

DIFFICULTY IN RAISING CAPITAL
The small business does not normally enjoy as high a credit rating as a larger firm because its chance of failure is greater. Thus, **long-**

> *"The probability of success of a small company is inversely proportional to the size of the president's office."*
>
> FREDERICK R. ADLER

---

[5]*INC.*, June 1980, 30.

term capital (*money needed for extended periods*) is difficult to secure and is usually lent at a high interest rate. Under these circumstances, business expansion is difficult.

SENSITIVITY TO ECONOMIC FLUCTUATIONS
Because the small business has difficulty raising capital, it is particularly sensitive to economic fluctuations. During a recession, for example, a large business can ordinarily operate for months or years without making profits, by spending money it earned previously. A small business, however, cannot continue operations for long without earning a profit. Paradoxically, the small business sector as a whole has continued to prosper in times of economic expansion and stress—perhaps because individual businesses can spring up quickly in response to changing conditions.

Why Do Many Small Businesses Fail?

Small businesses do have a high failure rate, maybe because they are so easy to start. You only need to have a little capital and to file a few papers; and there are always small businesses for sale. Because people can enter the field easily, small businesses attract many people who lack the training, education, personality, energy, or experience to succeed. Incompetent management is one of the major factors in the high failure rate of small businesses.

Dun & Bradstreet, which reports annually on business failures, consistently lists lack of managerial ability as the principal cause of business failure. Various studies on small business failures conclude:

- The rate of closures relates inversely to the age of the firm's owner: Older persons are less inclined to fail.

- Female business owners are about as likely to survive as male owners.

- Owners with less education (measured in years of schooling) have a higher rate of business closure. Inexperienced and uneducated managers are the least likely to succeed, whereas educated and experienced managers have the highest success rate.

- There is little relationship between previous experience in the same line of business, taken by itself, and the closure rate.

- Individuals who previously owned a business have a much lower failure rate than those who have never been in business before. Thus the single experience factor that appears to matter most is not experience in the same occupation but rather whether the person has had *entrepreneurial* experience.

- Management teams of two, three, or four persons have a much higher success rate than single managers.
- In general, the larger the amount of invested capital, especially in the $1,000–25,000 range studied, the lower the failure rate. Further, the source of initial capital appears to have a bearing on failure rate. One study found lower failure rates among firms where owners had invested a great deal of their own capital.

Which Is Better, Buying an Established Business or Starting from Scratch?

It depends. Generally speaking, unless you intend to go into something really new, it's better to buy an established business when a suitable one is available at a fair price. With an established business you can analyze past records and deal in specifics, like known prices, volume of sales, and operating expenses. When starting a business, you can only estimate these things.

The problem lies in finding a desirable established business. One good search method is to approach a leading supplier who deals with the kinds of businesses that interest you. Chances are the supplier will know when partners are quarreling and want to get out, when owners are getting old and want to retire, or when owners have other interests to which they want to devote their time. Assuming that you are an attractive prospect, the supplier has a vested interest in your success and will help you get established. After all, presumably, the more you prosper, the more the supplier sells.

WHAT ARE THE ADVANTAGES OF PURCHASING AN ESTABLISHED BUSINESS?

- You acquire existing customers.
- The location has been selected.
- Employees may be in place already.
- Suppliers of the business already exist.
- Much of the equipment you need is present.
- At least some of the needed inventory is on hand.
- You can benefit from the previous owner's mistakes.

WHAT ARE THE DISADVANTAGES OF ACQUIRING AN ESTABLISHED BUSINESS?

- It could be a loser. Some business locations, for example, never support a successful business.
- You may inherit undesirable employees.
- The equipment may be obsolete.

- Change and innovation could be difficult. Often it is easier to start from scratch than to remodel an enterprise.
- Inventory may be outdated.
- The business may be overpriced.
- You may suffer from the previous owner's mistakes.

How the Small Business Administration Can Help

People considering going into business for themselves frequently ask, "Where can I get advice?" and "How can I learn more about the business I want to start?"

A major source of assistance is the **Small Business Administration (SBA),** *a permanent, independent government agency created by Congress to advise and assist small business enterprises.* The law that established the SBA says in part:

It is the declared policy of the Congress that the Government should aid, counsel, assist, and protect insofar as is possible the interests of small-business concerns in order to preserve free competitive enterprise, to insure that a fair proportion of the total purchases and contracts for supplies and services for the Government be placed with small-business enterprises, and to maintain and strengthen the overall economy of the Nation.

The SBA also provides the following services.

FINANCIAL ASSISTANCE

What do you do when you want to buy or start a small business but you cannot find a bank willing to grant a loan? Go to the local office of the SBA. The SBA may be able to grant you a loan or to guarantee a bank loan. The requirements are that the proposed business be small (as defined by the SBA), and that your loan application at a bank has been rejected (in cities of 200,000 people or more, rejections from two banks are necessary).

The SBA offers two basic types of aid: guaranteed loans and direct loans. With a guaranteed loan, a bank holds a lien against the business; however, the SBA agrees to guarantee or "insure" that bank loan for up to 90 percent of the loan's value, or a maximum of $500,000, whichever is less. The SBA regularly sets the maximum allowable interest rate that banks can charge on guaranteed loans.

If you can't get a loan under the SBA's guarantee plan, you may still qualify for aid. The SBA occasionally makes direct loans of up to $150,000. Interest rates on direct loans depend on the current cost of money to the federal government. In general, direct SBA loans carry interest rates slightly lower than those in the private financial markets. The term of both guaranteed and direct loans may not exceed seven years for working capital loans and 25 years for regular business loans. For more information on how to apply, visit or call the local office of the SBA (or use the toll-free telephone number that follows) and ask for the pamphlet, *Business Loans from the SBA.*

Recognizing that its resources are limited, in recent years the SBA has worked with the private sector to widen assistance and to make more funds available. The SBA has urged lenders to participate in its guaranteed loans and to create their own loan programs to meet the needs of small business. In the years ahead, the SBA plans to become more a "wholesaler" of lending, with private lenders assuming the role of "retailers."

MANAGERIAL AND TECHNICAL ASSISTANCE

The SBA provides managerial advice through administrative-management courses, supplies pamphlets covering a wide range of practical business problems, and offers management counseling.

Particularly helpful are the SBA's publications. The SBA has prepared bibliographies of articles, books, and reports on how to start and operate many kinds of businesses. It also publishes a series of "Starting and Managing" booklets designed to help small entrepreneurs "look before they leap" into a business. The first volume in the series—*Starting and Managing a Small Business of Your Own*—deals with the subject in general terms. Each of the other volumes deals with one type of business in detail. For a complete list of SBA publications or to order any SBA publication, call 202-653-6565.

The SBA also maintains more than 100 field offices. Many of these offices conduct management training seminars at little or no cost to participants.

ADVOCACY

Since 1976 the SBA has worked to further the cause of small business through its Office of Advocacy. The **Office of Advocacy,** or Advocacy for short, *represents small business in policy decisions and serves as an omsbudsman for individual small businesses trying to resolve their problems with other federal agencies.* Through its toll-free SBA answer desk, Advocacy makes sure that people can get answers to questions quickly and easily. The telephone number of the Office of Advocacy is 800-368-5855. (A better understanding of the needs and benefits of small businesses, by the way, resulted in congressional authorization of a Small Business Innovation Research Program. Under the SBIR program, if a government agency has a budget of more than $100 million for outside research and development, it sets aside a percentage of its budget to go to small R&D firms. Started in 1983, the program will grow to provide an estimated

Women and minorities are getting help from the Small Business Administration. Here an owner of a men's clothing shop discusses inventory with her store manager.

$362 million for small business research in fiscal 1987 and each year following.[6])

Advocacy is also working to improve the flow of information about small business. Since 1982 it has helped the President prepare an annual report on the state of small business, and Advocacy develops and maintains a small business data base. This data base provides a systematic examination of the small business community's contribution to the economy, and it allows the government to measure accurately the effect of programs and policies on small businesses.

HELPING WOMEN AND MINORITIES GET INTO BUSINESS

The SBA offers special programs to assist women and members of minority groups who want to start small businesses or expand exist-

---

[6]Mendel Gragg, "New Opportunity in Washington for Small Firms," *Nation's Business*, October 1983, 34.

ing ones. Its Office of Minority Small Business and Capital Ownership Development and its Office of Women in Business administer these programs. The 1984 report on the state of small business notes that from 1972 to 1982 the number of minority self-employed workers increased 43 percent; the comparable increase for whites was 35 percent. The report also notes that younger and better-educated minorities are entering business now, and the businesses they enter have greater growth potential and better prospects for earnings. The report notes as well that in recent years, female-operated businesses have increased more rapidly than either male-operated firms or the total number of businesses.

FRANCHISING

One way to merge the strengths of small business with the strengths of relatively large business is through franchising. In **franchising** *a parent company grants an individual or a company the right or privilege to do business on its behalf, subject to prescribed conditions.* The **franchisor** is *the parent company;* the **franchisee** is *the receiver of the privilege to do business;* and the **franchise** is *the right or privilege.*

Franchising isn't new. Widespread application of the concept has been with us since 1950, and Coca-Cola bottlers, automobile dealerships, and gasoline stations have long been operated as franchises. Today franchises include many fast-food restaurants (like McDonald's and Wendy's), motels (like Days Inns and Ramada Inns), and service establishments marketing everything from weight reduction to dry cleaning to income tax preparation.

Familiar Franchised Operations

CONTEMPORARY ISSUE

Is This the Decade of the Woman Entrepreneur?

In the second half of the 1980s, what experts hailed at the outset as "the decade of the woman entrepreneur" still holds the same promise of greater personal and financial independence for women who run their own businesses. Statistically, however, the verdict is still out on the advances made.

When *Business Week* looked at the issue in 1980, it reported a big change. Previously, women entrepreneurs had succeeded mainly in businesses like cosmetics and only rarely in a "mainstream" industry. Now the number of women entrepreneurs was rising and their operating styles had changed dramatically, the report said. "Equipped with advanced degrees and management experience acquired at major corporations, many women are moving aggressively beyond their traditional industries into high-technology and manufacturing businesses. They are fending off merger and acquisition partners, recruiting seasoned male executives, and winning the backing of bankers and occasionally venture capitalists."* The article then examined a number of success stories to prove its point.

There are good reasons why women consider entrepreneurship. Women who start their own businesses are able to solve two common problems: frustrated corporate careers and inadequate child-care. When a mother is her own boss, she does have greater flexibility to arrange her schedule so she can rear her children in a satisfying way, says Phyllis Gillis, author of *Entrepreneurial Mothers* (New York: Rawson, 1984).** The woman who entered a major corporation in the 1970s, only to find her career at an unacceptable plateau in the 1980s, will have no alternative

The Franchise System Is Important

In 1984 there were 462,000 establishments operating as franchises in the United States. These businesses did over $436 billion in business and employed more than 5 million people. Average sales volume per establishment was almost $1 million, which is much larger than the average nonfranchised small business. Franchises account for about one-third of all retail sales.

How Does Franchising Work?

Typically, the franchisor sells the franchisee a franchise which gives the franchisee the right to market the franchisor's product or service in a specified geographical area. As part of the franchise, the franchisor supplies a complete business format including use of a trade name, the particular facilities required, methods of operation, a marketing plan, advertising, a quality control procedure, a communication system, and the required training to operate the business.

In return for the franchise, the franchisee pays the franchisor a but to strike out on her own, says Charlotte Taylor, a management consultant who headed the 1979 Interagency Task Force on Women Business Owners.[†] Taylor has elsewhere written of women as "the new immigrants," who (like the Irish, Italian, and Jewish immigrants before them) will turn to creating their own businesses because they lack access to traditional channels of success.[‡]

Women today are better prepared to succeed in small business, what with higher enrollments in technical and business classes, more role models of successful, self-made women, and grudging male acceptance of women in all fields of business. In none of these areas, however, is progress as great as it could be.

What do the numbers say? One strong trend of the 1970s continues into the 1980s. According to the U.S. Bureau of Labor, the number of self-employed women increased by 56 percent from 1970 to 1979—more than five times the rate of men. From 1980 to 1982 the number of self-employed women rose by ten percent, compared to a one percent gain for men. There was not, however, an equivalent increase in the size or earnings of firms operated by women. Even the major types of female-operated businesses remained in the traditional areas of retail trade and services.[a] But make no mistake: the change is on its way. *The State of Small Business* optimistically concludes that "Gradually women are entering new fields of education and different occupations that will assist their transition to high growth, unfamiliar, and more profitable business ventures."

---

[*]"Working Women Rise as Entrepreneurs," *Business Week*, Feb. 25, 1980, 85.
[**]As quoted by David E. Gumpert, "The Other Bottom Line," *Working Woman*, July 1984, 76.
[†]"Women Rise as Entrepreneurs," 86.
[‡]*Women and the Business Game: Strategies for Successful Ownership* (New York: Cornerstone Library, 1980), 20.
[a]*The State of Small Business: A Report of the President* (Washington, D.C.: Government Printing Office, 1984), 347, 350.

---

certain sum which ranges from a few thousand dollars to a half million or more. The franchisee also pays the franchisor a royalty or percentage of sales, some of which may be used for national advertising. More importantly, the franchisee agrees to operate the franchise according to the franchisor's specifications. Tight control over operations is essential to the success of the franchise.

Advantages for the Franchisor

Franchising enables a franchisor to expand fast because (a) most of the capital needed is supplied by the franchisee, and (b) on-site management is provided by the franchisee. Many successful entrepreneurs have used franchising as a tool to build a small business into a large one. See, for example, the profile on Ray Kroc on page 82.

Advantages for the Franchisee

Entrepreneurs approaching a franchise from the other side should ask themselves, "What can a franchisor do for me that I can't do for

PEOPLE WHO MAKE THINGS HAPPEN

A PROFILE OF RAY KROC

By the time he was 50 years old, Raymond A. Kroc had been—among other things—a Florida real estate salesman, a piano player, music director for a Chicago radio station, and a paper cup salesman. But, as Kroc approached middle age, he "discovered" hamburgers and developed a way to sell them by the billions.

In 1954 Kroc was selling milkshake "multimixer" machines. One customer, McDonald Brothers in San Bernardino, California, ordered eight machines. When Kroc observed the efficiency of the McDonald Brothers operation (limited menu, fast service), it occurred to him that if McDonald's opened up more stores, he could sell them more milkshake machines. So Kroc persuaded the McDonald Brothers to let him sell franchises for them.

Gradually, Kroc became more interested in selling franchises than in creating a market for his milkshake machines. He began to see the large profit potential in a franchise business.

Soon Kroc had franchised 200 stores whose combined volume was $37 million annually. At this point Kroc was receiving 1.9 percent of the gross revenues. He discovered he could earn more if McDonald's would lease a site, develop it, and then release the whole operation to the franchisee. This would give them a profit from the lease in addition to the profits from the franchise fee. With this idea in mind, Kroc bought out the McDonald Brothers' interest for $2.7 million.

At first Kroc confined McDonald's stores to suburbs. In recent years, restaurants have also been opened in inner cities and small towns. The menu has been expanded to attract breakfast customers. Today, the McDonald's chain has more than 6,833 outlets in the United States and in 31 foreign countries.

Ray Kroc believed in old-fashioned hard work as an essential ingredient for success. He emphasized that neither education nor talent alone is sufficient to ensure success. "Nothing is more common than unsuccessful men with talent," he said, "and the world is full of educated derelicts. Nothing in the world can take the place of persistence."

When Kroc died at the age of 81 in 1984, he was worth an estimated $500 million. Kroc owned the San Diego Padres baseball team. Dedicating the 1984 season to his memory and wearing the initials RAK in black on the sleeves of their uniforms, the Padres played their way to their first-ever World Series.

---

myself as well or better?" The advantages claimed for franchising are many and include:

1. *Brand-name recognition.* A buyer of a Kentucky Fried Chicken franchise knows that virtually everyone is familiar with the name, product, and method of operation.

2. *Standardized quality and service.* Ideally, the franchisor works to ensure that the produce and service are identical in all outlets. Standardization builds consumer confidence.

3. *Management training.* To ensure standardized products and services, franchisors go to great lengths to train their franchisees. McDonald's, for example, requires franchisees to attend Hamburger University for 14 days of concentrated training in all details of how to operate a franchise successfully.

4. *National sales promotion.* Typically, the franchisor advertises regionally or nationally. Because the promotion benefits all franchisees, each contributes a certain amount of sales (usually one to two percent) to the advertising campaign.

5. *Business location assistance.* Franchisors either pick the location for the franchise or issue tight guidelines for its selection. This is an important advantage because the wrong location can make failure certain.

Other advantages of franchising to the franchisee may include (a) help in financing the business, (b) centralized buying, and (c) better odds for success. The SBA says that 80 percent of all franchises succeed, while 90 percent of all strictly independent businesses fail!

What Are the Disadvantages of Franchising?

No business arrangement is perfect. To the franchisee, key limitations are:

1. *Franchise costs and fees may be high.* A franchise with good potential is expensive. People with limited capital, for example, find it very difficult to raise the capital needed to purchase a well-known franchise. Fees for promotion, in some cases, are greater than profits earned.

2. *Independence of action is restricted.* Successful franchisors insist that franchisees follow their prescribed methods or forfeit the right to operate. Highly innovative people may prefer to operate a truly independent business.

3. *Restrictions on purchasing.* Franchisors often require franchisees to purchase supplies and fixtures from the franchisor or an approved vendor. This practice, which has been challenged in court, still prevails. Franchisors argue that purchasing must be restricted to ensure quality standards in all locations and thereby protect the franchisor's reputation.

APPLICATION TO PERSONAL AFFAIRS

How to Evaluate a Franchising Opportunity

Franchising is a popular way of going into business for yourself. And statistically, your chances of success as a franchisee are many times greater than if you go into business on a strictly independent basis. Nevertheless, many thousands of franchises fail each year. If you do the following, you will give yourself the best chance for success.

1. Study the product or service and the merchandising concept.
   - ☐ Is it a fad? Luxury item? Staple?
   - ☐ To what extent is demand for it seasonal?
   - ☐ What is the pricing structure?
   - ☐ At what point would you break even?
   - ☐ Has the soundness of the marketing plan been proven?

2. Investigate the franchisor.
   - ☐ Get the opinion of your banker and accountant.
   - ☐ Check with the Better Business Bureau or chamber of commerce.
   - ☐ Obtain a detailed and certified profit-and-loss statement.
   - ☐ How long has the franchisor been in business?
   - ☐ Who are the principals? What is their reputation?
   - ☐ What are the franchisor's plans for expansion?

3. Check with several existing franchisees.
   - ☐ Ask to see their income and expense statements.
   - ☐ Ask franchisees about such things as (a) how many hours per week are involved, (b) employee turnover, (c) theft, (d) advertising and promotion costs, (e) the main problems they have had.

4. Determine exactly what you will receive for your franchise fee and how much other money you will pay the franchisor.
   - ☐ Does the franchisor pay for all or part of the advertising?
   - ☐ Is the franchise fee competitive with those of similar franchises?

5. Review the franchise agreement carefully with your lawyer.
   - ☐ Is the contract equitable to both parties?
   - ☐ What are the provisions for renewing, terminating, or transferring the contract?
   - ☐ Can the franchisor buy back the franchise? Under what conditions?
   - ☐ Can unsold merchandise be returned for credit?
   - ☐ Does the agreement restrict other economic activities of the franchisee?
   - ☐ Does it provide exclusive rights for a given area?

6. Never be in a hurry to sign a franchise agreement. Take at least 30 days to make up your mind.

7. Do your homework thoroughly before making a decision. The guidelines above are just starting points for a thorough investigation.

THE OUTLOOK FOR FRANCHISING

Although franchise operations have a much lower failure rate than small, independently owned businesses, you should take great care in signing up with a franchisor. "The business is loaded with come-ons—for every good franchise opportunity there are five bad ones," according to one knowledgeable observer. The future of franchising has become clouded legally because of certain questionable practices on the part of some franchisors. The following practices have received particular criticism:

- Canceling franchise agreements for minor contract infringements
- Limiting the right of the franchisee to transfer ownership of the franchise
- Charging franchisees excessive fees and demanding royalty payments out of proportion to sales
- Requiring franchisees to buy merchandise, supplies, and equipment from franchisors at prices above what the franchisees would have to pay elsewhere
- Demanding control of the selling price regardless of local conditions

Franchisors, for their part, may have serious problems with franchisees. Some companies operate under two systems: They own and operate outlets where they want strict control, and they use franchisees where they are convinced that good managers are available.

To achieve maximum success, both parties must make concessions. The franchisor must accept that complete control over the franchisee is impossible because the business is independent. Franchisees must be willing to sacrifice some independence and to conform substantially to the franchisor's methods. Despite the problems associated with franchising, it will continue to be important in the years ahead, for it combines the advantages of both big and small business.

BIG BUSINESS REDISCOVERS ENTREPRENEURSHIP

The social trend to independence in the 1980s affects big business too. We see this trend in the increase of large public corporations "going private" through leveraged buyouts, in the rise of the corporate entrepreneur, and in the response of business schools and consulting firms to the new demand for managers with entrepreneurial abilities.

Leveraged Buyouts

In a **leveraged buyout (LBO),** *a new owner will borrow heavily to buy out public stockholders of a corporation.* Often the new owners are the managers themselves. The new owners then have the freedom to run the company without worrying about reporting to stockholders. A recent LBO was the sale of Dr. Pepper to its chief executive, W. W. Clements—for $650 million. Although controversial,

LBOs are likely to remain popular, because on balance, "an LBO gives [a company's] managers—and in some cases, its workers—a big equity stake in the business, unleashing their entrepreneurial energies and providing huge incentives to run a tight, efficient operation."[7]

Corporate Entrepreneurs Are in Demand

Opportunities are increasing for a new breed of corporate employee called the corporate entrepreneur. A **corporate entrepreneur** is *a person with drive and initiative who wants to run a small business within the structure of a large business.*

Demand for self-starting, high-energy employees is growing because senior executives in large enterprises have come to realize, in the words of one observer, "almost without exception, the revolutionary inventions and the businesses to exploit them have come from small enterprises led by venturesome entrepreneurs. 'Why not us?' the big companies have been asking. 'Why do an average nine out of every ten enterprises we try to develop end in failure?' "[8]

Corporate entrepreneurs are particularly needed to develop new products and market them successfully. "IBM, for example, is implementing a number of IBU's (independent business units) as vehicles for its corporate entrepreneurs."[9] Other major companies that are integrating the corporate entrepreneur concept into company operations include 3M, General Electric, General Foods, and Citicorp.

By giving individuals with initiative the freedom to act as entrepreneurs within the corporations, managers may avoid seeing former employees become their competitors. Many independent entrepreneurs got their start working in large corporations. Then, equipped with experience and contacts, these individuals started their own businesses. Founders of many high-tech firms once worked for IBM. Most entrepreneurial heads of accounting firms, advertising agencies, law firms, engineering organizations, and construction companies began their careers working for an established company in their chosen field—and some entrepreneurs have become very wealthy. (See Table 3–1.)

Schools and Consultants Teaching Entrepreneurship

As managers demand the benefits of entrepreneurship for their large companies, campuses and consultants appear eager to meet the de-

---

[7]"Leveraged Buyouts: How Real Are the Dangers?" *Business Week*, July 2, 1984, 73.

[8]Hanan, 75.

[9]Hanan, 77.

mand. More schools offer entrepreneurial classes than ever before. And some entrepreneurs have discovered that teaching corporations how to nurture innovation is itself a new growth industry.

TABLE 3-1 Computer Wealth—America's Richest Computer Entrepreneurs

NAME	COMPANY	ESTIMATED NET WORTH
David Packard	Hewlett-Packard	$1,000,000,000
William Hewlett	Hewlett-Packard	650,000,000
An Wang	Wang Labs	620,000,000
H. Ross Perot	Electronic Data Systems	325,000,000
Mandel Brothers	Newark Electronics	250,000,000
Max Palevsky	Scientific Data Systems	200,000,000
Kenneth Olsen	Digital Equipment	157,000,000
Pat McGovern	International Data	150,000,000
Howard Vollum	Tektronix	135,000,000
Saul Steinberg	Leasco	130,000,000
Gordon Moore	Intel	125,000,000

SOURCE: *Business and Society Review*, Spring 1984, 38.

AMERICA'S REEMERGING CREATIVITY

Teaching Entrepreneurship

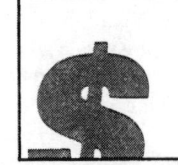

Is entrepreneurship a skill you can learn? Schools and consulting firms appear to believe the answer is yes—with qualifications.

Karl H. Vesper, a professor at the University of Washington and an authority on entrepreneurs and education, estimates that the number of universities with courses or research centers on entrepreneurship grew from six in 1967 to 150 in 1984.* If we include colleges and community colleges, we estimate that the number of campuses teaching entrepreneurship—corporate or otherwise—is now over 500.

Company chiefs aren't always waiting for the graduates to arrive. Many companies are turning to a new crop of consultants who specialize in helping large organizations develop an atmosphere that will nurture the in-house entrepreneur. Clients seeking this advice include companies like AT&T, Tektronix, Westinghouse, and Xerox. The consultants in turn are opening up their own schools to teach corporate managers and employees how to keep innovation from colliding with corporate culture.** And of course, some companies are encouraging entrepreneurship without outside help.

But to return to the central question, can you teach any person to be an entrepreneur? As for the colleges, a recent article in *Forbes* raises a valid point:

Most businesses get started when the founder spots an opportunity others have overlooked. The best vantage point for such insights can be had by actually working in that field. If you are in a classroom as opposed to out working and looking, you increase the odds against finding that niche. Nor is an A+ in Entrepreneurship 101 likely to impress backers.[†]

The consultants who work with large businesses aren't obligated to turn every employee into an entrepreneur. Instead of inexperienced students, the would-be entrepreneurs in a large business are precisely those opportunists "working in the field" referred to above. At the least, the consultants have the easier time of it.

The cautious response to the question is that college classes in entrepreneurship can help a student who is already on the road to becoming an entrepreneur by providing a preview of the entrepreneurial process. For all students, these classes will widen their views on the role of the entrepreneur in businesses of any size. And large companies are continuing to turn to entrepreneurial consultants, recognizing that by fostering innovation, a company stands the best chances for growth and survival. Individuals and big businesses alike are attempting to recapture entrepreneurship—the magic spark that created American business.

Questions for Discussion

1. Why are many big businesses looking to business schools for corporate entrepreneurs?
2. Why would students choose classes for entrepreneurship over real work experience?
3. What can a small consulting firm teach a giant corporation about entrepreneurship?
4. How does it benefit American business to understand what encourages and what inhibits entrepreneurial behavior in a company?

---

[*] "B-Schools Try to Churn out Entrepreneurs," *Business Week*, March 5, 1984, 102.
[**] Sharon Nelson, "Finding Room for the Intrapreneur," *Nation's Business*, Feb. 1984, 50.
[†] Paul B. Brown, "Entrepreneurship 101," *Forbes*, Sept. 24, 1984, 174.

SUMMARY

- A small business is a business that is independently owned and is not dominant in its field. The Small Business Administration, for loan purposes, sets guidelines as to what constitutes "small" in different industries.
- Big business could not exist without small business because (1) small businesses link big businesses to the consuming public, and (2) small businesses act as suppliers to big businesses. Small businesses now employ one-half the private labor sector and are the source of all net new jobs.
- Small businesses have advantages over big businesses when the market is limited, craftsmanship is important, service is personal, convenience is important, and demand is irregular.
- Principal strengths of small businesses are (1) freedom to act quickly, (2) ability to adapt to local needs, (3) public favor, and (4) lower operating costs. Main weaknesses are (1) difficulty in attracting the best employees, (2) lack of specialized management, (3) difficulty in raising capital, and (4) sensitivity to economic fluctuations.
- Most small businesses fail because of poor management.
- The Small Business Administration is an independent government agency that provides the following services: financial assistance, managerial and technical assistance, advocacy, and special programs for women and minorities.
- Franchising ideally combines the advantages of large and small business while avoiding the weaknesses of either. Franchising employs more than 5 million people and accounts for about one-third of all retail sales.
- Despite legal problems, the outlook for franchising is good.
- Big business has rediscovered entrepreneurship in the increase of leveraged buyouts, in the rise of the corporate entrepreneur, and in the rapid growth of classes in entrepreneurship offered by colleges and by consulting firms.

KEY TERMS YOU SHOULD KNOW

corporate entrepreneur	Individual Retirement	Office of Advocacy
entrepreneurship	Account (IRA)	small business
franchise	Keogh Plan	Small Business
franchisee	leveraged buyout (LBO)	Administration
franchising	long-term capital	
franchisor	market	

QUESTIONS FOR REVIEW

1. How does the Small Business Act define small business?
2. In terms of size, what is a small business in retailing? the services industry? wholesaling? agriculture? general construction? manufacturing?
3. Why does the Small Business Administration set limits on size in its classification of small businesses?
4. What facts show that many small businesses are part-time or one-person operations?
5. What are the distinguishing characteristics of small businesses?
6. Under what specific conditions does small business have advantages over big business?
7. What are the strengths of small businesses?
8. What are the weaknesses of small businesses?
9. Why do small businesses fail?
10. What are the pros and cons of purchasing an established business?
11. How can the Small Business Administration help small businesses?
12. What is franchising? a franchisor? a franchisee? a franchise?
13. What are the advantages and disadvantages of franchising to the franchisee?
14. How does the franchisor benefit from the franchising system?
15. What is a corporate entrepreneur? Why are corporate entrepreneurs in demand?

QUESTIONS FOR DISCUSSION

1. "All giant enterprises once were small." Explain why this is so.
2. How do entrepreneurs who succeed in making fortunes benefit society?
3. Why do many college students look forward to owning and operating their own businesses?
4. Does the large number of part-time businesses suggest that some people don't make enough money in their regular jobs? Or does it indicate many people need an outlet for their creative energies?
5. Some experts have said that franchising ideally combines the advantages of both the large business and the small business. Do you agree? Explain.
6. Review recent issues of the *Wall Street Journal* and study the advertisements for franchises. Make a list of those offered, the products involved, and the prices of each (if they are given). What conclusions can you draw about (a) the variety of franchises available, (b) the types of product suitable for franchising, and (c) the capital required?
7. Is a corporate entrepreneur as defined in the text a true entrepreneur in your opinion? Why or why not?

CASE STUDY

Positive Thinking and Working on the Side

Millions of Americans go into sideline ventures believing that a positive attitude is all it takes for success. Here we follow the discussion between Sue Wilicki and Darrel Sanchez, both about 30 years old and employed in the personnel department of a large corporation. Darrel believes he can find happiness and fulfillment—and the income to support a better lifestyle—by starting a sideline venture.

Darrel: I can't lose. In two years I'll be earning twice as much as now and working half the hours—working for an outfit with the right attitude.

Sue: You mean you're going to quit here?

D: Not so loud, okay? Anyway, the answer is no—not yet. I'm going to start by working this job on the side, and let it grow. When things take off, I'm saying goodby to this eight-to-five prison.

S: What is this outfit you're talking about?

D: Urban Pro Cosmetics, Inc.

S: What? You're going to sell soap door-to-door?

D: Wrong. My product is the right attitude. The soaps and cosmetics sell themselves, because they promote the success-oriented attitude of the urban professional.

S: No one gets rich selling Urban Pro.

D: Wrong. Thousands of engineers, lawyers, doctors, and architects are in the business because it pays prime rates for spare time.

S: I think the guy who started Urban Pro is the only one who makes real money.

D: Wrong, wrong, wrong. Urban Pro is just taking off. If I play my cards right, I can build a network of sales leads that will take care of itself. Then I can branch out into new little market niches that no one else has thought of. When you build enough sales in any one area, Urban Pro gives you added responsibility. In a few years I'll become my area's district representative, and I'll get a percent of every dime my people bring in.

S: I think you're crazy. When you work on your sideline, you won't have the energy for work here. Most likely you'll be passed over for raises and promotions. And your sideline will fizzle because you won't be able to work on it full-time.

D: My sideline will *help* my work here, because I'll be around a lot of people who are highly motivated. And I'll be a better employee because I'll have the right success attitude. I truly believe that I can succeed at anything I want to do. And that includes working two jobs at once.

Questions

1. Darrel Sanchez offers little in the way of hard data to support his enthusiasm. What should Sanchez know about Urban Pro *before* he starts working two jobs?

2. If you were an employer, would you discourage or prohibit your employees from establishing sideline ventures? Why or why not?

3. Which side of this argument do you support? Why?

EVOLUTION OF A BUSINESS

Acquire a Franchise? Start from Scratch? Or What?

The next time Sara and Ray got together, Ray brought up an idea they hadn't considered before.

Ray: We've been talking about *starting* a business from scratch. What about buying a business that's up and running?

Sara: Good idea. Somehow, when you think of going into a business you automatically think of starting your own. But I think we should consider every option.

Ray: Maybe we could find an agency with a good reputation that's for sale.

Sara: Or a franchise. I remember glancing through the "Business Opportunities" section in the *Wall Street Journal*—and noticed some franchises offered in the travel agency field. Franchising companies were looking for investors who would manage their own agencies.

Ray: What are the advantages in that? Travel agencies are so personalized. It doesn't seem there'd be much to gain by tying ourselves to a franchising arrangement.

Sara: Obviously there are some advantages we aren't aware of, or the franchisor wouldn't be so successful. I think we should look into it before we reject the idea.

Ray: Okay. So we need to investigate buying an ongoing business *and* buying a franchise. How do you want to split the research chores?

Questions

1. What are the advantages and disadvantages of buying a going business versus starting one from scratch?
2. How can Sara and Ray best find out about what going businesses are available? How can they judge whether a business is a good buy?
3. What would be the advantages and disadvantages of a franchise arrangement?
4. Which approach is least risky—acquiring a business, acquiring a franchise, or going it on your own?
5. How should Sara and Ray go about deciding which approach to take?

CON/AGG '8
CONCRETE & AGGREGATES
CHICAGO U.S.A.
29-Feb. 2, 1984
SEAL OF THE PRESIDENT OF THE UNITED STATES

4

BUSINESS, GOVERNMENT, AND SOCIETY
Who's Responsible for What?

READ THIS CHAPTER SO YOU CAN:

Discuss the social responsibilities of business.

Describe three major social movements affecting business.

Discuss the history of government regulation of business, and the four major laws created to promote competition.

Explain how federal regulatory agencies affect business.

Describe the role of the Department of Commerce.

Define the major federal and state taxes.

Discuss tax revolts, tax evasion, and "bracket creep."

Explain the effect of the large amount of paperwork required of business, and the need for business and government to cooperate.

Business affects each of us directly. Business provides our jobs, and makes and markets the shelters we live in, the foods we eat, and the beverages we drink. It supplies the clothes we wear, the cars we drive, the recreation we seek, the books and magazines we read, and the medicine we consume.

But business does more. It pays taxes and determines to a great extent how the nation's land is to be used. It also determines the location and design of buildings, manufacturing plants, and other physical structures. Business directly affects the quality of the air we breathe, the purity of the water we drink, and the attractiveness of the landscape we see.

By any measure, business is our dominant social institution. Because of the prominence of business, society—all of us—is interested in what business does and how it does it. In evaluating the role of business in society, we must ask ourselves whether the welfare of society takes precedence over the welfare of business, or if the welfare of business supersedes the welfare of society. In other words, is a businessperson primarily a member of society or a member of the economic community?

To understand the obligations of business as the primary employer of people, user of land, water, air, and other natural resources, and maker and marketer of the products we consume requires that we examine its social responsibility.

WHAT IS SOCIAL RESPONSIBILITY?

Social responsibility is *the duty of business to promote (or at least not damage) the welfare of society*. For example, a business that makes safe products, carefully disposes of its wastes, and provides equal employment opportunities is socially responsible. A business that makes unsafe products, pollutes the environment, and discriminates in employment is not.

Many people question the honesty and social responsibility of businesspeople. One reason is that much business is transacted in public. Another factor is that each of us has on occasion been cheated or treated unfairly.

Another reason for the public's dim view of business is negative publicity. Newspapers and the broadcast media devote considerable space and time to businesses accused of bad practices. When a business does something illegal or unfair, news of it quickly becomes public.

Most businesses try to act responsibly. Enlightened businesspeople know that in the long run the surest way to earn profits is to play fair with consumers, protect the environment, and maintain fair employment practices.

Unfortunately, not all businesspeople are enlightened. Some do try to take advantage of consumers, some do damage the environment, and some do discriminate. In response to the irresponsible behavior of a comparatively few businesses, three major movements occurred: the consumer movement, the environmental movement, and the civil rights movement. These movements, in turn, helped bring about much greater government involvement in business. In this chapter, we discuss the relationship between business, government, and society.

MAJOR SOCIAL MOVEMENTS AFFECTING BUSINESS

Three major movements have had a great impact on the conduct of business. The *consumer movement* is largely concentrated on how business behaves in the marketplace. The *environmental movement* deals mainly with how business handles waste, pollutes the air, and uses the land. And the *civil rights movement* is focused mainly on employment problems.

The Consumer Movement

Consumerism is *a loosely organized movement of private individuals and citizens' groups formed to protect the public from various business malpractices.*

THE THREE WAVES OF CONSUMERISM

Historically, consumerist agitation can be roughly divided into three waves. The first, occurring in the early 1900s, gathered momentum from scandals in the prescription drug field and from publications like Upton Sinclair's book *The Jungle*. This was an exposé of unsanitary conditions in the meat-packing industry. The first wave reached its peak with the passage of the Pure Food and Drug Act of 1906, which prohibited interstate commerce in adulterated or mislabeled foods and provided for government inspection of meat products.

The second wave was an outgrowth of the Great Depression of the 1930s. In 1938 Congress passed the Food, Drug, and Cosmetics Act to tighten loopholes in the Pure Food and Drug Act. It also amended the Federal Trade Commission Act to provide penalties for manufacturers who falsely advertised food, drugs, or cosmetics.

The third and current wave of consumerism arose in the early 1960s. Investigative teams under the leadership of Ralph Nader, a lawyer who is still one of the consumer movement's chief organizers and spokespersons, uncovered corporate abuses of consumer rights in many fields. Nader's book, *Unsafe at Any Speed* (1965), called public attention to the many dangerous defects in Corvair automobiles. Later, a Senate subcommittee uncovered the fact that General Mo-

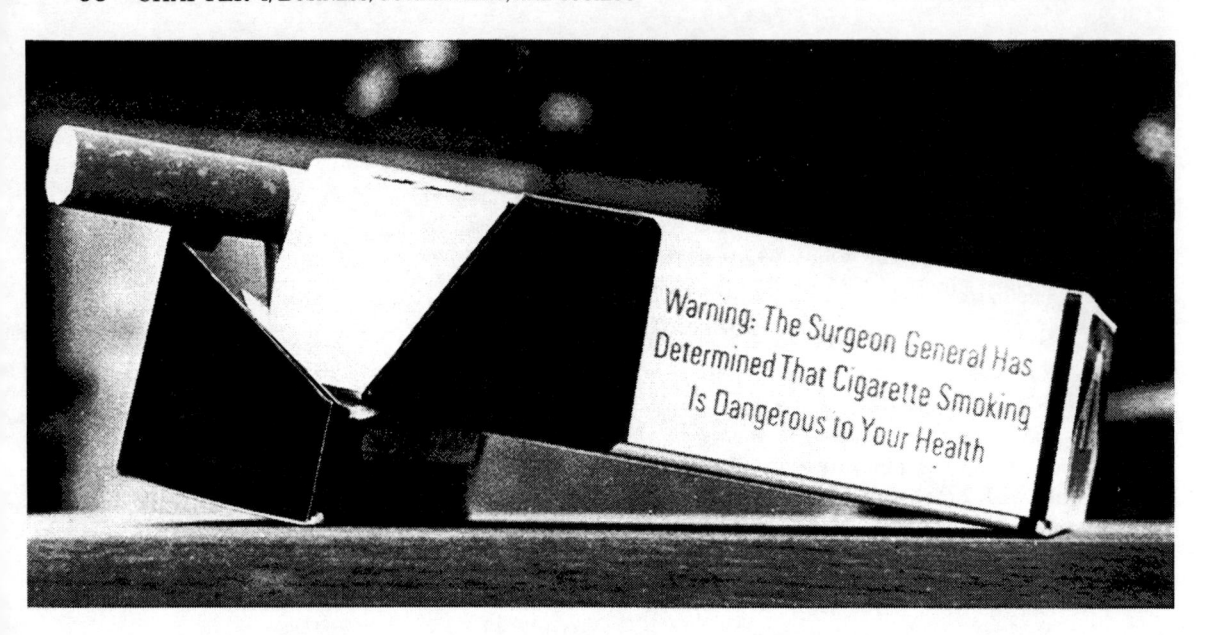

Consumers have the right to know when products are dangerous or can produce harmful effects.

tors had hired private detectives to put Nader under surveillance shortly after publication of the book. As a result of scandal caused by this disclosure, the president of GM publicly apologized to Nader. The resulting adverse publicity forced GM to take the Corvair out of production.

Consumerism continued to gain momentum. Today a host of laws and regulations helps protect the consumer. And manufacturers recognize that it is in their own best interest to provide their customers with safe and reliable products.

THE CONSUMER BILL OF RIGHTS

In 1962 President John F. Kennedy established a Consumer Advisory Council, which published a report that included a "bill of rights" for consumers. These rights include the following.

<u>The right to safety.</u> Consumers have the right to be protected against hazardous products. Thus there are laws concerned with safety. If the potential exists for dangerous misuse, consumers must even be protected from themselves. A clear warning must be provided by the manufacturer, as in the case of the warning that smoking tobacco products is injurious to health. Despite government guidelines, some marketers successfully advertise harmful products as being safe. The following comments from the Federal Trade Commission about cigarette advertising illustrate a form of deception which is legal but considered by many to be irresponsible.

The right to be informed. Information directed at consumers should not be fraudulent, deceitful, or misleading. The Federal Trade Commission polices advertising and has determined that an advertising claim, even when actually true, deceives if it falsely implies that a claim is unique for the advertiser's product. When Wonder Bread advertised that its bread "builds strong bodies 12 ways," the claim was considered deceptive, not because it was untrue but because the same claim is true of other breads as well. People exposed to such advertising might assume that the claim was unique. In a landmark decision, Wonder Bread was forced to run remedial advertising to correct any false impressions the original advertising may have created.

A wide range of legislation related to information has been enacted. The Truth-in-Lending Act of 1969 is designed to ensure that consumers are clearly informed about the interest rates they are required to pay for consumer credit. Care labeling laws require clothing manufacturers to provide labels explaining how to take care of garments.

The right to choose. The right to choose dates back to the Sherman Antitrust Act of 1890, which legislated against monopolies. Today, the Federal Trade Commission and the Antitrust Division of the Justice Department seek to ensure that companies do not have agreements or practices that restrain competition. Many people argue that the consumer benefits from free competition in the marketplace, since market pressures force companies to provide satisfactory products and services.

The right to be heard. Consumers have the right to receive full and sympathetic consideration by governmental agencies. One of the problems of the consumer movement has been its loose organization and lack of strong influence with legislators. To help consumers gain a larger voice in the nation's affairs, President Johnson in 1964 created the Office of Special Assistant to the President for Consumer Affairs. And in 1975 Congress passed the Consumer Protection Act and established the Agency for Consumer Advocacy, which provides consumer information to government agencies.

Misleading Marketing

"Cigarette ads associate smoking with good health, youthful vigor, social and professional success and other attractive ideas, individuals and activities that are both worthy of emulation and distant from concerns relating to health.... Thus the cigarette is portrayed as an integral part of youth, happiness, attractiveness, personal success and an active, vigorous, strenuous life style."

—*Federal Trade Commission, May 1981*

SOURCE: Darmstader, Ruth, *Snuff and Chaw: The Tobacco Industry Plugs Nicotine by Osmosis*, as reported in *Business and Society Review*, Fall 1983, volume 47, page 24.

NONGOVERNMENTAL PROTECTIVE AGENCIES

Nonfederal organizations are also involved in protecting the consumer. Some states and cities, as well as trade and credit unions, have offices of consumer affairs. **Better Business Bureaus**—*voluntary organizations composed of businesspeople in a community—seek to prevent illegal and unethical practices through self-regulation.* There are hundreds of local Better Business Bureaus throughout the country, financed by member businesses. These organizations try to ensure that their members follow sound ethical standards in their advertising and selling, provide a complaint service for consumers, and mediate in disputes between buyers and sellers.

Another well-known organization is Consumers Union, which tests products and rates them as "best buys," "also acceptable," and "not acceptable." The results are reported in *Consumer Reports,* a widely read and influential magazine that is published monthly.

THE FUTURE OF THE CONSUMER MOVEMENT

Ralph Nader was asked in 1980 to confirm press reports that the consumer movement in the United States was losing steam.[1] He replied that the media do not realize how outnumbered consumer groups are in terms of staff and resources. He stated that the total budget of consumer groups in the United States is probably less than $2 million annually, whereas there are 15,000 full-time business lobbyists in Washington spending $2 billion a year. Nader compared this to "... two football teams with only one person on one side and 11

Citizens have the right to demonstrate against rate increases and higher prices of goods and for safety.

---

[1]This section is based on information from an interview with Ralph Nader reported in *International Management* (July 1980).

people on the other.... [You] would hardly ask the one-man team whether he was slipping."

Businesses also lobby extensively through trade associations to seek passage of legislation they feel is favorable and to block passage of laws they feel are antibusiness. The following chart shows how much trade associations spent in one year to elect people to Congress to advance the interests of their members.

Two new consumer strategies for the 1980s are emerging. One calls for concentrating more on state legislatures because of the feeling that more can be accomplished in individual states than in Washington. For example, because of the efforts of Nader's group, a law in Wisconsin now states that public utilities must insert in monthly bills invitations for consumers to join their own statewide consumer action group. Nader says this is an important breakthrough and asks, "How else can millions of consumers with common objectives get in touch with one another and coordinate their efforts?"

A second emerging strategy is to focus on multinational companies. Says Nader, "I think that we in the United States have an obli-

---

Making Friends on Capitol Hill

TOP CONTRIBUTORS TO CONGRESSIONAL CAMPAIGNS

Political Action Committee	1981–1982 Contributions
1. Realtors PAC	$2,045,092
2. American Medical PAC	1,638,795
3. United Automobile Workers PAC	1,470,354
4. Machinists Non-Partisan Political League	1,252,209
5. National Education Association PAC	1,073,896
6. American Bankers Association PAC	870,110
7. National Association of Home Builders PAC	852,745
8. Associated Milk Producers PAC	842,450
9. Automobile and Truck Dealers Election Action Committee	829,945
10. A.F.L.- C.I.O. Political Contributions Committee	823,125
11. Seafarers Political Activity Donation	802,261
12. Engineers Political Education Committee	651,535
13. Associated General Contractors PAC	651,125
14. Active Ballot Club	634,357
15. National Rifle Association Political Victory Fund	612,137

—Federal Election Commission

SOURCE: Reported in *Business and Society Review*, Spring 1983, volume 45, 85.

gation to alert people around the world to how multinationals are affecting them."

The Environmental Movement

Prior to the 1960s, there was so little concern over "environmentalism" that the term did not even exist. Many people thought that there was an endless supply of raw materials, fresh air, and clean water.

Public awareness began to change—and the environmental movement began—with the publication of Rachel Carson's book *Silent Spring* in 1962. This book described the effects of the widespread use of pesticides and projected a future in which most wildlife would be unable to survive. There was an increased recognition that the lives and health of all human beings depend on the maintenance of a complex balance of interlocking systems (see Figure 4–1).

Problems concerning pollution are frequently international in scope. Spread by wind and air currents, pollution in one area can affect the population in other, nonpolluted areas. For example, pollu-

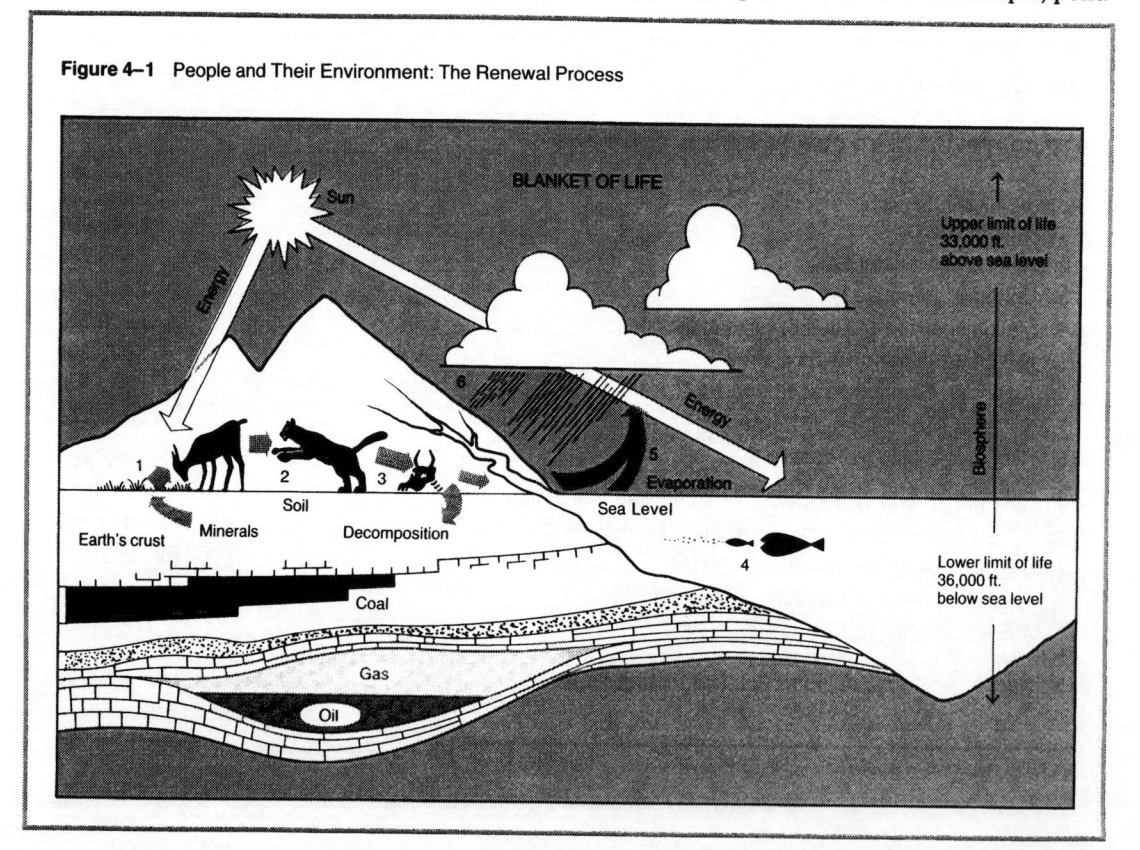

Figure 4–1 People and Their Environment: The Renewal Process

tion from the factories and mills of the industrial northeastern United States produces the acid rain that is destroying the forests of New England and eastern Canada.

And pollution can sometimes have deadly consequences. In 1966, a high concentration of sulfur dioxide in the air over New York City was blamed for the deaths of 168 people. Methyl mercury from industrial wastes dumped into the waters of a bay in Japan claimed the lives of 110 people and permanently crippled many others.

To guard against disasters such as these—and to prevent longer-term environmental damage—the U.S. government has passed a series of acts. In addition, in 1970 the **Environmental Protection Agency (EPA)** was established. The EPA was *given the power to develop and enforce standards for clean air and water; to regulate pollution from pesticides, noise, and radiation; and to approve state pollution abatement plans.* Later laws set deadlines for community and industrial compliance with federal pollution standards.

Today, business executives must deal with complex and wide-ranging legislation designed to restore the physical environment of the United States and prevent exhaustion of its resources. But we must always remember that industry is not the sole polluter of the environment. Each of us shares part of the responsibility and each of us bears part of the responsibility to help prevent further damage to nature's delicate balance.

The Civil Rights Movement

The civil rights movement for equal employment opportunities goes back more than a century. Traditionally, blacks, Hispanics, Native Americans, and other minorities have held the lowest paying jobs. Women, while now a majority in terms of population, have been typically included with the minorities because they were subject to the same kind of employment discrimination. If women were allowed to work at all, they were expected to be nurses, teachers, or secretaries, or to work in occupations where they had little chance for advancement.

Many Americans feel it has always been the social responsibility of business not to discriminate. But it took legal action to guarantee minorities equal employment rights.

Protests by minorities and by other concerned Americans led to the passage of the **Civil Rights Act of 1964.** Title VII of the act *prohibits discrimination in employment based on race, religion, national origin, or sex by any employer with 15 or more employees who engages in interstate commerce.* The **Equal Employment Opportunity Commission (EEOC),** *a federal agency that reports directly to the president, enforces the act.* Under Title VII, businesses are required to take **affirmative action**—that is, to make *special efforts to increase the proportion of women and minority-group mem-*

> **Affirmative Action at Sears**
>
> The 1985 annual report of Sears, Roebuck pinpoints the dramatic changes that have taken place in the company's work force over the past fifteen years by publishing a table showing utilization of minorities and women in nine different job categories, 1966 contrasted with 1984. The table below speaks for itself.
>
> **PERCENTAGE OF FEMALE AND MINORITY EMPLOYEES IN EACH JOB CATEGORY**
>
> | Job Categories | Female (%) Feb. 1966 | Female (%) Dec. 1984 | Black (%) Feb. 1966 | Black (%) Dec. 1984 | Hispanic (%) Feb. 1966 | Hispanic (%) Dec. 1984 |
> |---|---|---|---|---|---|---|
> | Officials and managers | 20.0 | 35.6 | .4 | 6.8 | .7 | 3.0 |
> | Professionals | 19.2 | 53.4 | .8 | 10.3 | .4 | 3.3 |
> | Technicians | 48.1 | 55.1 | 1.1 | 20.1 | .7 | 5.6 |
> | Sales workers | 56.9 | 63.7 | 3.2 | 16.7 | 1.5 | 5.6 |
> | Office and clerical | 86.0 | 84.0 | 3.1 | 17.6 | 2.0 | 6.2 |
> | Craft workers | 3.8 | 8.1 | 2.8 | 11.1 | 2.8 | 6.4 |
> | Operatives | 12.0 | 12.3 | 13.8 | 24.0 | 3.5 | 8.6 |
> | Laborers | 34.3 | 35.0 | 18.4 | 29.4 | 6.5 | 8.2 |
> | Service workers | 32.3 | 33.1 | 44.9 | 24.7 | 2.0 | 7.2 |
> | All categories | 50.7 | 54.6 | 5.9 | 17.8 | 2.1 | 6.1 |
>
> SOURCE: Sears, Roebuck Annual Report, 1985, 26.

bers who hold positions of responsibility in a company.

At first, the EEOC had little real impact because it could only pressure businesses through verbal complaints or informal meetings to persuade them to change discriminatory practices. Minority-group members complained that companies were satisfying the EEOC through tokenism and promises. Minority leaders felt that the government needed to be tougher in forcing compliance with the laws concerning discrimination that Congress had passed in the 1960s.

Compliance with civil rights legislation required many businesses to adjust their policies regarding hiring, work assignments, pay, and promotion. Discrimination still exists, but it is an issue that government and business leaders are working to resolve. Sears, Roebuck & Co. is an example of a firm that has gone far beyond government guidelines in complying with civil rights legislation (see above).

WHAT ROLE DOES GOVERNMENT PLAY?

All business is influenced in a number of ways by federal, state, and local governments. Government regulations stipulate the procedure for organizing a business and determine in part its location; they also dictate various construction specifications for reasons of safety, community zoning, and employee working environment, and specify minimum ages, hours, wages, and standard working conditions of employees. Government regulations influence advertising and selling practices; they regulate the sale of corporate securities and attempt to maintain free competition; and they specify procedures for dissolving a business.

History of Government Regulation

One of the first moves to regulate business was the establishment of the Interstate Commerce Commission in 1887. The original purpose of the commission was to prevent rate discrimination by railroads. Shortly thereafter, in 1890, the Sherman Antitrust Act was passed to curb the growth of trusts and monopolies, which threatened free competition.

In 1913 another step toward government regulation was taken with the passage of the Federal Reserve Bank Act, which resulted in a variety of controls over the banking system.

It was during the Great Depression, however, that government regulation of business took its greatest leap forward. The election of Franklin Roosevelt as president in 1932 marked the introduction of the **New Deal**—*a sweeping program of government-directed economic actions designed to lift the country out of the Depression.* Extensive controls were placed on the economy: Agricultural production was regulated, rigid restrictions were placed on banking and finance, public works were instituted on a gigantic scale, and extensive labor legislation was enacted. The government changed from a passive force in the economy to an active promoter and controller of economic welfare.

The period from 1933 to 1980 was an era of steadily increasing regulation of business. The three movements already discussed—consumerism, environmentalism, and civil rights—were important elements that caused more restrictions to be placed on the way in which business was conducted.

In the early 1980s the pendulum swung from more regulation to less. Voters decided that more government was not the answer to the nation's ills. High interest rates, low productivity, lack of capital available for business, high unemployment, erosion of the value of the dollar, deficit spending, and deficit trade balances were among the reasons the public appeared to want less government control over business. While business leaders constantly complain loudly about the evils of too much government regulation (as they have for decades), it is doubtful that many of them would care to revert to the pre-1933 period. Business leaders recognize that:

- Considerable government regulation of economic activity is essential in today's complex world.
- The government, as an instrument of the people, can guide and assist business in many useful ways.

> *"It is truly enough said that a corporation has no conscience; but a corporation of conscientious men is a corporation with a conscience."*
>
> HENRY DAVID THOREAU

APPLICATION TO PERSONAL AFFAIRS

Uncle Sam's Agencies and Offices That Stand Ready to Help

The single most important printed guide to government information is the annual *U.S. Government Manual,* which describes and gives telephone numbers of all government agencies. In an interview for this book, George Mu, an American embassy commercial attaché, told how best to get information from the government. He advised that questions should be carefully thought out, written in advance, and as specific as possible. The government employee you are dealing with should be told why you want the information—you may not be asking the right question or may be talking in language that is not customarily used in government.

The following are numbers of *public affairs offices:*

Commerce, Department of—(202) 377-2000
Consumer Product Safety Commission—(800) 638-CPSC
Energy, Department of—(202) 252-5000
Environmental Protection Agency—(202) 382-2090
Equal Employment Opportunity Commission—(202) 634-6922
Federal Deposit Insurance Corporation—(202) 389-4221
Federal Reserve System—(202) 452-3000
Federal Trade Commission—(202) 523-3598
Interstate Commerce Commission—(202) 275-7252
Labor, Department of—(202) 523-8165
Occupational Safety and Health Review Commission—(202) 634-7943
Overseas Private Investment Corporation—(202) 653-2920
Securities and Exchange Commission—(202) 272-3100
Small Business Administration—(202) 653-6565

The following numbers are for *recorded messages* on recent developments; most are updated daily:

Commerce, Department of
  Economic news—(202) 393-4100
  News highlights—(202) 393-1847
  Weekend feature—(202) 393-4102
Consumer Product Safety Commission News—(800) 638-CPSC
Joint Economic Committee of U.S. Congress—(202) 224-3081
Energy, Department of—(202) 252-5000
Environmental Protection Agency—(202) 382-2090
Federal Trade Commission—(202) 523-3598
Housing and Urban Development, Department of—(202) 655-4000
Interior, Department of—(202) 343-3171
Labor, Department of—(202) 523-8156
Transportation, Department of—(202) 426-4000
Treasury, Department of—(202) 566-2000
White House Office—(202) 456-1414

These toll-free *hot lines* will connect you to people who provide information to the public:

Consumer Product Safety Commission
  Product recall information, complaints, and fact sheets—(800) 638-CPSC
Energy, Department of
  Alcohol fuels and gasohol information—(800) 525-5555
  Solar heating and cooling information—(800) 523-2929
Environmental Protection Agency
  Industry assistance on the Toxic Substances Control Act—(202) 382-2090
Export-Import Bank
  Financial aid for exporters—(202) 566-8990
Federal Deposit Insurance Corporation
  Banking complaints and information—(202) 389-4221
Small Business Administration
  Business publications—(202) 653-6565

By gathering in front of government buildings, farmers not only alert government officials to their needs but also get publicity for their cause from the media.

Government Action to Promote Competition

Economic theorists and pragmatic businesspeople alike believe that the result of unregulated competition would be a **monopoly**, or *a firm that controls such a large part of the total business done in an industry that it can dictate or control the market prices for the output of that industry.* Americans have traditionally feared monopolies and have therefore accepted laws to prevent them. The four most important antimonopoly acts are: the Sherman Antitrust Act, the Clayton Act, the Federal Trade Commission Act, and the Robinson–Patman Act. These laws, passed decades ago, guide today's competitive practices.

THE SHERMAN ANTITRUST ACT

During the 1880s, powerful monopolies developed in the sugar, oil, whiskey, tobacco, shoe machinery, harvesting machinery, and cash register industries—monopolies that were working against the public interest.

Accordingly, Congress passed the **Sherman Antitrust Act** in 1890. This act declared that *"every contract, combination . . . or conspiracy in restraint of trade or commerce among the several states . . . is hereby declared to be illegal"* and that *"every person who* shall monopolize or ... combine or conspire to monopolize ... shall be deemed guilty of a misdemeanor."

THE CLAYTON ACT

The **Clayton Act,** passed in 1914, *supplemented and strengthened the Sherman Antitrust Act.* The Clayton Act is much more specific, stating that practices that tend to lessen competition substantially or create a monopoly are unlawful. Practices specifically condemned in the Clayton Act and its amendments are:

- Discrimination in price between purchasers of like grade, quality, or quantity of a commodity
- **Interlocking directorates** in directly competing corporations (that is, *a director of one company also serving on the board of a competitor*)
- Acquisition by a corporation of more than a limited amount of stock in a directly competing corporation

THE FEDERAL TRADE COMMISSION ACT

While the Sherman Antitrust Act prevents combinations in restraint of trade and the Clayton Act deals with specific unfair trade practices, the **Federal Trade Commission Act** was *passed to control unfair trade practices generally.* Enacted in 1914, this law provides that "unfair methods of competition in commerce are hereby declared unlawful." Examples of practices that the commission has found to be unfair are:

- Advertising in a false or misleading way
- Misbranding goods as to quality, durability, composition, ingredients, origin, and so on
- Making false statements to the disadvantage of a competitor's products, services, financial status, and similar matters
- Advertising and selling rebuilt, reconditioned, or old merchandise as new

THE ROBINSON–PATMAN ACT

The **Robinson–Patman Act,** passed in 1936, *regulates marketing activity.* The Sherman Antitrust Act was intended primarily to curb monopolistic practices of manufacturers. But with the appearance of giant marketing establishments, mainly chain-store systems, it became clear that unfair competition also existed in marketing.

The most important provision of the Robinson–Patman Act prohibits "discrimination in price between different purchasers of commodities of like grade and quality, where any of the purchases involved are in interstate commerce, and where the effect may be

> *"Economic performance is no longer enough. Business is properly expected to act in the public interest as well as the shareholders' interest."*
>
> REGINALD JONES
> —GENERAL ELECTRIC COMPANY

substantially to lessen competition or tend to create a monopoly in any line of commerce, or to injure, destroy, or prevent competition with any person who either grants or knowingly receives the benefit of such discrimination or with customers of either item."

Federal Regulatory Agencies

The main contact businesses have with government is through **federal regulatory agencies,** of which there are currently more than 70. Those most important to business are described in Table 4–1. Their main activities are to *maintain competition, protect the consumer, and provide advice and counsel to business.*

Although business tends to be critical of most government regulatory agencies, the Occupational Safety and Health Administration (OSHA) and the Environmental Protection Agency (EPA) are especially controversial.

Established in 1970, OSHA had more than 2,900 employees and a budget of almost $230 million by 1984. Businesspeople agree that a safe and comfortable work environment increases the productivity of workers, but feel that OSHA regulations are at times arbitrary and interfering. OSHA's section in the Code of Federal Regulations fills nearly 1,500 pages.

The government protects employee working conditions through OSHA. Those engaged in hazardous jobs, such as construction, must use reasonable care and must wear protective shoes, gloves, and headgear.

TABLE 4-1 Major Federal Agencies That Regulate Business Activities

AGENCY	PURPOSE AND FUNCTIONS	LEGISLATIVE AUTHORITY
Consumer Product Safety Commission (CPSC)	Protects the public against unreasonable risks of injury from consumer products. Assists consumers to evaluate the comparative safety of consumer products.	An independent federal regulatory agency established in 1972.
Environmental Protection Agency (EPA)	Seeks to protect and enhance our environment today and for future generations. Controls and abates pollution in the areas of air, water, solid waste, pesticides, noise, and radiation.	Established in the executive branch as an independent agency in 1970.
Equal Employment Opportunity Commission (EEOC)	Works to end discrimination based on race, color, religion, sex, or national origin in hiring, promotion, firing, wages, testing, training, apprenticeship, and all other conditions of employment.	Created by Title VII of the Civil Rights Act of 1964. Title VII was amended by the Equal Employment Opportunity Act of 1972.
Federal Trade Commission (FTC)	Works to maintain strongly competitive enterprise as the keystone of the American economic system. Seeks to prevent monopoly, restraints on trade, or unfair or deceptive trade practices.	Basic purpose finds its primary expression in the Federal Trade Commission Act and the Clayton Act, both passed in 1914.
Food and Drug Administration (FDA)	Seeks to protect the health of the nation against impure and unsafe food, goods, drugs, and cosmetics and against a variety of other potential hazards.	Authorized under the Food and Drug Act of 1906.
Occupational Safety and Health Administration (OSHA)	Works to provide safe and healthful working conditions for both the employer and the employee.	An independent agency established by the Occupational Safety and Health Act of 1970.
Interstate Commerce Commission (ICC)	Regulates interstate surface transportation, including trains, trucks, buses, inland waterway and coastal shipping, freight forwarders, oil pipelines, and express companies.	Created as an independent establishment by the act to regulate commerce of February 4, 1887.

SOURCE: Adapted from the *United States Government Organization Manual,* Office of the Federal Register, National Archives and Records Service, General Services Administration.

The EPA, also established in 1970, had a budget of about $4.2 billion and employed over 12,000 persons in 1984. The cost of cleaning up such traditional heavy polluters like the steel industry is enormous, and some factories and mills have been forced to shut down because they could not afford the expensive equipment necessary to make themselves environmentally sound. People who lose their jobs as a result of such plant shutdowns may consider this too high a price to pay for a clean environment. Business and the government must work together to find a solution to this problem.

The Department of Commerce

The role of the **Department of Commerce** is *to encourage, serve, and promote the nation's economic development and technological advancement.* This work was carried out in 1984 by 119,000 employees with a budget of $2 billion.

The Department of Commerce gets high praise from U.S. business leaders. U.S. presidents traditionally appoint distinguished and seasoned business veterans to this cabinet post. The commerce secretary's job is very complex. Former Secretary of Commerce Juanita Krebs has said that among the department's main goals are to expand U.S. exports and to assist in reindustrialization. The Department of Commerce is also particularly concerned with corporate responsibility, ways to improve the economic climate, and ways to increase the amount of oil that American ships carry.

TAXATION

Taxation concerns each of us. Many people feel that taxes are too high and that the government spends our tax dollars unwisely. There is also growing sentiment that the tax structure is unfair and places a heavier burden on individual taxpayers rather than large corporations. The Reagan administration in late 1984 was preparing a new tax plan for submission to Congress in early 1985. This new plan was to be more equitable and was expected to increase tax revenue by eliminating many of the loopholes through which the government annually loses millions of dollars.

The power to tax is granted the federal government by Article I, Section 8, of the Constitution. Federal tax laws can be enacted only by Congress. Since the states may exercise any powers not delegated to the federal government, not prohibited to them, or not reserved for the people themselves, the state governments also levy taxes. The power of local government units to tax is determined by their state constitution. Federal taxes must be equal throughout the United States, but state and local taxes vary widely in kind and amount.

Even Americans living abroad usually need to file U.S. tax returns. Here Fred Fredericks, an American tax consultant in Hong Kong, kneels next to the stack of books he refers to in preparing U.S. returns. The pamphlet provides all the information needed for Hong Kong returns.

Uses of Taxes

Tax revenues allow the government to provide a wide range of services for the American people. Our tax dollars pay for the schools we attend, the highways we drive on, and the national parks we visit

TABLE 4–2 The Public's Attitude Toward Taxation

CHANGING AMERICAN ATTITUDES TOWARD THE UNFAIRNESS OF DIFFERENT TAXES
QUESTION: Which do you think is the worst tax, that is, the least fair?

	INCOME TAX FEDERAL	INCOME TAX STATE	STATE SALES TAX	LOCAL PROPERTY TAX	DON'T KNOW
1972	19%	13%	13%	45%	11%
1973	30	10	20	31	11
1974	30	10	20	28	14
1975	28	11	23	29	10
1977	28	11	17	33	11
1978	30	11	18	32	10
1979	37	8	15	27	13
1980	36	10	19	25	10

SOURCE: Surveys by the Opinion Research Corporation for the Advisory Commission on Intergovernmental Relations, and published in *Changing Attitudes on Governments and Taxes*, latest that of May 1980.

PERCENT OF RESPONDENTS WHOSE CONSCIENCE WOULD NOT BE BOTHERED "A LOT"
QUESTION: The following questions ask you about things some people do when filing their tax return. For each one, show on the scale (respondent shown scale running from 1 to 5, with 1 = "Not at all" and 5 = "A lot") whether your conscience would bother you if you did it. Circle one of the 5 numbers on the lines to show whether your conscience would be bothered.

BEHAVIOR

Behavior	%
Not declaring the value of a service that you traded with someone else	61.6%
Not declaring large gambling earnings	52.6
Padding business travel expenses	48.9
Overstating your medical expenses	46.4
Understating your income	42.2
Not filing a return on purpose	30.7
Claiming an extra dependent	29.0

SOURCE: Survey by CSR, Inc., for the Internal Revenue Service, March 1980.

Both tables reprinted from *Public Opinion* (August–September 1980), pp. 15, 16, and *Across the Board* (January 1981).

during our vacations. Tax dollars allow the government to provide low-cost medical care for the elderly, and food and reasonable rent for the needy. The government pays its enormous defense bill with tax dollars, and NASA's Space Shuttle program, which has civilian as well as military uses, is funded by tax revenues.

Taxation is also used to influence the economy. For example, to stimulate private investment in energy development or some other needed but risky venture, the government may give tax breaks to encourage people to invest. Adjustments in income tax rates are sometimes made to stimulate spending by consumers and investment by business. Tariffs are levied to restrict the amount of foreign goods sold in the country to protect domestic businesses from foreign competition.

Are We Taxed Enough?

No one likes taxes (see Table 4–2). But some economists argue that the federal government should place heavier taxes on individuals and corporations. Two observations support this view. First, the per capita federal debt in 1972 was $2,037. But by 1985, the average debt for every man, woman, and child in this country was $6,629. Some, but not all, of this increase was caused by inflation. Second, in 1972 the federal government paid out 9.4 percent of its revenue as interest on the national debt. In 1985, only 13 years later, the percent of total government receipts paid out as interest on the national debt was 18.6 percent. When the government takes in less revenue than it spends, a deficit results.

The National Debt

To finance expenditures not covered by tax revenue, the government sells certificates of debt, mostly bonds (discussed in Chapter 5), to insurance companies, banks, mutual funds, pension plans, and individuals. When the government sells bonds, it is in competition with private industry for investment dollars. Since the laws of supply and demand determine the price of bonds or debt certificates, government demand for money pushes up the rate of interest.

Since large deficits are a contributing factor to inflation, many people feel that the government must balance the budget by reducing expenditures or by raising taxes to produce more revenue, or both.

Federal Taxes

The four major taxes imposed by the federal government are individual income tax, social insurance tax, corporate tax, and excise tax (see Figure 4–2).

INDIVIDUAL INCOME TAX

The **individual income tax** is *a federal tax on personal income and the government's largest single source of revenue.* Employers are required by law to withhold a certain portion of wages and remit it directly to the Internal Revenue Service. Individual taxes, with similar withholding requirements, are also levied by many states and cities.

112 CHAPTER 4/BUSINESS, GOVERNMENT, AND SOCIETY

Figure 4–2 Predictions of Federal Revenue and Spending

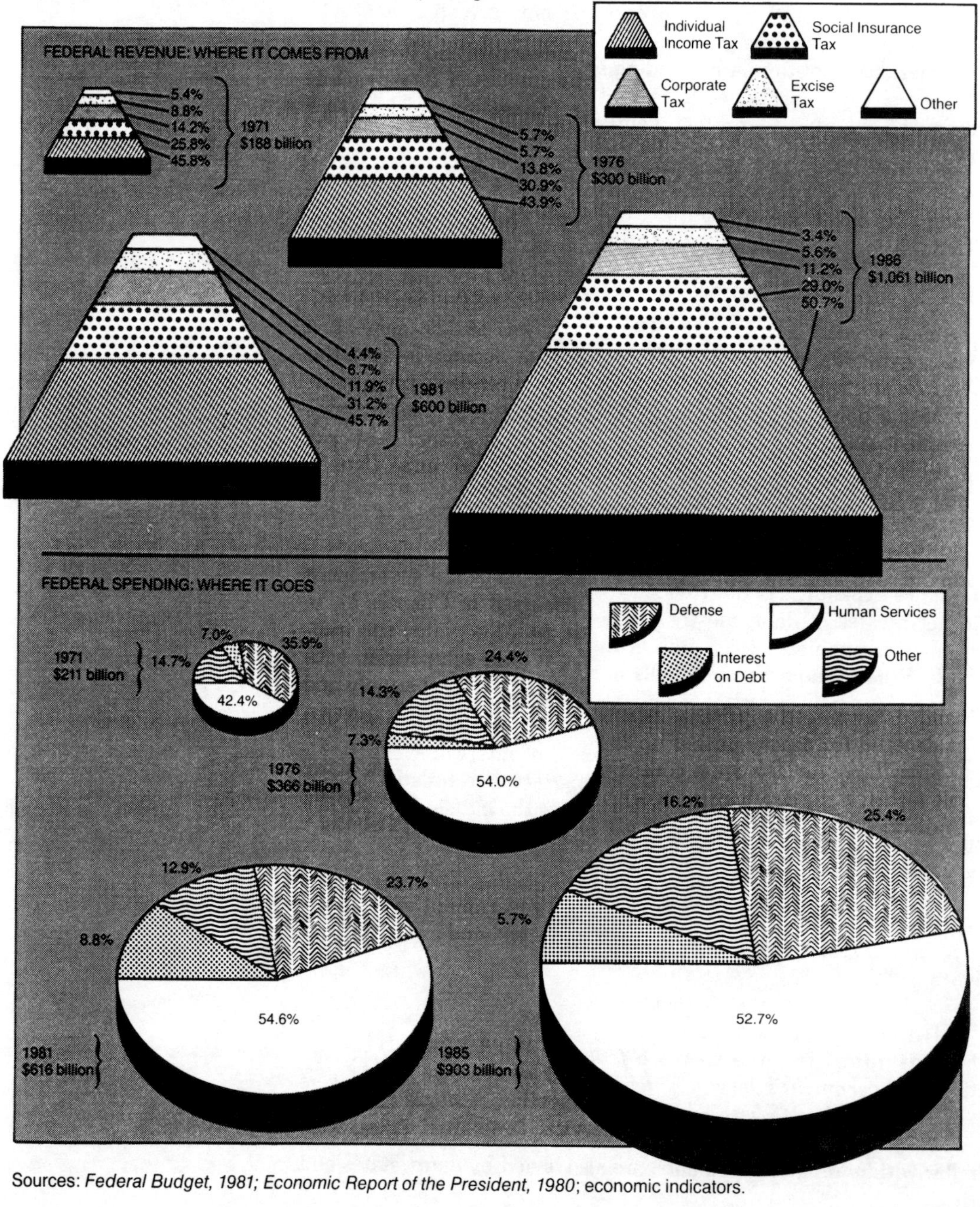

FEDERAL REVENUE: WHERE IT COMES FROM

Legend:
- Individual Income Tax
- Social Insurance Tax
- Corporate Tax
- Excise Tax
- Other

1971 $188 billion:
- 5.4%
- 8.8%
- 14.2%
- 25.8%
- 45.8%

1976 $300 billion:
- 5.7%
- 5.7%
- 13.8%
- 30.9%
- 43.9%

1981 $600 billion:
- 4.4%
- 6.7%
- 11.9%
- 31.2%
- 45.7%

1986 $1,061 billion:
- 3.4%
- 5.6%
- 11.2%
- 29.0%
- 50.7%

FEDERAL SPENDING: WHERE IT GOES

Legend:
- Defense
- Human Services
- Interest on Debt
- Other

1971 $211 billion:
- 7.0%
- 14.7%
- 35.9%
- 42.4%

1976 $366 billion:
- 24.4%
- 14.3%
- 7.3%
- 54.0%

1981 $616 billion:
- 12.9%
- 23.7%
- 8.8%
- 54.6%

1985 $903 billion:
- 16.2%
- 25.4%
- 5.7%
- 52.7%

Sources: *Federal Budget, 1981; Economic Report of the President, 1980*; economic indicators.

Social Insurance Tax

Commonly referred to as **social security, social insurance tax** is *a federal tax earmarked for retirement, medical care, disability, and other related benefits and is the second largest source of federal revenue.* It differs from all other taxes in that its use is specified. People are entitled to social security only if they made payments into the program. Social insurance taxes are withheld on wages and are paid by employees and employers. They have risen more rapidly than any other tax. Because of a declining birth rate and the fact that people are living longer, the nation's social security program faces serious difficulties.

Corporate Income Tax

Corporate income tax is *a federal tax on a corporation's profits.* All corporations must file corporate tax returns. Profits or losses made by sole proprietorships and partnerships must be reported by the owners of these businesses on their personal income tax returns.

Corporate profits are taxed by the federal government at the rate of 17 percent for the first $25,000, 20 percent for $25,000– $50,000, 30 percent for $50,000–$75,000, 40 percent for $75,000– $100,000, and 46 percent for over $100,000. Often, state and local governments also levy corporate income taxes, but at lower rates. If a corporation operates overseas, it must pay income taxes in foreign countries as well. The U.S. government allows American corporations a tax credit (a deduction from its U.S. taxes) for amounts paid to foreign countries.

Excise Tax

Excise taxes are *federal taxes levied on commodities or services that are regarded as luxuries.* Most often, the *tax is levied on the manufacturer, who adds it to the cost of the product.* Such a tax is often called a **manufacturer's excise tax.** The consumer is often unaware that the prices for tires, radios, automobiles, and electric appliances might include one or more excise taxes.

Some excise taxes are collected by the retailer, and for that reason they are called **retailer's excise taxes.**

Types of State and Local Taxes

State and local (county and city) taxes are levied on property owned, money spent, gasoline purchased, personal income earned, and profits earned by corporations. In 1984 Americans paid about $1,382 to state and local governments, more than three times the average amount paid in 1970. Figure 4–3 shows how widely taxes differ among states.

All but five states and the District of Columbia levy a **sales tax,** or a *tax on retail sales.* Usually these taxes total from 2 to 8 percent of the selling price.

114 CHAPTER 4/Business, Government, and Society

Figure 4–3 State and Local Taxes, 1984, per Capita

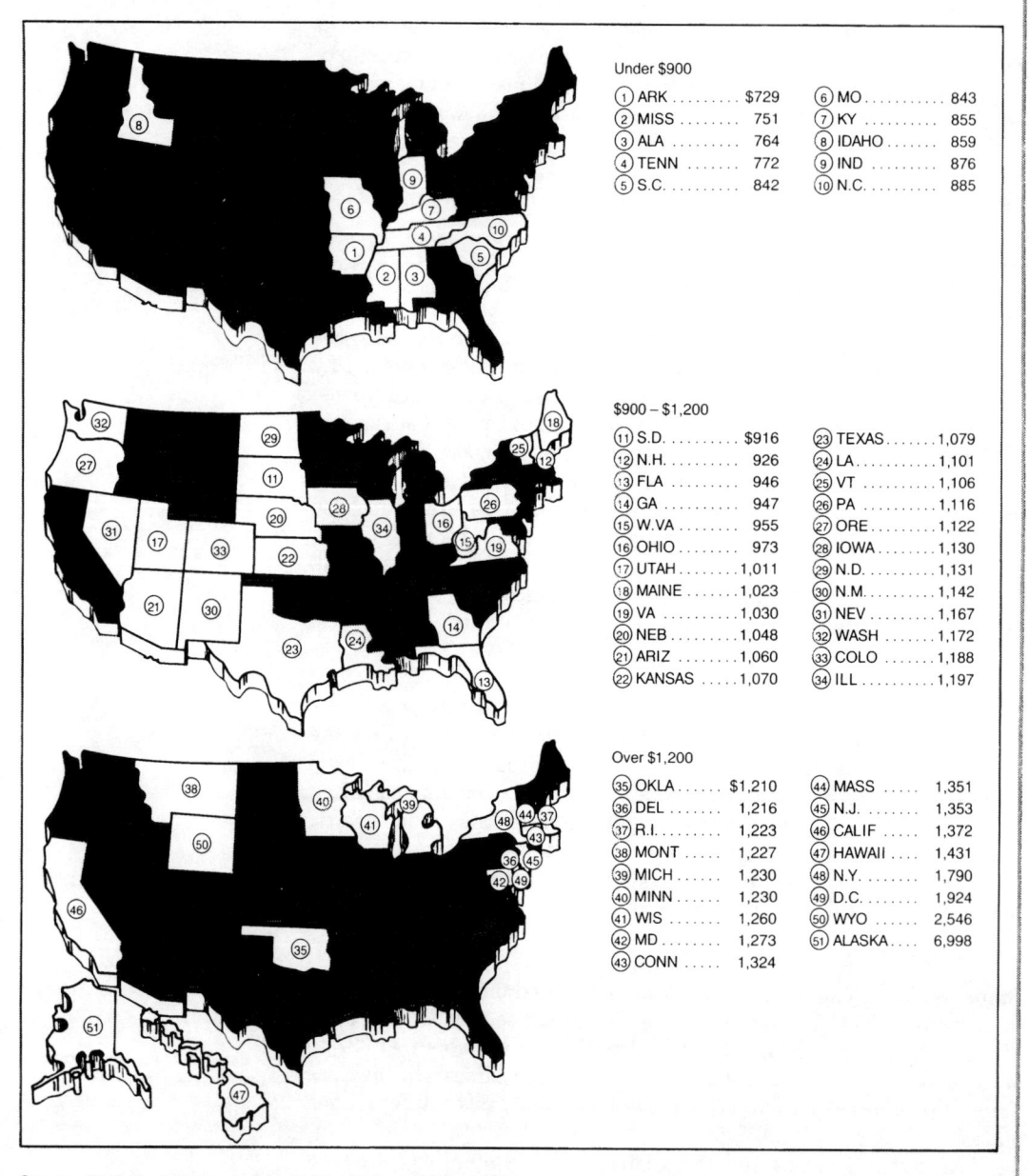

Under $900

① ARK $729
② MISS 751
③ ALA 764
④ TENN 772
⑤ S.C. 842
⑥ MO 843
⑦ KY 855
⑧ IDAHO 859
⑨ IND 876
⑩ N.C. 885

$900 – $1,200

⑪ S.D. $916
⑫ N.H. 926
⑬ FLA 946
⑭ GA 947
⑮ W.VA 955
⑯ OHIO 973
⑰ UTAH 1,011
⑱ MAINE 1,023
⑲ VA 1,030
⑳ NEB 1,048
㉑ ARIZ 1,060
㉒ KANSAS ... 1,070
㉓ TEXAS 1,079
㉔ LA 1,101
㉕ VT 1,106
㉖ PA 1,116
㉗ ORE 1,122
㉘ IOWA 1,130
㉙ N.D. 1,131
㉚ N.M. 1,142
㉛ NEV 1,167
㉜ WASH 1,172
㉝ COLO 1,188
㉞ ILL 1,197

Over $1,200

㉟ OKLA $1,210
㊱ DEL 1,216
㊲ R.I. 1,223
㊳ MONT 1,227
㊴ MICH 1,230
㊵ MINN 1,230
㊶ WIS 1,260
㊷ MD 1,273
㊸ CONN 1,324
㊹ MASS 1,351
㊺ N.J. 1,353
㊻ CALIF 1,372
㊼ HAWAII .. 1,431
㊽ N.Y. 1,790
㊾ D.C. 1,924
㊿ WYO 2,546
㊀ ALASKA .. 6,998

Source: *Statistical Abstract of the United States, 1985*, p. 472.

TABLE 4-3   Identical Compliance Costs Hit Small Firms Harder
Assume that compliance with a government regulation requires a capital expenditure of $50,000 and annual operating expenditures of $5,000. The table shows the effect of this cost on firms of varying sizes.

FIRM SIZE	SALES	REGULATION COST PER DOLLAR OF OUTPUT YEAR 1	YEAR 2
10 employees	$500,000	$0.11	$0.01
100 employees	$5 million	$0.011	$0.0011
1,000 employees	$50 million	$0.0011	$0.00011
10,000 employees	$500 million	$0.00011	$0.000011

The company with 10 workers pays 10 times as much per sales dollar as the company with 100 workers. If you assume that employee productivity rises with company size, which is generally the case, the burden of a fixed cost of compliance on a smaller company is still more disproportionate.

SOURCE: *INC.*, June 1980, 54.

City, county, and other local governments obtain most of their revenues from a general **property tax,** or *a tax levied against privately owned property.* Both personal property and real estate are taxed after valuation is determined by a tax assessor.

Because business owns much property, it must also pay property taxes.

Paperwork

Reacting to pressures to reduce the inroads of government, Congress in 1980 passed the Paperwork Reduction Act, and established the Office of Information and Regulatory Affairs (OIRA). The federal bureaucrats assigned to ease the paperwork burden found that in 1981 Americans spent about 1,276 billion hours filling out 5,000 kinds of government forms. At $10 an hour, the cost of the job would have been $12,760 billion. This works out to five and a half hours for every American.

The bureau with the biggest appetite for filled-in forms is the Internal Revenue Service, which requires half the total. The IRS is followed by the Department of Transportation (20 percent), and the Department of Agriculture (about 10 percent). Not surprisingly, the amount of paperwork required is especially heavy in business.

Further studies revealed that the burden of paperwork falls heaviest on small businesses (see Table 4–3). To counter this, Congress passed the Regulatory Flexibility Act of 1980. Among other things, it requires federal agencies to exempt or simplify rules for small business wherever possible.

> ## CONTEMPORARY ISSUE
>
> ### How Life and Health Insurance Companies Help Meet Social Needs
>
> The insurer's report card shown below illustrates how insurance companies are cooperating to help meet social needs. Note that significant contributions are made to charity, minority employment is on the rise, women are being promoted, companies are lending managers to work for social causes, and large investments are made for socially desirable purposes.
>
> **Insurer's Report Card**
>
> Not every insurance company participates, but enough do to make the annual "Social Report" of the life and health insurance business a valid indication of social responsibility activities in the insurance industry. The "Social Report" has been issued annually for the past ten years by the Washington-based Center for Corporate Public Involvement (it used to be called the Clearinghouse for Corporate Social Responsibility). This year 228 companies returned the questionnaires sent to them (compared to 148 the first year). There are 556 member companies of the American Council of Life Insurance and the Health Insurance Association of America but the 228 participating in this survey account for 85 percent of all the assets of all companies (so you know that the most responsive companies are the big ones).
>
> Here are some highlights of the most recent survey:
>
> - Charitable contributions reached $72 million in 1981, up 9 percent over 1980.
> - Minorities now represent 18 percent of the total work force.
> - Women received more than two-thirds of all promotions made by the companies during 1981.
> - Over 225,000 volunteer man-hours were contributed by the companies through loaned executives or released-time arrangements.
> - Investments for "socially desirable purposes" totaled $1.4 billion in 1981. One-third was for housing.
>
> A copy of the complete "Social Report" is available, free of charge, from the Center for Corporate Public Involvement, 1850 K Street, N.W., Washington, D.C. 20006.
>
> SOURCE: As reported in *Business and Society Review*, Winter 1983, volume 44, 66.

Cooperation Between Government and Business

Business has nothing to gain by viewing government as an adversary. Walter E. Hoadley, then an executive vice-president of the Bank of America (the nation's largest), aptly summarized the situation: "Government at all levels across the United States is now widely recognized to be in varying degrees of trouble—financial, administrative, operational, as well as in public esteem. . . . There is now a major need and opportunity for business to lend a hand to government.... It is important for business executives to place their main focus on helping government... while insisting growth in government spending be held at or below the growth rate of the economy. Businessmen should not get caught in the political cross fire of helping select which services are more important."

An objective review of the interrelationships of society and business suggests the goals of each are parallel. What is good for society helps business. And what helps business also helps society.

SUMMARY

- To meet its social responsibilities, business is expected to make safe products, carefully dispose of its wastes, and provide equal employment opportunities.
- Most businesses act responsibly. Because of the socially irresponsible behavior of a comparatively few businesses, three major movements occurred: the consumer movement, the environmental movement, and the civil rights movement.
- The consumer movement is largely concentrated on how business behaves in the marketplace. It has helped consumers win the right to safety, to be informed, to choose, and to be heard.
- The environmental movement is concerned with improving the way waste is disposed of and with the use of land.
- The civil rights movement seeks equal employment opportunities for blacks, Hispanics, other minorities, and women.
- To promote competition, four important laws were passed: the Sherman Antitrust Act, the Clayton Act, the Federal Trade Commission Act, and the Robinson–Patman Act.
- The main contact business has with government is through regulatory agencies, which enforce legislation. Business is especially critical of two agencies: OSHA and EPA.
- The federal government imposes four main taxes: individual income tax, social insurance tax, corporate income tax, and excise tax.
- State and local taxes are levied on property owned, money spent, gasoline purchased, income earned, and profits made by corporations.
- Business must do much paperwork for the government.

KEY TERMS YOU SHOULD KNOW

affirmative action
Better Business Bureau
Civil Rights Act of 1964
Clayton Act
consumerism
corporate income tax
Department of Commerce
Environmental Protection
    Agency
Equal Employment
    Opportunity Commission

excise tax
federal regulatory agency
Federal Trade
    Commission Act
individual income tax
interlocking directorate
manufacturer's excise tax
monopoly
New Deal

property tax
retailer's excise tax
Robinson–Patman Act
sales tax
Sherman Antitrust Act
social insurance (social
    security) tax
social responsibility

QUESTIONS FOR REVIEW

1. Why is business our dominant social institution?
2. Why do many people have a low opinion of business behavior?
3. What are the three major social movements that have had an impact on business?
4. Define consumerism. What are the three waves of the consumer movement?
5. How did President John F. Kennedy help consumers? What are the four provisions of the consumer bill of rights?
6. What nongovernmental agencies also aid the consumer?
7. How did the environmental movement get started? What is the EPA?
8. Specifically, what does the Civil Rights Act of 1964 say about discrimination in employment?
9. What was the main purpose of the Sherman Antitrust Act of 1890? The Clayton Act of 1914? The Federal Trade Commission Act of 1914? The Robinson–Patman Act of 1936?
10. What is the purpose of the Department of Commerce?
11. Why are we taxed? What is the source of government authority to levy taxes?
12. What is the individual income tax? The social insurance tax? The corporate income tax? The excise tax?
13. How do sales taxes differ from property taxes?
14. How can business help government perform more effectively?

QUESTIONS FOR DISCUSSION

1. The argument is often made that competition will eliminate businesses that deceive or cheat consumers. People will simply stop patronizing a business if they believe that a firm is taking unfair advantage of them. The business will either shape up or fail. How valid do you feel this argument is?
2. Do you think that media attacks on business are indicative of more unethical behavior by business people today or of more in-depth probing by modern reporters? Explain.
3. In your opinion, is there really a need for a consumer movement? Explain.
4. What brought about the environmental movement? Do you believe the environment has improved over the past decade? Explain why or why not.
5. Do you think the trend toward less government regulation will continue? What actions might cause a return to increased regulation?
6. Which would be better for business: a cut in individual income taxes to stimulate buying or a cut in corporation taxes to stimulate investment in plants and equipment? Why?
7. Assume the tax commissioner in your county must raise taxes to provide services. You are given a choice between an increase in the sales tax or an increase in property taxes. Which would you prefer? Why?
8. Are you disturbed because a large amount—perhaps 10 percent—of the GNP goes untaxed? Why or why not?

CASE STUDY

Should Pressure Be Put on Employees to Contribute to the We Help People Campaign?

Walter Pride is president of Computer Engineering Systems. Pride is also this year's state vice-chairman of the We Help People Campaign (WHPC), a national charitable organization that provides a wide range of services to people in need. The following discussion took place at a Friday meeting between Pride and his four department heads, Bob, Mary, Sam, and Herman.

Pride: Before we adjourn, I'd like to discuss this year's WHP campaign. As you are probably aware, I'm vice-chairman for the state, and I want to see us do a good job.

Mary: How good?

P: OK. This year I'm thinking big. I want to see 100 percent of our employees participate.

Sam: What size contribution are you shooting for?

P: I think each of our 260 employees should contribute at least one week's income to WHPC. And I'm counting on you people to get this level of commitment.

Herman: You mean you want us to talk our people into giving up what amounts to 2 percent of their incomes for a cause they may not really believe in?

P: Now, rest assured, it's a good cause. All you have to do is show them what WHPC does. As I see it, Computer Engineering has social responsibilities to meet, and the one week's contribution is a way to meet them.

S: It's not easy to sell something you don't believe in. I'm sure you think WHPC is a great organization. But I have my doubts. I looked at its budget and found that 50 percent of all the money collected as contributions went for travel and salaries of professional staff and volunteers.

P: I know 50 percent overhead looks high, but it's needed. And most employees won't look at the budget. Just stress what projects WHPC funds.

Bob: This is going to be difficult to put across. If we asked the employees to make a modest, one-time contribution of, say, $10 or $20, we could come close to getting 100 percent involvement. But asking them to contribute 2 percent is a lot. That means an employee earning $20,000 would contribute $400.

M: What happens if an employee doesn't contribute?

P: The campaign is four weeks long. Keep asking. Let him or her know that I personally am interested. Then, during the last week of the campaign, I'll talk personally with each holdout.

H: Mr. Pride, I think this is a mistake. It's going to cause me to give up time I need to do my job. It's going to make a lot of people mad. And I don't think it's a good cause. Can't you reduce the level of contribution?

S: I agree with Herman. It's going to be resented by a lot of our people. They are professionals, and don't want to be pushed around. This is unfair.

M: Why not make the contribution in behalf of the corporation? It could be 2 percent of the payroll budget.

P: The board of directors would never approve that. Besides, I want people to get involved with WHPC. OK. Meeting is adjourned.

Questions

1. How would you, as an employee of Computer Engineering Systems, react if your supervisor asked you to contribute one week's pay to WHPC?
2. Why do you think Pride is so eager to get the employees to contribute so heavily?
3. Is there any way the department heads can get Pride to change his mind?
4. Is Pride's plan a good way for a firm to meet its social responsibility? Explain.

EVOLUTION OF A BUSINESS

What Is and Is Not Ethical?

As Sara and Ray continued to talk about their hypothetical travel agency, they found themselves quickly into the matter of ethics.

Sara: I think bad ethics was the underlying reason for a lot of our dissatisfactions with the travel agencies we used.

Ray: How do you figure that?

Sara: Well, for example, take that hotel I was so disappointed with, the Grand Hotel. I'll bet the woman at the agency recommended the Grand to me because they wine and dine her lavishly. I know this happens because I see it on income tax returns I audit. Resort hotels deduct entertaining of travel agents and their employees as a business expense.

Ray: So the government is actually subsidizing an unethical practice.

Sara: Well, some people see it that way. At the IRS they only think it's unethical if it's excessive.

Ray: This is making me suspicious about some things that happened on *my* tour. Once, when we were on a bus tour we seemed to spend more time stopping at shops and handicraft places than we did seeing the countryside. We spent ten minutes sightseeing a waterfall and a full hour at a glass factory—so-called—where one man was making a bottle. Now that I think about it, there were probably some kickbacks going on.

Sara: Sure. And I also wonder about why we got steered into taking this airline rather than the one we first asked to be booked on.

Ray: Probably because the kickbacks are better.

Sara: It certainly couldn't be the food and service—or should I say, what there *is* of the food and service.

Ray: You know, we're feeling ripped off now, but this wouldn't all be so bad for us if we went into the agency business. If we just operated honestly and did what was best for our customers, they'd be loyal to us and tell all their friends about us.

Sara: But would people really know the difference? And if they did, would they care?

Ray: Sara, what a negative attitude. I think you've spent too many years being an auditor.

Questions

1. What do you think about the ethics of the situations described?
2. Do you think the government, by allowing entertainment deductions as a business expense, is subsidizing unethical practices?
3. Could a travel agency operate at all if it didn't accept free transportation, accommodations, and so on?
4. What policies could a travel agency adopt to keep itself ethical?
5. Would customers support an honest agency, as Ray thinks, or wouldn't they notice the difference, as Sara thinks?

ન
USING MONEY IN BUSINESS

5 LONG- AND SHORT-TERM FINANCING

6 FINANCIAL INSTITUTIONS

7 SECURITY MARKETS AND BUSINESS NEWS

8 RISK MANAGEMENT AND INSURANCE

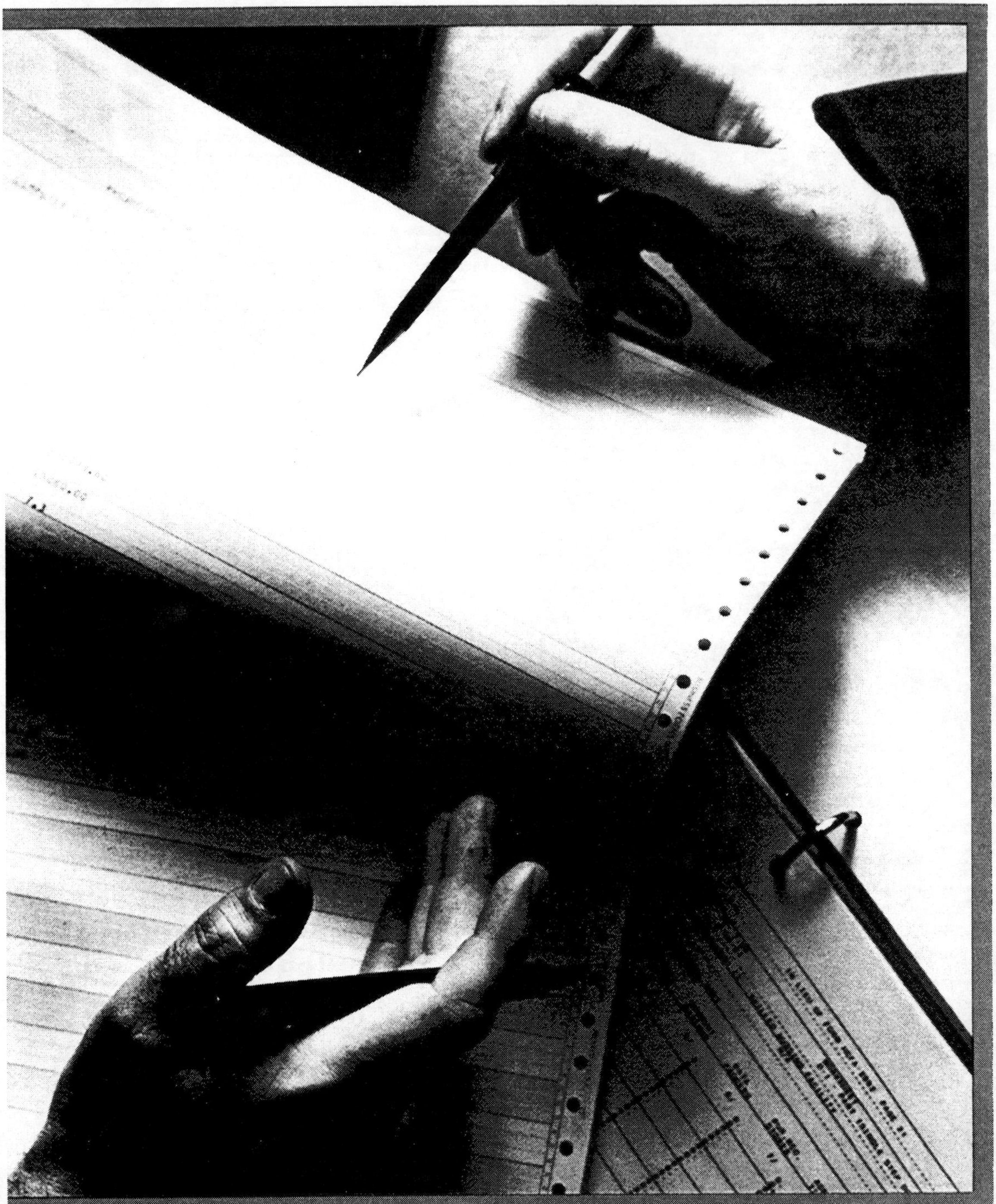

5

LONG- AND SHORT-TERM FINANCING
Coming Up With the Money

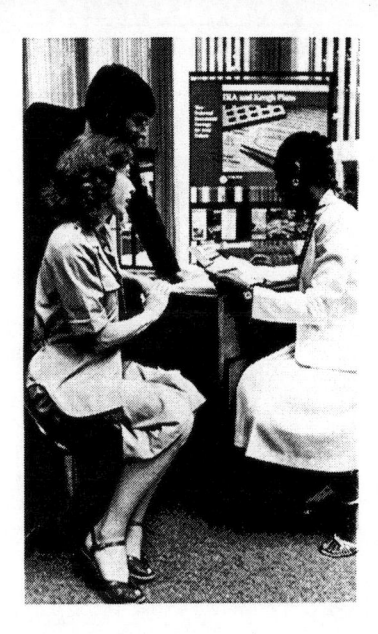

READ THIS CHAPTER SO YOU CAN:

Explain how a small business obtains long-term financing.

Describe how large businesses use common and preferred stock and bonds for long-term financing.

Discuss the pros and cons of issuing stock and selling bonds to the issuing company and to the investor.

Explain short-term financing and the methods used to accomplish it.

Evaluate the advantages and disadvantages of leasing as it relates to financing.

Describe what financial management involves, the importance of cash flow, and why idle money should be put to use.

All businesses need money, or capital, to operate. We can divide the money a business needs into two categories: long-term and short-term. **Long-term capital** is *money used to acquire permanent assets needed in the business*—that is, buildings, machinery, equipment, and other property that has a useful life of one or more years. **Short-term,** or **working, capital** is *money needed to purchase raw materials and goods to resell, pay wages and salaries, and meet other obligations of debts that fall due in the short term (usually 12 months or less).*

Most of this chapter deals with the methods of financing that larger established businesses use. However, every big business begins as a small one, so it is worthwhile to consider also how the entrepreneurs obtain the capital they need to launch an enterprise.

LONG-TERM FINANCING FOR SMALL BUSINESSES

Raising capital is the first hurdle the potential entrepreneur faces. This challenge is often so discouraging that the entrepreneur decides not to start the business.

Main sources of long-term or permanent capital for a small business are: (a) personal savings, (b) friends and relatives, (c) using personal assets or collateral for loans, and (d) government agencies.

Personal Savings

Personal savings provide the most common source of long-term capital for a small business. Regardless of what form of ownership entrepreneurs select (proprietorship, partnership, or corporation), good business practice usually demands that they invest some of their own money, usually at least 50 percent of the initial capital. Two reasons for the 50 percent rule are, "If the entrepreneur is not willing to risk his or her money, other potential investors are not likely to risk their money in the business either. And if the owner contributes any less than half of the initial capital requirements, an excessive level of borrowing is required to fund the business properly, and the high repayment schedule puts intense pressure on cash flows."[1]

Friends and Relatives

Friends and relatives are sometimes willing to invest capital in a new business. A problem with this source is that if the business fails, friends may no longer be friends.

---

[1]Scarborough, N. M., and Zimmer, T. W., *Effective Small Business Management*, Charles L. Merrill Publishing Company, Columbus, Ohio, 1980, 268.

Partners

As Chapter 2 explains, one of the primary reasons for forming a partnership is access to more capital. Adding a general partner to the enterprise naturally results in sharing profits the company earns. However, many entrepreneurs do not necessarily want to share.

Personal Assets as Collateral for Loans

Banks, insurance companies, pension funds, and savings and loan institutions may be willing to make long-term loans to a small business if the business pledges sufficient assets as **collateral,** *property pledged by a borrower to protect the interests of the lender.*

An entrepreneur may be able to refinance his or her home to obtain capital. For example, assume a person owns a house worth $100,000 which already has a mortgage of $50,000. The home owner may be able to borrow $25,000 more using the house as collateral. (Most savings banks will loan up to 75 percent of the appraised value of a residence). The problem with borrowing against the value of a home is that mortgage payments will increase.

Other assets a new business may use as collateral to obtain capital are stocks, bonds, automobiles, cash value of life insurance policies, trust funds, and retirement plans.

Government Agencies

The Small Business Administration, as Chapter 2 explains, makes long-term loans to qualified small businesses. Another government agency, the Federal Land Bank, makes loans of up to 40 years for the purchase of land.

Assuming a new business grows and prospers, it will begin using the sources that big business relies on for long-term capital: stock and bonds.

LONG-TERM FINANCING FOR LARGE BUSINESSES

Large businesses obtain long-term capital by issuing **securities**—*either common stock, preferred stock, or bonds.* The first two of these are called **equity capital**—*the owner of a stock has part ownership, or equity, in the corporation.* Bonds are considered **debt capital**—*they represent a debt owed by the corporation to the bondholder.*

Deciding which type of security to issue involves many factors. For example, consider the following questions:

- Which type of security—stock or bonds—will be easiest to sell in the current money market (that is, the market for stocks and bonds)?

Major firms issue securities—stocks and bonds—to obtain the long-term capital they need to finance expansion. Here, members of the New York Stock Exchange check prices on stocks.

- How do the different types of financing compare in long-run and immediate costs?
- Which financing plan will achieve the company's goals and, at the same time, be acceptable to those who already have a financial interest in the corporation?
- How will the financing program affect ownership control of the business?

Financing Through Stocks

When a corporation wishes to expand, it may sell **stock,** or *shares of ownership.* Purchasers of stock become owners of the business. If, for example, a company sells 100,000 shares and Mary Livingston buys 1,000 shares, Ms. Livingston owns exactly 1 percent of the company. The corporation will never refund money invested by stockholders, although investors can sell their stock to other investors if they wish.

Shareholders, as part owners in the business, are entitled to *a share in the corporation's profits.* The business distributes such profits as **dividends,** usually quarterly. However, since a company may not earn any profits in a certain year or, if it does, may wish to plow back some or all of its earnings into the business, it may not always declare dividends.

Authorized, Issued, and Unissued Stock

Authorized stock is *the maximum number of shares that a company can issue, as specified in its corporate charter.* If, at a later date, management wishes to increase the amount, law requires that it secure the approval of the stockholders. In practice, newly formed corporations authorize considerably more stock than they plan to issue when they start so that if additional financing eventually becomes desirable, they can conveniently sell more stock in the future.

Do not confuse authorized stock with issued stock. **Issued stock** is *that portion of authorized stock that a company has sold.* **Unissued stock** is *authorized stock that a company has not yet offered for sale.*

Par-Value and No-Par-Value Stock

Par-value stock is *stock that a company has assigned a fixed dollar value,* which is printed on the stock certificates. This printed value may be any amount, ranging from one cent to $100 or more. Originally, the par value was the price at which buyers purchased the stock. Today par value represents only a fictional value. Thus many corporations now issue **no-par-value stock,** which is *stock that has no printed value on the certificates.*

Sale of Stock and Preemptive Rights

A new corporation either sells stock openly or restricts sales to limited numbers of investors. Companies usually *offer subsequent stock issues first to current stockholders.* This privilege, called the stockholders' **preemptive right,** protects stockholders from losing their proportionate interest in the corporation. For example, if David Grant owns 5 percent of the stock in a corporation that later doubles its outstanding stock, David's proportionate interest drops to $2\frac{1}{2}$ percent if he does not purchase any of the new stock. Preemptive rights exist only when required by state law or when provided for in the company's corporate charter.

Common Stock

Common stock is *equity shares in a corporation whose owners share in dividends after debts are paid.*

Common stock is often referred to as "risk capital" for two reasons. First, it does not specify a definite rate of return. Whether or not a company pays dividends depends largely on the amount of net profit earned and the decision of the board of directors on how much profit it shall declare as dividends.

If the corporation fails, common stockholders may lose their entire investment. In effect, their shares may have no value. When a business fails, claims against any assets remaining are in the following order: employees, bondholders, suppliers, and other creditors and preferred stockholders.

The price investors are willing to pay for a stock may vary widely as the data in Figure 5-1 show. Only a small number of stocks traded on the New York Stock Exchange go up or down by only 10 percent in just one year.

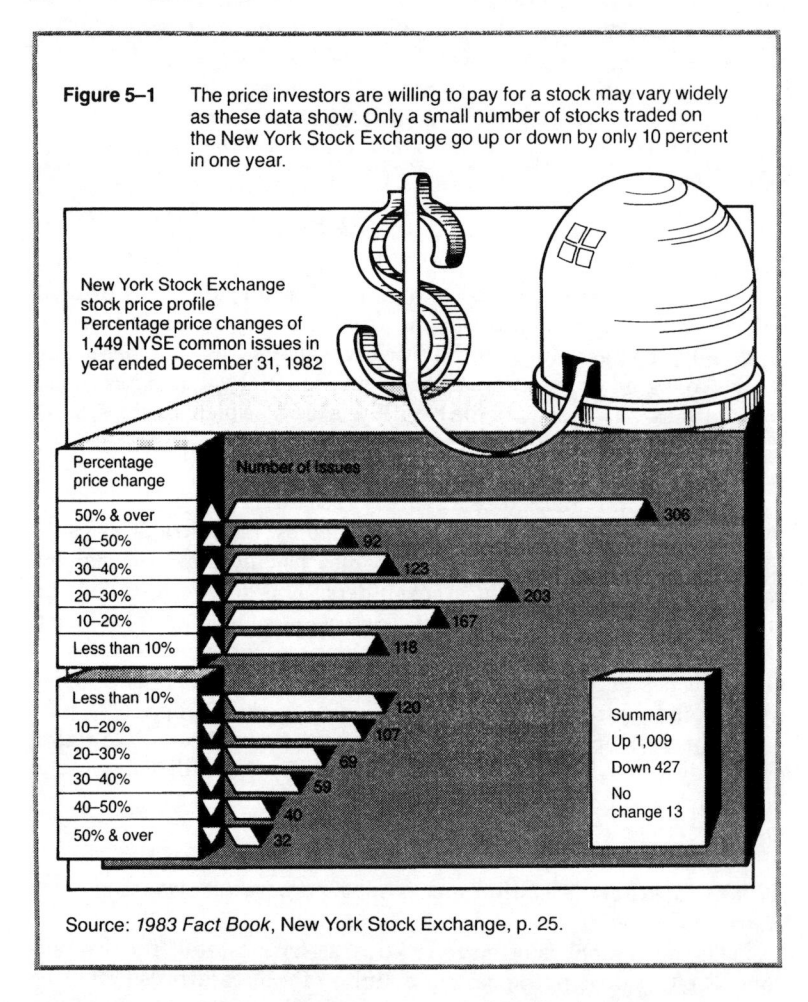

Figure 5-1 The price investors are willing to pay for a stock may vary widely as these data show. Only a small number of stocks traded on the New York Stock Exchange go up or down by only 10 percent in one year.

New York Stock Exchange stock price profile
Percentage price changes of 1,449 NYSE common issues in year ended December 31, 1982

Percentage price change	Number of issues
50% & over ▲	306
40–50% ▲	92
30–40% ▲	123
20–30% ▲	203
10–20% ▲	167
Less than 10% ▲	118
Less than 10% ▼	120
10–20% ▼	107
20–30% ▼	69
30–40% ▼	59
40–50% ▼	40
50% & over ▼	32

Summary
Up 1,009
Down 427
No change 13

Source: *1983 Fact Book*, New York Stock Exchange, p. 25.

What Are the Advantages and Disadvantages of Common Stock?

Common stock has advantages and disadvantages to the investor, or shareholder, and to the issuing corporation.

To the investor, the main advantages of common stock are:

1. *The stock may appreciate in value.* Many investors buy shares in companies they feel will grow and become more profitable. It is not unusual for stock in a growth company to increase 1,000 percent or more in market value over a 10-year period. Many investors are not interested in owning stock for a decade or longer but are interested in short-term appreciation in value. As Figure 5–1 suggests, short-run appreciation can be considerable.
2. *Certain companies may pay dividends.* Successful corporations usually pay dividends, and dividends may increase as time passes. Table 5–1 shows corporations listed on the New York Stock Exchange that have paid dividends since the nineteenth century.
3. *Stocks are easily transferred.* Common stock, especially in major corporations, is easily bought and sold. Security exchanges, discussed in Chapter 7, exist to facilitate transfer of ownership.

To the investor, the main disadvantages of owning common stock are:

1. *The stock may decline in value.* Lack of demand for the company's products, increased competition, uncontrollable production costs, and strikes are just some of the problems that may cause the price of a stock to decline.
2. *The investor may have to forego other investment opportunities.* When an investor has purchased stock in a company, he or she cannot use the same money to invest in another stock, bonds, real estate, or some other investment opportunity.
3. *Common stock is considered risky because it has a fluctuating* **market value** *(the price offered on the market at a given time).* The price others are willing to pay depends on a host of factors, all related in some manner to corporate earnings.

Preferred Stock

A second type of equity capital is **preferred stock,** or *stock that has a preference.* Usually preferred stockholders receive the following preferences:

- The right to receive a fixed or stated dividend before common stockholders receive any.
- A specified claim on assets (prior to that of common stockholders) in the event the corporation is dissolved.

Not all corporations issue preferred stock. Corporations that issue it do so for two major reasons. First, it is often easier to sell than common stock because it is less risky. Thus it provides a method of

TABLE 5–1 Annual Dividend Payments Since the Nineteenth Century

BEGAN IN	STOCK	BEGAN IN	STOCK
1784	Bank of Boston Corporation	1882	Bell Canada Enterprises Inc.
1784	Bank of New York Co., Inc.	1883	Carter-Wallace, Inc.
1791	Fleet Financial Group, Inc.	1883	Chesebrough-Pond's Inc.
1804	Norstar Bancorp Inc.	1883	Exxon Corporation
1813	Citicorp	1885	Consolidated Edison Co.
1813	First Nat'l State Bancorporation	1885	Eli Lilly and Company
1827	Chemical New York Corp.*	1885	UGI Corporation
1840	Morgan (J.P.) & Co. Inc.	1886	United Water Resources Inc.
1848	Chase Manhattan Corporation	1889	West Point-Pepperell, Inc.
1850	Connecticut Energy Corp.	1890	American Brands, Inc.
1851	Connecticut Natural Gas Corp.*	1890	Boston Edison Co.*
1851	Manhattan National Corp.	1890	Commonwealth Edison Co.*
1852	Bay State Gas Co.*	1890	Hydraulic Company
1852	Manufacturers Hanover Corp.	1890	Procter & Gamble Co.*
1852	Washington Gas Light Co.*	1891	Southern New England Tel. Co.*
1853	Cincinnati Gas & Electric Co.	1892	Times Mirror Company
1853	Continental Corporation	1892	Westvaco Corporation*
1856	Scovill Inc.	1893	Coca-Cola Co.
1863	Pennwalt Corporation	1893	Fidelity Union Bancorporation
1863	Singer Company	1894	Rexnord Inc.
1865	Irving Bank Corp.*	1894	Standard Oil Co. (Indiana)
1866	First Atlanta Corp.	1895	Burroughs Corp.*
1866	Travelers Corporation*	1895	Colgate-Palmolive Co.
1867	CIGNA Corporation	1895	Mellon National Corp.*
1868	American Express Co.	1898	General Mills, Inc.
1875	InterFirst Corporation*	1898	"Shell" Transport & Trading Co., Public Ltd. Co.
1877	Stanley Works*	1898	Springs Industries, Inc.
1879	Cincinnati Bell Inc.*	1899	Borden, Inc.
1880	Bancal Tri-State Corp.*	1899	General Electric Co.*
1881	American Tel. & Tel. Co.*	1899	Nabisco Brands, Inc.*
1881	Corning Glass Works	1899	PPG Industries, Inc.*
1881	Security Pacific Corp.	1899	Washington Water Power Co.

SOURCE: *1983 Fact Book*, New York Stock Exchange, 30.

*Unbroken quarterly record since the nineteenth century.

acquiring capital from the more cautious investors who would not invest in common stock.

Second, because preferred stock has a specific dividend, the company knows the cost of paying dividends in advance. Third, a company can issue preferred stock that carries no voting rights. Thus, this kind of stock does not jeopardize control of the corporation when preferred shares transfer from one owner to another. In a typical year, 25 to 30 percent of new stock issues are preferred stock.

Cumulative and noncumulative preferred. Dividends on preferred stock may be either *cumulative* or *noncumulative*. **Cumulative** means that *if a company skips a dividend, the obligation to pay the dividend in the future continues.* **Noncumulative** means that *the company has no obligation to pay skipped dividends.*

For instance, suppose a corporation fails to earn a profit one year but in the following year earns $120,000, just twice the amount needed to pay one year's dividends on the preferred stock. Under the noncumulative arrangement, the preferred stockholders receive only one year's dividend—$60,000—just half the earnings of the company. The common stockholders are then entitled to receive the remaining $60,000, less any amount the directors feel should be reinvested in the business or held as a cash reserve. If the stock is cumulative, however, the preferred stockholders receive the entire $120,000, and those owning common stock receive nothing.[2]

Voting privileges. Holders of preferred stock may have full voting rights, voting privileges limited to important company matters, or (rarely) no voting rights. Stock with limited voting privileges is the most customary. With this type of stock, the right to vote is usually restricted to proposals that affect the stock value directly, such as selling or mortgaging company property, changing preferred stock provisions, and voluntarily dissolving the company.

Financing Through Bonds

Bonds are another major source of long-term financing. Unlike stock, bonds are a method of borrowing money. A **bond** is *a certificate indicating that the corporation owes money to the bondholder.* With bonds, an organization promises (1) to repay *the amount borrowed*—called the **principal**—to the bondholder at a specified future date, and (2) to pay a specific rate of interest until it repays the principal (that is, when it redeems the bond). An example that meets these requirements is a $1,000 bond paying 12 percent interest each year un-

---

[2]Don't infer that corporations distribute all their profits to stockholders; they almost always retain a certain percentage for use in the business or hold it as reserve.

til 2000 (the maturity date), at which time the company would repay the loan. In the event the corporation dissolves, the bondholder—being a creditor—has a claim to the company's assets before either common or preferred stockholders.

Many types of corporations (especially industrial, transportation, and utility) as well as municipal, state, and federal governments use bonds extensively to raise capital. Legally, there is no reason a sole proprietor or a partnership could not issue bonds. However, because only the corporation has continuity of life, bond financing is almost exclusively a corporate method of financing.

From the viewpoint of the corporation, bonds have four important advantages:

- The sale of bonds does not affect control of the corporation, because bondholders, unlike stockholders, have no equity in the business. Stockholders are *owners,* while bondholders are *creditors.* Bondholders cannot vote on matters affecting the company.

- Although federal legislation prohibits many of the largest corporate investors, such as bank pension plans, and insurance companies, from buying certain stocks, they can buy bonds. The corporation that sells bonds can therefore tap these large sources of capital.

- Because company assets generally secure (back) bonds, companies can frequently sell them at comparatively low interest rates. Thus, money obtained by bond sale may cost the corporation less than that obtained by other methods.

- Bonds have great tax advantages to the corporation, because interest on debt is a cost of doing business and is deductible from taxable income.

Most bonds are **negotiable,** which means that *the original purchaser can sell them to someone else.* During the course of its life, a bond may be bought and sold many times.

THE BOND INDENTURE

Before a corporation issues bonds, it must prepare a **bond, or trust, indenture,** which is *a detailed statement describing the rights and privileges of bondholders and the rights, privileges, and responsibilities of the issuing corporation.* The indenture details (1) specific information about the purposes of the bond issue, (2) the denomination of the bonds, (3) the number of bonds to be issued, (4) the security behind the bonds, (5) the rate of interest and method of payment, (6) action to be taken in the event the corporation defaults payment, and (7) the name and responsibilities of the trustee.

PEOPLE WHO MAKE THINGS HAPPEN

A PROFILE OF FREDERICK W. SMITH

As Les Seago of the Associated Press put it, "They laughed when Frederick W. Smith sat down to build an airline with the family fortune. After all, the skeptics said, the bankruptcy courts are full of people who have tried to make money in aviation."

Federal Express Corporation, which Smith founded when he was 27 years old, began operations in April 1973. After losing $29 million initially, Federal Express has been very profitable since July 1975. In just a few years, the company jumped from nothing to become the leader in the air express industry. Its jet airplanes fly about 125,000 small packages and documents nightly and generate revenues of approximately $800 million a year.

Chairman of the board and chief executive officer Smith got the idea for Federal Express while doing research for a term paper at Yale University. He presented a plan for setting up an express company that specialized in door-to-door, nationwide, overnight transportation of small packages and documents.

Smith got hooked, as he puts it, on transportation during childhood, for he was the son of the founder of a Memphis company that grew into Dixie Greyhound Lines. Smith had a bone disease as a child. While confined and recovering, he dreamed of the day when he could fly. This he accomplished when he was 15. Later, after he joined the Marines, he flew more than 200 combat missions in Vietnam and won two Purple Hearts and Silver and Bronze Stars.

Following his Vietnam experiences, Smith helped his stepfather, retired Air Force General Fred Hook, run a company in Little Rock that modified aircraft and overhauled their engines. Difficulty in getting delivery of parts when he wanted them sent Smith back to his concept of Federal Express. With $4 million inherited from his father, Frederick W. Smith, who died when young Fred was four, the young entrepreneur set about finding venture capital. He raised $72 million and chose Memphis as the company's home base because of its central location and fine weather.

Starting out with an air taxi certificate and a fleet of Falcon fanjets, Smith quickly recognized the need for air cargo deregulation that was passed through Congress and signed into law by President Jimmy Carter in November 1977.

The company quickly added larger Boeing 727s to its fleet and since has put into service McDonnell-Douglas DC-10s. Federal Express now serves more than 281 major markets and 17,600 communities. It employs about 11,200 people throughout the system, all of them nonunion. The company has been able to maintain less than a 6 percent annual employee turnover because of its constant emphasis on state-of-the-art working conditions and benefits, which include hospitalization, medical and dental insurance, retirement benefits, and profit sharing.

Asked why Federal Express has such good employee relations, a company official said, "We're very people-oriented. We care about people because it's just good business." The employees are, indeed, the basis for the company's slogan, "People-Service-Profits."

The Bond Trustee

Individual bondholders would be almost powerless to enforce their rights and privileges were it not for the *trustee*. The **bond trustee** *may be an individual but is usually a bank or other financial institution specializing in bonds that the issuing corporation appoints to represent the bondholders.* The trustee:

- Certifies the bonds—that is, verifies that the bond issue is in accordance with the indenture. This certification affords protection against overissue or forgery of bonds.
- Sees that the property backing the bond is in safe custody.
- Sees that the corporation carries out its obligations to the bondholders. The trustee studies bondholder complaints and, if necessary, can bring action against the corporation.
- Represents the bondholders should the issuing corporation default in payment of interest or principal or engage in some activity that jeopardizes the ultimate repayment of the bonds.

Denominations

Most corporate bonds are of $1,000 denomination, although larger bonds of $5,000 or $10,000 are not uncommon. Small denomination bonds have not been popular because the more certificates that are issued, the larger are the expenses incurred in handling the issue.

Interest Payments

All bonds bear an interest rate expressed as a percentage, such as $7\frac{7}{8}$ percent, $11\frac{1}{4}$ percent, or $15\frac{1}{4}$ percent. Companies usually pay interest semiannually. Interest payments on bonds are a fixed charge to the company and so are not dependent on fluctuations in company earnings; nor does payment require action by the board of directors as in the case of stock dividends.

The Maturity Date

The **maturity date,** always stated on the bond certificate, is *the time at which the principal of a bond is due.* Bonds may have a life ranging from two to thirty years or more.

Methods of Retiring Bonds

The issuing corporation must provide for the eventual repayment of its obligation. The bond indenture may indicate one or more general provisions for redemption:

- The **call option** *gives the issuing corporation the right to retire bonds at any time before the maturity date.*

- The **sinking-fund plan** *calls for periodic deposit with the trustee of an amount that will ensure that money is available to retire bonds at maturity.*
- The **serial-plan method** *stipulates that bonds will be retired each year according to the numbers on them.*

MAJOR TYPES OF BONDS
Major types of bonds are:

- **Mortgage bonds**—*Secured by a mortgage on fixed assets owned by the corporation*
- **Debenture bonds**—*Unsecured obligations of corporations*
- **Convertible bonds**—*Can be exchanged for other securities, usually common stocks*
- **Municipal (tax-exempt) bonds**—*Issued by state and local governments* which use the proceeds to build schools, roads, and so on. The tax-exempt feature enables municipalities to secure money they would otherwise have difficulty obtaining.

WHAT DETERMINES BOND INTEREST?
In general, two factors determine the interest rate paid on borrowed money: conditions in the money market and the financial condition of the business. Suppose Company A wishes to borrow money by selling bonds secured by company assets. *The price it will have to pay to borrow the money*—that is, the **interest rate**—will depend on conditions in the money market (whether or not money is in short supply) when the bonds are offered for sale. Bonds offered one year may have to pay a rate of 12 percent in order to sell. The same bonds offered two years later might require a rate of 14 percent to sell. Finance managers try to time the securing of funds to take advantage of the cheapest interest rates.

Financially profitable corporations can sell bonds at lower interest rates than financially weak companies. The price (interest rate) a company must pay to borrow money is related directly to its risk rating. A **risk rating** is *a determination of how able the issuer is to meet the promises specified on the bond.* In the United States, several independent rating agencies—Fitch's, Moody's, and Standard & Poor's—assign risk ratings.

WHY DO BOND PRICES FLUCTUATE?
Even though bonds have a stipulated interest rate, prices paid for outstanding bonds may vary significantly even if the company's basic financial standing is constant. Prices of outstanding bonds tend to fall when money is in great demand and to rise when money is plentiful.

Assume that a company found the going interest rate to be 9 percent a few years ago and issued a bond under agreement to pay that rate. A few years later, interest rates have advanced, and the same company now has to pay 14 percent to borrow money under identical terms. Of course people would rather have the new 14 percent bond than the old 9 percent bond. As a result, the market price of the old bond moves downward so that its yield approaches that of the new bond.

The financial pages of a newspaper give the daily prices of bond issues listed on the stock exchanges (see Chapter 7).

Which Method of Long-term Financing Is Best?

The decision as to which type of security to issue—common stock, preferred stock, or bonds—depends entirely on the individual circumstances. A business will need to consider the long-term implications of each mode of financing, the amount of control it is willing to relinquish, current money-market conditions, and so on. A summary of the most important characteristics of each method follows.

Financing with Stock

- With common stock the amount of dividends, if any, is not fixed but is up to the board of directors. However, companies do have to pay fixed dividends on preferred stock.
- Paid dividends are not considered a business expense, and so they are not tax-deductible.
- Dividends paid reduce the amount of money available for expansion, modernization, retirement of bonded debt, and other business purposes.
- Selling additional common stock may reduce the ownership share each existing shareholder has in the business.
- Money obtained from the sale of stock need never be repaid to investors, since it is equity capital.
- In some years selling stock is more difficult because the public interest in buying new issues rises and falls.

Financing with Bonds

- Since bondholders are not owners, sale of bonds does not affect control of the company.
- Bond expense is fixed, and so management can plan accordingly.
- The cost of bond financing can be high if the company is weak financially.

- Bonds, being debt, *must* be repaid by a set date. The company must pay from earnings, sell more stock, or float a new bond issue to pay off its indebtedness.
- Companies cannot skip or postpone interest payments during periods of economic stress.
- Interest payments are tax-deductible.

SHORT-TERM FINANCING BY BUSINESS

We have seen how small and large businesses obtain capital to purchase buildings, land, equipment, and other assets for long-time use. Now we turn our attention to methods by which businesses, both large and small, finance inventories, raw materials, rent, and other short-term expenses.

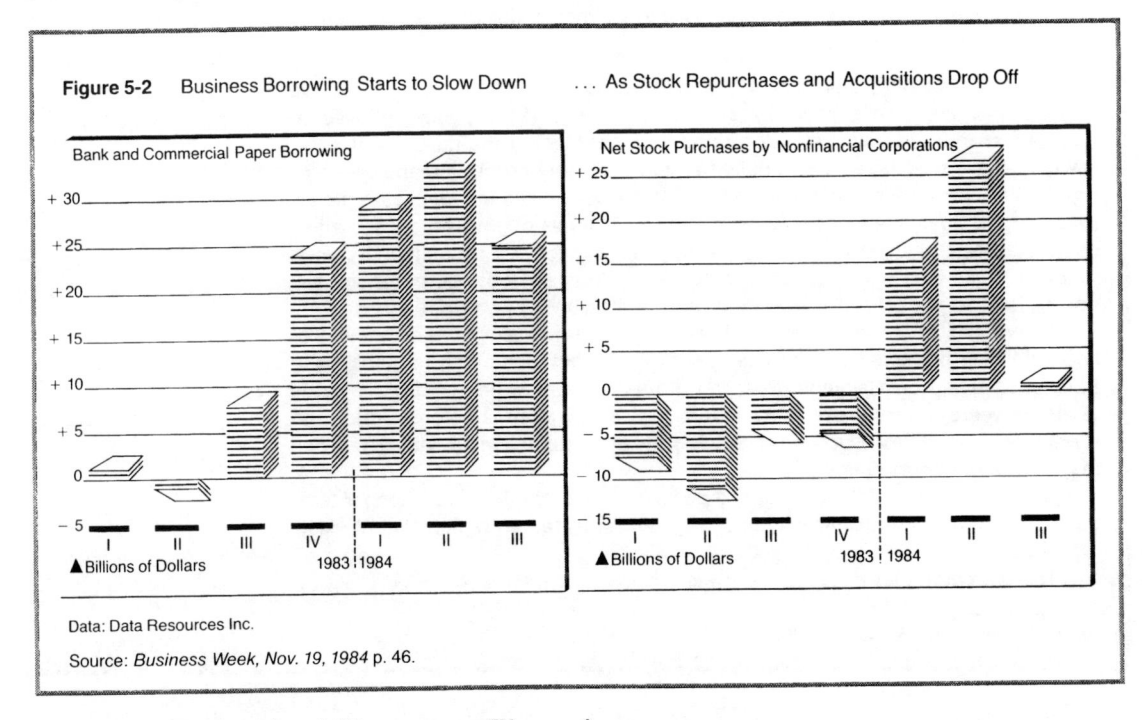

Figure 5-2 Business Borrowing Starts to Slow Down ... As Stock Repurchases and Acquisitions Drop Off

Data: Data Resources Inc.
Source: *Business Week*, Nov. 19, 1984 p. 46.

Why Firms Need Short-term Financing

Several reasons account for the widespread borrowing of short-term capital, usually borrowed for periods of 30 days to one year. First, nearly every business has seasonal peaks of activity. In the off-sales periods companies must hold unusually large inventories of raw materials or merchandise pending sale. Retailers, for instance, may have to buy large quantities of goods between August and October that

CONTEMPORARY ISSUE

Converting Short-term into Long-term Debt

In an article on reducing short-term debt in the early and mid-1980s, *Business Week* pointed out one measure that business and government can take to reduce the discomfort of short-term debt.

> For corporate treasurers, the recovery never seemed to bring an end to recession-caused pain. The economy snapped back so vigorously that interest rates spurted to levels normally associated with a credit crunch. And the stock market rally stalled before all but a handful of companies could raise new capital. For many companies, recovery meant being stretched thin by costly short-term debt.*

The reduction of economic growth and the cooperation of the Federal Reserve Board both lowered rates radically. These factors caused companies to invest in the bond market as a way of fixing rates and lengthening the duration of debt. Fewer takeovers occurred and reduced an extraordinary credit demand (see Figure 5-2). Capital spending then could become better aligned with cash flows. According to *Business Week* economist, David M. Jones of government securities dealer Aubrey G. Lanston & Co., "It's what you'd expect in a disinflationary environment. It now pays to be out of debt rather than in debt. Corporations will borrow long to pay off short-term debt, but net borrowing won't rise much."

Companies have discovered that borrowing via bonds is a more stable way of financing their projects than short-term options. In fact, according to statistics in *Business Week,* from Salomon Bros., in October, 1984, new bonds with due dates of eleven years or more rose to 37% from 27% a few months before. During the same time, companies issued short-term bonds at a rate of almost half as many as they had only a short time earlier.

Business Week points out that one positive aspect of this trend in longer term bonds is that much of this activity has been concentrated on refinancing of existing debts.

This indicated that a stabilization was occurring at the end of 1984.

---
*Business Week, November 19, 1984, 46.

---

they will not sell until the Christmas season.

Second, producers may lack funds to prepare their products for market. Farmers, for example, may have cattle that they cannot fatten unless they borrow money for feed.

Third, an unforeseen event may throw a business into temporary financial difficulty. A strike, for example, may make shipping goods impossible. In such an event, short-term capital enables the organization to weather income curtailment.

Companies could meet unexpected or seasonal financial needs by holding cash in reserve. However, as we will see later, keeping large amounts of cash on hand is not good management.

Types of Short-term Obligations

Short-term obligations are either unsecured or secured. **Unsecured obligations** *involve no collateral and thus are usually available only if the firm has a high credit rating.*[3] **Secured obligations** are *loans backed by the pledge of some asset.* A discussion of the major types of short-term obligations follows.

OPEN-ACCOUNT OR TRADE CREDIT

Sometimes called **trade** or **mercantile** credit, **open-account credit** supplies part of the working capital for most firms. This form of credit is not a cash advance; rather, it is *the sale of goods by one business to another, with payment expected at a later date.* Since no security is required, the lender usually investigates the business seeking credit carefully. Most transactions among producers, wholesalers, and retailers take place on an open-account basis. Thus most firms both grant credit and receive it.

In selling goods on open-account credit, vendors normally detail **credit terms,** or *stipulations of the length of the credit period and the cash discount for prompt payment.*

The length of the credit period, though usually 30 days, depends on industry custom. Generally, it is roughly equal to the time buyers require to convert the goods into cash. The **cash discount** specifies *the amount that buyers can deduct from a bill if they make payment on or before the designated due date.* A very common credit term is 2/10 net 30. The "2/10" means that buyers are entitled to a 2 percent discount if they pay for the goods within ten days; "net 30" signifies that if they don't take the discount they must pay the entire bill within 30 days. Assume that Barbara Smith, the owner of a medical supplies store, receives a $100 shipment of goods billed 2/10 net 30. If she pays for the merchandise before the tenth day, she deducts 2 percent, or $2, and remits $98. If she waits until after the tenth day, the full $100 is due on or before the thirtieth day.

Sellers offer cash discounts because (1) the sooner they receive the money, the sooner they can put it to use; (2) less billing and collection expense is necessary when buyers pay for goods promptly; and (3) losses from bad debts tend to be lower.

The buyer also benefits from cash discounts. If a merchant buys $100,000 worth of merchandise from a manufacturer and the terms are 1/10 net 30, the merchant saves $1,000 by paying within 10 days. The manufacturer is saying in effect, "If you pay me 20 days before

To obtain short-term loans, firms often apply to commercial banks. Here, two company executives discuss such loans with a bank officer.

---
[3]We discuss credit management in greater depth in Chapter 6.

the bill becomes due, I will give you a 1 percent discount for paying promptly." It is the same as saying, "I will give you 1 percent for the use of that money for 20 days." This is equivalent to an annual interest rate of more than 18 percent (360 divided by 20 equals 18). Buyers who take cash discounts are regarded as preferred customers. If they have temporary financial difficulty, the vendor is likely to be especially understanding.

COMMERCIAL BANK CREDIT

Commercial banks *specialize in making short-term (three to twelve months) loans to businesses.* A commercial bank loan may be secured or unsecured.

Unsecured loans are loans that have no assets or security pledged as collateral. A commercial bank will often grant such a loan if it feels confident of the firm's financial soundness and if the bank has had a continuous relationship with the firm.

Commercial banks make some loans only if the borrower pledges collateral, which the bank can seize if the borrower fails to repay the loan. Most lending agencies insist that the marketable value of the collateral leave a margin of at least 20 percent more than the amount of the loan. Thus, if a business wants to borrow $1,600 on a secured loan, the lender would probably require at least $2,000 worth of collateral.

A bank is likely to require collateral if (1) the borrower has only a fair credit rating; (2) the lending agency doesn't know the borrower; (3) an unusually large sum is involved; (4) the lender questions the use the borrower will make of the money; or (5) the bank requires collateral on all loans as a matter of policy. Stocks, bonds, accounts receivable, bills of lading (see page 145), warehouse receipts, and chattel mortgages are all used as collateral.

What Is a Line of Credit?

A line of credit is a predetermined amount of money a bank agrees to loan a business. Usually, a line of credit is granted for one year and is unsecured. Both banks and borrowing businesses benefit from a line of credit since it saves time and is convenient. Borrowers need not make a new application every time they need a loan and the bank need not investigate the creditworthiness of such borrowers each time they request money.

Floor Planning

Retailers of expensive or "big ticket" items, such as automobiles and home appliances, may be able to finance their purchases with money a bank advances. Under **floor planning,** the *lending agency holds*

ISSUE FOR DEBATE

Should Commercial Banks Be Allowed to Engage in Interstate Banking?

Since 1933 commercial banks have not been allowed to open branches outside the states in which their headquarters are located. Some banks have found loopholes in the law and are, in fact, engaging in interstate banking. Interstate banking, however, remains a controversial issue.

PROS

Interstate banking would promote competition and lead to better, more efficient service and lower interest charges.

State boundaries are an artificial barrier to commerce. Virtually all other products are sold in all states to the benefit of everyone.

The absence of full permission to engage in interstate banking has caused some companies to find ways to get around the law. Legalizing interstate banking would stop this manipulation.

Nonbanks, such as credit card companies, operate in all states and have been well-accepted and successful.

Modern day technology such as ATMs and other computer services would enable people to choose any bank in the nation—or even the world.

CONS

Much thought went into prohibiting banks from engaging in interstate banking. Why throw a good law away?

Big banks in rich states would acquire savings and other forms of capital from poorer states. This would unbalance national economic development.

Too much of the nation's wealth would be concentrated among too few banks. This might be harmful to small businesses.

Most local banks are managed by people who know the community. The needs of local people might be overlooked or ignored by big absentee-managed banks.

Interstate banking would eliminate the "personal touch" people have come to appreciate from smaller bank corporations.

Questions

1. Do you feel that interstate banking is a good idea? Why or why not?
2. Do you foresee a time when the number of banks will be greatly reduced? Why or why not?

title to the car or appliance as collateral. When the retailer sells the item, it repays the bank.

Pledge Accounts Receivables for Loans

Under this method of obtaining short-term capital, a business pledges its **accounts receivable** *(money customers owe the busi-*

ness) as collateral for a loan. The lender, usually a commercial bank, will not loan an amount equal to the face value of the accounts receivable because some of a business' creditors may not pay their debts. As a firm receives payment from its customers on the accounts receivable, it repays the bank.

Lease Instead of Buy

Increasingly, businesses subscribe to the adage, "Never own it if you can lease it." A **lease** *is a contract whereby one party, the lessor, lets another party, the lessee, use property for a certain period of time for a specified fee or payment.*

Leasing has long been a common way for businesses to acquire the use of offices, stores, and other real estate. In the past two decades, leasing has also been widely used to acquire equipment such as computers, copy machines, trucks, and automobiles used in a business.

Businesses can operate on less initial capital by leasing large equipment. Companies save on insurance, can deduct leasing expenses from their taxes, and do not have to sell the old equipment.

Advantages of Leasing

The main advantage of leasing to the lessee is that a business requires less initial capital to operate. For example, a business (or an individual) can lease an automobile without making a substantial down payment, which provides capital for other uses in the enterprise. Other advantages of leasing are: a) the leasing company usually provides the insurance and maintenance or upkeep of the leased property; b) the cost of leasing is a business expense that is deductible from income taxes; c) the lessee has no problem disposing of the leased equipment once the term of the lease expires; and d) in some cases, the business can apply lease payments to the purchase of the property.

Disadvantages of Leasing

One disadvantage of leasing is that the lessee does not build up equity or ownership in the leased property. A company that leases an automobile, for example, has no cash value in the vehicle when the lease terminates. Another disadvantage of leasing is that the lessee cannot claim depreciation of the leased property on his/her income tax return. This limitation may offset the advantage of claiming the cost of the lease as a business expense. A third disadvantage of leasing is that the lessee cannot use the property as collateral for a loan.

Credit Instruments Used in Short-term Financing

To obtain short-term capital, a business may use several documents or credit instruments.

BILLS OF LADING

A **bill of lading** is *a receipt issued by a transportation agency for merchandise to be transported from a named shipper (the consignor) either to a specified consignee or to the order of any person.* A bill of lading stating that the goods are being shipped to a specific person is called a **straight bill** and is nonnegotiable. *If the bill of lading does not specify the consignee,* it is called an **order bill** and is negotiable. The holder of either type of bill holds the title to the merchandise and can offer it as collateral.

WAREHOUSE RECEIPTS

One of the most common types of collateral is the **warehouse receipt,** which is *a receipt a warehouse issues that serves as title to the stored merchandise and that the owner of the merchandise can use as collateral.* For example, a business stores products in a public warehouse that specializes in storage for a fee. The warehouse issues a warehouse receipt, which is title to the stored merchandise described in the receipt. If the business needs funds, it can present the receipt to a bank and usually obtain a loan for up to 70 or 80 percent of the goods' market value. Until the loan is repaid, the borrower cannot withdraw the merchandise from storage. If the borrower defaults in payment, the bank takes possession of the goods. Warehouse receipts are usually negotiable.

CHATTEL MORTGAGES

A legal device by which movable property is pledged as collateral is a **chattel mortgage.** Almost any movable property that has a fairly large market—such as motor vehicles, bulldozers, furniture, livestock, appliances, or grain—can serve as collateral in this way. Chattel mortgages are especially common in the financing of motor vehicles. A business purchasing a truck, for example, can make the customary down payment and then sign a note backed by a chattel mortgage on the truck for the balance.

FINANCIAL MANAGEMENT

Financial management *involves advising the business on how to obtain the money needed to operate and how to control its use.* Some of the specific activities a financial manager performs are:

1. Estimating how much money the business will need over a period of time for payroll, inventory, equipment, interest, expansion, maintenance, and other purposes.
2. Arranging to obtain the capital needed to operate the business at the lowest cost.
3. Investing financial surpluses to obtain the highest return.

> *"The use of money is all the advantage there is in having it."*
>
> — BENJAMIN FRANKLIN

In addition to these activities, the financial manager controls the granting of credit to customers, supervises the company's use of credit, prepares and submits budget proposals, invests idle company funds, polices inventory levels and purchasing policies, and handles stock and bond issues.

PUTTING IDLE MONEY TO PRODUCTIVE USE

So far, this chapter has dealt with the different means companies have for securing funds and credit. While it is important to have enough money on hand, it is uneconomical to have too much money. Unused cash is just as unproductive as an employee playing cards instead of working, a machine gathering dust instead of producing, or a building sitting empty instead of earning rent.

When a business is not using excess funds profitably, the efficient manager will invest those funds to earn interest. This is particularly important for businesses in which short-term capital needs fluctuate widely, often because of seasonal factors.

Assume a corporation has $500,000 in idle cash that it does not need for a few months or even a few weeks. This sum invested at 13 percent would produce $5,417 per month in interest. The company can put the money to work in several profitable ways: (1) It can lend the funds to a bank and receive a promissory note; (2) it can buy some commercial paper, such as short-term negotiable promissory notes; or (3) it can deposit the money in the bank by buying certificates of deposit. Investments such as these provide, in effect, short-term financing to other businesses.

SUMMARY

- Businesses need long-term capital to acquire permanent assets, and they need short-term capital to finance ongoing operations.
- Small businesses may obtain long-term capital from personal savings, friends and relatives, partners, personal assets used as collateral for loans, and government agencies.
- Large businesses may obtain long-term capital by selling common and preferred stocks and bonds. Stocks represent ownership in the business. Bonds are debt capital which must be repaid to the bondholders.
- For the investor, the advantages of owning common stock are (a) possible appreciation in value, (b) possible dividends, and (c) ease of selling or transferring ownership. Limitations of owning common stock are (a) the value of the stock may decline, and (b) the investor may have to decline other investment opportunities.
- Advantages of common stock to the issuing company are (a) it need not pay dividends, and (b) it need not repay the investor the money raised through the sale of stock.
- Limitations of selling stock are (a) the value of the original shares may be diluted, (b) dividends paid common stockholders are not a business expense and are, therefore, taxable to both the corporation and the shareholder, and (c) public interest in buying new issues of stock is uncertain.
- Advantages of issuing bonds to obtain long-term capital are (a) bondholders have no voting power and cannot exercise control over the management of the company, (b) interest paid bondholders is a business expense and is, therefore, tax-deductible, and (c) interest paid on bonds is a known cost. Disadvantages of selling bonds are (a) they must be repaid, (b) if the company is weak, the interest rate paid bondholders may be high, and (c) the company cannot skip interest payments during periods of economic stress.
- Large and small businesses need short-term financing to meet seasonal needs for operating capital and unusual drains on capital.
- Sources of short-term capital include (a) open-account or trade credit, (b) commercial bank credit, (c) floor planning, and (d) pledged accounts receivables.
- Increasingly, businesses are leasing equipment rather than purchasing it because (a) the business does not have to tie up its own capital, (b) the leasing company usually takes care of maintenance and upkeep, and (c) the cost of leasing is a business expense and therefore tax-deductible. Some firms prefer not to lease because leasing does not create any value or equity in the equipment, and the firms cannot use leased equipment as collateral for loans.
- Credit instruments used in short-term financing include promissory notes, drafts, bills of lading, warehouse receipts, and chattel mortgages.
- Financial management includes: (a) estimating financial needs and (b) arranging to obtain financing and investing financial surpluses.
- Cash flow management includes collecting money due the business as quickly as possible and delaying payment of obligations as long as possible.
- Companies should invest idle money to earn interest.

CHAPTER 5/LONG- AND SHORT-TERM FINANCING

KEY TERMS YOU SHOULD KNOW

accounts receivable	dividend	par-value stock
authorized stock	equity capital	preemptive right
bill of lading	financial management	preferred stock
bond	floor planning	principal
bond indenture	interest rate	risk rating
bond trustee	issued stock	secured obligation
call option	leasing	security
cash discount	long-term capital	serial-plan method
chattel mortgage	market value	short-term capital
collateral	maturity date	sinking-fund plan
commercial bank	mortgage bond	stock
common stock	municipal bond	straight bill
convertible bond	negotiable bond	unissued stock
credit term	noncumulative dividend	unsecured obligation
cumulative dividend	no-par-value stock	warehouse receipt
debenture bond	open-account credit	
debt capital	order bill	

QUESTIONS FOR REVIEW

1. What is the difference between short-term and long-term capital? Give examples of expenditures that include each.

2. Give pros and cons for using each of the following to raise long-term capital for a small business: personal savings, friends and relatives, partners, use of personal assets as collateral for loans, and government agencies.

3. What is the main difference between stocks and bonds?

4. Explain the differences among authorized, issued, and unissued stock.

5. What are the differences between common stock and preferred stock?

6. From the investor's view, what are the advantages and disadvantages of common stock? What are the pros and cons from the company's standpoint?

7. Why may a company sell bonds? What are the disadvantages of financing through bonds?

8. What is a bond indenture? A bond trustee?

9. Why do prices of bonds fluctuate?

10. Explain how each of the following is used in short-term financing: commercial bank credit, floor planning, and pledging accounts receivables.

11. What are the advantages and disadvantages of leasing?

12. Explain how each of the following credit instruments is used: promissory note, draft, bill of lading, warehouse receipt, and chattel mortgage.

13. What functions are involved in financial management?

14. What is cash flow? Why should idle money be put to productive use?

QUESTIONS FOR DISCUSSION

1. Find an advertisement offering to lease an automobile or other product. What specific advantages are claimed for leasing instead of buying?

2. According to the New York Security Exchange, convertible bond issues (bonds which may be converted into stock some time after purchase) are outnumbered 15 to 1 by nonconvertible bond issues. What factors may account for this?

3. How are problems of short-term and long-term financing made difficult during periods of inflation?

4. Assume you sell securities for a brokerage company. How are prospective buyers for tax-exempt municipal bonds likely to differ from prospects for regular corporate bonds?

5. New corporations generally issue shares to a small number of "inside" investors. Then, when the business decides to "go public" with a new issue, the original investors usually keep control of at least 50 percent of all outstanding shares. In your opinion is this fair to outside investors?

6. "Idle money kept in a noninterest-bearing bank account is just as wasteful as an employee being paid for not working." Explain why this is so. How can a business avoid this kind of waste?

CASE STUDY

How to Finance the Purchase of a Laboratory

Three young physicians, Drs. Brown, Jordan, and Harris, operate a medical clinic in a city of 500,000. One month ago, Harold Yaker, owner of a medical laboratory, died suddenly. Yaker's lab does blood analyses for the clinic and many other physicians in the area.

Harold Yaker's widow, Janis, now owns 100 percent of the laboratory. Members of the medical clinic want to buy the laboratory from Mrs. Yaker. They meet to devise a plan.

Brown: I talked to Mrs. Yaker about selling the lab.
Jordan: How much?
B: $750,000. And she wants cash.
Harris: Is it worth that?
B: Mrs. Yaker let our CPA examine the books carefully. He feels that $750,000 is a fair price. And the lab shows excellent growth potential.
J: National Medical—that big lab chain—also wants to buy the Yaker operation. My source told me that it is prepared to offer $375,000 cash and $375,000 worth of their stock. And since their shares have been going up, they think that Mrs. Yaker may go for their deal.
B: We've got a problem. The most cash we can come up with is $250,000. That leaves us $500,000 short.
H: The three of us know quite a few physicians in the area. Maybe we could sell stock to raise the $500,000? It would be good for the business because any doctor who owned stock in the lab would use its services.
B: But if we sold stock, we'd have to share the profits and the anticipated appreciation of the lab's value.
J: I know Mrs. Yaker wants cash. But maybe she'd accept something almost as good.
B: Like what?
J: Why not offer her $250,000 cash and a note for $500,000? We could tie the interest rate on the note to the prime rate. That would be fair to her and to us.
B: How long a note?
J: I'm thinking of a ten-year payout in ten equal annual installments. I believe that we could handle the payments easily out of profits. And the interest would all be tax-deductible.
H: I think your idea has a lot of merit. But there's another possibility. Suppose we offered Mrs. Yaker less money for the lab and let her keep 20 or 25 percent of the stock?
B: If we followed your plan, we would also have the advantage of Mrs. Yaker's expertise. She knows the lab business inside and out.
H: Right. And if we offer her an attractive management contract in addition to some of the stock, she might accept a much lower price.
B: Mrs. Yaker promised me she would not accept an offer from National Medical for two weeks. Let's get together this weekend and decide how to structure an offer.

Questions

1. What are other ways to finance the purchase of the laboratory?
2. Evaluate the Jordan plan. Evaluate the Harris plan. Which do you prefer? Why?

EVOLUTION OF A BUSINESS

The Ins and Outs of Raising Capital

After investigating the possibilities of acquiring a franchise or an established business, Ray and Sara decide to start a business from scratch. They plan to form a partnership on a 50–50 basis, with each person working full-time in the new business. In estimating their capital needs they conclude that they need a minimum of $87,000 to acquire the lease on the space they want, to furnish and decorate it appropriately, and to meet operating and promotional expenses for the first year. Ray has $15,000 and Sara $17,000 in personal savings that they are able to invest. Thus they need to raise an additional $55,000.

Sara: The loan officer I spoke to at the bank said we'd need at least half of the total amount—that's $43,000 or so—before he'd consider lending us the rest. He pointed out that a service business like ours doesn't build up assets after it's established. Also, he said that in the bank's experience, it often takes a business like ours a couple of years before it gets on its feet.

Ray: Have you come up with any other ideas?

Sara: Well, my brother's pretty well off, so I talked to him about it. He said he could lend us about $5,000 for a year at the prime rate.

Ray: My mother said she'd let me use her house as collateral for a loan if I wanted to do it that way. But the house is practically the only asset she has, and I hesitate to expose her to that kind of a risk.

Sara: I talked to an equipment supplier who said he could lease us the furniture and other equipment we'd need for the first couple of years. We could buy it later, and apply the rental fees to the purchase price. That would reduce what we'd need right away by about $7,000, but it would raise our expenses by $200 a month.

Ray: I have a life insurance policy that I could borrow $5,000 on.

Questions

1. Which arrangements would cost the least in terms of interest?
2. What about the advisability of getting funds from friends and relatives?
3. How do you size up the various possibilities? What combination of possibilities would you consider most feasible?
4. As far as capital requirements are concerned, how do buying a going business, acquiring a franchise, and starting a business compare?

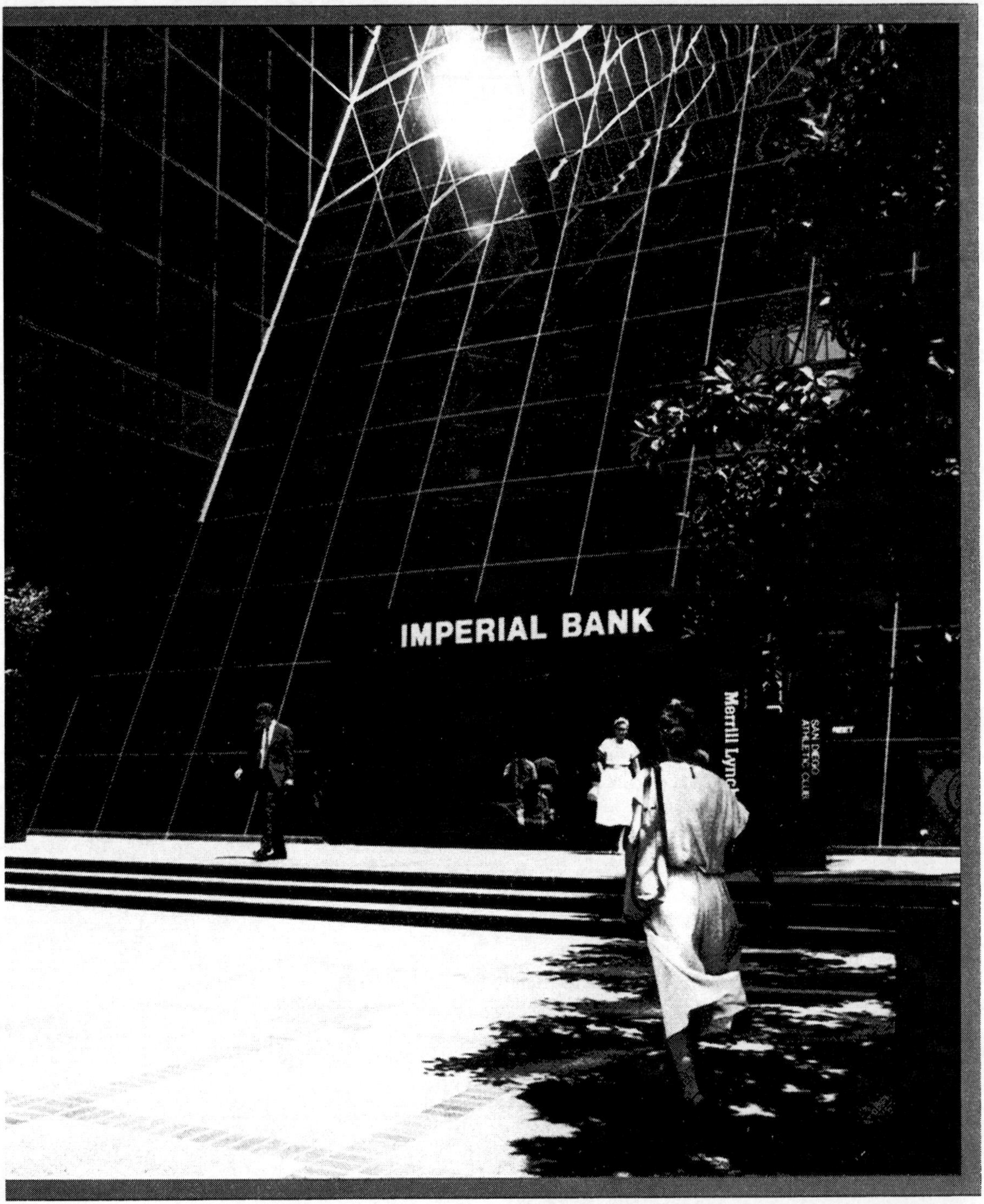
IMPERIAL BANK
SAN DIEGO ATHLETIC CLUB

6

FINANCIAL INSTITUTIONS
The Money Pipeline

READ THIS CHAPTER SO YOU CAN:

Explain how financial institutions serve business and society and discuss why the financial industry is both competitive and dynamic.

Know and understand the nature and services of the various types of financial institutions.

Understand how the Federal Reserve System works.

Describe Supercompany Financial Institutions and explain why they emerged.

Explain credit management and how business and consumer credit applicants are evaluated.

Financial institutions are an important part of our everyday lives. Though there are many types of financial institutions, they all serve businesses and individuals in at least one of three ways. First, they are a source of loans or credit. Businesses often must borrow money to pay for inventories, supplies, and other operating expenses or to expand and modernize their facilities. As individuals, we sometimes need to borrow money to finance automobiles, pay personal expenses, buy homes, and purchase a vast variety of consumer goods and services. Obtaining a loan from a bank, credit union, or other such financial organization helps us meet these goals.

Instead of loaning money, some financial institutions serve businesses and individuals by providing a means for investing money. Savings and loan associations and credit unions and some other financial companies pay interest on money people deposit. For example, you may have an interest-bearing checking or savings account. Financial institutions or "money companies" may also sell securities, stocks and bonds, Individual Retirement Accounts (IRAs), and other investments to business or private consumers.

Finally, financial institutions make it convenient for us to transact business on a daily basis. They allow us to store our money and retrieve it whenever we need it. They provide us with methods of payment—credit and checking accounts—that virtually make cash obsolete. Credit cards, for example, enable us to pay for merchandise and services a little at a time. Checks allow us to pay bills, buy goods, and transfer money from one party to another easily.

THE FINANCIAL SERVICES INDUSTRY IS COMPETITIVE

Traditionally, banks and other financial institutions operated under clearly defined government regulations. Each type of financial institution offered a specific range of services. A commercial bank, for example, did not make real estate mortgages; in turn, a savings and loan association did not finance the purchases of automobiles.

Because of this specialization, a financial company competed directly only with similar financial companies. This trend changed drastically, however, in the late 1970s and early 1980s. Extensive government deregulation allowed many financial institutions to expand the types of services they may provide. Consequently, banks and savings and loans are in direct competition for home improvement and auto loans and for checking and savings account services. Many different types of financial institutions now compete vigorously for the patronage of businesses and individuals.

In addition to more competition within the financial services industry, a new competition from nontraditional financial institutions is emerging. Many security brokerage companies, credit card companies, insurance companies, and manufacturers offer ways to borrow, invest, or handle money without utilizing the traditional banking organizations. Today, for example, the largest grantor of consumer credit for automobiles is the General Motors Acceptance Corporation, a division of General Motors.

THE FINANCIAL SERVICES INDUSTRY IS DYNAMIC

Increased competition, brought about by deregulation, has forced banking institutions to become more dynamic in providing services (called financial products). Three other forces, however, are also at work to make the industry more dynamic. The first is technology. The advent of computerized banking has greatly altered the way we spend our money, invest our funds, and pay our bills. As one observer notes, "The computer is to the financial services industry what the mass production line was to manufacturing. It gives financial service firms the capacity to handle more transactions at declining unit cost and has created large-scale enterprises."[1] Individuals with home computers and telephone hook-ups can even do their banking without leaving their own living rooms!

An inevitable result of computerization, the automatic teller machines (ATMs) have greatly influenced the financial industry. First introduced in 1977, ATMs are now available in virtually all banks and handle many standard financial transactions quickly and efficiently. Some banks are experimenting with micro-branches that have a number of these machines but only one employee to answer questions.

A second force that is strongly affecting financial institutions is the continuing shift from a production-based economy to a service-oriented economy. Service businesses tend to be much more liquid (with a large share of assets in cash) than manufacturing companies. Financial institutions must change to meet the investment needs of businesses that have greater assets.

The third force causing financial companies to become more dynamic is the availability of an international market. As communication and technology increase, the financial markets—securities, corporate lending, consumer borrowing, and investments—expand beyond U.S. borders. Large financial institutions already conduct

---

[1]George J. Vojta, "New Competition and Its Implications for Banking," *The Magazine of Bank Administration,* July 1983, 36.

banking operations in many parts of the world. This trend toward internationalization of financial activities seems certain and is likely to gain momentum in years to come.

In this chapter we will discuss the various conventional financial institutions—commercial banks, savings and loan associations, mutual funds, investment banks, and credit unions—and examine how nonbanks, such as credit card companies, insurance companies, and manufacturers, contribute to the financial services industry. We will also explore the Federal Reserve System and analyze credit management.

MAJOR FINANCIAL INSTITUTIONS

Commercial Banks

A **commercial bank** is *a public corporation* (that is, it is owned by private stockholders) *that accepts demand deposits and specializes in making loans to businesses and individuals.* Commercial banks are either **state banks,** which are *chartered or authorized by a state,* or **national banks,** which are *chartered by the federal government.*

Over the years, commercial banks have expanded their services, and today they strive to provide every possible financial service their customers can use. In 1984 there were 15,440 commercial banks operating 59,050 offices. The total assets of these commercial banks exceeded 2.4 trillion dollars, making them the dominant financial institution. In the past decade, commercial banks have established a record of safety for depositors. Between 1977 and 1984, for example, only 133 commercial banks were closed because of financial difficulties, and all depositors were insured by the Federal Deposit Insurance Corporation (explained on pp. 162–163).[2]

Active international markets have caused many American banks to establish branches around the world. This branch is in Hong Kong.

DEMAND DEPOSITS

A **demand deposit** is *a deposit that can be withdrawn by the depositor at any time, with no advance notice.* Commercial banks accept deposits in cash, notes, drafts, or similar forms. *The depositor can withdraw or transfer money at will by writing checks* against a **checking account.** On December 31, 1980, banks, credit unions, and savings and loan associations were all given the right to offer *interest-bearing checking accounts,* called **NOW (Negotiable Order of Withdrawal) accounts.**

The procedure for opening a checking account varies, depending on whether the applicant is an individual, a corporation, or a partnership. For individual checking accounts most commercial banks sim-

---
[2]*Statistical Abstract of the United States, 1985.*

ply require the individual's address, place of employment (if any), credit references, and a signature that can be used to identify checks written on the depositor's account.

For a corporate checking account, the bank requires the corporation to prepare a formal resolution that (1) authorizes the opening of the account, (2) specifies the officer or officers who are authorized to sign checks, and (3) indicates which officers have authority to borrow money in the name of the corporation. Sample signatures of the authorized officials are also required.

Partnership accounts are opened in much the same manner as individual accounts. However, the bank requires signatures of all persons who are authorized to sign checks for the partnership.

COMMERCIAL LOANS

Commercial loans are *loans made to businesses.* Interest charged on these loans is the bank's chief source of income. Traditionally, commercial bank loans have been for 90 days or less; in recent years, however, banks have frequently made loans for much longer periods. For a discussion of secured versus unsecured commercial loans, see page 142.

Recently, corporations have begun to compete within the commercial loan market by serving as both lenders and borrowers. This is because corporations with excess funds can loan money at lower interest rates than commercial banks can offer. Dealers called investment bankers unite corporations that are short on funds with those that have extra funds.

CONSUMER LOANS

A loan made by a commercial bank directly to consumers is a **consumer loan.** Commercial banks make more consumer loans than any other financial institution. These banks also indirectly finance consumer loans made by sales finance and consumer finance companies because these lenders obtain most of their capital from commercial banks. They borrow from commercial banks "at wholesale," then "retail" the money to consumers.

CHECKING ACCOUNTS

Commercial banks and savings and loans provide checking accounts for depositors. These may pay interest, but banks usually require a minimum balance.

SAVINGS ACCOUNTS

Commercial banks encourage the opening of **savings accounts** (also called **time deposits**). These are *accounts that earn interest and from which withdrawals are permitted only on presentation of a*

> *"Money is a handmaiden if thou knowest how to use it; a mistress if thou knowest not."*
>
> HORACE

AMERICA'S REEMERGING CREATIVITY

Electronic Funds Transfer Systems

Great strides are being made in transferring money electronically. Doing so means more convenience for consumers and less human labor in handling financial transactions.

An **electronic funds transfer (EFT)** is *a transaction initiated through an electronic terminal, a telephone, a computer, or a magnetic tape for the purpose of ordering, instructing, or authorizing a financial institution to debit or credit an account.* There are four basic types of electronic funds transfer systems: automated clearinghouses, automated teller machines, point-of-sale terminals, and bill payment by telephone.

Automated clearinghouses (ACH) do away with individual paper postings of deposits or payments. The basic concept is simple—when several similar transactions are initiated and sent to one institution, an automated clearinghouse can combine the transactions to speed the process.

The best example of an automated clearinghouse is the direct deposit program carried out by the federal government to pay Social Security benefits. A recipient of Social Security can sign up at his or her bank to have the check sent for direct deposit to an account.

Automated teller machines (ATMs) are the best known type of electronic funds transfer system. An ATM is basically a cash dispenser that permits withdrawals from checking and savings accounts and cash advances from lines of credit on charge accounts. It also enables transfers between accounts, payments on loans or charge accounts, and balance inquiries. Most basic transactions that can be handled through a teller can be handled by an ATM.

The automated teller machine gives an individual privacy and access to banking for up to 24 hours a day, seven days a week. Also, financial

---

passbook. The bank reserves the right to require a notice, usually of 30 days, of intention to withdraw funds, although this rule is seldom enforced.

CERTIFIED CHECKS

A **certified check** is *guaranteed by the bank that issues it.* An officer of the bank writes "accepted" or "certified" on the face of the check and then signs his or her name. A sum equal to the amount of the check is withdrawn from the depositor's account and held by the bank pending cashing of the check. Certified checks are used when personal checks might not be accepted—for example, when large amounts are involved, as in auto, real estate, and securities transactions.

TRUST SERVICES

Many banks maintain a **trust department,** which *manages funds of individuals or businesses,* primarily of estates and pension plans. When a bank is named trustee of an estate, it carries out the provisions of an individual's will and invests the money left in the estate.

institutions are beginning to locate ATMs in areas away from their premises—such as at service stations, shopping malls, and amusement parks—giving customers a chance to bank at more locations.

Point-of-sale (POS) terminals are another type of electronic funds transfer system. Computerized cash registers or terminals in a store can authorize a customer's credit card or debit card purchase. Similar to a credit card, a debit card is presented at the point of purchase. The debit card automatically deducts the amount of purchase from the customer's standing account through an on-line terminal at the merchant's location. Merchants not using such systems must now call authorization centers, such as the National Data Corporation, to approve purchases.

Bill payment by phone (BPP) is a system whereby customers dial directly into the computer of their financial institution and authorize payments or transfers to or from their accounts. When applying for the telephone bill pay option, a checking account holder supplies the bank with a list of names and addresses of each creditor he or she wishes to pay by phone. The bank returns this information in the form of a vendor list. Each vendor's name is accompanied by a three-digit vendor number, which has been properly recorded in the computer and can be referenced by the account number, and a personal identification number (PIN).

After receipt of the vendor list, the customer can use the account. The only further requirement is a touch-tone telephone. It is then possible to key in, in a predetermined sequence, the account number, PIN, vendor number, amount to be paid, and date to be paid.

Use of EFTs will increase dramatically in this decade. The cost to the bank for processing a check is about a dollar—far more than the cost of an electronic fund transfer. We are ready for a "less check" society.

Questions for Discussion

1. Many older people are afraid to use EFTs. Why? How can their fears be relieved?

2. Why would financial institutions be eager to see EFTs become universally accepted?

When the bank is trustee of an employee pension plan, it invests funds to obtain the best possible income.

Investment Banks

Investment banks—unlike commercial banks—do not accept deposits, make loans, or provide services associated with commercial banking. Instead, an investment bank is *a specialist in helping corporations acquire long-term capital; it is an intermediary between a corporation that wants to sell securities and the investing public.* The bank purchases stocks or bonds from the issuing corporation, then resells them to private investors. Investment banks also sell bonds for government units that issue them for public improvements such as new schools or sewage systems.

Here's how it works. A business or government wishing to raise capital by issuing securities contacts the investment bank. The bank's analysts then determine if the company's proposed security issue is sound. They review the company's financial status, profit possibilities, products manufactured or sold, legal status, labor relations, competitive strength, and the qualifications of its executives.

If the investment bank is satisfied that the issuing corporation is sound, it may bid on the entire issue of securities. *When the amount involved is large, however, the bank usually invites other investment banks to join in the venture.* Such an arrangement, called a **purchase group** or **underwriting syndicate,** spreads the risk among all participating parties.

Next, a selling price for the securities is set, based on the judgment of the investment bank's analysts, prices of similar offerings, general market conditions, and the prominence of the issuing firm. When the deal is closed, the investment bank pays the issuing corporation the full price of the securities less a **spread** (*the bank's commission for selling the securities*). On very high-grade bond issues, the spread is often less than 1 percent. On other issues—depending on their size, type, and quality—the spread may be anywhere from 2 to 10 percent.

Investment banks maintain a sales department to sell securities to institutional investors, such as commercial banks, insurance companies, pension plans, and mutual funds. Part of any issue may be sold to individual investors.

Mutual Savings Banks

Mutual savings banks have no stockholders and are owned by depositors, who receive their share of earnings as interest. A mutual savings bank *accepts deposits of individuals, pools them, and then channels them into real-estate mortgages and other productive loans and investments.* The savings depositor is given a passbook in which deposits and withdrawals are entered. Interest on savings is paid regularly. Depending on provisions of state laws, mutual savings banks may invest in residential and nonresidential mortgages, corporate stock, and corporate and government bonds.

Mutual savings banks, formed in Philadelphia and Boston in 1816, are the nation's oldest type of savings institution. They have retained their popularity, for at the end of 1984 there were 393 mutual savings banks located in 18 states; at that time these banks had total assets in excess of $183 billion.

Savings and Loan Associations

Traditionally, **savings and loan associations** *were organizations that accepted deposits from savers and invested this capital in local home mortgages.* They operated in much the same manner as mutual savings banks. The Garn–St. Germain Depository Institutions Act of 1982, however, granted savings and loan associations new powers. They may now make commercial loans, finance the purchase of commercial real estate, and lend funds for automobiles and other personal property. The act also permitted savings and loans to switch from a mutual to a stock form of ownership, thereby making it easier to raise capital for expansion.

Funds for qualifying savings and loan associations are protected by Federal Savings and Loan Insurance. This ensures solvency in much the same manner as the Federal Deposit Insurance Corporation (FDIC) protection that is available to commercial banks (see p. 162).

Approximately 43 percent of all savings and loan associations are incorporated under federal law; the remaining 57 percent have state charters. There are approximately 3,872 savings and loan associations in the United States, with combined assets of more than $907 billion.

THE FEDERAL RESERVE SYSTEM

Because the banking industry exerts a strong influence on our country's economy, banks must be subject to certain laws to avoid creating financial havoc. To this end, all national banks and many state banks belong to the **Federal Reserve System.** This is *a federally controlled system set up to regulate the supply of money and credit so as to contribute to a high level of employment, economic growth, and price stability.* This system, established by the Federal Reserve Act of 1913, is managed by a Board of Governors, the seven members of which are appointed by the President. The nation is divided into 12 districts with a Federal Reserve Bank in each.

The Federal Reserve Banks are owned by the commercial banks that belong to the system. However, the commercial-bank members cannot "control" the Federal Reserve System as stockholders normally control a corporation. Management of the system is under the direction of the executive branch of the federal government.

The Federal Reserve System has an enormous influence not only on commercial banking but also on economic affairs in general. The Reserve System uses the following three tools to control the economy: regulation of bank reserves, regulation of the discount rate, and open-market operations.

Regulation of Bank Reserves

In banking, **reserves** are *the portion of deposits that a bank keeps on hand to meet the withdrawal demands of depositors.* The Federal Reserve System determines the size of cash reserves that member banks must maintain, thereby fixing the percentage of deposits that banks can loan to borrowers. Reducing reserve requirements gives banks more money for loans and investments and inflates the economy. Increasing reserve requirements decreases the money available for credit purposes and, in turn, deflates the economy.

Regulation of the Discount Rate

The Federal Reserve acts as the bankers' bank. It loans money to banks in much the same way that a bank loans money to us. And like a bank, the Federal Reserve demands payment for borrowed funds. Known as an interest rate in public banking, this charge is called a **discount rate** when dealing with the Reserve bank. This is because *the charge for the loan is deducted ahead of time,* instead of being paid out later.

If the Reserve sets the discount rate high, it discourages member banks from borrowing. It also causes prime rates to rise, since banks must pay more for the money they put out on loan. The **prime rate** (which affects all interest rates) is *the lowest rate that Federal Reserve member banks charge borrowers with the highest credit ratings.* When the Reserve wishes to slow down the economy, it raises discount rates, which discourages loans. If it wishes to stimulate the economy, it lowers discount rates, which encourages loans and puts more money into the economy.

Open-market Operations

Sometimes the Federal Reserve wishes to cause the supply of money to increase or decrease to stabilize the economy. It does so by *buying or selling short-term government securities on the open market.* These **open-market operations,** as they are called, alter the nation's cash flow. When the Reserve purchases government securities, for instance, its payment for them in effect puts new money into circulation. When the Reserve sells government securities, they are bought primarily by insurance companies, banks, mutual funds, and other businesses that have idle funds. This in effect takes money out of circulation.

It may be said that the three tools the Federal Reserve System uses deal directly with the supply of money. The government can add to or subtract from it, and can indirectly influence the demand for it by making money cheaper or more expensive to secure.

THE FEDERAL DEPOSIT INSURANCE CORPORATION

The federal government not only controls the economy; it also attempts to protect the economy and consumer from financial failure. In the depression of the 1930s, many banks became insolvent—that is, they were unable to pay depositors who all demanded their funds at once. In 1933, to prevent a recurrence of this and to restore public confidence in our banking system, the government established the **Federal Deposit Insurance Corporation (FDIC),** which is *a federal organization for banks that insures depositors' accounts.* All banks belonging to the Federal Reserve System are required to belong. Nonmember banks may join if they can pass a careful examination conducted by the FDIC.

The FDIC insures each deposit account for up to $100,000. In the event a member bank fails, the FDIC pays off each account up to that amount and takes the bank's assets. The FDIC finances this procedure by charging each member bank an annual fee that equals one-twelfth of 1 percent of all money on deposit in that bank. In a given year, after costs, losses, and so on are computed, member banks receive a credit that usually reduces this fee by over 50 percent.

MAJOR SOURCES OF CONSUMER CREDIT

Consumer credit is *credit extended to an individual to finance the purchase of consumer goods.* Paying on credit is a way of life in America.

There are two forms of consumer credit available from retailers. **Charge-account credit** *resembles the open-account credit extended by business firms. At the end of a given period, usually 30 days, consumers are billed for purchases.* **Installment credit** dif-

Most retailers accept credit cards because they simplify business transactions for retailers. Credit card companies earn money from such retailers and from the fees and interest charged card holders.

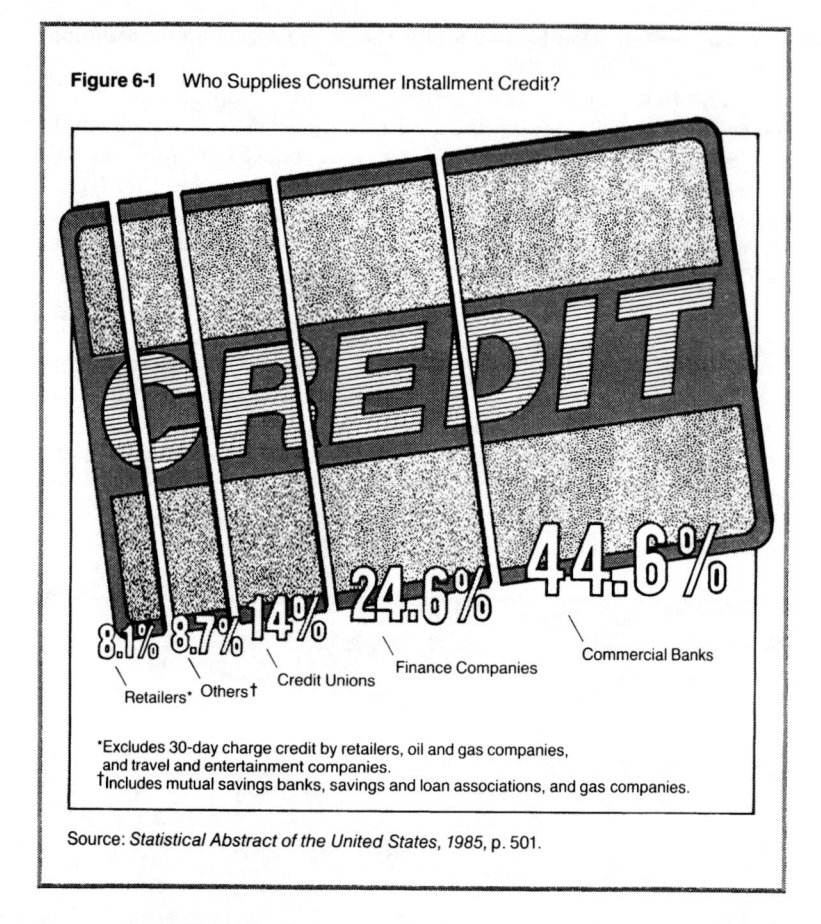

Figure 6-1 Who Supplies Consumer Installment Credit?

- Retailers*: 8.1%
- Others†: 8.7%
- Credit Unions: 14%
- Finance Companies: 24.6%
- Commercial Banks: 44.6%

*Excludes 30-day charge credit by retailers, oil and gas companies, and travel and entertainment companies.
†Includes mutual savings banks, savings and loan associations, and gas companies.

Source: *Statistical Abstract of the United States, 1985*, p. 501.

fers from the charge account in that *the customer's obligation is repaid in fractional amounts at stated intervals after the purchase is made.* This method is known by various names—"easy-payment plan," "budget plan," and "deferred-payment plan." About one-third of the total installment debt in this country is owed to automobile dealers.

As Figure 6–1 shows, most installment credit is granted by commercial banks and finance companies. Many retail and service establishments also extend credit, both charge account and installment, to their customers. In the following section we discuss the main sources of consumer credit.

Credit Card Companies

In recent years an ever-increasing share of *consumer credit has been supplied by outside agencies,* or **credit card companies,** such as American Express, MasterCard, and VISA. Today, there are about three credit cards for every person in the United States. Retailers who honor these cards receive payment from the credit card companies minus a certain percentage that goes to pay the credit card company for its risk, operating costs, and profit. Credit card companies simplify the retailer's credit-granting problem, since the credit card company pays off quickly and thus provides more working capital for the retailer. Furthermore, the retailer bears no risk and does not have to incur the expenses of credit investigations, billing, and other items of credit department overhead. Some say credit cards are unfair to nonusers. The Issue for Debate in this chapter discusses this matter.

Sales Finance Companies

Sales finance companies *specialize in financing the sale of automobiles and other durable goods, such as sewing machines and refrigerators.* They relieve businesses of the financing burden. Besides the larger General Motors Acceptance Corporation (GMAC)—which does most of the financing of General Motors' cars—and the CIT Financial Corporation, there are hundreds of smaller sales finance companies.

Some sales finance organizations make cash loans directly to individuals. Most of them, however, engage chiefly in buying consumer installment contracts from dealers and providing financing for these dealers at the "wholesale" level. For example, say a motorcycle dealer sells a bike for $3,000. The dealer might offer the customer an installment plan that calls for a down payment of 20 percent, or $600, leaving a balance of $2,400. To this balance the dealer adds a finance charge of 18 percent per year, or $432. Then the customer signs a contract to pay a total of $2,832 ($2,400 + $432) in 12 monthly payments of $236 per month. The motorcycle dealer then sells this contract to a financing organization for $2,400—which, with the down payment, equals the full price of the bike. By selling the customer's $2,832 account for $2,400, the dealer gets the full amount of the sale in cash and thereby maintains the working capital needed to operate the business. The sales finance company, in turn, earns a profit of $432 on the deal when the customer completes the total payment of $2,832.

Consumer Finance Companies

Consumer finance companies, often called **small loan companies,** *specialize in making cash loans to consumers for almost any worthwhile purpose.* These loans are repaid in installments. Frequently they are **signature loans**—*loans made with no cosigners.*

ISSUE FOR DEBATE

Should Credit Card Customers Pay More than People Who Pay Cash?

In 1984, there was an outstanding balance of over $85 billion on the more than 600 million credit cards in use in America. Each credit card requires an annual user fee, and card owners pay additional money in interest charges when they don't pay off their entire balance within 30 days.

Aside from these up-front expenses, customers pay an invisible fee for credit: the cost of the merchant discount, or the amount the seller must pay the credit card company for all sales made with the credit card company's card. This merchant discount averages 3 percent, and the merchant must take it out of his profits.

For example, if one customer pays for a $100 purchase in cash, the merchant keeps the entire $100. But if the customer uses a credit card, the merchant keeps only $97, remitting the other $3 to the credit card company. In effect, the merchant keeps more money from the cash customer than from the credit card customer.

Many sellers wish to avoid these expensive credit fees. Some retailers, such as service stations, offer cash discounts to people who pay cash. Another proposal, to charge a card holder extra each time the card is used, would also discourage credit card use and decrease credit fees for the merchant.

With this system, the merchant would charge a cash customer $100 for a product, but would charge a credit card customer $103 for the same product. This would allow the merchant to keep $100 from each sale. The credit user, however, will have paid more. The proposal is controversial; some pro and con arguments follow.

PROS	CONS
An explicit surcharge makes it clear to credit card users that they are paying extra for the chance to use credit cards. While a discount to cash buyers has the same effect, its message is not as explicit. Therefore, a surcharge would probably induce more credit card customers to save the cost of the surcharge by paying cash.	Issuers sold the American consumer on the fact that credit cards were an easy, convenient, and ultimately essential way to make purchases. Now that credit is an intrinsic part of the household economy, consumers are told that they must pay even more for the opportunity to use credit. Simply stated, this is not fair.

Consumer finance companies charge considerably higher interest rates than other financial institutions because their risk is greater and because the size of the loan is small.[3]

---

[3] Higher rates for small loans are a matter of business economics and not bias against small borrowers, as some people think. To understand this, compare a $10,000 loan with ten $1,000 loans. Ten $1,000 loans require ten sets of paperwork, ten credit investigations, ten sessions with the loan officer, and so on. One $10,000 loan requires no more work and overhead than one $1,000 loan.

PROS

The argument over surcharges really boils down to who is going to pay for the merchant discount. Currently, both cash and credit customers pay because the merchant must raise his prices to allow for the credit fees. These hidden charges amount to more than $1.5 billion for the top three credit card companies. Since cash sales account for more than two-thirds of total sales, cash customers pay more than $1 billion for credit services they never receive. In effect, $1 billion is transferred from the pockets of generally less affluent cash customers to the more affluent credit card customers.

Many, possibly most, consumers do not know that cash customers are in effect subsidizing credit card customers. A surcharge would make credit users the only ones who pay for the credit option, and would make everyone aware that credit costs.

Credit card companies are making huge profits from consumers. These companies (a) charge very high interest rates on the customer's unpaid balance (b) charge high annual fees for the cards and (c) make big profits on what they charge retailers in the form of a merchant discount.

CONS

Members of all segments of society, not just the rich, use credit cards. Retail charge volume on bank cards has increased six-fold in the past ten years. In many instances, credit cards provide a means to purchase school clothes, medicine, and other necessities when stretched household budgets cannot provide the cash. They are no longer a rich person's luxury. To many, they are a daily necessity. Tacking on an extra surcharge would only strain budgets further.

Making credit users pay extra would mean that they are paying *three* times over for their credit cards. In addition, the acceptance of credit cards is only one of the many services stores offer their patrons. As with the option of using the parking lot or the layaway plan, all customers actually pay for its *availability*. That the merchant is currently responsible for the "hidden" fee is also reasonable: He pays for the chance to increase sales by offering credit when customers do not have ready cash.

Use of credit cards is an economic stimulant. A surcharge would reduce the use of credit cards and thereby reduce consumer spending. The American economy would suffer.

Questions
1. Suppose a surcharge on credit cards were enacted. Each time you purchased an item for $100, three or four dollars would be added to the amount. Would you be likely to use your card less? Why or why not?
2. Credit card companies, banks, and most retailers are opposed to a surcharge on credit card purchases. Why?

Credit Unions

Credit unions *are nonprofit financial institutions organized as cooperatives and owned, controlled, and managed by their members.* Each member has one vote, regardless of how much money the member has on deposit. Credit union members share a common bond, such as working for the same employer or belonging to the same professional group. There are more than 20,000 credit unions with a membership of 47 million people.

Credit unions are either federally or state-chartered. The National Credit Union Administration, established in 1970, supervises federally-chartered credit unions. State-chartered credit unions are regulated by their respective state supervisory authorities.

Credit unions are member-supported. They pay interest on money deposited by members; the credit unions then loan these deposits to members or invest them. The credit unions return interest paid on loans, along with income from investments, to members in the form of dividends on savings, interest rebates on loans, and membership services. Since credit unions are nonprofit, investors avoid most taxes. Money that members deposit is insured up to $100,000 by agencies of the state or federal government.

Credit unions make loans for a wide variety of purposes, the most important being automobile financing and home improvement. As shown in Figure 6–1 (p. 164), credit unions accounted for 14 percent of all installment credit in 1984.

SUPERCOMPANY FINANCIAL INSTITUTIONS EMERGE

In recent years, **financial supercompanies,** sometimes called **financial supermarkets,** have emerged to *serve the consumer's total needs in banking, insurance, credit cards, security investments, and real estate* (see Figure 6–2). The leading financial supercompanies are Sears, Roebuck & Company, Prudential-Bache Securities, BankAmerica Corp., American Express, Citicorp, and Merrill Lynch & Company (see Figure 6–3). Other major financial supercompanies that are emerging include Travelers Insurance, Aetna Life & Casualty, and Transamerica.

Nonbanks Have Joined the Financial Industry

A **nonbank** is *an enterprise whose primary business is to provide a variety of financial services,* such as marketing installment consumer loans, business loans, brokerage services, insurance, real estate mortgages, and credit card loans.

Of the six major super financial companies shown in Figure 6–3, only BankAmerica Corp. and Citicorp have roots in the banking industry. All others are nonbank establishments. One of the leading nonbanks is General Motors. Through one of its divisions, General Motors Acceptance Company (GMAC), GM has become the largest consumer lender in the United States.

Nonbanks have entered the financial industry because (a) deregulation of banking and consumer lending permitted them to do so; (b) the market for financial services is growing; and (c) increased use of technology in the form of toll-free 800 numbers, automatic teller machines. Sophisticated computer software has made financing a broad and competitive field.

Supercompany Financial Institutions Emerge 169

Figure 6-2 A Brief Comparison of the Scope of the Six Leading Supercompanies. (Figures as of December 31, 1982).

THE SUPERCOMPANIES

BANKING

American Express
None domestic

BankAmerica
Offices: 1,085
Location: California
Accounts: 2.73 million
ATMs:* 475

Finance America (finance subsidiary)
Offices: 290
Location: 42 states

Citicorp
Offices: 310
Location: New York

Accounts: 3 million (est.)
ATMs:* 525

Citicorp Person to Person (finance subsidiary)
Offices: 106
Location: 24 states

Citicorp Savings (formerly Fidelity)
Offices: 60
Location: California
Accounts: 300,000 (est.)
ATMs:* none

Merrill Lynch
None

Prudential Insurance
None

Sears, Roebuck (Allstate S&L)
Offices: 87
Location: California
Accounts: 300,000
ATMs:* 10

*Automated teller machines

CREDIT CARDS

American Express
15 million T&E* Cards

BankAmerica
4.5 million Visa and MasterCards

Citicorp
1.4 million Carte Blanche* and Diner's Club* Cards (est.)
4.9 million Visa and MasterCards

Merrill Lynch
986,000 Visa debit cards

Prudential-Bache Securities
30,000 Visa debit cards

Sears, Roebuck
25 million Sears credit cards
96,000 Visa debit cards

*T&E—travel and entertainment

INSURANCE

American Express (Fireman's Fund)
Independent Brokers: 11,000
Life Insurance in Force: $10 billion
Property/Casualty Premiums: $2.6 billion

BankAmerica
Credit insurance only

Citicorp
Credit insurance only

Merrill Lynch (Family Life Insurance Co.) Company
Agents: 662
Offices: 274
Life Insurance: $8.5 billion

Prudential Insurance Company
Agents: 25,000
Offices: 1,700
Life Insurance: $482 billion
Property/Casualty Premiums: $659 million

Sears, Roebuck (Allstate Insurance Group) Company
Agents: 11,600
Independent Brokers: 2,250
Offices: 3,150

Life Insurance: $41.1 billion
Property/Casualty Premiums: $5.8 billion

REAL ESTATE

American Express (Balcor/American Express)
Syndications: $300 million raised

BankAmerica
Home Mortgages: 109,953

Outstanding: $15.3 billion

Citicorp
Home Mortgages: 300,000 (est.)
Outstanding: $9.3 billion

Merrill Lynch (Merrill Lynch Realty Associates)
Transactions: 35,000 (est.)*
Revenue: $251 million
Agents: 5,000
Offices: 340
States: 15

Syndications: $159 million raised

Prudential Insurance
Home Mortgages: 86,000
Outstanding: $2 billion

(withdrawing from the business)

Sears, Roebuck (Coldwell Banker Real Estate Group)
Transactions: 65,000 (est.)*

Revenue: $533 million
Agents: 9,000
Offices: 350 owned, 200 franchised
States: 30

*Source: Intercommunity Relocation (Kansas City)

SECURITIES

Shearson/American Express
Commissions: $444 million
Account Executives: 4,500
Offices: 334

BankAmerica (Charles Schwab & Co.)
Commissions: $53 million
Account Executives: 280
Offices: 52

Citicorp
Test marketing with discount brokers Quick & Reilly

Merrill Lynch
Commissions: $1.1 billion
Account Executives: 9,000
Offices: 430

Prudential-Bache Securities
Commissions: $250 million (est.)
Account Executives: 3,900
Offices: 190

Sears, Roebuck (Dean Witter Financial Services)
Commissions: $400 million (est.)
Account Executives: 5,000
Offices: 330

Source: "The Supercompanies Emerge," *Dun's Business Month*, April 1983, pp. 46–47.

170 CHAPTER 6/FINANCIAL INSTITUTIONS

Figure 6-3 The Relative Sizes and Strengths of the Six Major Financial Supercompanies. (Figures as of December 31, 1982.)

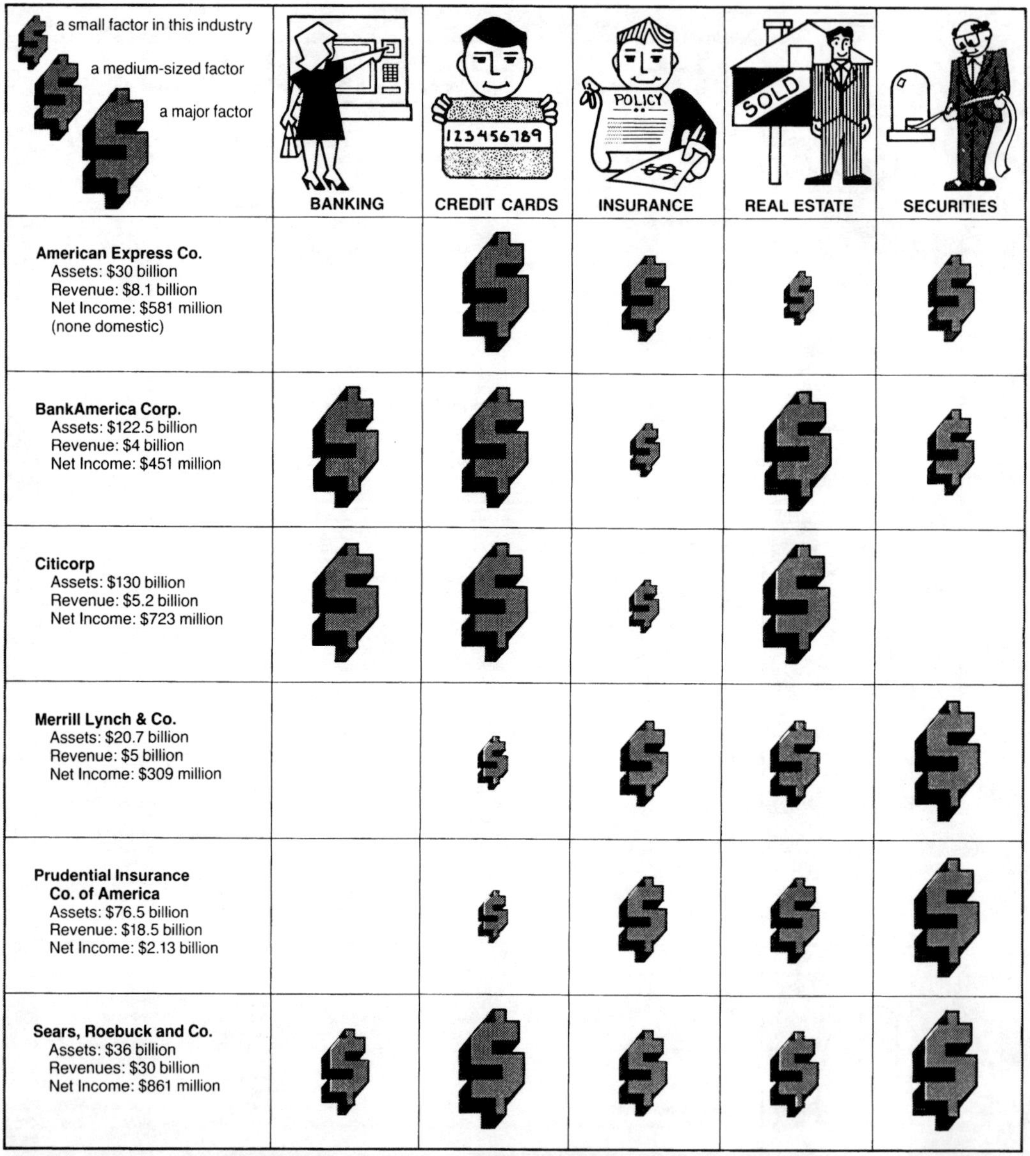

Legend:
- $ — a small factor in this industry
- $$ — a medium-sized factor
- $$$ — a major factor

Company	Banking	Credit Cards	Insurance	Real Estate	Securities
American Express Co. Assets: $30 billion; Revenue: $8.1 billion; Net Income: $581 million (none domestic)		major	major	small	major
BankAmerica Corp. Assets: $122.5 billion; Revenue: $4 billion; Net Income: $451 million	medium	major	small	medium	medium
Citicorp Assets: $130 billion; Revenue: $5.2 billion; Net Income: $723 million	major	major	small	medium	
Merrill Lynch & Co. Assets: $20.7 billion; Revenue: $5 billion; Net Income: $309 million		small	medium	medium	major
Prudential Insurance Co. of America Assets: $76.5 billion; Revenue: $18.5 billion; Net Income: $2.13 billion		small	major	major	major
Sears, Roebuck and Co. Assets: $36 billion; Revenues: $30 billion; Net Income: $861 million	medium	major	major	major	major

Source: "The Supercompanies Emerge," *Dun's Business Month*, April 1983, p. 45.

Supercompany Financial Institutions Emerge

Large retailers have been either entering the financial services industry or expanding their current holdings. Sears, Roebuck & Company, for example, broadened its financial services in the early 1980s. In 1981 Sears acquired Dean Witter Reynolds, a stock brokerage company, while in 1983 it formed the Sears World Trade, Inc., to market worldwide financial products offered by other Sears Financial subsidiaries. Also in 1983, Sears opened its first financial centers, called the Sears Financial Centers, outside of the company's retail stores. These centers provide services offered by other Sears subsidiaries.

Kroger Company, a large supermarket chain, has also entered the supercompany field. In 1982 Kroger opened financial centers that offer a wide range of insurance products, mutual funds, IRAs, and other services. Kroger has also added commercial banking to its holdings.

Supercompany financial centers, such as Sears, provide customers with services including insurance, real estate, investment, and credit. Such centers are forcing banks and credit unions to expand their services.

How Banks Are Responding to Supercompany Competition

Deregulation of the financial industry and new competition from nonbanks have begun to threaten commercial banks. To survive, banks must take new measures to ensure their influence in the financial services industry. In effect, they are becoming like supercompanies themselves.

- Efforts are being made to legalize interstate banking. Attaining this goal would enable banks to branch out into previously untapped markets. The idea, however, is controversial, and is discussed in the Issue for Debate in Chapter 5.
- Many commercial banks, savings and loan associations, and credit unions are offering discount brokerage operations as a new service. A discount broker buys and sells securities on the organized exchanges for a lower fee than regular brokerage firms charge because the discount broker provides fewer services. This puts financial institutions in direct competition with firms such as Merrill Lynch and Dean Witter Reynolds.
- Commercial banks are also attempting to sell property, casualty, and life insurance to compete with insurance companies.

Supercompany financial institutions are the trend of the future. As competition within the financial services industry grows, these financial supermarkets are likely to expand their operations and services.

CREDIT MANAGEMENT

Since nearly all businesses both buy and sell on credit, and since consumer use of credit is growing steadily and the cost of money has risen, credit management has become an increasingly important function. Larger companies generally establish a separate credit department headed by a credit manager. In the small business, credit decisions are made by the manager or the manager's assistant.

Credit management has two basic, sometimes conflicting, objectives: *to minimize bad debt losses and to maximize sales volume.* To minimize losses, credit applicants must be carefully screened to avoid business firms or individuals who may not meet their obligations. To achieve maximum sales, however, a credit company must be reasonably lenient in extending credit; if credit policies are too rigid, customers will take their business elsewhere. Realizing both objectives—that is, both minimizing bad debts and maximizing sales—is not easy. Credit managers, who want strict control, and sales managers, who want lax control, frequently lock horns! To make wise credit decisions, therefore, it is necessary to investigate credit applicants and establish credit limits.

How Credit Applicants Are Investigated

The credit investigation determines whether the applicant can pay for goods bought on credit. Investigations differ, depending on whether the applicant is a business or an individual.

BUSINESS CREDIT APPLICANTS

When a business applies for credit, it is normally evaluated in view of what are popularly known as the "four Cs" of credit:

- *Character*—The applicant's reputation for honesty, integrity, and responsibility
- *Capacity*—The applicant's business ability as measured by efficiency, methods, and history
- *Capital*—The applicant's ability to pay (collateral, cash reserves, and so on)
- *Conditions*—The probable economic trends and competitive position of the credit applicant

To evaluate the creditworthiness of a business, creditors may use many sources.

Dun & Bradstreet. One such source is Dun & Bradstreet. This service specializes in gathering credit information about businesses throughout the United States and in many foreign countries. D & B's National Business Information Center houses current, comprehensive data on over 4 million companies. Reports for determining creditworthiness would include type of business; history and how long it has been operating; credit history; names of principals and an evaluation of their past performance; banking connections; assets and liabilities; net worth; sales volume; and any financial problems. D & B gives each business two credit ratings: one indicating financial strength and one indicating overall creditworthiness.

The computer and telephone have greatly sped up and improved credit checking procedures. Subscribing companies simply dial the Center and explain their information needs to one of the over 120 D & B men and women. These people then question the computer, which projects answers and information onto deskside screens. Information given by phone is later confirmed in mailed printouts.

Creditors and other sources. The most specific information concerning a credit applicant's paying habits can be obtained from businesses that have made credit sales to the applicant. Larger organizations often employ credit investigators, whose main job is to inquire about an applicant's paying habits. Groups of businesses selling to the same accounts sometimes form credit exchange bureaus for the purpose of sharing credit information. Other sources of credit information are financial statements, personal interviews, banks, and the sales representatives who call on applicants.

CONSUMER CREDIT APPLICANTS

Managers of consumer credit rely heavily on two main sources of information about the creditworthiness of consumers: Equifax and retail credit bureaus. Equifax, formerly the Retail Credit Company, can supply credit-related information on virtually anyone. The type of information supplied depends on the creditor's needs. An in-depth report, for example, may cover the credit applicant's entire credit history since high school. Retailers, companies reviewing job applicants, and life insurance companies making sure insurance applicants are not hiding something that might make them poor risks all depend heavily on Equifax reports.

Credit bureaus, another source of credit information, are *organizations of various businesses that extend considerable consumer credit.* Each member is required to furnish information on each of its credit customers to the bureau. In this way credit files are established for all consumers who buy on credit. The various bureaus in the United States and Canada cooperate closely, and so people's credit histories tend to follow them wherever they go. Many people assume that credit bureaus give credit ratings. They do not. They simply supply a credit history, which the lender evaluates to determine a credit rating.

The Fair Credit Reporting Act. To protect against falsified credit records, Congress passed the **Fair Credit Reporting Act** in 1970, which *protects consumers from inaccurate or obsolete information in reports used to determine eligibility for credit or employment.* The law guarantees the consumer's right to know what personal data is being reported by a credit bureau, and it gives the applicant the right to correct false information. Applicants must be told if an unfavorable credit report is the reason for rejection of a loan, job, or insurance application.

The act also states that credit information may be given only to those who have a bona fide business interest in the individual's financial background. Retail stores are acceptable; lawyers seeking evidence for a divorce case are not. The FBI and Internal Revenue Service must secure a court order to get access. The congressman who sponsored the bill explained, "At some point, the individual's right to privacy must take precedence over the creditor's right to obtain information."

In 1975, further legislation in the form of the **Equal Credit Opportunity Act** *made it illegal to discriminate against anyone because of sex or marital status in the granting of credit.*

<u>The privacy issue.</u>   Consumer groups are pushing for further legislation to protect the consumer's right to privacy. Many people are upset that financial institutions can so easily obtain their financial histories. A University of Illinois survey revealed, for instance, that all banks supply information to government agencies and credit grantors, such as department stores, and that one bank in four supplies data to landlords. Bank managers tend to say that although they are concerned that new legislation would add to costs, they agree that some safeguards may be needed and that they can live with the type of legislation proposed.

Meanwhile, some businesses are making attempts at self-regulation. IBM, for example, has developed what it calls the Four Principles of Privacy.[4]

- Individuals should have access to information about themselves in record-keeping systems. There should be some procedure for individuals to find out how this information is being used.
- There should be some way for an individual to correct or amend an inaccurate record.
- An individual should be able to prevent information from being used for other than authorized purposes without his or her consent, unless required by law.
- The custodian of data files containing sensitive information should take reasonable precautions to be sure that the data are reliable and not misused.

Establishing Credit Limits

Credit investigations reveal, in a general way, how much credit can safely be granted to the applicant once he or she has been deemed a safe risk. *The fixed maximum amount of credit permitted to be outstanding at any given time* is called the **credit limit.** While numerous formulas have been designed to fix such limits on a semiscientific basis, the judgment of the credit manager remains the most important factor in deciding the limit. This limit is not a permanently fixed amount, however, and usually changes as the credit applicant's circumstances change.

---

[4]Retail Credit Company (now Equifax), *Inspection News* (Summer 1975), 13.

SUMMARY

- Major financial institutions in the United States are commercial banks, investment banks, mutual savings banks, savings and loan associations, and mutual funds.
- Commercial banks provide the widest variety of services. They accept demand deposits, make commercial and consumer loans, offer checking accounts, issue certified checks, and provide savings accounts, payroll services, and trust services.
- Investment banks specialize in helping corporations acquire long-term capital.
- Mutual savings banks and savings and loan associations specialize in making home loans.
- Major supplies of consumer credit are commercial banks, credit card companies, sales and consumer finance companies, credit unions, and retailers.
- In recent years, large and diverse financial institutions have emerged. These companies provide comprehensive financial services including banking, insurance, credit cards, security investments, and real estate.
- The Federal Reserve System regulates the supply of money and credit through (1) regulation of bank reserves, (2) regulation of the discount rate, and (3) open-market operations.
- Credit management is an important function in business. It involves appraising applicants for credit in terms of character, capacity, capital, and conditions. Dun & Bradstreet and Equifax are the leading credit-investigating companies.

KEY TERMS YOU SHOULD KNOW

certified check	electronic funds transfer	open-market operations
charge-account credit	Equal Credit Opportunity Act	prime rate
checking account	Fair Credit Reporting Act	purchase group
commercial bank	Federal Deposit Insurance Corporation	reserves
commercial loan		sales finance company
consumer finance company	Federal Reserve System	savings account
consumer loan	financial supercompanies	savings and loan association
credit bureau	financial supermarkets	signature loan
credit card company	installment credit	small loan company
credit limit	investment bank	spread
credit management	mutual savings bank	state bank
credit union	national bank	time deposit
demand deposit	nonbank	trust department
discount rate	NOW account	underwriting syndicate

QUESTIONS FOR REVIEW

1. In what three ways do financial institutions serve businesses and individuals?
2. What facts suggest that the financial services industry is both competitive and dynamic?
3. What is a commercial bank? What two basic functions do commercial banks perform? What services do commercial banks provide?
4. Explain how each of the following institutions serves the economy: investment bank, mutual savings bank, and savings and loan association.
5. What is the Federal Reserve System? Who owns it? Who controls it? What services does it provide?
6. How does charge-account credit differ from installment credit?
7. How does each of the following financial institutions function: credit card company, sales finance company, consumer finance company, and credit union.
8. What are examples of supercompany financial institutions?
9. What is a nonbank?
10. What is credit management? How are business credit applicants evaluated? Consumer credit applicants?

QUESTIONS FOR DISCUSSION

1. The financial services industry has been deregulated to the point that nonbank institutions can now provide most of the services that banks and other financial companies provide. In the long run, what are the advantages of this trend? What possible disadvantages may result?
2. The Board of Governors of the Federal Reserve System is appointed by the president. The governors are expected to be objective in their judgments and to regulate the supply of money and the discount rate. Ask three people whose opinions you respect whether they feel decisions made by the Federal Reserve Board are always nonpolitical.
3. In recent years many commercial banks have installed automatic teller machines that let customers obtain cash and make deposits automatically, for up to 24 hours a day. Some observers believe that electronic devices will become so sophisticated in the future that both checks and cash will be virtually unnecessary. What would be the pros and cons of a cashless/checkless economy to (1) business, and (2) consumers?
4. Evaluate the following case according to the "four Cs" of credit (see p. 173). Under each "C," rate the prospective borrower as a good, fair, or poor credit risk. After you have made the ratings, give your decision as to whether or not you would grant the credit requested.

The Bar X Lumber Company, a lumber yard and mill supply house established five years ago with a net worth of approximately $400,000, has received a request for credit for a period of 90 days from J. C. John & Company, a carpenter contractor for lumber and mill supplies. The credit would amount to $70,000. J. C. John & Company has been a customer of the yard for three years, has had credit for amounts up to $20,000, and has always paid its bills promptly. There is no credit record previous to the three-year period because, until then, Mr. John and his employees always worked for someone else rather than contracting for themselves. They have just received a contract, from a large company with a good credit standing, that is approximately five times larger than any handled before. Mr. John lives in his own home, which is worth $90,000 and which carries a mortgage of $25,000. He has approximately $12,000 in the bank and owns a late model car, a company truck, and tools that have a total market value of $9,000. There are no other assets. Mr. John is well thought of by his neighbors.

CASE STUDY

Is an Economic Doomsday Inevitable?

The Conglomerate is a combination of over 50 subsidiaries with combined annual sales of $12 billion. One day the president of The Conglomerate, Jay Levy, calls in his two senior economists, Richard Fiedler and Susé Hendricks, to discuss the economic future.

Jay: I just finished reading another one of those books predicting an enormous economic collapse in the next two to five years. The economist who wrote the book said it will be even worse than the economic crash of the 1930s. I'd like your opinion because our company is heavily in debt and I don't want us to be caught off guard.

Richard: Well, the author and others who share his view may be right. If enough financial institutions get into deep financial trouble, a chain reaction that could be disastrous would result.

J: But the deposits are insured. Even if a bank fails, the depositors get their money.

R: Up to a point. There is only a fraction of one penny's insurance for each dollar on deposit in federally insured banks. If bank failures become common, the government would have only two alternatives: not pay all the claims or literally print more money. And the latter choice would fuel inflation, which in turn would compound the crisis.

Susé: I'm not pessimistic about the future. Authors of panic books know that fear is an important emotion and they get rich playing up to it. Look at the nation's assets: new technology, better educated people, large-scale demand, some evidence that the work ethic is returning, and less evidence that people depend on the government to run their lives.

J: But less government control may be only temporary. People vote their pocketbooks, not their economic sense. If we go into a deep recession, people will demand more aid from the government and that means more government debt. Even now, each newborn infant inherits over $5,000 of federal debt.

S: It's true that the national debt is about $5,000 per capita. But it's also true that every newborn also inherits a lot of assets—public lands, highways, dams, and so on. But I can't agree with your observation that people vote their economic self-interest.

R: Historically, economic collapses have occurred periodically since the beginning of the Industrial Revolution. Economic upheavals are inherent in capitalistic systems. I feel that we should consider survival in everything we do.

J: I do too. Preventive medicine is always a good idea. Here's what I want you two to do. As you know, we've invested in many industries. Prepare a report in which you rate our divisions in terms of their resistance to a deep recession. Have it ready for our September board meeting.

Questions

1. Do you think another 1930s-style recession is possible? Why or why not?
2. Rate these industries in terms of resistance to a deep recession: automobile, paper products, food processing, public utilities, and entertainment. Explain your logic.
3. Do you feel that our capitalistic system would survive another great depression? Why or why not?

EVOLUTION OF A BUSINESS

Owning Real Estate—Pros and Cons

Sara considered what the bank loan officer had told her—that most service businesses do not accumulate assets that increase in value. She realized that without assets, getting loans would always be a problem.

Sara had a friend who was a builder. She decided to talk to him about the possibilities of constructing a four-unit office building on an attractively located lot she knew could be acquired. Her friend thought her idea was sound, provided they could get tenants with good credit ratings to sign long-term leases. He assured her that he could arrange to borrow funds and build them an office building valued at $400,000 with just $40,000 of their own capital. The rent income from the three other office suites in the building would pay expenses, taxes, and also mortgage payments.

Ray: (When Sara told him about the scheme) That's a great idea, Sara, but raising an extra $40,000 would stretch us to our absolute limit.

Sara: Well, it wouldn't take $40,000 extra. We'd be saving about $22,000 the first year on rent. So we're committing only an additional $18,000. Besides, it isn't such a big gamble because a building is a physical asset. The banks wouldn't go into it if it weren't sound. Our equity in the building would grow each month, so our credit standing would increase as time went by. Also, our Dun & Bradstreet report would look better if it said we owned our own building.

Ray: Don't you think you're looking a little too far into the future? Many businesses prefer not to own their own real estate because property can become a burden if the neighborhood deteriorates. It would also give us less flexibility in changing our location.

Sara: (Ignoring the remarks) Now all we have to do is decide what to call the building. How does "The Excel Travel Building" sound?

Ray: "Excel Travel"?

Sara: Don't you think that would be a good name for our company? I also thought of calling it "Sara's Travel Bureau," but I had a feeling you wouldn't care for that.

Questions

1. What do you think of this new turn of events?
2. What risks do you think would be involved in the real estate venture?
3. Give some other reasons—besides potential property deterioration and limited flexibility—why a business may prefer not to own real estate.

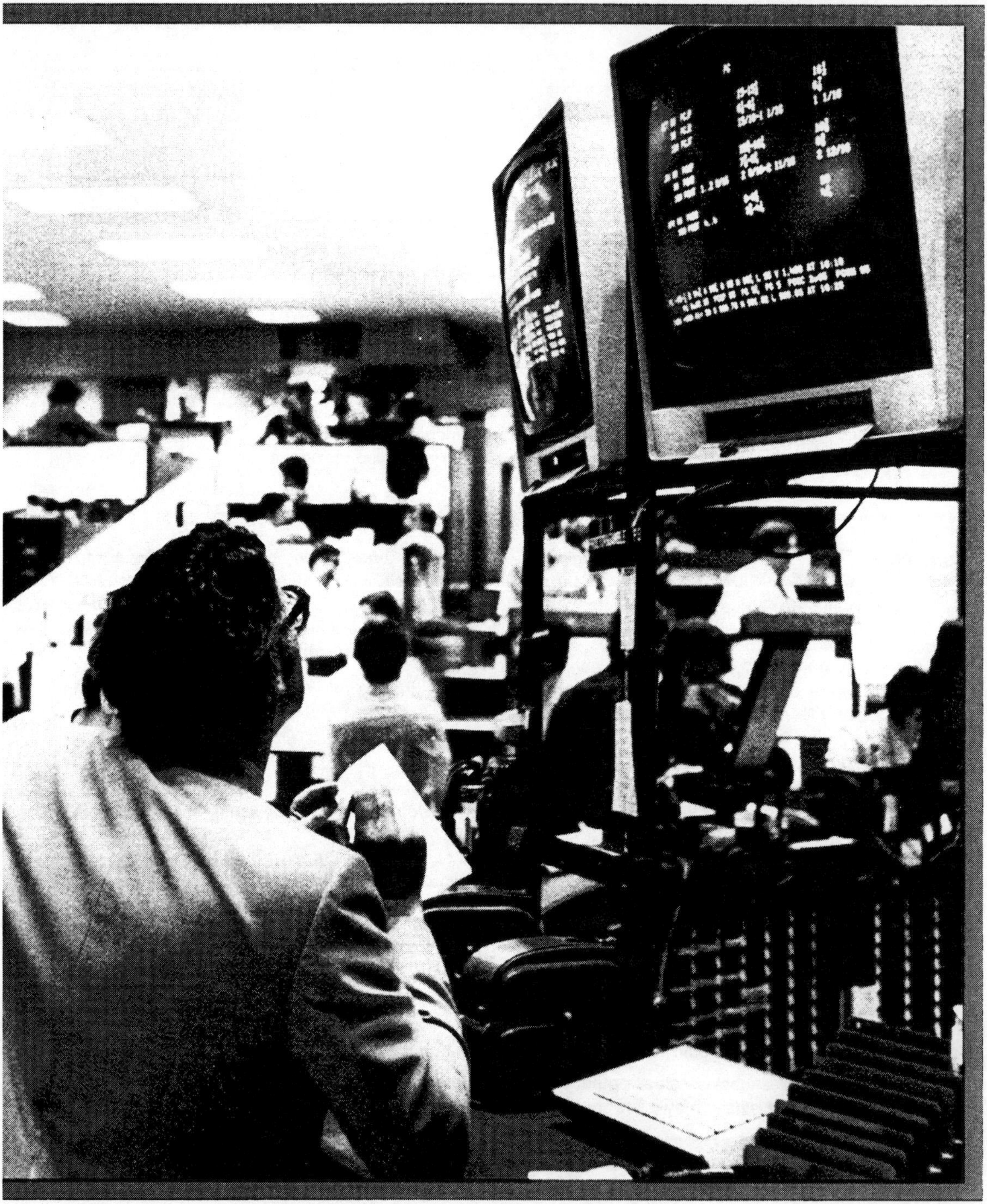

7

SECURITY MARKETS AND BUSINESS NEWS
Using Sense to Make Dollars

> **READ THIS CHAPTER SO YOU CAN:**
>
> Explain why business news is important.
>
> Describe how the New York Stock Exchange, the American Stock Exchange, and the over-the-counter markets function.
>
> Explain why the over-the-counter market is growing in popularity.
>
> Discuss how mutual funds work and serve investors.
>
> Interpret security quotations as they appear in the *Wall Street Journal* and other media.
>
> Understand the basic legislation that regulates securities trading.
>
> Discuss the benefits of reading and understanding business news about consumption, government, politics, marketing, and international business.

Almost every day, most of us come in contact with some form of business news: We read about it in the *Wall Street Journal* and in the financial sections of other daily newspapers, we hear of it on radio and television newscasts, and we talk about it with our friends. In one form or another, business news reaches us—and for good reasons: Our economic well-being—and many of our important personal decisions—depend on what happens in business.

Like other types of news, business news can be good or bad. We react positively to news of tax cuts, high employment, low inflation, and reduced interest rates. Such news makes us feel "bullish" and confident, and can make us bold in career choices and investment decisions. But we react negatively to news of additional taxes, increased unemployment, high inflation, and high interest rates. Such news makes us "bearish" about the economic future, and it can make us feel insecure about our jobs, income, and investments.

In the same way that we as individuals hear and react to business news, so do millions of private investors, managers of pension plans, bankers and other lenders, and security analysts. The information that such people receive is translated almost immediately into decisions about the worth of corporations and their securities—and those decisions become news in themselves, determining the value of goods and services on the market. The most immediate expression of these decisions, and, consequently, one of the most significant business news devices, is the security exchange.

WHAT ARE SECURITY EXCHANGES?

Security exchanges (often called **stock exchanges**) are *organized markets that provide a meeting place for buyers and sellers of stocks and bonds.* Security exchanges perform two useful functions. First, they make available an immediate market for the purchase and sale of securities. This accessibility gives people confidence in making investments, because they realize they can sell their securities for cash in a very short period of time. Second, security exchanges provide a marketplace where investors' opinions determine stock prices. Someone is always ready to buy if the price is low enough, and someone is always ready to sell if the price is sufficiently high. This results in prices being set on a free-market, or supply-and-demand, basis.

The three most important security markets, in terms of the volume of shares traded, are the New York Stock Exchange (NYSE), the over-the-counter market (OTC), and the American Stock Exchange (AMEX). The NYSE and the AMEX are basically similar in that they both have physical locations in New York City; generally, the

AMEX represents lesser known companies, and its average transaction is smaller. The OTC market, unlike the two New York based exchanges, has no central, physical place of business—its operations are conducted through telephones linked with computers.

Trading Procedures on the NYSE and AMEX

MEMBERSHIP

To the investor, there is little difference in trading procedures between the NYSE and the AMEX. The NYSE, often called the "big board," is the older exchange, and in 1984 had 1,439 members. The AMEX had 781 members in the same year. *Most members are partners or officers in a brokerage firm, which, by virtue of its connection with the exchange, is known as a* **member firm.** Each firm has a **floor member** (or **floor broker**), *who trades securities for the firm.*

To become an exchange member, a member of a brokerage firm must purchase a membership, called a "seat," from an existing exchange member or from the estate of a deceased member. Prices paid for seats on an exchange vary greatly, depending mainly on the vol-

Investors can follow the program of their common & preferred stock by reading the market quotations from the New York Stock Exchange, the American Stock Exchange, the over-the-counter market, and the smaller exchanges in a variety of daily newspapers. Other financial news investors want to check on includes options trading, bond prices, mutual fund offerings, futures, credit markets, and foreign exchange rates.

ume of business transacted. In 1984, the price for a NYSE seat ranged from $237,000 to $403,000.

How Securities Are Listed

Securities that have been approved for trading on an organized securities exchange are called listed securities. All three securities markets set requirements for listing. Those of the NYSE are the most difficult to meet, followed by those of the AMEX; the requirements of the OTC are the most lenient. In determining eligibility for listing, the NYSE considers (a) the earning power of the company, (b) the company's net worth, (c) the market value of the shares, and (d) public interest in the company as demonstrated by the number of shareholders. In 1984, 1,598 stock issues were listed on the NYSE and 1,058 were listed on the AMEX.

Why a Business Wants Its Shares Listed

Most businesses want their shares to qualify for listing and trading in one of the three markets, for the following reasons:

- Listing improves corporate visibility, making it easier to acquire additional capital.
- The price of a security is set by the interplay of supply and demand. Thus, through listing, a company knows what its real value is at any given time.
- Listed companies are perceived as less risky for investment than unlisted companies.
- Listing broadens stock ownership and gives the company a broader ownership base, which (a) supports the sale of company products and services, and (b) helps prevent undesirable takeovers of the corporation.

How a Trade Takes Place

Buyers and sellers of securities place their orders through **brokers,** *who trade on a securities exchange for their clients.* The broker's office is connected with the trading floor of the exchange by a direct telephone and computer terminal.

For example, suppose Ethel Churchill, an investor who lives in Albany, decides to purchase 100 shares of Coca-Cola stock. She telephones a local brokerage house and places her order. The account executive may ask, "Do you want to buy this at the market?" (meaning *at the current market price*). If the customer says yes, the order, called a **market order,** is transmitted directly to the floor of the exchange. Since it is a market order, *the brokerage firm's floor member buys immediately at the prevailing market price.* Often the entire transaction is completed in minutes (see Figure 7–1).

What Are Security Exchanges? **185**

1. An account executive receives a round-lot market order from an investor by telephone.

2. The order goes to the wire room of the local office, where it is sent by teletype to the New York headquarters . . .

3. . . . and simultaneously to the floor of the New York Stock Exchange, . . .

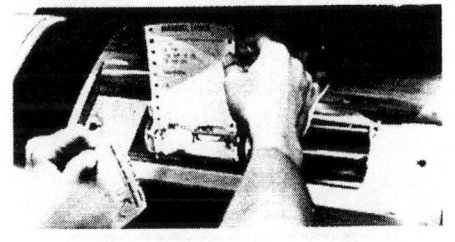

4. . . . where it is given to the firm's floor broker, . . .

5. . . . who executes it, bargaining for the best possible price, at the appropriate trading post.

6. Confirmation is teletyped to the local office, . . .

7. . . . where it is received . . .

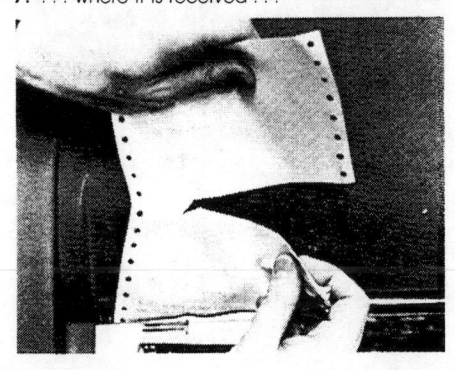

8. . . . and relayed to the account executive so that he can notify the customer of the price he paid—or received—for the stock. It takes only two or three minutes to buy or sell a popular stock.

Source: Merrill Lynch, Pierce, Fenner & Smith, Inc.

If the customer wants to buy the 100 shares of Coca-Cola not at the current price of, say, 35 (that is, $35), but at, say, 32, he or she may place a **limited order,** which is *an order to a broker to purchase securities at a specified price on that day only, unless a longer time period is specified.* The shares will not be purchased unless the price goes down to 32. *An order made at a specific price but with no specified time limit* is called an **open order** and is held until the purchase is made or the order canceled.

It is not necessary for the customer to visit the brokerage house in person to buy or sell; orders can be given at any of the exchanges by telegraph, telephone, or mail.

WHAT DOES IT COST TO TRADE SECURITIES?

For many years, all brokerage houses charged the same commissions. In 1975, however, commissions became negotiable—that is, different brokers may now charge different prices for their services. A distinction can be made between two kinds of brokers: full-service and discount. **Full-service brokers** *research investments for clients, advise them when to sell or buy, and give advice at no charge.* **Discount brokers** *execute buy or sell decisions made by a client.* Because they provide no other services, their commissions are signifi-

So You Want to Buy Some Stocks
● A GLOSSARY OF TERMS A BEGINNER NEEDS TO KNOW

Odd lot: THE PEOPLE YOU'LL BE DEALING WITH.

Point: THE WAY YOU'LL PICK YOUR FIRST STOCKS.

Convertible: WHAT YOU WANT WHEN YOUR STOCKS GO UP.

Broker: WHAT YOU'LL SOON BE BECAUSE YOU BOUGHT THE WRONG STOCKS.

Big Gains: WHAT YOUR STOCKS REGISTER AFTER YOU SELL THEM.

Net Value: YOU'LL UNDERSTAND AFTER YOU READ ABOUT THE Big Gains.

Institutional Investor: WHAT YOU ARE NOW.

Big Board: YOU'VE INSTALLED IT, BUT THEY WON'T LET YOU USE IT. Turnover Rate: ABOUT 25,000 TIMES PER NIGHT.

TOLES UNIVERSAL PRESS SYNDICATE ©1982 THE BUFFALO NEWS

cantly lower than those of full-service brokers—hence the name "discount brokers."

Generally, the larger the transaction, the lower the commission rate (see Table 7–1). Thus investors buying a few shares pay considerably more per share for securities than big volume buyers.

TABLE 7-1   Typical Costs for a Stock Sold at $10 per Share by a Full-Service Broker

TRANSACTION SIZE (NO. OF SHARES)	TOTAL VALUE OF STOCK PURCHASED	TOTAL FEE	AVERAGE BROKERAGE FEE AS A PERCENTAGE OF PURCHASE PRICE
100	$ 1,000	$ 20.80	2.08
500	5,000	86.50	1.73
5,000	50,000	545.00	1.09
50,000	500,000	2,250.00	0.45

WHAT IS BUYING ON MARGIN?

Most brokerage houses will arrange to buy securities **on margin.** Buying on margin means that *the customer pays for a certain portion of the purchase and secures credit through the broker for the balance.* Margin requirements are subject to regulation, and they change from time to time because of federal credit policies. If, for example, the current margin requirement set by the Federal Reserve Board is 50 percent, $50 in credit may be secured through the broker for each $100 worth of stock purchased.

Under a margin arrangement, the securities are held by the brokerage firm until full payment is made. In the meantime, if the price of a stock drops to a certain point, the broker will ask the client to supply additional margin (funds). If the buyer does not come up with this additional margin, the brokerage house will sell the security. Low margin requirements encourage speculation, while high margin requirements discourage it.

Trading in the Over-the-Counter Market

In the securities markets, OTC stands for "over-the-counter." But stocks traded OTC are not literally traded over a counter. Nor are they traded on the floor of an exchange, as on the New York Stock Exchange and the American Stock Exchange. There is no physical location for the OTC market. Instead, the **OTC market** *is an intricate web of telephones and computers that connect stockbrokers regionally, nationally, and internationally.*

In all, the OTC market consists of an estimated 30,000 issues ranging from very small companies to giants, such as MCI Telecommunications Corporation.

Of the 30,000 OTC stocks, about 10,000 companies are local, because they are so small they are of interest only to investors in the immediate area. Trading in these issues is infrequent and receives little if any public attention. Another 16,000 companies, with larger revenues and promises of growth, are listed on what brokers call "pink sheets." These offers to sell or buy are mailed to interested brokers across the United States by an organization called the National Quotation Bureau.

The remaining 4,000 issues are the most prominent OTC stocks and are traded by the National Association of Securities Dealers (NASD) through its National Association of Securities Dealers Automated Quotation system (NASDAQ).

WHAT IS THE NASD?

The NASD is an organization of brokers and dealers who trade over-the-counter securities. NASD's objectives are to "adopt, administer and enforce rules of fair practice and rules to prevent fraudulent and manipulative acts and practices, and in general to promote just and equitable principles of trade for the protection of investors." The Association has the power to expel members who have been found guilty of unethical practices.

The Association maintains an automated information network that provides brokers and dealers with price quotations on 4,000 principal securities traded over the counter. This network, called NASDAQ (an acronym for National Association of Securities Dealers Automated Quotations), provides current information on the prices that sellers are offering and the prices that buyers are willing to pay.

In 1984, the NASDAQ market further consolidated its position as the second-largest and fastest-growing stock market in the U.S. NASDAQ share volume in 1984 was 61 percent of NYSE volume and more than six times AMEX volume. The numbers of NASDAQ issuers and issues were greater than those of the NYSE and the AMEX combined. Over the seven-year period 1977–84, NASDAQ volume more than quadrupled, while NYSE volume grew 2.7 times and AMEX volume grew 1.6 times.

REASONS FOR THE GROWTH OF THE NASDAQ

Four reasons account for the rapid growth of the OTC market operated by the NASD, compared to the small growth, or decline, in the volume of issues traded on the NYSE and the AMEX.

First, the NYSE and the AMEX carry less prestige than before. *Business Week* notes,

Time was when a growing company confirmed its coming of age by getting its stock listed on the New York Stock Exchange. Today, however, increasing numbers of companies whose shares trade in the over-the-counter market see little mystique and no compelling advantage to a Big Board listing.[1]

More than 600 companies meet the size and other requirements for listing on the NYSE but see no advantage in doing so. Among them are companies such as MCI Telecommunications Corporation (one of the most actively traded issues in the nation), Apple (computers), and Intel (computer chips).

Second, listing requirements in terms of company size, profitability, and public interest in the company, are lower for NASDAQ than for either the AMEX or the NYSE. Smaller and newer companies, therefore, can gain national visibility sooner by listing with NASDAQ.

Third, listing is less expensive on the NASDAQ than on the

Floor brokers at the New York Stock Exchange try to get the highest price for clients selling stock, the lowest price for those buying stock.

[1] "Why the Big Board is Fishing for Small Fry," *Business Week*, September 26, 1983, 61.

AMEX or the NYSE. The initial cost for a company to be listed on the NYSE is $30,000, on the AMEX $15,000, and on the NASDAQ $5,000. Additionally, listing on the NASDAQ requires less legal work.

Fourth, the NASDAQ has become increasingly efficient. As recently as 15 years ago, trading stocks over-the-counter was awkward and expensive. One observer notes, "It was a backwater of the securities business. Linked by phone calls and buried in price quotation sheets, it was known for its high mark-ups on stocks."[2] Today the NASDAQ is noted for its efficiency. Instantaneous information on more than 4,000 issues traded is accessible to 80,000 computer terminals in the United States and foreign nations. Each dealer in the NASDAQ securities is required to complete a trade within 90 seconds. The terminals display the latest trading information, and constantly update the bid and asked prices for the securities traded. A terminal and a telephone are all that is required to buy or sell on the NASDAQ system.

IS THERE AN INTEGRATED, CENTRALIZED SECURITIES MARKET IN THE FUTURE?

In 1975, Congress directed the Securities and Exchange Commission (SEC) and the securities industry to work together to develop a system to integrate the NYSE, the AMEX, and the OTC markets into a centralized securities market. Obviously the need for such a system exists based on investor interest and desire for greater convenience.

Progress on developing such a system has been slow. Some observers contend that the NYSE and the AMEX do not want a centralized securities market because it may adversely affect their interests. It seems likely, however, that a truly integrated securities market will eventually emerge. Advances in electronic technology will help to encourage progress.

INVESTING IN THE MUTUAL FUNDS MARKET

A **mutual fund** is a common term for *an investment company that sells shares to individuals, pension and profit-sharing plans, and other investors, and that uses this capital to buy shares in the securities of other companies.* Mutual funds do not facilitate the exchange of securities, like the NYSE, AMEX and OTC. They do, however, act as an investment medium.

To the investor, a mutual fund has several advantages.

1. *Professional Management* Securities are selected and traded at the discretion of fund managers who are experienced in making investments.

---

[2]Laurie Cohen, "OTC: Backwater To Mainstream," *Chicago Tribune*, October 16, 1983.

APPLICATION TO PERSONAL AFFAIRS

Guidelines for the Beginning Investor

Many college students already own stock or will become investors in the future. Here are ten guidelines that may help in making security investments:

- *Know your investment objective*—Have a clear idea of what level of risk you can tolerate and whether you are looking primarily for dividends (that is, high yield) or for long-term growth. To compute the **yield** of a security, *divide the dividend by the price.* (A stock selling for $50 that pays a dividend of $5 is yielding 10 percent.) Some securities pay only a small dividend or no dividend at all but show promise of substantial growth in the years ahead. Still other securities are pure speculation.

- *Investigate before investing*—Before you buy or sell a stock, study the company's financial reports and obtain the advice of experts. Do not buy or sell on the basis of tips that have not been checked.

- *Invest only in stocks listed on organized exchanges*—These must comply with various government and exchange regulations designed to protect the investor.

- *If you insist on putting your money into speculative situations, discipline yourself to hold the amount to no more than 20 percent of your total investments*—Then be prepared to lose it. If you can't afford to lose, don't speculate!

- *Do not become enchanted with a stock*—If you do, your decisions about it will be based on emotion instead of logic, and you will soon be separated from some of your money.

- *Review your portfolio regularly*—Sell those stocks that appear weakest, *even at a loss,* and replace them with stocks that show more promise.

- *Invest in different companies in different industries*—Don't put all your money into a single firm or even a single industry.

- *Do not buy just because you happen to have some extra cash*—Wait until the right opportunity presents itself or until the market is depressed.

- *Consider your aggregate gains or losses and what they will be in a year's time*—Do not worry about daily ups and downs of individual stocks or become disenchanted with a broker if the stock he or she recommends drops the day after you buy it. Jumping in and out of the market may make a broker rich on your commissions, but it will not help you! In the long run, if the decision is sound, the investment will pay off.

- *Regularly read respected financial publications*—The *Wall Street Journal, Barron's,* and *Forbes* are good ones. Also, consult an advisory service such as Value Line or Moody's.

2. *Diversification* A mutual fund typically invests in 100 or more securities, thereby reducing risk.
3. *Convenience* It is easy for an investor to buy and sell shares in a mutual fund.

4. *Automatic Reinvestment Privilege* Most mutual funds will automatically reinvest dividends earned by the securities in the fund, as well as profits or capital gains earned when shares are sold.

How Does a Mutual Fund Produce a Profit?

A mutual fund makes money in three ways. First, it charges fundholders a fee for managing the fund. Second, it earns a small commission when it trades securities owned by the fund. Third, *some funds charge a commission,* called a **load,** when shares in the fund are sold to investors. Typically the load is 8.5 percent. When an investor buys $1,000 worth of funds, the investment company with a load fund keeps $85 for its services.

Many funds do not charge a sales commission, and are called **no-load funds.** There is no conclusive evidence that load funds are better investments than no-load funds.

Mutual funds have specific investment objectives. Some funds invest primarily in growth companies—businesses believed to have above-average prospects for growth and profitability. Other funds may invest in income securities—securities that pay high dividends. Still other funds may specialize in investing in government securities, municipal bonds, corporate bonds, and gold and precious metals securities.

Mutual funds are growing in popularity. In 1984 there were more than 600 separate funds owned by an estimated 22 million investors.

How Well Do Mutual Funds Perform for Investors?

Each mutual fund has different objectives, invests in a different combination of securities, and has different managers. Therefore, no two mutual funds perform in exactly the same way. Table 7–2 shows the 25 best-performing mutual funds over a ten-year period. A $10,000 investment in the Fidelity Magellan Fund, the top performer, grew to $116,600, assuming all dividends and capital gains had been reinvested in additional shares. Funds not shown in Table 7–2 generally were worth two to four times the original investment during this period.

REGULATION OF SECURITIES TRADING

Securities trading, appealing as it does to investors' get-rich-quick dreams, has often caused dishonesty. As a result, federal and state legislation arose to protect investors.

TABLE 7-2 Percentage Increase in Value of the Top 25 Mutual Funds, 1974 to 1984

Fidelity Magellan Fund	1166.00%
Oppenheimer Special	963.26
Lindner Fund	934.07
Twentieth Century Select	855.54
Twentieth Century Growth	835.48
Evergreen Fund	838.69
Amer Capital Pace	821.96
Mutual Shares Corp	712.36
Amer Capital Comstock	712.11
Amer Capital Venture	701.83
Pennsylvania Mutual	694.75
Sequoia Fund	688.22
Fidelity Destiny	635.09
Quasar Associates	624.57
Over-The-Counter SEC	582.51
Pioneer II	548.50
Security Ultra Fund	537.38
Sigma Venture Shares	523.97
St Paul Growth	513.23
Tudor Fund	510.90
Fidelity Equity-Income	501.31
Value Line Lvge Growth	496.28
Nicholas Fund	486.85
Valley Forge Fund	485.78
Mass Capital Development	481.32

SOURCE: *Barron's,* May 24, 1984, 48.

The Securities Exchange Act of 1934

The wild speculation of the 1920s, which ended in the stock market collapse of 1929, led Congress to pass the **Securities Exchange Act of 1934** to prevent abuses. The act, amended several times, requires:

- *Registration of securities*—All securities for trading on national exchanges must be registered with the Securities and Exchange Commission (SEC). This gives the investor pertinent and reliable information about the securities.

- *Accounting and financial reports*—Corporations listing securities on the exchanges must submit periodic reports that describe their current financial condition. This gives investors information concerning the financial condition of companies in which they have invested or may invest.
- *Registration of security exchanges*—Each interstate security exchange must file information concerning its constitution, by-laws, requirements for membership, and regulations.
- *Prohibition of unfair dealings*—The SEC is especially concerned with the exchanges' commission rates and methods of soliciting business. Dissemination of false or misleading information about securities, price fixing, and collusion in stock transactions are prohibited. The SEC can compel the exchanges to adhere to desirable practices.
- *Regulation of brokers*—Brokers' activities are subject to SEC controls. Thus the Board of Governors of the Federal Reserve System regulates how much credit brokers may extend to purchasers of stocks.

Regulation by the State

Many securities are sold by companies that do not meet the rigid requirements imposed by the Securities and Exchange Commission for trading on the organized exchanges. If not SEC registered, a company can only sell securities on an intrastate basis (within its own state) if approved by the appropriate state agency, usually the office of the secretary of state. There may be a greater risk in buying such issues because state requirements are less strict than those established by the SEC.

HOW TO INTERPRET BUSINESS NEWS

Business news is essential for anyone involved in business activity—for professional managers who must decide how much to expand or contract production, for entrepreneurs who must determine whether there is a market for their intended products, and for private individuals who must make the wisest choice among many possible investments.

Most daily newspapers provide business news, much of it of special interest to local business people. The nation's most widely read daily newspaper, the *Wall Street Journal,* is devoted exclusively to business information. A host of magazines, such as *Fortune, Dun's Business, BusinessWeek,* and *Forbes,* provide in-depth coverage of what is happening in business. Figure 7–2 lists some terms that the reader will probably encounter in a regular reading of financial reports.

Figure 7-2 Terms Used Frequently in Financial News

Aftermarket: A market for a security (either over-the-counter or on an exchange) after an initial public offering has been made.
Annual report: A formal statement issued yearly by a corporation to its shareowners. It shows assets, liabilities, equity, revenues, expenses, and so forth.
Automatic reinvestment of distributions: A feature of certain mutual-fund plans by which shareholders can reinvest dividends and/or capital gains by acquiring new shares.
Bear market: A declining securities market in terms of prices.
Big board: A popular slang term for the New York Stock Exchange.
Bull market: A rising securities market in terms of prices.
Capital gain (or loss): Profit (or loss) from the sale of a capital asset. Capital gains may be short-term (12 months or less) or long-term (more than 12 months). Capital losses are used to offset capital gains to establish a net position for tax purposes.
Dollar cost averaging: A long-term investment plan in which fixed dollar amounts are invested at periodic intervals, regardless of security price fluctuations.
Dow Jones average: A market average indicator—usually either (1) the average of 30 industrial stocks, (2) the average of 20 transportation common stocks, (3) the average of 15 public utility common stocks, or (4) a composite average of all of the above.
Ex-dividend date: (synonymous with "Without dividend"): A date, set by a stock exchange, on which a given stock will begin trading in the marketplace without the value of a pending dividend included in the contract price. It is often represented as "X" in the stock listing tables in newspapers.
Odd lot: An amount of stock less than the normal trading unit of 100 shares.
Prime rate: The interest rate that is currently being granted to corporate borrowers with the highest credit standing on large-volume loans.
Prospectus: A document that describes a company, its financial status, and an impending offering of securities.
Round lot: A unit of trading or a multiple thereof. On the NYSE, stocks are traded in round lots of 100 shares for active stocks and 10 shares for inactive ones.
Short sale: The sale of securities not owned at the time of the trade. A buyer puts up collateral and asks his broker to "borrow" the shares and sell them for him. Later he makes the actual purchase of the shares ("covers" the sale). If the stock price goes down, the buyer will make a profit because he sold the stock for more than he paid.
Split: A division of the outstanding shares of a corporation into a larger number of shares. Each outstanding share entitles its owner to a fixed number of new shares. The shareholder's overall equity remains the same, because the total value of the shares remains the same.
Standard & Poor's Index: A market average indicator that covers 500 leading common stocks.
Tax-exempted securities: Obligations issued by a state or municipality whose interest payments (but not profits via purchase or sale) are exempted from federal taxation. The interest payment may also be exempted from local taxation if the security is purchased by a state resident.
Yield (rate of return): The dividends or interest paid by a company on its securities, expressed as a percentage of the current price or original acquisition price.

Privately circulated newsletters written by economists, financial analysts, and trade association executives, are another source of business news and analysis. The follower of business news should also pay attention to radio and television broadcasts that supply background information on business activities and current reports on stock prices.

How to Read Market Quotations

Price quotations of securities and commodities traded on the NYSE, AMEX, and OTC markets are an important part of business news. These quotations indicate the investors' opinions of the value of secu-

PEOPLE WHO MAKE THINGS HAPPEN

A PROFILE OF
CHARLES DOW AND EDWARD JONES

One hundred years ago, Charles Dow and Edward Jones launched a little company in a room behind a soda fountain in the basement of a building next to the New York Stock Exchange. It's a safe bet the two founders would be flabbergasted to see how far their shaky little enterprise has come.

Dow Jones, which started life by delivering hand-written summaries of financial news to subscribers in the Wall Street area, has matured into an international organization whose varied activities include publishing, business and financial information services, newsprint production, and telecommunications equipment manufacturing and leasing.

Charles H. Dow, an intense young newspaperman from Providence, R.I., was still in his twenties in 1880 when he arrived in New York City and landed a job as a reporter for one of the daily newspapers. His new employer soon discovered that young Dow had a rare talent for turning routine financial reporting into expert analysis. Taking shorthand notes on the cuffs of his shirts, he soon earned a reputation for reliability.

It wasn't long before Dow accepted an offer from the Kiernan News Agency, a firm whose messenger-delivered bulletins brought subscribers news of the stock exchanges, brokerage houses and other financial happenings. As the work load there increased, he convinced a New England journalist friend, Edward D. Jones, to come to New York and join him at the agency. In the fall of 1882—experienced and with their own ideas about how financial news should be reported—the intrepid pair took their leave of Kiernan (along with a third employee, Charles M. Bergstresser) and formed their own company.

What was it like at Dow Jones in the beginning? Dow and Bergstresser (the reporters) would submit their stories to Jones for editing. He, in turn, would dictate the edited versions to four or five "manifold writers"—scribes who bent diligently over books of tissue-and-carbon-paper sandwiches, using agate-ware styluses to produce up to 24 "flimsies" at a time. Messengers would then rush the bulletins to customers; a day's service might amount to 800 words.

In November, 1883, the growing young news agency introduced its first publication: the "Customers' Afternoon Letter," which summarized the bulletins issued throughout the day. A year later, the Letter published the first Dow Jones Average of stock prices, a popular index that increased the demand for the Dow Jones service. To meet that demand, the company found a faster method of producing its bulletins—a slotted revolving cylinder that could hold and print up to 16 lines of type.

But the subscriber list kept growing, and a more radical change was needed to keep up. On July 8, 1889, The Afternoon Letter was converted into a daily newspaper, with the printing of the first issue of the *Wall Street Journal*. All of the company's 50 employees gathered around to see the new paper come off the press. (The official account of the occasion fails to mention whether anyone cheered.)

Today, the *Wall Street Journal* is a vital part of a worldwide publishing and communications organization whose 5,000 employees gather, distill and distribute news and information in a multitude of ways. Satellites, multiple printing centers, radio broadcasts, computerized communications systems—all contribute to the success of the company, listed on the New York Stock exchange under the ticker symbol DJ.

SOURCE: Adapted from the *Wall Street Journal*, Educational Edition, vol. IV, no. 1, 1984.

rities and commodities. Investors form their opinions of what specific securities are worth by digesting a wealth of information about the economy, including prospects for specific industries and companies, developments in technology, changes in marketing strategies and consumption patterns, and the effects of government actions.

SECURITY QUOTATIONS

Security quotations are listed in the *Wall Street Journal* and in the financial pages of most large daily newspapers. Figure 7–3 explains how to interpret security quotations for the New York Stock Exchange and the American Stock Exchange, as they appear in the *Wall Street Journal*.

Figure 7–3 How to Read NYSE and AMEX Stock Quotations

[1]52 WEEKS HIGH	LOW	[2]STOCK	[3]DIV.	[4]%	YLD P-E [5]RATIO	SALES [6]100s	[7] HIGH	LOW	[8]CLOSE	NET [9]CHG.
51¼	30	duPont	2.40	5.1	13	1227	47¾	47	47¼	−½
37	27⅝	duPont	pf3.50	10	..	4	35	34	34 ..	..

1. **52-week High/Low Range**
   The first two columns show the highest and lowest closing price reported for DuPont Co. for the preceding 52-week period.

2. **Company Name and Type of Stock**
   a. Common Stock—No qualifier following the company name indicates it is common stock (shares without a fixed rate of return of investment).
   b. Preferred Stock—"pf" indicates the listing is for preferred stock (shares that have a fixed rate of return). These shares of stock receive preference over common stock in the distribution of dividends.

3. **Dividend Rates**
   This indicates the payment per share designated by the Board of Directors of DuPont Co. to be distributed among the shares outstanding. On preferred shares, it is generally a fixed amount. On common shares, it varies with the business condition of the company and it is up to the discretion of the directors. When a letter follows the dividend rate, this refers to a qualifying footnote that can be found in the Explanatory Notes section of the stock listings.

4. Percent Yield

This figure represents the return an investor can expect on each share of stock he owns. It is calculated by dividing the dividend each share pays by its current market value, and is expressed as a percentage. Percent yields appearing in the *Wall Street Journal* are based on cash dividends only; though stock dividends are paid by some companies, these are not included except when a company pays only stock dividends, or has a history of paying stock and cash regularly.

5. Price Earnings Ratio (P-E)

This calculation acts as a barometer for evaluating market prices. It is computed by dividing the stock's selling price by the company's per share earnings for the most recent four quarters.

6. Trading Volume

This figure shows the total number of sales for the day, listed in hundreds. Here, the column shows 1227, which means 122,700 shares were traded that day. Whenever a "z" precedes the volume number, the figure that follows represents the actual number of shares traded. For example z20 means 20 shares were traded, not 2,000.

7. High/Low, Previous Day

This indicates the trading price range of the security on the previous day.

8. Close, Previous Day

This is the last trading price recorded when the market closed the previous day.

9. Net Change

This indicates the difference between the last closing price reported for the day and the last closing price reported for the preceding day.

SOURCE: Educational Service Bureau, Dow Jones and Company, Inc.

Figure 7-4 explains how to read quotations of securities traded over-the-counter.

Figure 7-4 How to Read Over-the-Counter Stock Quotations

[1]STOCK & DIV.	SALES [2]100s	BID [3]	ASKED	NET [4]CHG.
Pioneer Gr .48	6	47	48	−1

1. Name and Dividend

Cash payouts are shown on an annualized basis when possible, the same as the New York and American exchanges. But there are differences. Most of them are minor and covered in separate footnotes for the OTC tables.

2. Volume

Sales are shown in 100's. If 25 appears, for example, in the volume column, it means 2,500 shares traded. The "z" footnote used in the NYSE and AMEX lists applies to the OTC table. Thus, z25 means just 25 shares changed hands, not 2,500.

> **3. Bid and Asked**
> Issues fluctuate throughout the day just as issues traded on the exchanges. The bid and asked quotations show the best prices at which dealers are willing to buy and sell as of 4 P.M. of the previous trading day.
>
> **4. Net Change**
> Gain or loss from the previous close. The change is calculated on the bid quote.
>
> SOURCE: Educational Service Bureau, Dow Jones and Company, Inc.

BOND QUOTATIONS

Many bond issues (see Chapter 5) are listed on the stock exchanges. For quotation purposes, bonds are generally classified as domestic, foreign, utility, or U.S. Other classifications, such as world bank bonds, municipal bonds, and federal land bank bonds, are given in some financial publications. Figure 7–5 shows how to interpret bond quotations.

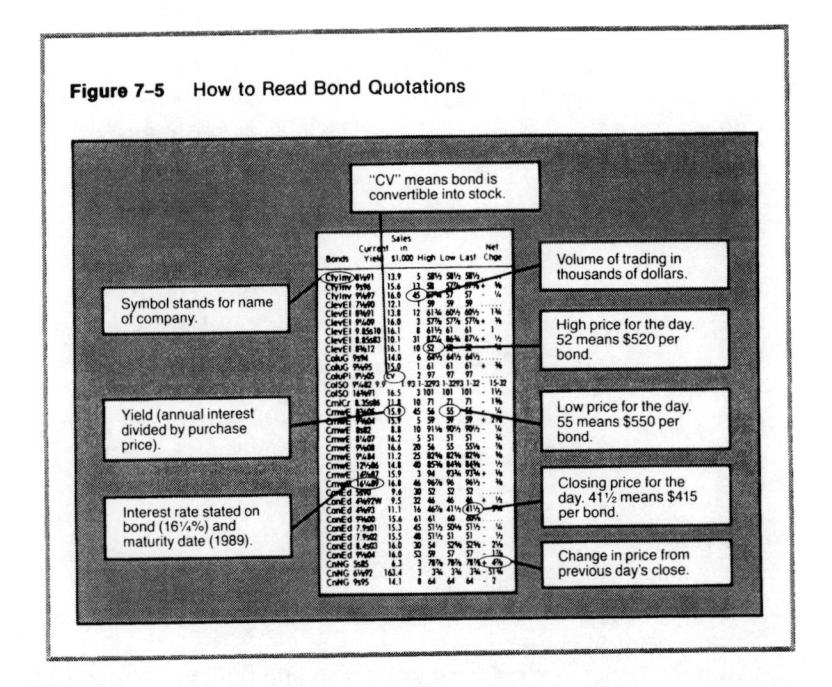

Figure 7-5 How to Read Bond Quotations

Bond prices are quoted somewhat differently from stock prices. Bonds generally have a par, or stated, value—usually $1,000. The price quotation is given as a percentage of the par value. Therefore, a quotation at 96 means that the current price of the bond is 96 percent of $1,000—in other words, $960. Any interest that has accrued since the time of the last interest payment is always added to the price of the bond. U.S. government bonds are quoted in thirty-seconds of a point. Practically all other bonds are regularly quoted in eighths of a point.

Bonds—as noted in an earlier chapter—are rated according to risk. Table 7-3 shows the ratings used by the most prominent independent rating agencies.

TABLE 7-3 Risk Ratings for Municipal Bonds

FITCH'S	MOODY'S	STANDARD & POOR'S
AAA	Aaa	AAA
AA+		AA+
AA	Aa	AA
AA−		AA−
A+	A1*	A+
A	A	A
A−	Baa1	A−
BBB+		BBB+
BBB	Baa	BBB
BBB−		BBB−
BB+		BB+
BB	Ba	BB
BB−		BB−
		B+
B	B	B
		B−
CCC	Caa	CCC
CC	Ca	CC
C	C	C
DDD		
DD		
D		D

But do not let safe risk ratings lull you into thinking that bonds are safer than they really are. During periods of inflation, bonds lose purchasing power. If inflation gets worse after you buy a bond, then interest rates will rise and the value of your bond will drop. It is true that bonds will give you back the number of dollars you invested if they are held until maturity. However, the dollars you get back may not have the purchasing power of the dollars you used to buy the bond.

COMMODITY-MARKET QUOTATIONS

A number of commodity exchanges are located in the United States. Any commodity for which there is an active demand—such as grains, eggs, hide, butter, cattle, cotton, wood, and silver—may be traded. Like stock markets, commodity markets are membership organizations. Most members are people who produce, market, or process commodities, or they are brokers who execute orders for others.

The mechanics of trading are similar to those for the purchase and sale of securities. However, there are three key differences. First, trading is done in large lots, called **commodity contracts,** which are *commitments to buy or sell a commodity at a specified time and place in the future.* For example, grain is traded in 5,000-bushel lots, coffee in 37,500-pound lots, and eggs in 22,500-dozen lots.

Second, prices fluctuate much more because weather and other environmental factors greatly affect the commodity markets. An unexpected drought, for example, can cause prices of grain to change significantly and swiftly.

Third, margin requirements are small, usually amounting to about 10 percent of the value of the commodity. This encourages speculation. People can both make and lose money much faster in trading commodities than in buying and selling securities.

Commodity-market quotations give the name of the commodity, the market on which it was traded (for example, CBT for Chicago Board of Trade), the minimum contract size, the high and low prices for the day, the closing price for the day, the change in price from the previous day, and the highest and lowest prices for the season.

Commodity trading is much more complex than securities trading, and novice investors should not engage in it.

Topics of Business News

In addition to market quotations, business people must analyze a wealth of information in areas that have both direct and indirect effects on business activity.

HOW MUCH ARE PEOPLE BUYING?

For high production to be maintained, high consumption is essential. Much consumption news is statistical. Wholesale sales, retail sales, carloadings, and inventories show movement of goods into the hands of users. In addition to current consumption data, there is information that gives a clue to future consumption—for example, savings deposits, consumer debt, consumer incomes, and unemployment statistics.

The **Consumer Price Index (CPI),** considered to be a measure of inflation and the erosion of the dollar, is perhaps the most highly publicized and closely watched economic series in the United States. It is *a measure of the average change in prices over time in a fixed market basket of goods and services.* For some years, the base year has been 1967; in 1982, the base year was changed to 1977. The CPI is expressed as a percentage. For example, a CPI of 275 indicates that prices have risen 275 percent since the appropriate base year. The CPI is released monthly and furnishes the basis for automatic wage increases for thousands of wage earners under contracts tied to the cost of living. It is based on price information gathered in 85 areas across the country.

WHAT IS THE GOVERNMENT DOING?

No business is exempt from the influence of government. The actions of government agencies directly affect pricing, investment, production, marketing, and financial decisions. Product quality standards, waste disposal methods, employee and environmental safety, and IRS tax rulings are examples of government activities that directly affect business decisions. Consequently, news of government actions, as reported in daily newspapers and weekly news magazines, is of significance to business people.

WHAT IS GOING ON IN POLITICS?

Since political changes have an effect on governmental policies, political news is also business news. Accordingly, business news reports devote much attention to what elected political leaders are doing in relation to economic activity. Sponsorship and endorsement of new legislation or repeal or modification of existing laws and regulations is of interest to business, because, directly and indirectly, such political action affects business success.

WHAT IS NEW IN MARKETING?

Much business news reports how specific companies are changing their marketing strategies in an attempt to increase their sales. News about new products, packages, advertising campaigns, distribution channels, and similar information helps executives evaluate what they are doing to reach their target customers.

WHAT WILL BE THE EFFECTS OF NEW TECHNOLOGY?

Business people depend on business news for information about developments in computers, communication, energy, and other technology-based companies and industries. Managers want to know how changes in technology and science will affect their companies.

WHAT IS HAPPENING IN INTERNATIONAL BUSINESS?

News about international business is of increasing interest for practical reasons. The *Wall Street Journal* notes:

> The increasingly international quality of economic and business issues presents new challenges. Inflation and energy prices are truly world problems. The making of autos, steel and pharmaceuticals are world industries. Corporations buy and sell, invest and compete on a global scale. This has led us to open new foreign bureaus in Europe and Asia, to improve and expand foreign coverage.[3]

Business people have a strong and growing interest in news that concerns foreign markets, for several reasons:

- In recent years, the United States has had huge trade deficits. Consequently, the government has vigorously promoted exports, making businesses increasingly alert to foreign developments.
- Many Americans own stocks and bonds in foreign corporations, and many investors in other countries own shares in American corporations.
- Foreign countries purchase a significant volume of U.S. products and materials.
- U.S. corporations purchase large quantities of foreign-produced raw materials and manufactured articles.

Because of the interdependency between the United States and other countries, the business pages sometimes allocate as much space to foreign economic developments as they do to domestic ones. International business is intricate and complex, since foreign countries differ greatly in their trade regulations, some foreign governments are unstable, and our own government's policies regarding imports and exports change frequently.

Business News Is Interesting

Clearly, business news is valuable to people making investment and business decisions. But there is another benefit to keeping up with what is happening in the world of commerce—business news is interesting. The efforts of one company to take control of another company that doesn't want to be acquired, methods used by a once unknown company such as Apple Computer to gain international prominence in less than a decade, and the uphill battle of Chrysler to survive and prosper, make interesting reading.

---

[3]The *Wall Street Journal,* Educational Edition, Dow Jones and Company, Inc., 1984, 13.

ISSUE FOR DEBATE

Are Adjustable Rate Mortgages (ARMs) a Good Idea?

Changes in laws affecting home mortgages make it possible for interest rates to fluctuate over the life of the loan.

In its simplest form, an adjustable rate mortgage is a long-term loan agreement under which a buyer promises to pay interest at a base rate plus periodic adjustments tied to the rate of inflation.

Some argue that ARMs are good for lenders, the housing industry, and home buyers. Others say ARMs are bad for all concerned.

PROS

It simply is no longer possible for a lender to commit mortgage money for up to 30 years at a fixed rate of interest—anymore than you'd agree to sell your goods or services for the next 30 years at the price you're charging today.

Adjustable mortgages represent the only way home-lending institutions will be able to pay competitive interest rates to consumers who save when all savings-rate ceilings are removed.

CONS

For the economy as a whole, ARMs will serve to worsen the problem they are designed to counteract: inflation. The traditional fixed rate mortgage acts as a drag on inflation because its payments are constant and predictable, irrespective of inflation. In contrast, the adjustable rate mortgage tracks present inflation and helps cause future inflation because of its critical effect on price expectations. As long as people anticipate that their mortgage costs will increase, they will act accordingly in planning their economic lives. Inflation will follow suit.

Negative amortization occurs when the monthly payment is not sufficient to cover the interest charge, and the payment shortfall is added to the loan balance. Under the ARMs now being made, the loan balance can increase by 7, 8, or 10 percent a year or even more. If the value of the homeowner's property does not increase at a rate to offset such loan balance increases, the homeowner's equity would be eroded and even eliminated. The erosion of homeowner equity would dramatically increase default rates. In many cases the borrower could end up owing more than the house is worth—a "negative equity" situation. If this happens, massive numbers of defaults could occur.

PROS

Today 60 percent of all deposits in savings and loan associations are in savings instruments whose initial rates change according to the money market—and the proportion is getting bigger all the time. If savings associations are to be able to attract money for new mortgages, this must be matched with flexible rates on the mortgage side.

The vast majority of mortgages held by savings associations are old fixed rate loans, many made at interest rates now far below the market. Obviously if associations earn 10 percent or less on many old mortgages but must pay 15 percent or more to attract new savings, their operating margin is greatly curtailed.

Because decreases in the interest rate are mandatory when market rates come down, potential homebuyers shouldn't have to wait until interest rates come down to buy a home. They can obtain an adjustable mortgage today, even in the midst of high interest rates, and be assured that when inflation and interest rates moderate, so will the rate they pay on their adjustable mortgage loan.

CONS

Most people's income does not adjust to increases in the price of money (inflation). Why should savings and loan associations be permitted to adjust the price (interest rate) they charge on mortgages?

Consumers' freedom to choose is being eliminated. Even though adjustable rate lending is just beginning, some lenders appear to be abandoning traditional fixed rate mortgages. Three of New York City's largest savings banks are making only adjustable rate mortgage loans. Five out of six savings and loan associations surveyed in Akron, three out of five in Rochester, and 12 out of 25 in Cleveland have stopped fixed rate mortgage lending.

Questions

1. Assume you are buying a house or condominium. Would you prefer a fixed rate mortgage or an ARM? Why?
2. Which form of mortgage carries the most risk? Why?

SUMMARY

- Business news dominates information in our society. People are interested in business news because it affects their jobs, incomes, and investments, and shapes their standard of living.

- Security exchanges help people buy and sell stocks and bonds. The three most important security exchanges are the New York Stock Exchange (NYSE), the American Stock Exchange (AMEX), and the over-the-counter market (OTC).

- Advantages to a corporation of having its securities traded on an exchange are (a) listing gives greater corporate visibility, (b) prices on an exchange are set quickly by the interplay of supply and demand, (c) listed securities are perceived to be less risky, and (d) listing gives a corporation a broader ownership base.

- The over-the-counter market is growing more rapidly than other security exchanges because (a) the NYSE and AMEX carry less prestige than before, (b) listing requirements are less stringent on the OTC, (c) listing costs are lower on the OTC, and (d) OTC trading is more efficient.

- Mutual funds investment companies offer investors professional management, diversification, convenience, and automatic reinvestment of capital gains and profits from the sale of securities.

- The Securities Exchange Act of 1934 requires registration of securities and security exchanges, and requires accounting and financial reports from corporations that list securities. It prohibits unfair dealings by exchange members, and regulates the activities of brokers.

- Business news sources, which include both the print and broadcast media, provide specific information on the prices of stocks, bonds, and commodities. Other useful business news includes background information about consumption, government, politics, marketing, technology, and international business.

- Stock quotations give the 52-week high and low price of the security, its type (common or preferred), dividend rates, yield, price-earnings ratio, trading volume, high and low price for the previous day, close for the previous day, and net change.

KEY TERMS YOU SHOULD KNOW

broker	listed security	open order
commodity contract	load	over-the-counter (OTC)
Consumer Price Index	market order	market
discount broker	member firm	Securities Exchange Act
floor member	mutual fund	security exchange
full-service broker	no-load funds	yield
limited order	on margin	

QUESTIONS FOR REVIEW

1. Why are we interested in business news?
2. What is a securities exchange? What are the three most important securities exchanges?
3. Why may a company want its shares listed on an exchange?
4. Describe how a purchase of a security takes place.
5. How do full-service brokers differ from discount brokers?
6. What is buying on margin?
7. What are the main differences among the NYSE, AMEX, and OTC?
8. Why is the NASDAQ growing rapidly?

9. What are mutual funds? What advantages do they offer an investor?
10. How is the yield of a security computed? Its price-earnings ratio?
11. Why was the Securities and Exchange Act of 1934 passed? What are its main provisions?
12. How can one benefit from consumption news? Government news? Political news? Information about marketing? News about international business?

QUESTIONS FOR DISCUSSION

1. Suppose a friend told you security exchanges are nothing but legalized gambling establishments. How would you answer this charge?
2. Assume you are a stockbroker. Next week you have appointments with the following people to help them devise investment programs to suit their needs.
   a. Abe Brown, age 27. Single. Income, $16,200 per year. Amount available for investing, $6,000.
   b. Janet and Fred Green, ages 46 and 47. Three teen-age dependents. Combined income, $42,500. Amount available for investing, $40,000.
   c. Ida Blue, age 66. Widowed. Income from other investments and Social Security, $10,200. Amount available for investing, $75,000.

   For each person or couple, explain what general types of securities you would suggest. Why would the same investment program not be wise in all three cases?
3. There is an old adage for making money in the stock market: "Buy low, sell high—fast." Why is this advice so difficult to apply in practice?
4. The *Wall Street Journal* is one of the fastest-growing national newspapers and can be found on many newsstands all over the United States, at a time when many daily newspapers in large cities are disappearing. Why do you think this is so?
5. A problem the government has in promoting exports is that Americans have been disinterested in foreign countries and news about them. What is the cause of this? What can be done to make Americans more interested in foreign business?
6. There are three securities exchanges—the NYSE, AMEX, and OTC. Would you favor one stock exchange that would provide trading facilities for all stocks owned by corporations? Why or why not?

CASE STUDY

What Should Ted Do with a $50,000 Inheritance?

Six weeks ago, Ted Williams, age 21, single, and a junior in college, inherited $50,000 from a distant relative. Ted is ignorant about investing, and he seeks advice from Phyllis Brown and Fred Adams about how to solve his "problem." Both of them are going to be financial planners when they finish school.

Ted: I've got a problem. Six weeks ago I inherited $50,000. I'm an art major and I know next to nothing about money management. How should I invest the money?

Phyllis: I wish I had your "problem"!

Fred: So do I!

P: Seriously, I think the first thing you should do is list the alternatives—stocks, bonds, mutual funds, real estate, limited partnership in ventures such as oil exploration, and perhaps your own business.

T: Well, I know I don't want to go into business for myself. Art is my life. But you're not answering my question—which alternative do you recommend?

F: Ted, making an investment decision is not easy. For each of the alternatives Phyllis named there are literally thousands of choices. In the case of stocks, for example, there are issues that vary greatly in terms of risk, yield, and possibilities for appreciation in value. The same is true of bonds, mutual funds, and other investments.

P: Beside listing and evaluating your investment alternatives, I think it's important that you also evaluate your emotional makeup.

T: What does my emotional makeup have to do with my investments?

P: A lot! You see, few investments are guaranteed, and those that are provide relatively low returns. Simply put, if you fear risk, then you should invest conservatively. If you don't, then you may want to take chances and either gain a much bigger return or lose some of what you invest.

T: Well, I guess I'm pretty conservative. I don't want to worry about my money. From what little I know, I think low-risk common stocks or mutual funds might be best for me.

F: In that event I suggest you spell out clearly your investment objectives as low risk and a reasonable rate of return. Then visit three brokerage houses and ask them to recommend a portfolio. From the three recommendations, choose the one that you feel is best for you. And don't hurry in making your decision.

P: By the way, where is your $50,000 now?

T: In my checking account.

P: Ted, do you realize there are safe places for you to keep your deposit that pay interest? At 12 percent, you are losing $500 per month!

Questions

1. If you were Ted, what would you do with your $50,000? Explain.
2. "A fool and his money are soon parted." Why? How?
3. Explain the relationship between risk and return.

EVOLUTION OF A BUSINESS

Sizing Up the Travel Market

Sara and Ray decided to build their own building. They liked the idea of building up assets by having tenants pay off the mortgage. While the building was under construction, they spent many hours discussing the details of how they planned to run the business. One evening the talk turned to their potential clients. Their first step is to analyze the market—to discuss who their customers will be, and what services they will demand.

Sara: The travel agency business is so competitive that we'll not only have to offer good travel packages, we'll have to be sure to reach the biggest markets for travel.

Ray: Which are...?

Sara: Well, I haven't researched it in depth, but they seem to be business executives and their families, the singles market, and retired people. Every business publication I read—the *Wall Street Journal, Barron's, Forbes*—carries news indicating that business executives travel a lot. And since they're in high income brackets, they're probably interested in recreational travel too.

Ray: What about singles and retired people?

Sara: I read in the daily paper yesterday that the number of adults under 35 who live alone has more than doubled since 1970, even though rents have been going up and up. And last week I read in the financial section that elderly and retired people are the fastest-growing segment of the travel business.

Ray: Then I guess we should cater to those three groups.

Sara: Yes. I'm planning to do more research to make sure about all this. But I'm tentatively thinking we should divide up the responsibility for studying these different markets. How about if you took on the retired and business-executive markets, and I tried to find out more about what singles are looking for in travel.

Ray: Sounds fine to me. A good starting point, I think, would be for us to read regularly what our segment of the market reads.

Questions

1. What do you think of Sara's plan to try to reach specific markets?
2. Can a small company specialize in three such large and diverse markets? Would it be better if they specialized in only one? Why or why not?
3. What other kinds of reading and investigating could Sara and Ray do to learn about each particular market?
4. What other groups do you think would be good prospects for travel?

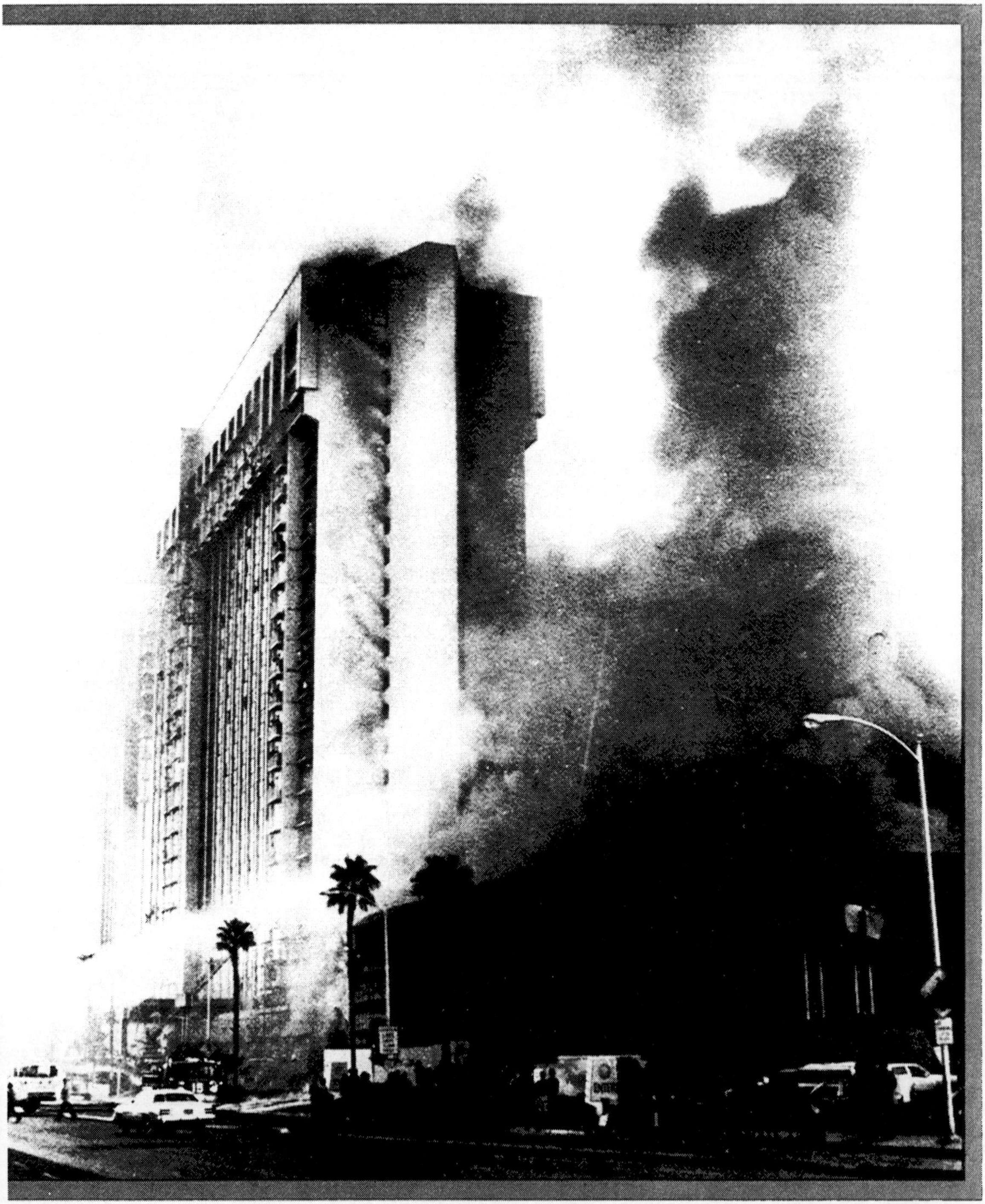

RISK MANAGEMENT AND INSURANCE
Reducing the Odds

READ THIS CHAPTER SO YOU CAN:

Discuss the four methods of meeting risk: (a) reducing the chance of loss, (b) good management, (c) selling insurance, and (d) insurance.

Explain the law of large numbers and why it is essential to the insurance industry.

Describe what constitutes an insurable risk.

Contrast stock insurance companies and mutual insurance companies.

Define and explain the various types of insurance.

Discuss the role of the risk manager.

Perhaps the only certain thing in business is uncertainty. Since uncertainty, or risk, can at any time weaken or destroy a business, risk must be managed by carefully anticipating and providing for it.

Business risk is, in simplest terms, *the chance that something will happen to cause a financial loss.* The following are examples of common business risks:

- Property may be damaged or destroyed by fire, windstorm, flood, hail, explosion, riot, vandalism, or earthquake.
- Merchandise and other property may be stolen by employees, customers, or others.
- Company funds may be stolen or embezzled by employees.
- Accidents may injure employees, customers, or others, posing a threat of lawsuit.
- Goods may spoil or deteriorate, or they may become obsolete because of changes in customer preferences.
- There are a large variety of miscellaneous risks, such as the death of key executives, drought in the grain and cattle areas, strikes, changes in the price of goods, credit losses, new competition, new legislation, and decrease in demand for a firm's products.

Lack of preparation for such contingencies is both a major cause of business failure and a significant factor in reducing profits. Wise managers face risks realistically and minimize the chances of loss in every way possible.

METHODS OF MEETING RISK

Reducing the Chance of Loss

The chance of loss can be reduced through preventive and protective measures. Automatic sprinkler systems, regular inspection of movable equipment (such as elevators), employment of guards in industrial plants and detectives in stores, special locks on safes and vaults, adequate lighting, electronic surveillance systems, and careful selection of employees who will handle money are all calculated to reduce risks.

Such measures, while helpful, do not eliminate the chance of loss. Numerous "guaranteed fireproof" buildings burn; shoplifting goes on in stores staffed with security guards; thieves break into "unbreakable" vaults; "unsinkable" ships sink; and machines "just inspected" break, injuring employees. A business, therefore, must do more than take preventive and protective measures against risks.

Good Management

All business organizations face a number of risks that can be met only through good management. For example, risks of product obsolescence, population shifts that reduce the value of a given business location, price changes, and economic recession can be dealt with only if the organization anticipates these changes and prepares for them. Many large organizations maintain research departments to study trends and guide management decisions. For example, research can measure whether potential customers would buy a proposed new product and what segments of population watch which TV shows, and thus help management reduce the possibility of making costly mistakes in spending money.

Self-insurance

A third method of meeting risk is to *set aside a financial reserve that can be drawn on when losses occur.* This is known as **self-insurance, or underwriting one's own insurance.** Self-insurance is simple and appeals to some businesses; it is not, however, a practical method for most. Suppose, for example, that the owner of a $300,000 building decided to put $1,000 per year into a reserve to protect the building against fire. It would obviously take more than a lifetime before sufficient funds could be accumulated to cover a total loss.

Self-insurance is sometimes used successfully by organizations that operate several hundred similar, widely scattered establishments. A contribution by each unit to a general fund might be sufficient to meet the losses that occur.

Self-insurance can be used for protection against only some risks. For example, a taxicab company operating a large number of cabs may self-insure against the risk of collision, because this risk is reasonably easy to predict. The same company would not, in all probability, self-insure against the risk of injuring a passenger, because losses from such an occurrence are much more difficult to estimate. Thus, even for large organizations, self-insurance is usually not a complete answer to the problem of risk. (See the debate on self-insurance in the case study at the end of this chapter.)

Insurance

The methods of meeting risk just discussed provide only partial protection against the chance of loss. The most popular and effective method is to transfer the risk to insurance companies.

Insurance *is an agreement by a company to compensate a person or organization for specific losses that may occur. In return, the person or organization (also called the insured) agrees to pay the insurance company a sum of money (the premium) on a periodic basis.*

Suppose that A owns a building worth $300,000. B, the insurance company, agrees, for a $1,000 annual premium paid by A, to insure against the risk that A's building may be destroyed by fire. If the building should burn, B will pay A the amount of loss up to $300,000. If the building does not burn, B keeps the premium and uses it, together with premiums from other insureds, to reimburse those who do experience losses and to pay B's operating expenses. Thus, insurance does not *prevent* loss. Rather, it *transfers the risk* to someone better able to assume it.

Insurance companies will not insure for amounts greater than the value of the property. For example, a claim for a burned-down building cannot be for more than the value of the building, since this would encourage the unscrupulous to destroy property deliberately for money gain. All insureds would then suffer in the long run through higher premiums. (See the discussion of arson in the section on fire insurance on page 219.)

THE LAW OF LARGE NUMBERS

How can an insurance company afford to assume a $300,000 risk for only $1,000? The explanation lies in the **law of large numbers,** often called the **law of averages.** According to this mathematical law, *out of a very large number of similar risks, only a certain number of losses will occur.* By studying the experience of, say, 10,000 similar buildings over a period of years, actuaries [1] are able to predict with surprising accuracy how many of these structures will be damaged by fire in any one year. When this number is known, the insurance company can determine how much money it must collect in premiums to have a sufficiently large fund to pay all losses, meet its own operating expenses, and realize a profit.

If, for example, of the 10,000 insured buildings it was determined that 250 would be damaged by fire to the extent of $30,000 each in a normal year, the company would need to have $7.5 million available to cover losses. Suppose the company also required $2.5 million to cover operating expenses and profits. It would then need to collect $10 million that year. Prorating this cost equally among all those buying the insurance would mean that each would pay a $1,000 premium.

Losses can be estimated accurately only when large numbers are involved. The same actuaries who can predict almost the exact number of fires in a group of 10,000 buildings could not predict the number of losses in a group of 100 buildings.

---

[1] An **actuary** is *a person who calculates insurance premiums by estimating expected claims, interest that the premiums will earn, and the like.*

WHAT CONSTITUTES AN INSURABLE RISK?

A number of qualifications must be met before an insurance company will insure a given risk.

First, the chance of loss must be predictable with reasonable accuracy. Without such predictions, companies simply do not know how large the premium should be. For example, in the 1960s, State Farm Insurance pioneered a good-student discount on car insurance when research showed that students with averages of B or above had a lower claims incidence than other students. Actuarially sound, this breakthrough provided State Farm with a competitive and public relations coup as well as profitable business.

Second, risk must concern possible financial loss. Sentimental losses, such as the destruction of a child's painting, cannot be insured because there's no objective way to evaluate sentiment.

Third, insurance concerns itself only with **pure risks**—that is, *risks where there is a chance only to lose.* **Speculative risks,** *where there is a chance to gain or lose,* as in horse races or fluctuations of stock prices, cannot be insured.

Fourth, to obtain insurance, the applicant must have an **insurable interest,** or *a clear interest in the property insured.* Ownership of property is an obvious example of insurable interest. One cannot, for example, purchase insurance on property belonging to someone else under most circumstances.

Fifth, the company or individual that applies for insurance must not be a **moral hazard.** A moral hazard *exists when there is danger that the property will be deliberately destroyed by the insured to collect the insurance.* The moral hazard is particularly important in fire insurance. During recessions, the number of business properties that burn increases greatly, indicating that people are setting fire to or hiring others to set fire to their businesses to get themselves out of debt. When the interstate highway system was built, for instance, insurance commissioners noted an increase in fire losses in businesses located along older highways that were bypassed by the system.

State insurance commissioners estimate that 25 percent or more of all fires involving business property are intentionally started. In terms of amount of damage done, arson leads the list of known fire causes.[2]

To minimize the moral hazard, insurance companies conduct investigations of applicants. Companies give particular attention to the applicant's character, the applicant's previous insurance-loss record, and the profitableness of the present business operation. Sudden eagerness for large insurance coverage by a hard-pressed business

---

[2]Insurance Information Institute, *Insurance Facts* (1980–81 ed.), 44.

not previously heavily insured would be suspect. Life insurance policies generally include a **suicide clause,** which *states that in the event the insured commits suicide within two years after purchasing the policy, the company will pay the beneficiary only the amount of the premiums paid, not the face value of the policy.*

TYPES OF INSURANCE COMPANIES

In terms of ownership there are two types of insurance companies: stock and mutual. A **stock company** is *a corporation owned and operated by stockholders for profit.* The stockholders are not necessarily purchasers of insurance. Rather, they act in the capacity of investors hoping to gain from dividends and from appreciation in the value of their stock. Stock companies write most of the insurance for all types except life. Mutuals write a majority of the life insurance policies, which we will discuss later.

Mutuals are *a form of cooperative. There are no stockholders, and the companies are owned by the policyholders;* hence there can be no dividends on stock.

Some Mutuals May "Demutualize"

The nation's largest mutual life insurance companies, however, are considering converting from policyholders to stock ownership. Prob-

TABLE 8-1 The Ten Biggest Mutuals
Their surpluses, experts say, give a conservative idea of their book value as stock companies.

LIFE INSURANCE COMPANY	ASSETS IN BILLIONS 12/31/83	SURPLUS IN BILLIONS
Prudential	$72.2	$3.0
Metropolitan	$60.6	$2.5
Equitable	$43.3	$1.2
New York Life	$24.2	$1.4
John Hancock	$23.5	$1.0
Northwestern Mutual	$14.5	$.8
Massachusetts Mutual	$12.2	$.8
Bankers Life	$11.4	$.3
Mutual of New York	$9.3	$.5
New England Mutual	$8.5	$.5

SOURCE: Eleanor Johnson Tracy, "The Top Life Insurers Weigh Going Public," *Fortune*, June 25, 1984, 96.

able reasons for the "demutualization" are that (a) new legislation may tax mutuals at a higher rate than stock companies; (b) mutual companies want access to more capital which could be acquired through the sale of stock, and thus new capital could be used to diversify into other industries; and (c) to compete with the supermarket financial institutions (discussed in Chapter 6), life insurance companies need to offer broader services.

To demutualize, mutual life insurance companies must obtain approval of two-thirds of their policyholders and issue stock to their policyholders.

Mutual life insurance companies control vast amounts of assets (see Table 8–1). When they become public corporations, investors will have new opportunities for investments.

Both stock and mutual insurance companies invest their **reserves** (*funds set aside to meet future obligations*) in a variety of ways to earn money. Figure 8–1 shows how life insurance companies invest their assets. Insurance companies are, of course, insurers; however, in investing their funds they become a chief source of equity capital for other businesses.

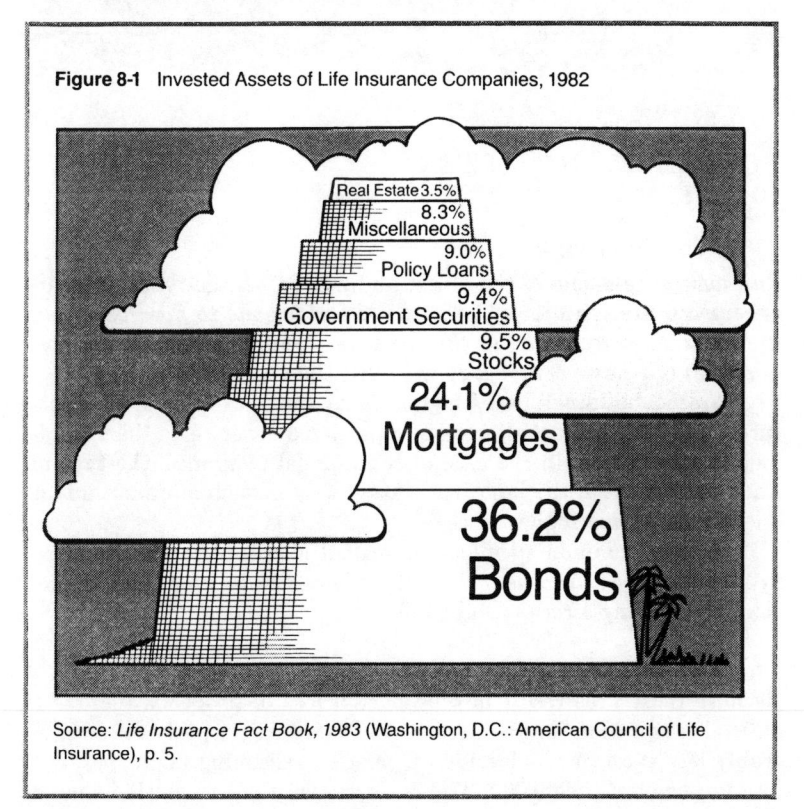

Figure 8-1 Invested Assets of Life Insurance Companies, 1982

- Real Estate 3.5%
- Miscellaneous 8.3%
- Policy Loans 9.0%
- Government Securities 9.4%
- Stocks 9.5%
- Mortgages 24.1%
- Bonds 36.2%

Source: *Life Insurance Fact Book, 1983* (Washington, D.C.: American Council of Life Insurance), p. 5.

Arson-caused fires are now the most costly crimes: Few arsonists are caught, and even fewer convicted. Therefore, companies have difficulty getting insurance or may find it very expensive.

PROPERTY AND OTHER RELATED INSURANCE

Fire Insurance

Fire insurance is one of the oldest and most essential types of insurance. **Fire insurance** policies are *written for one to five years, and the rates vary according to the risks involved.* The policies are prepared on one *basic contract form* called the **standard policy.**

Frame buildings carry higher rates than brick or steel structures, and well-protected areas in cities have lower rates than buildings in rural areas. In the case of commercial insurance, the type of work performed in the building is also a factor, with more hazardous operations paying higher rates.

A very common *supplement* (called a **rider**) to the standard fire insurance contract is one covering losses from wind, hail, explosion, riot, falling aircraft, and smoke.

THE COINSURANCE CLAUSE

Because most fires result in only partial loss of property, there is a natural temptation for business people to insure property for considerably less than its total value. A person's reasoning might be, "My building is worth $200,000. The odds are very great that if I should have a fire it would destroy only part of the building. So I'll purchase only a $100,000 policy and take my chances that a total loss will never occur."

The reasoning tends to work to the disadvantage of the insurance company, for it results in insufficient premium income to pay for losses. Insurance companies have therefore adopted the **coinsurance clause,** which *states, in effect, that if the insured person has insured the property for less than a certain percentage (usually 80 percent) of its value, the insurance company will not pay the full value of a partial loss.*

The coinsurance clause operates as follows. Assume that the owner of a building worth $200,000 insures it with a fire insurance company under a contract containing an 80 percent coinsurance clause. A policy is written for $160,000. Later, a $120,000 fire occurs. Since the property owner has met the requirements of the 80 percent coinsurance clause (that is, had insured the property for at least 80 percent of its value), the full amount of the loss, $120,000, would be paid. However, if the owner in this case had obtained insurance for only $100,000, and a $120,000 fire had occurred, the owner would receive only $75,000 in settlement of the loss. This amount is arrived at in the following manner: The owner holds $100,000 worth of insurance, which is five-eighths of the amount ($160,000) needed to be fully insured against partial losses. Therefore, the owner is reimbursed for only five-eighths of the $120,000 loss, or $75,000.

Arson and Fire Insurance

Fire insurance is a major concern of business. It is often either hard to get or prohibitively expensive because arson has become America's most costly crime. Each year, arson kills 1,000 people and destroys $3 billion worth of property, a much greater amount than the $1.9 billion lost in car theft, the second-place crime.[3]

The reason arson is so widespread is that chances of getting caught are slim, and only 1 percent of those who are caught are convicted. Law enforcement agencies, with the assistance of the federal Law Enforcement Assistance Administration, are stepping up their efforts to increase arrests and convictions. Also, there is a major movement to remove the profit motive from arson, since at least one in four fires is set for profit. The standard fire policy states, "It shall be the option of this company to repair, rebuild, or replace the property destroyed or damaged with other of the like kind and quality." Few insurance companies ever use that option, but that is changing. Companies that rebuild property, especially in cases that are suspected to be the work of an arson ring, find that the incidence of arson in the area they serve is reduced.

---

[3]*Business Week,* May 21, 1979, 68.

Ocean marine insurance protects shipping companies against losses incurred from many risks, including bad weather, theft, and sinking.

Marine Insurance

Marine insurance, sometimes called **transportation insurance,** took its name from the fact that it was first used to insure ships and cargoes at sea. It has the distinction of being the oldest type of insurance; it existed in an elementary form 5,000 years ago. Marine insurance covers two broad areas: ocean marine and inland marine.

OCEAN MARINE

Ocean marine insurance is *used to protect shippers while goods are on the sea or temporarily in port.* Protection is against losses resulting from sinking, capsizing, stranding, collision, bad weather, and theft. While all ocean marine policies tend to follow the same form, there is no standard policy as there is in fire insurance. Time policies are used when shipments are made regularly, while single-voyage policies are issued when shipments are made at infrequent intervals. Rate-setting is complicated, because many variables must be considered: route traveled, season of the year, type of cargo, and so on. Rates are usually established by management judgment rather than through mathematical calculations.

INLAND MARINE

Of more significance to most businesses is **inland marine insurance,** which *comprises primarily inland transportation insurance.*

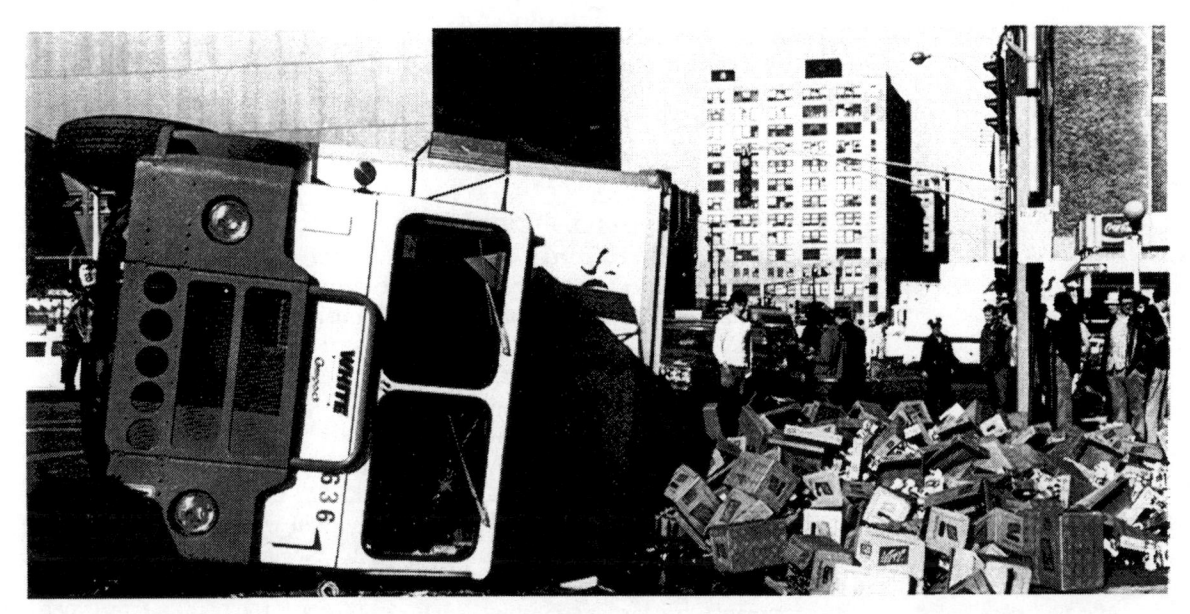

Inland transportation insurance is *not restricted to inland water transportation but covers risks while goods are being transported by truck, plane, and railroad.* Inland insurance contracts were originally very similar to ocean marine, but with the extension of coverage to many new risks the contract has been modified substantially to cover plate glass, signs, bridges, and other things indirectly related to transportation.

Inland marine insurance protects companies against risks that occur during transportation by truck, plane, and inland waterway ships.

Automobile Insurance

Automobile insurance is *held by automobile owners to protect themselves from collision, fire and theft, and liability.*

COLLISION

Collision insurance *protects against damages to one's automobile resulting from collision with other automobiles or with other objects, either moving or fixed.* It may be either full-coverage or deductible. Under **full-coverage insurance,** *the insurance company indemnifies (compensates) for all losses up to the present value of the car;* under **deductible coverage insurance,** *the insurance company is liable (responsible) only for losses over a specified sum,* such as $100 or $500. The premium rate decreases as the size of the deduction increases. An important point to remember with collision insurance is that you should consider dropping it when the value of your car depreciates to the point where you can stand the loss yourself.

FIRE AND THEFT

Fire-and-theft coverage *indemnifies for losses caused by fire or theft.* This coverage can, for an additional premium, be *extended to cover losses resulting from windstorm, riot, flood, or almost any other risk not covered under the collision policy.* Such additional coverage is called **comprehensive coverage.**

AUTOMOBILE LIABILITY

Automobile liability insurance is *issued to cover bodily injury to another person or damage to the property of another person.* If the driver of a car is found to be responsible for an accident, a very expensive lawsuit can result. The insurance company investigates claims made by the parties, defends the insured in lawsuits when required, and pays damages to the limit of the policy.

Standard policy limits are set by each state. For example, they may be $20,000 for death or injury to one person and $40,000 for death or injury to more than one person. The maximum that could be collected for one accident by one individual would be $20,000. Frequently, however, this is insufficient to pay the costs of damages; accordingly, for a higher premium, the automobile owner can get insurance for larger amounts, such as $50,000/$100,000 and $100,000/$200,000.

Automobile lawsuits have been so serious that most states now have financial responsibility laws. These laws specify minimum liability coverages automobile owners must carry unless they can prove they have sufficient financial resources to pay for the costs of accidents their negligence may cause.

Insurers have rendered judgments as high as several hundred thousand dollars in automobile liability cases, and in recent years the trend has been for jury awards to increase.

HOW INSURERS DETERMINE PREMIUMS

To arrive at equitable rates, automobile insurance companies classify drivers according to risk. Rates depend on a number of factors: usage of car (business or pleasure), city versus rural driving, age, sex, marital status, occupation, number of miles driven, and value or age of the auto itself. Insurance studies have shown measurable differences in the potential for accidents according to these factors. The rate structure thus reflects these risks. For example, since young drivers have a higher percentage of accidents than older drivers (see Figure 8–2), insurance companies must charge the young drivers higher premiums to compensate for the greater risk.

Some states have mandated insurance companies to adjust the premiums on the basis of the driver's record and not on the person's age, sex, or marital status. The legislation corrects the unfairness of

Figure 8–2 Age and Driving Accidents, 1979

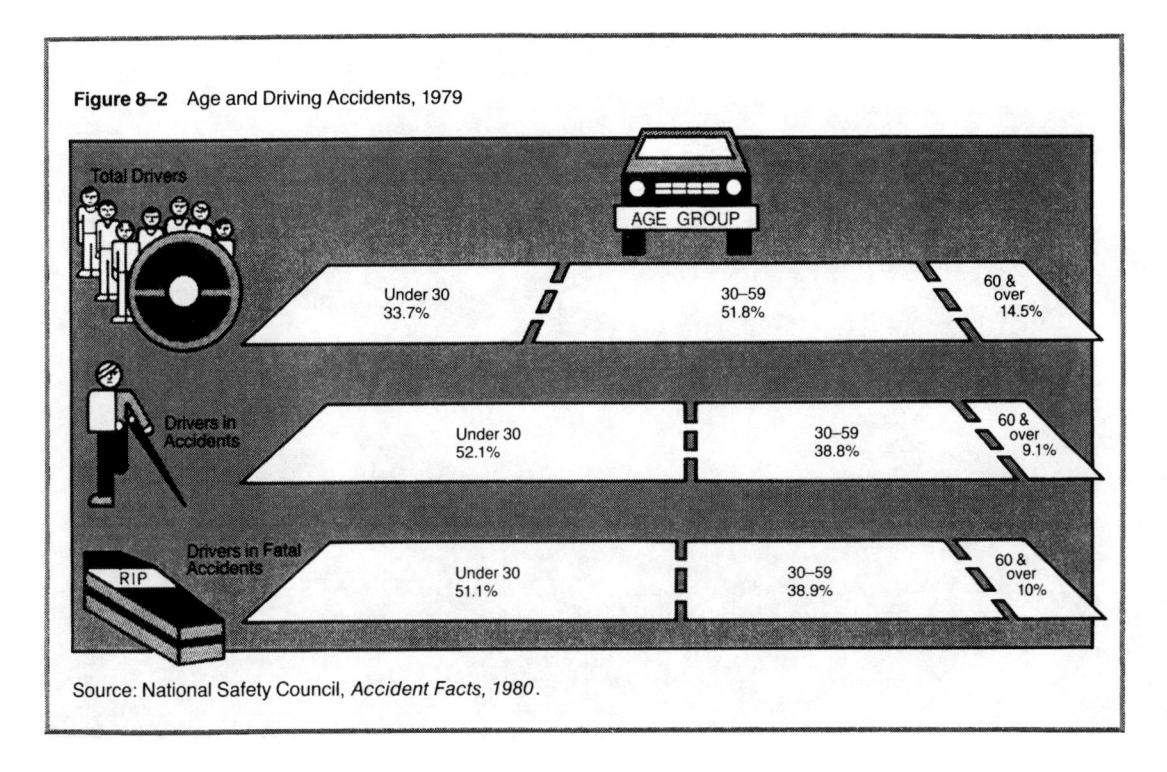

Total Drivers: Under 30 33.7%; 30–59 51.8%; 60 & over 14.5%

Drivers in Accidents: Under 30 52.1%; 30–59 38.8%; 60 & over 9.1%

Drivers in Fatal Accidents: Under 30 51.1%; 30–59 38.9%; 60 & over 10%

Source: National Safety Council, *Accident Facts, 1980.*

the higher premiums charged to *all* young drivers—particularly unmarried men up to age 25, who must pay the highest rates—regardless of their driving records, because a few in their age group are involved in the majority of accidents.

Most insurance companies, however, do offer premium reductions such as the following:

- Driver training—10 percent for drivers up to age 20 who have taken acceptable driving courses
- Good student—15 to 25 percent for young drivers whose school grades average B or better
- Multicar—15 percent for the second car insured on the same policy
- Bumper—10 percent on the collision premium for cars with safety bumpers

THE MOVE TOWARD NO-FAULT

Until recently, the costs of automobile accidents were always allocated on the basis of **fault,** or **tort, law.** Fault law *involves deter-*

Motorists carry insurance to protect themselves against loss through collision, fire and theft, and liability. Insurance companies base rates on risk factors of the insured, such as age, driving record, what the driver uses the car for, and occupation.

mining who is legally responsible for the losses suffered. Criticisms of the system are (1) it assumes that driver error is the only cause of accidents; (2) when the system pays off, it is inequitable—some are overpaid, others underpaid; (3) many automobile accident victims go unpaid entirely; (4) it is incredibly slow in paying benefits because of litigation, which may take four to five years; (5) it is inefficient and wasteful—legal and administrative costs are so high that, on the average, only 40 cents of every dollar paid goes to the victim; and (6) it encourages routine exaggeration of claims, with the result that premiums are unnecessarily high.

In 1970, Massachusetts enacted the nation's first **no-fault insurance** plan. The principle of the plan is that *the victim is entitled to receive specified benefits from his or her own insurance company without regard to fault.* Theoretically, no-fault systems result in lower insurance premiums because costly lawsuits to determine who is at fault in accident cases are eliminated. Thirty-nine states have now passed laws switching to variations of no-fault. However, laws differ in each state, and so there is a movement afoot for a national no-fault law. In cases of serious liability, such as death or disfigurement, cases still sometimes go to court in no-fault states.

Experience with no-fault so far is mixed. It is not clear whether the system results in lower insurance costs. Inflation makes it necessary for no-fault states to legislate premium increases periodically, so that no one knows whether no-fault is producing cost benefits. It can be said that no-fault is firmly entrenched in states that have it.

Liability Insurance

Liability insurance, also called **third-party insurance,** is *insurance against the chance of loss resulting from injury to another person or damage to that person's property.* Automobile liability insurance, discussed earlier, is the best known type of such insurance.

Under our legal system, one is liable for any damage done to another person through some negligent act. Exactly what constitutes negligence is usually a matter for the courts to decide. In general, "failure to exercise caution or prudence" is considered negligence, but this definition obviously leaves much room for legal interpretation.

Some of the more common instances in which liability may arise are the following: Restaurants may be liable for illness resulting from spoiled food. Farmers may be liable for accidents caused by livestock that wander onto a highway. Pharmacists who make a mistake in filling a prescription might be sued. Homeowners may be liable for injuries suffered by guests from accidents. Manufacturers may be liable if the public suffers injury from using their products. Contractors erecting a building may be liable for injury caused by materials that fall and strike someone. Doctors are sometimes held liable under malpractice charges.

There are many different liability coverages. Most of the policies have fairly uniform, standardized provisions. The insurance company agrees to indemnify the insured, up to the amount of loss or limit of the policy, for liability claims on the insured adjudged by the courts. Legal defense for the insured, when he or she is accused of causing a loss to another, is provided automatically by the insurance company.

To protect themselves against false claims, insurance companies maintain the National Casualty and Surety Underwriters Bureau, which, in addition to other activities, keeps a record of all liability claims.

Criminal Loss Protection

Criminal loss protection is *insurance against burglary* (forcible entry), *robbery* (taking of property by violence or threat of violence), *and theft* (stealing of property while it is unprotected). Businesses face many risks both from dishonest employees and from criminals.

Fidelity bonds *indemnify employers against theft, forgery, and embezzlement by employees.* They can be purchased for either individuals or groups. That is, the amount of coverage may be either the maximum amount of cash or property an employee may have access to at any time or the maximum amount that might be misappropriated by several employees acting in collusion.

Insurance policies are also available to protect businesses from other crime-related losses, including (1) robbery of money and securities inside company premises, (2) robbery of money and securities outside company premises, (3) depositor's forgery and use of counterfeit paper currency, and (4) burglary and robbery of store keepers.

Surety Bonds

Surety bonds *insure against the failure of a second party to fulfill an obligation.* They are used to insure the completion of contracts made with building contractors, suppliers, and other parties. If the second party does not carry out the agreement, the bonding company then pays the amount specified in the bond.

LIFE INSURANCE

All insurance contracts discussed thus far indemnify the insured only when some uncertain event happens. Life insurance, however, deals with a certain event: death.

Life insurance *provides financial benefits to the beneficiary—or to a company—when death of the insured occurs.* It should not be concluded, however, that one must "die to win" in life insurance. Many life insurance policies contain investment features that provide for the policyholder's retirement or that can be used (assuming a sufficient amount was purchased) to provide a monthly income for the family, to pay for the education of children, or to repay long-term loans such as home mortgages.

Figure 8–3 shows how the premium income of life insurance companies was used in 1982. (Figure 8–1, as you recall, shows how reserve funds were invested.) The largest operating expenses were for home- and field-office expenses and agents' commissions.

The Commissioners' 1980 Standard Ordinary Mortality Table shown in Table 8–2, which is the official table used by the insurance industry in determining premium rates, is an excellent example of the practical application to life insurance of the "law of large numbers." The table is based on actual death rates and shows how many deaths will occur at each age each year. At age 20, for example, 1.90 men and 1.05 women per 1,000 will die. The further life expectancy at this age is 52.37 and 57.04 years, respectively. The death rate gradually in-

Figure 8-3 How the Life Insurance Company Dollar Was Used, 1982

3.4¢ Taxes and dividends‡

15.7¢ Operating expenses†

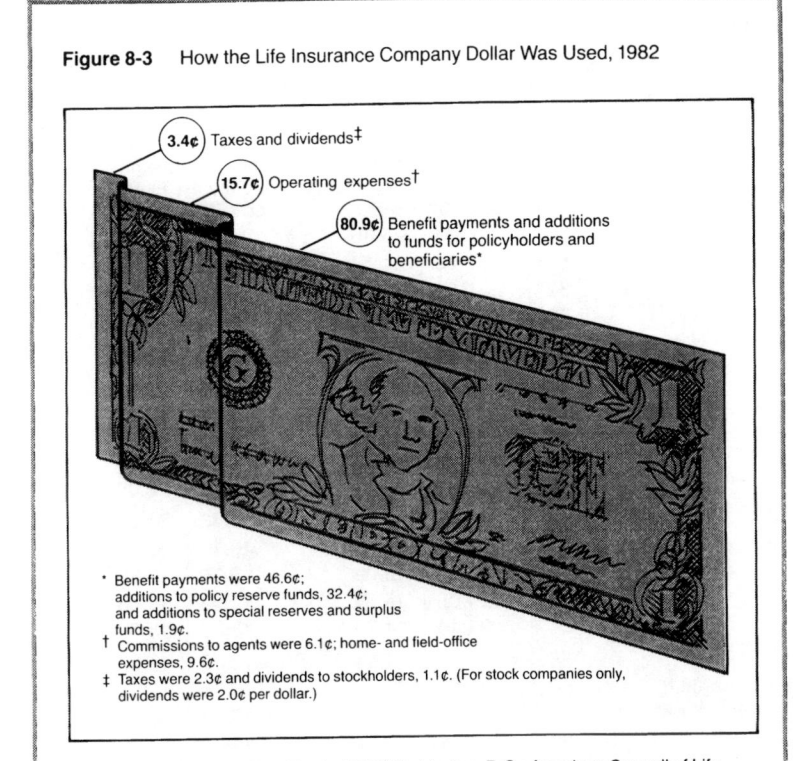

80.9¢ Benefit payments and additions to funds for policyholders and beneficiaries*

* Benefit payments were 46.6¢; additions to policy reserve funds, 32.4¢; and additions to special reserves and surplus funds, 1.9¢.
† Commissions to agents were 6.1¢; home- and field-office expenses, 9.6¢.
‡ Taxes were 2.3¢ and dividends to stockholders, 1.1¢. (For stock companies only, dividends were 2.0¢ per dollar.)

Source: *Life Insurance Fact Book, 1983* (Washington, D.C.; American Council of Life Insurance), p. 45.

creases as age advances. While a few individuals will live to be 100 or more, the table assumes that no one will reach this age, although the mortality table has been revised to reflect the increased life expectancy due to preventive medicine and the discovery of new cures for illness. Longer life expectancy will mean lower premiums at each age. In addition, some companies offer discounts on life policies according to a buyer's lifestyle, such as being a nonsmoker.

A simple illustration will indicate how a mortality table is used to compute life insurance premiums. Suppose that 100,000 college students, all 20 years old, decide to form an insurance company, with each student purchasing a $10,000 policy. Reference to Table 8–2 shows that an average of 1.48 persons (men and women combined) per 1,000 in this age group will die. So, 148 persons in the 100,000 student group can be expected to die during the first year. Claims will total $1,480,000, for which each of the 100,000 students would be

TABLE 8-2 1980 Standard Ordinary Life Insurance Mortality Table

COMMISSIONERS 1980 STANDARD ORDINARY

Age	Male Mortality Rate Per 1,000	Male Expectancy, Years	Female Mortality Rate Per 1,000	Female Expectancy, Years	Age	Male Mortality Rate Per 1,000	Male Expectancy, Years	Female Mortality Rate Per 1,000	Female Expectancy, Years
0	4.18	70.83	2.89	75.83	50	6.71	25.36	4.96	29.53
1	1.07	70.13	.87	75.04	51	7.30	24.52	5.31	28.67
2	.99	69.20	.81	74.11	52	7.96	23.70	5.70	27.82
3	.98	68.27	.79	73.17	53	8.71	22.89	6.15	26.98
4	.95	67.34	.77	72.23	54	9.56	22.08	6.61	26.14
5	.90	66.40	.76	71.28	55	10.47	21.29	7.09	25.31
6	.85	65.46	.73	70.34	56	11.46	20.51	7.57	24.49
7	.80	64.52	.72	69.39	57	12.49	19.74	8.03	23.67
8	.76	63.57	.70	68.44	58	13.59	18.99	8.47	22.86
9	.74	62.62	.69	67.48	59	14.77	18.24	8.94	22.05
10	.73	61.66	.68	66.53	60	16.08	17.51	9.47	21.25
11	.77	60.71	.69	65.58	61	17.54	16.79	10.18	20.44
12	.85	59.75	.72	64.62	62	19.19	16.08	10.96	19.65
13	.99	58.80	.75	63.67	63	21.06	15.38	12.02	18.86
14	1.15	57.86	.80	62.71	64	23.14	14.70	13.25	18.08
15	1.33	56.93	.85	61.76	65	25.42	14.04	14.59	17.32
16	1.51	56.00	.90	60.82	66	27.85	13.39	16.00	16.57
17	1.67	55.09	.95	59.87	67	30.44	12.76	17.43	15.83
18	1.78	54.18	.98	58.93	68	33.19	12.14	18.84	15.10
19	1.86	53.27	1.02	57.98	69	36.17	11.54	20.36	14.38
20	1.90	52.37	1.05	57.04	70	39.51	10.96	22.11	13.67
21	1.91	51.47	1.07	56.10	71	43.30	10.39	24.23	12.97
22	1.89	50.57	1.09	55.16	72	47.65	9.84	26.87	12.28
23	1.86	49.66	1.11	54.22	73	52.64	9.30	30.11	11.60

assessed $14.80 for the one-year policy if there were no costs involved.

The company, however, has other expenses beyond just paying claims—such as salaries, commissions, travel costs, printing and postage, office costs—and it must pay taxes and dividends. Let us assume these *operational costs* (called **loading**) are typical; if so, the company will spend $287,200 for operating expenses and $62,200 for taxes and dividends. These amounts must be added to the $1,480,000 needed to pay the claims. The company now must collect $1,829,400 in premiums, distributed evenly among the 100,000 policies. Thus each student must actually pay $18.29.

TABLE 8-2 (continued)

24	1.82	48.75	1.14	53.28	74	58.19	8.79	33.93	10.95
25	1.77	47.84	1.16	52.34	75	64.19	8.31	38.24	10.32
26	1.73	46.93	1.19	51.40	76	70.53	7.84	42.97	9.71
27	1.71	46.01	1.22	50.46	77	77.12	7.40	48.04	9.12
28	1.70	45.09	1.26	49.52	78	83.90	6.97	53.45	8.55
29	1.71	44.16	1.30	48.59	79	91.05	6.57	59.35	8.01
30	1.73	43.24	1.35	47.65	80	98.84	6.18	65.99	7.48
31	1.78	42.31	1.40	46.71	81	107.48	5.80	73.60	6.98
32	1.83	41.38	1.45	45.78	82	117.25	5.44	82.40	6.49
33	1.91	40.46	1.50	44.84	83	128.26	5.09	92.53	6.03
34	2.00	39.54	1.58	43.91	84	140.25	4.77	103.81	5.59
35	2.11	38.61	1.65	42.98	85	152.95	4.46	116.10	5.18
36	2.24	37.69	1.76	42.05	86	166.09	4.18	129.29	4.80
37	2.40	36.78	1.89	41.12	87	179.55	3.91	143.32	4.43
38	2.58	35.87	2.04	40.20	88	193.27	3.66	158.18	4.09
39	2.79	34.96	2.22	39.28	89	207.29	3.41	173.94	3.77
40	3.02	34.05	2.42	38.36	90	221.77	3.18	190.75	3.45
41	3.29	33.16	2.64	37.46	91	236.98	2.94	208.87	3.15
42	3.56	32.26	2.87	36.55	92	253.45	2.70	228.81	2.85
43	3.87	31.38	3.09	35.66	93	272.11	2.44	251.51	2.55
44	4.19	30.50	3.32	34.77	94	295.90	2.17	279.31	2.24
45	4.55	29.62	3.56	33.88	95	329.96	1.87	317.32	1.91
46	4.92	28.76	3.80	33.00	96	384.55	1.54	375.74	1.56
47	5.32	27.90	4.05	32.12	97	480.20	1.20	474.97	1.21
48	5.74	27.04	4.33	31.25	98	657.98	.84	655.85	.84
49	6.21	26.20	4.63	30.39	99	1000.00	.50	1000.00	.50

SOURCE: *1984 Life Rates & Data,* The National Underwriter Co. Cincinnati, Ohio, Copyright 1984 by The National Underwriter Company.

Based on experience of years 1970–1975.

The main types of life insurance are as follows.

Ordinary Life Policies

The **ordinary life policy,** also known as **whole-life** or **straight-life,** *requires the insured to pay premiums from the date of purchase until death of the insured.* The *amount of the premium is the same from one year to the next,* which is known as a **level-premium plan.**

In addition to providing death benefits, the ordinary life policy acts as a form of savings plan, in which the insurance company places part of each premium in an investment fund. This fund, which increases each year, is the cash surrender value of the policy. The insured can terminate the policy at any time and receive this amount in a lump sum or, alternatively, can borrow the amount from the insurance company.

Limited-Payment Policies

The **limited-payment policy** resembles the ordinary life policy in all respects but one. *The insured pays premiums not for an entire lifetime but for a specific number of years*—usually 20. Limited-payment policies appeal to people who prefer to complete payment for their insurance during the prime of life, when income is at its peak, rather than to continue to pay premiums after the beginning of old age. Further, policyholders know exactly how many payments they must make as with a loan, although, of course, the insurer does not pay the policy until the insured dies.

The cash surrender value of the policy also builds up more rapidly than for ordinary life policies, but this is because the premiums are higher. What an insurance company would expect to receive in premiums over a period of, say, 30 to 40 years would now be squeezed into a 20-year span. This is an important consideration for those who have heavy financial responsibilities, such as a large family or a large mortgage.

Group Policies

Group policies are the fastest growing type of life insurance protection. As its name indicates, this form of insurance is *sold on a group rather than an individual basis. Most is purchased by companies for their employees.* A master policy is issued for the group and each individual receives a certificate. Premiums are lower because many individuals are insured simultaneously and, often, because no health examinations are required.[4]

Sound personal advice, when buying insurance, is to try to buy insurance on a group plan through your employer or an organization of which you are a member, for that is where you will get the best value. Some group plans also provide coverage for the dependents of group members.

Term Policies

Term policies *pay a given sum of money to the insured's beneficiary if death occurs during the term of the policy.* No savings accu-

---

[4] A medical examination, paid for by the insurance company, is usually required when life insurance is sold to an individual.

mulate; the policy pays benefits only in the event of death. Most term insurance is sold in the form of group policies.

Term-insurance policies are generally issued for five to ten years and usually carry the stipulation that they can be renewed (at a higher premium) or that they can be converted into other types of policies if desired. Premiums on term insurance continue to rise in direct proportion to the buyer's age, in contrast to the ordinary life policy in which the premium is fixed. It should be noted that agents get higher commissions for selling ordinary life. Therefore there is greater incentive for an agent to sell modest amounts of ordinary life insurance even though the insured can purchase a larger term insurance policy for the same amount of money.

One type of term insurance is **credit life insurance,** which is *used to pay a debt if the borrower should die.* This way, both the lender and the borrower's family are protected. Of course the amount of coverage decreases as the loan is repaid. Life insurance companies sell this type of insurance through lenders such as banks, credit unions, small loan companies, and retailers.

Term insurance appeals to people who want the maximum amount of insurance protection at the lowest possible cost. Its main advantage lies in giving inexpensive temporary protection during times when greatest protection is needed—for example, when children are young or when a business is being started. The policy offers "pure protection"; no cash values are created.

PRIVATE HEALTH INSURANCE

The purpose of **health insurance** is to *pay the insured for expenses resulting from sickness and for lost earnings.* Many types of private health insurance plans are available, but in general they provide the following benefits:

1. Payment of all or part of medical, hospital, and surgical expenses

2. Loss-of-income payments for a certain period of time when the insured is unable to work

3. A specified sum for the loss of an eye, hand, foot, and so on

Like life insurance policies, health insurance can be purchased on an individual or a group basis, though more than 90 percent of all health insurance is written under group policies. The costs are greatly reduced for these group plans because the insurer doesn't need to process and administer the members' applications individually. For the remaining 10 percent of the health policies written—the individual plans—the cost for each individual can be prohibitive.

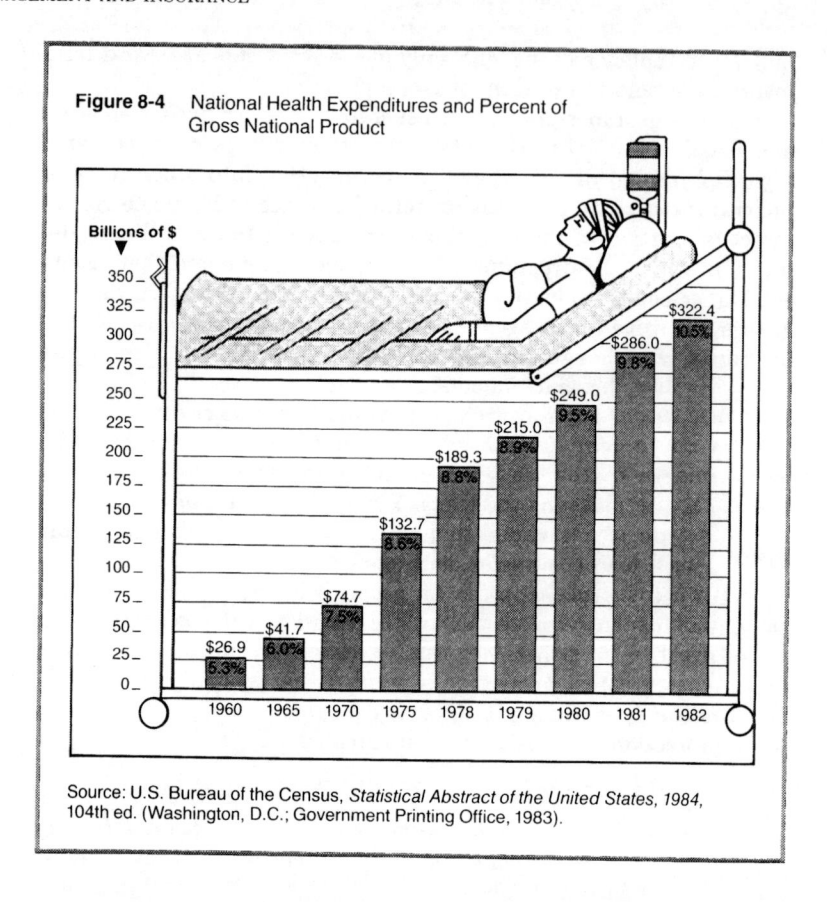

Figure 8-4 National Health Expenditures and Percent of Gross National Product

Billions of $

Year	Expenditure	Percent
1960	$26.9	5.3%
1965	$41.7	6.0%
1970	$74.7	7.5%
1975	$132.7	8.6%
1978	$189.3	8.8%
1979	$215.0	8.9%
1980	$249.0	9.5%
1981	$286.0	9.8%
1982	$322.4	10.5%

Source: U.S. Bureau of the Census, *Statistical Abstract of the United States, 1984*, 104th ed. (Washington, D.C.; Government Printing Office, 1983).

Americans spend more money for health insurance than all other forms of insurance combined. As shown in Figure 8–4, health expenditures in 1982 were greater than 10 percent of the nation's gross national product. About 58 percent of health care expenditures is paid for by private insurers, and the other 42 percent comes from government funds.

Health insurance plans are written in six categories:

Hospital Expense Insurance

Hospital expense insurance protects against the cost of hospital care resulting from illness or injury of the insured person.

Surgical Expense Insurance

Surgical expense insurance provides benefits toward the physician or surgeon's operating fees. Benefits may consist of scheduled amounts for each surgical procedure.

Private Health Insurance **233**

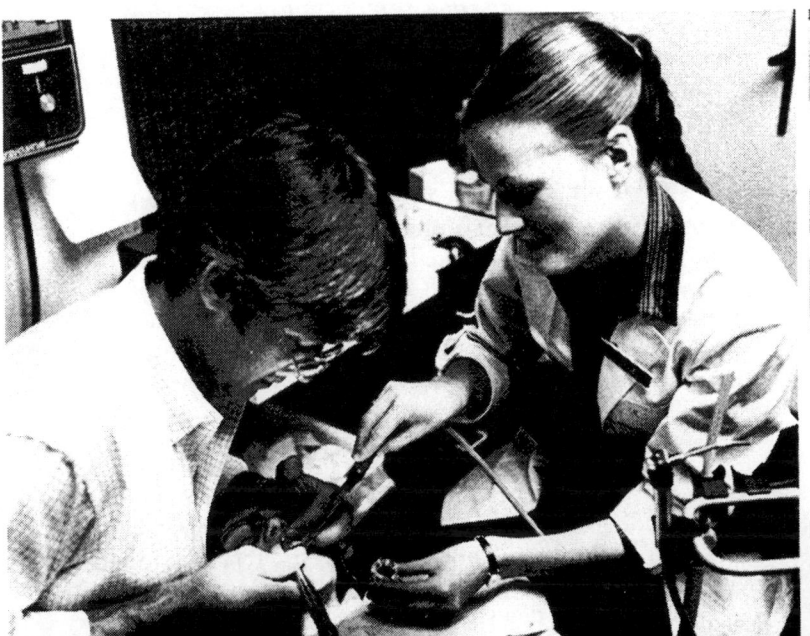

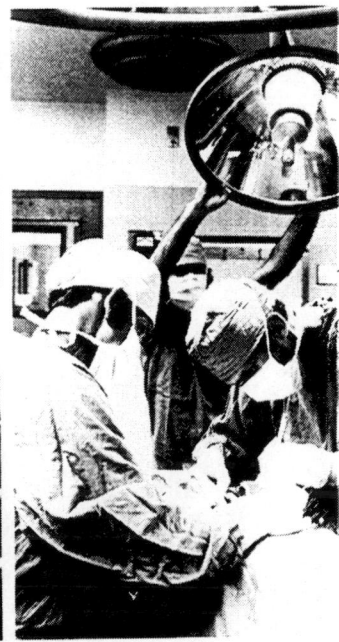

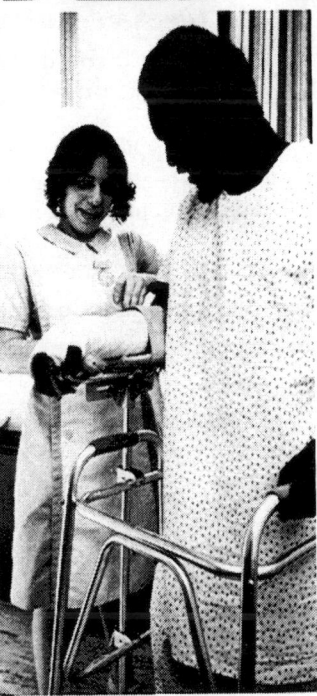

Private health insurance plans provide medical coverage for illness, surgery, accidents, and disability. Among the kinds of coverage are benefits for hospital, surgical, physician, major medical, and dental expense as well as disability income.

Physicians Expense Insurance

Physicians expense insurance *provides benefits toward the cost of such services as doctor's fees for nonsurgical care in a hospital, at home, or in a physician's office and for X-rays and laboratory tests performed outside the hospital.*

Major Medical Expense Insurance

Major medical expense insurance *finances the expense of major illness and injury, and the large benefit maximums ranging from $250,000 to no limit at all.* The insurance, above an initial deductible, reimburses the major part of all charges for hospital, doctor, private nurses, use of medical equipment, prescribed out-of-hospital treatment, and medicines. The insured person, as coinsurer, pays the remainder.

Dental Expense Insurance

Dental expense insurance *reimburses the insured for dental services* including oral examinations, fillings, extractions, inlays, bridgework, and dentures, as well as oral surgery, root canal therapy, and sometimes orthodontics. As with major medical coverage, the insured usually must pay a deductible each year.

Disability Income Expense

Disability income *provides benefits to replace income when an insured person is unable to work as a result of illness, injury, or disease.*

Table 8–3 shows the number of people covered by these six types of health insurance plans. Approximately five adults in six have some form of health insurance.

TABLE 8–3 Number of Persons with Health Insurance Protection by Type of Coverage, 1983

TYPE OF HEALTH INSURANCE	NUMBER OF PEOPLE COVERED (IN MILLIONS)
Hospital Expense	191.1
Surgical Expense	180.3
Physicians Expense	171.6
Major Medical Expense	160.9
Dental Expense	88.2
Disability Income Expense	83.1

SOURCE: *Source Book of Health Insurance Data, 1983–84* (Washington, D.C.: Health Insurance Association of America, 1985), 15.

Nonprofit Health Insurance Organizations

BLUE CROSS AND BLUE SHIELD PLANS

The Blue Cross and Blue Shield Associations and similar organizations provide much of the private health insurance. Blue Cross is an independent, nonprofit organization that provides hospital care benefits. Through a contract with member hospitals, it reimburses the hospital for covered services provided to the insured. Blue Shield complements Blue Cross by providing benefits for surgical and medical services performed by a physician. Independent plans run by labor unions, fraternal societies, and cooperatives also provide certain types of health insurance.

Table 8–4 compares these nonprofit plans with profit-seeking insurance companies and lists the premiums charged and the benefits paid. As you can see, the nonprofit organizations and the corporations paid their insureds about the same amounts in benefits, $42.5 billion versus $41.6 billion, respectively, but the nonprofit plans charged considerably less in premiums, $45.2 billion, than the profit-seeking companies, $49.0 billion.

TABLE 8–4   Premiums Charged by Private Health Insurers and Benefits Paid to Insureds (in billions of dollars)

	PREMIUMS CHARGED	BENEFITS PAID	BENEFITS AS A PERCENT OF PREMIUMS
Blue Cross/Blue Shield and other Nonprofit Plans	45.2	42.5	94.0
Profit-seeking Insurance Companies	49.0	41.6	84.9

SOURCE: *Source Book of Health Insurance Data, 1982–83* (Washington, D.C.: Health Insurance Association of America, 1983), 23, 27.

HEALTH MAINTENANCE ORGANIZATIONS

For more than a decade, medical costs have been increasing faster than the gross national product and the rate of inflation. A possible solution to this problem is the **health maintenance organization** (HMO), which has developed as another form of nonprofit health insurance organization. An **HMO** *provides a wide range of comprehensive health care services for a specified group at a fixed periodic payment.* A group of physicians and surgeons, and sometimes dentists and optometrists as well, furnish needed health services on a contractual basis. The insured will often have to pay no more than $10 for each office visit; the fixed payment covers the balance of the doctor's fee. The government, medical schools, hospitals, employers,

AMERICA'S REEMERGING CREATIVITY

Health Maintenance Organizations

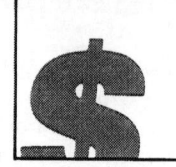

The HMO concept is not new. Its roots began in 1933 when a small group of doctors, organized by Dr. Sidney Garfield, provided health care for workers at a construction project in the Mojave Desert for five cents a day per worker. Industrialist Henry J. Kaiser asked Dr. Garfield to establish a similar program, which later became known as the Kaiser Foundation Health Plan, for Kaiser workers at other construction sites. The plan was opened to the public after World War II. Today, the Kaiser Foundation Health Plan has 27 hospitals, 85 clinics, and serves more than 4 million members.

Other group health plans sprang up in the 1930s and 1940s, usually in response to the needs of an organized group of people. Development was slow because medical ethics prevented advertising, thus limiting public awareness. Medical associations promoted passage of state laws that discouraged prepaid medicine. County medical societies refused membership to group health physicians and prevented them from gaining admission privileges at hospitals.

These roadblocks were removed in 1943 when the Supreme Court ruled that the actions were an unlawful restraint of trade. But the HMO idea did not catch on until the 1970s, when the government promoted the idea as a possible solution to rapidly rising health costs. As a result of a federal law enacted in 1973, many more people have an opportunity to choose between a prepaid plan (HMO) and the traditional fee-for-service practice. By 1981, a number of employees were required to offer a certified HMO (if one is available) as an option to the health insurance they provide.

The problems of fee-for-service practice are many: difficulty in finding satisfactory medical care, widely separated office locations, high cost, lack of communication among specialists treating the same patient, scattering of the patient's records in several locations, double payment by the patient having the same test performed by two doctors, physicians' lack of information regarding the previous treatment, and limited insurance coverage for outpatient and preventive services but rich reimbursement for hospitalization. Under these circumstances, the more services doctors provide, the more they earn—whether the patient really needs all of them or not.

An HMO addresses these problems. By joining an HMO, a member gains access to a team of doctors. The HMO guarantees around-the-clock medical care, 365 days a year. A primary-care doctor coordinates all of the patient's health care, including referral to specialists outside the organization if needed. The HMO team of doctors, laboratory technicians, and administrative staff work together in a central location. The main offices or clinics usually contain laboratories. In addition, many HMOs have treatment rooms for minor surgical procedures that might otherwise require hospitalization.

HMOs are viable alternatives for containing runaway health costs, both for the individual and the employer, and at the same time provide quality care consistent with the highest standard of medical practice.

Questions for Discussion

1. Would you consider joining an HMO? Why or why not?
2. Besides the growth in the number of HMOs, what other trends do you see emerging in the delivery of needed health services?

labor unions, consumer groups, insurance companies, and hospital medical plans often sponsor the HMOs.

The development of the health maintenance organization has caused a 10 percent reduction in the escalation of health costs. HMOs are the most efficient and economical delivery system of medical services, and they are growing in popularity. From 1972 to 1982, for instance, the number of HMOs increased from 39 to 377, and the number of subscribers increased from 3.5 million to 10.8 million. The accompanying box on "America's Reemerging Creativity" provides a history of the HMO.

PUBLIC OR SOCIAL INSURANCE: SOCIAL SECURITY

Over the years the government has been increasingly involved in providing insurance through the Social Security system. **Social insurance** programs established by the Social Security Act of 1935 *provide protection against wage loss resulting from old age, prolonged disability, or death, and protection against the cost of medical care during old age and disability.* The Social Security program, officially known as the Old-Age, Survivors, Disability, and Health Insurance program (or OASDHI), provides health, retirement, and disability coverages. An outline of each follows.

Health Insurance

The two main forms of government-sponsored health insurance are Medicare and Medicaid.

MEDICARE

Medicare *is a hospital insurance system and supplementary medical insurance for the aged* created by 1965 amendments to the Social Security Act and operated under provisions of the Act. In 1984, expenditures for Medicare were $64.4 billion.

MEDICAID

Medicaid *is a system of state public health assistance to persons, regardless of age, whose income and resources are insufficient to pay for health care.* The Social Security Act provides matching federal funds for financing state Medicaid programs. Expenditures in 1984 for Medicaid were $20.5 billion.

Other federal government health care programs include military personnel and their dependents, veterans' medical care, federal civilian employees, Indian Health Services, and worker's compensation medical care. The states pay for most of worker's compensation insurance which covers work-related injuries and benefits for dependents of workers who are killed because of their employment.

The cost of federal health insurance programs financed through taxes, like the cost of health care in general, is rising much faster than the gross national product and the rate of inflation. Reasons for the increase include: (a) increasing life expectancy resulting in more older people, (b) more costly and sophisticated medical technology, (c) more lenient interpretation of eligibility for government services, and (d) greater demand for the best possible health care.

Retirement, Disability, and Survivors Benefits

The normal retirement age under Social Security is 65, although a worker can retire at age 62 at reduced monthly benefits. The amount of benefits a person receives depends mainly on his or her years of covered employment, age, and average earnings over a period of years. Social Security benefits are adjusted to the cost of living so that a person's real income is unaffected by inflation.

RETIREMENT OR DISABILITY

If a worker is receiving **retirement** or **disability benefits**, monthly benefits also can be provided to his or her dependents as follows:

- Unmarried children under 18 (or under 19 if full-time high school students).
- Unmarried children 18 or over who were severely disabled before age 22 and who continue to be disabled.
- Wife or husband age 62 or over.
- Wife or husband under 62 if she or he is caring for a child under 16 (or disabled) who's getting a benefit based on the retired or disabled worker's earnings.

SURVIVORS

Monthly payments can be made to a deceased worker's dependents as follows:

- Unmarried children under 18 (or under 19 if full-time high school students).
- Unmarried son or daughter 18 or over who was severely disabled before age 22 and who continues to be disabled.
- Widow or widower age 60 or older.
- Widow or widower, or surviving divorced mother or father if caring for worker's child under 16 (or disabled) who is getting a benefit based on the earnings of the deceased worker.

- Widow or widower 50 or older who becomes disabled not later than seven years after the worker's death, or within seven years after mother's or father's benefits end.
- Dependent parents 62 or older.

In 1984, family benefits under Social Security exceeded approximately $1,400 per month.

How Social Security Is Financed

The employer and employee each pay an equal share of Social Security taxes, while self-employed persons must pay the entire assessed amount themselves. For example, for the years 1986–89, employers and employees will each pay 7.15 percent of the employee's income to Social Security on a maximum of $39,700 income; self-employed individuals for these years will pay 10 percent of their incomes up to the $39,700 maximum. This maximum income is refigured as income levels rise.

Death Benefit

Beneficiaries of a Social Security member who dies receive a one-time death benefit payment of $255.

Social Security in Perspective

Social Security is the nation's basic method of providing a continuing income when family earnings are reduced or stop because of retirement, disability, or death.

Social Security payments are not intended to replace all lost earnings. People should try to supplement Social Security payments with savings, pensions, investments, or other insurance.

Nine out of ten workers in the United States are earning protection under Social Security, and about one out of every six persons in the country receives monthly Social Security checks. Further, over 24 million people age 65 and over—nearly all of the nation's older population—have health insurance under Medicare. Another 3 million disabled people under 65 also have Medicare. In all, over 35 million people received Social Security checks in 1983, which means that almost every family has a stake in Social Security.

Unemployment Insurance

Enacted as part of the Social Security Act of 1935, **unemployment insurance** *guarantees people income for a period of time after becoming unemployed.* States individually determine the tax rate each employee must pay for this insurance. The national average is about 3 percent of the first $6,000 of wages earned each year. The state puts the collected money in the Unemployment Trust Fund of the United States and withdraws it as needed.

ISSUE FOR DEBATE

Is Social Security a Fair System for Providing Financial Security?

Legislation establishing the Social Security system was enacted in 1935 to help people with special hardships. Over the past half century, Social Security has become the nation's largest provider of both medical care and retirement benefits. Some feel the Social Security system is an excellent way to provide medical and retirement benefits. Others do not.

PROS

A large segment of the population cannot or will not purchase health insurance and will not provide for their retirement. Social Security is the only way to provide for these people.

Since costs of Social Security are met mainly through payroll deductions, most people do not miss the dollars they pay into the system.

Since virtually everyone is automatically covered by Social Security, costs of administering the system (loading costs) are very low. Under Social Security, there are no sales commission expenses, medical examinations to determine eligibility, or advertising expenses. Further, no profits need to be paid to investors.

The Social Security system is fair because all major changes must be approved by Congress, the elected representatives of all the people.

CONS

People now have the opportunity through **individual retirement accounts** (IRAs) *to use tax-free dollars to provide for their own retirement.*

Some people pay into the Social Security system many years. But, because they have no dependents or because of early death, they receive no benefits.

The great majority of people can obtain private health insurance and provide for their retirement. Those who choose not to should not expect society to take care of their health and retirement needs.

Young people can expect to pay into the system much more than they will receive in benefits. Employee and employer contributions now equal more than 14 percent of total payroll costs up to a maximum of over $5,000 per employee per year.

Questions

1. Do people age 20 to 40 tend to view the Social Security system differently than people age 40 to 60? Why or why not?
2. The maximum income per person on which Social Security deductions are made was $37,700 in 1984. Will this maximum likely be raised in the future? Why or why not?
3. What specific changes in the Social Security system might be made to make the system more equitable for younger people?

Most workers, including government personnel, are covered. Each state has different regulations governing benefits. But generally, if an employee is laid off and wishes to collect benefits, he or she must report to a state employment office to collect benefits and to show a willingness to accept employment. In most states the benefit that can be collected is 50 percent of the worker's average wages for the six months prior to becoming unemployed. The average maximum period for benefit payments is 26 weeks.

In 1983 approximately 87 million people were covered by unemployment insurance and $25 billion was paid to insured employees. Proponents of unemployment insurance claim that it helps stabilize the economy by guaranteeing income and reducing the miseries of unemployment. Opponents say it adds to the cost of doing business, creates more paperwork, and is frequently abused by people who don't really want to work more than is absolutely necessary.

Worker's Compensation

Worker's compensation laws *provide insurance protection in the event of work-connected injury or death.* Federal worker's compensation laws cover federal employees, private employees in the District of Columbia, and longshoremen and harbor workers. In addition, all states have some type of worker's compensation program. Most state programs exempt such employment as agriculture, domestic service, and casual labor; some exempt employers who have fewer than a specified number of employees. Under most laws, occupational diseases (or at least specified diseases) are compensable.

OTHER FORMS OF SOCIAL OR GOVERNMENT INSURANCE

Historically, when certain groups of people faced risks that private insurance companies would not insure, the government has stepped in with some form of insurance protection. The Federal Housing Administration, for example, insures many home mortgages. Bank deposits are insured by the Federal Deposit Insurance Corporation, and some government programs insure against floods, droughts, windstorms, and other "acts of God."

Sometimes government insurance is in the form of guarantees. For example, the only way some students may finance their education is through bank loans whose repayment is guaranteed by a government agency. The financial institution makes the student loan at comparatively low interest rates because the government guarantees or insures its repayment. The student loan program has been controversial, however, because a considerable number of students have failed to repay their loans after graduation.

WHAT'S NEW IN THE INSURANCE FIELD?

Viewed by those unfamiliar with it, insurance may seem boring and unchanging. But as with most things in business, there are actually frequent changes and discernible trends, such as those that follow.

The Corporate Risk Manager

Within the past few years, risk management at company headquarters has markedly changed character and has become more visible. The shock of massive product recalls, the kidnapping of top officials in foreign countries, product liability, and **class action suits**[5] have helped elevate the risk function to a top management position.

In the past, the head of risk management was usually someone with a strong insurance and perhaps accounting background, who headed a small department that most people in the company never heard about. Activities of the department were limited mainly to dealing with outside insurers.

Today the hazards of doing business have multiplied to a point where the risk manager's duties range from devising methods to combat vandalism to advising on whether to continue operations in unstable foreign countries. Thus the risk manager is someone with a broad background and the title of vice-president, who reports to the chief financial officer and has ready access to the CEO. The risk manager's job also includes keeping customer goodwill in mind: It is easy to overdo protection at the risk of creating customer illwill (see Figure 8–5).

---

[5]Lawsuits in which an award to a single consumer results in awards to all similarly injured parties.

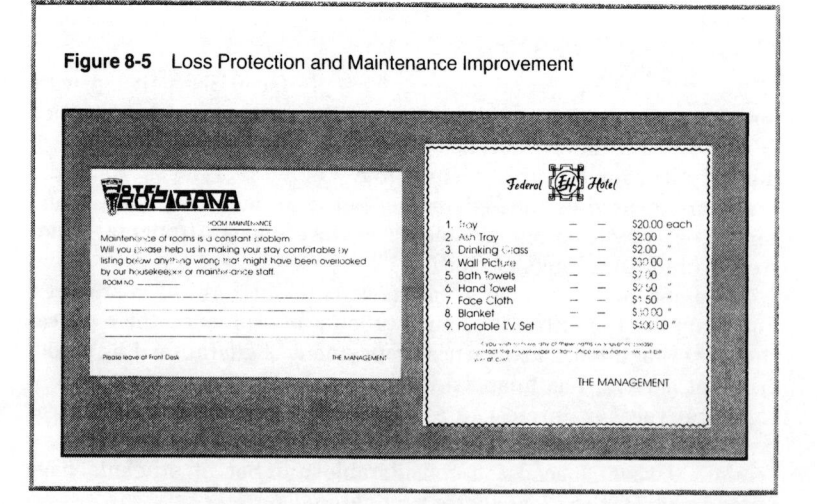

Figure 8-5 Loss Protection and Maintenance Improvement

The Growth of Self-Insurance

To protect the company's assets, the risk manager now has the company retain a larger share of risks, instead of transferring them to commercial insurers. Indeed, the risk manager acts more and more in the role of the **underwriter** *(the insurance company or agent that writes the insurance, or the insurance company employee who determines the acceptability of risks, the premium, and so on).* One reason for this is that inflation, the broader concepts of corporate liability, and high court awards have raised the price of insurance to unacceptable levels.

To self-insure, the risk manager must determine the financial capacities of the company and consider all feasible methods that could be used to protect it. Tax consequences also are involved and must be evaluated because insurance as a business expense is fully deductible from income taxes, whereas funds set aside as reserves may not be. As part of this self-insurance trend, the risk manager assumes many of the functions of an insurance company. These include such things as responsibility for loss control, claims negotiating, and even salvage.

Space Insurance

A newly developed and growing type of coverage is space insurance. By 1978, there were already 45 commercial communications satellites launched, using 13 different insurance programs.

The exciting new space shuttle is a major change in the concept of space vehicles (see "America's Reemerging Creativity," page 586). Instead of using one-time, throwaway vehicles, continuing-use vehicles are now being developed. The focus is now on the economics of space—the greatest number of launches for the cheapest price. This opens an era of routine commercial use of space, where multiple payloads are regularly lifted into orbit by shuttles.

The future of American industry in space is as limitless as space. Yet without insurance, the program could never get off the ground, for who would invest in a satellite worth millions of dollars if it were shot into space without insurance?

> Service companies can't allow the risk management function to become overzealous or customers will be offended. For example, no one wants to stay at a hotel that treats you as a dishonest person. The positive must at least outweigh the negative. In the service industry, constant problems are created by customer abuses and employee deficiencies, as these examples from the hotel industry illustrate. What do you think of management's attempts to solve each problem?

SUMMARY

- A wide variety of risks face businesses and individuals. Four ways of meeting risks are to reduce the chance of loss, practice good management, self-insure, and transfer risk to insurance carriers.

- For a risk to be insurable, (1) the chance of loss must be predictable with reasonable accuracy, (2) it must concern possible financial loss, (3) the risk must be "pure" rather than speculative, (4) the applicant must have an insurable interest in the property being insured, and (5) the applicant must not be a moral hazard.

- In terms of ownership, insurance companies are classified as either stock companies (owned by investors) or mutual companies (owned by policyholders).

SUMMARY

- Fire insurance policies are written on a basic contract called the "standard policy." Rates vary according to the risk involved.
- Marine insurance is divided into two broad categories: ocean marine and inland marine.
- Automobile insurance is written to protect owners against collision, fire and theft, and liability. A number of states have enacted no-fault insurance laws.
- Liability insurance is used to protect the policyholder for damage done to another person through some negligent act.
- Criminal loss protection is used to protect against burglary, robbery, theft, embezzlement, forgery, and similar tasks.
- Surety bonds protect against failure of a second party to fulfill a contractual obligation.
- Most forms of life insurance provide benefits to beneficiaries when the insured dies. Policies may also be written to pay the insured upon reaching a certain age.
- Health insurance pays the insured for expenses resulting from illness. It may also be written to reimburse the individual for lost earnings.
- Social insurance is provided by the government through three main programs: Social Security, unemployment insurance, and worker's compensation.
- There are several new trends in the insurance field: increasing use of corporate risk managers, growth of self-insurance, and space insurance.

KEY TERMS YOU SHOULD KNOW

actuary
automobile insurance
automobile liability insurance
business risk
class action suit
coinsurance clause
collision insurance
comprehensive coverage
credit life insurance
criminal loss protection
deductible coverage insurance
dental expense insurance
disability benefits
disability income
fault law
fidelity bond
fire-and-theft coverage
fire insurance
full-coverage insurance
group policy
health insurance
health maintenance organization
hospital expense insurance
individual retirement account
inland marine insurance
inland transportation insurance
insurable interest
insurable risk
insurance
law of large numbers
level-premium plan
liability insurance
life insurance
limited-payment policy
loading
major medical expense insurance
marine insurance
Medicaid
Medicare
moral hazard
mutual
no-fault insurance
ocean marine insurance
ordinary life policy
physicians expense insurance
pure risk
reserve
retirement benefits
rider
self-insurance
social insurance
speculative risk
standard policy
stock company
suicide clause
surety bond
surgical expense insurance
term policy
underwriter
unemployment insurance
worker's compensation

QUESTIONS FOR REVIEW

1. What are examples of ways to reduce risk through (a) reducing or eliminating the chance of loss, (b) good management, (c) self-insurance, and (d) insurance?
2. What is the law of large numbers? How does it work? Why is the law essential to the insurance industry?
3. What conditions must be present for a risk to be insurable?
4. What is the different between a pure risk and a speculative risk?
5. How do mutual insurance companies and stock insurance companies differ?
6. What is fire insurance? What is the coinsurance clause?
7. Why do fire insurance claims increase during economic recessions?
8. How does ocean marine insurance differ from inland marine insurance?
9. Automobile insurance protects its insured against what kinds of losses?
10. Why is liability insurance often called third-party insurance?
11. What protection do fidelity bonds provide? Surety bonds?
12. Explain ordinary life insurance. Limited payment policies. Group policies. Term policies.
13. What is health insurance?
14. What is social government insurance? How does Medicare differ from Medicaid?
15. Explain risk management.

QUESTIONS FOR DISCUSSION

1. Choose a business you have some interest in starting. Then make a list of insurable and noninsurable risks the business may face. What do the two lists tell you about the importance of insurance as a way to meet risks? Of the role of reducing the chance of loss and of good management in dealing with risk?
2. In 1984 about 78 percent of all accidents involved improper driving. Excessive speed was a factor in about 30 percent of all fatal accidents and 17 percent of all accidents. About 64 percent of fatal accidents involved drinking drivers.
   a. Based on these facts, what actions do you feel lawmakers shoud take?
   b. How would a reduction in automobile accidents affect the cost of automobile operation?
3. Life insurance companies pay out only slightly more than 78 percent of premiums collected as benefits. Does this indicate that they are charging too much for premiums? Explain.
4. One partial solution to the problem of funding Social Security is allowing—and encouraging—employees to continue working after reaching age 65. People who work after age 65 will receive fewer Social Security benefits and thereby strengthen the system. Many corporations have already advanced their compulsory retirement age from 65 to 70. Do you think it is a good idea to permit people to work as long as they are physically and mentally competent? Why or why not?

CASE STUDY

Is Self-Insurance a Good Idea?

Advanced Technology, Inc., produces electrical components mainly for electrical utilities. The company employs 2,500 people in two divisions, one in California and the other in New York. In reviewing last year's expenditures, Si Elliot, company president, is surprised at the sharp increase in health insurance costs. Si decides to call in Jane Thurston, financial vice-president, and Keith Robbins, head of personnel, to discuss the matter.

Si: I notice that health insurance costs last year were up 19 percent over the previous year's. Why? Did we file a lot more claims?

Keith: Actually, the number of claims was down 2 percent. The reason for the increase was a jump in insurance premiums.

S: Well, these costs seem out of line. I think we should ask some other carriers to bid on our account.

Jane: Before we do that, may I suggest another approach to the problem?

S: Sure. All I want to see us do is get health care costs under better control.

J: I think we may be large enough to self-insure. We could set aside a reserve each month and use it to pay claims.

S: But we're in the component business, not health insurance.

J: I know. But it's not that complicated. And we already have several people in personnel who work with the insurance company.

K: Jane's right. We have to supply the insurance company with a lot of data about new employees, retirements, and various other changes.

S: How would we proceed? I don't want us to make a major blunder.

J: Step one would be to retain an actuarial firm. We have all the information in the computer it would be likely to need—age, sex, medical history—those sorts of things. The company could tell us whether self-insuring our health coverage would work.

S: But what would happen if we had several huge claims? We have no reserves.

J: The answer to that is to purchase a catastrophic policy to cover the very large claims—say $200,000 and up. Since claims of that size are very unusual, the cost of the policy would be low.

S: Give me a few days to think about it.

(A few days later, Si calls another meeting.)

S: The more I think about the idea of self-insuring our health care program, the better I like it.

K: Same here. I was amazed when I analyzed how much administrative support we give the carrier.

J: And keep in mind that the insurance company makes a profit off our business. In effect we would cut out a middleman.

S: OK. Jane, go ahead and authorize the best actuarial firm to make the study. And tell them to broaden the study to determine if we could also self-insure our life insurance coverage at the same time.

Questions

1. Why is the advice of an actuarial firm needed to avoid making a major mistake?
2. What other insurance coverages should Advanced Technology consider self-insuring? Explain.

EVOLUTION OF A BUSINESS

Reducing Risk, the Eternal Worry

In delegating responsibilities, it was decided that Sara, because of her accounting background, would be in charge of matters related to insurance. Sara spent several evenings with a Mr. Karcher, a representative of a large insurance agency. From the outset she was impressed that her area of responsibility was much more complicated and involved than she had ever suspected. Consider one conversation she had with Karcher:

Sara: So our biggest and most costly area of concern is customer liability insurance.

Karcher: That's right. As a travel agency, you're theoretically responsible for everything related to your clients' safety and well-being.

Sara: That's a frightening responsibility when you think of all the possible things that can happen on tours. Recently I've been working to set up a two-week package tour to Mexico. There are so many things to check out. For example, we're offering a morning boat trip to some islands in Acapulco Bay. We were about to sign up a particular boat operator but then found out his boat had only 40 life jackets for 60 passengers. Also, his reserve boat, in case anything went wrong with the first one, was only big enough to hold 35 people. I finally found an operator who had enough preservers and fire fighting equipment. He also has licensed equipment and operators, and has liability coverage of his own in a sound Mexican company.

Karcher: I suppose it's also complicated to arrange for the protection of your clients' property.

Sara: Right. We've had the usual hassles trying to find reliable, bonded agents to handle baggage at transfer points to hotels and terminals. There's nothing that spoils a trip more than losing someone's bags.

Karcher: Except maybe rain.

Sara: That's for sure! I wish rain was something we could insure against. Just let it rain for a couple of days when outdoor sightseeing is planned and see what happens to the morale of a group of 60 people who are beginning to get on each other's nerves. There's always the problem of planning something else in case it rains.

Questions

1. What are the various kinds of risk that Sara has to be concerned about? Which are insurable and which are not?
2. Why is it crucial for Sara to consider the morale of the people who sign up for tours?
3. What kinds of things can she do both to reduce risks and to assure customer satisfaction?

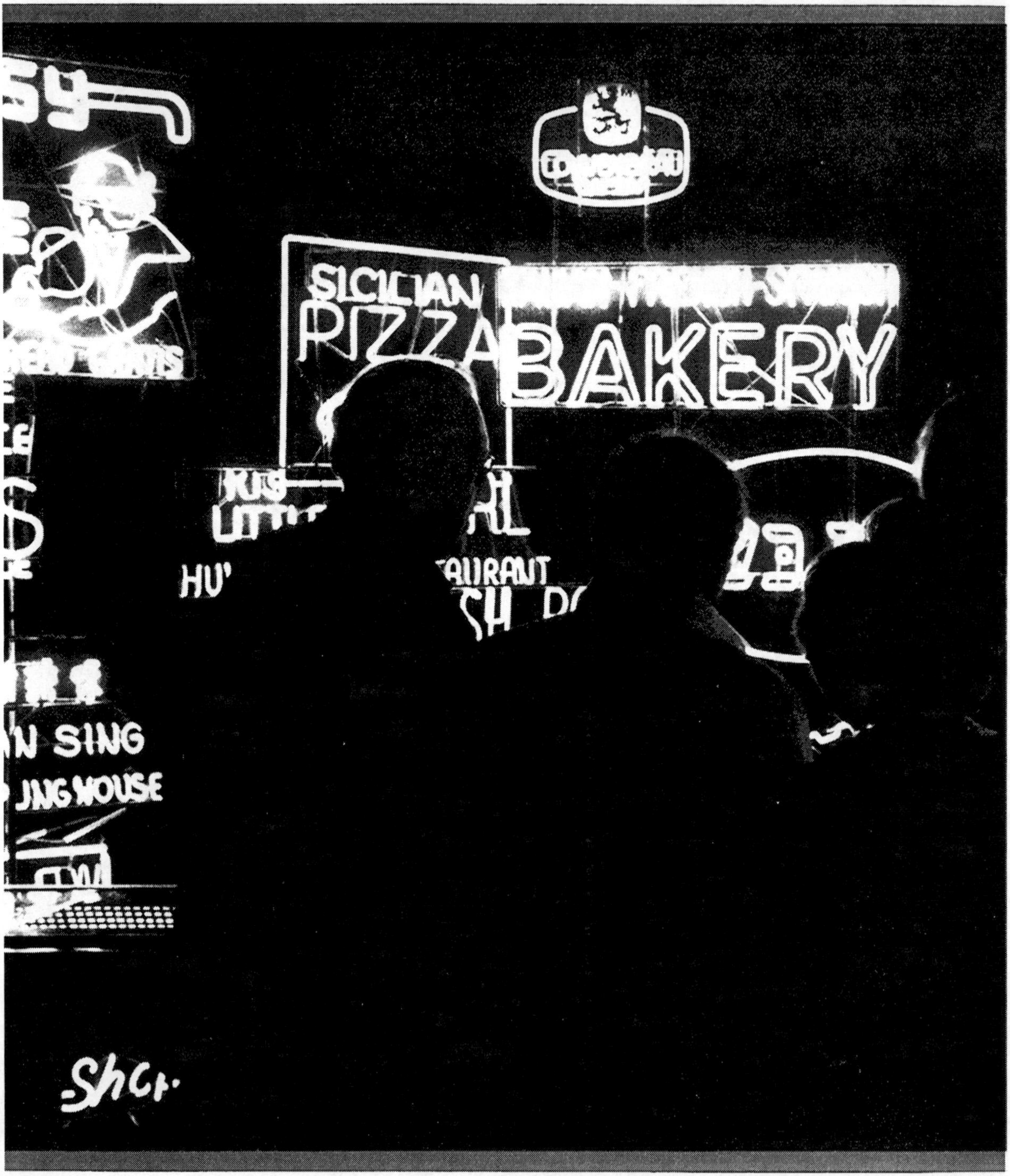
SICILIAN
PIZZA
BAKERY
N SING

GETTING PRODUCTS TO CONSUMERS

9 AN OVERVIEW OF MARKETING

10 THE CONSUMER: DEMOGRAPHICS, INCOME, AND MOTIVATION

11 PRODUCTS, PACKAGING, AND PRICING

12 MARKETING COMMUNICATIONS: SELLING, ADVERTISING, PROMOTION, AND PUBLIC RELATIONS

13 PHYSICAL ELEMENTS OF BUSINESS

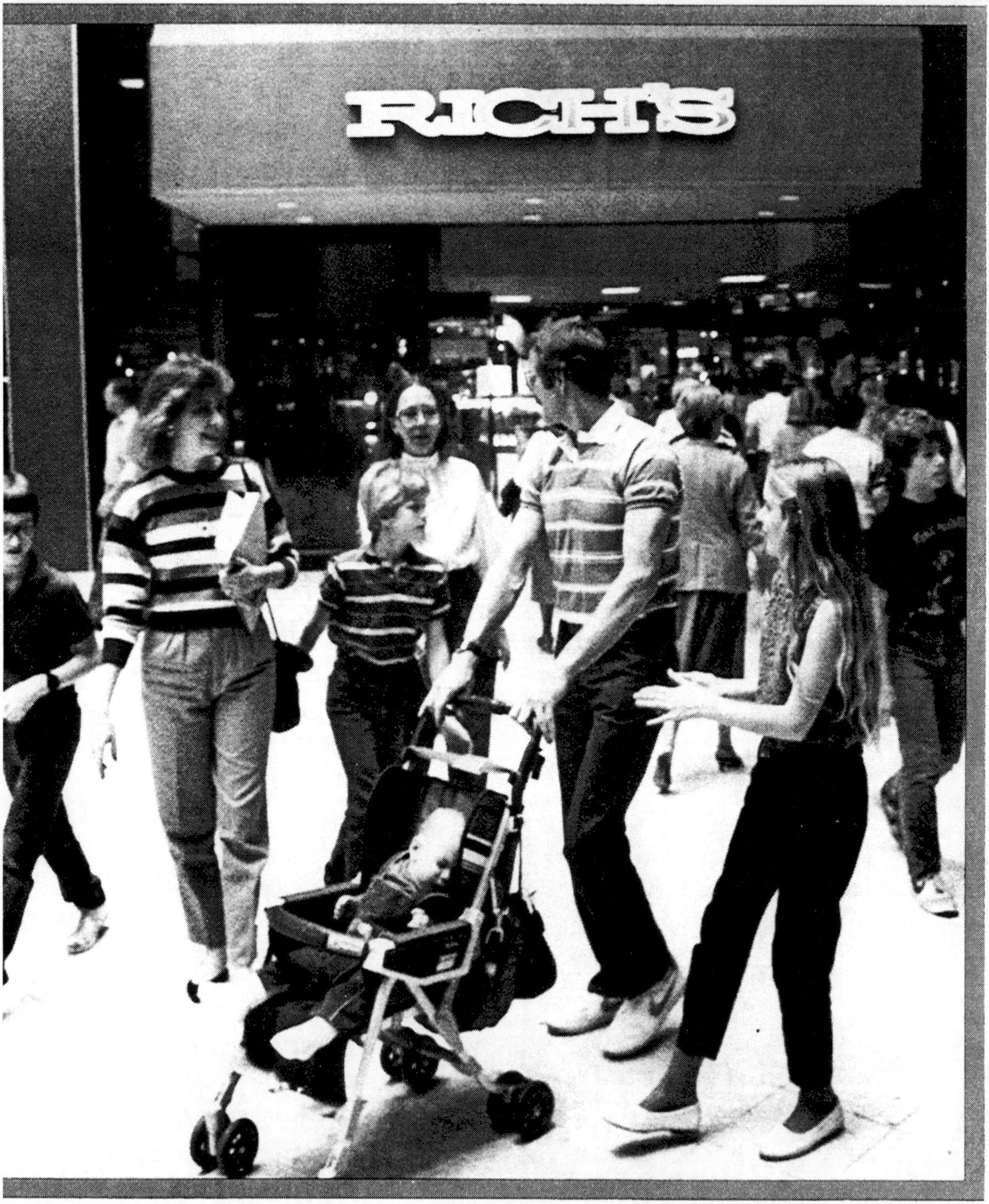
RICH'S

AN OVERVIEW OF MARKETING
Triggering the Sale

READ THIS CHAPTER SO YOU CAN:

Appreciate the importance of marketing to society and business.

Define marketing and describe what it does.

Explain the four Ps that make up the marketing mix.

Discuss the marketing concept and the four steps used to implement it.

Explain the differences between ultimate consumers and industrial consumers.

Understand distribution channels and what factors determine their length.

Define retailing and classify retailers by ownership and kind of business.

Explain how retailers combine efforts to increase profitability of individual stores.

Discuss non-store retailing.

Define wholesaling, explain its importance, and classify wholesalers by methods of operation.

Compare marketing of services with marketing of tangible products.

Marketing is expensive. An average of more than 50 cents out of every dollar we spend goes to pay for selling, advertising, packaging, wholesaling, retailing, transportation, and other marketing activities.

Marketing provides employment. More people work in marketing than in any other activity. Retailing and wholesaling employ more than 20 million people. Marketing of services—intangible products—employs another 20 million. And millions more have marketing jobs in the transportation, banking, insurance, and production industries.

Marketing is informative. It is our main source of knowledge about products and services. Through advertising, marketing people inform us about what to eat, drink, wear, and drive. Marketing suggests where we should spend our money, go on vacation, find a place to live, and even be buried.

Marketing is conspicuous. Retail stores line the thoroughfares of small towns and big cities. Large combinations of retail stores and service businesses called shopping centers cluster where major interstate highways intersect. Wholesale distribution centers locate where interstate highways and railroads meet. Daily we see trucks carrying products from manufacturers to retailers, and billboards seem to be everywhere.

Marketing does even more. It facilitates social interaction. Many people visit stores every day not only to buy products but to mingle with other people and perhaps share a few minutes of conversation. Some sociologists say shopping is both a major form of recreation and a cure for boredom. For millions, the real world is the marketplace.

> *"We shouldn't wait for a client to ask us about a problem or a development; we want to anticipate—not just react after the fact."*
>
> RAY GROVES

WHAT IS MARKETING?

The term **marketing** refers to *business activities that involve the movement of goods and services from producers to consumers.* Marketing includes not only physically transporting goods to where they are needed, but also determining what consumers want and seeking to satisfy those wants by providing appropriate products or services.

Sometimes people debate "Which is more important: marketing (selling) or production (engineering)?" While this argument raises some interesting points, it is impossible to resolve. It's like trying to decide which is more vital in football, offense or defense.

We need highly skilled engineers to design an automated production system, and we need highly skilled sales representatives to sell products and service the system. Ideally, engineering and marketing departments work together from the moment a new product is conceived until consumers use the product—and, indeed, even after that, to oversee the product's continued quality and salability and its possible improvement.

WHY IS MARKETING IMPORTANT?
Whether viewed from the economy as a whole or from the standpoint of an individual business, marketing is very significant.

Half Your Dollars Go for Marketing!
When we add all the marketing costs of producers, wholesalers, retailers, transportation companies, and advertising agencies together, they account for about 50 percent of the price consumers pay for products. A typical full-service department store spends 55 to 60 cents of each consumer's dollar to pay for the goods it retails. The remaining 40 to 45 cents pay for marketing. The manufacturers and wholesalers who sell merchandise to the department store also incur marketing expenses, ranging from 10 to 25 cents of each dollar they receive.

Over Two Million Businesses Are Directly Involved
All businesses in the United States are involved in some way with marketing. And in 1984 approximately 1.6 million retailers and 301,000 wholesalers—as well as other businesses, such as advertising agencies and transportation companies performed marketing functions exclusively.

Nonprofit Organizations Must Also Market
Marketing is also important for nonprofit organizations. While our discussion of marketing will focus on how profit-seeking enterprises practice marketing, nonprofit organizations also market their services. All organizations have "products" or services they want to deliver to certain "markets," and they employ a variety of marketing techniques to persuade people to accept their product or service. We discuss marketing by nonprofit organizations in Chapter 22.

Marketing Introduces New Products and Services
Marketing introduces new products and services to our economy. It helps to modify goods and services to suit constantly changing consumer tastes. Without an intelligent and aggressive marketing process, many of the products we enjoy would probably not be available.

Marketing Creates Demand
American businesses attempt to create demand in order to persuade people to purchase goods and services. Stimulation of demand is a

key not only to consumption but also to income and employment. Consider what happens when just one family buys a new television set. The family provides income directly to the salesperson (who gets a commission), to the retailer (who earns a profit), and to the manufacturer (who also makes a profit). The retailer and manufacturer stay in business and can continue to provide employment.

In addition, many other individuals and companies benefit indirectly from this marketing transaction—suppliers of components to the television manufacturer, transportation companies that handle the shipping of parts and finished products, owners of warehouses, advertising agencies, merchants who sell to the employees of the television manufacturer, and so on.

Although an individual purchase of a television set may not seem important to a large retailer or to the various indirect beneficiaries, the aggregate sales for all products are very important indeed. High-level prosperity and high-level consumption go hand-in-hand.

Marketing Creates Place, Time, and Possession Utilities

Oranges in Florida and automobiles in Detroit receive **form utility,** or *physical structure and properties people want,* from orange growers and car makers. But marketing organizations give these and countless other products **place utility** (make *products available where consumers want them*), **time utility** (make *products available when people want them*), and **possession utility** (make *ownership of products possible*).

Marketing Generates a Firm's Revenue

Over a period of time a firm must take in at least as much in revenues as it spends doing business. Inadequate sales, for whatever reason—bad management, recession, competition, and so on—are the basic cause. Effective marketing ensures that revenues are adequate to cover all expenses and to yield a profit.

All Businesses Must Engage in Marketing

All businesses market something. That "something" is a product, and may be as tangible as an airplane or as intangible as a vacation. Banks market financial services, insurance companies market insurance, consulting firms market advice, and motion picture companies market entertainment.

The "product" in marketing is a broad concept. It is the total package of benefits that customers receive when making purchases. In the case of tangibles, this includes delivery, warranties, credit terms, service facilities, and suggestions for using the product. In the case of intangibles, the package of benefits includes prompt and helpful service in handling claims (insurance); maintenance of an investor's portfolio of investments (stockbroker); or provision of airport layout maps, alternative menus, and adequate nonsmoking seating arrangements (airlines).

The product varies widely according to the type of customer. When the H. J. Heinz Company packages, delivers, and sells catsup for institutional use—to hospitals, restaurants, hotels, prisons, schools, and nursing homes—its product package is quite different from that of catsup bottles for home use.

It is the marketer's challenging job to think of the whole set of benefits that influence the customer's buying decision. An airline can fly passengers on time from one city to another yet lose out to a competitor because of poor baggage handling, or having poorly trained personnel at service desks.

THE FOUR Ps MAKE UP THE MARKETING MIX

A convenient way to study—and practice—marketing is to divide the decision variables into four Ps: product, place, price, and promotion. *The combination of the four Ps* forms the **marketing mix,** whose purpose is *to satisfy consumer demands.* Using the four Ps, a manufacturer of athletic shoes, for example, would make decisions such as:

- What kinds of shoes—tennis, running, soccer, and so on—should we make? (*product decision*)
- Where should we sell the shoes—sporting goods stores, discount houses, and so on? (*place decision*)
- Should we price our shoes above, at, or below the competition's? (*price decision*)
- How should we tell consumers about our shoes—radio, TV, magazines, and so forth? What features should we stress? (*promotion decisions*)

The marketing mix both simplifies decision making and results in better marketing plans, especially in conjunction with the marketing concept.

WHAT IS THE MARKETING CONCEPT?

For many years American businesses have operated under the **marketing concept,** *an approach by which producers consider consumer preferences before they design or manufacture the product.* Once industry could take mass production for granted, it could change the focus of its attention from producing what was adequate for most people to producing what was specifically desirable to meet

CONTEMPORARY ISSUE

The Four Ps in Practice: *Pollo*

The Business Week *article on* pollo *illustrates the importance of product, price, place, and promotion in marketing a new fast food concept.*

Just when it seemed that U.S. fast-food engineers had devised every possible menu "concept," a dish that originated in Mexico is stirring the enthusiasm of diners and merchandisers alike. It is spicy char-broiled *pollo* (Spanish for chicken). Marinated, splayed flat, and cooked on huge grills without breading or oil, *pollo* is seen by its backers as the Volvo of fast food: a fresh, wholesome dish—the American Heart Assn. endorses it for its low cholesterol content—that will appeal to the educated middle class. At least four companies are hatching plans for national fast-*pollo* chains.

Conventional fast-chicken chains refuse to worry. "It's a tiny, tiny segment," sniffs a Kentucky Fried Chicken official. "We don't see it becoming a major factor." He says KFC tested a similar Mexican-style chicken in Los Angeles last year and found little market appeal.

But *pollo* backers call this sour grapes. KFC stores, they say, lack room for *pollo* grills. As consumers grow more health-conscious, "that word 'Fried' in KFC's name is really going to hurt them," predicts a *pollo* chain executive. KFC is rumored to be working on a baked "light" chicken product. But KFC's biggest rival, Church's Fried Chicken Inc., has experimented with an all-*pollo* outlet, and its new growth-oriented management could jump into this market.

The top *pollo* chain is El Pollo Loco—"The Crazy Chicken"—the U.S. offshoot of a company by the same name that developed the concept nine years ago [1975] in Mexico, where it has 92 outlets. It opened stores in Hispanic areas of Los Angeles starting in 1980. They were so successful that more than 200 local imitators have cropped up, with such names as El Pollo Rico, El Rey Pollo, and El Pollo Mejor.

POLLO NETWORK. Last year, Denny's Inc., the coffee shop chain, bought El Pollo Loco's 20 Los Angeles stores. Now, Denny's is switching from *barrio* storefronts to classic suburban fast-fooderies. It unveiled its prototype restaurant in early November: a $400,000 tiled-roof unit with 60 seats and drive-up windows. Starting in the Southwest, Denny's hopes to build a national network of 500 outlets in five years. Next year, it will double its 24 California stores and open at least eight in Texas.

Capital constraints and a desire to limit franchising could slow Denny's, which is currently the object of a debt-burdening leveraged buyout. But other chains are ready to franchise fast. El Pollo Asado Inc. of Phoenix, run by Richard B. Lipson, co-founder of Garcia's of Scottsdale, a successful restaurant chain, has won licenses to sell *pollo* franchises in 39 states. It went public in October with five Arizona outlets. "I think this is the greatest new concept to come out of the chute in a long, long time," says Lipson.

HAMBURGER CONNECTION. *Pollo* is even invading the non-Hispanic heartland. A Cincinnati company called Marco Pollo Restaurants International Inc. opened its first outlet in Florence, Ky., in September. It has signed up franchisees to build five outlets each in Ohio and Florida. Marco Pollo plays down the chicken's Mexican heritage; all the same, it serves Ohioans tortillas. Manhattan's three Chirping Chicken restaurants are of Greek inspiration, but they offer *pollo*-style chicken— and have received rave reviews from connoisseurs of take-out food. Chirping Chicken, too, has big plans: It wants to franchise 50 outlets in the Northeast over the next two years.

There is nothing all that Mexican about *pollo*. The flavor is subtle, not fiery: The chains marinate it for 20 minutes in fruit juices, garlic, and aromatic spices. And it is priced to offer good value. El Pollo Loco sells a whole chicken with 10 tortillas for $6.29, a half-chicken for $3.10, and a two-piece serving with beans and coleslaw for $2.59.

If America takes to *pollo*, the dish could create ominous competition for fried fast food. But many observers feel it could give hamburger chains a new product to offer franchisees whose territories are saturated. Burger King, which already promotes the health qualities of its broiled burgers, would be a natural *pollo* franchiser, suggests Lipson of El Pollo Asado, and that would surely make fried chicken chains squawk.

By Stewart Toy in Los Angeles

SOURCE: Adapted from, "Fast Food for the Volvo Crowd," in *Business Week*, November 26, 1984, 57.

ISSUE FOR DEBATE

All Promotion of Cigarettes Should Be Banned

Experts officially recognize cigarette smoking as our number one health hazard. In the early 1970s, legislation banned all radio and television promotion of cigarettes. But cigarette companies simply stepped up promotion in newspapers, magazines, and billboards. Today some feel all advertising of cigarettes should be illegal. Others oppose such drastic action.

PROS

Cigarette smoking leads to premature death because it contributes to circulatory and lung diseases.

Even though smokers know smoking is a health hazard, most continue to smoke. In 1970 daily per capita consumption was 11 cigarettes. In 1984 it was eight cigarettes. We need a complete ban on promotion.

CONS

The cigarette industry makes profits for tobacco farmers, manufacturers and retailers. Why penalize them?

Cigarettes are heavily taxed. Banning promotion of cigarettes might reduce consumption and tax revenues.

PROS	CONS
Besides shortening lives, smoking results in more time lost from work, thereby reducing productivity.	In 1984, 29 percent of females and 35 percent of males age 17 and older smoked cigarettes. These people have a right to have information about different brands of cigarettes.
Health authorities say cigarette smoking does more harm to health than so-called hard drugs such as cocaine and heroin. Promoting and possessing hard drugs is illegal. Why shouldn't promotion of the most damaging drug of all—tobacco—also be illegal?	Banning cigarette promotion is another form of discrimination against smokers. Airlines, many restaurants, the federal government, and some private employers have already determined where people can and cannot smoke.

Questions

1. Which side of the argument do you feel is stronger?
2. What other points can you make to support each position?
3. Do you believe all promotion of cigarettes will be outlawed within a decade? Why or why not?

---

individual needs. Thus the emphasis changed from selling what manufacturers made (production orientation) to making what people wanted to buy (marketing orientation). Today, companies seek to determine market preference *before* manufacturing begins so that once they produce a product it will virtually sell itself. Table 9–1 shows the difference in management thinking when companies apply or do not apply the marketing concept.

Information collected annually by Dun & Bradstreet shows why businesses fail. Inadequate sales are the chief cause—and are the responsibility of the marketing manager. Thousands of products—appliances, clothing, stationery supplies, cosmetics—have not been marketed profitably because consumers did not like the color, design, price, durability, or quality.

To apply the marketing concept, any business—whether it is a manufacturer, a retailer, or a service establishment—should take the following four steps: define the total target market, segment the market, study each market segment, and develop a marketing strategy.

Step I: Define the Target Market

Broadly defined, the **market** consists of *all possible customers for a firm's goods or services.* However, the **target market**—*the most likely purchasers*—concerns the marketer. For a firm to be competitive, profitable, and efficient, companies must spend their marketing dollars in the most effective way possible.

What Is the Marketing Concept? 259

TABLE 9-1 Marketing Concept Applied and Not Applied

	MARKETING CONCEPT APPLIED	MARKETING CONCEPT NOT APPLIED
Product considerations	• We'd better do some research to find out which colors most consumers prefer • Let's show some experimental designs to some prospective buyers and get their views before we go ahead. • Let's check to determine how many different models consumers want and then see if we can produce that number profitably.	• We'll "give 'em any color they want, so long as it's black" (Henry Ford's famous quip). • Our engineers know how to design products. That's what we pay them for. Turn the whole job over to them. • The current model is fine. There's no point in spending money on research.
Place considerations	• Let's reappraise our outlets to see if they are as convenient as possible to the maximum number of consumers.	• We'll market this product through the same retail stores we've used in the past.
Price considerations	• What price will induce the maximum number of consumers to buy and yield the most profit?	• This is the price we'll set. We know our market from experience.
Promotion considerations	• We must make certain everything we say in our promotion and warranties is true.	• Don't worry about stretching a point. Consumers won't know the difference.
Results	• Management is aware of changes in consumer's preferences, knows people's wants vary, and is trying to keep abreast of them. Firm's continued success seems assured.	• Management is ignoring consumers, who will shift to competitors' products. Firm's continued success is in jeopardy.

Marketing managers first state a **market description**—or *a definition of the total target market for goods and services.* For example, an airline's market description may be "All people who fly at least once a year." Marketing managers usually start out with such a broad definition to make sure they do not overlook any important elements of the market.

Step II: Segment the Market

The marketer next divides the target market into **market segments,** or *submarkets.* Doing so helps in the later development of a marketing strategy. In the airline example, the market segments might be the military, students, business executives, vacationing families, or group tours. Similarly, a coffee shop may find out it attracts

"WE'RE JUST NOT REACHING THE GROUP BETWEEN YOUNG MARRIEDS AND SENIOR CITIZENS."

Marketing research, the gathering, recording, and analyzing of data, helps experts assess potential problems in marketing their company's goods and services.

three general types of customers: factory and construction workers at lunch, shoppers in midafternoon, and teenagers in the early evening.

Some descriptions of market segments are considerably more detailed. A manufacturer of lawn mowers might describe the market as follows: "Homeowners in middle- and upper-income brackets under the age of 50 who reside mainly in suburban communities in relatively new homes with lawns of at least 4,200 square feet." Publishers of a new magazine might describe their market segment as "Young, intelligent, single males and females, between the ages of 16 and 30, who either are students or work in a professional field."

Sometimes considerable market research is necessary to define market segments. **Marketing research,** is *the systematic gathering, recording, and analyzing of data about problems relating to the marketing of goods and services.* Marketing research may determine who currently buys a firm's products or services or who might potentially buy them, the motivation behind consumer purchases, or any other type of information relating to marketing. We discuss various types of research in Chapter 18.

Descriptions of market segments should be as clear and specific as possible. The more accurately researchers define a target market, the more efficiently they can reach it. A cloudy market description often results in wasted advertising efforts, incorrect pricing, or incorrect decisions on which retail establishments should handle the product.

Step III: Study the Market Segments

Next the marketer must study each target market to learn more about the wants, needs, buying patterns, and motivations of the potential consumers. Someone doing personal selling will study individual behavior patterns. An advertising executive will identify motives for purchasing certain products or find out what characteristics the members of the market segment have in common. Researchers may study such issues informally, but often they use marketing research extensively in this phase.

A manufacturer tries to tailor its selection of retailers to the market descriptions it has researched. For example, if a shoe manufacturer has the mass middle-income consumer in mind, it will seek outlets that cater to budget-conscious rather than style-conscious people.

Obviously, different strategies are necessary for different segments. A firm would not use *Time* magazine to reach the majority of wrestling fans or advertise home furnishings in *Sports Illustrated.* A beverage manufacturer may, depending on the target market, set its commercials to music ranging from country to classical. A large bank in a major metropolitan area may use AM radio and local newspapers to reach its total target market (virtually all adults in the community). But it may use more specialized advertising (probably direct mail) to reach such market segments as college students, newcomers to the city, high-income families, teachers, or retirees.

Firms that sell mailing lists are specialists in helping companies reach their target markets. It is highly important that the client buying mailing lists describes as accurately as possible the type of people or businesses it wants to reach. Mailing to people who are not likely prospects is a needless waste.

Step IV: Develop a Marketing Strategy

A **marketing strategy** is *the overall plan a business creates to market its product.* Examples of questions managers ask in developing a marketing strategy are:

- What channel of distribution (we discuss this later) should we use?
- How shall we price our product—above, at, or below the competition?
- What specific appeals will work best in selling the product to our target market?

> *"The will to win is important, but it isn't worth a nickel unless you also have the will to prepare."*
>
> ANONYMOUS

Business people develop a flexible marketing strategy by considering channels of distribution, pricing, specific appeals for the target market, and product differentiation. Marketing research and computers assist firms in preparing their strategies.

- What kinds of sales promotion devices should we use?
- How can we best differentiate our product from those that competitors offer?

A strategy, like any kind of plan, should be flexible. A firm may need to change its strategy, for example, when competitors change theirs.

Marketing research and computers greatly facilitate defining the target market, segmenting it, analyzing the market segments, and developing a marketing strategy. They can analyze such variables as consumer income, employment, product preferences and age by state, county, metropolitan area, zip code, and even telephone number. Also, libraries provide much information useful in developing marketing strategies.

HOW ARE INDUSTRIAL GOODS MARKETED?

Ultimate consumers are *all of us who purchase products for personal or family use. The products we buy* are called **consumer products** or **goods**. The goal of our economic effort is to satisfy ultimate consumers.

Industrial consumers are *businesses that purchase* **industrial goods,** or *products used in making other products,* such as steel and component parts, *or to operate a business,* such as computers and machine-lubricating oil. The public generally thinks that marketing relates only to goods sold for personal use, but marketing also involves industrial goods. Characteristics of industrial-goods marketing are:

- *Industrial purchasers require technical assistance*—The industrial purchaser expects the seller to furnish information such as performance standards, tolerance rates, tensile strengths, and heat-resisting properties. Such knowledge is difficult to pass on reliably through an intermediary. Thus, direct selling predominates in the marketing of industrial goods.
- *Units of purchase are large*—Manufacturers purchase industrial goods in varying quantities, but almost all their purchases are large when compared with quantities of consumer goods purchased.
- *Purchase contracts cover deliveries over long periods of time*—A purchase may cover a season, a year, or even longer.
- *Many people enter into purchasing decisions*—Often the purchasing decision is not vested in a single person. While the contract for the supplier seeking an order is the company purchasing manager, other people in the company, including engineers, company officers, designers, and plant superintendents, may have a voice in purchasing decisions.
- *The market is concentrated geographically*—Industrial business is often concentrated in a few concerns, a fact that further encourages direct selling. For example, a supplier of products used in the manufacture of glass will find the bulk of its market located in just three states—Ohio, West Virginia, and Pennsylvania.

WHAT ARE DISTRIBUTION CHANNELS?

The route taken in the transfer of ownership of a product as it passes from producer to consumer is known as the **channel of distribution.** *People who perform most marketing functions along that route and bridge the gap between producer and consumer* are known as **marketing intermediaries** or **middlemen.** Most of these are retailers and wholesalers. However, intermediaries need not own or physically handle the goods in which they deal. They may do no more than negotiate contracts for purchase or sale.

Why Are Intermediaries Needed?

Some manufacturers advertise: "Buy from us and eliminate the middleman's profit." While this is the best arrangement in certain cases, in many more an intermediary is necessary. Producers are, by and large, experts only in producing. Modern business is not simple, and markets are complicated and distant. Since many producers must give their full attention to production, they turn the functions of distribution and sales over to others.

The existence of large numbers of intermediaries proves that they perform economically justifiable functions. Wholesalers or retailers simply could not sell their services to a shrewd manufacturing firm if the manufacturer felt it could do the job better itself. Of course, some manufacturers say, "I'm going to organize my own sales force," and some retailers say, "I'll buy in carload lots, direct." And some do find these procedures economical or advisable. However, intermediaries—that is, manufacturers' agents, brokers, auction companies, commission merchants, wholesalers, and retailers—flourish because they are doing a necessary job; otherwise they would be eliminated by the natural competitive forces of our private enterprise system.

From the viewpoint of the consumer, intermediaries are valuable because they make products available at the place and time the consumer wants them, as well as provide many important services. Often, people appreciate the contribution of retailers and wholesalers to the economy less fully than they do the contribution of manufacturing. Manufacturing converts raw materials, such as wood or steel, into finished products, such as furniture or appliances. Intermediaries perform a less tangible service.

Major Distribution Channels

The channels of distribution vary greatly depending on the nature of the product, the financial strength of the manufacturer, the number and kinds of consumers, and the marketing experience of the manufacturer. We can, however, distinguish four major channels:

- Manufacturer ▸ Consumer
- Manufacturer ▸ Retailer ▸ Consumer
- Manufacturer ▸ Wholesaler ▸ Retailer ▸ Consumer
- Manufacturer ▸ Agent intermediary ▸ Wholesaler ▸ Retailer ▸ Consumer

Table 9–2 helps explain factors that determine the length of a channel. Usually, a combination of these factors enters into a channel decision.

TABLE 9–2 What Determines the Length of a Channel?

FACTOR	GENERALIZATIONS ABOUT CHANNELS
Type of product	Industrial products tend to have shorter channels than consumer products, because they are often made to buyer specifications and because conditions favor personal selling.
Value of product	Costly consumer products such as furniture and major appliances have shorter channels than inexpensive products such as thread.
Size of retailer	Large retailers, because they have greater purchasing power and buy more units, often buy directly from the manufacturer or in some cases make their own products.
Size of manufacturer	Large manufacturers generally have shorter channels than small manufacturers. Sometimes they own their own retail outlets.
Number of related products sold by a manufacturer	Generally, the more closely related the products produced by a manufacturer are (food, drugs, and so on), the shorter the channel, since sales representatives can sell many products at one time.
Perishability of product	The more perishable the product (meat, vegetables, fruit, fashion apparel, and so on), the shorter the channel.
Degree of marketing control desired by manufacturer	Manufacturers that want close control over the retailing of the product try to sell directly to retailers.
Geographical concentration	If customers are highly concentrated in one area, the channel may be short, since a sales representative can visit many customers with a minimum of effort. Conversely, widely scattered customers tend to make for longer channels.

RETAILERS

Retailing consists of the *activities involved in selling directly to the ultimate consumer.* A **retailer** is *a business outlet that sells principally to ultimate consumers.* (Some retailers do make sales to other firms, but the total amount of such transactions is small.)

In size, retailers range from one-person operations with no full-time employees, to the giant Sears, Roebuck, with 167,000 employees. In products carried, retailers range from those who handle only one product or a few closely related products to department stores that may carry 10,000 or more different items. Retailers are in planned shopping centers, in shopping districts that grew naturally along highways and interstates, and in small towns. Retailing is even done in the home or from trucks or vending machines.

Retailing is significant to our economy for four reasons. (1) It is an indispensable part of our distribution system; (2) most personal income is spent at retail; (3) it is a major source of employment; and (4) it accounts for a large portion of marketing costs. Figure 9-1 shows retail sales by type of merchandise. Food, automotive products, and general merchandise account for well over half of all retail sales.

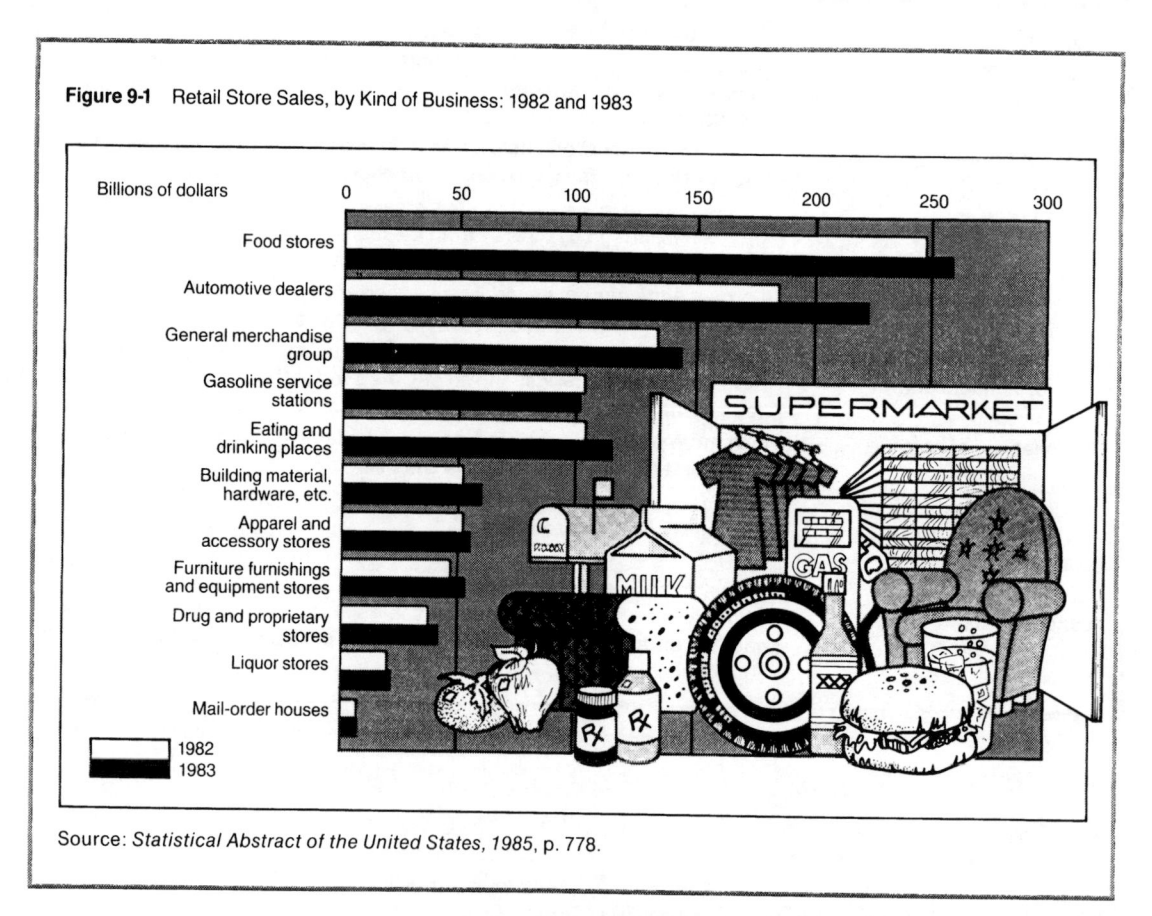

Figure 9-1 Retail Store Sales, by Kind of Business: 1982 and 1983

Billions of dollars

- Food stores
- Automotive dealers
- General merchandise group
- Gasoline service stations
- Eating and drinking places
- Building material, hardware, etc.
- Apparel and accessory stores
- Furniture furnishings and equipment stores
- Drug and proprietary stores
- Liquor stores
- Mail-order houses

☐ 1982
■ 1983

Source: *Statistical Abstract of the United States, 1985,* p. 778.

Retailers Classified by Ownership

INDEPENDENT RETAIL STORES

An **independent retail store** is *a retail store that is separate from any other store in operation and ownership.* Usually the independent retail store is small; frequently it is small enough to be a family business with no other employees. (Key advantages and disadvantages of independent retailers are those of the small business, explained in Chapter 3.)

CHAIN STORES OR MULTI-UNIT OPERATIONS

A **chain store** is *a retail store that operates on the principle of mass (large-scale) merchandising* and responds to a large demand for standardized merchandise, as opposed to technical or personalized goods that require the services of specially trained personnel. Even though modern chain stores may sell quality merchandise, they make every effort possible to keep costs down so that their appeals can be made on the basis of low or moderate price.

Chain stores, such as Woolworth's and K mart, are particularly important in variety retailing. Chains are also widespread in the drug, food, ready-to-wear, and shoe fields.

Major advantages of chains, compared with independent stores, include (1) large-scale buying power, (2) spread of risk over a number of units, (3) use of highly skilled executives, and (4) more capital for modernization and expansion. Among the disadvantages are (1) difficulty in adjusting to local conditions, (2) impersonal relationships with customers, and (3) less motivation on the part of the store manager, because the manager is usually not the owner.

Retailers Classified by Kinds of Business

SINGLE-LINE STORES

Appliance stores, automobile dealers, heating and air-conditioning concerns, and other *retail stores that specialize in only one basic product* are termed **single-line retailers.** Most hardware, food, and furniture stores are considered single-line operations.

LIMITED-LINE STORES

Limited-line retailers, often called **specialty stores,** are *retailers that carry only part of a broader merchandise line.* However, they carry a wider selection in their specialty than a department store. Examples include retailers of apparel, shoes, gifts, and decorative accessories.

SUPERMARKETS

A **supermarket** is *principally a self-service food store, although it sells fast-moving non-food items as well.* It is departmentalized and carries a full line of food products, as well as such household items as paper towels, cleaning aids, and drug sundries.

AMERICA'S REEMERGING CREATIVITY

The Spread of the Self-service Concept

An ongoing revitalization remedy is the trend toward the self-service, or "do the work yourself and save," movement. The self-service concept first became popular in food retailing in the 1930s. Until then, consumers went to the grocery store (which was about the size of today's delicatessen) and told the merchant what they wanted. The storekeeper would then find the merchandise, bring it to the cash register, put it in a bag, and charge the customer.

The introduction of self-service to food retailing had a revolutionary impact. Gross margins were soon cut in half—from 34 percent to 17 percent. Self-service in effect "paid" the consumer in the form of lower prices.

In the 1940s and 1950s, the self-service concept spread to drugstores and discount houses. People liked saving money by doing some of the work of retailing themselves. They also enjoyed the open form of shopping and the wider availability of merchandise.

In the 1960s and 1970s, the self-service concept continued to find new applications. Fast-food operations have continued to grow in importance at the expense of full-service restaurants. Food-vending centers became commonplace in factories and colleges and on the interstate highways.

Self-service laundries do more business each year. Many of them have no "on-premises" personnel. Self-service banking via machine tellers is now commonplace on virtually all college campuses and at thousands of other locations.

The self-service concept is helping elevate productivity and thereby is reducing costs—and prices in other ways, too. The most dramatic use of self-service in the 1970s was in retailing gasoline. Self-service gas stations were operating in California in the 1940s; but the major oil companies soon had them outlawed. In 1970, there were very few self-service gasoline retailers. Now, however, many stations are self-serve.

The future for self-service is excellent. Today, mothers of newborn infants receive financial incentives for leaving the hospital and caring for themselves as soon as possible after delivery. Self-service auto repair centers are becoming common: The vendor supplies the tools and equipment, and the customer supplies the know-how and sweat. Some brokerage houses now offer lower commissions on securities trading when you, the investor, make the investment decision (self-service) without help from the broker. And those of us who travel know fewer baggage handlers work at baggage claim areas in airports. And we see far fewer bellmen in hotels than a decade ago.

Self-service is a continuing way for increasing productivity in the United States. Many people prefer serving themselves. And self-service is an important way to fight inflation.

Questions for Discussion

1. What new applications of self-service do you think will appear in the next decade? Why?
2. Would you personally prefer having a computer or a real librarian give you the information you need at the library? Based on experience, explain.

DISCOUNT STORES

A **discount store** is *a retailer that sells a large selection of well-known merchandise at below* **list** *(manufacturer's suggested)* **prices.**

It has some or all of the following characteristics: (1) limited customer services, (2) unpretentious facilities, (3) ample parking, (4) a low-rent location, and (5) self-service displays.

DEPARTMENT STORES

Department stores are *retailers that carry an unusually wide variety of merchandise*—ready-to-wear clothing, fabrics, home furnishings, appliances, housewares, and a host of other items. Most department stores provide more customer services than other retailers.

CONVENIENCE FOOD STORES

The growth of suburban communities, increasing demands on consumers' time, and the resulting need for a convenient place to "pick up just a few items" gave birth, in the 1950s and 1960s, to **convenience food stores**. These are *retailers that carry a limited line of food products, give fast service, and are open long hours*. The appeal is not price but convenience.

Consumers have many choices in where they can shop. Although some shoppers prefer grocery stores where the clerk waits on them, many shoppers prefer to wait on themselves in self-service supermarkets.

HOW RETAILERS COMBINE OR UNITE

Three ways retailers cooperate or work together in an effort to improve the profitability of individual units are planned shopping centers, voluntary groups, and franchising (discussed in Chapter 3).

Planned Shopping Centers

A **planned,** or **controlled, shopping center** (commonly known as a **mall**) *is a group of retail stores developed as a unit and usually located in a suburban shopping area.* Modern shopping centers include as few as ten to more than 100 stores which are carefully selected to combine for maximum consumer drawing power. Many centers include banks, brokerage houses, theaters, restaurants, and other service enterprises.

Shopping center management is separate from the management of stores that make up the center. This management leases space to the stores, arranges center promotions, and sets hours of operation and other guidelines member stores must meet. Very importantly, shopping center management decides what stores will locate in the center.

Voluntary Groups

A **voluntary group,** sometimes called a **voluntary chain,** *consists of independently owned retail establishments that band together to purchase products, establish common product brands, promote jointly, and give their stores a standardized physical appearance.* To the consumer, voluntary chains look and function like regular corporate chains.

Usually, a voluntary group is organized by a wholesaler who sets operational guidelines, supplies the merchandise, and arranges for group promotion. Voluntary groups are very important in food retailing and, to a lesser extent, in drug and hardware retailing.

WHAT IS NON-STORE RETAILING?

Vending machine retailing is a *non-store, non-personal, self-service type of retailing used extensively to market soft drinks, candy, cigarettes, sundry items, and similar products.* Vending machines operate in high traffic locations and are popular for selling products when retail establishments are closed.

Direct-to-the-consumer retailers *specialize in soliciting, billing, and delivering merchandise to consumers in their homes.* The most common are door-to-door salespeople who sell cosmetics, encyclopedias, and a variety of other products. Many direct-to-the-consumer retailers work only part-time. Less than one percent of all retailing is done in this manner.

Mail-order retailing *is a form of retailing by which consumers order merchandise through a catalog and receive it by mail or by delivery service.* Businesses who use mail order retailing can pinpoint target markets effectively by analyzing which consumers are logical prospects for the items sold. For consumers, mail order retailing may save time and the expense of visiting stores.

Telemarketing *is a non-store type of retailing whereby consumers see a product advertised on television and order it either by calling an 800 (toll-free) number or by writing to an address.* Products retailed through telemarketing include insurance, cookware, health and beauty aids, hardware items, and books. Telemarketing is increasing in popularity because of expansion in cable television. Many stations charge television marketers a percentage of the retail price of the items sold in this manner.

APPLICATION TO PERSONAL AFFAIRS

Tips for Shopping by Mail

Shopping by mail can save time and energy. The Federal Trade Commission and the Direct Mail Marketing Association has prepared certain how-to guidelines.

1. Before ordering, check the company's return policy; when placing an order, fill out the form with care.
2. If you return merchandise to a company, get a return receipt from the shipper.
3. Keep a record of your order, including: the company's name, address, and phone number; information identifying the item you purchased; your cancelled check or a copy of your money order; and the date you mailed the order.
4. Never send cash through the mail. Send a check or money order. Some companies also accept credit cards, but special credit rules may apply.
5. If merchandise is damaged, contact the mail order company immediately. If you're asked to return it, get a receipt from the shipper.
6. If you don't receive your order and your package is lost in transit, the mail order company will probably take responsibility for tracing it.
7. If your prepaid order doesn't arrive when promised, you may cancel the order and get a full refund. If the company didn't give you a delivery date in its solicitation, the company must ship your order within 30 days of receiving it.
8. If you cancel a mail order purchase charged on your credit card, the seller must credit your account within one billing cycle following receipt of your request.
9. If you ever get something in the U.S. mail you didn't order, you can keep it without paying for it. It's your legal right.

Catalog, showroom, and/or warehouse operations are not strictly forms of non-store retailing, but they are emerging as significant retailing trends. The merchandise catalog—often bulky and once the mainstay of shopping by mail—simplifies shopping in the store. The customer preselects goods from a catalog at home or at the showroom and either picks up the product at the warehouse or has it delivered to his/her home.

WHOLESALERS

Wholesalers are *businesses that sell to customers who buy for resale or for industrial and institutional use.* Wholesale transactions include sales to retailers; other wholesalers and institutions; manufacturers and processors of all kinds of goods; building contractors; railroads; public utilities; service establishments, such as dry cleaning shops and hotels; farmers (for supplies and equipment used in farm production); and federal, state, and local governments.

Wholesale sales ordinarily are in quantities much larger than retail sales, but the *motive* of the buyer, not the *size* of the transaction, generally determines whether a sale is wholesale or retail. If the purchaser plans to resell the goods, use them in the manufacture of other goods, or use them in the operation of a business or institution, the transaction is wholesale. The sale of combs, clippers, and tonics to a hair stylist, for instance, is a wholesale transaction, since the motive of the stylist is to use these supplies in the business.

The volume of goods sold at wholesale is approximately 50 percent larger than the total retail volume because (1) much merchandise sold to manufacturers and businesses is used for business operations, (2) wholesale sales are often to other wholesalers. For instance, one wholesaler may sell a carload of oranges to another wholesaler, who in turn sells it to retailers. In this example, oranges have been sold twice at wholesale, but as is always the case, only once at retail. In addition, wholesale trade includes export sales under the definition established by the U.S. Census Bureau whereby, (3) all sales to the government are wholesale sales, and (4) all sales to foreign buyers are wholesale transactions.

What Are Merchant Wholesalers? What Do They Do?

We distinguish **merchant wholesalers** from other intermediaries because *they take title to the products with which they deal and assume the risks of ownership.* The two types of merchant wholesalers are full function and limited function. **Full function wholesalers** *perform all wholesale activities* such as (a) assemble merchandise from many sources, (b) store merchandise, (c) break bulk goods, (d) deliver merchandise, and (e) extend credit. **Limited function wholesalers** *also take title to products, but they do not perform all wholesaling functions.* Cash-and-carry wholesalers, for example, do not extend credit or make delivery. Truck jobbers, important in selling snack foods, beverages, and drug sundries, combine the functions of delivery and selling but often do not extend credit.

How Do Wholesalers Serve Retailers?

Consider for a moment what the retailer would encounter without the services of the wholesaler. For example, the ordinary independent retail drugstore stocks from 1,000 to 2,500 different merchandise items which as many as 350 manufacturers produce. Utter confusion (to say nothing of the extra expense) would result if the druggist had to do business with each of 350 manufacturers! The druggist would receive each month about 350 separate shipments of merchandise, each with invoices requiring individual attention—separate bookkeeping, check-writing, correspondence, and so on.

Besides simplifying retailers' buying problems, wholesalers help them by storing merchandise until needed, delivering merchandise, extending credit, and supplying market information and advice.

How Do Wholesalers Serve Manufacturers?

The functions that wholesalers perform for manufacturers are (1) assuming responsibility for selling, transporting, and storing merchandise, and (2) extending credit to the retailer, which enables the manufacturer to concentrate on production.

The Wholesaling Function Is Essential

A business axiom says, "You can eliminate wholesalers, but you cannot eliminate the functions they perform."

Not all retailers buy from wholesalers. Large retailers such as Sears, J. C. Penney, and K Mart eliminate the wholesaler by buying directly from manufacturers and operating their own distribution centers which supply products to their stores. But large retailers do not eliminate the wholesaling function; they simply perform it themselves.

Nor do all manufacturers sell to wholesalers. Large manufacturers such as General Motors and General Electric operate their own sales branches which supply their retail dealers. Like large retailers, large manufacturers eliminate the wholesaler but not the wholesaling function. They perform it themselves.

WHAT ARE AGENT WHOLESALE INTERMEDIARIES?

Another major group of intermediaries—*those who do not take title to the goods in which they deal, who normally perform few services, and whose chief function is to negotiate a sale*—are **agent intermediaries,** or **agent wholesalers.** They include brokers, selling agents, and manufacturers' agents.

Merchandise Brokers

Brokers *are agent intermediaries who negotiate transactions for merchandise without having either title to or physical possession of the goods.* Sellers usually retain brokers to dispose of goods, but occasionally buyers employ them to acquire products. Brokers never, however, represent both buyer and seller in the same transaction. The broker receives a commission only on sales made. Usually the broker's **principal** (*the party retaining the broker's services*) carefully specifies the price, terms of sale, and delivery arrangements, leaving the broker with relatively little authority.

Brokers are valuable because they have intimate knowledge of a limited and highly specialized market. For example, a broker may deal only in sugar and arrange sales only in the Philadelphia market. Brokers are important in the distribution of food specialties, grain, fresh fruits, cotton, and similar products. As experts, they give valuable advice on market prospects in their field.

Who Are Selling Agents?

Selling agents differ from brokers: They are *agent intermediaries who handle the entire output of the principal they represent, have a continuous contractual relationship with the principal, and sell in unlimited territories.* Selling agents have few restrictions placed on them by their principals with regard to selling price and terms of sale. Often they provide financial assistance to their principals.

Selling agents are important in the distribution of coal, textiles, and food. They sell to wholesalers, industrial consumers, and occasionally retailers. Using the services of selling agents is advisable when the principal is small or produces merchandise that needs wide distribution. Usually, selling agents are aggressive promoters with many connections among regular wholesalers and industrial consumers, and they take the place of a manufacturer's sales force. One agent often represents several manufacturers.

What Are Manufacturers' Agents?

Manufacturers' agents are frequently confused with selling agents. Unlike selling agents, however, **manufacturers' agents** are *agent intermediaries who sell only a part of a producer's output, are limited as to the territory they can cover, have less authority over price and terms of sale, and rarely finance their principals.* Manufacturers who wish to free themselves from marketing problems but retain close control over distribution use manufacturers' agents. They are important in the distribution of machinery, equipment, supplies, steel, and chemicals.

Marketing by Service Establishments

Consumers spend slightly more than 50 percent of their incomes for services or intangible products. Unlike tangible products, we cannot see, touch, handle, wear, smell, taste, display or store services products.

When we have our clothes dry-cleaned; attend a movie, concert, or sporting event; have our car, TV or computer repaired; hire someone to baby-sit; sleep in a motel; retain a lawyer; have our teeth cleaned; take an airplane trip; or have our hair styled, we are purchasing intangible or service products.

Main types of service establishments appear in Table 9-3. Note that the number of establishments, paid employees, and sales volume increased significantly between 1977 and 1983. While not shown in Table 9-3, major industries such as banking, insurance, real estate sales and management, transportation, and health care are also service businesses.

TABLE 9-3 Service Industries—Establishments with Payroll, 1977 and 1983

KIND OF BUSINESS	ESTABLISHMENTS WITH PAYROLL (IN THOUSANDS) 1977	1983	RECEIPTS (IN BILLIONS OF $) 1977	1983	PAID EMPLOYEES (IN THOUSANDS) 1977	1983
Hotels, motels, and other lodging	44.7	41.9	18,127	33,554	918.7	1,112
Personal services	170.2	168.2	15,297	23,163	910.4	981
Business services	154.8	215.9	49,999	111,414	2,297.4	3,233.5
Auto repair services, garages	106.2	115.4	19,659	31,054	483.2	558.4
Miscellaneous repairs	55.0	54.5	9,558	14,409	279.1	305.2
Amusement, recreation services, including motion pictures	61.8	67.2	19,756	32,715	660.3	790.6
Health services, except hospitals	277.7	346.5	50,764	94,516	1,821.0	2,418.3
Legal services	94.9	115.4	17,147	34,338	392.0	569.3
Selected educational services	6.8	7.4	1,382	2,717	61.2	71.4
Engineering, architectural, surveying services	34.4	45.2	14,049	33,532	373.2	566.5
Accounting, auditing, bookkeeping services	39.3	51.8	7,277	14,596	230.9	329.6
Social and other services	26.4	33.4	2,559	4,596	191.4	243.4

SOURCE: *Statistical Abstract of the United States, 1985,* p. 795.

HOW MARKETING SERVICES AND TANGIBLE PRODUCTS DIFFER

Many similarities exist between marketing tangible products and services. In both areas, marketers consider the four Ps—product, place, promotion and price—in developing strategies. But some important differences include the following:

- Production and consumption of services take place simultaneously. While the basketball team plays the game, or produces it, the spectators watch the game, or consume it.

- Producers of services cannot store or inventory their products. Airlines cannot sell vacant seats after the flight has taken off;

PEOPLE WHO MAKE THINGS HAPPEN

A PROFILE OF FRED BUREAU

Fred Bureau has definite ideas about what it takes to succeed in business. He says "Success, first and foremost begins in the mind. It demands that you be a *positive, self-confident person* who sees obstacles and roadblocks as things that you go over, under, or around. They are certainly not things that stop you."

Mr. Bureau's parents were of modest means. With the aid of the GI Bill and part-time jobs, he obtained a Bachelor of Science degree in General Business from Marquette University. He notes, "My grades were Cs (and I was glad to get them!). But I did have confidence, motivation, persistence, and a positive outlook (which I got through reading self-help books in the service)."

"Self-confidence is a trait that enables you to start a business and make things happen. It gets you out of the pack. A lack of self-confidence forces you to sit around and think about a business—for years. If you don't have self-confidence—get it."

Mr. Bureau graduated in 1962. He worked for the Travelers Insurance Company in Milwaukee and Phoenix Insurance Company in Denver as an insurance adjuster for five years. In 1967, Mr. Bureau started a Data Base Publishing Company in Denver. After struggling for four years, the company developed into a national company with regional publishing in Denver, San Antonio, and Atlanta. While the company was in the process of setting up for a fourth plant in Washington, D.C., it was sold to McGraw-Hill. By the time McGraw-

---

hotel operators cannot market empty rooms for a time in the past. A barber cannot store haircuts, and a dentist cannot put his or her services on a shelf.

- Producers of service products are more likely to use free promotion than producers of tangible products. People often see a movie because friends or critics recommend it; football teams and other athletes receive extensive free publicity in the media. Legal, medical, dental, and accounting firms also rely mainly on word-of-mouth promotion.

- The skills, training, and professional experience of service establishment proprietors and employees are especially important in marketing services.

- Marketing services often requires less capital than marketing tangible products since renderers of services require relatively modest physical inventories. Often they can locate their establishments in low rent districts.

Hill bought the company, it was publishing weekly Multiple Listing Catalogues for about 190 cities in about 30 states.

Mr. Bureau places great emphasis on two qualities that lead to success: "You can be short on cash, production knowledge, management ability, even product knowledge; but if you're properly motivated, if you believe in something enough, you will work hard, and you will achieve it. Believing will motivate you."

Mr. Bureau believes that motivation and persistence are the forces that will get business people through in the darkest hours even if it looks as if only a miracle can save the business. Actually motivation is like a miracle drug that gives people inner strength and determination. Mr. Bureau believes that the motivated person, drawing on a secret supply of will power and energy, remains fired up at a time when most people become burned out. The most successful business people are enthusiastic and highly motivated and often throw caution to the wind and go all out.

He says, "If I were looking for a person to run my company and the choices were between a rich Harvard graduate with a 4.0 grade point average and masters degree or a C student from a small town university who, unlike the Harvard graduate, was a positive, self-confident, highly motivated and persistent person, I would hire the small town university person every time." Mr. Bureau believes that a good business education is a must; but when a person can combine education with confidence, persistence and a decent business idea, that person can become a winner. "I am probably a good example of the preceding illustration," he says.

Fred Bureau's ideas about making money reflect wisdom. He says, "I do not think that you must have a burning desire to make money to be successful in business. The dream of wealth is not a good indicator of entrepreneurial success. In fact, those who see entrepreneurs as money-hungry and greedy do not know the true entrepreneur's personality." He continues, "Growth, challenge, opportunity, competition, success and risk—not money—move the entrepreneur who remains, at heart, a dreamer. He is not greedy, but neither is he a social worker obsessed with a strong desire to cure society's ills through the creation of jobs." And he concludes, "*Money is the result of success and fulfillment, but money is not the goal.* Money is the result of action, not the cause of action. It's an excellent by-product."

- Establishments marketing services are more difficult to franchise than businesses marketing tangible products. For example, standardizing service products such as weight reduction or legal assistance is more difficult than standardizing fried chicken or roast beef sandwiches.

FUTURE OF SERVICE MARKETING IS EXCELLENT

The marketing of service products will probably become more important than the marketing of tangible products for three reasons. First, as consumer income rises, people will have more money left over after purchasing tangible items, such as food, clothing, automobiles, appliances, and other products many regard as necessities. Second, the development of tangible products, such as computers, creates the need for service businesses to maintain them. Third, the increasing complexity in many fields, such as electronics, technology, health care, accounting, law, and money management, will create demand for experts who can provide specialized services.

SUMMARY

- All organizations perform the marketing function. Many of them—such as retailers, wholesalers, transportation companies, and advertising firms—engage exclusively in marketing.

- Marketing is important to our economy because half of the consumer's dollar is spent on it; many institutions are involved; nonprofit organizations must also market. Marketing introduces new products and services, creates demand, creates time, place, and possession utilities, and it generates a firm's revenue. All businesses must engage in marketing.

- The marketing mix consists of the four Ps: product, place, price, and promotion.

- Four steps are essential to effective marketing: define the total target market, segment the market, study each market segment, and develop a marketing strategy.

- Industrial marketing supplies customers with technical assistance, facilitates large units of purchase, involves several people in the purchase decision, supervises products over long periods of delivery, and provides expertise on geographic concentration of the market.

- A channel of distribution is the route taken in the transfer of ownership of a product as it passes from producer to consumer. Various intermediaries may stand between the producer and the consumer.

- Retailers, who may be either independents or chains, can be classified as single-line stores, specialty stores, supermarkets, discount stores, department stores, convenience-food stores, planned shopping centers, voluntary groups, vending machines, catalog/showroom/warehouse operations, nonstore retailers, and mail-order operations.

- Wholesalers buy from manufacturers and sell either to (1) retailers, who buy for resale; or (2) industrial and institutional buyers, who purchase products for their own use.

- Full-service wholesalers take title to goods and perform all functions normally associated with wholesaling. They serve *retailers* by simplifying buying problems, storing and delivering merchandise, extending credit, and giving advice. They serve *manufacturers* by selling, transporting, and storing merchandise, and extending credit to retailers.

- Agent intermediaries do not take title to merchandise they sell and normally perform few services except to negotiate sales. The main types of agent intermediaries are brokers, selling agents, and manufacturers' agents.

- In marketing of services, production and consumption take place simultaneously, services cannot be stored, free publicity is important, skill of the provider of the service is a key factor, relatively little capital is necessary, and franchising is difficult.

KEY TERMS YOU SHOULD KNOW

agent intermediary
broker
catalog/showroom/
   warehouse operations
chain store
channel of distribution
consumer product
convenience-food store
department store
direct-to-the-consumer
   retailer

discount store
form utility
full function wholesaler
independent retail store
industrial consumer
industrial good
limited function wholesaler
limited-line retailer
list price
mail-order retailing
manufacturer's agent

market
market description
marketing
marketing concept
marketing intermediary
marketing mix
marketing research
marketing strategy
market segment
merchant wholesaler
place utility

planned shopping center	selling agent	time utility
possession utility	single-line retailer	ultimate consumer
principal	supermarket	vending machine retailing
retailer	target market	voluntary group
retailing	telemarketing	wholesaler

QUESTIONS FOR REVIEW

1. Explain each of these statements: marketing is expensive; marketing provides employment; marketing is informative; marketing is conspicuous; and marketing facilitates social interaction.
2. Specifically, why is marketing important?
3. What are the four Ps of the marketing mix?
4. Explain the term marketing concept; and describe each of the four steps used to implement it.
5. How do ultimate consumers differ from industrial consumers?
6. What is a distribution channel? Why are intermediaries often needed?
7. What is retailing? How can retailers be classified by ownership? By kinds of business?
8. What may retailers combine or unite to achieve goals?
9. Explain non-store retailing. Give some examples.
10. What do wholesalers do? Why is wholesale sales volume larger than retail sales volume?
11. How do merchant wholesalers differ from agent wholesalers?
12. What do brokers do? selling agents? manufacturers agents?
13. "You can eliminate wholesalers, but you cannot eliminate the functions they perform." Explain.
14. In what ways does the marketing of services differ from the marketing of tangible products?

QUESTIONS FOR DISCUSSION

1. Give an example of a local firm that you feel applies the marketing concept and of one that does not. Compare the firms in terms of product, place, price, and promotion decisions. Which firm appears to be more successful?
2. Productivity, or output per employee, is much lower for marketing personnel than for production personnel. How do you account for this?
3. Some supermarkets remain open 24 hours, seven days a week. What do you think are the advantages and disadvantages of this policy? On balance, do you think the advantages outweigh the disadvantages? Why?
4. About every decade or so a new form of retailing becomes popular. The 1930s saw the rise of department stores, the 1940s the supermarket, the 1950s the discount house, the 1960s the planned shopping center, and the 1970s the convenience-food store. What innovation or innovations in retailing do you foresee in the 1980s?
5. Typically, agent intermediaries pay their own expenses and are compensated on a straight commission basis. The more they sell, the more they make. You are a manufacturer's agent representing an apparel maker. You work hard and spend much time and money to acquire the business of a leading department store. In 1985, commissions on that account were $51,500. Your manufacturer thinks that's too much, and tells you he will not renew your one-year contract and will handle the account himself. What could you do?

CASE STUDY

Is Valerie's Idea for an Apparel Firm Feasible?

Valerie Henkel, age 27, studied fashion design in college. Her instructors considered her highly talented, and the awards she received proved it. Valerie dreams of someday owning her own apparel firm, but she "knows" she can't afford it. One day Robert Dryer, a sales representative, visits the boutique where Valerie is employed as a buyer. They decide to have lunch together. The following discussion takes place.

Valerie: You know, Robert, I like my job as a buyer, but it's not what I *really* want to do.

Robert: Well, what *do* you want to do?

V: When I was going to the Fashion Institute I used to dream of someday having my own apparel company. But now I know that's impossible.

R: Why?

V: Money, mainly. The guy I date tells me it would take between $500,000 and $1 million just to get started. And there is no way I could raise that much.

R: What does your friend do?

V: He's an engineer.

R: I see. But maybe he is overestimating the money needed. The biggest apparel firm right here in New York—I believe in the nation—was started with only $7,500. That was quite a few years ago, but I think it would cost only a small fraction of what your friend estimates.

V: I don't see how. I'd need money for a factory, personnel, salespeople, advertising, and raw materials. Little people like me don't have a chance to get started.

R: Well, to begin with, forget about manufacturing. You can contract that out to apparel makers. There are lots of manufacturers who could do that for you. Initially, you concentrate on design.

V: I know I'm good at design, but I can't afford to pay for an inventory.

R: You told me before that you feel you are a great designer of blouses. So here's what you could do. Make up a line of, say, 12 blouses. Next have some samples made of each.

V: OK, now I have some samples. I can't sell enough by myself to make it worthwhile. And I sure can't hire salespeople. Their salaries alone would break me.

R: Valerie, don't hire salespeople on salary. Salaries are a fixed cost. Instead, retain manufacturer's agents. They work on commission—like I do. They make money only when they make sales.

V: How do I find them?

R: Advertise in the trade press. Many agents are looking for new lines and most of them cover several states. Work out an agreement with them, and send them your samples.

V: But what about money I have in inventories? Suppose the samples don't sell?

R: Don't create an inventory until you know how well your line is selling. As the orders come in, you'll be able to judge how many blouses to make.

V: You make it sound so simple.

R: I have skipped over some things like promotion, shipping, and pricing. But I do hope I've shown you how you can go into business without a lot of money. In the beginning, keep production and marketing costs variable as far as possible.

Questions

1. Why is it important to keep production and marketing costs variable depending on volume of business done?
2. Agent intermediaries are very important in the apparel industry. In what other industries can they be used effectively? Why?
3. Finding salespeople who will work on a straight commission is often difficult. Why?

EVOLUTION OF A BUSINESS

The Travel Industry's Wholesale Practices

Ray and Sara are considering whether Excel Travel should offer package tours organized by wholesalers, who either purchase blocks of seats from scheduled airlines at significant discounts (about 50 percent) or hire planes from charter companies. Wholesalers also buy hotel rooms at volume discount prices, often at less than half the going rate.

The question is: By offering such tours, would Sara and Ray be departing too greatly from their company's policy of personalized service?

Sara: The fact is, groups like that aren't geared to the personalized requirements of our customers. We'd have little or no control over how they were handled. For example, on our own package tours we use only scheduled airlines. We don't use charters because charters have the lowest priority for airport clearance. If the weather is bad, the charter goes to the end of the line and is the last to leave. Also, charters rarely have more than one crew available, which can also cause delays.

Ray: Everything you say is true. But prices are often so low that clients should expect some inconveniences. If we explain these shortcomings, our clients can decide. It's just like buying the cheaper or trimmed-down model of something in a store. You don't expect it to have all the features of the standard or deluxe model. Offering cheaper tour deals would just be an additional service we render. After all, some of the most expensive department stores have bargain basements and their image doesn't suffer.

Sara: But isn't travel different? Once people buy it they simply expect good treatment. If they discuss poor or shabby experiences with their friends, they neglect to tell them they bought a cheap deal—they just mention the name of the travel agency they're angry with.

Questions

1. Do you think the handling of cut-rate package tours would detract substantially from the high-service image the Excel Agency wishes to project?
2. Is it necessary to tell clients about the shortcomings of wholesale package tours?
3. If they wish to grow in the future, shouldn't Ray and Sara think in terms of forming a separate wholesale division?
4. In terms of overall travel industry policy, don't wholesaling practices discriminate against the individual traveler? Doesn't the individual traveler make discounting possible?

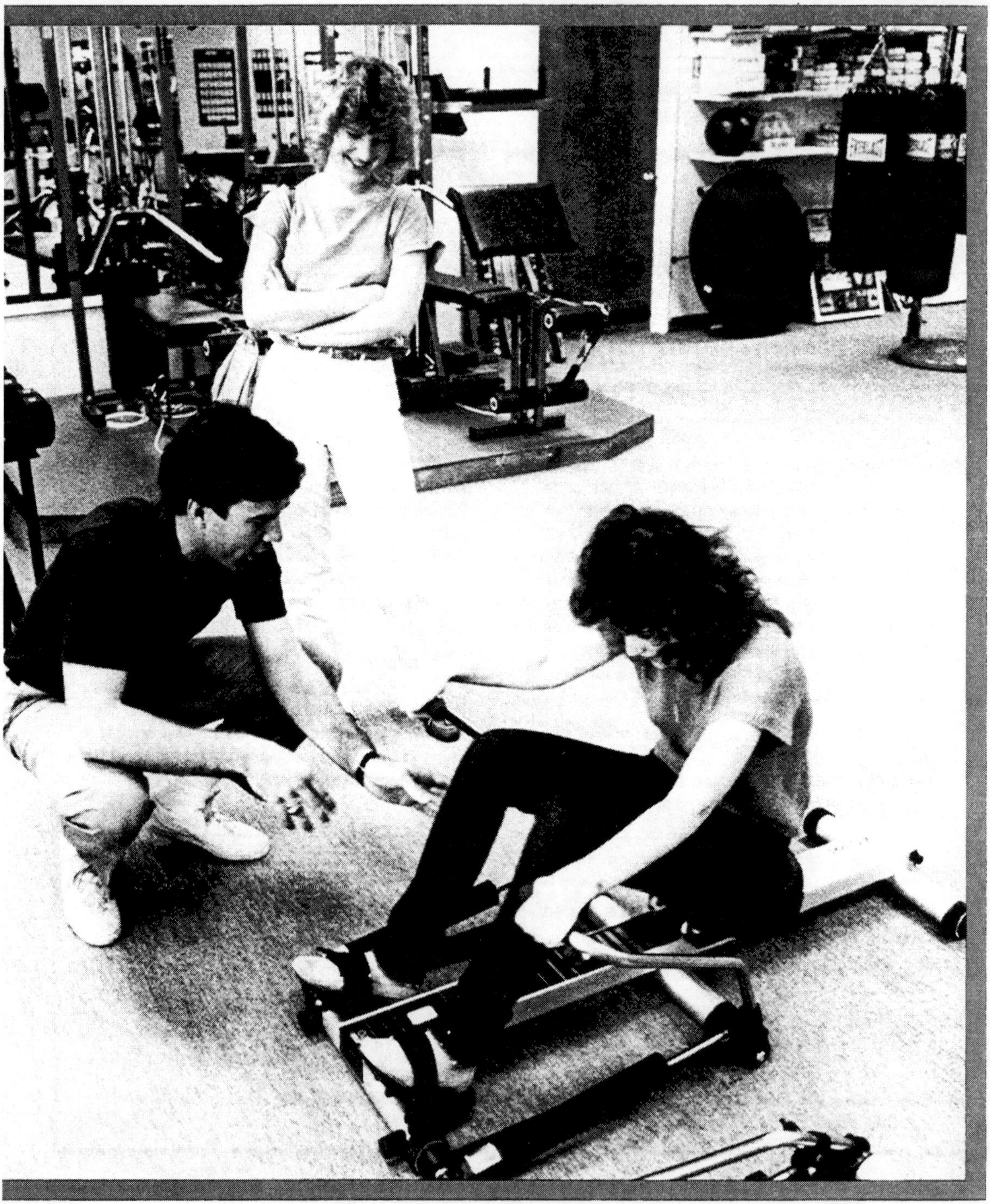

10

THE CONSUMER: DEMOGRAPHICS, INCOME, AND MOTIVATION
Who Buys How Much and Why?

READ THIS CHAPTER SO YOU CAN:

Explain each element in the equation, "people + income + motivation = a market."

Describe the changes and shifts in population that affect consumption.

Understand how changes in population due to births, deaths, and immigration, the average household size, and the ethnic composition of the population affect consumption.

Describe income distribution differences by region and state and among the general population.

Explain how consumer motivation helps explain what people buy.

Explain these emotional buying motives: to feel superior, to gain distinction, to overcome fear, to escape routine, to imitate important people, to give loved ones advantages, and to get a bargain.

Describe the rational motivations for buying: price, quality, and utility.

Understand why people buy where they do: seller's reputation, seller's services, seller's location, and buyer's habits.

Define and explain psychographics.

Consider a market as an equation:

people + income + motivation = a market

A market is a demand for products and services. It consists of three parts: people, income, and motivation to buy. *People*, or consumers, buy products and services. To do this, they need an *income*, or money, including credit. They spend their money only on the products and services that fulfill their needs and satisfy their *motivations*. These three requirements—people, income, and a motivation to buy—must be present for a market to exist.

Consumers can buy products and services wherever they are available. By deciding *what* products and services to buy, and *where* to buy them, consumers can determine which products and services succeed and which fail to catch on.

For this reason, businesses want to know as much about consumers as possible. They strive to find out what and where consumers buy. Factors such as how many people live in an area, how big the area is, how much money the average person in that area makes, the size of the average family in the area, and the number of people living in a household all affect consumers' needs for products and services. Since businesses cannot ask each person these questions, marketers must rely on demographics to help them learn more about their target markets. A **target market** *is a group of consumers with similar characteristics and buying habits that a business thinks will buy its product or service*. **Demographics** *is the statistical study of human populations as markets based on their size, density, distribution, and vital characteristics*. This chapter explains how businesses use demographics to learn more about consumers in general and target markets in particular.

Table 10–1 summarizes what businesses must know about consumers in order to market their products successfully. We examine these aspects in detail in this chapter.

POPULATION AND CONSUMPTION

A **marketing area** is *the territory from which a business draws most of its customers*. Generally, the more populated a marketing area is, the larger the market will be. For example, a fast-food retailer, whose store attracts customers from an area of only a few square miles, is interested in whether more or fewer customers live in that small area. On the other hand, department store executives are concerned with population changes in an entire metropolitan area, because their many customers usually come from all parts of a city. Executives of companies that sell nationwide watch changes in the

TABLE 10-1 What Managers Must Know About Consumers

POPULATION CHARACTERISTICS (PEOPLE)	INCOME CONSIDERATIONS (MONEY)	REASONS FOR BUYING (MOTIVATION)	

Number of households
Average age
Birth and death rates
Population shifts (rural to urban, growth of urban areas, central cities to suburbs, region to region)
Average education level
	How much money there is in the area
	How it is distributed (who has money and who does not)
	How it is spent
		What People Buy
		Emotional reasons
		  Superiority
		  Distinction
		  Fear
		  Escape routine
		  Imitation
		  Welfare of loved ones
		  Bargains
		Rational reasons
		  Price
		  Quality
		  Utility
			Where People Buy
			Reputation of seller
			Services of seller
			Location of seller
			Habits of consumer

nation's population. Knowledge of population shifts helps them decide in what area of the country to open new stores, which existing outlets to close, where more sales representatives are needed, and whether or not to appoint new dealers in an area.

Marketing managers get much of their information on populations from the United States Bureau of the Census, which takes a national census every ten years. Census data is available for regions, states, cities, counties, and subdivisions of major cities. Between census years, the Department of Commerce updates yearly information gathered from the latest census. Key data that interest marketing managers include statistics about total population change, births, deaths, and immigration; changes in where people live; and changes in the average age, the number of people who are married and single, and the average number of people in a household. This and a wealth of other statistical information are found in the *Statistical Abstract of the United States,* published yearly, and in "Current Population Reports," published monthly.

Changes in Total Population

The total U.S. population grew 99 million between 1940 and 1982. Conservative population estimates suggest that the population will grow by 59 million by the year 2020. These estimates reflect a slowdown in growth due to birth control and restrictions on immigration. Nevertheless, increases in total population through 2020 should be substantial. Knowing this helps marketing managers plan their marketing strategy for market growth.

Changes in Births, Deaths, and Net Immigration

Figure 10-1 illustrates changes in the number of births, deaths, and net immigrations from 1960 to 1982. In the figure, net immigrations means the surplus of non-United States citizens coming to the United States to live permanently (*immigration*), over the number of people leaving the United States to live in other countries (*emigration*). The number of deaths in the United States increased slightly during the period, and the number of births decreased. The portion of the population increase that immigration caused rose significantly.

Marketing managers can use this information to target products to the ages and backgrounds of the population. For example, the increase in the number of deaths compared to births could eventually change the average age of the population. This trend affects sales of

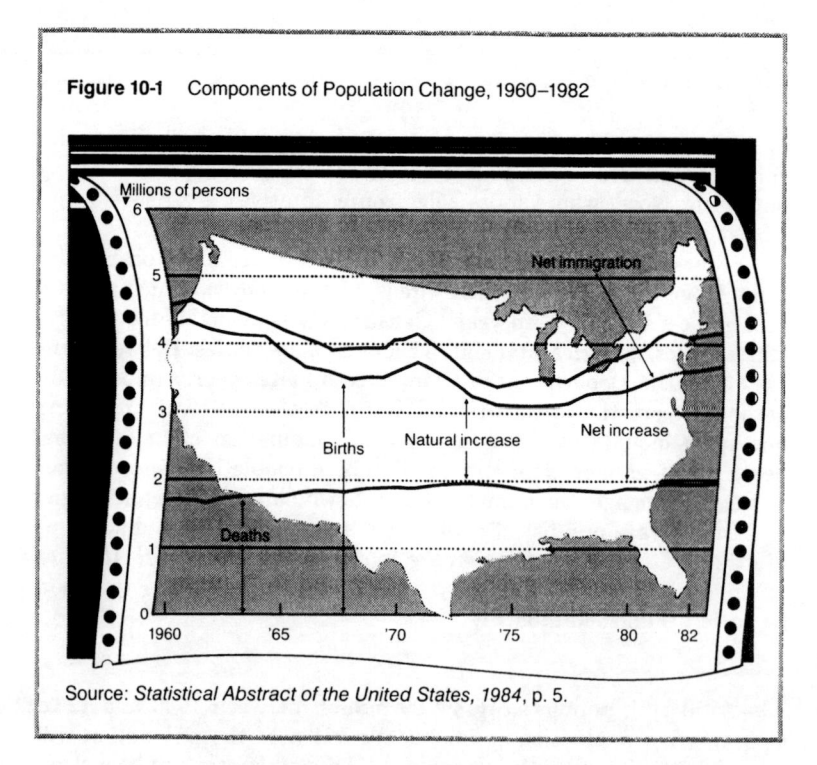

Figure 10-1 Components of Population Change, 1960–1982

Source: *Statistical Abstract of the United States, 1984*, p. 5.

products targeted to younger or older people. Immigration figures could affect the sales of products targeted to or bought by those who are new to the United States.

Changes in Number and Size of Households

These statistics for the total population are important, but the household, not the individual consumer, is the real buying unit. A household comprises all persons who occupy a housing unit such as a house, an apartment or other group of rooms, or a single room used as separate living quarters. A person living alone is considered a household. People not living in households are classified as living in group quarters, which include prisons, military barracks, rooming houses, and college dormitories.

An increase in the *number* of buying units or households, not an increase in the overall population, is what marketing managers watch for most closely. Here is an example of how the number of buying units can increase and how they affect the market for goods and services. A family of two parents and three teenage children is one household. When the three children leave home and establish living quarters of their own, there are now four households. Each new family must furnish their new household with such items as a television set, a dishwasher, a stove, and many other appliances and products.

Figure 10-2 illustrates the increase in the number of households since 1970.

There are additional factors that may contribute to the increase in the number of households. The marriage rate has dropped since 1960, significantly since 1969. The divorce rate has risen steadily during this period. (See Figure 10-3.)

The *size* of the household can determine the types of products that the members of the household buy. A woman living alone or with another person would probably spend much of her earnings differently than would a woman of the same age living in a family of five. The single woman may have a career and, therefore, choose to spend more on work clothes, entertainment, and fine furnishings. The woman with the large family may be concerned with "stretching" available income five ways, so her purchases may be mostly basic supplies for household upkeep. Lifestyles and income may differ in each case, but the size of households largely determines the buying requirements of each woman.

In 1984, one household in five was occupied by only one person, and half the households had only one or two members. Figure 10-4 illustrates how average household size has been dropping in recent years. This is good news for marketers of dwelling units, appliances, automobiles, telephones, and many other products whose sales corre-

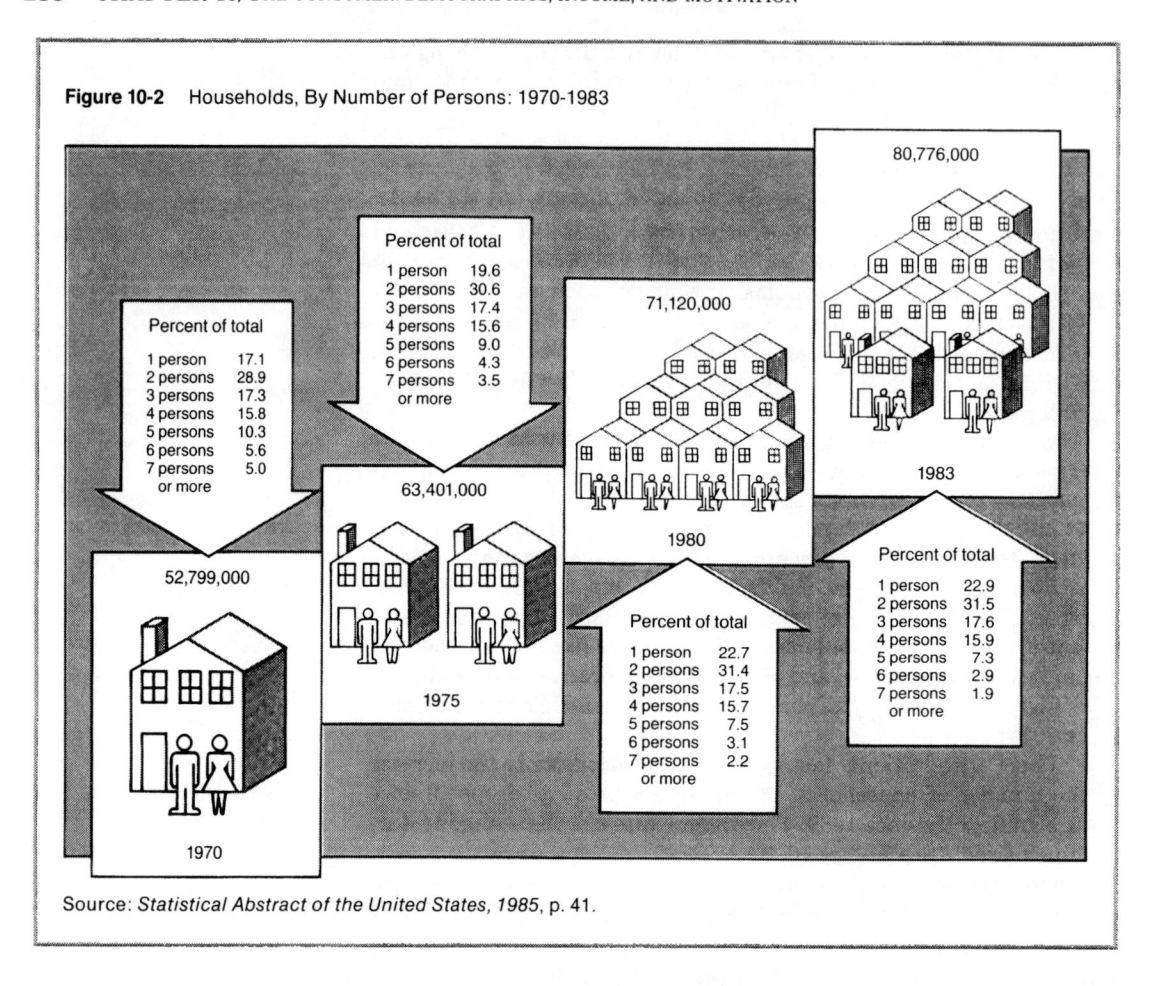

Figure 10-2 Households, By Number of Persons: 1970-1983

1970 — 52,799,000

Percent of total
1 person	17.1
2 persons	28.9
3 persons	17.3
4 persons	15.8
5 persons	10.3
6 persons	5.6
7 persons or more	5.0

1975 — 63,401,000

Percent of total
1 person	19.6
2 persons	30.6
3 persons	17.4
4 persons	15.6
5 persons	9.0
6 persons	4.3
7 persons or more	3.5

1980 — 71,120,000

Percent of total
1 person	22.7
2 persons	31.4
3 persons	17.5
4 persons	15.7
5 persons	7.5
6 persons	3.1
7 persons or more	2.2

1983 — 80,776,000

Percent of total
1 person	22.9
2 persons	31.5
3 persons	17.6
4 persons	15.9
5 persons	7.3
6 persons	2.9
7 persons or more	1.9

Source: *Statistical Abstract of the United States, 1985*, p. 41.

late more with the number of households than with the number of people per household. Also, a trend toward single-person households affects sales of smaller housing units.

AVERAGE AGE OF HOUSEHOLD MEMBERS

The age composition of the population is important to marketing managers because age influences what people want and the money available for spending. The two household age groups that will have the most impressive growth rates by 1990 are the 25- to 34-year-old bracket, which should grow by 36 percent, and the 35- to 44-year-old bracket, which should grow by 62 percent. Both age groups, approach-

Figure 10-3 Marriage and Divorce Rates, 1960–1983

Source: *Statistical Abstract of the United States, 1985*, p. 60.

ing the height of their earning potential, rank high on spending scales.

Figure 10-5 illustrates the large increase in the working-age population, 18 to 64, and the over-65 groups. Meanwhile, the under-18 group has declined as a percentage of the total population. These trends suggest more people in the labor force and more purchasing power as well as increases in demand for products that senior citizens need.

290 CHAPTER 10/THE CONSUMER: DEMOGRAPHICS, INCOME, AND MOTIVATION

Figure 10–4 Persons per Household, 1960–1982

Average Family Size: 3.33 (1960), 3.14 (1970), 2.76 (1980), 2.72 (1982)

Source: *Statistical Abstract of the United States, 1984*, p. xviii.

The trend toward active retirement has enabled merchants to count on senior citizens as a major purchasing group. Here cyclists pedal through Sun City West, a retirement community.

Figure 10-5 Age Distribution of Resident Population, 1982

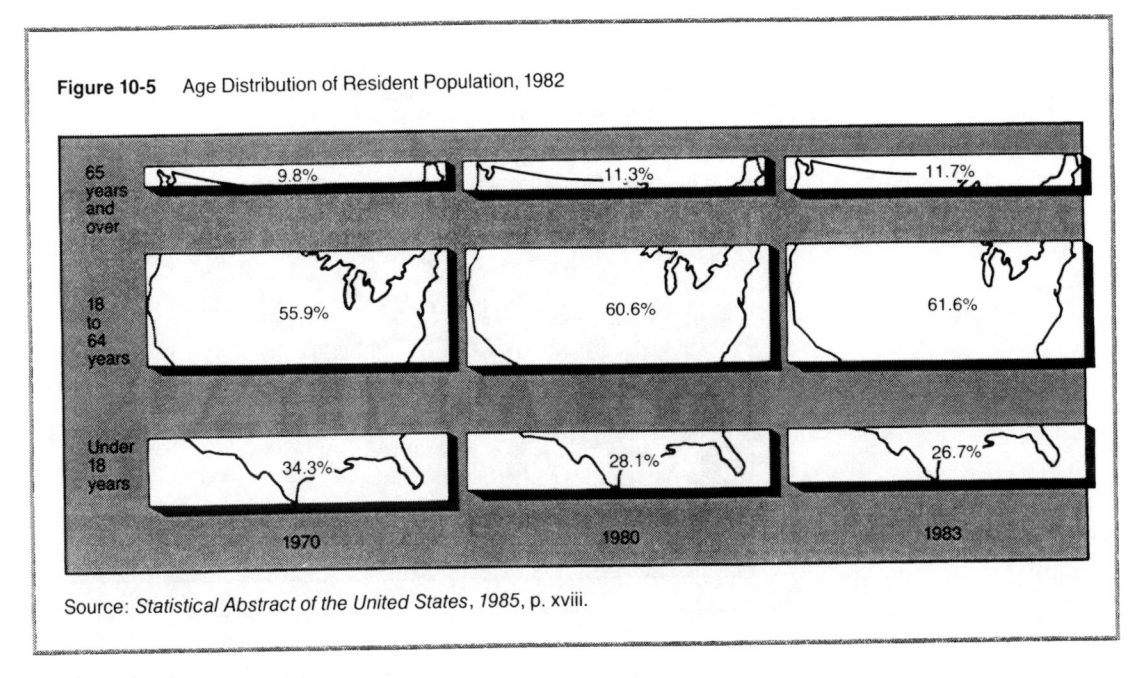

	1970	1980	1983
65 years and over	9.8%	11.3%	11.7%
18 to 64 years	55.9%	60.6%	61.6%
Under 18 years	34.3%	28.1%	26.7%

Source: *Statistical Abstract of the United States*, 1985, p. xviii.

Population Shifts

Several population shifts have taken place over the last 25 years that directly affect the marketing of goods and services.

DECLINE IN RURAL POPULATION

The drop in rural population has resulted mainly from the mechanization of agriculture. Fewer people than ever are necessary to fulfill our agricultural needs. For example, a steep decline in the farm population has occurred in the last 30 years, from just over 23 million in 1950 to less than 7 million in 1984. In turn, the size of the average farm has increased greatly, from 213 acres in 1950 to 437 acres in 1983. The number of farms has dropped to almost 2.4 million from over 5.6 million in 1950.

GROWTH OF URBAN AREAS

Most of the population lives in urban areas. In 1984, 76 percent of U.S. households were located in 321 Standard Metropolitan Statistical Areas[1] widely distributed throughout 21 states and Puerto Rico. Therefore, most of the nation's business is conducted in urban areas.

---

[1]**Standard Metropolitan Statistical Areas (SMSAs)** are used for reporting vital U.S. statistics. An SMSA is *an integrated economic and social unit with a large population nucleus.*

As the farm population in the United States has dropped sharply since 1950, the size of the average farm has more than doubled and the total number of farms has fallen significantly.

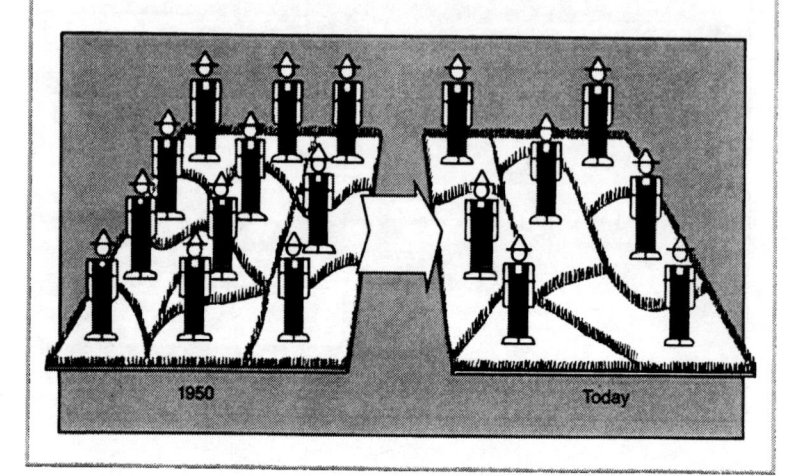

1950   Today

SHIFT FROM CENTRAL CITIES TO SUBURBAN AREAS

The rush to suburban communities has been one of the most important population trends of recent decades. The rapid formation of new households, congested living conditions in the central cities, racial unrest, and urban decay have been the main factors responsible for this trend. Today, the suburbs are the most important single market in the nation—a fact that accounts for the proliferation of shopping centers. Many companies concentrate their marketing efforts in suburban areas because incomes there are higher, and households have more money to spend on such items as fashion apparel and other luxuries.

REGIONAL CHANGES IN POPULATION

Population does not increase at the same rate in every region of the United States. Some areas grow more quickly, some remain about the same population between censuses, and some areas actually lose population. Figure 10–6 shows the percentage of population change for the 25 largest metropolitan centers from 1970 to 1984. All of the centers showing growth rates of 10 percent or more were in the South or West.

Study of population trends is of great importance to businesses that distribute their products nationally. The story goes that the favorite reading of General Robert Wood, who charted the expansion program of Sears, Roebuck & Company, was the *Statistical Abstract*

Population and Consumption   293

Figure 10–6   Population Change of the 25 Largest Metropolitan Areas

AREA ▼
New York–Northern New Jersey–Long Island, N.Y.–N.J.–Conn. CMSA
Los Angeles–Anaheim–Riverside, Calif. CMSA
Chicago–Gary–Lake County (Ill.), Ill.–Ind.–Wis. CMSA
Philadelphia–Wilmington–Trenton, Pa.–N.J.–Del.–Md.–CMSA
San Francisco–Oakland–San Jose, Calif. CMSA
Detroit–Ann Arbor, Mich. CMSA
Boston–Lawrence–Salem, Mass.–N.H. CMSA
Washington, D.C.–Md.–Va.
Houston–Galveston–Brazoria, Tex. CMSA
Dallas–Fort Worth, Tex. CMSA
Cleveland–Akron–Lorain, Ohio CMSA
Miami–Fort Lauderdale, Fla. CMSA
Pittsburgh–Beaver Valley, Pa. CMSA
St. Louis–East St. Louis–Alton, Mo.–Ill. CMSA
Baltimore, Md.
Atlanta, Ga.
Minneapolis–St. Paul, Minn.–Wis.
Seattle–Tacoma, Wash. CMSA
San Diego, Calif.
Cincinnati–Hamilton, Ohio–Ky.–Ind. CMSA
Denver-Boulder, Colo. CMSA
Tampa–St. Petersburg–Clearwater, Fla.
Milwaukee–Racine, Wis. CMSA
Phoenix, Ariz.
Kansas City, Mo.–Kansas City, Kans. CMSA

Percent change   −10   0   10   20   30   40   60

Note: Metropolitan statistical areas (MSAs) defined as of June 30, 1983.

Source: *Statistical Abstract of the United States, 1984*, p. 894.

of the United States. Because Wood learned to anticipate population shifts, he influenced Sears to expand in those areas in which population seemed likely to increase and to reduce its mail-order efforts in declining rural areas.

Average Educational Level

A higher level of education in a population affects consumer demand in two ways. First, it increases the *number of our wants.* Until people know that a product or service exists, they have no desire for it. Education brings us into contact with different customs, ideas, and ways of doing things, and these new horizons increase our desire for material as well as nonmaterial things. Second, a higher level of education changes the *character of our wants.* It tends to make us more discriminating, harder to please. Preferences in music, reading, recreation, and style change with education. Even color preferences may be affected. Research has found that college graduates tend to prefer

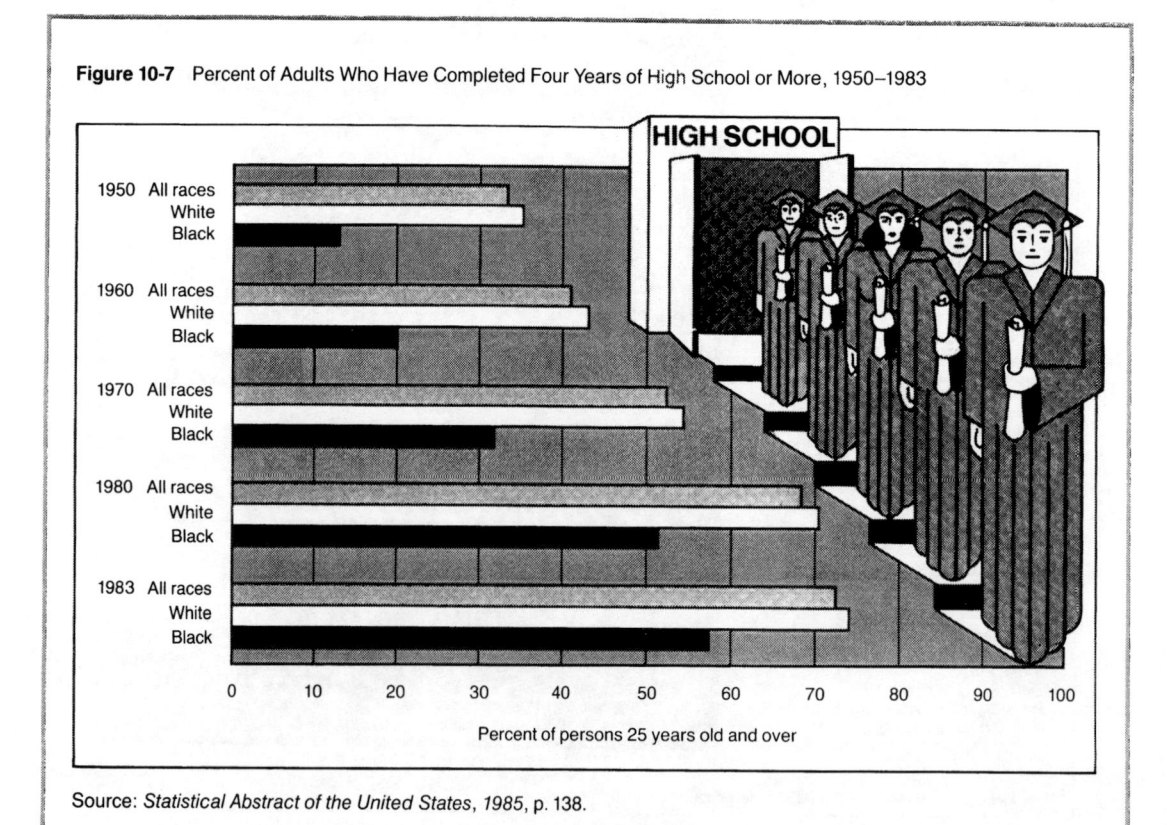

Figure 10-7 Percent of Adults Who Have Completed Four Years of High School or More, 1950–1983

Percent of persons 25 years old and over

Source: *Statistical Abstract of the United States, 1985,* p. 138.

pastels and subdued colors; those with less schooling usually like bright primary colors best. Figure 10-7 illustrates the long-term trend toward a better-educated population. Also, in 1950 only 6.2 percent of the population over 25 years of age had four years of college. In 1984, 17.9 percent had that many years of college education.

Ethnic Makeup of the United States

The population of the United States is a diverse mixture of ethnic and racial backgrounds. In recent years, the percentage of people of Spanish and Oriental origins has increased significantly. The Hispanic population is growing rapidly in New York, Florida, Texas, and California. This has prompted some businesses to use Spanish newspapers, magazines, and radio and television stations to reach that important marketing segment with their products. Each culture has an influence on the ever-changing customs and mores that make up American society.

Population Distribution by Sex

More males are born than females. For the population as a whole, however, there are more females than males. After age 24, there is a steadily declining ratio of males to females. For those over age 65, the ratio becomes highly significant. Since at this age there are far more women than men, housing units, apparel, health care, and recreation are among the products marketed primarily with older women in mind.

U.S. and World Population in Perspective

For most of history, world population grew slowly. The birth rate was high, but so was the death rate, due to epidemics, famine, chronic malnutrition, and inadequate medical care. The industrial revolution, advances in agricultural production, and better medical care resulted in rapid population gains, especially in underdeveloped nations. And movement of population from rural areas to urban centers is taking place throughout the world.

Figure 10-8 summarizes the projected growth between 1984 and 2025 for selected nations and the world. In 1950, only seven urban centers had a population of five million or more. By 1984 the number was 34. By 2025, demographers predict that 93 urban centers will have populations of over five million.

Total world population is expected to increase from almost five billion in 1984 to 8.3 billion in 2025. The share of world population living in the United States will decline from 4.9 percent in 1984 to 3.4 percent in 2025.

The population explosion in some parts of the world means a greatly increased potential for marketing all kinds of goods and ser-

People of Spanish and Oriental origin add variety to American culture and spur merchants to cater to their specific needs and tastes.

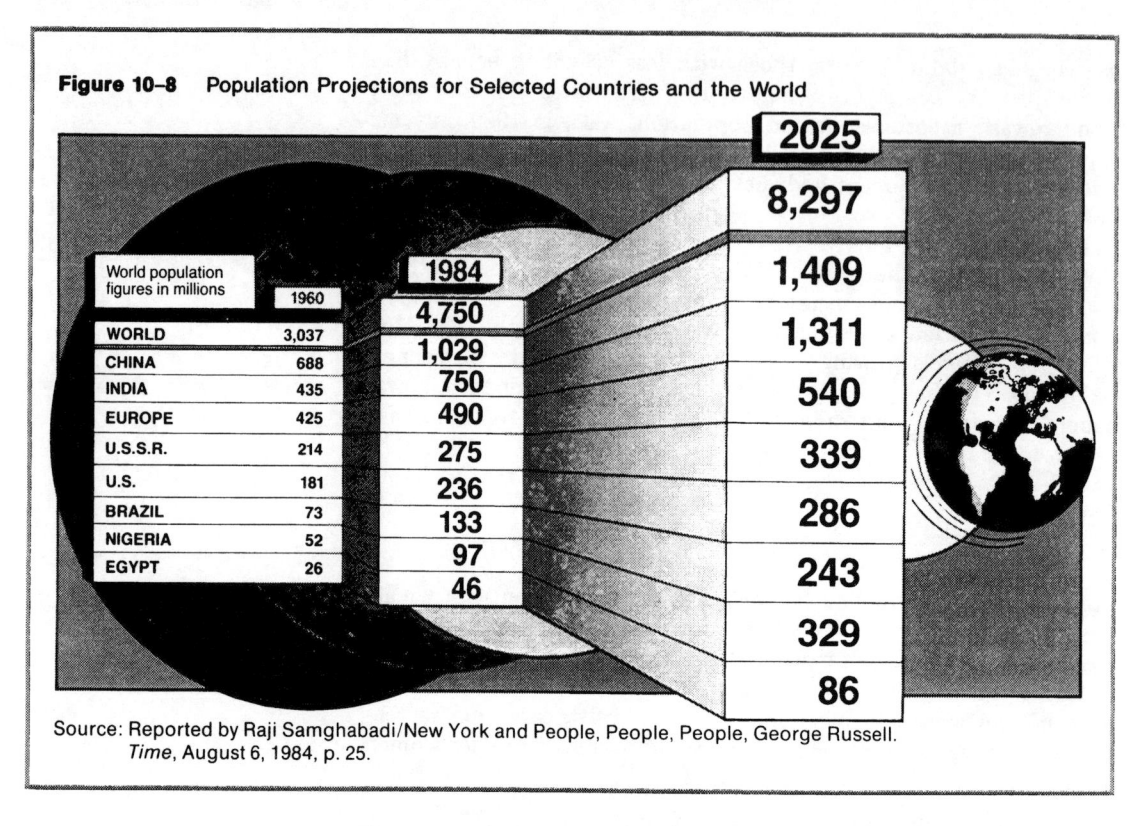

Figure 10-8 Population Projections for Selected Countries and the World

World population figures in millions	1960	1984	2025
WORLD	3,037	4,750	8,297
CHINA	688	1,029	1,409
INDIA	435	750	1,311
EUROPE	425	490	540
U.S.S.R.	214	275	339
U.S.	181	236	286
BRAZIL	73	133	243
NIGERIA	52	97	329
EGYPT	26	46	86

Source: Reported by Raji Samghabadi/New York and People, People, People, George Russell. *Time*, August 6, 1984, p. 25.

vices targeted to these populations. But the problems associated with rapid growth, such as unemployment, inadequate health and education facilities, food shortages, and low productivity, may be too severe to allow much cash flow. As our equation suggests, people who want and need products and services do not alone constitute a market. They must also have income.

INCOME AND CONSUMPTION

Income is the second element in the equation, "people + income + motivation = a market." Business people look closely at the amount of income per capita in a population (that is, average income per person). They are also interested in how total income is distributed throughout the population and the way income is spent.

Business people are concerned mainly with **disposable personal income,** which is *the income a person receives after tax and other deductions have been made.* So important is this income as an economic factor that the U.S. Department of Commerce, trade associations, business people, marketing-research organizations, and others analyze it as an aid in making economic and marketing decisions. Knowledge of the distribution of income among the population, of regional variations in income, and of trends in family and per capita income is essential to successful marketing.

Business people are also concerned with **real income,** or *the amount of goods and services a dollar will buy compared with what a dollar would purchase during a previous year.* Figure 10-9 shows how a dollar has decreased in real purchasing power from 1946 to 1984.

"Ignore tomorrow's customers and you might not have any."

ANONYMOUS

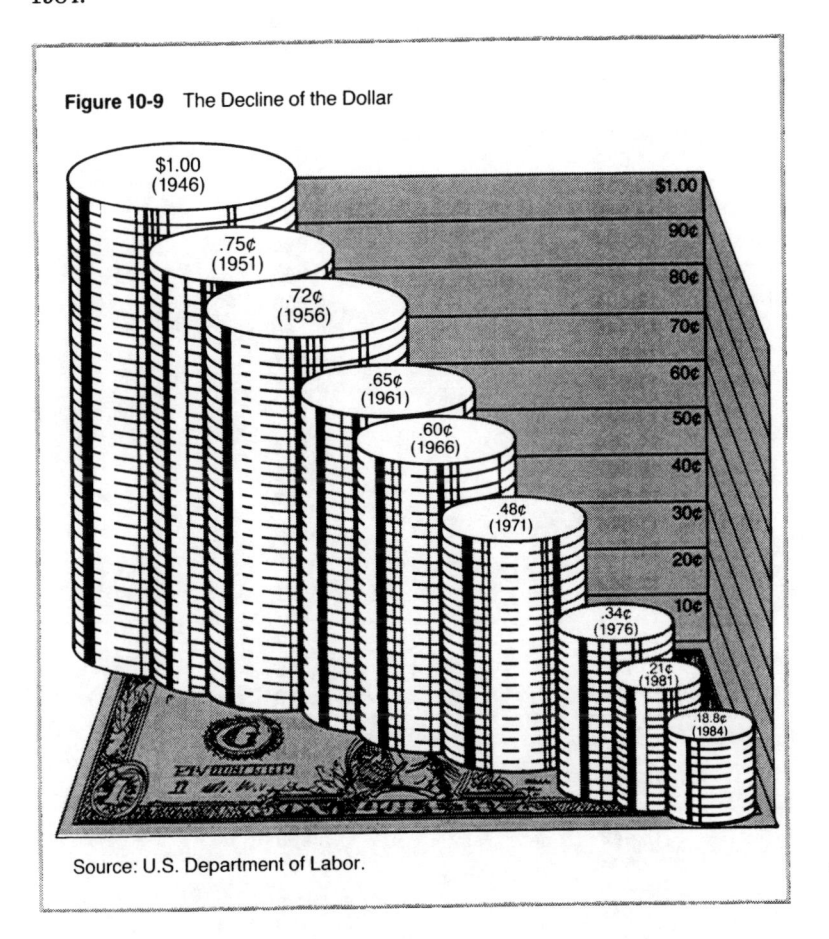

Figure 10-9 The Decline of the Dollar

$1.00 (1946)
.75¢ (1951)
.72¢ (1956)
.65¢ (1961)
.60¢ (1966)
.48¢ (1971)
.34¢ (1976)
.21¢ (1981)
.18.8¢ (1984)

Source: U.S. Department of Labor.

Per Capita Income and Distribution of Income

Table 10-2 summarizes per capita income by state and region in current dollars for 1983 and in constant 1972 dollars. The difference between figures for current dollar income and for constant dollar

TABLE 10-2 Personal Income Per Capita in Current and Constant (1972) Dollars by State and Region, 1983

REGION, DIVISION, AND STATE	CURRENT DOLLARS 1983	CONSTANT (1972) DOLLARS 1983
U.S.	11,675	5,471
Regions:		
Northeast	12,814	5,471
Midwest	11,493	5,386
South	10,700	5,014
West	12,368	5,796
New England	12,845	6,019
Maine	9,619	4,507
N.H.	11,620	5,445
Vt.	10,036	4,703
Mass.	13,089	6,134
R.I.	11,504	5,391
Conn.	14,826	6,947
Middle Atlantic	12,804	6,000
N.Y.	13,146	6,160
N.J.	14,057	6,587
Pa.	11,510	5,394
East North Central	11,599	5,435
Ohio	11,254	5,274
Ind.	10,567	4,952
Ill.	12,626	5,917
Mich.	11,574	5,424
Wis.	11,132	5,216
West North Central	11,242	5,268
Minn.	11,666	5,467
Iowa	11,048	5,177
Mo.	10,790	5,056
N. Dak.	11,350	5,319
S. Dak.	9,704	4,547
Nebr.	10,940	5,126
Kans.	12,285	5,757
South Atlantic	11,020	5,164
Del.	12,442	5,830
Md.	12,994	6,089
D.C.	16,409	7,689
Va.	11,835	5,546
W. Va.	8,937	4,188
N.C.	9,656	4,525
S.C.	8,954	4,196
Ga.	10,283	4,819

TABLE 10-2 (continued)

REGION, DIVISION, AND STATE	CURRENT DOLLARS 1983	CONSTANT (1972) DOLLARS 1983
Fla.	11,592	5,432
East South Central	9,056	4,244
Ky.	9,162	4,293
Tenn.	9,362	4,387
Ala.	9,235	4,328
Miss.	8,072	3,783
West South Central	11,173	5,236
Ark.	9,040	4,236
La.	10,406	4,876
Okla.	11,187	5,242
Tex.	11,702	5,484
Mountain	10,864	5,091
Mont.	9,999	4,686
Idaho	9,342	4,378
Wyo.	11,969	5,609
Colo.	12,580	5,895
N. Mex.	9,560	4,480
Ariz.	10,719	5,023
Utah	9,031	4,232
Nev.	12,516	5,865
Pacific	12,920	6,054
Wash.	12,051	5,647
Oreg.	10,920	5,117
Calif.	13,239	6,204
Alaska	16,820	7,882
Hawaii	12,101	5,671

SOURCE: U.S. Bureau of Economic Analysis, *Survey of Current Business*, April 1984; and unpublished data. In: *Statistical Abstract of the United States, 1985*, 440.

income is largely accounted for by inflation. In addition to such regional and state differences in income, income is also distributed in the population by age, ethnic group, occupation, and education. Such data help businesses target their products and services based on economic factors as well as on consumers' motivations.

Income is distributed unequally from family to family (see Table 10-3). As of 1984, the two-fifths of all families which had the highest incomes received a proportionally larger share of total income—67 percent—than did the other three-fifths, who received only 33 percent. This means that a small percentage of families received a larger share of the total family income than did most other families.

TABLE 10-3 Percentage of Total Family Income Received by Each Fifth and Top 5 Percent of Families, 1984

ITEM
Total income, all families (1,000) — $61,997

PERCENT DISTRIBUTION OF AGGREGATE INCOME	ALL FAMILIES
Lowest fifth	4.7
Second fifth	11.1
Third fifth	17.1
Fourth fifth	24.4
Highest fifth	42.7
Top 5 percent	15.8

SOURCE: *Statistical Abstract of the United States, 1985*, 448.

TABLE 10-4 How Consumers Spend Their Money

	TOTAL (IN BILLIONS OF $)	PERCENTAGE OF TOTAL
Durable Goods		
Motor vehicles & parts	129.3	6
Furniture & household equipment	104.1	5
Other	46.4	2
Nondurable Goods		
Food & beverages	444.8	21
Clothing & accessories	150.0	7
Gasoline & oil	90.0	4
Other	116.9	5
Services		
Housing	363.3	17
Household operations	153.8	7
Transportation	73.5	4
Other	483.8	22

SOURCE: Adapted from Table 724, *Statistical Abstract of the United States, 1985*, 435.

How Income Is Spent

Table 10–4 illustrates the percentages of total expenditures in the United States made for different classes of items. Note that the consumption pattern of any one household may vary from this, depending on income, the size of the household, occupations, ages, personal preferences, and other factors.

CONSUMER MOTIVATION: WHY PEOPLE BUY WHAT THEY DO

Consumers' reasons for purchasing are called **buying motives**. They can be classified as either emotional or rational. **Emotional buying motives** are *subjective, often impulsive, and are not based on logical thinking*. Such is the case when a couple buys an attractive sports car that is uncomfortable to ride in, expensive to insure, and costly to repair. Emotional buying motives are ego-related. That is, they stem from the human urge to protect and enhance one's self-image or self-concept. Many of our buying decisions are related to the conscious or subconscious question, "How will this product influence the way others see me?"

One emotional buying motive is that people like to feel superior: Purchasing expensive items like crystal and bone china can fulfill the need.

Consumers use **rational buying motives,** *based on a logical analysis to determine if they should or should not make a purchase.* The couple's decision to buy a pickup truck because the family can use it for both personal transportation and for hauling in connection with the couple's work is an example of a rational buying motive.

The study of consumer motives is complicated because each consumer is an individual with his or her own motivations. What may be a rational motive to one person may be emotional to another; the determining factor is what goes on in the consumer's mind at the time of the purchase. Further, most purchase decisions involve a combination of emotional and rational motives. For example, a man decides to buy a certain personal computer with small-business software. He bases his decision on his feeling or his projection that someday he will need to start his own small business for extra income. He may have come to his buying decision rationally, based on an assessment of his needs, or emotionally, to achieve superiority over his friends who have less expensive home computers and use them mostly to play games. In fact, he probably decided to buy the computer for a combination of rational and emotional reasons: in part, to achieve the working sense of superiority he feels will spur him to success in his new venture.

What Are Emotional Buying Motives?

Seven emotional buying motives are discussed in this section. Note that some of them may also be rational, depending on the product and the particular consumer.

TO FEEL SUPERIOR

Most people want to feel superior to others and enjoy being admired and respected. Sellers often capitalize on these desires. A stereo salesman may tell a prospect, "This amplifier has such power and such low distortion that it will make you the envy of all your friends." A proud mother is told by a salesperson that a certain outfit will make her daughter the prettiest girl at the party. Community colleges urge adults and young people to enroll in their self-help courses to "move ahead" of their peers. Purchases of expensive automobiles, custom-made or designer clothing, exotic perfume, and certain tobaccos and magazines are often based on the consumers' desires to feel superior.

TO GAIN DISTINCTION

Related to the desire to feel superior is the motivation to be different. Many consumer products attempt to satisfy the craving for individuality. For example, automobiles, even in the lower price ranges, are manufactured in a number of different body styles and in numerous colors to cater to individual whims. To help the motorist gain even more distinction, a wide choice of accessories is usually available.

Also, many marketers emphasize that simply buying the product confers individuality on the consumer. Such products include men's cologne, men's designer fashions, some types of audio equipment, accessories such as watches and leather products, and four-wheel-drive vehicles.

TO OVERCOME FEAR
The buying motive of fear assumes many forms: fear of loss of life or health, fear of losing one's job, fear of social disapproval, fear of accidents. Some such purchases are quite rational; they are simply part of self-preservation. For example, consumers may buy insurance to eliminate financial fears associated with loss of life or health, invest in education to ensure themselves better job security, or buy good-quality tires to relieve fear of accidents. However, many fear-motivated purchases are more emotional. Advertisers of deodorants, toothpastes, and personal hygiene items use fear of social disapproval.

ESCAPE ROUTINE
People make certain purchases to escape routine. Movies, sports events, and other forms of recreation are sold on the basis of this motive. Sellers of vacation travel, musical instruments, and sporting equipment urge consumers to buy in order to enjoy life. Age, education, occupation, sex, and income are factors that help determine what pleasures people purchase based on this motive.

TO IMITATE "IMPORTANT" PEOPLE
Consciously or subconsciously, people imitate those who have attained prominence. Advertising testimonials appeal to this motive. The implication is that if a movie star or famous athlete endorses a product, anyone who uses it will have something in common with that person. A picture of a beautiful model applying face cream suggests that anyone who uses the preparation can be beautiful also.

The compulsion to "keep up with the Joneses" is another manifestation of this motive. Often, consumers may not actually want a product but buy it because their neighbors or members of their social set own it.

TO GIVE LOVED ONES ADVANTAGES
Sellers capitalize on the fact that most people want to give their families advantages. Home computer commercials try to make parents feel that being without the computer will jeopardize their children's education. Insurance agents show how "for just a few pennies a day" parents can guarantee a child's college education. New homes, appliances, vitamins, recreational services, and toys are sold on this basis.

To Get "The Bargain"

Mark Twain relates how superior a boy finds the flavor of a watermelon he has stolen. Adults as well as children experience a special delight in the feeling that they are getting "something for nothing"—or, by extension, getting something for less than it ought to cost. Merchants know this and tempt us continually with mark-down sales. We may buy a lamp marked down from $60 to $30 not because we need it (we were probably doing very well without it before the sale came along) or because it is really worth more than we are paying (we seldom stop to analyze a sale, anyway). Instead, we buy it for basically the same reason that made the watermelon taste so good to Mark Twain's boy.

What Are Rational Buying Motives?

While many rational motives exist for buying products and services, the three major ones are price, quality, and utility.

Price

Appeals to economy influence buyers. Discount stores owe their existence to this buying motive. Examples of economy appeals are "compare and save," "down-to-earth prices," "prices you can afford," and "easy on your pocketbook."

Businesses often use appeals to economy to induce consumers to purchase in large quantities: "two for the price of one," "save three cents on each package when you buy six," and "buy by the dozen and save." Both the seller and the consumer have a valid interest in selling and buying in larger quantities. The buyer may realize a saving. For the seller, an increase in the amount sold to each customer tends to reduce selling costs and thus to increase profits. Selling in large quantities is good marketing policy, also: In theory, the customer who buys a larger quantity uses the produce over a longer period of time and is more likely to develop the habit of using the brand. Also, tests made by a soap manufacturer showed that products bought in larger quantities are used more freely. We are inclined to put more toothpaste on the brush when we use the larger tube than when we use a small one.

Quality

A strong rational buying motive is the desire for quality—a motive that arises when consumers decide which make or model to purchase. For example, after a customer has made the primary decision to buy a television set, he or she may then compare the dependability and color accuracy of various makes before actually purchasing the set.

Advertisers appeal to the quality motive by showing details of product construction. "Built to stand up under the hardest use" and "superior workmanship" are common claims. To satisfy the desire for dependability, sellers frequently offer guarantees. Warranties on appliances, automobiles, and other durable goods are customary. Even hair sprays, breakfast cereals, and cooking oils may be guaranteed to satisfy, or the manufacturer will refund the purchase price. In general, guarantees do increase consumers' confidence in goods and services.

Advertisers may simply *imply* quality in their appeals to consumers' emotional motives of distinction and superiority; or they may base their appeals on a past record of quality without giving present evidence of it. These appeals are not rational ones; they are really emotional ones in disguise.

UTILITY

The intended use of the product frequently plays a major role in buying decisions. This is why most manufacturers make a careful study of the possible uses for their product. For example, a do-it-yourself homeowner wishes to paint a damp basement wall. His deci-

Manufacturers must gear production to the need of consumers. This family obviously needs a truck to transport its source of income. A sports car or limousine would not do.

sion about which paint to buy hinges entirely on solving this problem. Similarly, if someone wishes to fix a drawer that sticks, he or she will go to the store in a rational frame of mind and make a buying decision on the basis of what product can solve the problem best.

The business people who are most successful develop marketing programs based on what the *customer* feels is important rather than on what the manufacturer believes is important. Such programs may not only address the consumer's existing needs; they may create needs for their products to fill.

Combinations of Buying Motives

Both rational and emotional motives are usually involved in a buying decision. In order to appeal to different motives, advertisers influence different types of buyers. Although an advertisement may seek to stimulate only one buying motive, a series of advertisements, run over a period of time, may try to stimulate several motives for buying the product or service.

WHY PEOPLE BUY *WHERE* THEY DO

Two service stations are on opposite sides of an intersection. One does twice as much business as the other. Why? The answer lies in **patronage motives**—that is, *the reasons people buy where they do*. The most important patronage motives are the seller's reputation, the seller's services, the seller's location, and the buyer's habits.

Reputation of Seller

The seller's reputation is an important patronage motive. Merchants who back up claims made in their advertising, give good value, and are ethical become known as reliable business people.

The importance of reputation varies with the type of goods sold. When buying jewelry and furs, consumers often inquire about the reputations of various sellers before deciding where to buy. When purchasing staples, such as food, usually consumers are more concerned with the reputation of the manufacturer than with that of the retailer.

Consumers may pay higher prices because they enjoy personalized attention. Large stores try to develop a favorable image by training salespeople to be friendly and courteous and by encouraging executives to participate in community activities.

A national food chain helps build and maintain its reputation by hammering away continually on what it calls its eight magic words for pleasing customers. These words constitute a company policy: freshness, cleanliness, value, variety, uniformity, convenience, quality, and courtesy.

> *Reputations are made by searching for things that can't be done and doing them.*
>
> FRANK TYGER

Services Rendered

Cashing checks, extending credit, and delivering purchases at no cost are examples of services that help build a clientele. Although services add to the cost of doing business, they are justified when they attract customers. For example, because of the advent of discount fashion clothing outlets, which offer few amenities in exchange for low prices, many department stores now emphasize personalized customer service, help with selection and fitting, and gift services to make buying easier for customers.

Location

The convenience or fashionable atmosphere of a location is an important patronage motive, even though the customer may not be aware of it. A business may be efficient in all other respects and yet not succeed if it is not conveniently located. The success of quick-service food stores, which price their products much higher than supermarkets, is due mainly to their convenient locations. Retail stores may also flourish if other stores offering the same quality of goods to the same clientele are nearby.

Habit

Much consumer behavior is simply habitual. Generally, people develop a habit of buying personal services such as hair styling and legal, medical, and dental services from the same establishments. They also tend to develop habitual behavior in patronizing restaurants and movie theaters. Marketers can use consumer habits to boost sales by cultivating regular customers.

PSYCHOGRAPHICS, LIFESTYLE CHANGES, AND CONSUMPTION

Psychographics

People who share similar demographic characteristics (age, sex, income, place of residence, and so forth) often have extremely different lifestyles and different product desires. **Psychographics,** or *the study of how a person's lifestyle affects his or her consumption pattern,* is a useful tool for marketers.

For example, one psychographic study divided men into eight different groups, ranging from the quiet family man (quiet, shy, life revolves around the family), to the pleasure-oriented man (very masculine, self-centered, seeks immediate gratification of his needs); to the sophisticated man (intellectual, cosmopolitan, wants to be the leader).[2] Women were likewise divided into eight groups, ranging

---

[2]*Psychographics: A Study of Personality, Life Style, and Consumption Patterns* (New York: Newspaper Advertising Bureau, 1973), 14–17.

PEOPLE WHO MAKE THINGS HAPPEN

A PROFILE OF **THE GUCCI FAMILY**

Where would you buy a $10,000 piece of luggage with gold hardware "for traveling on your own plane" (according to a salesperson who works there)? Yes, Fifth Avenue. But *where* on Fifth Avenue? Gucci's, of course.

Gucci is a brand name that has become synonymous with upper-class appeal throughout the world. It belongs to a fascinating family business with headquarters in Florence, Italy. It was founded in 1906, when a prosperous straw merchant and his wife insisted that it was time for their playboy son, Guccio Gucci, to settle down and go to work. Learning his father's business was an unlikely playboy-substitute activity for Guccio. Straw was used chiefly to bed down horses! Guccio decided that other aspects of horses were more exciting, so he started making saddles. He became so absorbed working in leather that his saddles soon became a symbol of perfection. Well-designed and impeccably crafted, the saddles were eventually stamped with a "GG" to assure customers that they were riding the best saddle available. The same "GG" is now carried on all Gucci goods; it announces to the world that customers can afford to buy Gucci.

When horses lost their importance after World War I, Gucci began making leather accessories. Soon the fame of Gucci leather handbags spread throughout Europe. World War II brought a shortage of leather; Gucci, in desperation, experimented with using canvas, the material originally used for horses' feedbags. The famous GG was stamped on the drab canvas to give it chic. A colored stripe was added to brighten it up, and the famous Gucci bag was born. The company seal shows a knight in armor, holding luggage in one hand and a handbag in the other. The rose symbolizes the poetic spirit, the wheel creativity and leadership.

Gucci's invasion of America's luxury-goods stronghold, New York City, began in 1953, when the first leather-goods boutique opened. Quickly successful, this shop was followed by others at posh New York locations. Their success spawned more stores in Palm Beach, Bal Harbour, Fla., Chicago, Beverly Hills, San Francisco, Honolulu, Miami, and Dallas. The opening of the elegant $12 million Gucci's Galleria on Fifth Avenue in 1980 provided the operation with a shopping temple of art. In addition to merchandise, the Galleria holds millions of dollars worth of art masterpieces. Customers can enter the exclusive shopping area freely if they are fortunate enough to have one of the gold elevator keys issued to Gucci's best customers. Others must be escorted by a manager. Customers may caress furs or inspect jewelry while sipping champagne and looking at the art that adorns the walls. Gucci has developed a unique method of retailing that breaks most conventional business rules. Gucci has grown to 20 shops and about 200 franchises worldwide.

There are three generations active in the business, which is headed by Dr. Aldo Gucci, chairman of the board.

from the conformist (resists change, likes the familiar, hunts bargains); to the natural, contented woman (likes simple things, enjoys the outdoors, is casual); to the career seeker (rejects the role of housewife, feels liberated, likes to cultivate her intellect).

Once consumers are segmented on the basis of lifestyle, it is easier to prepare promotional messages that will influence them to buy. The female career seeker and a housewife will probably react differently to the same advertisement for a luxury car, for example.

Lifestyle Changes

New lifestyles and values have emerged in the 1980s that affect and are affected by the market for goods and services.[3] The demographic statistics of later marriages, fewer children being born, and more women in the work force only tell part of the story of the nation's new market profile. These are five groups of lifestyles that are becoming prominent in the 1980s and may be a factor in the changing market of the next decade:

- *Voluntary simplicity.* The propensity for increased consumption is diminishing as a basic motive for consumer behavior.
- *Self-fulfillment.* People want to express themselves by purchasing goods and services which are meaningful to them rather than symbols of conspicuous consumption.
- *Lowered expectations of standards of living.* There will be a growing propensity to consume less costly products and services.
- *Poverty of time.* The increased number of women in the work force who now have less time to spend at home will affect consumption habits.
- *Mature tastes.* As the population grows older, consumption patterns will reflect this demographic shift.

Voluntary simplicity is a legacy of the 1960s and 1970s and the concerns for ecology, energy shortages, and personal realization. The emphasis is on handmade or simple products that have a do-it-yourself purpose and promote self-sufficiency. Self-fulfillment lifestyles are centered on physical and psychological improvement, indulgence of one's desires for pleasure and for "getting more out of life." Marketers may target a wide range of books, exercise, culinary, and pleasure-oriented products, and travel to this market. Those whose lifestyles revolve around lowered expectations for the future are interested in "less is more" products. They are concerned about such matters as levels of energy consumption and job status and obsolescence in a changing economy. Those who suffer from lack of time include the emerging large group of career women whose husbands now share the homemaking and child care roles. Men and women in this group make buying decisions together, and career women look

---

[3]Michman, Ronald D., "New Directions for Lifestyle Behavior Patterns," *Business Horizons* 27, July–August 1984, 59–64.

for ways to appear young and attractive in an aggressive job market. The last group, those with maturing tastes, reminds us that by the year 2000 one-quarter of the population will be between 45 and 64. Adult tastes will begin to re-emerge, and this may mean an increase in sales of comfort- and health-related items, such as spas, vitamins, cosmetics, and health foods.

Many of these lifestyle changes reflect a rising educational level and a sophistication concerning product worth and the usefulness of products to enhance a lifestyle. According to Faith Popcorn, marketing consultant, "Clever catch words aren't enough. [Marketers] have to give some real value."[4]

[4]Nelton, Sharon, "Adapting to a New Era in Marketing Strategy," *Nation's Business*, August 1984, 18–20, 22–23.

SUMMARY

- Consumers are one focal point in the study of marketing. By deciding what products to buy and where to buy them, consumers determine which products and services succeed.
- Business people are interested in the relation of the population to consumption. Of special interest are the number and size of households, average age, birth and death rates, population shifts, and education level.
- Total population continues to increase but at a decreasing rate. By 2020, U.S. population is expected to increase by more than 59 million.
- Population growth in the United States is uneven. Most growth is in the southern and western regions.
- World population, particularly in underdeveloped nations, is increasing much faster than in the United States, Europe, and Japan.
- Income is the most important factor determining how much people buy. When total income drops, total sales also drop.
- Business people who study income are concerned with distribution of income, and how income is spent.
- Consumers may buy what they do for emotional or rational reasons—to feel superior, to gain distinction, to overcome fear, to escape routine, to imitate "important" people, to give loved ones advantages, and to get "the bargain" are emotional buying motives. Price, quality, and utility are rational buying motives. Often, purchasing decisions are based on a mixture of emotional and rational motives.
- Patronage motives explain why people buy *where* they do. The seller's reputation, the seller's services, the seller's location, and the buyer's habits are the main patronage motives.
- Marketers must study lifestyles and their changes to determine how best to market their products and services.

KEY TERMS YOU SHOULD KNOW

buying motive
demographics
disposable personal income
emotional buying motive

marketing area
patronage motive
psychographics
rational buying motive

real income
Standard Metropolitan
   Statistical Area
target market

QUESTIONS FOR REVIEW

1. Explain why each element in this equation is important: people + income + motivation = a market.
2. What happened to total population between 1940 and 1984? Why is population increasing at a lower rate than in previous periods?
3. Why is the increase in households more important to marketers than the increase in population?
4. How does the increasing number of people in the working-age population affect consumption? The increase in people age 65 and older?
5. How does the shift of population from the Northeast and North Central regions to the South and West affect demand for housing, roads and utilities, education, and consumer products?
6. How does the diverse composition of our population affect marketing?
7. In what ways is income unevenly distributed in our economy?
8. What is the difference between emotional buying motives and rational buying motives?
9. What are the most common emotional buying motives? Rational buying motives?
10. Why is a combination of emotional and rational buying motives usually present in most advertisements?
11. Define patronage motives. What are the four most common patronage motives?
12. Explain psychographics. What are four major lifestyle changes in the 1980s?

QUESTIONS FOR DISCUSSION

1. How might projected increases in world population affect Americans? Think in terms of our standard of living, international trade, immigration, and political changes.
2. What factors may reverse, or at least modify, the trend toward (a) lower birth rates, (b) higher divorce rates, (c) increased immigration, and (d) the shift of population to the South and West?
3. Many of our largest metropolitan areas in the North and Midwest (New York, Chicago, Detroit, Boston, Cleveland, Buffalo, Cincinnati, Pittsburgh, Philadelphia, and others) are experiencing a decline in population. A decline in population means less new construction, more urban decay, and reduced tax revenue. Assume you work for the chamber of commerce of a large city that is experiencing a decline in population. What programs would you recommend be developed to reverse the population decline?
4. Select what you think would be the three most important appeals for selling (a) life insurance, (b) sports cars, (c) spring topcoats, and (d) cake mixes.
5. Some critics believe that it is wrong to use emotional appeals such as sex, "keeping up with the Joneses," and fear of not being accepted, since this creates a nation of neurotics. "Madison Avenue," these critics say, "sets goals for the nation, and Madison Avenue is sick." (Madison Avenue is where the main offices of many advertising agencies are.) What do you think of this criticism?
6. Find an advertisement that appeals primarily to each of the following emotional motives: superiority, distinction, fear, pleasure, imitation, and welfare of loved ones. Do the same for these rational motives: price, quality, and utility. Do some advertisements appeal to more than one emotional or rational motive? Why?

CASE STUDY

Making Practical Use of the Marketing Formula

Market area:
Walker State University (WSU) is located on only 20 acres near the center of a large city. Since WSU has no living quarters, all students commute by car, bus, or rail from the city and suburbs.

Potential market:

- PEOPLE About 12,000 students attend morning classes, 4,000 students go to classes in the afternoon, and 8,000 attend evening classes.
- INCOME Eighty-five percent of the students work full- or part-time.
- MOTIVATION Most students are shuttling from home to school to work.

The following conversation takes place between John Wilson and Brenda Smith as they drive to their homes after marketing class.

John: Studying that chapter on getting products to people who need them got me to thinking about my sandwich-shack idea again.

Brenda: Why? You said the university wouldn't lease you space because it already has a cafeteria and two vending operations.

J: Well, its "no" decision made me give up. But in going over the chapter, I had a new and better idea on where to place the sandwich shack.

B: What is it?

J: Most of the students enter campus from the back side, where the parking lots are located—also near the bus and rapid-transit stations. Now, two of the parking lots are privately-owned. I'm going to try to make a deal with the owner to let me put up a sandwich shack in each one. The shacks would be small, less than the size of one car space. I'll open up at 7:00 A.M.

B: But you can't sell ham on rye at 7:00 A.M.

J: There again, the chapter helped open my eyes. Before, I visualized only one target market. Now I see three distinct groups: students who arrive between 7:00 A.M. and 9:00 A.M., those who leave or arrive between 11:00 A.M. and 1:00 P.M., and those who leave or arrive between 4:00 P.M. and 6:00 P.M. Each needs a similar yet different product.

B: Well, you can immediately scratch one target market. Everyone will have already eaten breakfast. Nobody wants sandwiches at 7:00 A.M.

J: Did *you* eat breakfast this morning?

B: Well, I had some coffee. . . .

J: You're making my point—many of the early shift students don't eat breakfast. A lot of them would be tempted by sausage and biscuits or a sweet roll. I can adapt the product to the target market.

B: But what about the second target group? I don't see much demand at lunchtime. They can eat away from the campus. There are plenty of places three or four blocks from school. And students who arrive around noon will have eaten.

J: That's true. But a lot of the students work miles away from the campus. They can buy a sandwich and a drink and eat on the way to their jobs.

B: Okay, there are no laws that say you can't eat in a car. But it is against the law to eat on buses and trains. And keep in mind that the university prohibits carrying food and drinks into the classroom. I think some, maybe most, students are smart enough to walk and eat at the same time. But doing so is difficult if you're carrying books.

J: You've got a point there. But maybe I can figure out a way to package the product conveniently so that consumers can carry it to a place where eating is legal. Only a few instructors enforce the regulation about no food in the classroom.

B: Here's another problem—there are laws against street vending. Are you sure there are no laws against selling food even on private property?

J: I'm going to find out.

Questions

1. Based on the description of the student body and the campus' physical environment, do you feel that the demand for sandwiches and related items justifies John's idea? Explain.

2. Would the place decision be a better one if it called for using special vans instead of shacks?

3. Many downtown carry-out shops around the university do a lot of business during lunch. Where do *their* customers consume the food?

EVOLUTION OF A BUSINESS
Targeting a Market Segment

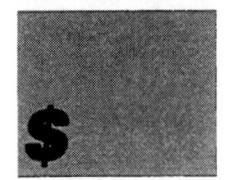

Sara's efforts to reach the business-executive market were going well. Now she began concentrating on another market segment: retired people.

Sara: You know, Ray, this looks like quite a promising market. The population in general is growing older. And more and more retired people want to use their spare time to travel.

Ray: Have you come up with any specific ideas for reaching them?

Sara: Well, I thought I would offer to give special presentations at church groups, social clubs, fraternal organizations, and maybe national associations of retired people. I could get some good travel films from overseas airlines and government tourist bureaus. I would combine the films with lectures about different countries, then hand out brochures about trips to the areas I discuss.

Ray: Sounds like a good idea. What approach do you think you'd use in the lectures?

Sara: According to a study I read, the reason older people don't travel abroad more is that they're afraid to. For example, they hear about the highly publicized crime incidents in Mexico, then they conclude that other foreign countries will be just as unsafe. And they're concerned about lack of sanitation, tainted and indigestible food, and difficulty in getting good health care in an emergency. My plan would be to emphasize our personalized service and stress the fact that travel abroad is safe and easy.

Questions

1. What do you think about Sara's plan? Is there anything you can suggest to make it more effective?
2. Why does this particular market segment hold such attractive potential?
3. How could Sara publicize the fact that she has movie and lecture programs?

Valuable aids to demographic research include:

American Demographics Magazine. (1984). *Population Profiles of the 50 States.* Homewood, Ill.: Dow Jones–Irwin.

Surveys, Polls, Censuses, and Forecasts Directory, 1st ed. (1984). Detroit, Mich.: Gale Research Co. (published three times per year)

U.S. Bureau of the Census. (1985). *County and City Data Book.* Washington, D.C.: U.S. Government Printing Office. (published yearly)

Wasserman, Paul, Jacqueline O'Brien, Daphne Grace, and Kenneth Clansky (eds.). (1983). *Statistics Sources,* 8th ed. Detroit, Mich.: Gale Research Co.

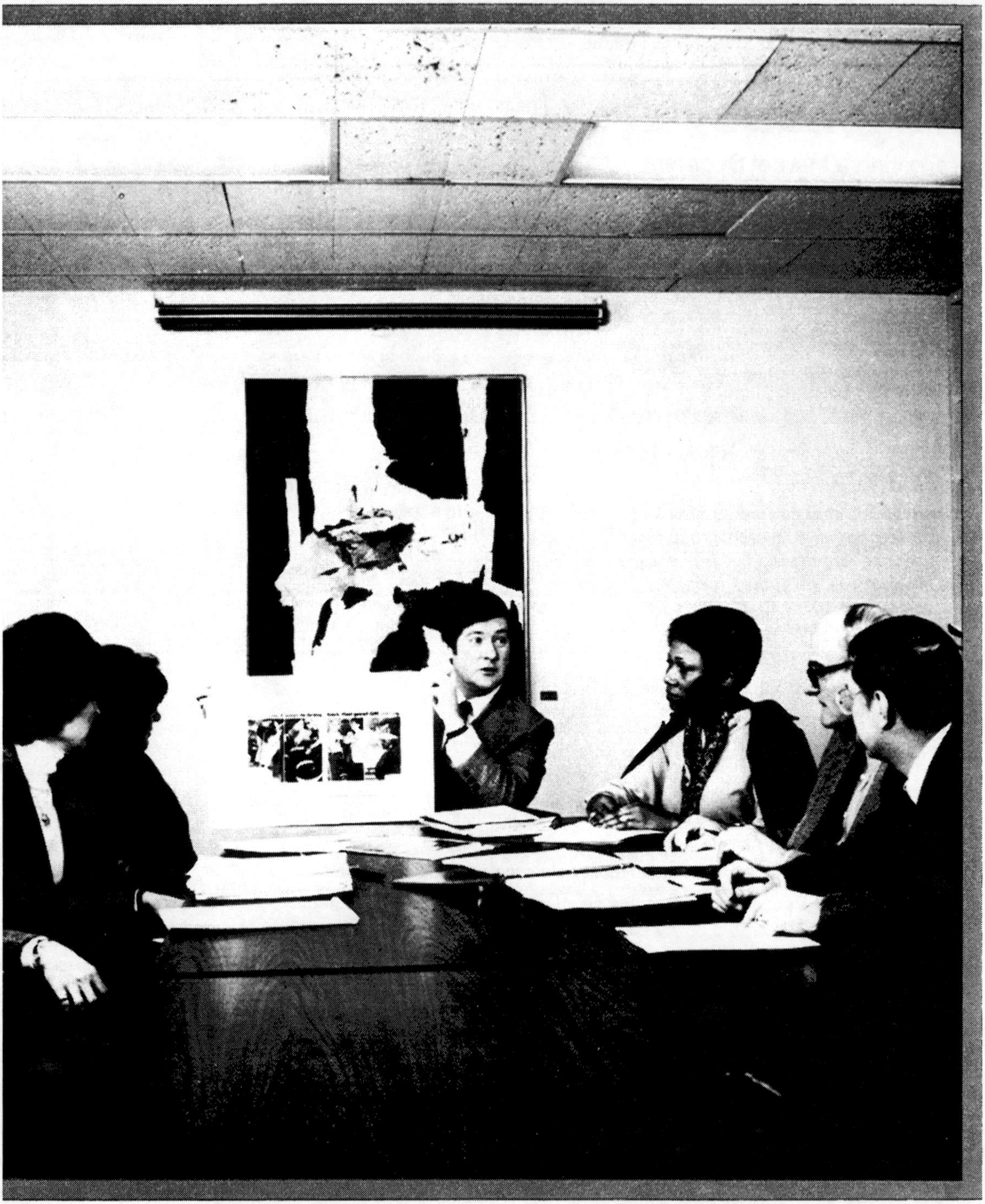

PRODUCTS, PACKAGING, AND PRICING
Deciding the Basics

READ THIS CHAPTER SO YOU CAN:

Define product and differentiate between consumer goods and industrial goods.

Explain the roles of the product life cycle, the product mix, and the product line in the marketing process.

Define packaging and explain its goals, explain what a label should do, and understand the advantages of branding.

Describe what a good brand name is and why some products do not have a brand name.

Discuss the theoretical considerations in pricing, including law of supply and demand, elastic and inelastic demand, pure and imperfect competition, profit maximization, and inflation.

Describe the practical considerations in pricing, including price policies, break-even analysis, manufacturers' suggested prices, markups, and geographic price policies.

Explain how discounts are used in pricing.

Understand how to figure markups and explain why retail markups often seem high.

Describe how pricing of services differs from pricing of tangible products.

Developing a product that people want and getting it to the right place at the right time is only part of the marketing process. The marketing manager must also monitor how the product is selling to determine whether modifications in the product or the marketing approach are necessary. Further, the company must price the product appropriately—high enough to provide a reasonable profit yet low enough to be competitive. The manager must also package the product well, both for protection and in terms of attractiveness, to grab customer attention and create a positive impression.

In this chapter, we consider the marketer's primary decisions related to products, packaging, and pricing.

WHAT ARE PRODUCTS?

In broadest terms, a **product** is *anything that a business sells.* It may be tangible (such as a car, boat, or television set), or it may be intangible (such as a movie, life insurance policy, or ocean cruise). Some products, such as jetliners, cost millions of dollars; others, such as bubble gum, are still sold for as little as five cents. Some products are highly perishable (newspapers last about one day), while others are durable (houses are designed to last a half-century or longer).

The term **product** also includes *all the peripheral factors that contribute to a customer's satisfaction.* For example, when you eat in a restaurant, the product is more than just the food. It includes the quality of the service and the atmosphere.

This chapter discusses primarily the marketing of *tangible products,* or **goods.** Goods classifications are of prime importance, for they affect many marketing decisions, such as through which channels the good will flow, in what department in a store it will be displayed, how it will be advertised, and so on. Misclassification of a good can make or break its market acceptance. For example, when *Granola* first appeared on the market, marketers considered it a specialty food and retailed it through health food stores, where it was a limited-volume item. After marketers reclassified it as a convenience good, they sold it through supermarkets, where it has become a standard high-volume item.

We can divide goods into two categories—consumer and industrial.

What Kinds of Products Are Available?

CONSUMER GOODS

As noted in Chapter 9, *ultimate consumers purchase* **consumer goods** *for personal and household use.* Every person is *potentially*

> *"Always remember that someone, somewhere, is making a product that will make your product obsolete."*
>
> GENERAL GEORGES F. DORIOT

part of the market for such products. Basically we can talk about three classes of consumer goods, each based on the buying habits of the purchaser: convenience, shopping, and specialty goods.

Convenience goods. **Convenience goods** are *purchased frequently, in small quantities, and with a minimum of effort.* Common examples are candy, staple groceries, and gasoline. Convenience goods generally have a low unit value and are easy to carry.

Shopping goods. **Shopping goods** differ from convenience goods in that they are *of relatively high unit value, purchased less frequently, and often bought only after the customer has compared several offerings as to price, style, quality, and general suitability.*

Examples of shopping goods are furniture, clothing, shoes, china, and rugs. Like convenience goods, shopping goods are often advertised nationally, but some personal sales effort is usually necessary.

Specialty goods. **Specialty goods** are for consumers willing to make a special purchasing effort. Compared with convenience and shopping goods, specialty products are *found in few retail outlets, command much more customer loyalty, and are higher priced.* Examples are furs, expensive tobaccos, automobiles, and pianos.

What determines consumer-good classification? What may be a convenience item to one person may be a shopping item to a second and a specialty item to a third. The *intention* is the determining factor. Take the example of a person shopping for roast beef for a dinner party. To many people, this is a simple convenience-goods

The three classes of consumer goods are convenience, such as food products; shopping, such as clothing; and specialty, such as expensive clocks.

purchase, which they make at a conveniently located store. Some people, however, may be price conscious and visit several stores to compare prices and quality before making the purchase. In this case, the beef becomes a shopping item. To another homemaker, the dinner party may be a special event for some important guests. This person may drive all the way across town to purchase the beef, regardless of cost, at a store that handles only the finest-quality aged beef. Such a purchase would fall into the specialty-goods classification.

Goods tend to fall into the same classification for most people, however. This is important, since store location, decor, arrangement of goods, and marketing methods must be suitable for the classification of goods.

INDUSTRIAL GOODS

Industrial goods are *used in the production of other goods or in business and industrial operations.* Oil purchased for a truck or by the General Electric Company to lubricate gears on an assembly line is an industrial item. However, oil sold at a service station for a motorist's car is a consumer item. Again, the intention of the buyer determines the classification of the good.

We can divide industrial goods into two broad categories:

- Goods that are used in the production of other goods and/or become a physical part of another product: raw materials, semimanufactured goods, components, and subcontracted production services.

- Goods that are used to conduct business and do not become part of another product: capital goods (for example, machinery, desks), operating supplies, and services for which the user contracts.

HOW DO CONSUMER- AND INDUSTRIAL-GOODS MARKETING COMPARE?

Producers market consumer and industrial goods very differently (see Table 11–1). Marketers sell these two kinds of goods through separate sets of channels and agencies. Consumer goods are sold through a much larger number of outlets and tend to have a longer channel of distribution (that is, they go through the hands of more intermediaries).

Consumer-goods marketing is the phase of marketing with which the public most often comes into contact. Most people are familiar with consumer-goods marketing terms, such as "retail outlet" and "discounts," but they have only a hazy impression of such industrial-goods terms as "steel broker," "installations," and "zone

TABLE 11-1   Key Comparisons Between Industrial-Goods Marketing and Consumer-Goods Marketing

MARKETING ASPECT	CONSUMER GOODS	INDUSTRIAL GOODS
Reason for buying	Personal satisfaction	To make other goods or to operate a business
Is product made to buyer's specification?	Rarely	Often
Buyer knowledge of product	Limited	Often considerable
Value per transaction	Comparatively small	Comparatively large
Length of channel	Often long	Usually short-often producer to user
Promotion	Nontechnical	Highly technical
Price	Usually one price to all	Often negotiated
Buying motive	Emotional	Rational
Seller backup support	Limited	Considerable

pricing." The distinctions between the two fields are significant for those considering careers in marketing.

Industrial marketing places emphasis on inanimates—production, materials, and technical services. The successful executive in this field is usually stimulated by dealing with things in a precise manner and is adept at making judgments based on facts and analyses.

Consumer-goods marketing places emphasis on animates—that is, on people: how they respond and what they require. Consumer-goods selling relies on emotional appeals to a large extent, whereas industrial-goods selling relies on rational buying motives. Ultimate consumers often buy because they "like" a product or it "looks nice"; industrial consumers buy because the product will enable them to manufacture efficiently—because they can "depend on deliveries" or because "quality control specifications are maintained."

Ultimate consumers usually have only limited knowledge about the products they buy. The industrial-goods buyer, on the other hand, is often a trained purchasing manager who requires concrete facts concerning the performance of a product before buying.

What Are Product Life Cycles?

Some products are introduced on the market and continue to sell well for years—even decades. Examples are Kellogg's Corn Flakes, Coca-Cola, and Crest Toothpaste.

ISSUE FOR DEBATE

Should doctors and lawyers be considered businesses and market their services like other commercial enterprises?

Traditionally, lawyers and doctors have said through their professional organizations, "We're special. We are not businesses and should be allowed to regulate ourselves." Self-regulation included rules that forbid advertising, price competition, and other competitive marketing practices.

In 1977 the Supreme Court held in *Bates v. State Bar of Arizona* that lawyers can market their services like other commercial enterprises.

Whether lawyers and physicians are, in fact, businesses and should market their services is an important issue.

PROS

Advertising promotes price competition which lowers costs to the consumer. For example, now, because of price competition, consumers can find eyeglasses 25 to 40 percent cheaper than earlier when optometrists were able to prohibit honest price advertising.

When professionals function as businesses and promote their services, lower costs to consumers will result because professionals will make greater use of modern technology and management methods.

When lawyers and physicians admit they are business people, public respect for them will increase. Today the public believes professionals want to limit competition and keep costs high. The public now thinks professionals are simply greedy.

Marketing by professionals will increase the volume of cases handled, thereby capturing the

CONS

Marketing of legal and medical services puts profits ahead of service. This is wrong. As Supreme Court Justice Potter said, "The practice of law is a profession. It is not like making shoes or making automobiles."

Justice Oliver Wendell Holmes said: "I should say that one of the good things about law is that it does not pursue money directly. When you sell goods the price which you get and *your own interests* are what you think about in the affair. When you try a case you think about the ways to win it and the *interests of your client*. In the long run, this affects one's whole habit of mind..."

There is a large segment of the public which cannot afford a lawyer or a doctor. As professionals, lawyers and physicians have traditionally given some of their services to those financially disadvantaged citizens. If lawyers and doctors regard themselves as business people rather than professionals, they will feel no more obligation to *pro bono* service commitments than a grocer does to supply free food to the poor or a clothier does to supply free clothing.

Each legal and medical problem is unique. Marketing techniques, as practiced in selling mass-

PROS	CONS
economies of scale. Larger volume will result in more income for professionals and lower cost to consumers.	produced identical problems, won't work for lawyers and doctors.
Through advertising and other forms of promotion, professionals can dispel the long-standing idea that the services of doctors and lawyers are available only for the well-to-do.	If physicians and lawyers act as regular businesses, consumer trust and confidence in them will decline, they may violate ethical codes, and quality legal and medical services may decrease.

Questions

1. Do you see any real differences between operating a medical or legal practice and other forms of services? If yes, what?
2. In your opinion, should legal and medical practices be regarded as businesses? Why or why not?

Others, such as fashion apparel, have a shorter life. A particular product may be popular for several months, but then demand may decline because consumer tastes have changed or a strong competitor has entered the market. In such a case, the product is said to have a distinct **product life cycle,** or *duration of popularity, during which there are four stages: introduction, growth, maturity, and decline* (see Figure 11-1). The length of each stage varies from product to product, but each stage is discernible.

The **introduction stage** *requires the greatest promotional effort,* and because companies must recover expenditures for research and development as well as promotion, it *is the riskiest segment of the product's life.*

A product enters the **growth stage** once *marketing establishes familiarity, and customers begin to seek it out.* During this period, profits usually increase, although perhaps not as fast as sales.

The **maturity stage** of a product's life cycle is one of increased competition from producers of nearly identical versions of the item. Product maturation should be an important signal for marketing management. At this point, often companies will wait to begin thinking about whether to (1) *look for ways to improve the product that will extend its life cycle (or start a new life cycle if the improvements are significant enough);* or (2) *gradually phase out the item and replace it with another product.*

The **decline stage** in a product's life cycle *occurs when the product's usefulness and profitability decrease.* This decline may

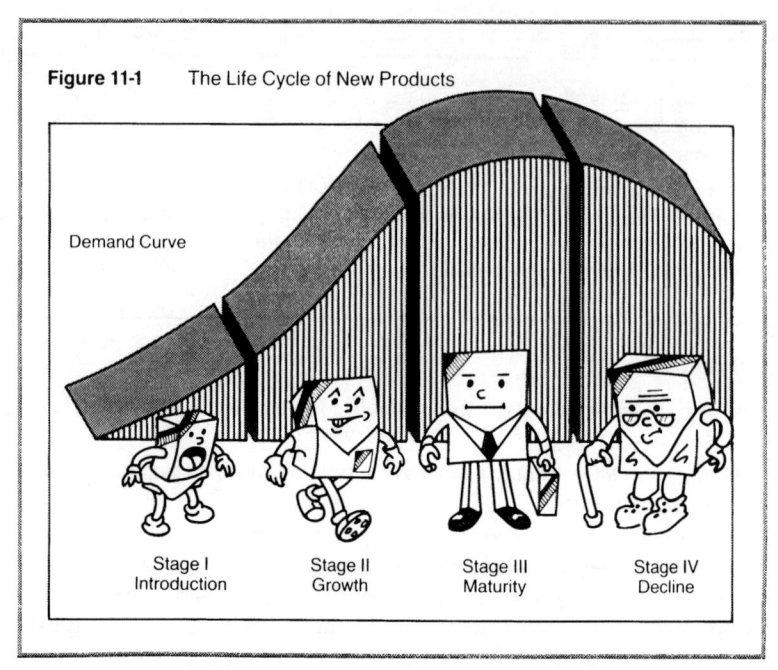

Figure 11-1 The Life Cycle of New Products

Demand Curve

Stage I Introduction
Stage II Growth
Stage III Maturity
Stage IV Decline

result from technological innovations. Automobiles replaced horse-drawn carriages. Ball point pens replaced fountain pens. The list of products made obsolete in this fashion is long.

Product Modifications Help Sell

Product modifications are *changes businesses make in their products in hopes of lengthening their life cycles.* A product modification may be made to satisfy the customers better, to equal or surpass product modifications made by competitors, to differentiate the product from those of competitors, or to meet government regulations. Most food products, for example, must meet certain government standards.

If we accept the broad definition of a product as "anything a firm sells," then only our imagination limits the ways in which producers can modify a product. Whether a specific modification is "right" depends on a host of marketing and engineering considerations. However, the opportunities for making changes are many, and the range of options is great.

Companies marketing intangible products can modify what they sell in many ways. An airline can modify its product (travel) by changing the uniforms of its flight attendants or by offering faster baggage service or different seat configurations, meals, or schedules. Similarly, a commercial bank can modify its product (various financial services) by establishing new, more conveniently located

Coca Cola, New Coke, and Coke Classic demonstrate that consumer satisfaction is important to businesses—who modify products to suit customers. But was diversification in this case a good idea?

branches or by offering gifts to those who open new accounts. Table 11-2 shows the types of modifications most commonly made.

Product Line and Product Mix

A **product line** is *any group of closely related products*. Such products may satisfy a certain class of needs, be used together, be sold to the same groups of customers, or be marketed through the same outlets. A **product mix** is *the mix of all products a business offers for sale*. Thus, in a drugstore lipstick is a product; cosmetics are a prod-

TABLE 11-2   Common Ways in Which Products Are Modified to Extend Their Life Cycle

PHYSICAL CHANGES		NONPHYSICAL CHANGES	
Accessories	Shape or design	Advertising claims	Price
Additives	Size	Advertising coupons	Retail outlets
Durability	Taste	Advertising media	Service facilities
Materials	Texture	Behavior of store personnel	Shelf space
Quality	Weight	Brand name	Trademark
		Packaging	Warranties

uct line; and the product mix might be drugs, magazines, cosmetics, and candy.

To the lipstick manufacturer, lipstick is a product; lipstick, face powder, mascara, and a variety of other items constitute a product line (that is, cosmetics); and, if the firm manufactures other types of products, those products plus its cosmetics (for example, razors, hair dryers, cosmetics) are its product mix.

All businesses must constantly ask themselves whether it is better to (1) add new products to the line or mix, (2) eliminate old ones, or (3) continue with the same line and mix.

PACKAGING, LABELING, AND BRANDING

The effectiveness of a product's package and brand name often determines its success. In fact, for some products—such as cosmetics, headache tablets, and soap—the package and brand may be more important than the contents in generating sales.

Packaging and branding decisions are important in marketing and often require much creative thinking on the part of design experts, advertising executives, and marketing managers. Packaging is so powerful a marketing tool that inferior products attractively packaged will outsell superior products poorly packaged. In a sense, packages are to marketing what spices are to cooking. Both are tricky to use, but properly applied, results can be phenomenal. The fact that packaging constitutes the second highest marketing cost (selling is the first) reflects its importance.

What Is a Package?

A **package** is *a covering or container that protects and identifies the basic product;* it is part of what a firm markets. Packages range from the simple to the complex—from the narrow paper band around a bunch of bananas to the heavy protective cases with styrofoam molds for expensive movie camera components.

Packaging is most important in the case of consumer convenience goods. Automobiles or major appliances—durable goods in general—are not packaged in the conventional sense. Most industrial goods are either not packaged or, if they are, the package is intended primarily to protect the product during shipment and storage. Raw materials, such as mineral products, lumber, and grain, are not packaged.

What Are the Goals of Packaging?

A package for a consumer product should:

- Protect the product so that it reaches the consumer in good condition
- Identify the product

- Be convenient to use (such as a carton for carrying soft drinks)
- Be attractive so that consumers want to buy the product (this point is especially important for products sold in self-service outlets)

The trend toward lighter, more convenient packaging materials has resulted in serious disposal problems. The ever-growing accumulation of indestructible plastic bottles, bottle caps, and beer and soft-drink cans has created demand for containers less damaging to the environment.

Attempts to solve the disposal problem have led to techniques for recycling many packaging materials. Crushed glass bottles are being used as an ingredient in paving highways. Aluminum cans are being resmelted. Paper is being recycled into new paper products. But we are far from solving this enormous problem.

One of the most promising solutions lies in developing **biodegradable packaging materials.** These are *materials that readily disintegrate when exposed to sun and rain and that enrich instead of contaminate the earth.* Here we are imitating nature: Discarded organic wastes, such as orange peels or peanut shells, soon deteriorate and in many instances enrich the earth because of the fertilizing qualities of the nutrients they contain.

What Is a Label's Function?

The most obvious and necessary function of a package **label** is to *identify the product. A complete label also identifies the producer, where the product was produced, the ingredients and weight, and instructions for use.*

Today, few products appear on the market without some form of identification. Even familiar food products, such as chicken parts and vegetables, often display a label testifying to their origins.

Labels help sell the products. Marketers choose type arrangement, illustrations, and colors with the consumer in mind. Marketing managers ask themselves, "What will encourage the consumer to buy *this* product over the many other products also on display?"

Distinctive package labels can also be useful for advertising the product through visual media.

How Do Laws Affect Packages and Labels?

The demand for greater safety in packaging is another major contemporary trend that we can expect to intensify. In 1966 the **Fair Packaging and Labeling Act** was passed. It *regulates all consumer commodities that are (1) packaged, (2) labeled but not packaged, or (3) unpackaged and unlabeled* (for example, a bar of soap that has no label other than the brand name impressed or molded on its face), unless they are specifically exempted.

AMERICA'S REEMERGING CREATIVITY

The Universal Product Code (UPC)

The idea of automated checkout stands in self-service operations goes back several decades. But it is just recently coming into wide use. The Universal Product Code will in time reduce labor costs in food, drug, and other types of stores.

In the **Universal Product Code (UPC)** system, *each manufacturer of consumer goods is assigned an identifying number. Each manufacturer, in turn, assigns a different number to each product it makes. The combination of manufacturer and product identification numbers is translated into a machine-readable symbol printed on packages.* No two symbols are alike. When the packages pass across an optical scanner designed to read the symbols, the encoded information is fed into a computer in the store that tells an automated checkout stand to print on a tape certain information such as the price, size, and name of the product. As it registers the sale, the computer flashes the price on an electronic display so that the customer can see it. The entire process occurs in a few seconds and is much faster than using the traditional cash register.

The UPC has several important advantages. It eliminates the waiting, noise, boredom, and tension induced by long lines and the constant ringing of the register. The time spent going through the checkout stand is shorter and more pleasant. Consumers are more certain that the checkout clerk is getting the price right. Consumers receive audited sales receipts that identify the product or category purchased, taxable and nontaxable items, refunds, coupons, change, bottle deposits, and so on—all printed to take home and study.

Because the computer tabulates sales information instantly, retailers have a better idea of which products may soon be out of stock. Thus, the consumer is less apt to find the brand of his or her choice not on the shelf. There are many UPC systems for the retailer to choose from, and the variety will dictate the benefits to the consumer.

With the decrease in checkout time, the retailer gains improved productivity and a considerable reduction in labor costs. Since prices are filled in the computer, labor cost for marking individual prices on products is cheaper. Also savings occur when fewer products are mispriced at the register. Checker training time is shorter because the system requires minimal learning time. The computer can produce store reports to improve store ordering potential.

Some believe that the UPC will revolutionize food retailing almost as much as the concept of self-service.

Questions for Discussion

1. Scanning devices and in-store computers are still expensive. How can a small retailer solve this problem?
2. Today, most UPC systems are used in food retailing. What other applications will likely develop in this decade?

Although the name of the product and the seller adequately identify some goods, various laws require that most labels give a more detailed description of the product. Processed foods, patent drugs, some cosmetics, textiles, and numerous other goods must carry a fairly complete list of ingredients. Labels on other products, such as furs, must provide information on their place of origin. Certain products must carry instructions for their use, giving, for example, recommended dosages.

Sometimes producers who do not have to furnish usage instructions do so anyway to increase sales. Manufacturers of canned soups, for example, provide recipes and serving suggestions.

Safety warnings must appear on labels of all potentially hazardous products or packages. If a substance is poisonous, the label must tell the user what steps to take if any is swallowed and list the antidotes.

Most over-the-counter drugs (nonprescription medications) must now have tamper-resistant containers. Actually, a more accurate term would be "tamper-evident," since the special packaging should make clear to the consumer if anyone has previously tried to open the package.

Over the years, Congress has enacted legislation that closely regulates the presentation of information on product labels, largely in response to consumer demands. These laws regulate wording; location of warnings or instructions on the label; and size of the type used in relation to the entire area of the principal display panel.

Brand Names and Trademarks: Are They Important?

A **brand name** is *a term a firm chooses to identify its products.* A **trademark** is *a brand name that has been officially registered and is legally restricted to the use of the owner or manufacturer.*[1] Coca-Cola is a brand name because it identifies a particular product and manufacturer; it is also a trademark because the Coca-Cola Company has registered it as such. The term "cola" is generic, referring to a type of soft drink.

ADVANTAGES OF BRANDING
Branding has two major advantages.

<u>Creates customer confidence.</u> One reason producers brand their products is to build customer loyalty and confidence. The consumer who can rely on a product tends to purchase it again and will buy it regardless of the reputation of the retailer who carries it. Many consumers are willing to pay a higher price (since most branded products cost more) for consistent dependability.

<u>Gives the producer control.</u> Producers like Procter & Gamble or intermediaries like Sears, Roebuck & Company which market their own branded products have more control over pricing, advertising,

---
[1] See Chapter 20 for a discussion of the legal aspects of trademarks.

Items within a product line often help to sell each other: If a consumer likes one item he or she may buy the complementary products.

and other promotional activities. Branding is frequently of great promotional value. For example, a number of producers manufacture washing machines for Sears, all of which are retailed under the brand name Kenmore. The manufacturers, however, cannot advertise that fact; Sears receives the customer's loyalty in this case.

What Makes a Good Brand Name?

In recent years the computer has taken on the job of "inventing" brand names by coining hundreds or thousands of new words and then selecting the most effective. Citgo is one of these brand names. The increase in this practice points up a growing difficulty in brand-name creation: The thousands upon thousands of brand names already in use or registered with intent to use make it more difficult to come up with fresh names.

The most effective brand names seem to be:

- Easy to pronounce but distinctive in sound (Brillo)
- Easy to recall (Kool)
- Closely associated with the product in meaning or spelling (L'eggs)
- Easy to translate into foreign languages for international marketing (Kodak)
- Appropriate to the target market and product (Barbie Doll)

No-name Brands

In recent years a new branding concept has emerged. The idea was, don't give the product a brand name, just tell what it is—toilet tissue, paper napkins, cream corn, detergent, flour, baked beans, and so on.

No-name (generic) brands are *unbranded products priced below branded products.* Consumer acceptance varies. Many who have tried these products believe they are of lower quality than the name brands. Nevertheless, no-name branding may become more important in the future if product quality is elevated to at least average for the product involved.

PRICING

Each business must price or set a monetary value on the product or service it offers. **Pricing** is *setting prices to generate sufficient revenues to cover all direct and indirect costs of doing business and to yield a profit so that the business can survive and prosper.* Pricing technique involves an understanding of accounting, economics, and, to a growing extent, psychology. Figure 11–2 shows some of the terms used to describe price.

Many businesses do not properly understand pricing. In many instances, a firm "priced itself out of the market" by charging too much. Conversely, many firms have underpriced to the point where they, too, were forced out of business.

Figure 11–2 Price by Any Other Name Means Money Paid

Anything of commercial value has a price. Below are a number of different ways price is expressed in the marketplace.

Price is all around us. You pay RENT for your apartment, TUITION for your education, and a FEE to your physician or dentist.

The airline, railway, taxi, and bus companies charge you a FARE; the local utilities call their price a RATE; and the local bank charges you INTEREST for the money you borrow.

The price for driving your car on Florida's Sunshine Parkway is a TOLL, and the company that insures your car charges you a PREMIUM.

The guest lecturer charges an HONORARIUM to tell you about a government official who took a BRIBE to help a shady character steal DUES collected by a trade association.

Clubs or societies to which you belong may make a special ASSESSMENT to pay unusual expenses. A lawyer you use regularly may ask for a RETAINER to cover his services.

The "price" of an executive is a SALARY, the price of a salesperson may be a COMMISSION, and the price of a worker is a WAGE.

Finally, although economists would disagree, many of us feel that INCOME TAXES are the price we pay for the privilege of making money!

SOURCE: David J. Schwartz, *Marketing Today*, 3rd ed. (New York: Harcourt Brace Jovanovich, 1981), 271.

To understand pricing it is best to view it first in terms of theoretical considerations and second from a pragmatic standpoint.

Theoretical Considerations for Pricing

PRICE AND THE LAW OF SUPPLY AND DEMAND

This economic law holds that the relationship of supply to demand considerably affects the general price level. The **law of supply** means that *a shortage will cause prices to advance while a surplus will cause prices to decline.* The **law of demand** means *more goods will sell at a lower price than at a higher price*—for example, we can expect more hamburgers to sell at $2 than at $4. Three factors influence the law of demand:

- *The principle of* **diminishing utility**—This principle states that *the more units we have of something, the less valuable each additional unit is.* A second car is less valuable to us than the first, the third is less valuable than the second, and so on.
- *Differences in consumer desire*—The degree to which consumers desire a product helps determine how much they are willing to pay for it.
- *Differences in consumer income*—Consumer ability to pay affects demand. Increased income strengthens demand; conversely, decreased income weakens demand.

The law of supply and demand is simply an economic theory and does not apply to all pricing situations. In fact, with increased government intervention in economic matters, many people feel that the theory is no longer applicable on a major scale. Table 11–3 shows some of the factors that can influence the prices of specific products and prices in general.

WHAT IS ELASTIC AND INELASTIC DEMAND?

While the law of demand generally applies, demand for some goods responds more freely to price changes than demand for other goods. *Demand for a given product is* **elastic** *if a change in price readily produces changes in demand for the product.* Demand for automobiles is elastic because more cars will sell at lower prices and fewer will sell at higher prices.

Demand for a product is **inelastic** *if it is comparatively insensitive to changes in price.* Demand for salt, for example, is considered inelastic since variations in price (within reason) do not change demand significantly.

TABLE 11-3 Forces That Tend to Push Prices Up and Down

FORCES THAT TEND TO PUSH PRICES UP	FORCES THAT TEND TO PUSH PRICES DOWN
Government action to increase the supply of money and reduce interest rates	Government action to decrease the supply of money and raise interest rates
Deficit spending by government	A balanced government budget or budget surplus
A small supply relative to demand	A large supply relative to demand
An increase in wages not matched by an increase in productivity	Stable wages as productivity rises
Buyers eager to acquire ownership (a bullish attitude)	Buyers resistant to purchasing, for whatever reason (a bearish attitude)
Sellers holding out for higher prices (a bullish attitude)	Sellers eager to sell (a bearish attitude)
Widespread speculation based on the belief that prices will rise	Fear that prices will go down
Rumors about shortages	Rumors about business

PRICING UNDER CONDITIONS OF PURE COMPETITION

A condition of **pure competition** exists when *no one seller controls enough of the supply of a product to influence its price in the marketplace.* Pure competition exists only in the case of some agricultural products, such as wheat, corn, and soybeans. No one farmer produces enough of these products to influence price. In industries in which there are a number of producers of homogeneous or very similar products, one firm might lower its prices to gain a competitive edge. However, in practice this action would cause producers of similar products to lower their prices also. And if one producer raised prices above industry levels, consumers would simply switch to a competitor's products.

PRICING UNDER CONDITIONS OF IMPERFECT COMPETITION

A product the consumer considers different in some way from all competing products has a market characterized by **imperfect,** *or* **monopolistic, competition.** A producer of such a product does not have a monopoly like a public utility; it must still compete for its share of the market. But, by making its product distinctive in the eyes of the consumer, such a producer does have a *degree* of control over price.

Imperfect competition characterizes markets for most products. In effect, this means sellers compete mainly on bases other than price. Auto makers, for example, compete more on such features as style, interior trim, and minor mechanical differences than on price.

PROFIT MAXIMIZATION

Three factors determine the amount of profit a business will make: number of units sold, price at which units sell, and cost of producing and selling this number of units. Choosing *a price that strikes the best balance between costs and revenue*—low enough to satisfy customers but high enough for the business to make money—is called **profit maximization.**

HOW INFLATION COMPLICATES PRICING

Inflation complicates pricing in two ways. First, when prices rise for an extended period, an inflationary psychology results. Buyer resistance, usually strengthened by rising prices, may weaken because consumers and businesses may think that even higher prices are inevitable. The result is even more inflation.

A second complicating factor resulting from inflation involves the negotiation of long-term contracts. Businesses that contract to build office complexes, shopping centers, and airplanes, for example, must try to anticipate what the costs of labor, raw materials, energy, and other items will be months—even years—later, before the project is completed.

Some businesses hedge against inflation through use of **price escalator clauses.** These clauses *call for automatic increases in price of a finished product linked to the seller's increase in costs.*

Practical Considerations

PRICE POLICIES

In setting a price for a product, a firm may follow any of the following policies.

Pricing to meet competition. Most businesses price their products at the "market," or prevailing, level. Charging the same as competitors is most common when (1) there is little product differentiation; (2) buyers are well aware of the market price; and (3) the seller can do little or nothing to control the market price. Detergents, for example, are usually priced to meet the competition.

Pricing below competition. Some firms deliberately set prices below competition to increase sales. Discount houses as a matter of policy price below department stores. Many independent service stations intentionally price their gasoline several cents below the "majors."

The term **penetration pricing** is applied to *the practice of pricing below competition to introduce a new product or expand the market for an old one.*

Pricing above competition. If a business markets a product that is unique, distinctive, or prestigious, it may elect to sell above the competitive price. Frequently this policy is followed by "name" restaurants, manufacturers of prestigious apparel, and hotels that have an excellent reputation.

Negotiated pricing. A one-price policy (charging everyone the same price) is practical for uniform, standardized products, but in the case of products that must be made to buyer specifications, **negotiated pricing** (*in which the seller and buyer bargain over price*) is used. Negotiated pricing is more important in the case of industrial products than for consumer goods. Consumers usually encounter negotiated pricing only in the purchase of real estate, a car, stereo equipment, or perhaps a major appliance.

Psychological pricing. **Psychological pricing** is *the use of price to suggest either that the product is a bargain or that it is of high quality.* Odd-amount pricing ($9.86 instead of $10 or $4.89 instead of $5) is often used to convey the impression of a bargain. To suggest high quality, dollars only—no pennies—may be used.

Another aspect of psychological pricing is the notion that price conveys image. Most consumers associate high quality with high prices. Exclusive retail outlets and specialty stores often price their products considerably higher than regular stores to help convey a "better" image. Discount stores, on the other hand, price below the competitive level and convey a "bargain" image.

How Discounts Are Used in Pricing

Businesses selling to other businesses often use discounts or reductions in normal prices although discounts are relatively unimportant in pricing products for ultimate consumers. Businesses have the option of several types of discounts:

- **Quantity discounts** are offered to encourage businesses to buy in larger quantities or to encourage a customer to concentrate purchases with one seller over a period of time. These discounts *rely either on the dollar value of the transaction or on the number of units involved* and are common in selling to both consumers and businesses. **Cumulative discounts** are *quantity discounts based on the total amount a customer purchases over a given period,* while **noncumulative discounts** are *quantity discounts used to encourage large single purchases.*

- **Trade discounts** *offer producers a way to reward wholesale and retail merchants for their help in performing marketing functions.* To illustrate: A manufacturer might quote its retail price as $100–40 percent–10 percent. The first figure ($100) represents the suggested retail price. The second figure (40 percent) is the trade discount to retailers, which means they pay $60. The third figure (10 percent) is the wholesaler's discount calculated on the retailer's price of $60. So, of the $100 retail price the retailer receives $40; the wholesaler, $6 (10 percent of $60); and the manufacturer, $54.

- **Cash discounts** are *inducements to buyers to pay promptly.* A common form is "2/10 net 30," which means that buyers may deduct 2 percent of the invoice if they pay within 10 days; otherwise they owe the full amount within 30 days.

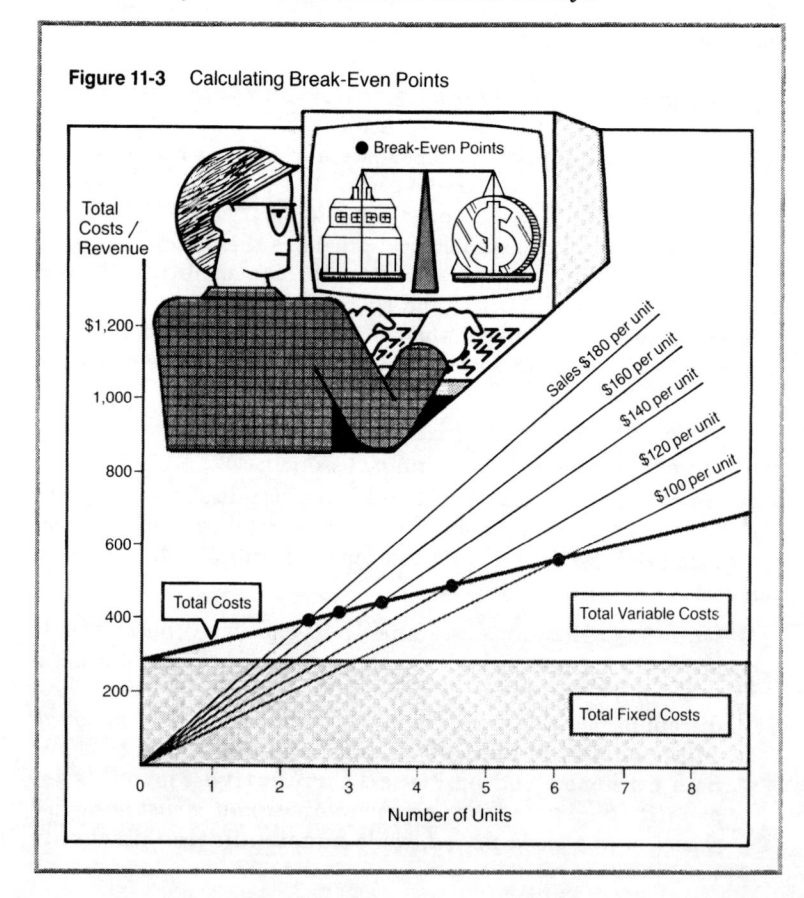

Figure 11-3 Calculating Break-Even Points

- **Seasonal discounts** provide businesses that market seasonal products *a method of selling more during the off-season.* Hotels in resort areas such as Miami Beach offer significant discounts during the summer.

MANUFACTURER'S SUGGESTED PRICE

When *a manufacturer who sells consumer goods to retailers suggests an appropriate price for his product* we call it a **manufacturer's suggested price.** Drug sundries, food staples, and wearing apparel frequently carry the manufacturer's suggested price. The retailer then sells either at or below that price.

Price lining. Many businesses use **price lining,** *a retail policy of selling all merchandise at one of a set number of prices.* For example, a store may sell dresses at $24.95, $29.95, and $39.95. All merchandise is priced at one of three levels.

WHAT IS BREAK-EVEN ANALYSIS?

No business wants to lose money on what it sells. So managers try to figure out how many units they must sell to break even. **Break-even analysis** *shows the relation between cost and revenue at various levels of sales volume and determines the point at which making and selling a product becomes profitable.* Manufacturers use break-even analysis primarily as a pricing tool.

To do a break-even analysis, you must consider two kinds of costs: fixed and variable. **Fixed costs** *do not vary with volume of business.* Examples are rent, energy, and equipment. **Variable costs** *do vary with business volume.* Examples are labor, raw materials, and administration.[2]

An example of break-even analysis appears in **Figure 11-3.**

MARKUP

Many businesses, especially retailers, use a standard markup percentage to price products. A **markup** is *the difference between what retailers pay for goods and what price they sell them for; we generally express the markup as a percentage of either cost or selling price.* **Gross margin** is another term meaning markup. The markup or gross margin must be large enough to cover all business expenses, such as merchandise, salaries, rent, insurance and advertising. The gross margin must also be large enough to yield a profit. The original markup must also include allowance for probable markdowns or price reductions so that the retailer can sell merchandise that is not selling well at higher prices.

---

[2]Some variable costs may be *semi*variable. If there are wide fluctuations in business volume, rent and energy and equipment costs will vary to some degree.

We use two methods to determine the percentage markup of a product's price:

Markup based on product cost. The formula for computing percentage markup based on a product's cost is:

$$\text{Percentage markup} = \frac{\text{dollar markup}}{\text{cost}}$$

To see how the formula works, assume that a product costs a merchant $100, and he decides to sell it for $150 by giving it a $50 markup. Inserting these numbers into the formula gives us:

$$\text{Percentage markup} = \frac{\$50 \text{ (markup)}}{\$100 \text{ (cost)}} = 50\%$$

Markup based on selling price. The formula for computing percentage markup based on the selling price is:

$$\text{Percentage markup} = \frac{\text{dollar markup}}{\text{selling price}}$$

To see how this second formula works, we again assume that the merchant paid $100 for a product and marks it up $50:

$$\text{Percentage markup} = \frac{\$50 \text{ (markup)}}{\$150 \text{ (selling price)}} = 33\frac{1}{3}\%$$

WHY DO RETAILERS HAVE RELATIVELY HIGH MARKUPS?

At first glance, some markups, or gross margins, may appear exorbitant. "Why," a consumer asks, "should a store charge $100 for a ring that cost it only $50?" Most manufacturers and wholesalers have gross margins in the neighborhood of only 5 to 25 percent. How do retailers justify such high gross margins when they typically make no changes in the finished product? Key reasons are high risk, low productivity, high operating costs, and customer and employee theft.

High risk. Retailing is a risky business, particularly for the small firm. A retailer who makes a major mistake regarding what consumers will buy or how much they will buy has little or no opportunity to realize a profit on the investment. Whenever a retail store fails to stock a preferred product line or mix at the price its particular market segment is willing to pay, the store's losses may be significant.

Further, many retailers face the problem of perishability. Foods cannot be stored for long periods because they decompose. Apparel and automobiles are perishable in that they lose much of their market values as time passes; the current model or style is more desirable

TABLE 11-4 Gross Margins of Retailers

TYPE OF RETAILER	GROSS MARGIN
Men's and women's wear	41%
Home furnishings	40
Department and specialty stores	40
Hardware stores	35
Appliances/electronic sales and service	24

SOURCE: "Expenses in Retail Business," Dayton, Ohio, NCR Corporation, 1981.

than last year's model or style. If retailers overestimate sales, they may overstock and then find themselves with spoiled or out-of-date merchandise on their hands. High gross margins help cushion retailers against such risks.

Low productivity. Low productivity is another reason for the relatively high markups in retailing. It is easier to reduce per-unit labor expenses in production than in retailing. Many forms of manufacturing use standardized production procedures, automated processes, and computers for a wide variety of tasks. In retailing it is much more difficult to standardize the work or to replace personnel with machines. Customers often require individual attention.

Consider the labor involved in a simple retail transaction we see daily. A customer approaches the clerk near a cash register and says, "Give me a package of gum." The clerk reaches for it, places it on the counter, punches the appropriate information into the cash register, accepts money from the customer, gives him the gum and his change, and says, "Thank you." Obviously this represents a large input of direct labor for such a small transaction.

High operating costs. Operating costs are in some ways higher for retailers than for manufacturers and wholesalers. Stores must usually locate in higher-rent districts convenient to consumers. The cost per square foot for decorating a retail establishment and outfitting it with appropriate furniture and fixtures is considerably higher than the cost of outfitting most manufacturing plants or wholesalers' warehouses.

The extra services offered by many retailers place a further burden on operating costs. Free parking, gift wrapping, delivery, credit, damage allowances, and liberal policies with respect to the return of merchandise all contribute to a need for high gross margins.

<u>Customer and employee thefts.</u> The financial loss resulting from thefts by employees and customers is a serious problem for retailers of nearly all types of merchandise. **Shoplifting** (*customer theft*) and **pilfering** (*employee theft*) are in some cases greater than net profits. The cost of stealing contributes to the need for high gross margins in retailing.

GEOGRAPHIC PRICE POLICIES

Transportation costs are an important variable cost for firms that sell products over a wide geographic area. Several geographic price policies are used: FOB, POE, uniform delivered pricing, and zone delivered pricing.

FOB, or **free-on-board, pricing** means that *the purchaser pays all shipping costs excluding loading charges.* A manufacturer in Chicago selling a product to a company in California bills the California buyer for all freight charges from Chicago.

POE, or **port-of-entry, pricing** means that *the buyer pays all shipping charges from the point of entry to the point of delivery.* A dealer of imported cars in Atlanta is required to pay transportation costs from Jacksonville, the point of entry.

Uniform delivered pricing *regards the entire country as one zone: manufacturers charge the same to ship goods anywhere in the country.* A Chicago manufacturer using this policy charges the same transportation cost to buyers in San Diego and Cleveland.

Zone delivered pricing *divides the nation into two or more zones and charges a flat transportation charge on a per-zone basis.* The Southeast may be one zone, the Midwest another, and so on.

Service Establishment Pricing Is Different

Service establishments market intangible products and therefore must employ different pricing strategies. In pricing services such as auto repair, hair styling and lawn care, the key pricing elements to keep in mind are labor, materials used, overhead (rent, utilities, equipment etc.), and desired profit.

Labor is usually the most important cost element in pricing a service. Often the seller of a service simply multiplies the hourly wage of employees by a certain percentage to arrive at a selling price. If the hourly wage paid a mechanic is $12, the owner of an auto repair shop may multiply $12 by 2 to arrive at the charge for labor. This figure plus the cost of parts is the price charged the customer. Accounting and law firms also generally multiply the hourly wages of employees by 2 or 2½ to arrive at the price charged clients.

Service businesses often charge the "going rate" for their products. Physicians, dentists, lawyers, accountants and other professionals in a given area generally charge about the same price. The main justification for charging a higher price than the competition is the reputation of the people who provide the service.

THE TIME FACTOR INFLUENCES SERVICE PRICING

Service businesses cannot "store" service products and sell them at a later date. Such businesses, therefore, have a special incentive to sell "now" or forever lose business. The time factor becomes important for service businesses. To sell their inventory of seats, most movie theaters charge lower prices during the afternoon; to fill rooms in the off-season, many hotels charge lower off-season rates; and many airlines charge lower fares at night. Even some hospitals charge less if patients have elective surgery when hospital staff and facilities are not fully utilized.

SUMMARY

- All businesses sell products. Products may be tangible or intangible, very costly or very inexpensive, perishable or durable.
- Products sold to ultimate consumers are consumer goods. Those sold to industrial consumers are industrial goods. We can classify consumer goods on the basis of the buying habits of the consumer as convenience, shopping, and specialty goods.
- Consumer and industrial goods are marketed very differently.
- Many products have a four-stage product life cycle: introduction, growth, maturity, and decline. Most businesses modify their products in efforts to extend their life cycles.
- Packaging is vitally important, especially for consumer convenience goods. Specific objectives of packaging are to protect the product, identify it, make it easy to use, and help sell it.
- A complete label identifies the product and producer, tells where the product originated, gives the ingredients and weight, and provides instructions for use.
- Branding has two main advantages: It helps to create confidence in the firm's products, and it gives the producer more control over marketing activities.
- Theoretical considerations in pricing are inflation, the law of supply and demand, elastic and inelastic demand, pure and imperfect competition, profit maximization, and inflation.
- Practical considerations in pricing are price policies (at, below, or above the competition; negotiated pricing; psychological pricing; discounts; and price lining), break-even analysis, manufacturers' suggested prices, markups, and geographic price policies.
- Service establishments market intangible products and therefore must utilize pricing strategies that differ from those used by firms that market tangible products.

CHAPTER 11/PRODUCTS, PACKAGING, AND PRICING

KEY TERMS YOU SHOULD KNOW

- biodegradable packaging materials
- brand name
- break-even analysis
- cash discounts
- consumer goods
- convenience goods
- cumulative discounts
- decline stage
- diminishing utility
- elastic demand
- Fair Packaging and Labeling Act
- fixed costs
- free-on-board (FOB) pricing
- goods
- gross margin
- growth stage
- imperfect competition
- industrial goods
- inelastic demand
- introductory stage
- label
- law of supply and demand
- manufacturer's suggested price
- markup
- maturity stage
- negotiated pricing
- no-name brands
- noncumulative discounts
- package
- penetration pricing
- pilfering
- port-of-entry (POE) pricing
- price escalator clauses
- price lining
- pricing
- product
- product life cycle
- product line
- product mix
- product modification
- profit maximization
- psychological pricing
- pure competition
- quantity discounts
- seasonal discounts
- shoplifting
- shopping goods
- specialty goods
- trade discounts
- trademark
- uniform delivery pricing
- Universal Product Code (UPC)
- variable costs
- zone delivered pricing

QUESTIONS FOR REVIEW

1. What is a product? Must a product be tangible? Explain.
2. What are consumer goods and how do we classify them?
3. What are industrial goods and how do we classify them?
4. What is a product life cycle?
5. Explain product modification. How may a product be modified physically and nonphysically?
6. What is packaging? What are its goals?
7. How does a label relate to marketing? To branding?
8. Define pricing and explain how it is important.
9. Explain the law of supply and demand, elastic and inelastic demand, pricing under pure and imperfect competition, and profit maximization.
10. Explain pricing to meet competition, pricing below competition, pricing above competition, negotiated pricing, and psychological pricing.
11. Explain quantity, trade, cash, and seasonal discounts.
12. What is break-even analysis?
13. Explain markup on cost and markup on selling price.
14. What does gross margin mean? Why is it so high for retailers?
15. How is pricing of services different from pricing of tangible products?

QUESTIONS FOR DISCUSSION

1. A department store carries all three of the basic classifications of consumer goods. Give an example of each type. Does the way in which a product is classified have anything to do with the product's location in the store? Explain.
2. From your viewpoint as a consumer, do you feel producers of consumer products such as headache remedies, food products, and detergents spend too much money advertising very superficial differences between their products and competitors' products? If you were the marketing manager for one of the products, in what ways would your viewpoint differ? Explain.
3. Some economists believe that the government should exercise no control over prices. They feel prices should be set on the basis of supply and demand alone. Other economists think prices of some basic products—such as oil, steel, agricultural products, and transportation—should be "administered" or set by government agencies. Prepare arguments for and against each of these viewpoints.
4. If inflation averages 9 percent per year, prices will double about every eight years. Using current prices for three products you are interested in buying, compute the price of those products 20 years from now. What factors other than inflation may affect the prices of these products in the future?

CASE STUDY

Should the College Cafeteria Buy No-name Brands?

Wilkie College is a community college in the Midwest. About 14,000 students attend, and most of them eat several meals a week in the college cafeteria. The Board of Regents did not increase the college budget this year, so all departments and support facilities have to hold the line.

Mildred Hofsteder is manager of the college cafeteria, which the college owns. Her assistant is Harold Henry. Concerned about the lack of a budget increase and the rising prices of food, Mildred asks Peter Hunsinger, a food broker who supplies most of the food products to the cafeteria, to discuss their problems.

Mildred: Peter, as you probably have heard, we've been ordered not to increase prices in the cafeteria this year. This seems impossible, since food prices keep going up. We thought maybe you could help us.

Harold: We've considered several solutions—smaller servings, fewer meat and vegetable alternatives, serving only two meals a day instead of three—but none of what we've talked about seems satisfactory.

Peter: Have you considered buying only no-name brands? Now, I know you buy in large quantities—catsup by the gallon, napkins by the gross, and beans by the hundred pound. But you have always bought well-known brand names. You could cut food costs by 15 to 20 percent if you switched to no-name brands.

M: I'm familiar with the no-name-brand concept, but only on the ultimate consumer level. Frankly, some of the no-name products I've tried at home lack the taste of the name brands. Some of them seem to be below standard.

P: Now I honestly don't know about that. But I can say that no-name brands are as safe and about as nutritious as the brand items. The lower price comes from the fact that the producers don't spend money on promotion. It takes a lot of money to make cornflakes and catsup household words.

H: I don't like to go with no-name brands. I want to know that when we serve food to the students here at Wilkie College we know exactly what we're serving. To me, a brand name implies that the producer stands behind its product.

P: I understand. But switching to no-name brands is a possible solution to your problem.

M: I agree. We really are under the gun this year. The price of what we sell is *going up* and the price we can charge is *fixed*.

P: Let me suggest this. Suppose I begin a gradual shift to supplying you with no-name brands. Meanwhile, you try to measure students' reactions. If there are only a few negative reactions, you're home free. And who knows, there may be no reactions at all.

Questions

1. What do you think about Peter's suggestion?
2. Do you believe no-name brands will become more popular in the future? Why or why not?
3. What has been your personal experience with no-name brands?
4. Does the exceptional emphasis on marketing branded products suggest marketing costs may, in fact, be too high? Explain.

EVOLUTION OF A BUSINESS

Solving Operational Problems with Pricing

After six months of operation, Sara and Ray were pleased with how well Excel Travel was doing. While they were not yet making a profit, they were breaking even. This is a good record for travel-agency businesses, which usually operate with deficits for a longer period of time.

As was to be expected, their operation was not without problems.

Sara: I've been reviewing the books and noticing differences in the amount of time devoted to handling various clients. Some require a lot of service, others very little. With client A, we make up just one itinerary and that's it. Client B, on the other hand, will change the stops he plans to make on his trip a dozen times, which means extra typings, telephone calls, and letters to cancel reservations and make new ones. Yet the client who requires a lot of service often buys little and contributes least to our net billings.

Ray: There's nothing we can do about that, is there? If we want to build our reputation on service, we can't give each client service according to what he or she spends.

Sara: Well, how about charging for itinerary changes?

Ray: It's an idea. But before we move on it, we'd better check to see what our competitors' policies are. We don't want to unknowingly give them an edge.

Sara: Another expense that's running high is the cost involved in making hotel reservations overseas at hotels that don't have U.S. representatives. The cable charges amount to quite a bit. In fact, if the reservation is for only one night, the cable costs often run as much as the commission we get on the room. I've heard that some agencies charge for cables—either the actual cost of the cable or a flat fee of $5. What about our doing that? Cables have been running us about $3.60 on the average.

Ray: Again, I'd move carefully. A charge like that might not be well-received. Say a couple traveling to Algiers buys more than $2,000 worth of airline tickets from us to get there. How would it look to add on a $5 cable fee? We don't know how our clients would react to various service charges. I'd say we need to do some experimenting or some research on other agencies' experiences.

Questions

1. What kind of policy would you adopt to reduce the number of itinerary changes?
2. Is adding cable charges to the client's bill good business?
3. How important is it to know what competitors' policies are? Do people evaluating travel agencies make these kinds of comparisons between agencies?
4. How can Ray and Sara find out how clients will react to the proposed changes?

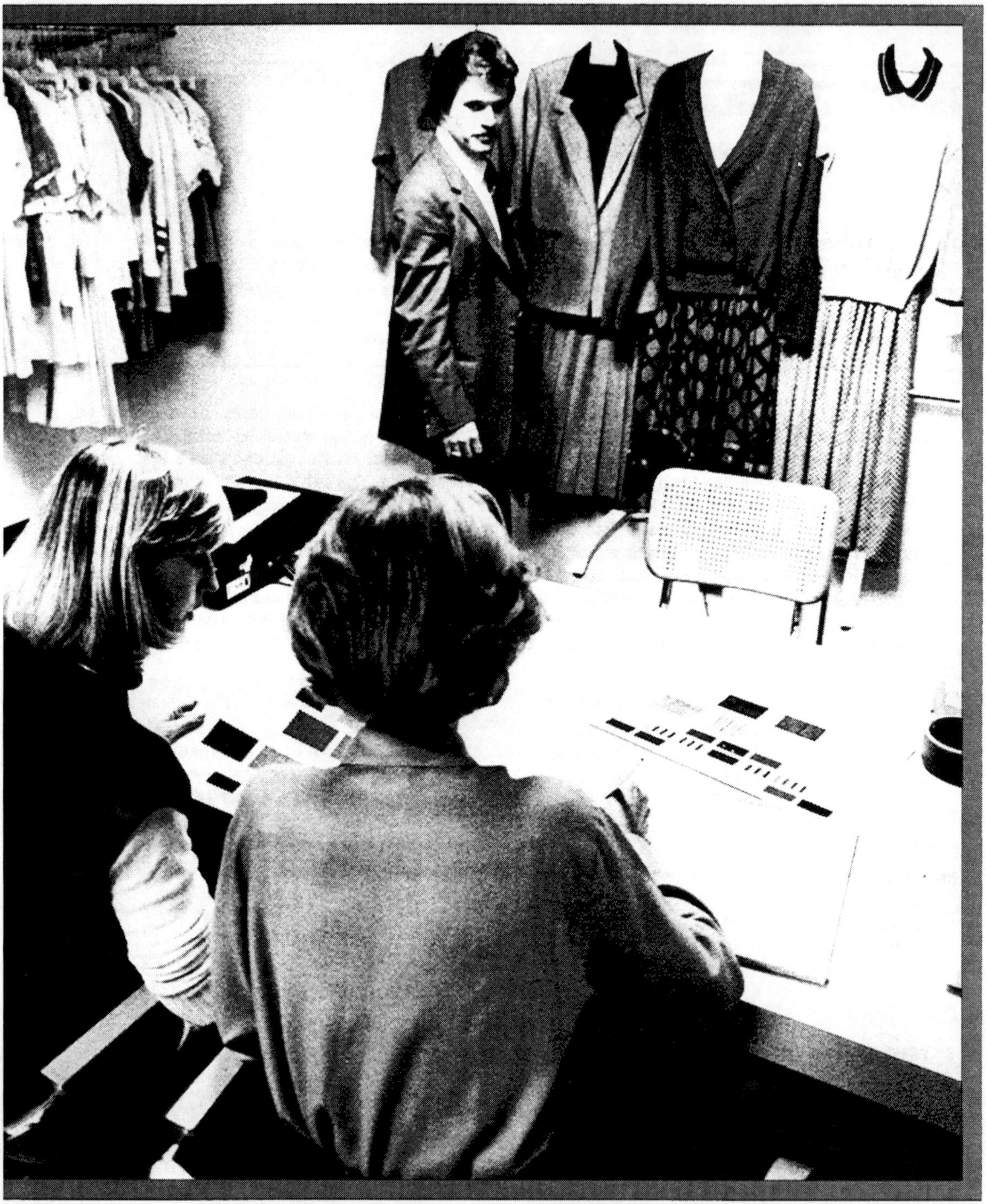

12

MARKETING COMMUNICATIONS: SELLING, ADVERTISING, PROMOTION, AND PUBLIC RELATIONS
Stimulating Interest

READ THIS CHAPTER SO YOU CAN:

Discuss personal selling and describe the steps in the selling process.

Explain what sales management involves.

Describe the role advertising plays in promotion, its specific purposes, and the kinds of available media.

Discuss what an advertising agency does and how it serves its clients.

Evaluate common criticisms of advertising.

Detail the role that samples; contests, sweepstakes, and games; premiums; coupons; and point-of-purchase displays play in sales promotion.

Explain how public relations fits into a company's promotional program.

Discuss ways to increase the productivity of marketing.

American business operates in an increasingly competitive and crowded marketplace. Each business is concerned with determining how it can increase sales and revenue and eventually come out on top or near the top. In any service or product industry, sales provide the bulk of total revenue and revenue is essential to business survival. The health of every business is measured by the ability to generate sales, and therefore revenue, in excess of expenditures. When sales equal or exceed projections, positive figures result. The business can meet its payroll, pay its suppliers, rent, utilities, interest, and other expenses, and make a profit. High sales volume encourages expansion, new product development, payment of dividends, and extra compensation for key employees. But when sales volume declines, the business is unable to cover operating costs, pay dividends, or expand. Inadequate sales can cause any business to fail. Seeing beyond their product or service and utilizing promotional activity to attract a profitable market is increasingly important for businesses.

WHAT GOES INTO THE PROMOTIONAL MIX?

Consider how Barb and Jack Williams use each element to promote "Cookie Delights," which they make in their small bakery and market through their on-site retail store.

Personal selling *involves personally assisting and convincing a prospective customer to buy a product or service.* Barb and Jack employ a retail salesperson to sell cookies over-the-counter. They also hire a person to make telephone sales calls to all businesses in the area suggesting cookies as a gift and party item for employees and customers. Their next plan is to visit delicatessens, food stores, and restaurants to develop wholesale business.

Advertising *is any paid, impersonal presentation of products, services, or ideas to induce people to buy or respond positively to the proposition presented.* Barb and Jack buy advertising space in the yellow pages and insert a small ad in the weekly suburban newspaper. After making telephone sales calls to area businesses, they follow up with a direct mail advertising campaign. In addition, if there's any money left in the advertising budget, they may consider buying ad time on a local radio station.

Promotion *consists of activities that stimulate buyer interest, such as displays, trade shows, demonstrations, and various nonrecurrent efforts.* As Barb and Jack's business grows, sales promotion becomes an increasingly important part of boosting sales and attracting a variety of customers. They may prepare attractive point-of-purchase window displays and counter cards to announce weekly specials; distribute matchbooks that give a brief message about Cookie Delights to area businesses; offer a dozen free cookies with each $10 purchase; employ students to give sample cookies to people passing by the store; include fancy napkins and balloons with every purchase; and buy a large, colorful neon sign in the shape of a cookie to identify the store.

Public relations *is planned efforts to obtain goodwill or favorable attitudes from the public* such as news items, plant tours, and interviews with the media. Public relations is used extensively to promote Cookie Delights. Each month a news release "What's New in Cookies?" which explains the production and marketing methods used by Cookie Delights is sent to the local newspapers, radio stations, and TV stations in hopes of getting free publicity. Local schoolchildren are invited to visit the bakery and see cookies being mass produced. Barb and Jack also decide to sponsor a little league soccer team—the players will wear Cookie Delights uniforms.

In this example of a small business, the owners give attention to each element in the promotional process. Larger businesses also use a four-point classification system for their marketing efforts but with greater sophistication and larger budgets. Now, let us look at each promotional element in more detail.

PROMOTION TOOL #1: PERSONAL SELLING

The retail employee who helps a customer select a pair of shoes is selling. The manufacturer's representative who persuades a wholesaler to stock a certain product and resell it to retailers is selling. And the newspaper representative who calls on firms to urge them to advertise in the paper is also selling. Personal selling affects each one of us, whether we are purchasing consumer or business products. It is essential to the general economic well-being of our country.

Who Sells?

Over 5 million peole have selling jobs in our labor force. Although they all sell, their jobs and titles differ greatly. Among the titles used are "salesperson," "sales representative," "executive representative," "account executive," "territory sales consultant," "sales engineer," "area manager," "professional sales representative," "communications consultant," and "key account sales manager."

Retail salespeople have the least complicated jobs, because customers come to the store. This is a good place for a person to get grass-roots experience in meeting, observing, and working with the public.

In many retail sales jobs, minimum selection standards are used and little training is provided. In contrast, sales representatives for wholesalers, banks, and manufacturers require more extensive quali-

Personal selling occurs on many levels—from wholesalers to jobbers and retailers. It affects us all and is essential to our economic system.

fications and training, since they call on professional buyers who want both technical data and information about how to resell what they buy.

What Is Selling?

If someone told you "I work in medicine," it might mean the person is a physician, nurse, administrator, orderly, or a lab technician. The statement "I work in medicine" is vague. And if someone told you "I work in sales," it could mean the individual is a manufacturer's representative, an intangibles salesperson, a salesperson for a wholesaler, or a retail salesperson. The statement "I work in sales" says little because the sales field is extensive and varied.

Table 12–1 shows nine basic job factors for five different kinds of selling. It is particularly difficult to be specific about income potential in selling, so the descriptions in the chart are generalized. However, one researcher has found that there are more salespeople than physicians who earn $75,000 or more per year.[1]

Regardless of the type of selling, salespersons follow similar basic steps in the selling process. The type of sales job determines how complex these steps are.

Selling Is a Five-step Process

The steps generally followed in making a sale are to (1) identify or locate prospective customers, (2) arrange to see the prospective cus-

---

[1] Dr. Thomas Stanley, Georgia State University—an Expert on Affluent Americans.

TABLE 12-1 Basic Requirements for Different Kinds of Selling Positions

KEY ASPECTS OF THE SELLING POSITION	RETAIL SELLING	WHOLESALE SELLING	MANUFACTURERS SELLING	INTANGIBLE SELLING	REAL ESTATE SELLING
Basic job	Sells products to ultimate consumers not sold through self-service.	Sells standardized products to retailers and wholesalers.	Sells equipment tools and installations to businesses; products are often tailor-made.	Sells financial services, insurance, advertising and other services; each customer's needs are unique.	Sells houses, lease arrangements, and commercial and industrial property.
Education required	Degree not needed.	Degree preferred but often not essential.	Degree required; technical background preferred.	Degree required; graduate degree helpful.	Degree preferred.
Compensation	Minimal; hourly and/or weekly wage.	Salary and some incentive reward.	Relatively high salary plus strong incentives.	Often straight commission.	Usually commission only.
Supervision provided	Considerable; day-to-day.	Considerable; usually on a weekly basis.	Little; self-management is stressed; creativity emphasized.		
Away-from-home travel requirements	None.	Considerable; over a route in a territory.	Considerable and to varied locations.	Considerable but usually confined to one area.	Little.
Self-motivation required	Average.	Average.	Considerable.	Considerable; often a key requirement.	Considerable.
Advancement potential	Fair.	Good.	Excellent.	Excellent; often leads to one's own business.	Good; may lead to one's own business.
Post-sale service	Usually none.	Continuous but routine.	Continuous and highly specialized.	Continuous.	Minimal.
Negotiation skills required	Little emphasis on negotiation.	Mainly fills orders; little negotiation.	Strong negotiation skills needed in pricing, special concessions requested, advertising allowances, service arrangements, etc.		

tomer under favorable conditions, (3) demonstrate or explain the value of the product or service, (4) answer the prospective customer's questions and meet his or her objections, and (5) close the sale by convincing the prospect that he or she should buy. The following illustrates how salespersons take these steps in actual selling situations.

Fred Brown, who sells securities for a brokerage firm, calls between 20 and 30 people each morning to find out if they are interested in investing. *The process of contacting potential customers to see if they are interested in buying* is called **prospecting**—Step 1 in the selling process. When someone indicates an interest, Brown arranges an appointment (Step 2). During the appointment, Brown explains the pros and cons of different securities in terms of the prospect's interests. In effect, this is Step 3 in the process—demonstration of the product. Next, Brown answers the prospect's questions (Step 4) and tries to close the sale by asking the prospect to open an account with the firm (Step 5).

In some fields—particularly industrial selling—salespersons make few personal visits on prospects. Because of greater dispersal of customers (who were once concentrated in central cities) and rising prices of transportation, it now costs an average of $168 to make a single industrial sales call. Thus, salespersons are making greater use of the telephone, catalogs, and automatic reordering systems.

What Does a Sales Manager Do?

The person who directs the activities of the sales force is the **sales manager.** The sales manager is responsible for the recruitment, selection, training, equipping, territorial assignment, and motivation of sales representatives.

RECRUITMENT

Methods of recruitment include advertising in newspapers and trade publications, visiting colleges and university placement offices, and asking present sales representatives to suggest likely candidates.

SELECTION

After recruitment, the next step is to select those applicants who show the most promise. Information from completed application forms and statements from previous employers, teachers, and others can help indicate the fitness of the applicant, though there is a tendency for such statements to be more laudatory than realistic. Many companies rely in part on tests to determine whether the applicant has the aptitude necessary for selling. Since ability to influence other people is necessary in selling, sales managers are interested not only in the courses taken by applicants while in school but in their extracurricular activities.

TRAINING

Sales representatives must have a knowledge of their company, the products sold, and the wants and buying motives of their customers. They also need skill in selling techniques. A major part of the sales manager's job, then, is to help sales representatives acquire the necessary product and service information and selling skills.

Equipping
The sales executive provides sales representatives with the necessary tools—automobiles, samples and sample cases, portfolios, advertising literature, displays, and the like.

Assignment of Territories
The sales manager divides the company's market area into individual sales territories. The purposes of territorial division are to:

- *Assign each sales representative an optimum number of customers and potential customers*—If a person's territory is too large, he or she is inclined to cultivate only the most important accounts and thus fail to get maximum sales volume. If the territory is too small, the person may be unable to earn an adequate income.
- *Avoid overlapping of territories*—Unless each sales representative has a clearly defined territory, two or more company representatives may call on the same customers. This confusion would result in excessive selling costs and could create customer dissatisfaction.

Motivation
Many kinds of selling require a great deal of self-motivation. For one thing, salespeople hear prospects say "no" far more often than "yes." For another, salespeople work alone and thereby lack the encouragement of other company people. For these reasons sales managers hold frequent meetings, devise contests, supply tapes and books on motivation, and in other ways try to keep morale of salespeople at a high level.

Figure 12–1 shows how the typical sales executive for a life insurance company spends his or her time. The time breakdown, of course, would differ with the type of product being sold.

PROMOTION TOOL #2: ADVERTISING

Advertising is one of the most conspicuous characteristics of American business. It is an exciting activity—sometimes loud and ludicrous, other times colorful, clever, and creative. As an economic force, advertising is both strongly condemned and solidly defended.

Advertising is most important in marketing consumer products such as soap, toothpaste, beverages, and automobiles. It is less important in marketing industrial products, since firms selling primarily to

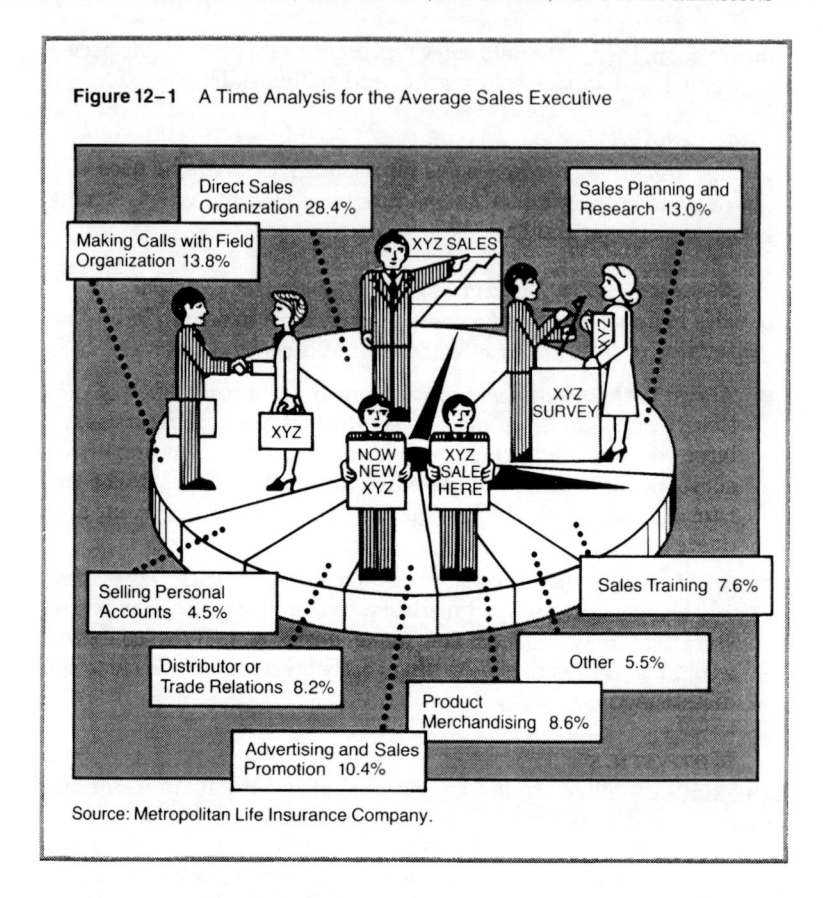

Figure 12–1 A Time Analysis for the Average Sales Executive

- Direct Sales Organization 28.4%
- Sales Planning and Research 13.0%
- Making Calls with Field Organization 13.8%
- Selling Personal Accounts 4.5%
- Sales Training 7.6%
- Distributor or Trade Relations 8.2%
- Other 5.5%
- Product Merchandising 8.6%
- Advertising and Sales Promotion 10.4%

Source: Metropolitan Life Insurance Company.

industrial consumers make greater use of personal selling. Table 12–2 shows advertising expenditures as a percentage of sales for 12 well-known companies.

Advertising is based on the assumption that producers must inform consumers about a product and its specific values before they will purchase it. An inventor may perfect a new device, but unless he or she can persuade the public to buy, quantity production may not result. Once demand has been created, advertising may help to maintain and possibly increase it.

How Do Advertising and Personal Selling Differ?

The basic distinction between selling and advertising is that *selling is personal, whereas advertising is impersonal*. The objective of both is the same—to sell. Advertising and selling are auxiliary to each other.

TABLE 12-2 Advertising as a Percentage of Sales

McDonald's Corporation	10.6%
Bristol-Myers Company	7.6
Procter & Gamble	6.6
Anheuser-Busch, Inc.	5.8
Philip Morris, Inc.	4.7
Polaroid Corporation	3.7
Coca-Cola Company	3.4
K mart Corporation	2.2
Sears, Roebuck & Company	1.6
General Motors Corporation	0.5
American Telephone & Telegraph Company	0.5
Ford Motor Company	0.5

SOURCES: "One Hundred Leading National Advertisers," *Advertising Age*, February 16, 1981; "The Forbes 500," *Forbes*, May 12, 1980.

Advertising informs, lessens buyer resistance, and paves the way for salespeople. Advertising presells the customer. For example, a computer company may advertise to make prospective customers aware of the advantages of using its computers. Salespeople, however, still must demonstrate the computer, answer the prospect's questions, and close the sale.

What Are the Specific Purposes of Advertising?

The overall aim of advertising is to sell products. More specialized goals of advertising are to:

- *Increase the number of units purchased*—"Buy by the case and save."
- *Introduce new products*—"See the new desk top computer today."
- *Suggest additional uses for the product*—"Here are four new recipes using our soup."
- *Increase sales in off seasons*—"Buy a new air conditioning system in January and save 25 percent."
- *Maintain brand loyalty*—"Don't accept substitutes."
- *Counteract competition*—"Tests prove our product is best."

Advertising agency executives discuss a campaign during the process of planning, preparing, and placing ads in various media.

Types of Advertising

NATIONAL ADVERTISING

National advertising is *used to sell nationally distributed, branded merchandise,* such as soft drinks, automobiles, appliances, and food products. To advertise nationally, a company may buy space in large-circulation magazines, such as *Newsweek,* or purchase time on television networks.

RETAIL ADVERTISING

Department stores, chain stores, automobile dealers, and other retailers, use **retail,** or **local, advertising** which is *much more specific than national advertising in describing price and terms of sale; it informs consumers exactly where and when the product or service can be purchased.* A retail advertisement often mentions a variety of different items, whereas national advertising is usually restricted to a single product or family of products.

INDUSTRIAL ADVERTISING

Advertising directed to telling manufacturers and other industrial users what to buy is **industrial advertising.** Because there are

Billboards provide just one of many advertising options. Others include print media, radio, and television.

relatively few industrial consumers compared with ultimate consumers, the volume of industrial advertising is smaller.

Trade Advertising

Trade advertising tells retailers and wholesalers what to stock and *conveys messages about price, markups, special offers, discounts, point-of-purchase materials and other information retailers and wholesalers want to know.*

Institutional Advertising

Attempts to enhance the image of a business are **institutional advertising.** Institutional advertising does not mention specific merchandise. Instead, it discusses the stability, reliability, and spirit of a business and its contribution to the public welfare. Banks, utilities, and insurance companies are some of the principal institutional advertisers.

Advertising Media Deliver Messages to Consumers

An **advertising medium** is *any device used to carry the advertising message to the people that the advertiser intends to influence.*

TABLE 12-3 Total Estimated Direct Advertising Expenditures (1977-1983)

(IN $ MILLIONS)

	1983	1982	1981	1980	1979	1978	1977
Coupons	182.1	127.1	94.6	84.2	72.0	61.0	84.0
Direct mail	12,692.2	11,359.4	10,566.7	9,998.7	8,876.7	7,298.2	6,966.7
Consumer magazines	188.7	167.0	150.0	135.0	123.0	99.8	86.2
Business magazines	73.9	66.0	59.0	53.0	47.0	49.4	49.4
Newspapers	80.5	70.6	73.0	60.6	54.4	58.0	42.8
Newspaper preprints	2,850.0	2,500.0	2,288.5	2,032.4	1,779.5	1,390.0	1,086.0
Telephone	13,608.3	12,935.6	11,467.0	9,845.0	8,555.6	8,555.6	7,699.0
Television	386.5	339.0	295.0	253.0	217.0	265.0	340.7
Radio	37.0	33.0	29.0	26.0	23.0	N/A	N/A
Total	30,099.2	27,597.7	25,022.8	22,487.9	19,748.2	17,777.0	16,354.8

SOURCE: Adapted from Direct Marketing Association.

NOTE: Creative costs not included in any of the above figures.

Sellers have a number of media at their disposal: newspapers, magazines, radio, television, direct mail, billboards, car cards, and many others of less importance. Table 12-3 shows advertising expenditures for each medium from 1977-1983.

The basic problem for the advertiser in selecting media is to find the best one for the desired market. The yardstick for advertising media is both quantitative (how many people will be reached) and qualitative (what type of people will be reached).

For example, an advertiser selling a product bought chiefly by women may have to choose between two newspapers. Newspaper A may be a typical daily newspaper, reaching all types of people, with an advertising rate of, say, $6 per line. Newspaper B may be of the shopping-news variety, reaching primarily homemakers, and may have a rate of $12 per line. The choice will depend on a number of factors, but it may well be that the medium with the higher rate will actually be the more economical, since it may be more effective.

Clearly, an advertiser has many choices as to how to spend advertising dollars. Standard Rate and Data Service provides detailed information about rates (costs) and circulation of advertising for specific newspaper, radio, television, and magazine media. This information is available in books that are published periodically and can be found at some business libraries.

How Advertising Agencies Function

An **advertising agency** is *a service organization composed of specialists who plan, prepare, and place advertising for companies.* Advertising agencies range in size from those employing one or two people to those employing several thousand and maintaining offices in major cities here and abroad. Some agencies specialize in preparing specific advertising, while others, known as **general agencies,** *prepare all kinds of advertising for many different clients.*

AGENCY INCOME

An agency receives an agency rate from the medium concerned when it purchases advertising time or space for its clients. The client pays the gross rate and the agency's commission usually amounts to 15 percent of the total cost. For example, if an advertisement in a magazine costs $10,000, the agency charges the advertiser $10,000 and pays the magazine $8,500. The $1,500 difference represents the agency's commission. This commission constitutes the major source of income for the agency.

This system is the most common one. However, some agencies simply charge a flat fee for each job.

HOW WORK IN AN AGENCY IS DIVIDED

The advertising agency usually divides work among several specialists. The account executive acts as a liasion between the agency and the advertiser, usually referred to as the client or account. The account executive is responsible for planning the advertising program and explaining the needs of the client to the agency staff. He or she should have a broad knowledge of advertising and an intimate understanding of the client's business. An account executive may handle several accounts or only one, depending on the size of the advertiser. The position of account executive pays well and is a coveted job in advertising.

Copywriters, artists, designers, and layout experts create the advertisements. Copywriters prepare text material for printed advertising and write commercials for radio and television. Artists and designers work closely with copywriters to visualize the ideas on which the advertisement is based. Their function is to make sketches, specify typography and color, and arrange the elements of the advertisement.

Actual production of the physical advertisement is the work of compositors and printers, but the agency production department performs the preliminary work for physical production. This department designates and oversees the printers and compositors.

The media director, or space buyer, is responsible for buying space in magazines and newspapers and time on radio and television.

This job is complicated because of the large variety of media from which to choose. To make wise selections, the media director analyzes circulation and audience size and studies the type of people reached by the media.

The Client's Advertising Department

In some cases, a business may have its own in-company, or in-house, advertising department. This is an important element of a business because some promotional activities must originate in-house. These activities include:

- Devising a broad advertising plan to incorporate into the overall marketing program
- Determining the size of the advertising budget and making sure funds are properly spent
- Selecting an advertising agency and acting as liaison with it
- Supplying information to the agency about the company, its products, and its marketing goals
- Preparing or purchasing various sales-promotion materials
- Coordinating advertising with personal selling, sales promotion, and public relations

Common Criticisms of Advertising

Advertising is a powerful, dynamic force in our economy. While some people feel it serves a valuable function in making people aware of available products and services, others criticize it severely. Following is a brief review of the major criticisms of advertising.

ADVERTISING COSTS TOO MUCH

A common criticism of advertising is that it increases the cost of goods and services. Many people are astonished to learn that the back cover of a national magazine may cost $100,000, a 30-second commercial on a network television program $200,000, and a one-page advertisement in a daily newspaper $10,000 or more. What most people do not know is that the cost of reaching one consumer may be only a fraction of a cent. The Super Bowl may attract an audience of 50 million people who see a commercial costing $250,000. The cost per person reached, however, is only half a penny.

ADVERTISING IS PURELY COMPETITIVE

This argument states that advertising simply enables one company to attract customers from another and does not bring new customers into the market.

To say advertising is purely competitive and hence wasteful is to suggest that competition as such is wasteful. As we have seen, competition results in efficiencies. Even if advertising did not enlarge the total market for a product, we can argue that society benefits from advertising competition. Firms must work to create better products—with more advertising features—if they are to surpass the advertising claims of competitors.

A joke common among advertising executives is, "We know 50 percent of our advertising is wasted. The only problem is we don't know which 50 percent." Remember that advertising is largely creative, and we cannot evaluate its effectiveness in a purely objective manner.

Advertising Makes People Want Things They Cannot Afford

There is undoubtedly some truth in this criticism: We can credit advertising with whetting the appetites of consumers for more and newer things. But is this harmful? The desire to enjoy a higher standard of living is a strong incentive to become better educated and to earn more money. A want-oriented society creates a desire in people to be ambitious. We can argue that, as a result, everyone benefits because the society produces more, which is potentially beneficial to the economy in the long run.

Advertising Misleads

Some advertisers do mislead. Exaggerated, if not erroneous, claims for curing colds, gaining or losing weight, and inducing sleep have worked to the detriment of society. Fortunately, legislation and the Federal Trade Commission and advertisers' own restraint have done much to correct these malpractices.

Advertising Offends

Certainly some advertising is annoying. For example, billboard advertising may spoil the beauty of a landscape. Television and radio commercials receive even more criticism. One frequently hears complaints that "Commercials are an insult to the intelligence of the viewer" and "TV programs today have more commercials than program."

Critics also often blame advertising for the content of radio and TV programs. They charge that advertisers determine—or at least approve—the content of the programs that they sponsor. Since advertisers are afraid of offending anyone and are seeking to appeal to the largest number of people, the resulting programs have little significance and in some cases (that is, violent TV programs) are potentially damaging. In addition, some controversy continues in the advertising business about the alleged use of subliminal advertising, which uses suggestive elements in design, particularly sexual elements and creates an image in the reader's mind which may cause him or her to respond emotionally rather than rationally.

What Can We Conclude About Advertising?

Some of the criticisms directed at advertising are valid. However, in evaluating advertising we should remember that advertising pays for most of our radio and TV entertainment as well as for our newspapers and magazines. And while many have tried, few magazine or newspaper publishers can stay in business without carrying advertisements.

A story told about Mark Twain offers an ironic comment on newspapers' desire to attract advertisers. In a letter to the editor that reached Twain during his editing days, a reader said he had found a spider in his newspaper and asked whether that was a sign of good or bad luck. Twain replied, "[The] spider was merely looking over our paper to see which merchant is not advertising, so that he can go to that store, spin his web across the door, and live a life of undisturbed peace ever afterward."

Keep in mind that advertising basically appeals to customers as they are now rather than attempting to change them. Ad agencies, like other businesses, are trying to do their jobs well—and their job is to help clients reach the largest possible audience with their advertising dollars. The criticisms of advertisers could just as well be directed against other people, such as sponsors of sports events or popular writers. We cannot blame advertisers if more people watch a football game than an opera or if more people read a sensational story than an academic article. Perhaps this type of criticism should more appropriately be leveled against our social attitudes and educational system. Right or wrong, advertisers are less interested in remaking society than they are in appealing to it as it exists.

PROMOTION TOOL #3: SALES PROMOTION

The boundaries of sales promotion are less clear-cut than those of personal selling and advertising. While some companies have sales promotion departments, responsibility for this activity is not clearly assigned in many organizations, and either sales management or the advertising department tend to take it over.

Sales promotion is important in marketing because it (1) increases the demand for new products, (2) helps differentiate similar products, and (3) is a substitute for price competition. The following examples are of common sales promotion activities.

Samples Encourage People to Try a Product

Samples are *products companies give away to consumers in an effort to build consumer demand.* Sampling is an old and widely used sales promotion technique, especially when the product is new or has a new feature. Soap, toothpaste, and cigarettes are examples of low-cost products that companies frequently have consumers sample.

Contests, Sweepstakes, and Games Create Interest

The purpose of contests, sweepstakes, and games is to get consumers to buy a product by creating involvement. **Contests** *offer prizes to consumers as a reward for analytical or creative thinking,* usually about a product. **Sweepstakes** *usually require only that the participant enter his or her name, which has a chance of being drawn from a "pot" containing all other consumer-entrants' names.* **Games** *are conducted over a longer period of time and do not require skill.* From the marketer's viewpoint, games have an advantage over sweepstakes and contests because the consumer must often make repeated visits to the outlet that carries the firm's products to continue playing—such as supermarket bingo games.

Premiums—Something of Value for Less

A **premium** is *a product offered free or at a lower price than usual to encourage consumers to buy another product*—generally one that they frequently purchase. China or glass tumblers given away with a specified purchase of gasoline and toy whistles attached to tubes of toothpaste are examples of premiums.

The objectives of premiums are to (1) induce consumers to switch from a competitor's product to the seller's, (2) induce consumers to try larger sizes of the product, (3) increase off-season sales, (4) introduce a new product, (5) obtain names of prospects, and (6) offset price competition.

Coupons Are Like Money

Manufacturers often issue **coupons,** which are *certificates consumers present to a retailer for savings or a cash refund on an item.* They are one of the most widely used sales promotion devices.

Manufacturers often use coupons for common food-store items. One premise of couponing is that a change in attitude does not necessarily have to precede a change in behavior. Consumers may be very loyal to one brand of detergent, but if a coupon for a competitive brand will save money, they may at least try it.

Point-of-purchase Displays Say "Buy Me"

Today, manufacturers retail most products through self-service. **Point-of-purchase displays** are *devices that display a product near where consumers make the purchase decision in order to stimulate immediate sales.* They tell consumers, "Here I am. Buy me

AMERICA'S REEMERGING CREATIVITY

Using Cash Rebates and Coupons to Stimulate Buying

When faced with a sales decline, American business people generally come up with creative ways to solve the problem. One technique widely employed in the late 1970s and early 1980s was the cash rebate.

A **cash rebate** is *the payment of cash by the seller to the buyer of the seller's product.* Cash rebates are most widely used by auto makers, who urge customers to buy a new car before a certain date and receive cash (usually $400 to $1,800, depending on the model).

Cash rebates are also used extensively in marketing appliances, furniture, and other costly consumer goods. It is difficult to measure the effectiveness of cash rebates as a demand stimulation device, especially over the long run. But the fact that all domestic auto makers have used them suggest that they do have a positive effect on sales.

Coupons are another sales promotion device that businesses are using to stimulate sales. While cents-off coupons go back a century, their popularity continues to grow as rising prices make consumers increasingly cost-conscious.

More than 1,000 manufacturers use coupons to stimulate sales. In 1984, more than 119 billion coupons were circulated in newspapers and magazines, and by direct mail. Coupons are used extensively in marketing cereals, dog food, soap, coffee, soft drinks, and other consumer convenience products. Some manufacturers feel that coupons are more effective than television ads in selling products.

Consumers like coupons too. An estimated 75 percent of American households clip and redeem coupons. Some consumers claim to save several thousand dollars a year by using them.

Coupons and cash rebates may not have been novel or great ideas, but they make a difference to many consumers who spend a lot of time and effort using them to save money.

Questions

1. Do you believe that giving cash rebates over a period of two to three years has any effect on total sales of a product? Explain the reasoning behind your answer.
2. When all cost factors are considered, do rebates and coupons actually reduce the cost of products to consumers? Explain.

---

now!" Some common point-of-purchase displays are floor displays, stands, interior overhead signs, wall signs, and posters. If they are attractive, show the product effectively, make the product look worth the price, and give needed information about the product, they help sell it.

PROMOTION TOOL #4: PUBLIC RELATIONS

All personal and impersonal business contacts with the public are aspects of public relations.

Specific purposes of public relations are to (1) interpret company policies and behavior to the public, (2) counteract distortion of facts caused by rumors, (3) "humanize" the business—give it a personality, and (4) win support from the various publics important to the business.

The "Publics" of Public Relations

We can break down the general public of a business into specific **publics,** or *special-interest groups*. The most important of these are:

- *Consumers*—This is the largest and most important public of a business, for no business can prosper without customer goodwill.
- *Community*—Like an individual, a business will operate in a more supportive environment if it earns the respect of its neighbors.
- *Stockholders*—Progressive companies recognize the owners of the business as a public and therefore maintain programs for stockholder relations.
- *Suppliers*—While often a public that is not large in size, suppliers are large in the power they wield. They tend to be most helpful to companies they respect.
- *Dealers*—The goodwill of the dealers who sell company products is very much worth cultivating.
- *Employees*—Employees are usually one of the smaller publics, but their importance is considerable. A public relations program that overlooks the importance of a company's own employees is shortsighted at best. Many corporations now give recognition to employees in their annual reports or feature them in print and media advertising.

Advertising vs. Public Relations

Advertising is a function of sales, or marketing, whereas public relations can be considered an extension of the executive branch of the company. Advertising is designed to capture a share of the market for the company's products, whereas public relations is a planned, continuing effort to create a positive attitude toward the company.

In some companies, advertising and public relations are considered separate functions. Large companies, particularly, have both an advertising department and a public relations department. However, many firms consolidate the two functions, with both public relations and advertising handled by one department (often called the communications department).

Publicity Is Part of Public Relations

Publicity, or *news items, about a business, its products and its personnel* is an important part of public relations. Increasingly, busi-

TABLE 12–4 Effective Public Relations in Action

J.C. PENNEY
The nation's third largest mass merchandiser donated its vacant store in downtown Seattle to the Seattle Art Museum.

SATURDAY EVENING POST
Cigarettes were bringing in $400,000 a year in advertising revenues, but the *Saturday Evening Post* said it would no longer accept these ads, effective with the March 1984 issue. The magazine is now owned by the Benjamin Franklin Literary & Medical Society, which decided that tobacco advertising was inconsistent with the health message of the society.

LEVI STRAUSS & CO.
This San Francisco-based apparel manufacturer adopted a plant-closing policy that calls, among other things, for the company to continue its support of local United Ways for one to three years after a facility has been closed. In addition, the company will consider making a special gift to a local agency addressing a critical community need. Levi Strauss & Co. closed 19 facilities in 1984.

COCA-COLA
Atlanta-based Coca-Cola became the first big corporation to mount a major program to expand ties with the Hispanic community. Called the National Hispanic Business Agenda, the Coke thrust calls for expenditures of $14 million to buy more goods and services from Hispanic firms, recruit more Hispanic employees and support educational and job-training programs. As part of its commitment, Coke will invest $5 million in Spanish-language ads, using Hispanic-owned ad agencies and broadcasting stations.

HONEYWELL
This international corporation, a leader in automation and control, received a 1983 President's Volunteer Action Award for its multifaceted volunteer programs. Honeywell maintains employee involvement programs at all its locations. It gives annual awards to employees for community service, placing these awards on a level with those given for sales and engineering achievements. It also has a volunteer program for retirees that in 1982 recruited 590 people who contributed more than 260,000 hours to various community efforts.

Only one other corporation received a President's Award at the White House luncheon. That was the Frito-Lay division of PepsiCo.

RICHARDSON-VICKS, INC.
If you have a cold this winter, you can help the Boy Scouts and the Girl Scouts by buying a passel of Vicks® products—NyQuil®, Formula 44D®, VapoRub®, Sinex®, Vicks® cough drops. If you will then mail four proofs-of-purchase to Vicks, the company will send you a $2 coupon good toward the purchase of any product at a local store and will contribute an additional $2 to the Boy Scouts and Girls Scouts. This is the repeat of a program Vicks ran in 1980. It worked then, so now it's being repeated. It's not open-ended. Vicks has put a maximum of $200,000 on how much it will contribute.

AVON PRODUCTS
This door-to-door seller of cosmetics and toiletries began a minority purchasing program in 1972. In that year it bought $172,000 of goods and services from thirty minority-owned companies. In 1981, Avon bought $12.5 million of goods and services from 300 minority firms.

SOURCE: *Business and Society Review*, Spring 1983, pp. 37–43.

nesses prepare news and release it to the media hoping to gain positive public reaction. Table 12–4 shows how seven companies have developed positive public relations. Actions like these build goodwill with the public and often produce more benefit to a firm than they

TABLE 12-5 Reputations on the Line

In the corporate reputations survey, *Fortune* polled 8,000 executives, outside directors, and financial analysts. About 52% responded—a good return. Those surveyed were asked to rate the ten largest companies in their industry, using a scale of 1 (poor) to 10 (excellent), on eight key attributes: quality of management; quality of products or services; innovativeness; long-term investment value; financial soundness; ability to attract, develop, and keep talented people; community and environmental responsibility; and use of corporate assets.

EXECUTIVES RATE AMERICAN CORPORATIONS

Most Admired	Least Admired
IBM	International Harvester
Dow Jones	Eastern Air Lines
Hewlett-Packard	Manville
Merck	Pan Am
Johnson & Johnson	American Motors
Time Inc.	Republic Steel
General Electric	Pabst Brewing
Anheuser-Busch	Trans World
Coca-Cola	Warner Communications
Boeing	U.S. Steel

SOURCE: *Fortune*, January 9, 1984.

cost. Table 12-5 shows the ten most and least admired companies in a recent year. Public relations always influences the way people feel about a particular company.

SOCIAL RESPONSIBILITY IN PUBLIC RELATIONS

How a business responds to an unforeseen, potentially damaging event is a key part of public relations. For example, when a gunman went berserk and killed 21 people in a California McDonald's restaurant, the famous chain donated a million dollars to the families of the victims and destroyed the building to help erase bad memories of the event. When cyanide-poisoned Tylenol killed several people, the drug company acted immediately by removing the product from the market and cooperating fully with the investigation. These actions, which may be described as *socially responsible* do much to maintain public goodwill and preserve that intangible asset called reputation.

EVALUATING THE PRODUCTIVITY OF MARKETING EFFORTS

Compared with marketing, measuring the efficiency of production is relatively easy. In production, the cost of labor, materials, supplies and other expenses can be measured precisely and therefore controlled. In marketing, however, costs for personal selling, advertising, sales promotion and public relations are more difficult to measure and control. Since marketing accounts for 50 percent or more of total business costs, companies are making special efforts to increase productivity and keep costs from rising even higher.

In *measuring* marketing productivity, managers seek to determine how well marketing activities are working and to pinpoint areas which need improvement. As Table 12–6 indicates, experts can measure marketing efficiency both objectively and subjectively.

The next step is to *improve* marketing productivity. For example, if a study of the efficiency of a firm's advertising program shows that promotional dollars are not producing the desired results, the firm must then take steps to make its advertising more effective. Marketing management concentrates on answering the following questions: "How can we do better?" and "How can we do more with our human and financial resources?"

TABLE 12–6 Sample Measures of Marketing Efficiency

MARKETING FUNCTION	OBJECTIVE MEASURES OF EFFICIENCY	SUBJECTIVE MEASURES OF EFFICIENCY
Advertising	The cost per 1,000 consumers reached by the ad; the number of first-time users per dollar of advertising.	Changes in popular awareness of the product as a result of advertising; changes in customer attitudes toward the product; consumer complaints.
Personal selling	The average cost of a sales representative's call; the selling cost per unit sold.	Customer satisfaction with the product; the goodwill created by sales representatives.
Sales promotion	Display costs per customer; shelf costs per product line; brochure cost per customer.	Customer's attitudes toward the company and the product; dealer's willingness to cooperate; consumer's desire to buy.
Product decisions	The contribution of each product to total profit; the percentage change in brand awareness over a previous period.	Customer attitudes toward the product's design; customer satisfaction with products.

SOURCE: Abridged from David J. Schwartz, *Marketing Today: A Basic Approach*, 2nd ed. (New York: Harcourt Brace Jovanovich, 1977), 718–19.

SUMMARY

- The objective of promotion is to sell. Elements in the promotional mix are personal selling, advertising, sales promotion, and public relations.

- Steps included in the selling process are (1) identifying prospective customers, (2) meeting with the prospect, (3) demonstrating the product, (4) answering the prospect's questions and objections, and (5) closing the sale.

- Sales management involves recruiting, selecting, training, equipping, assigning territories to, and motivating sales representatives.

- The purposes of advertising are to increase the number of units sold, introduce new products, suggest additional uses for the product, increase sales in off seasons, maintain brand loyalty, and counteract competition.

- The various kinds of advertising are national, retail, trade, industrial, and institutional.

- An advertising agency plans, prepares, and places advertising for clients. The client's advertising department works with the agency to develop and implement the advertising program.

- Critics frequently say that advertising is too costly, purely competitive, misleading, offensive and makes people want unaffordable things.

- Sales promotion increases demand for new products, differentiates similar products, and substitutes for price competition. Sales-promotion techniques include samples; contests, sweepstakes, and games; premiums; coupons; and point-of-purchase displays.

- Public relations seeks to interpret company policies to the public, counteract distortion of facts caused by rumors, humanize the business, and win support from the various "publics" important to the business.

- Marketing costs, which account for 50 to 60 percent of products' selling price will probably go even higher unless marketing managers find ways to increase marketing efficiency.

KEY TERMS YOU SHOULD KNOW

advertising	industrial advertising	public
advertising agency	institutional advertising	public relations
advertising medium	national advertising	publicity
cash rebate	personal selling	retail advertising
contest	point-of-purchase display	sales manager
coupon	premium	sample
game	promotion	sweepstake
general agency	prospecting	trade advertising

QUESTIONS FOR REVIEW

1. What four elements make up the promotional mix?
2. What five stages are involved in making a sale?
3. Compare retail, wholesale, manufacturers, intangible, and real estate selling based on the nine aspects of a sales position in Table 12–1.
4. What does a sales manager do?
5. What are the purposes of advertising? How does advertising differ from personal selling?
6. Explain how an advertising agency operates.
7. What are the major criticisms of advertising?
8. Explain these sales promotion techniques: samples, contests, sweepstakes, games, premiums, coupons, and point-of-purchase displays.
9. What are the objectives of public relations?
10. Name the specific publics, or special-interest groups, with which public relations deals.
11. How can marketing efficiency be measured?

QUESTIONS FOR DISCUSSION

1. Jan Brown has an excellent record as sales rep. Does this qualify her as sales manager?
2. Through which advertising media would you advertise a self-service laundry, canned soft drinks, typewriter ribbons, farm machinery, coffee? Give reasons for your selection.
3. Does the use of an advertising agency eliminate the need for an advertising department?
4. From your local newspaper clip four public relations articles. Write a paragraph about each in which you explain whether the article is good or bad public relations for each. Suggest how the company could encourage such publicity if it is good, or how it could prevent such publicity if it is bad.
5. The following changes in paid attendance for three major sports occurred between 1970 and 1984. Assume a major league baseball team employed you to "come up with some ideas to increase attendance." Suggest five ideas to increase attendance.

	1970	(000) 1984	INCREASE
Major League Baseball	28,747	46,269	60.1
Professional Basketball	7,113	10,262	42.2
Professional Football	10,071	13,953	38.5

CASE STUDY

How Can "Great Chicken" Stimulate Demand?

Great Chicken is a national fast-food franchisor with 875 stores. Under the franchise agreement, franchisees pay 4 percent of revenues for promotion. Great Chicken decides how to spend the promotional budget and what prices the franchisees charge.

Traditionally, sales for franchisees are lowest during the first quarter. Henry Elliot, senior marketing VP, asks Albert Clark, promotion VP, and Sheila Wilson, account executive from Great Wilson's agency, to formulate promotional plans for next year.

Henry: We're still in September, but I want to plan early to avoid the drastic decline we have in the first quarter. Our goal should be to make this period the best.

Albert: That's a great goal. But be realistic. People feel they're poor between Christmas and the income-tax time. Also, bad weather causes people to eat at home.

H: Now get off those excuses. Although sales for fast-food places fall in the first quarter, our sales don't have to be off.

Sheila: We have a huge potential market.

H: What do you mean?

S: The agency just completed a survey showing that 67 percent of Americans over 16 have never been to a Great Chicken. If 10 to 15 percent of those try our products, we have a record-breaking quarter.

A: People are very price-conscious. A price reduction—say 20 percent—would lure people. We could promote it on TV and radio in January.

S: I don't think stressing low prices is the answer. Although some people respond to the bargain motive, I think more respond to something for nothing or something for less.

H: I am lost. What do you mean?

S: Well, the agency thinks that we should build the promotional campaign around coupons, either give one of the 12 items on our menu free for a coupon or sell it at a reduced price—at cost.

A: I don't see how we can make money giving away products or selling at cost.

S: You've got a good point. But agency thinking is that a person redeeming a coupon—say for a free soft drink—will buy two or three other items. The free or at-cost items will be loss leaders, we will end up making more money.

H: We'll assess your idea further next week.

Questions

1. Which appeal would motivate you to buy a meal at Great Chicken—an overall price reduction or a coupon for one item free? Why?
2. Can a company in an extremely competitive industry go against industry trends and have record sales when other companies' sales decline? Why?
3. How can Great Chicken best distribute coupons to consumers?

EVOLUTION OF A BUSINESS

Is Ignorance Bliss?

Ray had quite a surprise as a result of doing some informal research on the young singles' market. He often visited a coffee shop where singles gathered, to try to better understand their values and viewpoints. While he was talking to a group of people about travel agents, he suddenly realized that many of them didn't really know what a travel agent did. Ray was shocked to find that he had overlooked something so basic. He had been assuming all along that people understood what services travel agents provided.

When he got back to his office he made up a list similar to the one that appears below. He decided to try to get local newspapers to feature the list from time to time in their travel section. Ray's reasoning was that it would be educational for readers and that newspapers that ran travel-agency ads owed it to the industry.

What does a travel agent do?*

A travel agent's business is to serve you, the consumer, in all major aspects of travel. Among the travel agent's responsibilities are:

1. Providing a wide range of unbiased travel advice—some clients will visit a travel agent with a specific plan in mind, while others are looking for ideas.
2. Arranging transportation (air, sea, rail, bus, car rental, etc.).
3. Arranging for hotel, motel, and resort accommodations, meals, sightseeing, transfers of passengers and luggage between terminals and hotels, and special features such as theater tickets.
4. Preparing individual itineraries, personally escorted tours, and group tours, and selling prepared package tours.
5. Arranging reservations for special-interest activities such as religious pilgrimages, conventions and business travel, student tours, and sporting trips.
6. Handling and advising on the many details involved in modern-day travel (visas, health and passport requirements, travel baggage, insurance, travelers' checks, and language study material).

*This list sometimes appears in U.S. newspaper travel sections.

Questions

1. Do you think that the public's not knowing what travel agents do is Ray's problem?
2. How might Ray go about getting newspapers to cooperate in his scheme?
3. Why do you think Ray overlooked the possibility that the public might not understand the nature of the travel-agency business?

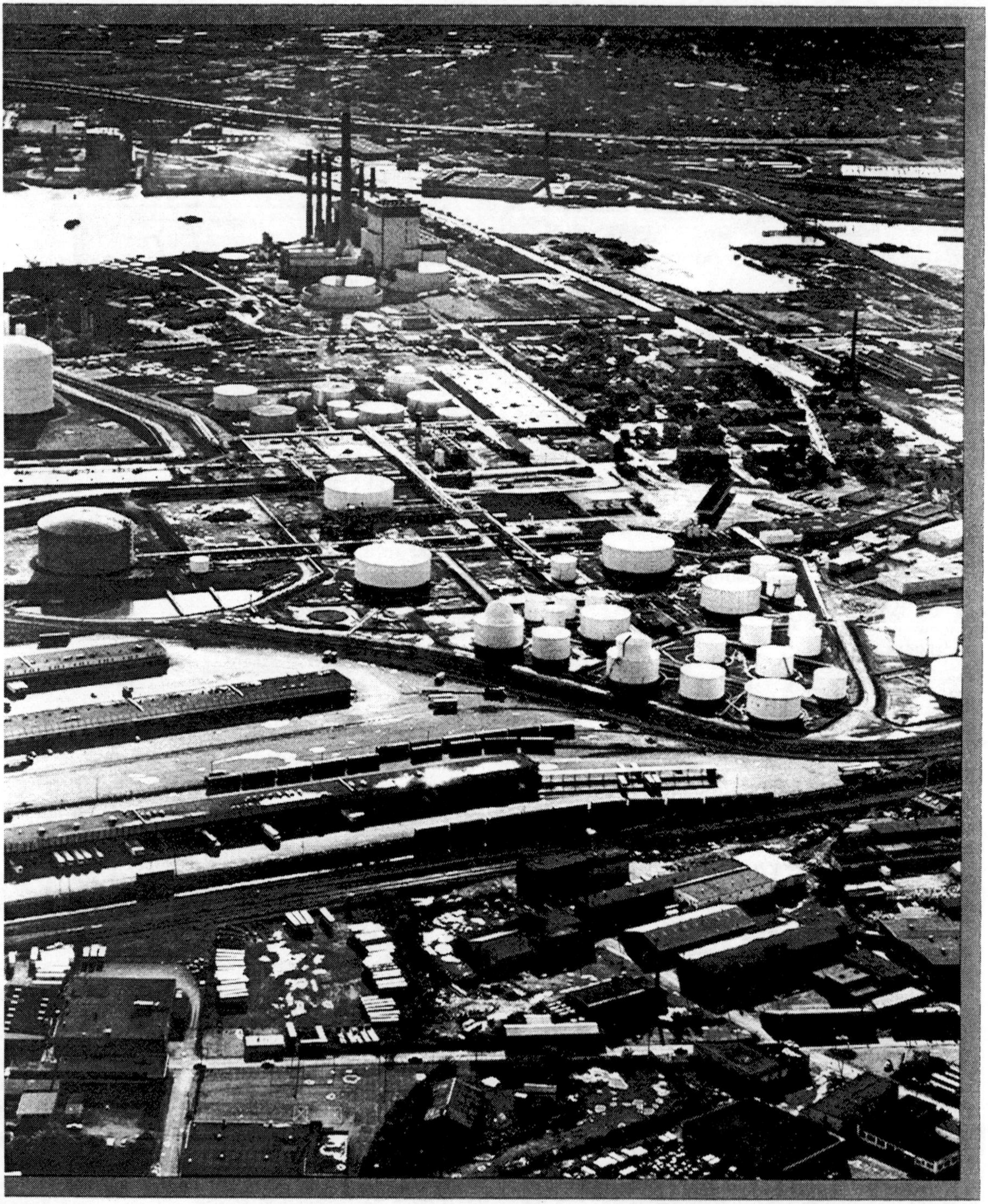

PHYSICAL ELEMENTS OF BUSINESS
Putting Things in Place

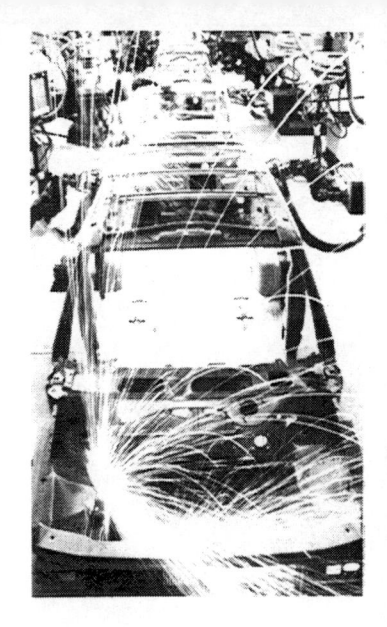

READ THIS CHAPTER SO YOU CAN:

Explain the five key physical elements of business.

Explain why each of the following factors is important in choosing an industrial location

- labor
- transportation
- energy
- proximity to raw materials
- proximity to markets
- local regulations
- special inducements
- quality of life

Describe why purchasing is important and understand the five questions purchasing people must answer.

Discuss mechanization, automation, product design, and production planning.

Define inventory, understand its importance, and tell why it is necessary and how it is managed.

Discuss what transportation is, list the five modes, and discuss their relative importance.

Explain how carriers are classified.

Explain what is involved in making transportation decisions.

A business truism is that "nothing happens until a sale is made," meaning that without income a firm can do nothing. A sale cannot take place, however, unless the business has a product to sell. Therefore to have an efficient marketing system, a company must first have an efficient production system.

The production system involves manufacturing, processing, assembling, converting and otherwise making products for private and industrial consumers. It is an inherent part of business activity.

Consider the construction of a house. Raw materials such as steel, aluminum, copper, and wood must first be converted into building materials, appliances, hardware, windows, and other components. The builder must then purchase these components and use them to build the house. Each major unit of construction requires hundreds of individual preliminary steps in production and many marketing transactions before the final home is complete.

In the same manner, when someone says, "General Motors makes cars," that person really means that General Motors combines and assembles hundreds of products—frames, batteries, computers, windows, locks, engines, tires, and other components—into one complete product: a car.

Often, products represent untold numbers of manufacturers, each producing a part of the whole. Even a simple product such as a candy bar includes ingredients from many producers located in various parts of America and the world.

In this chapter we consider five key physical elements of the production business: (1) selecting an industrial location, (2) purchasing, (3) production management, (4) inventory management, and (5) transportation.

PHYSICAL ELEMENT #1: CHOOSING AN INDUSTRIAL LOCATION

Where to locate an industry is important because geographical location affects costs of manufacturing, labor, transportation, and marketing. Because no perfect location exists, some compromise is always necessary.

In choosing a location managers should ask:

1. What region is best for us?
2. Which state within the region is preferable?
3. Which metropolitan area within the state would best serve our needs?
4. Which section of this metropolitan area is most desirable?

To answer these questions, managers focus on the area's availability of labor, transportation, and energy; its proximity to raw materials and markets; and its local regulations, special inducements, and overall quality of life.

WHAT ABOUT LABOR?

In selecting a plant location, a business manager must consider the quantity of labor and its skills and education. High technology industries, for example, seek locations near colleges, universities, and trade schools because these provide a greater pool of technologically skilled people.

Other labor factors to consider are prevailing wage rates and the strength of labor unions. If a company does not wish to become involved with union disputes, it will tend to stay away from areas that have organized labor. One of the main reasons for the gradual shift of industry from the North to the South and western parts of the nation is the relative weakness of organized labor in the latter regions.

AVAILABLE TRANSPORTATION

Manufacturers need transportation facilities to bring materials to the plant and to transport the finished products to wholesalers, retailers, or other factories. Thus, in selecting a site a company must review what transportation is available and how competitive the carriers are. A community served by several modes of transportation—water, air, rail, and truck—is preferred, because the company can ship goods by a variety of means.

AVAILABLE ENERGY SOURCES

The importance of available power varies with the type of industry. Electrochemical industries need large quantities of power, so they tend to locate near hydroelectric plants, where electricity costs less. Other industries, such as furniture factories, consume relatively little power, so this factor is often unimportant.

PROXIMITY TO RAW MATERIALS

Proximity to raw materials needed in manufacturing can be a major, sometimes decisive, factor in selecting locations for manufacturing plants. For example, the availability of raw materials is a main reason why some 90 companies have crowded onto the banks of the Mississippi from Baton Rouge to New Orleans (see Figure 13–1). Called the Chemical Corridor, this area has enormous supplies of raw-material resources at hand—water, oil, gas, sulfur, salt, and limestone—all obtainable via inexpensive water transportation. From New Orleans alone, 14,000 miles of inland waterways flow to two-thirds of the nation's markets for chemicals. A chemical plant not located on this

For many manufacturers, economical, plentiful energy sources are essential. Thus, many factories surround hydroelectric plants.

Figure 13–1 90 Miles Along the Mississippi: Baton Rouge–New Orleans

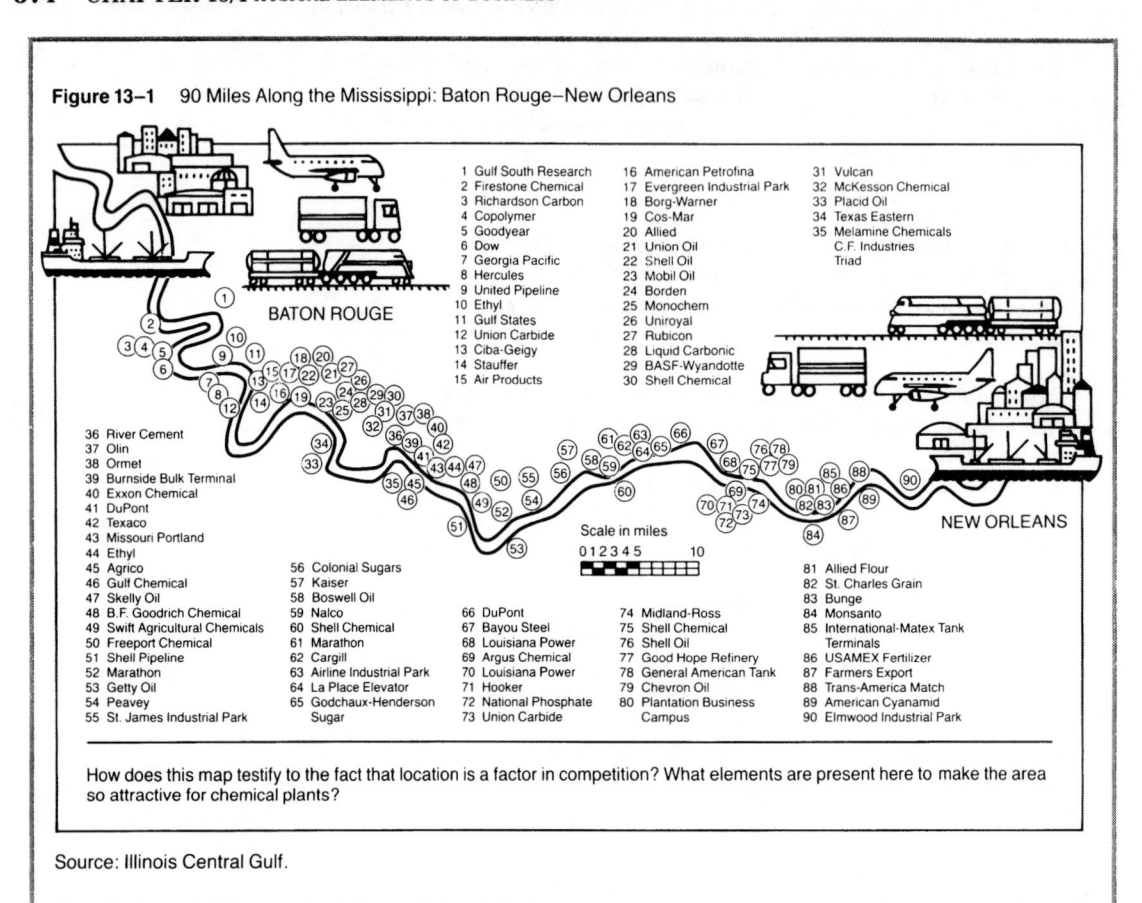

#	Name	#	Name	#	Name
1	Gulf South Research	16	American Petrofina	31	Vulcan
2	Firestone Chemical	17	Evergreen Industrial Park	32	McKesson Chemical
3	Richardson Carbon	18	Borg-Warner	33	Placid Oil
4	Copolymer	19	Cos-Mar	34	Texas Eastern
5	Goodyear	20	Allied	35	Melamine Chemicals
6	Dow	21	Union Oil		C.F. Industries
7	Georgia Pacific	22	Shell Oil		Triad
8	Hercules	23	Mobil Oil		
9	United Pipeline	24	Borden		
10	Ethyl	25	Monochem		
11	Gulf States	26	Uniroyal		
12	Union Carbide	27	Rubicon		
13	Ciba-Geigy	28	Liquid Carbonic		
14	Stauffer	29	BASF-Wyandotte		
15	Air Products	30	Shell Chemical		
36	River Cement	56	Colonial Sugars	66	DuPont	74	Midland-Ross	81	Allied Flour
37	Olin	57	Kaiser	67	Bayou Steel	75	Shell Chemical	82	St. Charles Grain
38	Ormet	58	Boswell Oil	68	Louisiana Power	76	Shell Oil	83	Bunge
39	Burnside Bulk Terminal	59	Nalco	69	Argus Chemical	77	Good Hope Refinery	84	Monsanto
40	Exxon Chemical	60	Shell Chemical	70	Louisiana Power	78	General American Tank	85	International-Matex Tank Terminals
41	DuPont	61	Marathon	71	Hooker	79	Chevron Oil	86	USAMEX Fertilizer
42	Texaco	62	Cargill	72	National Phosphate	80	Plantation Business Campus	87	Farmers Export
43	Missouri Portland	63	Airline Industrial Park	73	Union Carbide			88	Trans-America Match
44	Ethyl	64	La Place Elevator					89	American Cyanamid
45	Agrico	65	Godchaux-Henderson Sugar					90	Elmwood Industrial Park
46	Gulf Chemical								
47	Skelly Oil								
48	B.F. Goodrich Chemical								
49	Swift Agricultural Chemicals								
50	Freeport Chemical								
51	Shell Pipeline								
52	Marathon								
53	Getty Oil								
54	Peavey								
55	St. James Industrial Park								

How does this map testify to the fact that location is a factor in competition? What elements are present here to make the area so attractive for chemical plants?

Source: Illinois Central Gulf.

strip would be at a serious disadvantage when competing with these companies, for this particular blend of essential advantages does not exist elsewhere.

PROXIMITY TO MARKETS

Ideally, all manufacturers would like to be located near the markets for their products. For this reason, many small manufacturing firms that produce parts for major industries are located in the same cities as their largest industrial customers. This greatly reduces transportation costs, a major factor in choosing a plant's location. The Conference Board found that in plant expansions the desire to extend into new markets and the desire to improve customer services (quick shipments, replacement adjustments, and so on) were factors that had great bearing in one-third of all reported plant placements.

LOCAL REGULATIONS

A company must consider all facets of a community's rules and regulations for land use and construction. There are three categories: (1) **zoning regulations,** which *deal with land use*: (2) **subdivision regulations,** which *relate to such matters as sewage disposal and public facilities*; and (3) **building codes,** which *prescribe construction materials used, fire precautions, and the like*. In addition, the company must observe both federal and local antipollution standards, though local laws and often more stringent than federal ones.

Local taxes are another important consideration. A tax differential can mean the difference between meeting or not meeting the competition's prices. For example, even though practically all states levy a sales tax, some states exempt building materials, which substantially lowers industrial construction costs. Machinery, office equipment, and office supplies are also often exempt from taxes.

SPECIAL INDUCEMENTS

Many states and cities actively seek new industries because industry provides employment for local citizens and ultimately increases tax revenue. To attract manufacturers, some cities delay or minimize property taxes for several years, help arrange financing of plant construction, establish day care centers for parents of small children, and offer other inducements. Some major cities and states also send representatives to foreign nations to promote their area as an industrial site.

Quality of Life Is Important Too

The factors discussed above only indicate the economic feasibility of a location. Businesses must also seek a desirable place for their employees to live. Qualities such as the community's climate; recreational, educational, and cultural activities; sporting events; health services and similar characteristics are important. Quality of life helps determine whether key employees will accept transfers to the location and enjoy living there.

Industrial Concentrations, Industrial Parks, and Research Parks

Industrial concentrations, such as the Chemical Corridor shown in Figure 13–1, are *groups of similar companies located in one area because of the area's geographic advantages.* **Industrial parks** are *land areas with buildings planned and developed as optional environments for industrial occupants. When research dominates the activities in such areas,* they are sometimes dubbed **research parks.**

The nation's leading industrial and research parks, clustered around major universities, are the Stanford Industrial Park in Palo Alto, California, popularly known as the Silicon Valley (a nickname derived from the silicon computer chips produced there), and the Research Triangle Park, in the vicinity of Chapel Hill, North Carolina (see Figure 13-2).

A recent count revealed that the area contained 729 high-technology companies, mostly in electronics, accounting for over 66,000 jobs. *Science* reports another typical characteristic.[1] The Research Triangle ranks first in the number of Ph.D.s per capita—in the area there are now nearly 3,000 Ph.D.s who are scientists or engineers. *Science* also reports that the National Humanities Center has moved into the Triangle, evidence that effort is being made to overcome criticism that the humanities are neglected in the nation's technical centers.

PHYSICAL ELEMENT #2: PURCHASING

No business is self-sufficient: Each must buy products and services from other organizations to produce its own goods or services. Depending on the kind of business, the purchasing department spends 25 to 75 percent of every sales dollar. Careful purchasing of parts, supplies, components, and other materials, therefore, can determine a firm's ability to sell its products at a competitive price and greatly increase its profits. Even a 1 percent savings in purchasing can sometimes generate as much profit as a 10 percent increase in sales.[2]

---

[1] *Science,* June 30, 1978.
[2] U.S. Small Business Administration, "Purchasing for Owners of Small Plants," *Small Business Bibliography No. 85,* Washington, 1979, 22.

Figure 13-2 Research Triangle Park, North Carolina

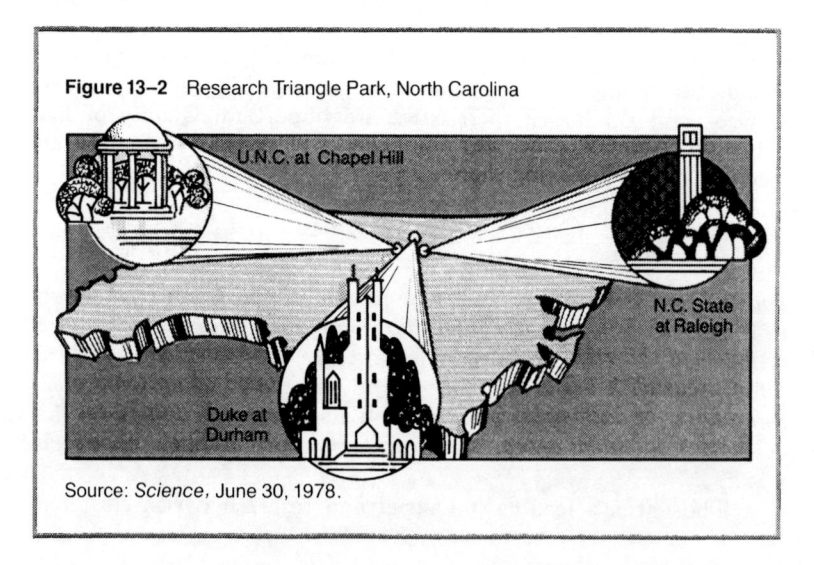

Source: *Science,* June 30, 1978.

APPLICATION TO PERSONAL AFFAIRS

How to Evaluate a Community Before You Move

Just as a business needs to choose a location, most of us will move a number of times to new communities. Since where we live helps to determine our level of satisfaction with life, it makes sense to evaluate a community carefully before deciding to become part of it. Following are some of the things that should be considered before a decision to move is made:

- *Are there a great many homes in the area for sale?* If the answer is yes, chances are that real-estate values in the community are declining. You should probably look elsewhere if you are planning to buy a home.

- *What is the local property-tax structure?* Usually, the closer a home is to a big city, the higher property taxes will be. Confer with a reputable real-estate agent and a banker before you buy.

- *What are the zoning regulations in the community?* There might be a time when you would like to build some new rooms, a garage, and so on. Are such additions permissible? What about regulations governing nearby undeveloped land? Are these regulations stringent enough?

- *Are the local schools good ones?* People with children may wish to visit local schools and observe teacher-student relations, find out how local per-pupil expenditures compare with the national and state averages, and find out what special services and facilities are offered.

- *How close is the local day-care center?* Parents with preschool-age children may wish to visit the center to study its method of operation, determine the child-to-teacher (and teacher's aide) ratio, and see whether the children currently there seem happy with their teachers, aides, and surroundings.

- *What types of public transportation are available?* If you plan to commute a sizable distance, how much will commuting cost you in time and money?

- *Do there appear to be adequate community services?* Is a hospital located nearby? Are police and fire protection adequate? Is sewage or garbage pickup a problem in the area? Are the streets well lit and free of potholes? Are there any chronic pipe or underground cable problems?

- *Are certain crimes, such as vandalism or burglary, common in the area?* Local police may be able to answer this question.

- *What community resources are easily accessible?* Is there a local library, park, playground, recreation center? Are any higher-education facilities available locally?

- *Is the community composed mainly of young, middle-aged, or older people?* How will the age mix affect your social life? Does the average age of the community's residents tell you anything about the community's future?

- *Would your pets pose a problem in the area?* Is there a leash law, a city tag law, a full-time dog catcher, and so on?

Despite its impact on profits, however, businesses often overlook the importance of purchasing because it is a behind-the-scenes activity. Business people can compare themselves fairly easily with

PEOPLE WHO MAKE THINGS HAPPEN

A PROFILE OF
BILL HEWLETT AND DAVE PACKARD

Many companies in industrial parks have exciting and inspiring histories. One such company is the electronics giant Hewlett-Packard, of Palo Alto, California. In 1984 its sales were almost $5.7 billion, and it employed 82,000 workers. But the firm had humble beginnings.

In 1938 Bill Hewlett and Dave Packard, classmates and engineering graduates from Stanford University, set up a business in a one-car garage behind Packard's rented house in Palo Alto. There they worked on the product that started their business venture. It involved circuitry that was the thesis subject Hewlett tackled while working toward his engineering degree.

Hewlett presented the product, a sound oscillator, at a West Coast meeting of what is now the Institute of Electrical and Electronics Engineers. The partners also sent information about the oscillator, which they called Model 200A "because the number sounded big," to potential customers. One that responded was Walt Disney Studios, which inquired whether the partners could build an oscillator with different specifications. Thus their second product, Model 200B was born. Disney bought eight and used them to produce the unique sound effects in its classic film *Fantasia*.

By 1950, Hewlett-Packard was a company with 200 employees, 70 products, and $2 million in sales. In 1956, HP broke ground for an engineering-manufacturing complex located in the nearby Stanford Industrial Park, which became the company's headquarters.

As HP grew, as is typical in high-technology fields, it expanded by making acquisitions buying smaller companies blessed with young managements with creative ideas. In 1959, on the twentieth anniversary of HP's incorporation, it made its first move overseas. Its first foreign plant was in West Germany, followed by a second plant in the United Kingdom, and then a joint venture in Japan.

By 1960, the problems of having become too big too fast were faced. HP was restructured. Each division was reorganized so that it operated much like a separate business. Each had its own research and development, manufacturing, marketing, and support operations, as well as its own line of products. One reason this was done was to retain the small-company atmosphere that had characterized HP at its inception. As the divisions grew, they were often split into smaller entities, in a format still followed by HP.

Bill Hewlett continues as chairman of the HP executive committee and Dave Packard remains as chairman of the board. One wonders what subject Hewlett would choose if he were assigned a thesis topic today!

---

competitors in selling, advertising, and many other business practices, but not in purchasing. Consequently, they often overlook the advantage a competing firm has if it does a better buying job.

What Is Involved in Purchasing?

We define **purchasing** as *the acquisition of needed materials, equipment, services, and supplies of (a) the right quality in (b) the right quantities for (c) the best prices at (d) the time needed from (e) reliable sellers.* Each element is important and relates to other elements.

WHAT IS THE RIGHT QUALITY?

The right quality is not always the same as the highest possible quality. The right quality of any item purchased means the quality does not exceed budgeted costs. Although a trade-off between quality and cost often occurs, the critical test is, "Does the product meet predetermined standards and specifications?"

WHAT IS THE RIGHT QUANTITY?

Buying the right quantity is a key purchasing consideration. Money tied up in too much inventory earns nothing. Not buying enough material or other items, however, may force the firm to shut down production, causing lost sales and lost time.

Other factors that affect the quantity-to-buy decision include the inventory's risk of spoilage or obsolescence, the possibility of a product's price increase, and the changes in supply availability due to overproduction by a supplier or underproduction resulting from a strike.

WHAT IS THE RIGHT PRICE?

The right or best price is the lowest price at which a firm can acquire products of a specified quality and quantity. Some sellers provide desired services, such as credit terms and discounts, which may modify what the buyer considers the right price.

WHAT IS THE RIGHT TIME?

Purchasing at the right time means that the materials are delivered soon enough to maintain production, but not so soon that supplies must be stored in inventory for a long time. The purchasing manager must therefore calculate reorder points for key materials based on their usage rate and how much lead time sellers require to produce the needed items.

WHO IS THE RIGHT SELLER OR VENDOR?

Purchasing managers usually consider several vendors before making purchases. They often rely on computerized records of vendor performance. In deciding which supplier gets an order, managers often give special attention to reliability. Specifically, does the seller's product meet promised specifications, and did the supplier make previous deliveries as agreed?

Criteria for the right seller also include service. Purchasing managers want to know if the vendor will repair and service purchased equipment as needed, accept returns of defective products, and help train workers in how best to use the product.

Purchasing Includes the Buying of Both Goods and Services

We can classify the types of purchases as follows:

- **Capital-investment goods**—*Products or facilities used to manufacture* (installations, tools, machines, computers).
- **Operating supplies**—*Things used to operate a business* (paper clips, lubricating oils, paper).
- **Raw materials**—*Natural and "nurtured" basics used in the manufacturing process* (iron ore, coal, lumber).
- **Semimanufactured goods**—*Processed materials that need further processing* (sheet steel for automobile fenders, cotton thread to be woven into cloth).
- **Components**—*Parts that need assembling to make up finished products* (tires for automobiles, crystals for watches, picture tubes for TV sets).
- **Subcontracted production services**—*Portions of a job one firm* (the **prime contractor**) *contracts to another, more specialized one* (a prime contractor for an apartment house complex would subcontract the installation of electrical, heating, air conditioning, and plumbing facilities to others).
- **Contracted industrial services**—*Industrial services performed on a contractual basis* (machine servicing and repair, cleaning, and remodeling).

The Purchasing Department

The **purchasing manager,** who is *in charge of orders for equipment, supplies, raw materials, and other goods, heads the purchasing department.* One industry spokesman explained the emerging role of the purchasing agent in this way:

Today's purchasing agent must be one of the most knowledgeable managers in his company. Unless he understands enough design, engineering, production, marketing, and related functions in sufficient detail, he can't possibly do his job. We insist that our purchasing people be brought into the picture in the earliest stages of design, engineering, and production. Frequently, they are able to make creative suggestions and studies that result in improved products, faster production schedules, even better design and appearance.[3]

The Make-or-buy Decision

A company does not always buy what it requires. When the production department plans to manufacture a product, it must resolve the **make-or-buy decision** (that is, *the decision about whether to make a part oneself or purchase it from another firm*). Sometimes a firm may want to use idle plant capacity, have an ensured supply (the Ford Motor Company, for example, makes its own steel and often has steel during a steel strike that may shut competitors down), or control quality.

Sometimes the make-or-buy decision is automatic. Many large companies, for instance, are conglomerates made up of smaller companies. Even though the firms that are part of the conglomerate may operate autonomously, they purchase needed products from other members of the same parent company if possible. In practice, then, we find divisions of a large business purchasing from other divisions. One of the principal motivations for a company to acquire other companies is to control sources of supply.

The purchasing and manufacturing departments cooperate in the make-or-buy decision. Purchasing furnishes prices from outside suppliers, and manufacturing calculates what the product will cost if the firm makes it itself.

PHYSICAL ELEMENT #3: PRODUCTION MANAGEMENT

The United States enjoys a high standard of living largely because of its tremendous industrial capacity. Further, manufacturing industries provide employment for approximately 20 percent of the total labor force.

Our production system functions on the concept of **mass production**—that is, *the large-scale production of goods using standard, interchangeable parts*. The objective of mass production is to lower the costs of production. The key factors that contribute to the efficiency of modern mass production include mechanization and automation.

Mechanization

The Machine Age is a relatively recent period in human history. In 1850, the average worker worked 70 hours a week and, chiefly with his muscles and those of animals, produced roughly 27 cents worth of goods per hour. The average worker in 1981, using virtually no animal

---
[3]W. F. Rockwell, Jr., former chairman of the board of Rockwell International.

muscle and a great deal less human physical effort, produced about $40 worth of goods per hour.

With the invention of machines, **mechanization,** *the substitution of mechanical effort for human effort and the process by which people and machines work according to systematic procedures,* dominated factories. The assembly line and motion-and-time study[4] became commonplace.

Automation

Automation is *the elimination of as much manual operation of machines as possible.* The goal of automation is to lower production costs by using mechanical or electronic devices to take the place of human effort, observation, and decision making.

Automation is an extension of mechanization. Mechanization substitutes mechanical effort for human effort, but people must still activate and control the machines. True automation eliminates the manual control of machines. Machines start and stop themselves automatically, and electric eyes check and correct the levels and weights of packages they fill. Under automation, then, the machine not only does the work but also controls and checks production.

The ultimate in automation is the industrial robot, which totally replaces humans. We discuss the expansion in the use of the industrial robot in the "America's Reemerging Creativity" feature in this chapter, on page 384.

Industrial robots apply nearly 3,000 welds automatically to Chrysler Corporation cars as they move through the Jefferson Assembly Plant line.

---

[4]**Motion-and-time study** *is a study of a specific act*—such as typing a letter, putting a fender on an automobile chassis, or picking a bushel of peaches—*to determine whether it can be performed more quickly and efficiently.*

Product Design

Product design *consists of two basic tasks: functional design and style design.*

FUNCTIONAL DESIGN

Functional design is *the phase of product design that gives the product its operational characteristics* (see Figure 13–3). The objective of functional design is to design a product that will provide the desired service and functional satisfaction. For example, the vacuum cleaner manufacturer is concerned with designing a product that picks up dust and dirt effectively, can be emptied easily, is light and easy to handle, will reach into corners and under furniture, has attachments to clean draperies and sofas, will fit in small closets, is

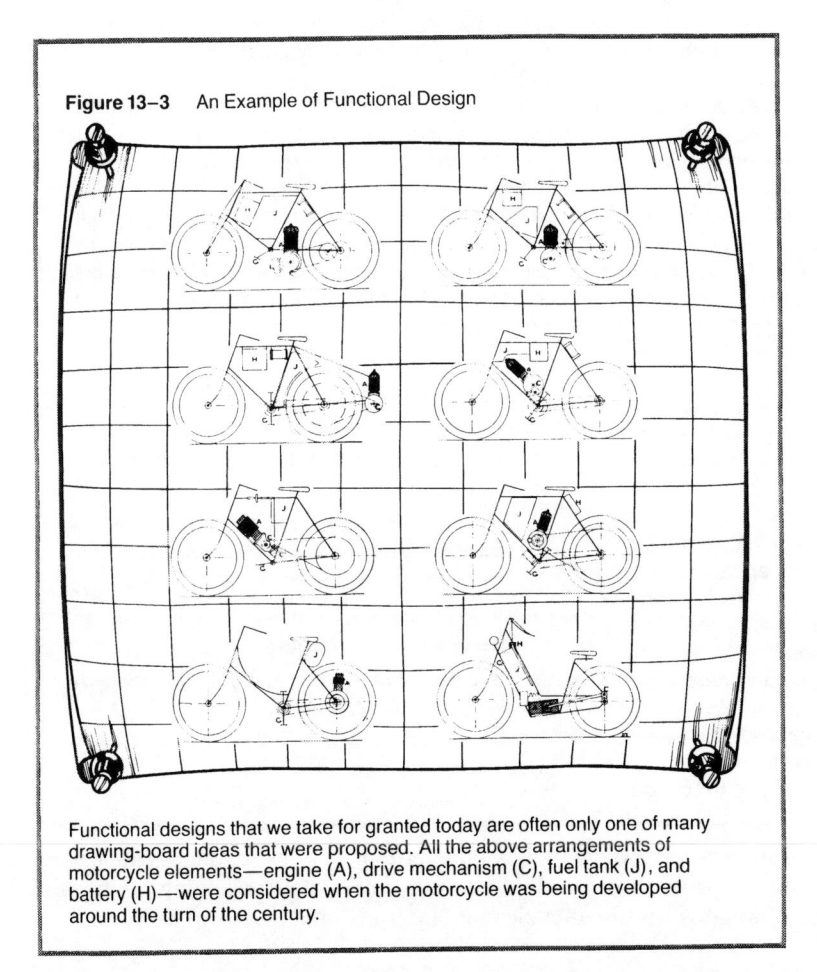

Figure 13–3 An Example of Functional Design

Functional designs that we take for granted today are often only one of many drawing-board ideas that were proposed. All the above arrangements of motorcycle elements—engine (A), drive mechanism (C), fuel tank (J), and battery (H)—were considered when the motorcycle was being developed around the turn of the century.

AMERICA'S REEMERGING CREATIVITY

The Industrial Robot Expansion in Perspective

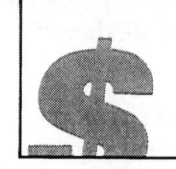

The Robot Institute of America defines an **industrial robot** as a *"reprogrammable multifunctional manipulator designed to move materials, parts, tools, or specialized devices through variable programmed motions for the performance of a variety of tasks."* The case for switching to robots is so convincing that a worldwide robot boom is occurring. A typical comment of those in the field is, "We are creating what is going to be an immense new industry, perhaps as big as the auto industry."*

New generation industrial robots are numerically controlled (NC) machines. Working three shifts a day, they are faster and more accurate than humans and do not take coffee breaks, get bored, go on vacation, call in sick, require overtime pay, or go on strike. Five such machines can do the work of ten skilled workers. Robots now on the drawing boards will be digging up ocean-bed minerals, spraying crops, and going into outer space to repair satellites.

With leading industrial nations rapidly adopting robots, a key question for America is, "What can be done to step up industry's investments in robots?" U.S. industry tends to drag its heels because of prevailing high interest rates and reluctance to scrap productive facilities before they are worn out. As robots grow in sophistication, perhaps the U.S. government should encourage their use as the government in Japan does. It leases robots to small- and medium-sized companies unable or unwilling to buy them.

Predictions are that "the human race is now poised on the brink of a new industrial revolution that will at least equal, if not exceed, the first Industrial Revolution in its impact on mankind."† People will hotly debate the impact of robots during the next decade. Though robots uproot people from factories, society does benefit from lower prices, increased production, and freedom from unattractive kinds of work. Difficult changeover and societal questions exist. Among them is the tendency for labor unions to resist the trend. But time for social considerations may be running out. If we are slow in embracing robot technologies, the United States may lose its ability to compete against faster-moving manufacturers in Europe and Japan.

The long-range future for robots is optimistic. While the Industrial Revolution freed humanity from the backbreaking, stoop-labor jobs of agricultural economies, it substituted the boring and tedious factory jobs that robots are now taking over. Isaac Asimov concludes cheerily that "Robots will leave human beings the tasks that are intrinsically human, such as sports, entertainment, science research."

Questions for Discussion

1. How can the United States try to lead in industrial robots and productivity?
2. Someone has said, "The perfect worker is a mindless idiot." Comment on and relate this comment to the issues presented.
3. What are the social implications of increasing use of industrial robots?
4. How do robots relate to America's ability to compete internationally?

*Time, December 8, 1980.
†Ibid.

safe, and is durable and capable of long service. If the designer does not provide these product characteristics, the consuming public will soon label the vacuum cleaner "inferior," and sales will drop.

In many industries, such as automobile manufacturing, functional design is extremely complicated, and several design groups usually perform it. Separate groups of designers may work on the chassis, engine, electrical assembly, body, and transmission.

The need for functional design is obvious in the so-called engineering industries, such as the aircraft industry. For producers of petroleum products, chemicals, or other nonassembled products, however, functional design is equally important. The oil refinery strives to "design" an oil that gives lasting engine protection; the textile manufacturer attempts to produce wrinkleproof and water-repellant fabrics.

STYLE DESIGN

Style design is *that phase of product design that adds attractiveness, distinctiveness, and aesthetic value to the product.* Just because a product is highly satisfactory from a functional standpoint does not ensure its public acceptance. Unless consumers are also satisfied with its appearance, the product will not sell well.

Instant recognition of a product design simplifies advertising, for when consumers see the product, they will recognize it without identification. Customers are much less apt to confuse that product with another, and competitors have more difficulty convincing customers to switch to their products.

One of the most successful product designs, recognized the world over, is the Coca-Cola bottle. Its design has managed to change with the times (see Figure 13-4). This ensured that younger generations would not avoid the product because it seemed old-fashioned.

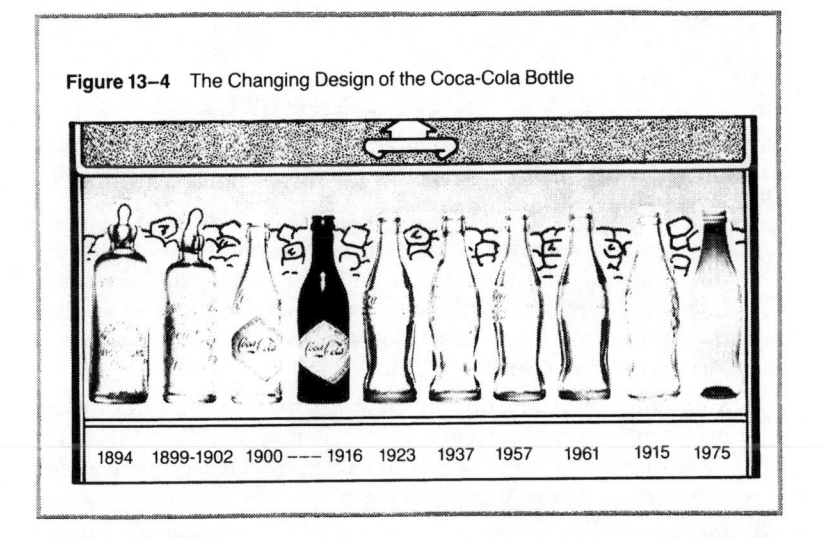

Figure 13-4 The Changing Design of the Coca-Cola Bottle

1894   1899-1902   1900 --- 1916   1923   1937   1957   1961   1915   1975

Production Planning

Production planning *involves determining where and how to manufacture a product.* Manufacturers estimate costs so that they can make make-or-buy decisions and select appropriate plant facilities.

KEY DECISION AREAS

Planning for production centers on the following key elements, sometimes called the "five M's." Companies ask such questions as

- *Methods*—Can we use present production lines to produce the new product, or must we provide other facilities?
- *Manpower*—Can we use present personnel or must we add new skills to the work force?
- *Machines*—What kind, capacity, and numbers will we need?
- *Money*—What will our long- and short-term money requirements be?
- *Materials*—How large should our inventories of parts, materials, and supplies be?

Production planning also includes (1) developing work standards and schedules to indicate length of manufacturing time, (2) anticipating what factory layout changes will be necessary, (3) diagramming methods for handling materials, (4) compiling lists of tools and machinery needed, and (5) conducting motion-and-time studies. Making sure that all production planning is careful and complete is essential because small errors can lead to large problems later on.

PHYSICAL ELEMENT #4: INVENTORY MANAGEMENT AND STORAGE

Inventory is *the stock of raw materials, parts, supplies, and other items held for use in the business or for resale.* Management of inventory is important for three reasons:

1. *Inventory represents money.* Inventory purchased with borrowed money means that companies must pay interest costs. Inventory purchased with cash means that the business has lost the use of funds for other purposes. Either way, excessive inventory results in expense to a firm.

2. *Maintenance of inventory also costs money.* Companies must insure products in inventory against fire, theft, and damage. Inventory items may also become obsolete, incurring lost funds and more expenses to replace them.

3. *Inventory allows production to continue.* If parts or other items

are not in inventory when they are needed, firms may have to shut down production and lose sales.

Why Is Inventory Necessary?

Inventory is essential to

1. *Balance seasonal production and year-round consumption.* Some products, particularly agricultural goods, are produced seasonally but consumed all year long. Storing items in inventory lengthens the period of the product's availability.
2. *Balance year-round production and seasonal consumption.* Manufacturers of snowtires, boots, and pesticide often operate manufacturing plants on a year-round basis and store products until the consumption season.
3. *Age or season the product.* Some products such as hides and lumber require time for seasoning before they can be used.
4. *Meet normal demand.* Businesses need products when customers want them. A business loses sales when products are not in stock, and the production process is interrupted when needed parts are not on hand.
5. *Take advantage of special purchase opportunities.* Sometimes a business may be able to purchase items at unusually low cost. If price savings exceed storage costs, the purchase is worthwhile.

What Does Inventory Management Involve?

Inventory management includes three tasks: (1) setting a reorder point, (2) deciding the quantity to reorder, and (3) arranging for storage.

The reorder point is the amount of inventory on hand when a new order is placed. To determine a reorder point, the inventory manager must consider lead time—the time between placement of an order and its delivery; and the usage rate of products—how fast inventory is used in the production process.

The quantity-to-order decision involves the purchasing manager. In this second inventory task, the manager must consider the costs of placing an order and the costs of carrying the inventory and balance them against the needs of production.

Storage or warehousing is the third function of inventory management. Its goal is to provide storage facilities that are convenient for inbound shipments, use in the business, and shipment to customers. Types of storage facilities are shown in Figure 13–5.

Storing inventory is expensive for manufacturers and distributors; so they try to keep enough material on hand to meet current demand, but not so much that they are paying excessive warehouse fees.

PHYSICAL ELEMENT #5: TRANSPORTATION

Transportation is *the movement of raw materials, components, parts, and other items from the point where they are produced to*

Figure 13-5 Many types of storage facilities are needed to accommodate the large variety of goods that must be stored in inventory.

Yard or Ground Storage Facilities
Used for lumber, coal, automobiles, stone, building materials, bricks, metal ores, airplanes.

Special Commodity Warehouses
Used for grains (grain elevators), fruits, computers, defense systems, cotton, leather, medical supplies, pharmaceuticals.

Bonded Warehouses
Used for liquor, imported goods, tobacco, furs, perfume (products subject to federal tax).

Cold Storage Warehouses
Used for meats, frozen foods, ice, flowers, eggs, certain types of drugs, butter, some medical supplies, cadavers.

Tank Storage Facilities
Used for petroleum products, gases, water, milk, vegetable oil, chemicals.

General Merchandise Warehouses
Used for furniture, appliances, clothing, paper, batteries, tires, books.

the point where they are processed or assembled and on to the point of ultimate purchase. Transportation is essential because few products are consumed where they are produced.

A key responsibility of a transportation manager is to select the mode or type of carrier to move products to other manufacturers, wholesalers, and retailers. Five modes make up the **transportation mix:** *Railroads, motor vehicles, waterways, pipelines,* and *airlines.* Figure 13-6 shows the relative importance of the various transportation modes and some of the typical products they carry. Table 13-1

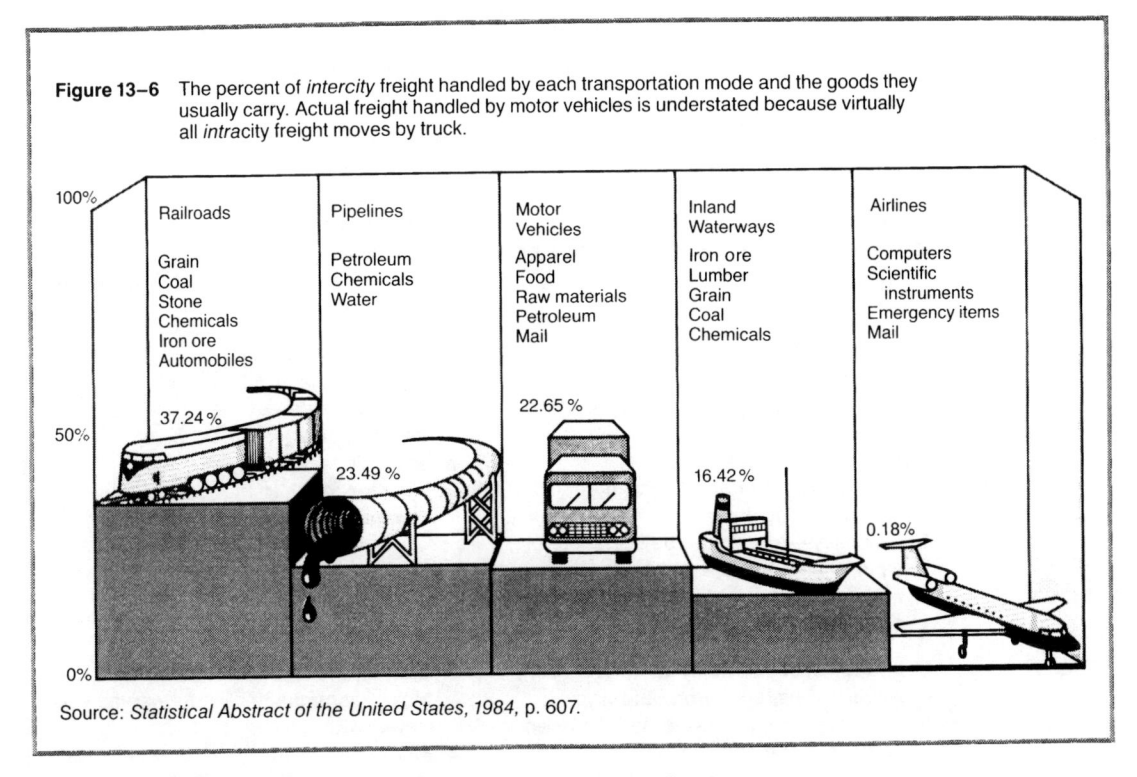

Figure 13–6 The percent of *intercity* freight handled by each transportation mode and the goods they usually carry. Actual freight handled by motor vehicles is understated because virtually all *intra*city freight moves by truck.

Railroads	Pipelines	Motor Vehicles	Inland Waterways	Airlines
Grain	Petroleum	Apparel	Iron ore	Computers
Coal	Chemicals	Food	Lumber	Scientific instruments
Stone	Water	Raw materials	Grain	Emergency items
Chemicals		Petroleum	Coal	Mail
Iron ore		Mail	Chemicals	
Automobiles				
37.24%	23.49%	22.65%	16.42%	0.18%

Source: *Statistical Abstract of the United States, 1984*, p. 607.

summarizes the advantages and disadvantages of each mode of transportation.

Auxiliary Freight Services

In addition to the five basic modes of transportation, a number of services are also available to help keep transportation costs to a minimum.

The *U.S. Postal Service* handles a large volume of small parcels; *express parcel services* such as Federal Express, Purolator, and United Parcel Services (UPS) pick up and deliver small packages overnight, and *bus lines* offer convenient, inexpensive, and fast transportation for products of high value and low bulk.

Coordinated shipping, when *a transportation company offers several modes of transportation to move products,* is increasing in popularity. Railroads, for example, offer a coordinated service of piggyback train travel by combining the pickup and delivery of trucks with the more economic long-haul travel by rail.

Many coordinated services involve **containerized shipping,** which is to *load many goods into large metal boxes and ship them as*

TABLE 13-1   Major Advantages and Disadvantages of the Five Modes of Transportation

MODE	ADVANTAGES	DISADVANTAGES
Railroads	• Low cost over long distances • Safe—few accidents • Reasonably reliable schedules • Large capacity—rarely a shortage of space for transport	• Slow speed • Often inaccessible because most businesses are not located near the railroad line • Many communities not served by railroad at all
Trucks	• Highly accessible—trucks reach all communities • Door-to-door delivery makes transfer of cargo unnecessary • Except for air, fastest mode • Lowest cost over short runs; moderate cost over long runs • Flexibility—trucks can be designed for almost any transport need, ranging from mixing concrete in transit to shipping fresh milk	• More expensive than rail for long runs, especially for products with high bulk and low value such as cement, fertilizer, and coal • Small capacity • Weather and traffic delays are still common
Water	• Lowest cost for bulky materials such as chemicals, coal, iron, and grain • Very large capacity—some ships can carry as much cargo as six to ten fully loaded trains • Only practical method for moving most raw materials and bulky products in international commerce	• Slowest mode of transportation • Most communities not served by waterways • Much water transportation is seasonal; the Great Lakes can be used only about 240 days a year
Pipelines	• Low maintenance and operating costs once construction is completed • No problem with empty equipment, since there is no return haul • Unaffected by weather	• High cost of initial construction • Limited almost exclusively to petroleum products • Highly dependent on other transportation modes to move refined petroleum products to points of consumption
Air	• Speed—any major city in the nation can be reached in only a few hours • Safety—products less likely to be damaged in transit than if shipped by water, rail, or truck • Packaging convenience—since items are handled personally and trips take less time, goods can be packaged more cheaply	• High cost • Lack of easy accessibility to small communities • Some other transportation mode is required to make delivery

one unit instead of as several. Containers are filled at the shipper's location, loaded onto trucks, taken to a railroad, and unloaded as one unit. Containerized shipping lowers transportation costs because it reduces the handling of many small quantities.

Legal Classification of Carriers

A **carrier** is *a company that engages in transportation.* Legally, the three types of carriers are common, contract, and private.

Common carriers *operate on regular schedules over definite routes.* Service and charges are the same for all shippers. Closely regulated, the law requires common carriers to give certain minimum service. Railroads, bus lines, most airlines, and some trucking companies are common carriers.

Contract carriers *engage in "for hire" transportation and do not offer the same service or the same price to everyone.* An individual contract is made with each shipper. Often, contract carriers specialize in transporting only certain kinds of products. The specialized rack and tank trucks commonly seen on highways, for example, are usually used to carry automobiles or chemicals on contract.

A **private carrier** is *part of a business that does not specialize in transportation.* Farmers, merchants, and manufacturers who operate their own trucks are private carriers. There are relatively few legal restrictions on private carriers.

Containerized shipping of goods saves firms time, manpower, and space. Goods packed at the factory travel by truck, train, ship, and/or plane and are unloaded only when they reach their final destination.

Key Transportation Decisions

In selecting the mode of transportation, shippers weigh the advantages and disadvantages of each (see Table 13-1 p. 390). The shipping decision hinges on the following factors:

- *Feasibility*—Does the carrier or transportation mode give service over the route the goods will travel? If so, is the carrier equipped to handle the product?
- *Safety*—Getting products delivered in good condition is especially important for certain types of goods, such as heavy machinery. Computers have long been transported by household goods movers because they are expert in careful handling.
- *Speed*—If time is critical, or if the product has a high value relative to its size, a fast mode may be desirable even if it is more expensive. When time is secondary and the materials transported are bulky, a slower, less expensive mode of transportation is generally used.
- *Cost*—Because air transportation is much more costly than other modes, it is used mainly for products of high value in relation to bulk and weight.
- *Services*—Some shipments require special services—for example, ready-to-pour cement may have to be delivered to a building site. Benefits must always be weighed against costs in making decisions about such custom services.

THE PHYSICAL ASPECTS OF BUSINESS IN PERSPECTIVE

In this chapter we have examined the physical elements of business: choosing a location, buying necessary raw materials, managing production and inventories, and transportation to other manufacturers or wholesalers and retailers.

The physical side of business may seem less challenging than promotion, finance, employee management, and other more visible aspects. But it is vital to the survival of the business itself.

Location of the production facility directly affects cost and efficiency. Purchasing often is the largest business expense and requires expert planning and negotiation skills. The production process is complex and must utilize the finest engineering and coordination talents available. Inventory control depends on increasingly sophisticated accounting and computerized methods to achieve goals, and transportation demands careful analysis to select the most effective and economic modes.

Attention to these physical elements of business is an important, challenging, and key part of economic activity.

SUMMARY

- Physical elements are location, purchasing, production, inventory management, transportation.
- Firms choosing an industrial location consider labor, transportation, energy, proximity to raw materials and markets, local regulations, inducements, and quality of life.
- Purchasing involves determining the right quality, quantity, price, time, vendor.
- We classify products purchased as capital-investment goods, operating supplies, raw materials, semimanufactured goods, components, subcontracted production services, and contracted industrial services.
- A make-or-buy decision involves deciding whether to make a product or buy it from a supplier.
- Mechanization and automation contribute to production efficiency.
- Product design involves (a) functional design, and (b) style design.
- Production planning includes "five M's," methods, manpower, machines, money, materials.
- Inventory represents money, needs maintenance, and is essential to production and sales.
- Inventory (a) balances seasonal production with year-round consumption, (b) balances year-round consumption with seasonal production, (c) involves age or season of product, (d) meets normal demands, and (e) takes advantage of special purchase opportunities.
- The transportation modes are railways, motor vehicles, waterways, pipelines, and airlines.
- Carriers or companies engaged in transportation are called common, contract, or private.
- Key transportation decisions involve feasibility, safety, speed, cost, and services.

KEY TERMS YOU SHOULD KNOW

automation
building code
capital-investment good
carrier
common carrier
component
containerized shipping
contract carrier
contracted industrial service
coordinated shipping
functional design
industrial concentration
industrial park
industrial robot
inventory
make-or-buy decision
mass production
mechanization
motion-and-time study
operating supply
prime contractor
private carrier
product design
production planning
purchasing
purchasing manager
raw material
research park
semimanufactured product
style design
subcontracted production service
subdivision regulation
transportation
transportation mix
zoning regulation

QUESTIONS FOR REVIEW

1. "Nothing happens until a sale is made." Explain.
2. What are the four questions managers should ask when choosing an industrial location?
3. Why is each of the following important in the location decision? (a) labor (b) transportation (c) energy (d) proximity to raw materials (e) proximity to markets (f) local regulations (g) special inducements (h) quality of life.
4. What is purchasing? What must a manager answer in making a wise purchasing decision?
5. What types of purchases are there?
6. Explain the make-or-buy decision.
7. What is mechanization? Automation?

8. Explain functional design and style design.
9. What are the "five M's"?
10. Why is inventory necessary?
11. Name the five transportation modes and rank them in order of importance.
12. Explain the differences among common, contract, and private carriers.
13. What five factors do managers consider when making transportation decisions?
14. Explain coordinated and containerized shipping.

QUESTIONS FOR DISCUSSION

1. What are the advantages and disadvantages of purchasing from a single supplier? Do the advantages outweigh the disadvantages?
2. "A dollar saved in purchasing may contribute as much to profit as $10 in additional sales." Explain. Why do many firms work to expand sales rather than to reduce purchasing costs?
3. It is fairly common for purchasing agents to accept "kickbacks"—expensive gifts or money—from suppliers. Aside from ethical questions, what are the economic consequences? What would you do to eliminate this if you had authority?
4. Recently, much industry has moved from the Northeast and Midwest to the South, Southwest, and West. Why has this occurred? Will the trend continue?
5. Less than 120 years ago, three of our five transportation modes—trucks, pipelines, and airplanes—were not even planned. What new transportation may exist in 100 years?

CASE STUDY

How to Plan for the Robots

Famous Fashion, a California apparel firm, manufactures low- to mid-priced garments and sells primarily to department stores. It employs 300 workers, mostly semi-skilled. Wardel Brown, president; Janet Jones, VP of finance; Maria Juarez, VP of personnel; Brad Phillipps, production manager; and Sandra Jarvis, legal counsel, are talking.

Wardel: I just received the feasibility study from Cleveland Electronics. They predict they can build 40 robots to replace 100 employees.
Janet: For how much money?
W: They want escalator clauses to cover inflation, of course. Their base price is $12.2 million.
J: That's $122,000 per employee replaced or payroll–fringe costs for three and a half years.
W: That's a lot of money to eliminate an employee, but benefits are no absenteeism, no accidents, no turnovers, fewer mistakes.
Brad: Robots are being used in assembly operations, but our business is more complicated. Apparel making requires a lot of hand labor.
W: Cleveland can design flexible robots.
Sandra: Before we sign the contract, I'll add protective clauses to bind Cleveland to perform.
Maria: I find this discussion inhumane. What about the 100 workers who will lose their jobs?
W: If we go ahead with the robots, you will help discharged workers get their benefits and new jobs.
J: Sir, you said *if* we go ahead. We don't have a choice. Our competitors are sure to use robots. Our higher costs will drive us out of the market.
W: I'm leaning toward the robots, but it's a big decision; we want to look at it carefully.
S: Better not wait too long.
W: What do you mean?
S: Our union contract comes up for renewal in five months. If we don't have the robot deal by then, the union will demand that we retain workers.
W: Good point. We'll decide in 45 days.

Questions

1. If the robots are purchased, what specific actions might Famous Fashion take to help the workers?
2. What are some advantages of "managing" robots compared with managing people?
3. What other information would you want before you decided about the robots?
4. Some observers say that robots will cause massive unemployment. What do you think and why?

EVOLUTION OF A BUSINESS

Overcoming Logistical Problems to Build Goodwill

Sara and Ray were discussing ways in which the Excel Travel Agency could achieve its goal of providing clients with exceptional, personalized service. The challenge was to provide service that surpassed the service provided by competing agencies without appreciably raising the cost of doing business.

Ray: You know, if we can make the process of traveling less vexing and more pleasant for people, they will appreciate and notice us. A lot of the problems of travel involve logistics—getting yourself and your baggage from one place to another, right?

Sara: Yes; what do you have in mind?

Ray: Well, the hotel/motel guide that we use contains maps of all the major airports. Wouldn't it be a good idea to provide a photocopy of the destination airport map with each airline ticket we sell? This would help people locate the parking lots, reception areas, customs offices, and so on. Also, it seems to me that people who are getting bored sitting in a plane would enjoy looking at a map of the airport where they're about to land.

Sara: Sounds like a good idea. How about also checking into executives' special interests when they order tickets? When we mail the tickets we could include appropriate brochures on, say, tennis club or golf courses nearest their hotel. If they're traveling with children we could give them suggestions about childcare facilities or information on where to take the kids for entertainment. What to do with children is often a problem when parents take them on a trip and have to spend part of their time working.

Questions

1. Is the idea of providing a map of the destination airport good enough to trigger word-of-mouth advertising? Are there other logistical difficulties that a travel agency could solve?
2. What about Sara's ideas? Do they relate to what business executives are interested in, or could something better be devised?
3. What else could Excel Travel do so that people would start praising it?

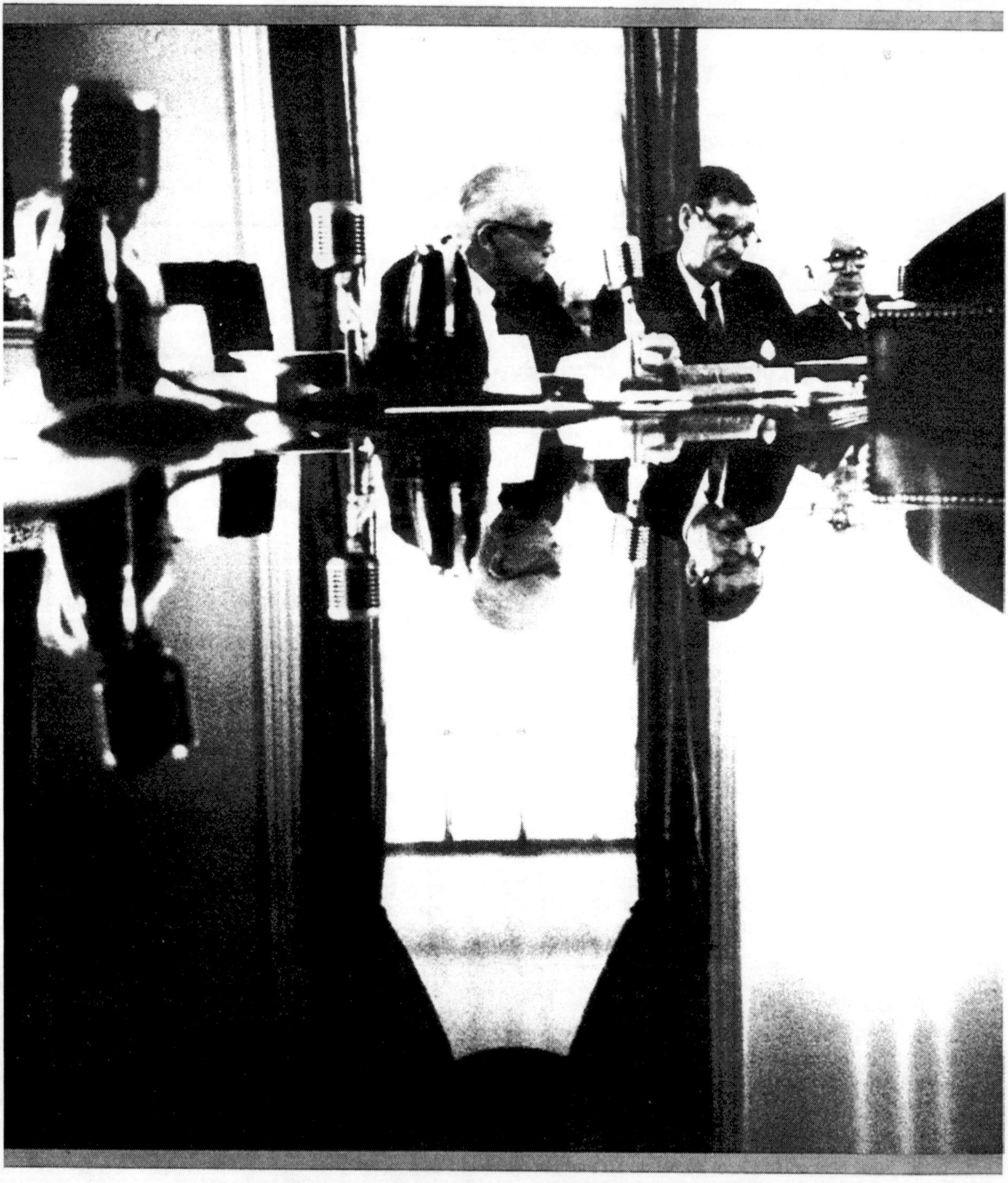

IV

MANAGING: MAKING THE BUSINESS WORK

14 PLANNING, ORGANIZING, AND CONTROLLING THE ENTERPRISE

15 HUMAN RESOURCE MANAGEMENT: STAFFING AND DIRECTING

16 MANAGEMENT AND LABOR RELATIONS

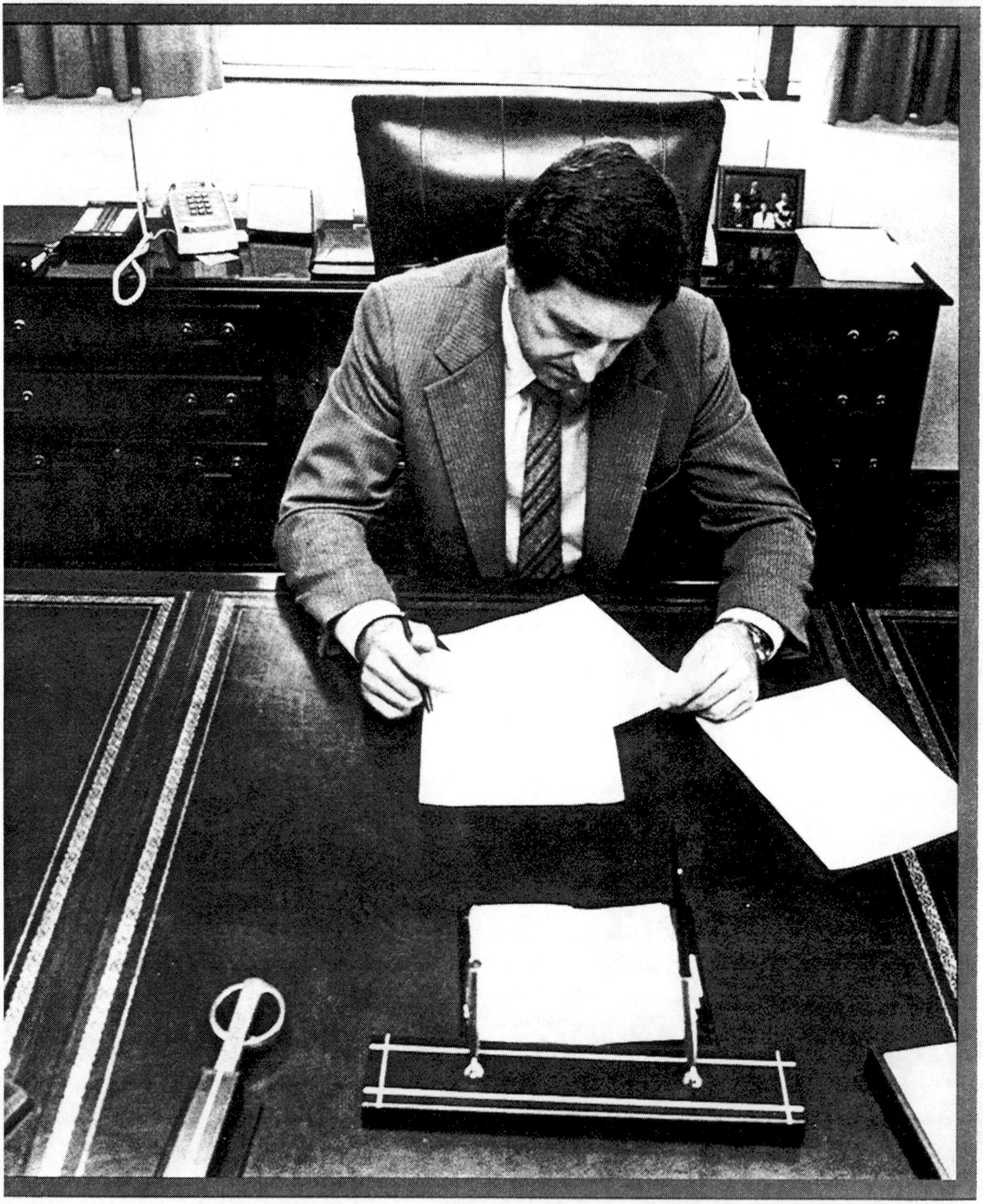

14

PLANNING, ORGANIZING, AND CONTROLLING THE ENTERPRISE

Getting Things Done: Ways and Means

READ THIS CHAPTER SO YOU CAN:

Define management and explain the universal need for management in all types of enterprises

Understand the power vested in managers

Demonstrate the importance of the planning function, define each type of plan, and list the characteristics of effective plans

Define organizing and explain why it is essential in all businesses

Explain how delegation of authority, levels of management, organization charts, chain of command, span of supervision, line and staff functions, and departmentalization enter into the organizing process

Describe the role of the informal organization

Discuss the three steps involved in the control process

Explain where management is headed

In all organizations, managers have authority: Consider the power managers have over people. Managers decide who has jobs, how much money employees receive, what their working conditions are like, and who their associates on the job will be. Managers have the power to transfer, promote, or dismiss employees.

Think also of the power managers have over resources. Managers decide how to acquire capital and how the company will use it. Managers also make decisions about what products to offer, where to locate branches, and when to expand.

And managers have power over change. Technicians, engineers, and scientists conduct research and contribute ideas, but managers decide whether their research and ideas are put to use.

When a business succeeds, people say, "The company has 'good' management." But when a business fails, people blame 'bad' management. Ultimately, in all organizations, members of management, not employees, are held responsible for results, good or bad.

WHAT IS MANAGEMENT?

All organizations, businesses, colleges, hospitals, and governments have goals or objectives. **Management** is *the process of achieving an organization's goals through the coordinated performance of five functions: planning, organizing, staffing, directing, and controlling.* Figure 14-1 shows how these functions interrelate.

Managers plan when they decide what to do and how to do it. Managers organize when they group work to be done into logical units or departments. Managers staff when they select and assign people to do the work. Managers direct when they communicate to personnel how to perform the work. And managers control when they determine if the work is accomplished as planned.

Management Means Making Decisions

Decision making, or *the selection of a course of action from available alternatives,* is inherent in managing; managers must make decisions. Table 14-1 shows examples of problems a manager may face and some alternative solutions. Managers make few, if any, decisions that please everyone. Even a decision to give everyone a $1,000 bonus may be disliked by some: "I'm a better employee than Greg, and he got just as much as I did." But managers, knowing that they will not be universally popular, must make decisions. The key consideration is whether or not the decision helps the organization achieve its goals.

Drawing by S. Harris; © 1979
The New Yorker Magazine, Inc.

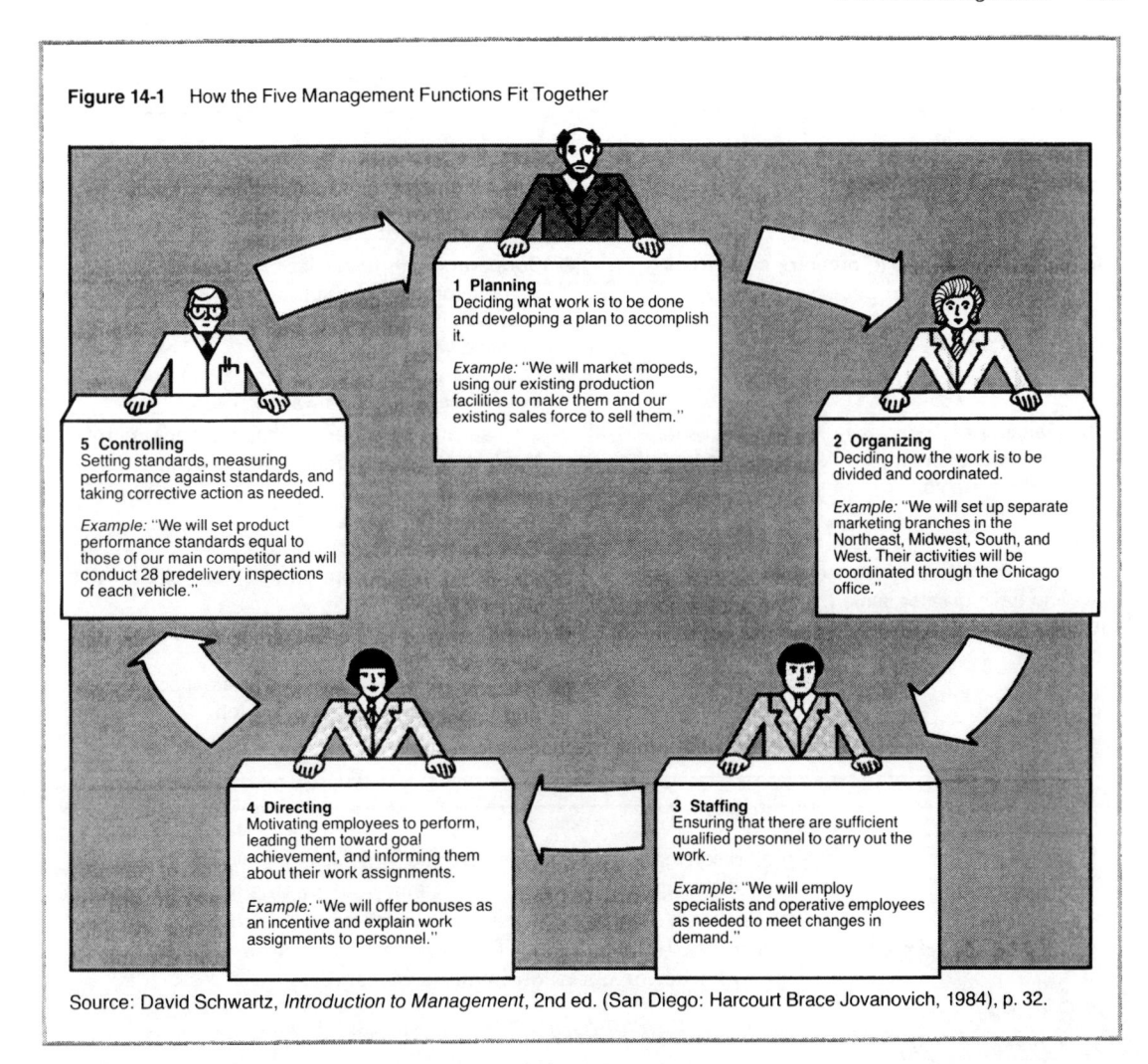

What Is Management? 401

Figure 14-1 How the Five Management Functions Fit Together

1 Planning
Deciding what work is to be done and developing a plan to accomplish it.

Example: "We will market mopeds, using our existing production facilities to make them and our existing sales force to sell them."

2 Organizing
Deciding how the work is to be divided and coordinated.

Example: "We will set up separate marketing branches in the Northeast, Midwest, South, and West. Their activities will be coordinated through the Chicago office."

3 Staffing
Ensuring that there are sufficient qualified personnel to carry out the work.

Example: "We will employ specialists and operative employees as needed to meet changes in demand."

4 Directing
Motivating employees to perform, leading them toward goal achievement, and informing them about their work assignments.

Example: "We will offer bonuses as an incentive and explain work assignments to personnel."

5 Controlling
Setting standards, measuring performance against standards, and taking corrective action as needed.

Example: "We will set product performance standards equal to those of our main competitor and will conduct 28 predelivery inspections of each vehicle."

Source: David Schwartz, *Introduction to Management*, 2nd ed. (San Diego: Harcourt Brace Jovanovich, 1984), p. 32.

What Is a Manager?

Job titles often describe what a manager manages. A marketing manager manages marketing, a production manager manages production, and a finance manager manages money.

But some management job titles do not contain the word manager. In a college, people with job titles such as dean, department head, and coach are managers because they have authority over peo-

TABLE 14-1 Representative Problems Encountered in Managing and Typical Solutions

PROBLEM	POSSIBLE SOLUTIONS
Sales slump unexpectedly.	• Lay off employees to cut outflow of funds. • Launch a new sales campaign. • Sell a division of the business.
A union is attempting to organize employees.	• Cooperate with union leaders and try to work out a favorable contract. • Improve the conditions that employees are dissatisfied with. • Launch a public relations campaign to convince workers they wouldn't want a union.
The manager of Department A has an absenteeism rate among employees that is double that of other departments.	• Counsel the manager, perhaps suggest enrollment in a short course on management techniques. • Terminate the manager. • Demote the manager.
A new supervisor is appointed over several people who have greater seniority. The supervisor's former co-workers deeply resent this action.	• Ignore the resentment on the theory that it will fade with time. • Send a memo to the workers to accept the new supervisor "or else." • Transfer the supervisor to another department, and appoint a stranger to the job.

In each case, what other alternatives can you suggest?

> *It's better to sleep on what you plan to do than be kept awake by what you've done.*
>
> ANONYMOUS

ple, resources, and change. In the military, job titles of managers include sergeant, captain, and general. And in nonprofit organizations, bureau chief, administrator, and executive director are job titles indicating managers. The work a person does, not the job title, tells whether or not a job involves managing.

Do You Want to Be a Manager?

Because managers exercise power or authority, they are generally better rewarded than nonmanagers in salary, fringe benefits, and prestige. But does everyone want to be a manager? The following exercise raises questions that you should answer if you are thinking about becoming a manager.

WHAT IS PLANNING?

The management process begins with **planning,** or *deciding what work will be done and how it will be accomplished.* Planning sets the stage for what the organization will do, both generally and specifically. Managers create five different kinds of plans: objectives, strategies, policies, procedures, and rules.

What Kind of Plans Are Objectives?

An **objective** is *any goal that an organization or group seeks to achieve.* Some objectives are large, such as "Install a pipeline," "Build an aircraft carrier," or "Operate a 2,000-room hotel at a profit." Others are small, such as "Get this report done by Friday" or "Sell more sewing machines than last quarter." Objectives should be established for the business as a whole, for each department, and for individual activities.

Company-wide objectives are *the general goals an organization wants to achieve.* Examples of such objectives are: "Earn an

---

APPLICATION TO PERSONAL AFFAIRS

Do You Want to Be a Manager?

If you think you are ready for the challenge of a career in management, answer the following questions. If your answers are positive, you are sincere about pursuing a career in management, and you have recognized some of the conditions which make management a challenge. It is a new world for those who have been in nonmanagement positions, and to accept the conditions is not always easy. *It takes a special type of person to succeed and be outstanding in the field of management, the most demanding of professional careers.*

Make this list of questions your starting point as you check your sincerity about that management career:

                                                                 YES   NO

1. Do you like being in charge of other people?
2. Do you like to have the responsibility for the actions of others?
3. Do you think you could take satisfaction in seeing employees under your supervision succeed?
4. Would you like being judged on results—good and bad?
5. Would you like a job where your bosses have little appreciation for excuses?
6. Do you enjoy being a "team" player?
7. Do you like visibility?
8. Do you think you can lead others positively toward objectives and do so consistently?
9. Would you enjoy setting the model for employee conduct on the job?

	YES	NO
10. Could you accept working 50–60 hours per week routinely when nonmanagement employees work 40?		
11. Are you confident you know the subject of management and know what managers are supposed to do?		
12. Do you thrive under a certain amount of stress caused by unusual demands, deadlines, schedules, and dealing with a multitude of different personalities?		
13. Do you enjoy problem solving and decision making and the risks that accompany implementing your decisions?		
14. Can you put aside personal interests and preferences and do what is best for the organization?		
15. Can you handle pressure from your peers, your bosses, and your subordinates?		

SOURCE: Francis J. Bridges, *So You Want to Be a Manager?* Atlanta: ESM Books, 1984, 7, 8.

annual return of 10 percent on our investment"; "Capture 22 percent of the market for Product A"; or "Develop a new product to compete with XYZ."

Departmental objectives are *the goals set for each department, which should relate to—and lead directly to the achievement of—the general company-wide objectives.* Some examples are: "Reduce departmental expenses by 17 percent"; "Develop and implement a new training program"; or "Hold departmental absenteeism to 7 percent."

Finally, **individual objectives** are *the goals that specific persons will have to achieve to meet departmental objectives.* Examples would be: "Increase my sales volume by 20 percent over last year" or "Process 10 percent more insurance claims per week."

MANAGEMENT BY OBJECTIVES

Management by objectives (MBO) is popular in many companies as a way to set goals. It is *a system by which managers let their subordinates participate in setting tangible, usually numerical, work objectives and then periodically discuss with subordinates what progress has been made, revising the goals if necessary.*

Key advantages claimed for MBO are:

- Each person knows the precise role management expects each to play.

- Morale improves because employees help define their goals.
- It is easier to evaluate an employee's performance because managers can compare results with the objectives set.

Two limitations of MBO are:

- MBO takes more time than if the manager alone sets the objectives for the employees.
- Some employees may resent MBO because they may see it as a way for management to get them to work harder.

MBO has been successful in many organizations. To make it work, however, managers need to understand thoroughly how to use the system.

What Are Strategies?

"Strategy" is a military term and comes from the original Greek meaning "the art of the general." Today, **strategy,** the second type of plan, means *a broad-based plan to achieve the objectives of an organization.* Consider the company-wide objective mentioned earlier: "Capture 22 percent of the market for Product A." One strategy might be, "We will enter the market with a medium-priced product designed for young couples, ages 22 to 35."

Managers such as these must determine strategies that will enable their firm to achieve preset company objectives.

Top managers generally develop strategies because they are so important. The other types of plans—policies, procedures, and rules—generally develop at lower levels. Strategies should have first priority. The other types of plans should fit the strategies, not vice versa.

What Are Policies?

A third type of plan is a **policy,** or *a broadly stated course of action, or guide, that individuals should follow in making decisions.* Note that a policy is a guide, and, thus, people do have some discretion in its implementation. An example of a policy is, business-school graduates will receive preference in employment. Note that this policy allows room for the employment of someone who is not a business-school graduate. Some other examples of policies that a company might adopt are:

- *Product policy*—"The product must meet quality specifications at least equal to those of competing products in its price range."
- *Credit policy*—"The company will extend credit to customers who, in the judgment of the credit manager, are eligible."
- *Price policy*—"Prices stated in the company's catalog are subject to change, at the discretion of the marketing manager."
- *Employment policy*—"Close relatives of present employees are usually not eligible for employment in this company."

Many policies are in effect in each company, and top management establishes those of a very broad character. Power to make specific policies for the guidance of each department is usually delegated to department heads.

Policies are essential to an organization for three reasons. First, they ensure that employees handle problems systematically and quickly. For example, a credit-department policy might be to send reminder letters to customers whenever an account is 30 days overdue. This ensures that employees review all accounts regularly for delinquent payments, so that slow payers receive prompt reminders.

Second, policies make for fairness in dealing with employees and the public. It is never wise, for example, to give one employee advantages denied to another who is equally deserving. Well-stated policies let everyone know what treatment to expect.

Third, policies increase the productivity of employees. Policies make it easier to train new people and help keep morale high, since employees have a clear idea of what they should do.

What Are Procedures?

The fourth basic type of plan is a **procedure,** which is *a detailed method for handling a specific situation.*

An example of a procedure for dealing with customer complaints follows:

The salesperson will listen carefully to the complaint, ascertain the problem, and try to solve it to the satisfaction of the customer. If this cannot be done, the salesperson will introduce the customer to the assistant manager, who in turn will listen to the complaint and make whatever proposals are within his or her defined limits of authority. If this fails, the assistant manager will escort the customer to the manager, who will make the final decision on the matter.

Procedures should be established for all activities in a business. The accounting department needs a procedure for classifying and recording income and expenses. A supply room needs a procedure for supplying other units in the organization with equipment, tools, paper, and other goods. Employees should handle the processing of incoming orders and the purchasing of raw materials according to a definite procedure. Procedures are necessary for recording the amount of time employees work, for handling correspondence and customer complaints, for greeting visitors to the company, and for dozens of other activities in the business.

Managers should use great care in developing procedures. Unless they are carefully conceived, they can result in needless paperwork and excessive red tape. Further, if no sound reason exists for a procedure, employees resent it. Therefore procedures should be (a) based on actual need, (b) easily understood by all employees, (c) revised only when necessary, and (d) provided to employees in written form.

Consider the value of the following written procedure as part of a discount store's security instructions:

No person other than a detective shall stop, question, or detain a person suspected of taking the store's property. All cases of suspicion must be immediately reported to the detective, either in person or over the phone. No person shall attempt to assist the detective unless called upon to do so. Employees should never acknowledge a detective when on duty; employees should always treat the detective as a "customer."

A clearly defined procedure like this spells out how an employee should behave in a specific situation. Problems and embarrassment can result if managers have not developed and applied workable procedures.

What Are Rules?

The fifth and *most detailed plan* is a **rule** (also called a **regulation**). Rules indicate in very precise terms whether, in a specific situation, employees are to do or not to do something. Rules are important for essentially the same reasons as procedures: They save time, since

TABLE 14-2 Managers Must Create Five Kinds of Plans

TYPE OF PLAN	QUESTION MANAGER MUST ASK	EXAMPLE
Objective	"What goals do we want to accomplish?"	"Our goal is to achieve a 10-percent share of the cowboy-hat business in three years."
Strategy	"What activities will we engage in to achieve our objectives?"	"Market a new style of hat."
Policy	"What guidelines will we follow to implement our strategies?"	"Sell our hats only to retailers who sell Western wear exclusively and when they express a deep interest in carrying our brand."
Procedure	"What action will we take under specific conditions?"	"If a retailer defaults on payment, no further shipments will be made."
Rule	"What precisely must employees do and not do?"	"Under no conditions may an employee gamble while at work."

people need not think through and ponder each new situation, and they give employees a clear sense of what they can and cannot do. Some examples of rules for various situations are: "Employees will be at their work stations by 8:30 A.M."; "No visitors or employees not authorized by a clearance badge will be permitted in Building 2401 at any time"; and "No product will be accepted for return more than 31 days after the purchase date."

Table 14–2 summarizes the five kinds of plans in the management process.

What Makes Effective Plans?

Every plan—an objective, a strategy, a policy, a procedure, or a rule—should be:

- *Written*—We are all familiar with the types of communication gaps that can arise when managers give instructions orally.
- *Comprehensive, yet also as simple as possible*—The plan should cover the main situations likely to arise but should not try to cover every possible situation. Such an attempt generally results in an overly complex plan, with the result that many people misinterpret or fail to grasp the essentials of the plan.
- *Flexible*—While flexibility will vary with the level of the plan,

even rules stated very explicitly should be modifiable in unusual circumstances.
- *Revised regularly*—Because conditions change, a good practice is to review all plans at least annually and to revise them when necessary.
- *Communicated*—While it seems obvious that managers should explain plans to the people who are to carry them out, often they do not. A good question for managers to ask themselves is, "Does everyone understand the message?"

WHAT IS ORGANIZING?

Organizing is *the management function of deciding how to divide and coordinate work. It is the process of logically grouping activities, delineating authority and responsibility, and establishing working relationships that enable employees to work with maximum efficiency and effectiveness.*

Why Is Organizing Important?

The organizing process is essential in all businesses, large or small. A food-store proprietor with only two employees is organizing the business when he says, "Janet, you're in charge of all meats and produce; handle them the best way you can. When you have problems, bring them to me. And when I'm not here, you're in charge of the entire store. Bill, your job is to handle all canned and packaged groceries. When I'm here, bring your questions to me; but when I'm gone, ask Janet what to do."

In the large company, where employees must perform hundreds or thousands of jobs, organization is naturally much more complicated. The manager must decide:

- Exactly what work each individual shall perform and apportion this work among the employees
- The responsibility of and authority for each employee
- How to coordinate the work done by individuals and groups of individuals
- To whom each employee will report—that is, establish the chain of command (see page 412)

When employees know exactly what management expects of them and to whom they report, they are much more likely to function as a team working toward common goals. When things are disorganized, employees are more likely to resemble a confused mob than a team. Though inefficient organization is not always obvious, it often causes friction among employees and may result in unsatisfactory service to the customer.

Delegate Authority to Get Results

Andrew Carnegie, one of America's early business successes, once wrote:

> Organizing power, upon the development of which my material success in my life has hung, [is] a success not to be attributed to what I have known or done myself, but to the faculty of knowing and choosing others who did know better than myself. Precious knowledge this for

PEOPLE WHO MAKE THINGS HAPPEN

A PROFILE OF **PETER DRUCKER**

Peter Drucker is to American business what apple pie is to American folklore. Indeed, one book about him, by John Tarrant, is titled *Drucker: The Man Who Invented the Corporate Society.** Few business people would dispute Tarrant's assessment: "Peter Drucker is a towering and controversial figure in the world of management ... well known to a large segment of the literate population of the world."

Drucker was born in Vienna and in German his name means "printer." This is a fitting name since he has written over 15 books and hundreds of articles.

Drucker held two jobs in Germany before getting a law degree from the University of Frankfurt. One was with an American banking firm. The other was with a large afternoon newspaper, the *Frankfurt General Anzeiger,* for which he wrote about many things, including business and finance. When the Nazis came to power, Drucker decided as a "conservative committed to constitutional government, the rule of law, and the tenets of Christianity" to leave Germany. In 1937 he came to the United States.

In 1950 Drucker became professor of management at New York University. In 1971 he took the chair of Clarke Professor of Social Science at Claremont Graduate School in California. Widely acclaimed, he has honorary doctorates from a cross section of the world's universities.

Drucker started his consulting career in 1943 when he undertook a huge study for General Motors. Since then he has worked with countless clients as one of the country's highest paid and most sought after consultants.

Drucker has brought new insights to organizational thinking, particularly with regard to the decision-making process. He has the rare ability to shake business thinkers out of their thought-pattern ruts. His gift for the witty, pithy remark is illustrated as follows:

> *Drucker shoots darts at entrenched management...*

Figure 14-2 The Management Activities Pyramid

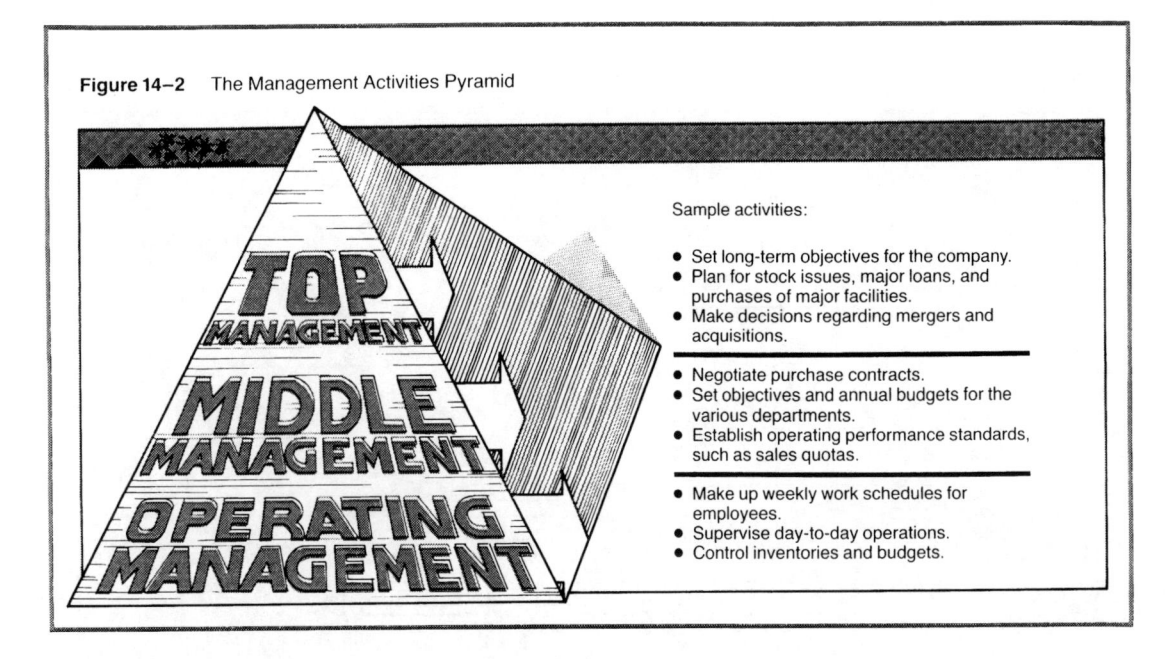

TOP MANAGEMENT
MIDDLE MANAGEMENT
OPERATING MANAGEMENT

Sample activities:

- Set long-term objectives for the company.
- Plan for stock issues, major loans, and purchases of major facilities.
- Make decisions regarding mergers and acquisitions.

- Negotiate purchase contracts.
- Set objectives and annual budgets for the various departments.
- Establish operating performance standards, such as sales quotas.

- Make up weekly work schedules for employees.
- Supervise day-to-day operations.
- Control inventories and budgets.

tions the chain is short, but in big companies it is usually very long. Ideally, each employee reports to only one supervisor. Otherwise an employee may be confused when given conflicting information by one or another boss.

What Is Span of Supervision?

Organizing also involves determining the **span of supervision,** or span of control—*the number of persons one manager can supervise effectively. When one manager supervises only a few people,* the span of supervision is **narrow.** In this case, *higher-level managers usually retain authority, and the company or unit is* **centralized.** *When one manager supervises many people,* the span is **wide.** In this case, *authority is granted to a greater number of subordinates,* and the company or unit is said to be **decentralized.** Figure 14-4 gives an example of wide and narrow spans of supervision for a vice president in charge of sales.

There is no ideal span. In some cases a narrow span of 3 to 5 people will be best, in others a moderate span of 6 to 14 people, and in some situations a wide span of 15 or even 50 people. Each management situation is unique and requires separate analysis. In general, however, spans can be fairly wide if the work is simple, the manager's subordinates are well trained, procedures and policies are well established, and the jobs supervised are highly similar and are grouped in close physical proximity.

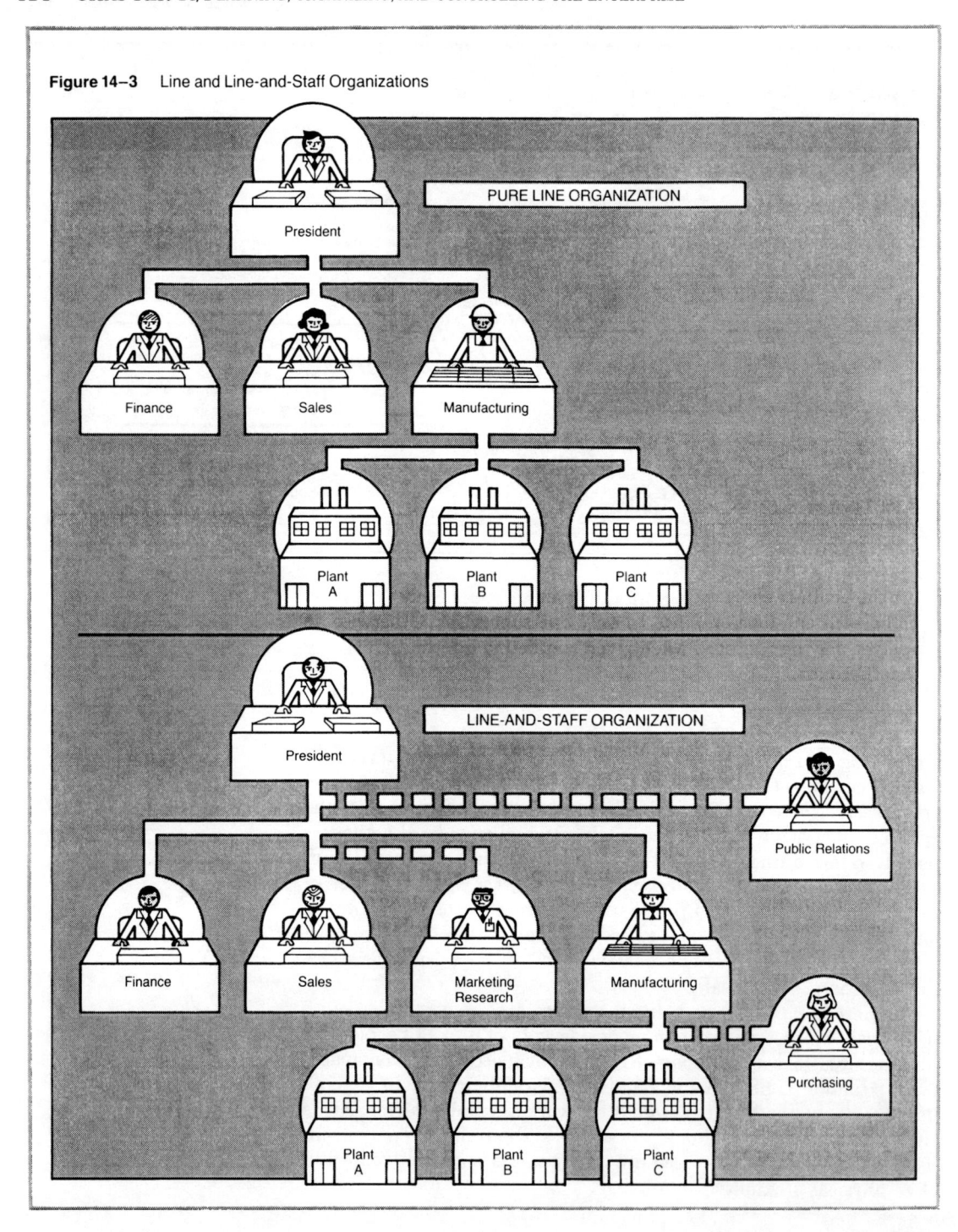

Figure 14–3 Line and Line-and-Staff Organizations

Figure 14-4 Examples of Wide and Narrow Spans of Supervision

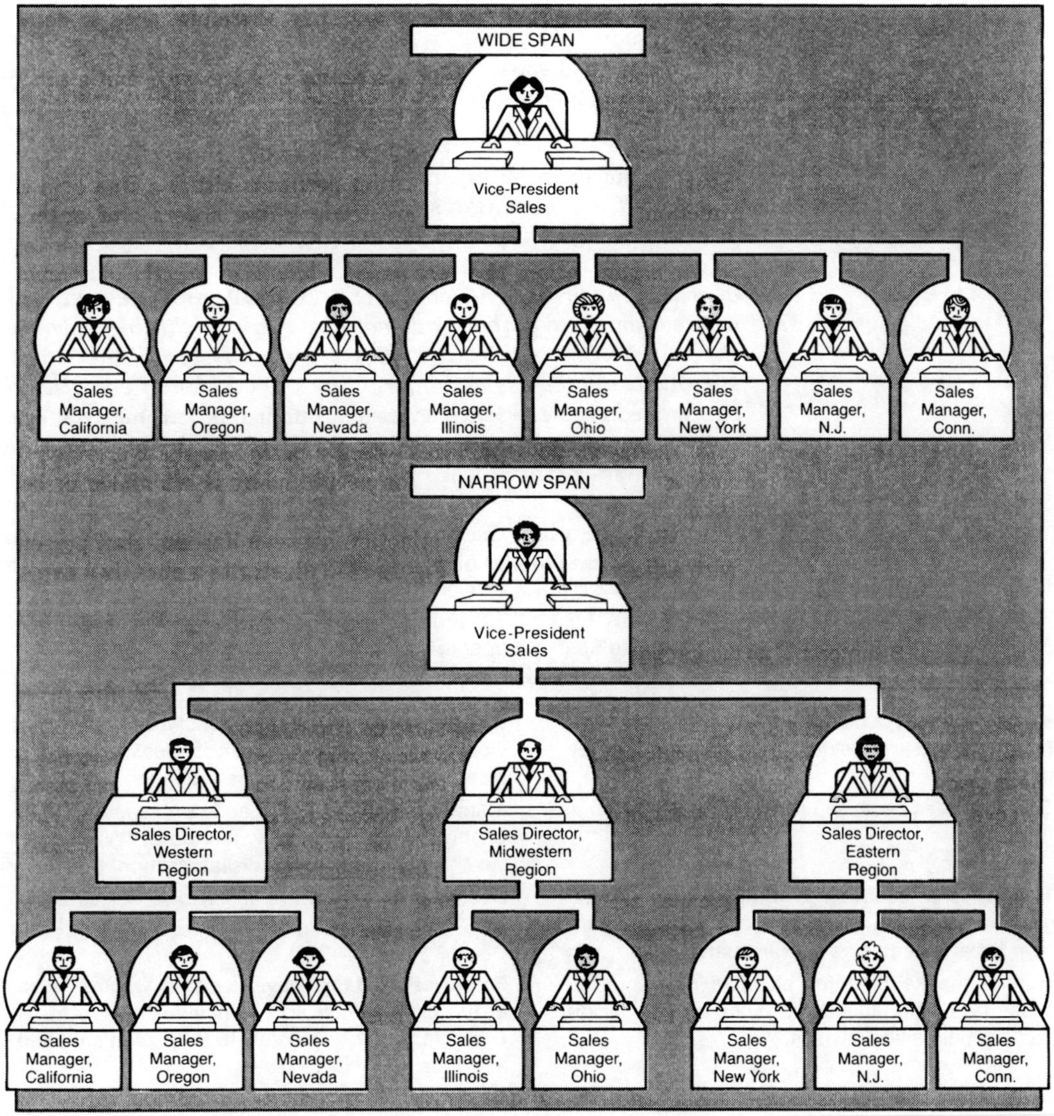

A narrower span is generally necessary if the work is complex, there is rapid turnover of subordinates, there are few formal rules and procedures, the jobs supervised are highly dissimilar, and the jobs supervised are far apart physically. When either of the last two conditions exists, the manager may not be able to spare the time to supervise each activity directly and may, therefore, need to delegate more authority.

Table 14–3 shows some symptoms of a too wide and a too narrow span of supervision.

What Is a Line Function? A Staff Function?

Every manager in an organization performs either a line or a staff function. **Line managers** are *those whose orders and authority flow in a straight line from the chief executive down to lower levels in the organization; they are usually involved directly in producing or selling the firm's products or services.* **Staff managers** are *those whose orders and authority do not flow in a straight line down from the top of the organization; they are usually technically trained specialists and advise and inform line and other staff executives on specialized problems,* such as legal or public relations matters. While staff managers do report to a specific person in the hierarchy, they may at times perform work for people many levels above or below them.

We can explain the distinction between line and staff personnel with a diagram. Part (a) of Figure 14–3 illustrates a pure **line organi-**

TABLE 14–3 Symptoms of an Inappropriate Span of Supervision

SYMPTOMS OF TOO WIDE A SPAN	SYMPTOMS OF TOO NARROW A SPAN
Personnel waste considerable time waiting to see the manager.	Communication up the organizational hierarchy is slow, and there seems to be too much red tape.*
Turnover rises because employees feel ignored.	Managers become bored and don't seem to have enough to do. They may, therefore, "oversupervise," causing employee dissatisfaction.
Training and counseling of personnel are neglected. Frequent mistakes occur because manager lacks time to give people instructions.	Overhead is excessive—much of it traceable to executive salaries.
Manager lacks time for effective planning because he or she spends so much of the day directly supervising activities.	Employees feel they have no say in what goes on in the organization and complain that top management is out of touch with their problems and activities.*

*These symptoms generally indicate that the company has become a *bureaucracy*, which is what occurs when managers keep narrowing their span of supervision by creating more and more organizational levels.

zation—*one in which all members perform line functions.* The concept of line organization stems from the military, where authority is based solely on rank—the corporal has authority over privates, the sergeant over both corporals and privates, and so on. The line organization in business works the same way: The president issues orders to subordinates, and so on down the line. The line form has certain advantages:

- The chain of command is easy to understand. No question can arise as to who is in charge of a certain segment of the business.
- Management can make and carry out decisions quickly.
- Executive overhead expense is low because no staff specialists are on staff.

Despite these advantages, pure line organization occurs only in small companies. As a business grows larger, certain weaknesses begin to appear in the line structure, chiefly because line executives often lack time to study problems and specialized training needed to make wise decisions on complicated business matters.

To compensate for these weaknesses, larger businesses use the **line-and-staff organization.** This structure illustrated in Part (b) of Figure 14–3 is *similar to the pure line arrangement in that line managers still make all major decisions and issue orders. However, in this case the line managers use the services of staff specialists, none of whom have direct line authority except in their own departments.*

Remember that line managers still make all basic decisions and issue all orders. Staff managers can only recommend; they cannot enforce.

The obvious advantages of the line-and-staff organization are that experts solve technical problems and that employees can carry out many functions (for example, purchasing) more efficiently because they are centralized. On the negative side, the line-and-staff organization results in slower decision-making and also increases the executive overhead expense.

Note that the organization charts shown in this section have been highly simplified. Figure 14–5 shows the many line-and-staff departments normally found in a large manufacturing company.

Departmentalization Groups Certain Tasks

The head of a company, division, or department must decide not only on how wide a span of supervision will be but also on **departmentalization,** or *the arrangement of work into manageable parts.* The three main ways of departmentalizing are:

- *Function departmentalization or type of work performed—*

Figure 14-5 Organization Chart of a Manufacturing Company

BOARD OF DIRECTORS

Committee on Audit

Bonus and Salary Committee

Executive Committee

President

Finance Committee

INDUSTRIAL (LINE) DEPARTMENTS

Electrochemicals | Elastomer Chemicals | Industrial and Biochemicals | Organic Chemicals | Photo Products | Textile Fibers

Fabrics and Finishes | Film | International | Pigments | Plastics

STAFF DEPARTMENTS

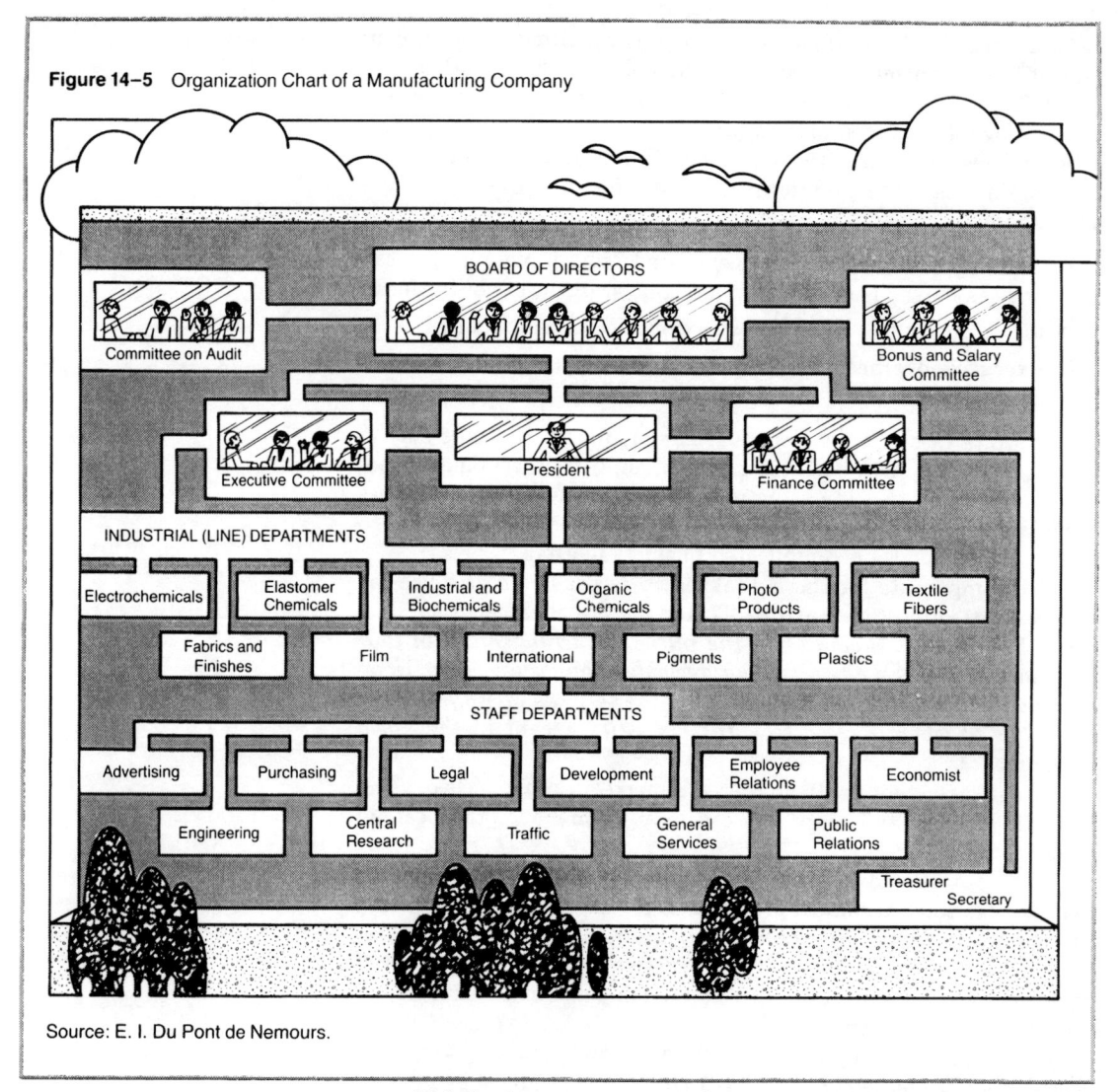

Advertising | Purchasing | Legal | Development | Employee Relations | Economist

Engineering | Central Research | Traffic | General Services | Public Relations

Treasurer
Secretary

Source: E. I. Du Pont de Nemours.

This is the most common basis for departmentalization. Typically, a business departmentalizes into production, marketing, and finance.

- *Geographic departmentalization or area where work takes place*—Some organizations have branch offices, divisional headquarters, or other geographic departments or units.
- *Product departmentalization or separate units for different*

products—General Motors, for example, is organized by product, with separate divisions for Chevrolet, Pontiac, Cadillac, and other product lines.

The objective of departmentalization is to group activities together skillfully to avoid waste, inefficiency, confusion, and duplication. In reality, however, most companies cannot achieve this goal completely. Further, the work of departmentalizing never ends because every business is dynamic. In a large business, for example, changes in consumer demand or other conditions may lead top management to create new departments or to combine or eliminate old ones.

What Is the Informal Organization? The Grapevine?

So far, our discussion of organizations has dealt with the formal structure of a business. Every enterprise also has an informal structure of organization.

Management creates the formal organization. But the members of the group create the **informal organization.** This group *consists of people who usually work together and elect their own leader.* This leader, of course, has no official standing in the company. Mutual trust and interests bind members of informal groups together.

Informal organizations exist for the following reasons.

- *To transmit information*—The **grapevine** is *the informal organization's communication channel.*
- *To reduce fear*—Members of the informal organization often gossip about management decisions, some of which they fear might hurt them. Sharing views can reduce members' anxiety.
- *To amuse*—Members of the informal organization enjoy talking about what is going on in the organization.

Management should try to use the informal organization to its advantage. For example, a manager can test opinions about a proposed change in working hours by mentioning it to a member of the informal organization who will pass this information along. The workers' feelings will eventually reach the manager.

Is American Business Overly Organized?

Some observers believe large American businesses are too organized. This overorganization, observers say, lowers productivity and increases costs. In some companies, nine or more levels of management separate a production worker from the top executive. In Japan, only four or five levels separate the worker from the senior executive.

AMERICA'S REEMERGING CREATIVITY

Growing Use of Employee Suggestion Systems

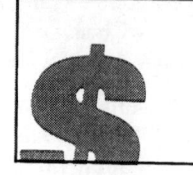

Employee suggestion systems are not new, but interest in them is. Suggestion systems are based on the concept that every employee thinks and, thus, can come up with ideas for saving money, increasing productivity, improving safety, and putting new vitality into a business.

For generations, companies have placed suggestion boxes in work areas. But these boxes were used mainly as receptacles for complaints and chewing gum wrappers—not for ideas for doing things better. Today, suggestion systems are a "formal communication vehicle through which progressive change can be brought to management's attention. They are a type of feedback system where people can innovatively participate in their organization."*

A formal suggestion has several characteristics:

- It requires that the person making the suggestion be identified.
- It provides for a committee to evaluate the idea.
- It actively encourages people to make suggestions.
- It compensates the employee for the idea if it is accepted.

The Bank of America was one of the first companies to use a formal suggestion system. "One of the earliest suggestions adopted by the bank came from Frank Risso, chauffeur for the founder of the bank.... In 1928, Risso suggested the bank issue travelers checks 'to accommodate those customers who are thinking of touring the state.' It has proven to be one of the most successful suggestions ever made by an employee. For his idea, Risso reaped a cool $1."†

Today, in some companies, awards between $1,000 and $25,000 are common. For example:

- A worker at Pacific Gas and Electric devised a new procedure for cleaning valves, which took four and a half hours less than the old one. For his idea, he was awarded $3,000, or 20 percent of the net savings for the first year.
- At Long Island Lighting, a worker who suggested a way to correct problems associated with fan maintenance procedures was awarded $15,600 for the suggestion, which resulted in a savings of $100,000 in the first year.

The National Association of Suggestion Systems (NASS) now has 750 member companies, who employ 12 million people. The age of revitalization through tapping the brains of all employees—from janitor to top executive—is finally here!

Questions for Discussion

1. Think of one idea for cutting costs at your school. Why do you feel your suggestion has not already been implemented?
2. Why do you think some employees are reluctant to make suggestions?
3. What problems is a company likely to incur in establishing a formal suggestion system?
4. Aside from money, what else can a firm do to motivate employees to make suggestions?

---

*"Suggestions Systems, An Answer to Perennial Problems," *Personnel Journal*, July 1980.
†Ibid.

WHAT IS CONTROLLING?

Controlling is *the managerial function of setting standards for work, measuring actual performance against the standards, and taking corrective action if performance does not meet the standards.* For example, if a standard says that eight units should be produced per hour but actual performance is only six units per hours, the manager must decide what should be done to raise actual performance from six to eight units.

Control Step #1: Set Standards

In Step 1 of the control process, a **standard** (*a preestablished performance level*) should ideally be set for every activity in the business, so that management knows how well things are going. Table 14–4 gives examples of standards for various types of activities.

A particularly important type of standard is product or service quality. Managers must ask themselves, "What level of quality should we supply—low, medium, high, or very high?"

Consider two companies that have decided to make potato chips. Company A sees its target market as the rank-and-file potato-chip eater who chooses a brand primarily on the basis of price and is not overly concerned about nutrition. This company will probably make a medium- to low-quality product. Company B, in contrast, seeks to appeal to people who are discriminating in food preferences, nutrition minded, and not price conscious. Therefore, it will probably make a product of high or very high quality.

Control Step #2: Measure Actual Performance Against the Standards

Step 2 in the control process is measuring performance against standards. It involves comparing what the standards accomplished with what managers hoped to accomplish with the standards. Performance measurement is always the middle step in the control process, following the setting of standards and preceding corrective action.

Measurement of performance is essential, for two reasons. First, a standard obviously serves no purpose unless we determine to what degree it is met. It is useless to set a per-unit production cost of $10 and then not measure actual costs.

Second, measurement of performance tells managers when corrective action, the third step in the control process, is necessary. Without measurement of performance, managers have no way of answering such key questions as, "How well are we doing?" and "What should we do to improve performance?"

In some cases performance can be measured objectively with

> **TABLE 14-4** Performance Standards for Different Types of Activities
>
> **CHIEF EXECUTIVE OFFICER**
> - Guide company to earn a 10 percent return on investment
> - Expand production facilities by 12 percent
> - Negotiate a satisfactory collective bargaining agreement with the union
> - Maintain company's share of the market
>
> **CHIEF ACCOUNTANT**
> - Prepare routine financial statements each month
> - Keep total accounting expenses to a specified level
> - Complete the company's annual report within 30 days of the end of the fiscal year
> - Get payroll checks out on the 30th of each month
>
> **SALES REPRESENTATIVE**
> - Make 18 calls per week
> - Make at least six sales per week totaling at least $3,000
> - Keep expenses to 8 percent of sales volume
> - Obtain one new customer per week
>
> **ASSEMBLY-LINE WORKER**
> - Attach 60 parts per hour
> - Report for work at 8:00 A.M.
> - Work overtime two days per month

considerable precision; in others it must be evaluated subjectively. Ideally, performance of every activity should be measured against the standard set for it. In practice, however, it is seldom possible or economically justifiable to check everything being done. What is very important in managing is the measurement of **strategic control points**—*those activities that can make or break the enterprise.* Examples of strategic control points are:

INCOME

In all organizations income is a strategic control point: business managers keep close tabs on income from sales; trade-association and union executives observe dues collected; managers of religious organizations and political parties monitor contributions. When income is off significantly, corrective action is necessary.

Measuring strategic control points can tell management whether standards are being met and if managers need to take corrective actions.

Expenses
Expenses over a period of time cannot exceed income, or the organization will fail. Thus, expenses are a strategic control point and are of primary concern. Some managers review key expense data every day.

Inventory
The level of inventory is significant in many organizations, especially those engaged in retailing, wholesaling, manufacturing, or processing. For a production enterprise, the size of inventory is a strategic control point because it helps determine whether production should be increased, cut back, or kept constant. For a merchant, inventory size may indicate whether to buy more, buy less, conduct special sales, or raise or lower prices.

Product Quality
Inspection of products to determine whether they meet quality standards is a strategic control point in many organizations, such as drug manufacturers, food processors, and auto makers. Quality control is especially important when the health and safety of the consumer is involved.

Absenteeism
In most organizations, absenteeism is important as a control point. In some situations it is exceptionally important. For example, "How many people are absent today?" is a critical control question a con-

struction manager must ask daily, because a minimum number of people is usually necessary for construction crews to operate. Absenteeism is also a strategic control point for airlines, since flights may have to be cancelled if absent crew members cannot be replaced.

Control Step #3: Take Corrective Action

The first two steps in the control process—setting standards and measuring performance against standards—have little value unless the manager takes **corrective action,** or devises *a plan to make performance meet the standards.*

Corrective action takes many forms. Consider, for example, the performance standard "No stealing." Evidence indicates that company property is being stolen by personnel. Unless something is done, the control process (inventory record-keeping) is pointless.

Consider another example: Janet Raymond sells office products. Her assigned quota is 1,000 units per month, but her results are 700 units. Some forms of corrective action are: lower the standard to 700 units; assign Janet a different territory; enlarge her present territory; give her more training; have her sell a different combination of products; or terminate her.

Quality control is important in industries where accuracy is essential. Products must be near perfect to maintain customer trust and ensure repeat business.

WHERE IS MANAGEMENT HEADED?

The concept of "management" will not change. The definition will always be achieving a firm's goals through the coordinated performance of five functions: planning, organizing, staffing, directing, and controlling. But managers will perform functions differently:

- Computerization will allow for managers to use more information in decision-making. Forecasting future events should improve because managers can analyze more relevant data.
- Work will be more decentralized. First level managers and employees will have more authority.
- Importance of staff managers may decline since computers will supply line managers with more specialized information.
- Businesses will give more emphasis to employee training and retraining as industry develops new technology.
- Work will be less structured: workers will have several skills.
- Firms will place greater emphasis on the quality of work life.

SUMMARY

- Management is the process of achieving an organization's goals through the coordinated performance of five functions: planning, organizing, staffing, directing, and controlling.
- Decision making is crucial in management.
- The management process begins with planning. Specific kinds of plans are objectives, strategies, policies, procedures, and rules.

- Organizing involves dividing and coordinating work among employees. It also entails grouping activities, delineating authority and responsibility, and establishing working relationships.
- As the work of an organization grows, managers must delegate more authority.
- Professional management consists of three levels: top, middle, and operating management.
- Organization charts show how people and jobs relate, and the chain of command tells people to whom to report or delegate authority.
- Span of supervision refers to the number of people who report directly to a manager. A narrow span produces highly centralized authority; a wide, decentralized authority.
- Line managers are usually directly involved in producing or selling a firm's products or services; staff managers handle specialized functions, such as accounting, law, and research.
- The three main ways to departmentalize are by function, geography, and product.
- Unlike the formal organization, members create their own informal organization to transmit information, reduce fear, and amuse.
- In controlling, management seeks to ensure that employees satisfactorily carry out activities. Management sets standards, measures performance against standards, and takes corrective action to bring performance in line with standards. To measure performance, managers pay particular attention to strategic control points—income, expenses, inventory, product quality, and absenteeism.
- Management trends include greater use of information, more decentralization, a decline in the importance of staff managers, a greater emphasis on the training and retraining of personnel, less structured work environments, and more emphasis on the quality of work life.

KEY TERMS YOU SHOULD KNOW

centralized organization	informal organization	planning
chain of command	line-and-staff organization	policy
company-wide objective	line manager	procedure
controlling	line organization	regulation
corrective action	management	rule
decentralized organization	management by objectives (MBO)	span of supervision
decision making		staff manager
delegation of authority	middle management	standard
departmentalization	narrow span of supervision	strategic control point
departmental objective	objective	strategy
first-line supervisor	operating management	top management
grapevine	organization chart	wide span of supervision
individual objective	organizing	

QUESTIONS FOR REVIEW

1. What specific powers do managers have?
2. What is decision making? Why are decisions often unpopular?
3. Is a manager always called "manager"? Explain.
4. What are the five kinds of plans involved in the management process?
5. Explain company-wide objectives, departmental objectives, and individual objectives.
6. What is management by objectives (MBO)? What are its advantages and disadvantages?

7. What is a strategy?
8. What are policies? Why are they needed?
9. Explain the purposes of procedures; of rules.
10. What does organizing involve?
11. Why is delegation important?
12. What does an organization chart tell?
13. How do line differ from staff managers?
14. What is controlling? What steps are involved?
15. Where does management appear to be headed?

QUESTIONS FOR DISCUSSION

1. Do you feel the administration could improve procedures for class registration and "dropping and adding" at your college or university? What are the procedural weaknesses? What would you change?
2. Draw an analogy between a good organization and a good athletic team.
3. Differentiate between line and staff executives. Which would you rather be? Give reasons.
4. Sometimes the informal organizational power structure in business is more effective than the formal. Why?
5. You have decided to go into the restaurant business. Financing is no problem; you are aware that profits do not always correlate with the level of standards. Would you direct your standard of service to high, middle, or low income clientele? Why?

CASE STUDY

Should the "Great Sounds" Record Store Develop Formalized Plans?

Mary and Bill Alden, married, in their late twenties, have just purchased a record store. They open in two weeks.

Mary: We must get off to a good start, so we should write out the plans and policies.
Bill: Why? We own the store.
M: But though we've worked in record stores, we've never owned one.
B: But why put plans on paper? We'll play it by ear until we learn more.
M: But we should put policies on paper. We're going to have part-time employees. Are they going to report to me, you, or both of us?
B: I don't know. But that's no problem.
M: I think it is. What policies will we have for funds? for honoring credit cards? for personal checks?
B: You make sense, but I still see no reason to write formal policies.
M: That management course you took did absolutely no good. We also need written guidelines to cover late employees, coffee breaks, smoking, merchandising, promotion.
B: Maybe after we've been operating we can reconsider. Wrong policies are worse than no policies.
M: Bill, we've put all our money into the store. We can't afford to open until we've got our act together.

Questions

1. Would you put your strategies, policies, procedures, and rules in writing? Why or why not?
2. Give two examples (not in the case) of policies and rules that the Aldens should develop.
3. Whose argument do you support? Why?

EVOLUTION OF A BUSINESS

How Systemized Should a Small Office Be?

Waiting for their building to be built and planning for it gave Sara and Ray plenty of experience working together before they finally opened the doors of their business. Sara had set up a number of attractive package tours that the agency could start selling as soon as it opened. Ray had established contacts with a wide range of hotel and transportation agencies. To start, they planned to hire two customer-contact people who would work in the office answering telephone inquiries and taking care of people as they came in.

Ray and Sara were concerned about how customer-contact work would be handled.

Sara: I think we should try to put some policies into writing before we hire employees. This would give them a clear idea of what we stand for as a company and how they should tackle their jobs.

Ray: Aren't we too small for that sort of thing? With only four people in our office, we'll all know pretty well what's going on. Furthermore, we can develop policies as we gain experience. We really don't know enough yet about the problems we'll be facing.

Sara: If you don't plan and set up systems ahead of time, you're not going to be efficient. You have to have policies for things, like using the telephone for personal use, and you have to keep standardized records for active customer accounts so someone can find things in the files in case the person handling the account isn't there. If you don't anticipate these things beforehand, you can cause a lot of unnecessary problems and customer ill will.

Ray: Well, I think things like that will work themselves out as a matter of course. There's such a thing as overplanning to the point where the system becomes more important than what we're trying to accomplish. People working in a small office shouldn't be the slaves of a system—if they are, you lose an advantage of being small.

Questions

1. Whose argument seems more sound, Ray's or Sara's?
2. Should policies be written out in some sort of company manual?
3. What did Ray mean when he said that they should not become slaves of a system?
4. In a small office do you think clients should be assigned to one employee, or should each employee be able to work on each client's account?

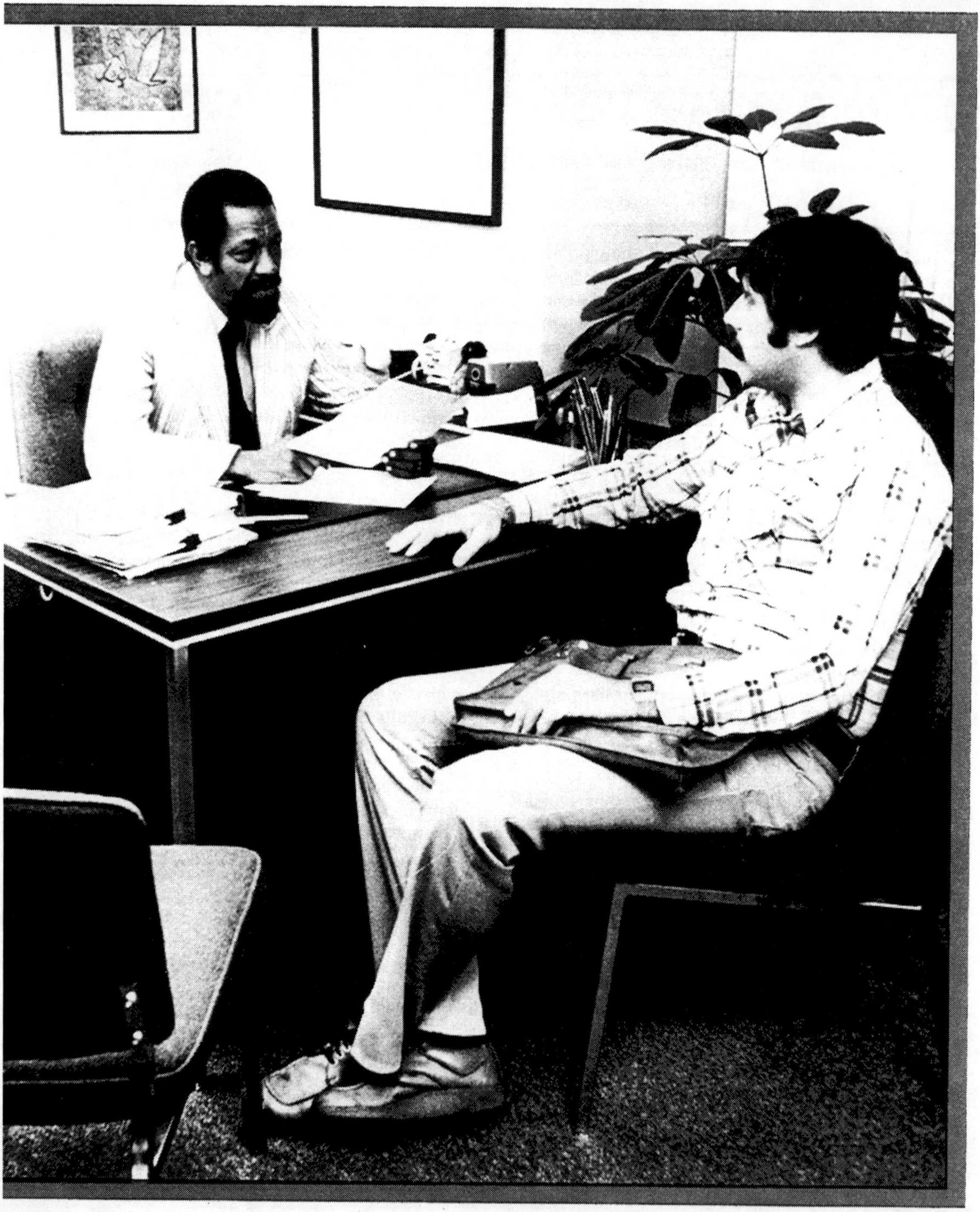

15

HUMAN RESOURCE MANAGEMENT: STAFFING AND DIRECTING

Beyond the Time Clock and the Paycheck

READ THIS CHAPTER SO YOU CAN:

Describe what the staffing function involves.

Explain the various tools used in the selection process.

Discuss the basic kinds of training provided employees.

Describe the methods of compensating personnel.

Explain what benefits and services other than money companies may provide their employees.

Discuss how employers evaluate their employees and for what purposes.

Define directing and list the indications of worker dissatisfaction.

Describe the basic theories of motivating employees.

Explain leadership and communication as aspects of directing.

429

All businesses consist of people who perform certain activities to achieve goals. People have always been the key resource in organizations, and recognition of their importance continues to grow. Technological advantages over competitors are not easy to maintain: Others soon copy one company's advances in production and materials. But human performance varies widely, and superior personnel performance is not easy to duplicate. It follows that the company with the most effective personnel has a competitive advantage.

In this chapter we discuss the managerial functions that have the most direct bearing on personnel: staffing and directing.

WHAT IS STAFFING?

Staffing is *the managerial function of selecting, training, compensating, and evaluating people so that they perform the work in an organization according to established standards.* The personnel department handles much of the work involved in staffing, and is also responsible for providing employee benefits and services and for maintaining health and safety programs.

Personnel management, sometimes called **human resource management,** is *the process of providing an organization with qualified employees and maintaining an atmosphere in which they will be productive and loyal.* Personnel management focuses on relating people to the work the firm expects them to do. The main concerns of the personnel department are to select, train, compensate, provide benefits to, and evaluate employees. It is a staff authority and, as such, concerns itself primarily with nonmanagement employees.

Tools Used to Select Employees

Personnel departments use various tools in the selection process (see Figure 15-1). The following sections describe these tools.

JOB ANALYSES, DESCRIPTIONS, AND SPECIFICATIONS

Before they can fill a position, personnel officers must define the jobholder's qualifications and the duties the employee will perform. To do this, they use three tools.

A **job analysis** is *a systematic detailed study of the work an employee is to do in a specific position.* While a job analysis tells us what a job involves, a **job description** is *a detailed statement explaining the specific tasks he or she will perform, the reporting relationships of the jobholder, and the results expected.* A well-written job description classifies the what, why, and how of the position.

Figure 15–1 The Employee Selection Process

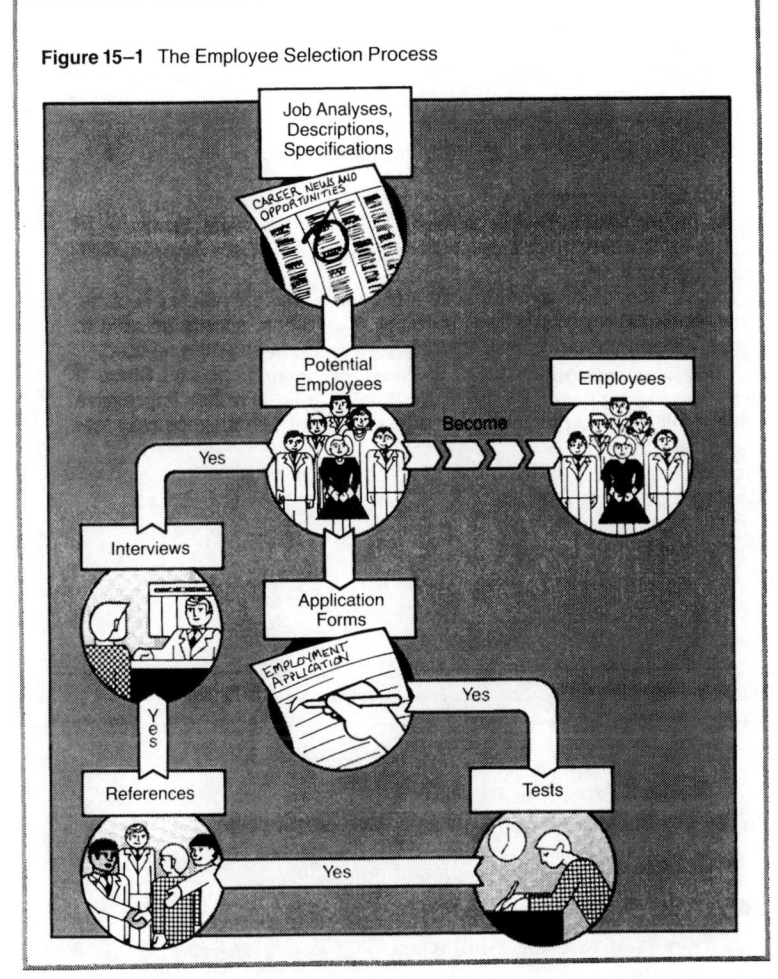

A **job specification** is *a statement of the qualifications a person must have to perform the work involved* (see Figure 15–2). It specifies such factors as education, experience, and health an employee needs to do the work satisfactorily.

Most small organizations do not prepare formal job analyses, job descriptions, and job specifications. However, as organizations grow in size and complexity, the need for them increases.

Once the personnel department knows as precisely as possible what kinds of people are to fill what kinds of jobs, it may begin its search for those people.

Figure 15-2 A Sample Job Specification

Job Title: Bookkeeper/Accountant
Salary: $18,000-20,000 depending upon experience and qualifications.
Hours of Work: 40 hours per week (8:30 A.M.-5:30 P.M., Monday through Friday).
Job Begins: September 1, 1985.
Qualifications: Two-year college degree in accounting.
Experience: Prefer person with one or two years of successful experience with a small firm.
Personal: Must enjoy working with people, meeting customers, and keeping accurate records. Reliability and dependability ess ntial.
Job Duties: Keep all financial accounts, accounts payable, accounts receivable, payroll, tax reports, fringe benefits reports, financial reports for government. In addition, should be able to run desk-top computer. Person should be willing to service customers when needed.
Opportunity for Growth: Person has unlimited opportunity to progress as firm grows. Since it opened in 1980, the firm has quadrupled its volume. Further impressive growth is anticipated. After one year of employment, employees may join profit-sharing plan.
Schedule for Interviews: Gregory Sharp, owner
Monday through Thursday
10:00 A.M.-1:00 P.M.
Beginning August 10

THE QUICK-COPY COMPANY
151 Main Street
Falls River, New Jersey 07418
(201) 555-3323

SOURCE: Karen R. Gillespie, *Creative Supervision* (New York: Harcourt Brace Jovanovich, 1981), 135.

SOURCES OF APPLICANTS

There are many sources of prospective employees:

- College and university placement offices
- Technical or trade schools
- Friends of existing employees
- "Walk-in" applicants
- Conferences or trade conventions
- Advertisements in newspapers and trade publications
- Employment agencies, government and private

Companies are making more and more use of **private employment agencies,** which are *businesses that seek out people who want jobs and match them with employers who need their skills.* Many private employment agencies specialize in placing people in specific fields, such as accounting, advertising, computer programming, and selling. In selecting management personnel, companies often rely on private employment agencies (also called executive search firms).

Generally there are far more applicants than there are jobs. The challenge facing the personnel department is to choose best-qualified individuals. Personnel managers use the following tools in making selection decisions.

APPLICATION FORMS AND RÉSUMÉS

A **job application** is *a form which generally asks the applicant for his or her name, age as being between 18 and 70 years, address, telephone number, work history, military record, education and training, and several references.* It may also request other information, such as membership in organizations, hobbies, and job goals. Applications for jobs in academic fields generally also provide a space for honors and publications.

The Civil Rights Act of 1964 and its amendments make it illegal for employers to request a picture or information on race, creed, religion, national origin, specific age, sex, or ancestry on either an application form or in a "help wanted" advertisement. However, the law makes an exception when such information relates to a **bona fide occupational qualification (BFOQ),** which is *a personal job requirement based on the nature of a specific job.* It is not illegal, however, for a prospective employee to voluntarily supply a picture or give information about his or her national origin, religion, etc.

For higher-level jobs, applicants also commonly provide employers with a résumé.[1] This is an outline of one's employment history, educational achievements, skills, and other job qualifications. An applicant may include career aspirations, references, and other information as well.

While the applicant will still have to complete a job application, the résumé provides an opportunity to personalize, to present significant details of one's accomplishments—something that is seldom possible within the confines of a standardized application form.

The completed application form and the résumé serve four purposes. First, the act of filling out an application or organizing a résumé is itself a test of the applicant's suitability since it reveals something of his or her ability to follow directions, communicate, and give facts neatly and correctly. Second, it is a guide for the interviews that follow. Third, if the firm hires the applicant, it will retain the forms as a part of the person's permanent work record and use them for reference when considering promotion, transfer, discharge, or similar actions. Last, if there are no immediate job openings for an applicant,

---

[1] A sample résumé is shown in the Appendix.

the personnel department may file the forms and refer to them when appropriate openings do occur.

TESTS

Tests attempt to measure the applicant's job-related mental and mechanical abilities, skills, and attitudes. The most common tests companies give to job applicants are:

1. **Intelligence tests,** which *try to measure mental abilities,* such as verbal comprehension, word fluency, memory, facility with numbers, and speed of perception.
2. **Achievement tests,** which *seek to measure an individual's ability to perform specific tasks.*
3. **Aptitude tests,** which *identify personal talents or capabilities,* such as mechanical aptitude.
4. **Personality tests,** which *try to measure personal characteristics,* such as maturity and temperament.

As part of the selection process, some companies—especially those that handle large amounts of cash and valuable merchandise, such as jewelry stores and banks—give **polygraph,** or **lie detector, tests.** These are *tests that try to measure honesty by revealing if stress is present when a person answers certain questions.* Organizations may find people unacceptable if they discover histories of gambling, drinking habits, or theft. They may also reject potential employees because of past arrest records or general unsuitability for the job. Companies often also use polygraph tests as a control device for existing employees who handle cash or expensive merchandise.

ARE TESTS ALWAYS A GOOD GUIDE?

Most personnel directors recognize that tests will not precisely predict the applicant's performance on the job. While tests may measure ability to do something, they do not measure whether someone wants to do something. The fact that a person can add and subtract without making mistakes does not necessarily mean that he or she will make a good bookkeeper. Tests are not good at measuring such intangibles as ambition, energy, boredom potential, or ability to work under pressure. Thus, the wise personnel director uses tests only as a guide.

REFERENCES

A **reference** is *a person or firm that an employer may contact to verify an applicant's claims.* Personnel departments often check references, or they ask outside investigators to do the checking. They verify educational claims, and question former employers to determine how the applicant performed on a previous job and how associates regarded him or her. If the applicant was convicted of a crime, personnel departments may check police and court records. A major falsification on an employment application or résumé is grounds for refusal to consider an applicant or immediate dismissal if the applicant is already on the job.

INTERVIEWS

Applicants usually have one or more interviews with the person for whom they will work if hired. There may also be interviews with other people, such as the next higher person in the department or a peer of the applicant (a person who holds a position similar to the one in which the applicant is interested).

In a typical interview, the interviewer asks the applicant to explain or expand on statements made on the application form or résumé. If the position requires the employee to meet the public, the interview will reveal what sort of general impression the applicant will make in personal-contact situations. In such cases the interviewer will probably take special note of the applicant's use of language, appearance, posture, and mannerisms. The interview also gives the applicant an opportunity to find out more about the job and working conditions. Interviews with the applicant's potential supervisor are particularly valuable, in that both parties get an idea of whether they would enjoy working together.

HOW TO PREPARE FOR A JOB INTERVIEW

Most of us will probably experience numerous job interviews in our careers. The Application to Personal Affairs on page 438 suggests some do's and don'ts for handling oneself during a job interview.

The interview is often the most important stage in the selection process. Unfortunately, it may also be the stage at which discrimination in hiring takes place. The Equal Employment Opportunity Commission (EEOC) and the courts have declared it illegal for employers to ask potentially discriminatory questions. Table 15-1 lists questions that may be discriminatory and why.

WHAT ABOUT OLDER EMPLOYEES?

In 1967, Congress passed the Age Discrimination in Employment Act, which made it illegal to discriminate against workers solely because they were over age 40. In 1977 Congress passed a bill that raised the mandatory retirement age from 65 to 70. Companies must now keep employees on until they are 70. The so-called gray power movement continues to push itself into the limelight more than ever because the retirement dream that every American once shared has become a financial nightmare.

Older Americans have legal protection against job discrimination because of age and do not have to retire until age 70.

TABLE 15-1 Questions That May Be Discriminatory

PROBLEM AREAS	POTENTIALLY DANGEROUS QUESTIONS	REASON FOR DISCRIMINATORY NATURE
Marital status	• Are you married? • What is your spouse's occupation? • What is your spouse's full name?	Questions of this nature tend to discriminate against women. Some firms do not like to hire married women, but will hire married men.
Dependents	• Do you have children? • What ages are your children? • Do you plan to have children?	This is another area in which discrimination against women may occur. The number of children and their ages would be of little significance in the hiring of a man, but many employers hesitate to hire a woman with small children because they fear frequent absenteeism.
Credit	• Do you have any debts? • Have you saved any money? • Do you have a good credit rating? • Do you own your own home?	Minority-group incomes tend to be lower than the national average; therefore, these questions may discriminate against minorities.
Age	• How old are you? • What is your birth date?	As a result of the Age Discrimination in Employment Act, it is unlawful to ask a person's age. The reason for this is to protect qualified applicants over 40 from being bypassed. However, if there is a minimum age requirement, such as 18 or 21, it is permissible to ask age of younger applicants.
Religion	• Do you attend church? • Can you work on Saturday or Sunday? • How do you usually spend Sundays?	Some religions forbid their members to work on Saturday or Sunday. This form of questioning could therefore be directly discriminatory. However, if there is a proven need for the employee to be available for work on weekends, the question can be asked.
Arrests or convictions	• Have you ever been arrested?	It is unlawful to ask about arrests, but not about convictions if they relate to specific jobs.
Bonding	• Have you ever been refused bond? • Are you bondable?	These questions are unlawful if they are used to elicit information about the applicant's character. However, they are permissible if the employee must be bonded.
Citizenship	• Are you an American citizen?	Lawfully immigrated aliens have every right to employment in the United States. Any questions designed to reveal a person's nationality are discriminatory and potentially unlawful. Direct questioning is permitted, however, if the job has national security implications.

TABLE 15-1 (continued)

PROBLEM AREAS	POTENTIALLY DANGEROUS QUESTIONS	REASON FOR DISCRIMINATORY NATURE
Lowest salary	• What is the lowest salary you will accept?	This question has frequently been directed toward women applicants, in the hope that they would accept lower pay than men for the same job. Discussion of salary is permissible, but to phrase the question in this manner is unlawful.
Garnishment	• Have your wages ever been garnished?	In some states, garnishment of salary is illegal. The answer in any case has no bearing on work performance and serves to discriminate against minorities.
Relatives working for same firm	• Do you have any relatives working in this firm?	Sometimes company policy prohibits more than one family member from working for the firm. This policy usually discriminates against women, as it is most often a male family member who is already employed.
Handicaps or health problems	• What is the state of your health? • Do you have any handicaps?	Only if these questions relate directly to the job may they be asked.

SOURCE: Mary Wilkes and C. Bruce Crosswait, *Professional Development: The Dynamics of Success*, New York: Harcourt Brace Jovanovich, 1981, 32–33.

Barbara Torrey, a federal expert on pensions, has commented: "Historically there has been an implicit social contract that the working generations will help support the retired generations either publicly or privately. But that contract may have to be renegotiated." The percentage of the population over 65 will have doubled between 1960 and 2020. Women outlive men by seven years and that gap may widen. The grim truth is that the gray population bulge threatens bankruptcy for both the Social Security system and many company retirement plans.

At present three workers contribute to support one retiree on Social Security, which is now barely able to collect enough taxes to cover benefit checks. In the year 2020 it will require two workers to support one retiree *if* the government increases worker contributions 50 percent. (Figure 15–3 projects the growing burden.) The government can avoid insolvency only by raising taxes, cutting benefits, or raising the eligibility age. Company pension plans are often not funded and increasingly become the largest single liability that a company shoulders. This trend away from early retirement is likely to continue because (1) Early retirement represents a waste of human resources; (2) People are living longer and receiving better health care; (3) Many people do not want to retire at 65 or 70.

APPLICATION TO PERSONAL AFFAIRS

Do's and Don'ts in Job Interviews

Most of you will be involved in many job interviews during your working life. And the job interview is usually the most important part of the job-getting process. Below are some general guidelines for making a good impression in interviews.

DO

- *Know as much as possible about the company.* Know such things as what it makes or sells, its size, its philosophy of management, and who its customers are. Try to read company literature before the interview. Talk to employees, customers, and suppliers if possible.

- *Know how your knowledge, training, experience, and education relate to the job you are applying for.* Explain how you feel you can contribute to the company. Bring letters of recommendation, a résumé, and any evidence you have of past performance that suggests you are qualified.

- *Act confident.* Remember that you too are an important person. Relax. Take the point of view that you and the interviewer are two people sitting down to discuss something of mutual importance.

- *Look employable.* Appearance is more important than many people think. It is a good idea to dress neatly and conservatively and avoid an extreme appearance.

- *Maintain eye contact with the interviewer.* Many interviewers feel that lack of eye contact suggests you lack confidence or aren't telling the truth.

DON'T

- *Be critical of your existing or former employers.* Criticizing your present or previous employer is negative. The interviewer will think less of *you,* not the other employer.

- *Dwell on fringe benefits.* Discussing at length such matters as paid holidays, vacations, or retirement programs suggests that you are more concerned with what the company can do for you than what you can do for it.

- *Overemphasize starting salary.* It is only part of the employment package. Instead, show more concern about the potential for advancement.

- *Act like a person who already knows everything.* Instead, demonstrate in the interview that you are a good learner, cooperative, and supportive of others. It is always a mistake to make elaborate, unrealistic promises. Never oversell yourself.

- *Discuss irrelevant personal matters.* Your goal in the interview process is to demonstrate how you can help the prospective employer achieve its objectives.

If you fail to get the job, evaluate your behavior. Correct any mistakes you made and get ready for the next interview. Keep in mind that in job interviews most of us hear "no" more often than "yes." Intelligent behavior in the interview process plus persistence will yield success sooner or later.

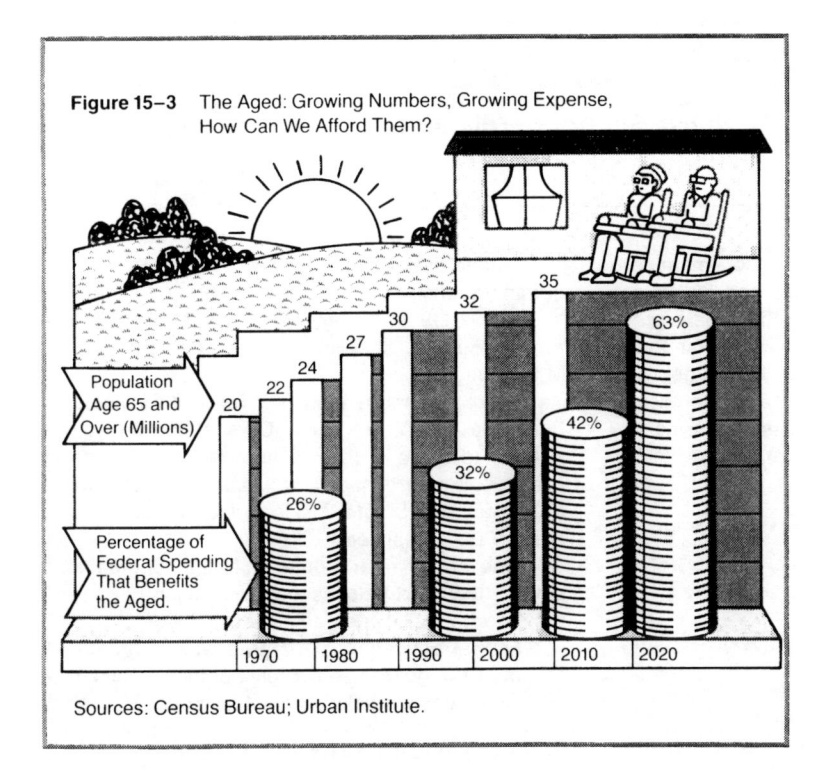

Figure 15-3 The Aged: Growing Numbers, Growing Expense, How Can We Afford Them?

Sources: Census Bureau; Urban Institute.

Training Employees

The personnel department frequently works with line managers to plan, organize, and control the company's training programs. The main objectives of training are to minimize the amount of time required to learn a job, increase the productivity of employees, improve the quality of their work, and prepare employees for more responsible positions.

MOST TRAINING IS INTERNAL

The personnel department may assist directly or indirectly in the following kinds of training, which take place within the organization.

Orientation. Typically the personnel department administers an **orientation program** *to introduce new employees to the organization.* Usually, the program covers:

- History of the company
- Reward system (compensation, overtime, insurance and other fringe benefits, vacations, pensions, and profit sharing)

AMERICA'S REEMERGING CREATIVITY

The Dramatic Increase in Business School Enrollments

Education in the basics of business—management, marketing, finance, production—is, over the long run, a most effective way to increase productivity. A business, after all, is no better than the talent that runs it. A trend that is helping to improve management talent is the increased enrollment in schools of business. In terms of degrees conferred, note the trend from 1973 to 1984:

YEAR	UNDERGRADUATE DEGREES IN BUSINESS
1973	126,800
1975	133,800
1978	161,300
1984	215,800

While college enrollments overall have leveled off, and in some areas are declining, the number of people attending business schools continues to increase.

The increase in the number of students seeking Master of Business Administration (M.B.A.) degrees is even more dramatic than the growth in numbers of students seeking undergraduate degrees. In 1960, only 4,400 M.B.A.s were conferred. By 1984, the number exceeded 61,000.

People with M.B.A. degrees seem certain to dominate business decision-making in the late 1980s and 1990s. A study made in 1981 of 12,000 top executives showed that 30 percent had M.B.A. degrees.

There are more than 500 business schools that have M.B.A. programs. Competition for admission to some of them is intense. In 1984, for example, Harvard had 6,200 applicants for 810 openings, and Stanford selected only 360 from the 4,700 who applied.

One incentive for getting an M.B.A. degree is pay. As the chart below shows, beginning pay for people with M.B.A. degrees is attractive.

Formal education, undergraduate or graduate, does not guarantee success. But when mixed with experience, it helps one achieve goals.

Questions for Discussion

1. From a personal standpoint, what are two pros and two cons of working toward an M.B.A. degree?
2. There is a widespread belief that the M.B.A. degree is a fad and that its value on the job market will decrease as the supply of M.B.A.s increases. Do you agree? Why or why not?

Starting Salaries for New M.B.A.s in 1985

SALARY BREAKDOWN BY RANGE	PERCENTAGE OF GRADUATES
$16,000—$20,999	8.2
$21,000—$25,999	49.4
$26,000—$30,999	22.3
$31,000—$35,999	14.1
$36,000—$40,999	4.8
$41,000 and over	1.2

Starting Salaries for New M.B.A.s in 1985 (*continued*)

EMPLOYMENT BY SELECTED FUNCTION AREAS	AVERAGE SALARY
Accounting	$22,500
Banking	$23,000
Consulting	$24,000
Finance	$24,500
General Management	$25,100
Sales/Marketing	$22,000
Information Sciences	$28,500
Industrial Relations	$20,500

EMPLOYMENT BY SELECTED TYPES OF EMPLOYERS	AVERAGE SALARY
Public Accounting	$24,500
Aerospace, Electronics and Instruments	$26,000
Commercial Banking and Financial Institutions	$28,500
Consulting Research	$28,000
Food & Beverage	$29,500
Merchandising/Service	$22,500
Transportation	$21,000
Nonprofit	$19,250

SOURCE: Graduate Business Placement Office, Georgia State University.

- Basic rules (work attendance, dress code, safety considerations, pregnancy leave, and grounds for termination)
- Key company policies (promotions, treatment of customers and visitors)

On-the-job training. Most employees receive their job training from the supervisor and/or other employees. The theory is "To do is to learn."

Coaching. **Coaching** is *informal person-to-person counseling about how to perform a job more effectively.* Usually, the employee's immediate supervisor provides the coaching. As an ongoing process, this kind of training can benefit both the individual and the company.

Rotational training. Companies use two kinds of rotation to help employees acquire knowledge and skill: functional and geographic. **Functional rotation** is *training that requires the employee to spend some time in different departments so that he or she will know what each department does and how it relates to the organization as a whole.* Functional rotation is especially important for people

On-the-job employee training is the most common way of learning a new skill. Most training is job-specific, although some companies provide general skills training as well.

being considered for management jobs in a company. Some companies take functional rotation beyond training. At one airline, for example, employees spend time behind the reservations counter, in the computer room, and in the air.

Geographic rotation is *training that requires the employee to work in several geographic locations as part of his or her development.* To move into the upper ranks in large companies, a person must usually work in several branches or divisions away from headquarters. People who move up in multinational companies will usually have worked in several nations.

Assessment centers. Some organizations have established **assessment centers,** sometimes called **evaluation centers.** These are *places where employees can practice their job-related skills through simulations.* Employees may work on solving specific problems, or role play job situations. Supervisors may also use these centers to evaluate candidates for managerial jobs.

A basic advantage of assessment centers is that supervisors can observe trainees operating in real-life situations. Two disadvantages are high cost and subjectivity, since the observers may be biased about the behavior they see.

SOME TRAINING MAY BE EXTERNAL

Increasingly, companies use external training services provided by universities, trade associations, and private companies. These institutions provide specialized training in many areas. Some companies pay part or all of the tuition costs for employees who attend college part time (provided they pass the courses!).

SHOULD TRAINING BE FOR THE LONG-RUN?

William Ouchi, the quality-circle consultant who wrote "Theory Z," concluded that:

Managers in U.S. companies, so universally accustomed to a short-term view of performance, have been forced to look at people and profits as opposites. In the short-run, an investment in employee training will reduce output; in the short-run, an unrealistic level of pressure on employees will increase output; and in the short-run oriented firm, of course, a manager who fails in the short-run will not be around to see the long-run.

Training is an expense. But it is a justifiable expense if, over time, it results in more productive employees. Anyone with even a little job experience has encountered supervisors who don't know how to lead employees, and managers who know little about setting poli-

Some companies pay tuition expenses at colleges and universities. Specialized courses that train for job skills benefit both employees and employers.

cies and procedures. For people in management positions especially, training for the long-run can benefit the firm in many ways.

Compensating Employees

The personnel department works in conjunction with line management to establish compensation levels for employees. Every compensation plan—whether for unskilled labor, office workers, sales representatives, or executives—should meet four objectives. It should:

- *Be competitive*—To attract well-qualified people, compensation should normally be at least equal to that paid by similar businesses in the area.
- *Be fair*—Compensation should vary with the difficulty of the job and the special qualifications required of the employee. People who do similar work should receive similar compensation.
- *Motivate employees to be productive*—To accomplish this, employers may use special wage incentives or bonuses.
- *Be based on performance*—Compensation should relate to the quantity and quality of work performed. Unfortunately, as Figure 15-4 suggests, pay does not always correspond to quality of performance.

There are several methods used for compensating employees, depending on the job and the custom of the industry or company.

WAGES

The simplest, easiest, and most common method of compensating employees is the payment of **wages,** which are *compensation based on the number of hours worked.* Thus, if the wage is $6.86 per hour and the employee works 40 hours, the gross income is $274.40. If the employee works more than the specified base number of hours (usually 35 to 40), he or she usually also receives overtime pay.

Employers pay wages when specific output is difficult to measure. For example, assembly-line workers, plant guards, and maintenance people generally earn a straight hourly rate. The disadvantage of wages is that there is no direct incentive for the employee to be productive.

SALARY

A firm generally uses the salary plan to compensate white-collar workers, such as office personnel, executives, and many types of professional people. **Salaries** are *compensation paid on a weekly, monthly, or annual basis.* Salaried employees usually do not receive overtime pay for hours worked above the normal number.

Salaried employees normally have considerably more job security than personnel paid hourly. In times of recession, for example,

Figure 15-4 Compensation Does Not Always Correlate with Performance

In tough times when employees and stockholders are taking cuts, top management salaries go up.

Corporation and CEO	1981 Salary	1980-1981 Salary Increase	1981 Corporate Earnings	1981 Stock Performance
ITT R. V. Araskog	$1,136,000	+15%	Down 10%	Down 1%
Revlon M. C. Bergerac	1,133,000	+5%	Down 89%	Down 43%
Exxon C. C. Gavin	992,000	+8%	Down 2%	Down 23%
Household International G. R. Ellis	912,000	+49%	Down 28%	Down 6%
Boeing T. A. Wilson	751,000	+16%	Down 21%	Down 49%
Phillips Petroleum W. C. Douce	715,000	+39%	Down 18%	Down 31%
Avon D. W. Mitchell	604,000	+10%	Down 9%	Down 12%
Reynolds Metals D. P. Reynolds	539,000	+18%	Down 52%	Down 32%
Bausch & Lomb D. S. Schuman	442,000	+13%	Down 10%	Down 16%
Ford Motor P. Caldwell	440,000	+10%	Loss	Down 16%
United Air Lines R. J. Ferris	371,000	+8%	Loss	Down 6%

Source: *Business Week*, "Supply Side Sacrifices," May 10, 1982.

firms may lay off hourly workers while keeping salaried employees—unless the recession becomes severe.

PIECE-RATE PLAN
Under the **piece-rate plan,** employers *pay workers a certain amount for each unit of work done.* Employees paid in this fashion are guaranteed a certain minimum hourly rate because of minimum wage laws. The piece-rate plan acts as an incentive, for the harder and faster the employee works, the more he or she earns. Companies use this plan when the work is standardized and when it is possible to measure the output of each employee. The piece-rate plan is common in apparel manufacturing, meat processing, and produce crating.

COMMISSION
A **commission**—used extensively in personal selling—*is a form of compensation by which a sales representative receives a certain per-*

CONTEMPORARY ISSUE

Should There Be a Minimum Wage Differential for Youth?

The problem of teenage unemployment is serious. This is particularly true among minority teenagers, where unemployment rates run as high as 40 percent. To fight this problem, a minimum-wage youth differential has been suggested. A **youth differential** is *a special minimum wage for employees under the age of 21 and for students.* These employees would receive 85 percent of the regular minimum age.

Jennifer, age 18; Alice, age 22; and Tim, age 26, are eating lunch together. Jennifer is upset.

Jennifer: Today I saw another item in the *Wall Street Journal* that said that some congressman is trying to get a law passed to set the minimum wage for teenagers at 85 percent of what people 21 and older get. That simply would not be right.

Tim: Look, Jennifer, I know how you feel because it would affect you. But let me cite some facts. A direct relationship exists between the minimum wage and teenage unemployment. When the minimum wage increases, teenage unemployment goes up. A youth differential holds down the minimum wage for teenagers, giving them greater employment opportunities.

Alice: But Jennifer has a point. The differential idea is unfair. Look what could happen. If the cost of teenagers is less than the cost of other employees, teenagers would displace older workers. Since a youth differential makes teenage labor cheaper, older workers, often with families to support, would lose their jobs. That result would not be fair to the older workers. So keep the minimum wage the same for all workers regardless of age.

J: I hadn't thought about that, but it makes sense.

T: But look at the problem from the employer's point of view. An employer cannot pay employees more than they are worth. Now, teenagers often lack any experience or skills; often they just aren't worth the minimum wage. A youth differential places the wage for teenagers more in line with their value to employers. All other approaches to the teenage unemployment problem haven't helped. I think we should try the youth differential.

A: That's just an old man of 26 talking. I work part-time in a dry cleaning store at the minimum wage, and I'm worth at least as much to the employer as one gal old enough to be my mother.

J: I agree all the way with Alice. And besides, the current minimum wage is not enough to live on—even for teenagers. A youth differential would make it even more difficult. Pay should not be related in any way to age.

Questions

1. Do you feel a differential minimum wage based on age is a good idea? Why or why not?
2. What other economic incentives could be designed to help reduce the problem of teenage unemployment?

centage of his or her sales volume. For example, if the commission rate is 5 percent of sales, the sales representative will receive $5 on each $100 sold. This plan is similar to the piece-rate system, for the more people sell, the more they earn.

BONUS
A **bonus** is *a cash payment used as an incentive.* Some firms use bonuses only to reward certain employees who make a better-than-average contribution to the business. Other firms may award bonuses to an entire group of employees when their overall performance exceeds expectations. Bonuses are a major portion of the pay package for senior managers in large companies. Typically, about one-third of a top manager's pay is in the form of a bonus.

PROFIT SHARING
Profit sharing is *a method by which qualified (usually management) personnel receive a predetermined share of profits.* Advantages of profit sharing plans are: (a) they serve as an incentive, (b) they help reduce turnover, and (c) they do not represent a fixed commitment. Limitations of profit sharing plans are: (a) they are often unfair since people who contribute little may receive as much as those who contribute a great deal, and (b) shareholders of the business may object.

Personnel Departments Arrange for Other Benefits and Services

The personnel department is responsible for planning and administering whatever programs the company provides to attract and retain qualified employees. It is also in charge of maintaining healthy and safe working conditions for all employees.

FRINGE BENEFITS
A **fringe benefit** is *a reward for labor in a form other than wages, salary, or other monetary reward.* Possible fringe benefits include paid holidays; vacation and sick pay; group health, life, and/or accident insurance; retirement plans; child care centers; psychological counseling; food services such as a cafeteria; plans whereby employees can obtain discounts on products; in-company athletic teams; and publication of a company magazine. The number and the variety of benefits are growing, and they account for an increasing percentage of the payroll dollar (see Figure 15–5).

HEALTH AND SAFETY PROGRAMS
Another major concern of personnel management is the health and safety of employees. The National Safety Council estimated that in

448 CHAPTER 15/HUMAN RESOURCE MANAGEMENT: STAFFING AND DIRECTING

Figure 15–5 Employee Benefits as Percent of Payroll, by Industry Groups, 1,454 Companies, 1983

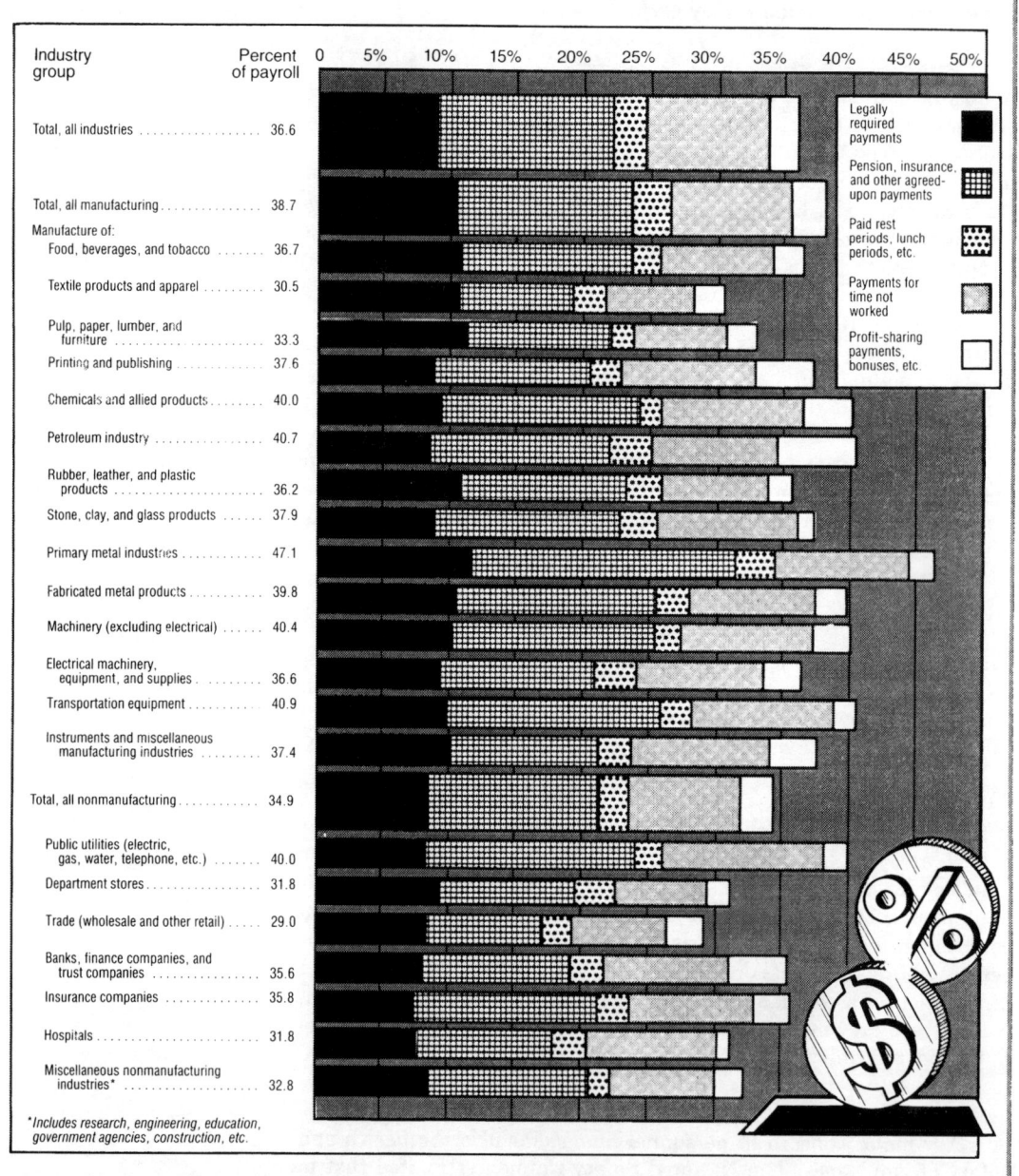

Industry group	Percent of payroll
Total, all industries	36.6
Total, all manufacturing	38.7
Manufacture of:	
Food, beverages, and tobacco	36.7
Textile products and apparel	30.5
Pulp, paper, lumber, and furniture	33.3
Printing and publishing	37.6
Chemicals and allied products	40.0
Petroleum industry	40.7
Rubber, leather, and plastic products	36.2
Stone, clay, and glass products	37.9
Primary metal industries	47.1
Fabricated metal products	39.8
Machinery (excluding electrical)	40.4
Electrical machinery, equipment, and supplies	36.6
Transportation equipment	40.9
Instruments and miscellaneous manufacturing industries	37.4
Total, all nonmanufacturing	34.9
Public utilities (electric, gas, water, telephone, etc.)	40.0
Department stores	31.8
Trade (wholesale and other retail)	29.0
Banks, finance companies, and trust companies	35.6
Insurance companies	35.8
Hospitals	31.8
Miscellaneous nonmanufacturing industries*	32.8

Legend:
- Legally required payments
- Pension, insurance, and other agreed-upon payments
- Paid rest periods, lunch periods, etc.
- Payments for time not worked
- Profit-sharing payments, bonuses, etc.

*Includes research, engineering, education, government agencies, construction, etc.

Source: Survey Research Section, Research Center, Economic Policy Division, Chamber of Commerce of the United States, 1615 H Street, N.W., Washington, D.C. 20062

1984 there were 13,600 workers killed while at work and 42,785 who died from off-the-job accidents—a death toll of 56,385. Worker injuries numbered about 2 million on the job and 3.5 million off the job.

In response to growing concern about job-related accidents and illnesses, the government passed the controversial **Occupational Safety and Health Act (OSHA)** in 1970. As *the nation's first federal safety and health law,* its stated goal is "to assure as far as possible to every working man and woman in the nation safe and healthful working conditions and a right to a workplace free from recognized hazards that are causing or are likely to cause death or serious physical harm." OSHA inspectors make surprise visits to workplaces, and an employee can complain to OSHA about a safety or health hazard without having his or her name revealed.

Some personnel departments also concern themselves with the general health of employees. They may have an infirmary or a first-aid center and may require an annual physical examination that is paid for by the company.

For example, personnel departments are accepting more and more responsibility for employee alcoholism, and view it as an occupational, rather than a medical, dilemma, according to a survey of more than 1,300 companies.[2] Authorities on alcoholism estimate that from 3 to 10 percent of the U.S. work force suffers from alcoholism and that another 10 percent has significant drinking problems. Two-thirds of the companies surveyed carry insurance that pays for a four-week rehabilitation program.

Evaluating Employees Is a Key Function

Personnel management works in conjunction with line managers to evaluate employees and decide what actions they should take to reward them or make them more productive. Employee evaluation can help answer questions about:

- *Promotions*—"Is the person promotable?" "Can he or she handle larger responsibilities?" "If so, in what areas and at what level?"
- *Transfers*—"Does the individual's performance suggest that he or she can be transferred to another position or geographic area?"
- *Compensation*—"On the basis of the evaluation, should the individual receive a raise?"
- *Development*—"What additional training does the individual need based on the evaluation?"
- *Terminations*—"On the basis of performance, is there reason to terminate the individual?"

---

[2]The Conference Board, Release 3004, September 24, 1980.

> *Someone else's achievement must act as inspiration, not as a standard.*
>
> M. A. K. GYSAI

METHODS OF EVALUATION

There are three bases on which to evaluate employees: results, traits, and informal observation.

Results, or **performance, evaluation** is the ideal. It *assesses what the employee actually accomplished over a period of time; it deals with measurable achievement, such as units produced, volume sold, and costs reduced.* Firms use results evaluation in conjunction with management by objectives (see Chapter 14).

Ideally, employers should evaluate all employees in terms of results achieved. Unfortunately, it is impossible to determine the precise accomplishments of some workers. How does one measure the performance of a receptionist or a security guard or a truck driver? Because of this difficulty, many companies rely on trait evaluation.

Trait evaluation (also called **attribute evaluation**) *assesses employees in terms of personal characteristics.* For example, the supervisor may rate the employee in terms of loyalty, cooperation, and likeability. Trait evaluation is simple, but it is also very subjective. It can be useful in companies where individual employee contribution to results is difficult or impossible to measure. The government uses trait evaluation for the vast majority of jobs.

Informal evaluation employs no structure or design. It is *based solely on observation of an employee's performance.*

TRANSFERS, PROMOTIONS, AND DISCHARGES

Using employee evaluations, the personnel department can help make decisions about transfers, promotions, and discharges.

Transfers. A **transfer** is *the assignment of a worker to another job;* it may be necessary for any of several reasons. Employees may have been placed originally in a job for which they were not suited, or they may be unable to get along with other workers. Management may also transfer employees to build a more flexible work force or to meet a change in work requirements. Transfer may be at the request either of the employee or of management.

Promotions. A **promotion** is *an upward move to a position of more responsibility and greater pay.* Promotions are a great incentive to employees and, when administered properly, favorably influence employee morale. Management must exercise extreme care, however, in awarding promotions, lest hard feelings result among employees who do not receive promotions but feel they deserve more recognition.

Usually, management awards promotions for a consistent display of ambition, initiative, high productivity, and ability to assume leadership. Sometimes promotions are automatic when an employee completes a specialized course of study or training. In any event, it is essential that all employees clearly understand the bases for promotion; otherwise, resentment, accompanied by lowered morale, results.

The **Peter Principle,** *a theory that holds that most people in organizations are promoted until they reach their level of incompetence,* has been advanced by management theorist Laurence Peter. People who believe this concept feel that promotions do not always reward merit. They feel that people move up because of seniority, politics, or personality—not ability or merit.

People who don't believe the Peter Principle point out that most managers—at any level—are competent, and while there may be exceptions, most promotions go to people who deserve that recognition.

Discharges. A **discharge** is *dismissal from a firm because of incompetence, intoxication on the job, insubordination, curtailed business, and so on.* One survey showed that 23 percent of all management-level vacancies come about because of discharges, which amounts to an estimated 100,000 executives a year.[3]

Because the firing task is distasteful, companies are increasingly turning to **outplacement counselors,** who are *outside consultants who assist companies in the "dehiring" process by helping discharged personnel find jobs elsewhere.* Outplacement experts agree that most discharges are a result of personality conflicts rather than poor performance. Discharge is a touchy matter, and is potentially troublesome in a society in which the number of lawsuits is growing.

Amusingly, the touchiness of the issue has spawned a hatful of euphemisms. Executives are never "fired" but are "separated" or "terminated." And they leave because of "policy differences."

WHAT IS DIRECTING?

Directing is *the managerial function of motivating, leading, and communicating with employees so that the goals of the organization can be most efficiently met.* Directing is a crucial function, since the best plans, organization, staff, and controls will not yield effective results without the presence of suitable motivation, leadership, and communication.

Motivating Employees Is Important

Fair wages, good working conditions, and short working hours—although important—do not guarantee the attainment of high worker productivity. Even companies that pay the highest wages, provide a comfortable working environment, and supply employees with many fringe benefits may have morale problems.

---

[3]As reported in Carl W. Menk, "What Are the Chances of Being Fired?" *New York Times,* June 18, 1978.

PEOPLE WHO MAKE THINGS HAPPEN

A PROFILE OF JOHN J. ALLEN

John J. Allen, one of five children, realized early that he would have to fund his college education. He began work as a part-time grocery clerk in 1964. John's parents, neither of whom had a college background, told him, "Education is something no one can ever take away from you. You can go bankrupt and lose everything, but a good education is yours forever."

In 1968 Mr. Allen received an Associates degree with a major in retail management from Columbus Technical Institute. After service in the army, he went on to earn a Bachelor of Science in Education degree from Ohio State University in 1973 with a major in Distributive Education.

Upon graduation from Ohio State, Mr. Allen went to work for HART Stores, a mass merchandising subsidiary of Big Bear, a supermarket chain. His first assignment was to do such special projects as determine how to better utilize payroll dollars, control inventory, maximize sales dollars per man hour, and make comparisons between stores.

Soon John began assisting the personnel department with store openings (interviewing, orientation, and training). At that time he set a long-term goal—to become personnel manager. He felt it would take about five to six years to accomplish this goal. In the meantime, John did extensive work on the Affirmative Action Program, writing policies and procedures and job descriptions.

He was soon promoted to personnel manager for Hart Stores. To strengthen his background in personnel management, John completed a Masters Degree, specializing in Personnel Management, from Central Michigan University.

Mr. Allen now owns his own personnel placement agency, John J. Allen and Associates. His company goal is to "make this agency one of the best search and placement firms in the country. This includes expansion into a multi-unit operation." He says, "The service we offer is important, but the people we deal with are more important. I want to build the kind of company I would want to work for—a company that is respected not only for its productivity and effectiveness but also for the professional and dignified way it handles its accounts." He continues, "I want to have a company that puts into practice the belief that only through the success of its clients does the business succeed. Such a company will be around for years to come."

Mr. Allen has some valuable advice for students who want to get ahead.

- Establish your goals and realize the discipline and sacrifices it will take to achieve them.

- Always try to do a better job than what you are being paid to do.

- Be a team player. Never forget the value of people. None of us succeeds alone. The people you come in contact with over the course of your career will contribute to your success or demise.

- If you have employees under your supervision, be fair—and make a special effort to communicate with all of them. Don't play favorites.

> - As a corporate employee, always look for a better way to serve your company. Keep the company's philosophy and interests in mind when making decisions or taking action. Do not hesitate to take on additional responsibility when given the chance. Be prudent and patient, but do not wait too long. Companies often are not aware of an individual's desire for advancement or the measures such a person may have taken to prepare themselves for more responsibility. You may have to find a way to let senior management know about you.
>
> Mr. Allen has always felt that success is a very personal experience. What each person considers success is determined by his or her personal values. Too often people are led to believe that a particular job or a certain position is what they should aim for to be a "success." *Success is what people want it to be.* It is different for each person. At times people tend to get caught up with other people's values and the pressures society imposes. Each person must decide what success means to him or her.

In a sense, company directors judge managers not by what they do but rather by what they cause others to do. A key part of a manager's job is to motivate people to *want* to perform activities so that the company can achieve its goals.

Indications of significant employee discontent include:

- *Decline of the work ethic*—Until the 1960s, the Puritan concept of work—that labor is good in itself and that the act of working makes the human being better—flourished. Today, the American attitude toward work has changed considerably. There is less tendency to consider work as virtuous in itself and as a necessity. Many people now feel that somehow the government will take care of them if all else fails.
- *Strikes*—In 1984, labor leaders called 3,550 strikes. This figure includes wildcat strikes (work stoppages not sanctioned by a union). While union-authorized strikes often are based on wages and other bread-and-butter issues, wildcat strikes almost always reflect what employees feel is unfair treatment by management.
- *Absenteeism*—If people *really* like their work, they make every effort to be on the job. The high rate of absenteeism tells us many don't.
- *Turnover*—Another indication of worker dissatisfaction is high voluntary turnover.
- *Dissatisfaction with routine jobs*—Growing numbers of working people feel they are underutilized—that their jobs have little variety and do not give them sufficient opportunity to use their skills. Dissatisfaction occurs not only among assembly-line workers but among white-collar and management personnel as well.

These indicators of worker dissatisfaction are evidence that employees do want more than money. What is it, then, that employees really want? What can managers do to **motivate** them—*cause them to want to put forth their best efforts to reach company goals?*

Following are some key ideas that shed light on the problem and suggest possible solutions.

WHAT THE HAWTHORNE STUDIES PROVED ABOUT MOTIVATION

G. Elton Mayo is often called the "father of human relations." In 1927 he directed a research project at the Hawthorne plant of Western Electric, located near Chicago. The Mayo research team studied the effects of lighting, temperature, and pay scales on worker productivity. Mayo discovered that, as a way to increase output, varying these factors was not as important as giving workers personalized attention. Based on his studies, Mayo advanced the idea of the **Hawthorne effect,** which proposed that *providing workers with self-esteem, positive co-workers, and status—not simply high pay and good working conditions—is the real key to improving employee productivity.*

HIERARCHY-OF-NEEDS THEORY

Abraham H. Maslow, a psychologist, developed *a theory of motivation based on the idea that people are motivated by five basic needs that form a hierarchy and as each need is satisfied the one at the next higher level emerges* (see Figure 15–6). These needs are, from lowest to highest:

- *Physiological needs*—The main physiological needs are to satisfy hunger, thirst, sleepiness, and sexual desire. They form the basis of the hierarchy. When a person is extremely thirsty, for example, he forgets all other needs.

- *Safety needs*—Safety needs are next to emerge. The obvious needs for safety—freedom from extremes of temperature, wild animals, and so on—are for the most part met in our culture. Beyond this point, we deal with safety needs in a modern society by buying life insurance, looking for a job with tenure, and in other ways seeking economic security.

- *Love needs*—When we have satisfied both physiological and safety needs, the need for affection, belongingness, and love emerges. The love need includes needs for both giving and receiving love.

- *Esteem needs*—The desire for self-respect and the respect of others is next in the hierarchy. People want to achieve, and they want others to recognize them for their achievements. Satisfaction of esteem needs leads to self-confidence and a feeling of worth.

Figure 15–6 Maslow's Hierarchy of Needs

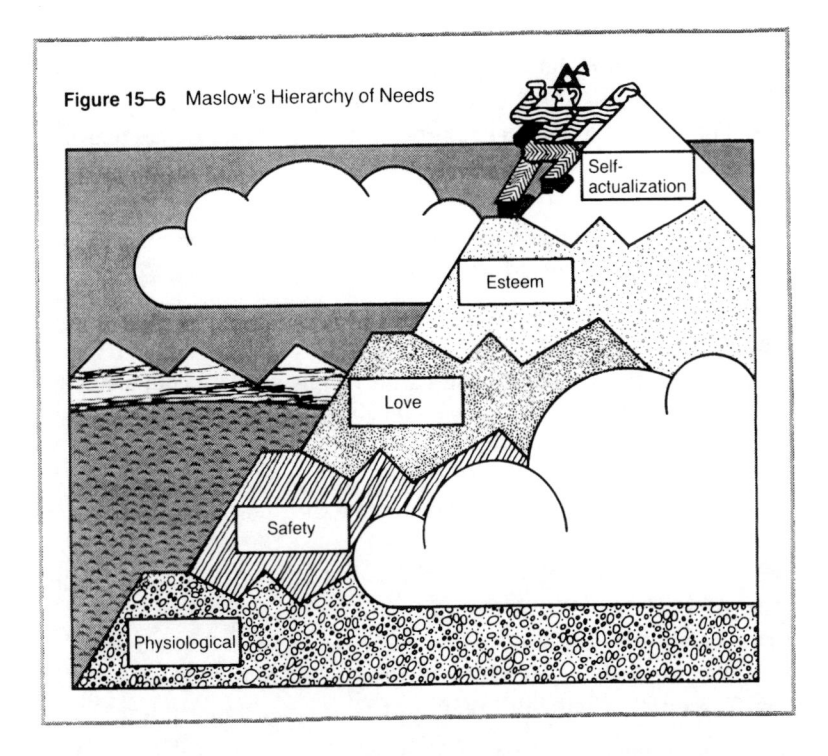

- *Self-actualization needs*—When physiological, safety, love, and esteem needs are satisfied, people will soon become discontented unless they are doing what they *want* to do. *Doing what one most wants to do with one's life* is called **self-actualization.**

Whether or not human needs fit this hierarchy is a question open to debate. What is of greater significance is that the Maslow model spells out what needs people have. When managers know people's needs, they are in a position to ask, "What can we do to satisfy those needs so that our personnel will enjoy greater satisfaction and be more productive?"

THEORY X AND THEORY Y

Douglas McGregor has identified two extreme styles of managing: Theory X and Theory Y. Each style involves certain assumptions concerning human nature. **Theory X** assumes that:

- The average human being has an inherent dislike of work and will avoid it if he or she can.
- Because of this human characteristic of dislike of work, most

people need a superior to coerce them or threaten them with punishment to get them to put forth adequate effort toward the achievement of organizational objectives.
- The average human being prefers to be directed, wishes to avoid responsibility, has relatively little ambition, and wants security above all.

Theory Y proposes directly opposite views concerning people and their attitudes toward work:

- Work is a source of satisfaction and is as normal as play or rest.
- Threat of punishment is only one way to induce people to work, and it is not usually the best way. People who are committed to achieving the organization's objectives will display self-motivation and self-direction.
- A person's commitment to objectives depends on the rewards he or she expects to receive when he or she and/or the firm meets those objectives.
- Under the right conditions, the average person will both accept and seek responsibility.
- The abilities to think creatively, to innovate, and to solve problems are widely, not narrowly, distributed among people.
- The intellectual abilities of most people are underutilized.

In a nutshell, the Theory X manager views the typical worker negatively, while the Theory Y manager thinks of the typical employee in a positive manner. Theory X managers see the worst in employees, whereas Theory Y managers see the best.

What Herzberg Discovered About Motivation

Frederick Herzberg, a psychologist, did extensive research to find out what job factors motivate people. He discovered that the **hygiene factors**—*good working conditions, fringe benefits, pay, and job security*—*are important but in themselves do not motivate.* Instead, Herzberg learned that *recognition, achievement, opportunity to advance, and the job itself*—which he called **motivator factors**—*are the true motivators.*

Job Enrichment: Specific Techniques for Motivating People

Employee job dissatisfaction has caused managers to experiment with a number of methods to improve motivation. **Job enrichment** is *the process of designing jobs to make them more interesting, challenging, and meaningful.* Following, we discuss three kinds of job enrichment.

Job redesign is *restructuring a job to make the work more appealing to the employee.* An example is letting a secretary decide what sequence to follow in handling typing and clerical tasks.

Job enlargement is *adding more responsibilities and tasks to an employee's present job.* An example is letting a receptionist act as both a receptionist and a typist.

Flextime is *letting workers decide when they will begin and end the workday.* Where used, management expects all employees to be on the job during a core period of time, such as 10:00 A.M. to 2:00 P.M., but the employees decide when to report to work and when to go home. The only requirement is that they work the necessary number of hours.

WHAT CAN WE CONCLUDE ABOUT MOTIVATION?

Higher motivation seems to result when superiors respect their employees, treat them fairly, recognize them for the work they do, and treat them as persons and not as pieces of equipment. A regressive climate gets low-level performance from people because it stems from *motivating them* with coercion. A progressive climate gets top performance by leading employees to *drive themselves.* We highly recommend creating a progressive climate.

Direction Includes Leadership

AUTOCRATIC VERSUS PARTICIPATIVE LEADERSHIP

At the extremes, we can identify two leadership styles: autocratic and participative. **Autocratic leaders** are *dictatorial; they make the decisions and issue all orders.* Autocratic leaders determine all policies, tend to be domineering, and impose their will on subordinates. Napoleon was an autocratic leader.

Participative leaders are *democratic; they invite subordinates to make suggestions in planning what to do and how to do it.* The participative leader tries to get employees to agree with a plan before he or she implements it. President Eisenhower generally exercised a participative leadership style.

Table 15–2 shows some specific differences between autocratic and participative leadership styles.

WHAT CHARACTERISTICS DO EFFECTIVE LEADERS HAVE IN COMMON?

Leadership is an art, and no exact prescription exists for developing that art. However, effective leaders seem to have the following six qualities:

- *Ability to inspire others*—Effective leaders can excite people about the task to be done.

TABLE 15-2 Autocratic Versus Participative Leadership Styles

AUTOCRATIC	**PARTICIPATIVE**
"If you want to keep your job, you'd better shape up."	"Let me help you improve your performance."
"I've got the answers, so why ask my subordinates?"	"I'll ask my subordinates for their input. Might get some good ideas."
"Our profits are down. It's because I've got some no-good people working for me."	"Our profits are down. I'm going to ask my staff what they think the problem is."
"Here's how I've decided you should handle that situation."	"What ideas do you have for handling the problem? You're usually pretty good at solving problems."

Questions

1. Would you expect to find any differences in employee performance under an autocratic leader versus a participative leader? Explain.
2. As you rise in an organization, which leadership style do you plan to follow? Why?

- *A good understanding of what makes people tick*—Effective leaders often resemble practical psychologists.
- *Ability to communicate effectively*—This is especially true of the spoken word.
- *Credibility*—Effective leaders come across so that people believe what they say.
- *Ability to set the example for others to follow*—Effective leaders work hard so that subordinates will work hard.
- *Ability to take full responsibility*—Leaders don't blame others when things go wrong.

Communicating with Employees

Communication is *the transmission of information.* Ineffective, inaccurate, false, misleading, or confusing communication costs business millions of dollars a day. To understand communication, think of it as a process with five elements:

- *The message sender*—Anyone who wants to transmit information to someone else. All people in business are message senders.
- *The message*—The information the message sender wants to

communicate. "Deliver this to the Smith warehouse by 1:00 P.M." is an example of a message.
- *The message vehicle*—The means by which a sender transmits a message: Telephone calls, computer printouts, memos, letters, and speeches are all message vehicles.
- *The message receiver*—The person or people the message should reach. A truck driver may have received the "deliver this" message.
- *The message feedback*—The response of a message receiver to a message. If the sender and/or vehicle made the delivery on time, the feedback is good. If the sender and/or vehicle makes the delivery to the wrong address, then the feedback is bad.

TYPES OF COMMUNICATION

Any attempt to convey information is a form of communication. Communication may be written (memos, letters, house organs), oral (face-to-face discussions, speeches, meetings), or transmitted by body language (gestures, facial expressions, mannerisms).

External communication *occurs with people outside the company*—the public, shareholders, and customers. **Internal communication** *takes place among people who work within the organization.* Internal communication may be **vertically downward,** *from a manager to a subordinate* ("John, please have this program written by Friday"), or it may be **vertically upward,** *from a subordinate to a manager* ("Here's the program, but it still has some bugs"). If in the process of preparing the program, John needs to *contact someone in another department,* the communication is **horizontal.**

HOW CAN WE MAKE COMMUNICATION MORE EFFECTIVE?

Communicating is difficult because many adults can't read. According to a Ford Foundation Report, 25 million Americans can't read at all, and another 35 million may be functionally illiterate.

According to one observer,

The workplace is becoming more complex, but that doesn't mean it's more efficient. The personnel staff at New York Telephone has to interview fifteen applicants for a skilled-job training program in order to get one who can read at an eighth-grade level. Many secretaries have $9,000 mag card machines that can triple their typing speed, but too many can't spell or punctuate and many can't read the instruction manuals to their exotic equipment. But the problem also spreads to executives as well though on a less obvious level. The *Wall Street Journal* reported that the "bizarre" situation exists where $30,000 M.B.A.s have to be enrolled in basic reading and writing courses because they can't compose clear reports and memos. The Conference Board study found that 34 percent of the companies they polled felt a need to supplement their employees' basic educations.[4]

More effective communication results in fewer mistakes, accidents, and disagreements. Improved communication translates into more sales and higher productivity. These guidelines are helpful:

- *Be brief*—The message should be no longer than necessary. When Lincoln was asked, "How long should a man's legs be?", he replied, "Long enough to touch the ground."

- *Be accurate*—Inaccurate information results in employees delivering packages to the wrong address, billing customers for the wrong amount, and making other costly mistakes.

- *Be empathic*—Good communicators ask, "If I had the intelligence, experience, and knowledge of the person I want to influence, would I understand the message I'm going to send?"

- *Use attention-getting devices*—Communication takes place when both parties pay attention. An interesting speaker gets messages across. Visual aids, such as charts, diagrams, and pictures, also make communication more effective.

- *Use a combination of media*—In teaching a worker how to operate a machine, for example, the trainer can use a combination of a written and verbal explanation, a visual demonstration, and a practice session, in that order.

[4]William McGowan, *Business and Society Review,* Winter 1983, 38.

SUMMARY

- People are the key resource that an organization uses to achieve its goals.

- The personnel department is responsible for staffing the enterprise with qualified employees and providing benefits and services for workers.

- Job analyses, descriptions, specifications; application forms, résumés; tests; references; interviews are used in the selection.

- The personnel department participates directly or indirectly in providing such training as orientation, coaching, on-the-job, rotational, and external training, and assessment centers.

- Compensation of employees should be competitive, fair, and motivational. Basic compensation methods are wages, salaries, the piece-rate plan, commissions, bonuses, and profit sharing.

- Many companies provide fringe benefits from insurance to retirement plans. Personnel also maintains health and safety programs.

- Employee evaluations are useful in making promotion, transfer, compensation, development, and termination decisions. Methods of evaluation are results, trait, and informal.

- Directing involves motivating, leading, and communicating, essential for achieving goals.

- The Hawthorne studies, Maslow's hierarchy of needs theory, McGregor's Theory X and Theory Y, Herzberg's research on hygiene and motivator factors, and job enrichment programs all shed light on what motivates workers.

- The two contrasting leadership types are autocratic (dictatorial) and participative (democratic).

- The communications process involves the message sender, message, message vehicle, message receiver, and message feedback.

KEY TERMS YOU SHOULD KNOW

achievement test	Hawthorne effect	personnel management
aptitude test	hierarchy-of-needs theory	Peter Principle
assessment center	horizontal communication	piece-rate plan
autocratic leader	hygiene factor	polygraph test
bonus	informal evaluation	profit sharing
coaching	intelligence test	promotion
commission	job analysis	results evaluation
communication	job description	salary
directing	job enlargement	self-actualization
discharge	job enrichment	staffing
external communication	job redesign	Theory X
flextime	job specification	Theory Y
fringe benefit	orientation program	trait evaluation
functional rotation	participative leader	wage
geographic rotation	personality test	youth differential

QUESTIONS FOR REVIEW

1. What is staffing?
2. Explain job analysis, description, and redesign.
3. What tests may personnel use in selection? What are their limitations?
4. Why is early retirement less popular?
5. Explain: orientation, on-the-job, coaching, rotational, and assessment center training methods.
6. What four objectives should a compensation program meet?
7. Explain the employee compensation methods.
8. What are the main kinds of fringe benefits?
9. Do performance and trait evaluation differ?
10. What did the Hawthorne studies tell us? What are the Hierarchy of Needs, the X and the Y Theories?
11. Define hygiene and motivator factors, job enrichment, redesign, enlargement, and flexibility.
12. Contrast autocratic and participative leadership. What traits do effective leaders share?
13. What is involved in communicating?
14. How can communication be more effective?

QUESTIONS FOR DISCUSSION

1. Personnel managers cannot ask job applicants about marital status, height, weight, arrest records, age, and financial status. Do you feel laws are too restrictive? Why or why not?
2. These questions are often asked in selecting management trainees. Explain why you think interviewers ask each question. How would you answer it?
   a. In past jobs, what changes would you have suggested?
   b. What is the most difficult situation you have ever worked in?
   c. What was your most creative achievement?
   d. How do you respond to criticism?
   e. What do you look for in a job?
   f. Why should we hire you?
   g. Why didn't you do better in college?
3. Most companies pay employees for time (wages, salary), not necessarily for results. Why? What compensation method would be ideal?
4. The ideal method for evaluating employees is results (performance) evaluation. Why, then, is results evaluation not the only method used?

5. Assume you really like your job—the work, co-workers, boss, general climate. If another company offered you a job paying 15 percent more, would you accept? Why? What factors would you consider?

6. Will the autocratic or participative leadership style be more popular in the future? Why?

7. Excerpts from a reader's letter to *Business Week* responding to a report on "The New Industrial Relations" (May 11, 1981), treating declining worker motivation, suggests that the decline started with the social revolt of the 1960s.

The younger... generation does have a different value system and set of work expectations than his predecessors did. Willing to work just as hard but on different terms, this new work force wants "meaningful" jobs—meaningful as workers define it, not as their organization would define it for them. Meaningful work, as often defined by this new work force, ... contributes both to the betterment of society and to workers' personal and professional growth.

The time has come when management must stop asking, "What's wrong with John?" and begin asking, "What's wrong with John's job?"

Which view do you support? Why? What could solve poor worker motivation?

CASE STUDY

Should Ace Electronics Pay Tuition for Employees?

The board of directors of Ace Electronics was holding its quarterly meeting. Ed Fowler, president of Ace, made a proposal to reimburse tuition and course-materials costs for employees who take college courses on their own time provided they earn a grade of "C" or better.

White: The way you state your proposal, we would reimburse educational costs to an employee regardless of the course. I see merit in paying expenses if courses relate to our work—engineering, electronics, information systems, business. But I question paying for liberal arts courses.

Fowler: I considered that, but I concluded that to be fair we wouldn't limit the policy. Some employees who have had little or no college have to take liberal arts subjects for a degree.

Henderson: Do you plan to limit hours an employee can take? We don't want people studying so hard they lose work effectiveness.

F: The maximum we are thinking of is eight. Based on a survey, I estimate that employees would take five hours.

Black: Tuition varies among the local colleges. Have you taken cost into consideration?

F: Yes, I have. But I feel it is best to let the employees choose the school they want to attend.

Mahoney: I'm opposed to the paying of employees to go to school. We're paying people for doing what they should do on their own. We pay them well. Let them pay for their own education.

Williams: I agree with Mahoney. I worked my way through school. If people have to be subsidized, college won't do them any good.

Gordon: I see good arguments in favor of the tuition reimbursement plan and some hard arguments against it. I move we postpone a vote until we've had a chance to think about it.

F: Is there a second motion?

Questions

1. From the company's standpoint, is a tuition reimbursement plan a good idea? Why or why not?

2. If you were offered a job with Ace Electronics, would tuition reimbursement be important in reaching a decision about joining the firm? Explain?

EVOLUTION OF A BUSINESS

Who's Boss? And What About Incentives?

Ray and Sara were concerned about hiring personnel and about being "bosses" because neither of them had ever been in that role before. They also were aware that conflicts of authority might arise.

Sara: There's a problem in a partnership. An employee really doesn't know who's boss.

Ray: How about having one of our employees report to me and the other to you? That might eliminate the conflicts, and it would give each of us a backup person who could handle our work area when we're not here.

Sara: Another possibility would be to designate one of us as the office manager. In that way, both employees would report to either you or me. That's a good basic arrangement for when we grow. Also, we're more apt to work as a team when a single person coordinates. It takes one person to see that someone is in the office at all times, to schedule time off and lunch hours, to assign workloads evenly, and so on.

Ray: Then there's the matter of incentives. Don't you think we should have some sort of commission system based on the amount sold to each client?

Sara: I'm not sure that would be in the client's best interests. Since we're planning to build our reputation on personalized pleasing of customers, that seems dangerous.

Ray: Still, I like the idea of building initiative into each employee. It keeps employees alert and interested when they're striving for a bigger paycheck.

Sara: What about a group bonus at the end of the year based on the total business produced by all of us for the year? In that way we would all share in what we produced together. It would also build team spirit.

Questions

1. What kinds of problems can arise in a partnership when employees aren't sure who the boss is?
2. What can be done to prevent partners from issuing contradictory orders?
3. Which system for assigning employees do you think should be adopted?
4. Is an incentive system in a travel agency a good idea? What kind of a salary system would you recommend—straight salary, salary with bonus, base salary with commissions, straight commission, or what?

TERMINAL
WALK IN THE
FRONT DOOR
& DRIVE A BUS
OUT THE BACK
NO TRAINING
REQUIRED
DON'T TRUST
YOUR LIFE TO-
GREYHOUND
SCABS and
STRIKEBREAKERS
GO
Trailways!

16

MANAGEMENT AND LABOR RELATIONS
It's a Delicate Balance

READ THIS CHAPTER SO YOU CAN:

Describe the changing makeup of the labor force.

Discuss the history of U.S. labor unions, how the AFL–CIO came about, and what the basic laws are that regulate labor-management relations.

Explain the tactics labor unions use to promote their interests.

Describe the methods management employs to protect its interests.

Discuss the collective-bargaining process and the elements covered in a union contract.

List factors responsible for the labor unions' decline in importance, and explain the concepts of QWL and co-determination.

CHAPTER 16/MANAGEMENT AND LABOR RELATIONS

A story about the late United Auto Workers' president, Walter Reuther, illustrates the interdependency of labor and management. When Reuther was being shown through an ultramodern Ford plant, a Ford official proudly pointed to some new robots and jokingly asked, "How are you union people going to collect union dues from these guys?" Answered Reuther, "How are you going to get them to buy Fords?"

Management needs labor to help produce its products and then, in labor's role as consumer, to purchase them. Labor needs management to provide jobs. Yet much U.S. business history has been characterized by antagonism between these two parties.

WHAT IS LABOR?

Labor in its *broadest sense, means human talent, skills, and energy used to make and market goods and services.*

When we use the term labor in business, we usually mean all nonmanagement employees. In bargaining sessions between management and employees, labor suggests unionized workers.

The **labor force** *consists of all people age 16 and over who are*

More and more women are joining the work force and entering job markets previously restricted to men.

willing and able to work and who are either employed or seeking employment. Executives, entrepreneurs, professional people, farmers, part-time employees, wage earners—anyone who receives a paycheck—is part of the labor force.

Why Is Labor Important?

Labor is important to our economy for two reasons. First, it is the major expense or cost in doing business. Second, it is the main source of income in our economy.

Labor as an Expense

As an expense, labor helps determine who succeeds and who fails in business. For example, in Japan labor costs are lower than in the United States. This is one of the reasons why Japanese car makers have a competitive edge over domestic producers. The price a business charges for what it sells always reflects the cost of labor, and higher than competitive prices usually result in reduced sales or revenue for a firm. Businesses, therefore, want to avoid excessive labor costs. Business' primary incentive for purchasing labor-saving equipment, automating, and increasing efficiency is reduction of labor costs.

Labor as Income

As the anecdote about Walter Reuther suggests, labor is also important as a source of income. Even a small increase in unemployment, resulting in less income for labor, soon translates into decreased demand for goods and services. This decreased demand or reduced consumer spending negatively affects profits. Unchecked, less income for labor leads to more unemployment, further sales declines, lower profits, business failures, and other economic problems.

Prosperity goes hand-in-hand with high levels of employment of productive, well-paid workers. Creating the climate for this to happen is a challenge facing business, labor, government, and concerned citizens.

How Is the Work Force Changing?

MORE WOMEN IN THE LABOR FORCE

The number of women who work outside their homes is increasing. In 1890, only 17 percent of women worked. By 1930 this figure had grown to nearly 30 percent; today over 44 percent of women work outside the home (see Figure 16–1). It is predicted that women will soon constitute 50 percent of the work force. The chairman of the National Commission for Manpower Policy has called this trend "the single most outstanding phenomenon of our century. It will affect women, men, and children, and the cumulative consequence will only be revealed in the 21st and 22nd centuries."

Figure 16–1 Women as a Percent of Total Labor Force for Major Occupational Categories

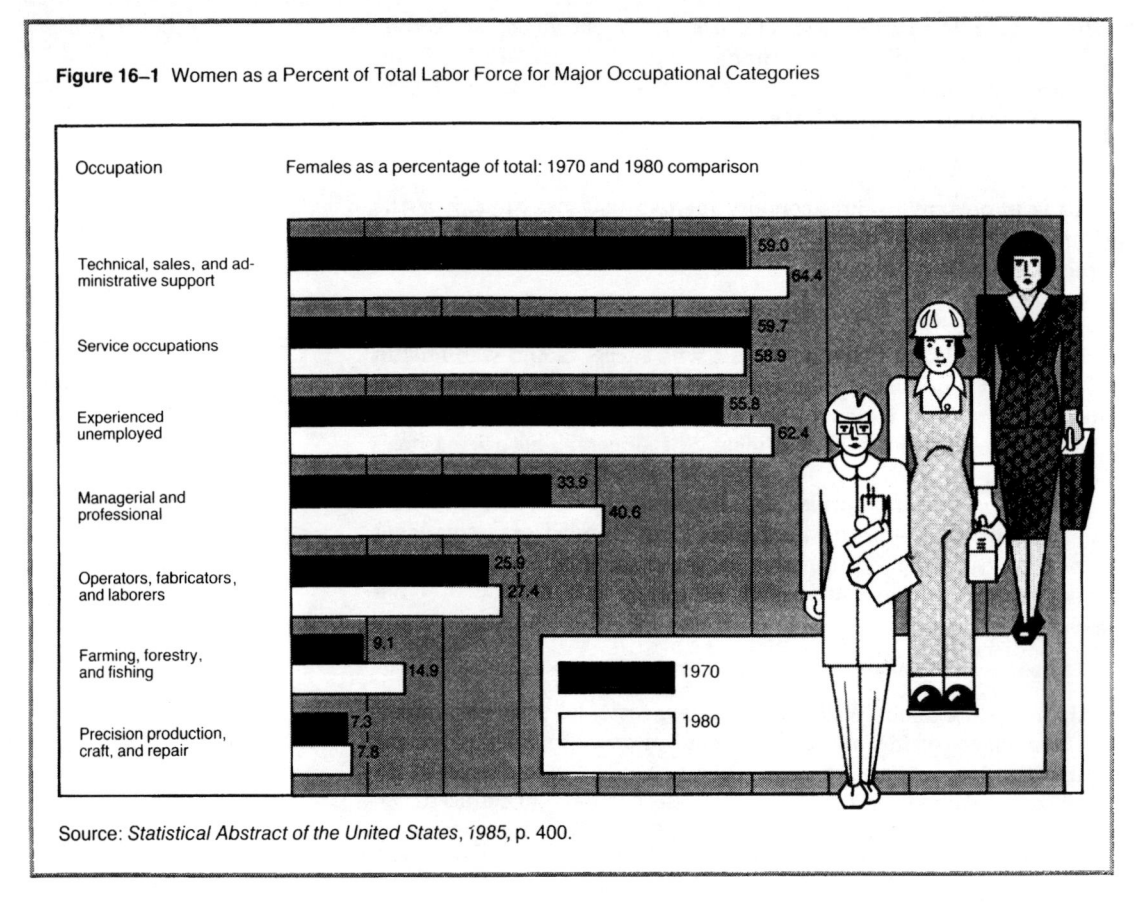

Occupation	Females as a percentage of total: 1970 and 1980 comparison
Technical, sales, and administrative support	1970: 59.0 / 1980: 64.4
Service occupations	1970: 59.7 / 1980: 58.9
Experienced unemployed	1970: 55.8 / 1980: 62.4
Managerial and professional	1970: 33.9 / 1980: 40.6
Operators, fabricators, and laborers	1970: 25.9 / 1980: 27.4
Farming, forestry, and fishing	1970: 9.1 / 1980: 14.9
Precision production, craft, and repair	1970: 7.3 / 1980: 7.8

Source: *Statistical Abstract of the United States, 1985,* p. 400.

Three reasons account for the increasing number of women who work. The first is necessity: The decline in marriage rates and the increase in divorce rates mean more women must support themselves. The second is inflation: Married couples often need two incomes to maintain their desired standard of living. The third is preference: When children are in school or have moved away, many women choose to spend their time working outside the home.

GROWTH OF THE PART-TIME WORK FORCE

In 1984, part-time workers accounted for almost 15 percent of the work force. Fifteen years ago the figure was just 11 percent. Now, 5 percent of the total labor force have second jobs, usually part-time.

Many retail stores and fast-food restaurants already employ from 50 to 75 percent part-timers, and the trend is growing. It is now common practice in these industries to replace full-timers lost through attrition with part-timers.

Employees have welcomed the opportunity to work part-time for a number of reasons:

- Flexible scheduling allows them to work at their convenience. Students can work late afternoons and evenings, for example.
- Older people can taper off on hours worked per week and may still collect Social Security.

Employers also welcome the trend because

- It is a good substitute for paying costly overtime.
- It reduces quality maintenance problems in jobs where the work is boring. A Venetian blind manufacturer who uses part-timers exclusively says full-timers could not stay interested in the tedious work that is required.
- It reduces absenteeism. One company reports an absenteeism rate of 3 percent for part-timers versus 8 percent for full-timers.
- A part-time work force is difficult to unionize.
- There is often no need to pay fringe benefits (which, as we saw in Chapter 15, are a rapidly growing wage element).

ISSUE FOR DEBATE

Is Domestic Content Legislation in the Best Interests of Business and Labor?

Congress has proposed legislation that would require foreign auto makers to use American-made parts in cars sold in the United States. Two major goals of domestic content legislation are (a) to force foreign auto makers to establish manufacturing plants in the United States, as Volkswagen, Honda, and Toyota have done, and (b) to prevent U.S. auto producers from buying parts or completely assembled vehicles from foreign nations.

PROS	CONS
Approximately 2.4 million jobs in the United States are directly or indirectly related to auto production. Auto production is important to the steel, rubber, glass, aluminum, and many of the high technology industries. Without domestic content legislation, half the workers in the auto industry will lose their jobs by 1990.	Consumers will lose by passage of domestic content legislation; they will be denied the benefits of competition. The essence of our free market system is that competition, including foreign competition, is beneficial in the long run.

PROS	CONS
The market share of foreign-made autos increased from 18 percent in 1978 to 32 percent in 1984. Of all imports, 81 percent come from Japan. Economists predict that, by 1990, foreign car makers will capture between 36 and 65 percent of the American market. In 1983, Japan sold 1.8 million cars in the United States; we sold only 3,149 cars in Japan.	If the government protects U.S. companies, their employees, and their suppliers from foreign competition, these firms will do less to improve quality control of performance overall. Consumers will end up paying more and getting less.
Other nations have almost unlimited access to the American market, but the Japanese market is severely restricted to American producers because of special taxes, government inspection procedures, and costly environmental modifications required.	Domestic content legislation would subsidize auto workers, who already receive wages 28 percent higher than the average for other manufacturing employees. Manufacturers would also receive subsidies. U.S. producers take about 200 hours of labor to build a subcompact car, while the Japanese use only 111 hours.
The United States, alone among major industrial nations, permits imports to overrun its domestic markets. Thirty-one other countries now enforce their own domestic content legislation or use quotas and tariffs to protect their manufacturing industries.	Protecting U.S. auto makers and workers would set dangerous precedents: It would tell the world we don't believe in free trade, and other major domestic industries would soon be demanding government protection.
The proposed domestic legislation is fair. It tells foreign car makers to sell as many cars as they want in the United States but lets U.S. workers and producers assemble and manufacture some of the parts.	Protection of domestic auto production would discourage efforts, already under way, to become more productive. Much progress toward greater efficiency will occur if the government does not subsidize domestic inefficiency and waste.

Questions

1. What other arguments, pro or con, can you offer regarding this issue?
2. Do you favor protecting the auto industry from foreign competition? Why or why not?

The Unemployment Problem and Its Causes

Unemployment is always a problem, although its severity varies greatly. Its causes include

- *Imports Exceeding Exports*—Union leaders contend that imported autos and other products take jobs away from Americans. When we import more than we export, jobs are lost. Figure 16–2 shows how imported products gained in market share between 1960 and 1982. During this period, 31 million new jobs were created, but only 1 million were in manufacturing, the area hardest hit by foreign products. To combat competition from foreign producers, unions urge passage of legislation to protect American jobs. For example, unions endorse the domestic content legislation discussed in the preceding Issue for Debate.

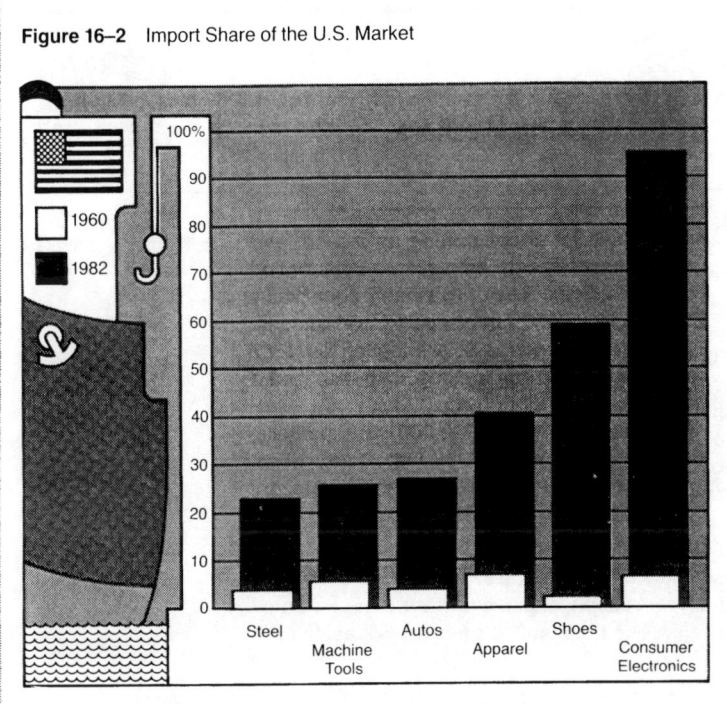

Figure 16–2 Import Share of the U.S. Market

[Bar chart comparing 1960 vs 1982 import shares for Steel, Machine Tools, Autos, Apparel, Shoes, and Consumer Electronics]

Source: *Rebuilding America: A National Industrial Policy.* Washington, D.C.: Industrial Union Department, AFL-CIO, 1983, p. 2.

Unemployment is unhealthy for individual workers, their families, and for the national economy: The unemployed become demoralized, their families must do without luxuries and even necessities, and businesses cannot sell them as many goods and services.

- *Recession*—Economic recession is by far the main cause of unemployment. A **recession** is *a period of well-below-average profits, economic activity, and sales, accompanied by well-above-normal unemployment.* As a recession deepens, it affects more businesses; they sell less, and must either discharge or furlough personnel.
- *Technology*—Computerization, development of labor-saving equipment, and automation are examples of technology that eliminates some jobs, particularly unskilled and semi-skilled ones.

- *Government Cutbacks*—The federal government and the state and local governments together are the largest consumers in our economy. When government cuts spending, unemployment results in affected industries.
- *Miscellaneous causes*—These include business failures, business mergers, company relocations, and catastrophes such as fires and floods.

CONTEMPORARY ISSUE

Mazda's Bold Embrace of the United Auto Workers

For a Detroit auto maker, there is nothing special about putting up a plant and inviting in the United Auto Workers to represent hourly employees. But nothing could be scarier to timid Japanese car companies. They have been agonizingly cautious about making cars in the U.S.—and petrified about dealing with unions.

That makes Mazda Motor Corp.'s plans to launch U.S. production by 1987 doubly daring. Its plant will be only the third built by a Japanese auto maker. And it will be the first of the three to start out with a UAW work force.

Mazda will build its plant, with the capacity to make 240,000 cars annually, just 24 miles southwest of Detroit—UAW headquarters—in Flat Rock, Mich. About half the output is expected to go to Ford Motor Co., a 25% owner of Mazda, for sale under the Ford name. Mazda bought the 500-acre site for its factory, along with a mothballed metal-casting plant, from Ford.

WARM RELATIONS. There are already close ties between the two companies outside the U.S. In Australia, Ford builds versions of Mazda's GLC and 626 models. And in Mexico, the Japanese company will supply engines and other major components for a $500 million Ford plant that, like the Flat Rock facility, will begin production in 1987.

But in announcing the Michigan plant, Mazda made clear that it will operate in the U.S. on its own. The new facility will receive its marching orders from Mazda headquarters in Hiroshima and nowhere else. Hirotaka Iida, a managing director of Mazda, says the Flat Rock plant will be "designed, built, operated, and owned" solely by Mazda. "We want to produce [our] products with Mazda's philosophy," he says.

The Japanese company has already managed to develop unusually warm relations with the UAW during the eight months of direct talks that led up to the project's announcement. The company has promised to recognize the union by agreeing to hire at least half the plant's 3,500-member work force from a pool of laid-off UAW workers. In exchange, the UAW promises to be "receptive" to flexible work rules similar to those agreed upon by the UAW and New United Motor Mfg. Inc., the joint venture between Toyota Motor Corp. and General Motors Corp. that begins producing a small car in California this month. Says Iida: "I am sure we can overcome all the hurdles." Adds UAW President Owen F. Bieber: "I look forward to a long and good relationship."

Such friendly talk contrasts sharply with the frosty relations between the UAW and both Honda Motor Co. and Nissan Motor Co. In 1982, Honda became the first Japanese company to build cars in the U.S., but so far the UAW has managed to organize only three workers—all boiler operators in the facility's power station. Nissan, which will boost production at its 18-month-old Tennessee truck plant in April, has been blunt in its distaste for the union.

Mazda claims it will not decide exactly which car to build in Flat Rock until mid-1985. But the company says the plant will surpass the remarkable flexibility of its manufacturing complex in Hofu, Japan. That facility has the capacity to produce nine models, including both front- and rear-wheel-drive cars, while most car plants are designed to produce only a few variations of one line. Mazda intends to buy or build at least half the parts for its American-made car in the U.S. and Canada. Engines, transmissions, and other major mechanical components for the car will be shipped in from Japan.

GENEROUS INCENTIVES. Company executives say they opted for a U.S. plant in part because they expect the limits on auto exports to the U.S. market to continue. Voluntary quotas are scheduled to expire on March 31, but many observers expect them to be replaced with slightly higher limits. A. Toriyama, president of Mazda (North America) Inc., figures that the plant will also give his company "more information" about the U.S. market than it can get by remaining an importer only.

By embracing the UAW and locating in a state with generally high costs, Mazda is flouting the wisdom that manufacturers ought to head south. But much of the difference that makes the Sunbelt so attractive was apparently offset by a generous package of tax inducements and other incentives offered by both state and local governments in Michigan. Moreover, company officials shrug off the notion that small cars cannot be produced profitably in the U.S. Executives are reluctant to comment on the widely held view that cars built in Japan and sold in the American market have a cost advantage of roughly $1,500 over similar products made in this country. Says Osamu Nobuto, manager of Mazda's office of international business development, "We wouldn't build a plant if there wasn't a prospect for profit."

By William J. Hampton in Detroit

SOURCE: *Business Week*, December 17, 1984, 40.

During our worst economic turndown, in the 1930s, the unemployed accounted for almost one-third of the work force. During the worst economic turndown of recent times, in 1980–82, unemployment reached about 12 percent of the total work force (see Figure 16–3).

WHO DOES UNEMPLOYMENT HIT THE HARDEST?

As Figure 16–4 shows, teenagers have by far the highest unemployment rate. Nonwhites have a higher rate than whites, and blue-collar workers a higher rate than white-collar workers. While not shown in the figure, there is also a relationship between education and employment. The more education people have, the less likely they are to be unemployed.

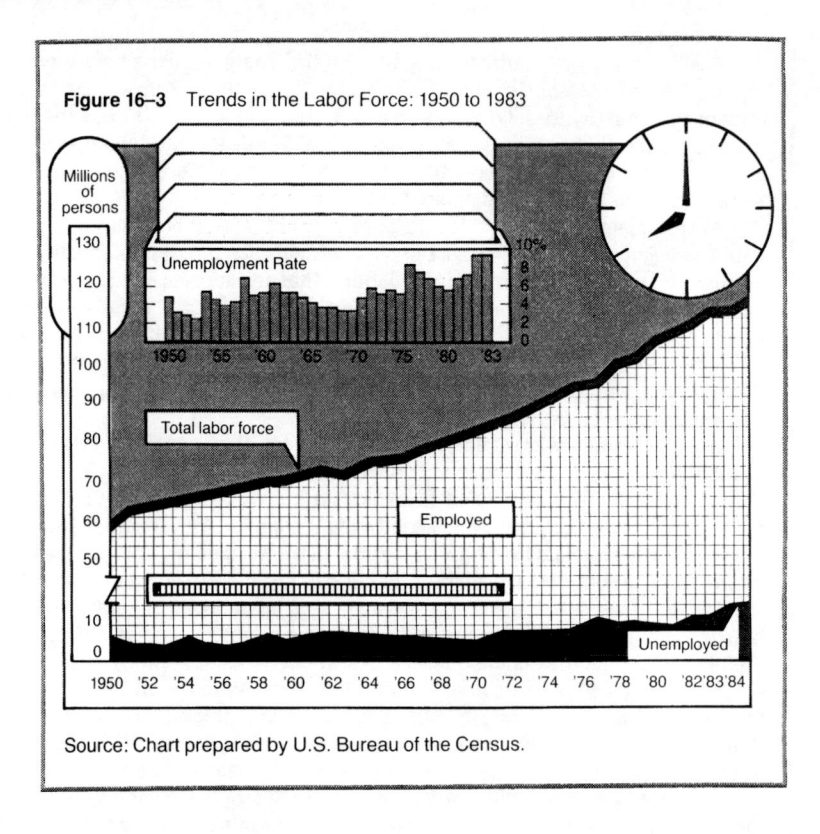

Figure 16–3 Trends in the Labor Force: 1950 to 1983

Source: Chart prepared by U.S. Bureau of the Census.

Unemployment adversely affects not only unemployed workers and their families but also, in an indirect way, many other people. We often refer to these *negative effects on society* as the **social costs of unemployment.** What happens is this: despite unemployment compensation, unemployed people have less income than they did when they were working. Since they have less to spend, they buy less. This hurts merchants, landlords, credit-granting organizations, and other firms that do business with the person out of work. These firms, in turn, are likely to have more trouble meeting their own obligations, and a chain reaction of negative consequences results.

In addition, to the extent that unemployment exists, it denies society the products that could have been produced. And since the government may provide income or welfare benefits for people who are out of work, unemployment is costly to taxpayers.

How Can We Solve the Unemployment Problem?
Experts disagree about who should be responsible for solving the unemployment problem:

Figure 16–4 Unemployment Rates for Persons 16 Years of Age and Older, 1984

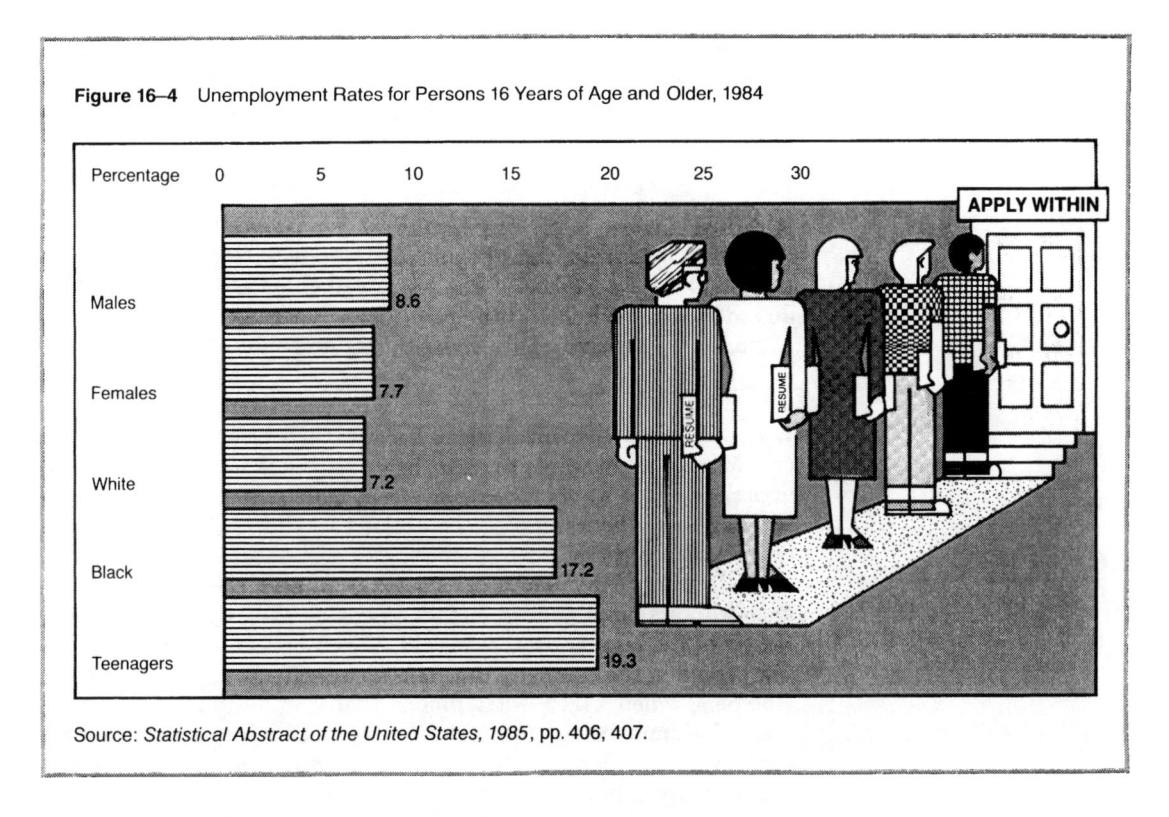

Category	Percentage
Males	8.6
Females	7.7
White	7.2
Black	17.2
Teenagers	19.3

Source: *Statistical Abstract of the United States, 1985*, pp. 406, 407.

- *Individuals are responsible for their employment*—Advocates of this view claim that (1) people who truly want to work can always find a job of some kind; (2) people who are unemployed because of foreign competition or technology should reeducate themselves for other kinds of work; and (3) people should be willing to move to wherever jobs are available.
- *Business is responsible for ending unemployment*—People who support this view believe that business-sponsored training programs and good management can help solve unemployment. Good management will result in economic expansion, creating more jobs.
- *Government is responsible for ending unemployment*—Some people feel that legislation and trade policy can solve the unemployment foreign competition creates. The government can also use its tax power to create more jobs by providing more incentives for business to expand. Finally, the government can ease unemployment directly by employing people who can't find work.

Solutions to the unemployment problem are not easy; nor, despite the periodic promises of politicians, are they imminent. Providing work for all who want to work remains one of the great challenges of our time.

HOW LABOR UNIONS RELATE TO BUSINESS

A **labor union** is *an association of nonmanagement employees formed to maintain and advance the economic status and working conditions of its members.* The principle behind labor unions is that an individual worker has little power, but that hundreds or thousands of workers collectively have strength that an employer cannot ignore.

Why Managers and Labor Often Disagree

Labor and management disagree because their basic goals are different. Management wants to earn the greatest possible profit, whereas organized labor wants concessions from management, such as higher wages, shorter hours, and better working conditions, that, if granted, often reduce profits.

Certainly labor wants the company to earn profits sufficient to keep workers employed. In fact, Samuel Gompers, a prominent labor leader of the last century, once said, "The worst crime against working people is the company that fails to operate at a profit." But Mr. Gompers, when asked what unions *really* want, replied instantly, "More." Commenting on this answer, AFL–CIO information sources explained that Gompers "compressed a great deal of meaning into that one word, but it sums up as well as any single word what trade unionism is all about. Unions have always wanted 'more' for their members. They want it now, and they will be seeking it long into the future."[1]

Unions and management are often at cross purposes. In unionized companies, management spends much of its time dealing with union representatives on wages, hours, working conditions, and other issues. In nonunionized organizations, management devotes considerable time to developing plans to keep the workers from joining a union.

Today the role of labor unions in our economy is a controversial one. Critics of organized labor claim that it is a primary contributor to inflation and that union demands, by reducing profits, make it difficult for business to compete, modernize, expand, or attract investment capital. While this charge undoubtedly contains some truth, we should keep the origins of labor unions in mind. Unions arose as a means of dealing with inhumane and unfair treatment by employers, who, without the constraint of a union, could take virtually any action they wished.

---

[1] *This is the AFL–CIO,* American Federation of Labor and Congress of Industrial Organizations, Washington, D.C., 1982, 23.

AMERICA'S REEMERGING CREATIVITY

Focusing on Long-run Results

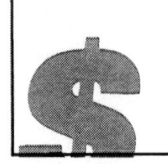

Management plays the key role in the success of individual companies. In a larger way, management also helps determine the nation's economic success.

As one observer notes, "No one seriously blames the country's corporate managers entirely. Government regulation, tax laws, pollution-control expenses, misguided economic policies, labor costs and the lofty price of imported oil have all played a part. Still, there is now a growing consensus, both at home and abroad, that the performance of American management of late has been sorely lacking; that, to some extent, the management policies, which served America so well and were admired the world over, are now being ignored in the country that created them."*

One important remedy often recommended is to pay more attention to long-run rather than short-run results. The following comment explains the problems of short-run evaluation of a managers' performance: "The verdict of Wall Street [short-term review]—and, hence, their [managers'] survival in office—depends on producing the steady quarter-to-quarter increases in profits that so please the financial community. This is known as the tyranny of Wall Street. Our top corporate managers are in the same boat as baseball managers," explained Norman E. Auerbach, chairman of Coopers & Lybrand, one of the so-called Big Eight accounting firms, which has mostly big corporations as clients. "You'd better win, produce those higher earnings quickly, or you're out."†

When a company measures a manager's successes quarter-to-quarter or year-to-year, the company will give less attention to research and development of new technology: Money that a company spends on research reduces short-term profits. This may make the manager seem inefficient. But if a company does spend money to develop or acquire successful new technology, the manager may look very successful over a three- to-five-year period.

The history of American business indicates that thinking for the long run pays off. And at least some leading American companies commit themselves to remodernization and the future. General Motors, for example, lost almost $600 million in the third quarter of 1980. Yet it announced it would keep a commitment to invest $40 billion in its reindustrialization program.

Questions for Discussion

1. What personal experiences have you had with companies that are profit-happy in the short run and will likely be profit-sad in the long run?

2. Do you believe that performance of low-level employees should be evaluated quarterly or annually? Explain.

3. Should managers think in both the short and the long run?

*Steve Lohr, "Overhauling America's Business Management," *New York Times Magazine*, January 4, 1981, 15.
†Ibid, 47.

Labor Unions Preceded the Nation's Birth

Labor unions existed even before the Declaration of Independence. Workers formed benevolent societies to help members who had suffered a financial or personal misfortune. These early unions were mainly friendship organizations; concern with wages, hours, and working conditions was secondary.

Employees soon realized that by organizing, they could bring about improvements in working conditions. By 1791, some skilled workers—printers, shoemakers, carpenters, and shipbuilders—organized for this purpose. However, these early unions were weak, poorly organized, and usually short-lived. Workers, by and large, saw little reason for cohesive organization. Small-scale farming and manufacturing predominated during this period, and if people were dissatisfied with the treatment they received from employers, they could, with very little capital, go into business for themselves or move west and farm.

During the 1820s, unionism spread rapidly. Local unions grew in power, and made loud demands for better wages, shorter hours, and improved working environments. Over the following decades, unionism tended to grow during good times but to suffer severe setbacks when times were hard and jobs were few.

How the AFL Came About

In 1881, several **craft unions**—that is, *labor unions that limit their membership to workers who practice one trade or a group of related trades, even though the workers may work for a number of different*

Before extensive union activity, owners of sweatshops exploited employees by working them long hours for very low wages.

employers—established the Federation of Organized Trades and Labor Unions. In 1886, it merged with several other unions. The new organization was called the **American Federation of Labor (AFL)**.

THE GROWTH OF THE AFL

Under Samuel Gompers' leadership, the AFL grew rapidly during the next three decades and became the dominant labor organization in the United States. The AFL was not interested in social or political change. Instead, it concentrated its efforts on gaining better working conditions for its members. It always believed in collective bargaining with employers (see page 486) and called strikes only when this method failed.

In the 1920s and early 1930s, however, the AFL met with difficulty. It became apparent that the principle of organizing labor along craft lines limited its further growth. Industry was becoming more mechanized, with fewer and fewer workers skilled in a craft. As a result, many could not qualify for AFL membership.

In the mid-1930s, a major controversy arose within the AFL over whether or not the organization should extend membership to unskilled, noncraft workers. Those who argued for extending membership pointed out three factors. First, the growth of the AFL was near a standstill, and therefore the entire labor movement was weakening. Second, entire industries, such as steel and automobiles, were unorganized. And third, almost no unskilled workers had union ties.

HOW THE CIO CAME ABOUT

As an outgrowth of this controversy, several unions belonging to the AFL formed the Committee for Industrial Organizations, with the stated purpose of promoting organization of the workers in mass-production and unorganized industries and encouraging their affiliation with the AFL. The committee organized workers in many industries without the approval of the AFL.

In 1938, the committee formally organized the **Congress of Industrial Organizations (CIO)**. The CIO was successful from the start. Workers were organized in the steel, automobile, newspaper, cannery, and communications industries, and soon the CIO was almost as strong as the AFL.

MERGER OF THE AFL AND CIO

Over the years, a number of efforts were made to unite the AFL and CIO. Success was finally achieved in 1955. George Meany, then president of the AFL, was named to head the huge consolidation of the two groups.

The AFL–CIO failed to grow significantly after the merger, for three major reasons. First, during the period in which the merger took place the labor movement was severely attacked for alleged corruption and pro-Communist activities. Second, expansion in U.S. mass-production industries, the best source of union members, peaked and began a decline that continues today. Third, an increasing share of the work force found employment in service industries, which are more difficult to organize. However, the AFL–CIO is still very large: In 1984 it had more than 14,800,000 members, or about 74 percent of all organized workers.

The AFL–CIO is not a union but a "union of unions"—103 affiliated unions comprised of 43,600 local unions. The affiliated unions are free to withdraw from the AFL–CIO at any time. Each has its own headquarters, officers, and staff, sets its own dues schedule, and carries on its own contract negotiations.

How the AFL–CIO Helps Member Unions

The AFL–CIO serves member unions by representing the entire labor movement before Congress, government agencies, and the public, helping organize workers, and settling disputes between affiliated unions.

WHAT ARE ITS GOALS?

The AFL–CIO seeks[2]

- To improve wages, hours, and working conditions for workers
- To bring the benefits of free collective bargaining to all workers
- To achieve equality of opportunity for all workers, regardless of race, creed, color, sex, or national origin
- To support legislation which will aid workers and to oppose harmful legislation
- To protect and strengthen democratic institutions and to preserve America's democratic traditions
- To aid in promoting the cause of peace and freedom in the world
- To protect the labor movement against corruption and racketeers
- To safeguard the labor movement from Communists, fascists, and other totalitarians
- To encourage workers to register and vote and to exercise fully their responsibilities as citizens

---

[2]*This is the AFL–CIO,* American Federation of Labor and Congress of Industrial Organizations, Washington, D.C., 1984, no. 20, 6, 7.

- To encourage the sale of union-made goods through the use of the union label

Labor Legislation

Federal legislation pertaining to labor unions dates back to the nineteenth century. Current labor policy, however, is based primarily on four important laws: the Wagner Act, the Fair Labor Standards Act, the Taft–Hartley Act, and the Landrum–Griffin Act.

THE WAGNER ACT

The severe economic depression of the early 1930s and a concurrent increase in union membership at that time gave impetus to the passage of the **National Labor Relations Act** of 1935. Popularly known as the **Wagner Act,** this law *assures workers the right to organize and bargain collectively with their employers*. The act strengthened the position of labor greatly. Specifically, the act declared it unlawful for employers to

- Interfere in any way with employees' right to bargain collectively
- Interfere with the formation or administration of a union
- Refuse to bargain collectively with employees
- Discriminate against employees because of their union affiliation

To administer the act, the government established the **National Labor Relations Board (NLRB)** and gave it two broad responsibilities. First, *the board certifies the appropriate bargaining representatives of employees;* it determines, in other words, whether the chosen leaders actually represent the majority of employees. Second, *it has authority to review and make decisions concerning alleged unfair labor practices.* When someone submits a complaint, the board holds a hearing. If the evidence that management has acted in bad faith is not sufficient, the board drops the case. If the board believes management is guilty, it issues a cease-and-desist order. The board can call on federal courts to enforce its decisions.

From the date of its enactment, management sharply criticized the Wagner Act on the grounds that it was slanted in favor of labor. Agitation for a new national labor law eventually resulted in passage of the Taft–Hartley Act.

THE FAIR LABOR STANDARDS ACT

The **Fair Labor Standards Act,** also known as the **Federal Wage and Hour Law,** was enacted in 1938. Amended many times, this law *sets the minimum wage and prohibits employment of people under age 16 in most jobs.*

The Taft-Hartley Act

The **Taft-Hartley Act**—officially titled the **Labor-Management Relations Act** of 1947—was *passed in an effort to equalize the rights and privileges of management and labor*. It gave management no new rights but sought to balance power by withholding some rights that had been extended to labor. The act reaffirmed the Wagner Act's provisions that management could not interfere with employees' rights to unionize and must bargain collectively with them. However, it also made it illegal for labor organizations to

- Seek to maintain a **closed shop**, that is, *a situation in which managers would only hire people who were already members of unions* (the act, however, continued to permit the **union shop**, that is, *a situation in which management may hire any employees it wishes but they must join the union within a certain period of time*)
- Discriminate against any employee who drops out of the labor organization or who is denied membership in the organization, unless the employee fails to live up to an agreement requiring membership in a labor organization as a condition of employment
- Attempt to cause the employer to discriminate against any employee in any way that would make the employer guilty of an unfair labor practice
- Attempt to *cause the employer to pay for services not performed* (commonly called **featherbedding**)
- Refuse to bargain collectively with the employer

The Taft-Hartley Act also contained a provision that gave states the right to outlaw the union shop if they wished. Out of this provision come the so-called **right-to-work laws:** In a state governed by a right-to-work law, *workers cannot be required to join a union in order to keep their jobs.*

The Landrum-Griffin Act

During the 1950s awareness grew that some unions were abusing their power. Charges of bribery, malfeasance, and other forms of corruption lead to a Senate investigation and, in 1959, to passage of the **Labor-Management Reporting and Disclosure Act.** This law, commonly known as the **Landrum-Griffin Act,** *mainly addresses the internal affairs of unions.* It requires unions to

- Make union leaders personally responsible for union funds
- Publish financial records so that all members can see them
- File their constitutions with the Secretary of Labor

The NLRB administers the Wagner Act, the Taft–Hartley Act, and the Landrum–Griffin Act. In effect, the federal government has more control over labor–management relationships than ever before. For instance, the President now has the power to ask for an injunction against strikers when the strike endangers the health and welfare of the citizens. This was the case with the Professional Air Traffic Controller's (PATCO) strike in 1981.

HOW LABOR ATTEMPTS TO FURTHER ITS INTERESTS

Labor uses lobbies, boycotts, and strikes to promote the welfare of union members.

Lobbies and Public Opinion

Labor relies extensively on **lobbies,** that is, on *groups of people who try to influence legislation at state and federal levels and gain public sympathy for their cause.* Unions are also active in political campaigns. Some labor organizations own newspapers and buy radio and television time to further the interests of labor.

Labor unions are an important voice in society. They take stands on issues, such as collective bargaining, minimum wages, unemployment benefits, worker safety, civil rights, and national and state labor legislation, that directly affect labor. But they also take strong positions on matters that indirectly affect workers, such as education, welfare programs, the ERA, foreign aid, Social Security, monetary policy, and environmental matters.

Boycotts

A **boycott** is *a concerted effort to have consumers stop buying goods or services from a company until it grants the boycotters' demands.* In a **primary boycott,** *union members refuse to buy their own employer's goods.* In a **secondary boycott,** *they refuse to handle, process, manufacture, or transport the goods of a second employer if that employer is accused of being unfair to its own union employees.* The secondary boycott is illegal, but occurs nevertheless.

Strikes

A **strike,** labor's ultimate weapon, is *a deliberate work stoppage or slowdown to force management to grant concessions.* Unions often call strikes during the busiest season of the year, on the theory that at such time labor can force management's hand more quickly. For example, newspaper employees might strike or threaten to strike in December, when the newspaper may lose the most advertising revenue.

Strikes are often very costly, both to companies and to their employees. Further, major strikes, such as those called by steel, rub-

Socially conscious citizens sometimes band together to boycott products either in support of workers' demands or to encourage consumers not to buy unsafe or expensive goods.

Generally, people associate strikes with factory workers, but other groups in society also use strikes to protest what they consider unfair treatment.

ber, and transportation unions, often have adverse spillover effects. If rubber workers stay out on strike long enough, the tire inventories of car makers become depleted, forcing auto companies to close operations.

Generally, however, less worker time is lost to strikes than most of us think. Of all contracts negotiated, 98 percent run their course without a strike or other interruption of work.

HOW MANAGEMENT ATTEMPTS TO RESTRAIN LABOR

Management tries to protect company interests against labor demands through employers' associations, lobbies, strikebreakers, and injunctions.

Employers' Associations

An **employers' association** is *a group of employers acting together to present a solid front in management's dealings with labor.* Employers' associations provide their members with research, publications, seminars, and other services showing how to prevent unionization, or at least how to negotiate contracts more favorable to the company.

Lobbies

Management may promote federal and state legislation designed to restrict union power and influence. When Congress is considering an important labor law, management, either through employers' associations or independently, exerts pressure on lawmakers to pass, defeat, or amend the proposed legislation. Some of the methods management uses to lobby for particular legislation are advertisements in magazines and newspapers, letters, telegrams, personal visits to influential people, and speeches on radio and television.

Retaining Management Consultants

In many companies, management retains consultants to restrain labor. (Labor leaders call the consultants union busters.) Consultants help management induce employees to (a) vote against attempts to unionize and (b) decertify or vote out an existing union. An estimated 400 management consulting firms, employing 6,000 people, work to restrain unions.

Labor leaders protest management's use of union busters to decrease the influence of unions: to keep unions out of companies or to urge workers to vote unions out of firms where they exist.

Management consultants help managers prevent unionization or get the union decertified by giving advice on how to avoid hiring pro-union employees and what tactics to use to create the fear that employees will lose their jobs if the business unionizes. Consultants also provide a variety of tools to help management preserve a union-free environment, such as letters to workers, radio and television spots, films, newspaper advertisements, and prepared speeches.

Management consultants claim great success in preventing unionization and obtaining decertification of existing unions. Labor unions file many complaints against management consultants with the National Labor Relations Board charging unfair labor practices. The Board dismisses most of them as unjustified or without merit.

Strikebreakers

While a strike is in progress, management may turn to **strikebreakers,** or *new employees hired in an effort to cause regular workers to return to work because they are afraid they will lose their jobs permanently.* Striking workers call the new employees "scabs." On occasion, managers attempt to operate the business by doing the work of the strikers, in the hope that the strikers will ultimately concede.

Injunctions

An **injunction** is *a court order directing a person or persons to refrain from a certain act or acts.* Injunctions against labor unions protect the employer's interests by holding off strikes, boycotts, or picketing that might cause injury to the employer's position and established relations with customers and employees. Courts can grant injunctions to either labor or management but generally grant them to management.

HOW COLLECTIVE BARGAINING WORKS

Despite the extensive publicity given to strikes, labor and management settle most of their disputes without interrupting production. They generally use **collective bargaining,** *a procedure in which both groups meet to discuss their differences and attempt to reach agreement on mutual responsibilities and activities.* The decisions they make together become part of a binding contract.

Most often, collective bargaining occurs between management and labor in a single company. In **area-wide collective bargaining,** *management and labor representatives from several companies in the same industry and geographical area meet.* The procedure is **industry-wide** if *an entire industry negotiates,* as with coal and steel.

Typically, both labor and management prepare themselves well for collective bargaining. Each side gathers information about working conditions, wages, fringe benefits, and other issues to justify its position.

Negotiations may go on for weeks or months. Despite the usually sincere efforts of both, labor and management may not reach agreement on certain issues. In this event, they can use one of two peaceful alternative methods of settlement: mediation or arbitration.

Mediation

Mediation is *an attempt to settle labor disputes with the assistance of a disinterested third party.* The third party, which may be one or several individuals, listens to the arguments of each side and attempts to reconcile the differences. The Federal Mediation and Conciliation Service, an independent agency of the federal government, has a staff of several hundred mediators to help settle disputes that threaten interstate commerce, national defense, or public health and welfare. Most states also provide mediation services.

The objective of mediation is not to *order* opposing parties to settle their disagreements, because neither is obligated to accept suggestions. Rather, mediators try to help labor and management reconcile their differences by suggesting compromises. Mediation is not always successful, and a strike may still occur. Even after a strike is under way, however, mediators may continue to work toward a settlement in order to prevent a long strike.

Arbitration

There is only one important difference between arbitration and mediation: The mediator can only *recommend* solutions to labor-management differences; the arbitrator is empowered to *determine* the solution. When **arbitration** is used, *the arbitrator plays the role of a judge, and both parties agree in advance to abide by the decision.* Labor and management jointly designate the arbitrator or arbitrators to ensure impartiality. Most frequently, union contracts call for the American Arbitration Association, an independent agency for arbitration of labor disputes, or the Federal Mediation and Conciliation Service to act as arbitrator.

The Union Contract

Successful collective bargaining results in a **union contract,** *a legal document that spells out the terms of and procedures for the relationship between an employer and a union.* Once adopted, both parties legally must abide by its terms and provisions for the life of the agreement, usually one, two, or three years. Table 16–1 shows some areas commonly covered in a union contract.

TABLE 16-1 Common Provisions in a Union Contract

WAGE BENEFITS	EMPLOYEE BENEFITS	OTHER PROVISIONS	
• Wages for regular hours • Wages for overtime and holidays • Wage differentials for different shifts • Automatic wage-increase provisions	• Group life insurance • Medical and disability insurance • Pension program • Paid vacations and holidays • Unemployment benefits	• Protection of seniority rights • Transfer policies • Promotion policies • Layoff and termination policies • Job redesign and employee evaluation policies	• Health and safety issues • Procedures for handling employee grievances • Management and union rights • Dues collection procedures • Provision for contract renewal

A particularly important provision concerns the **grievance procedure,** or *the union contract's specification for how to handle complaints (grievances)* (see Figure 16-5). Grievances are bound to arise over such matters as seniority, work assignments, transfers, and piecework rates.

A grievance procedure usually stipulates that union representatives first present an employee complaint to the employee's immediate superior. If the supervisor does not correct the grievance, the union official presents it to successively higher officials in the company. If the highest company official does not settle the grievance, the case is then appealed to an outside arbitration board, as described earlier. The arbitrator's decision is final and binding on both parties.

ORGANIZED LABOR TODAY

Since the Great Depression and the pro-labor presidency of Franklin Roosevelt, Americans have thought of themselves as a country of powerful labor unions. This image of labor is no longer appropriate. The proportion of nonfarm workers belonging to unions hit its peak in the early 1950s. It has declined ever since.

In certain industries, such as auto making, transportation, and steel, a large percentage of workers do belong to unions, but overall over three-quarters of the total work force is unorganized (see Figure 16-6).

Organized labor is still predominantly blue-collar and male. In 1978, there were 21.8 million union members nationwide, of whom

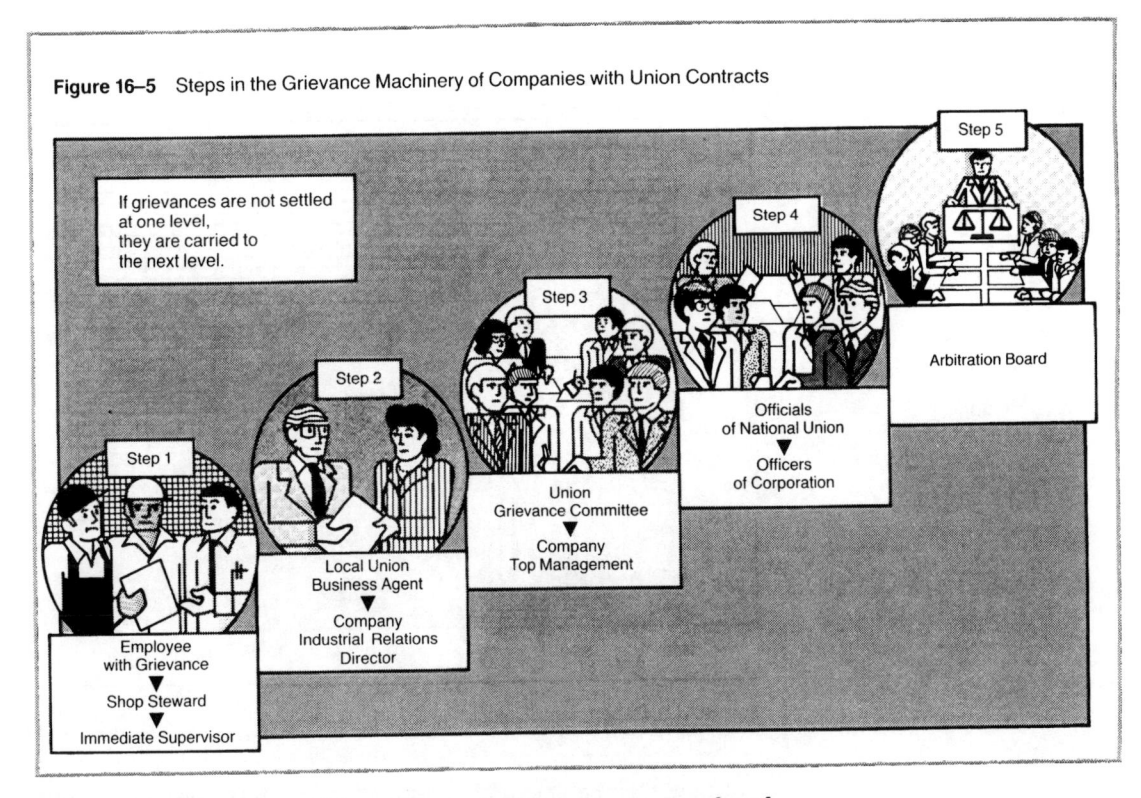

Figure 16–5 Steps in the Grievance Machinery of Companies with Union Contracts

If grievances are not settled at one level, they are carried to the next level.

Step 1: Employee with Grievance ▼ Shop Steward ▼ Immediate Supervisor

Step 2: Local Union Business Agent ▼ Company Industrial Relations Director

Step 3: Union Grievance Committee ▼ Company Top Management

Step 4: Officials of National Union ▼ Officers of Corporation

Step 5: Arbitration Board

only 18.7 percent were white-collar and 23.4 percent were female. However, the number of women in unions has been increasing, and more and more professional employees—particularly teachers—have organized. Furthermore, numbers of nurses and government employees at federal, state, and local levels have joined labor organizations in recent years.

What's Behind the Decline of Labor Unions?

Big labor is no longer Robin Hood in the eyes of the public. Once a mighty political force, its influence is decreasing.

Two problems in particular have contributed to the decline of labor unions. First, union membership is decreasing in proportion to the total labor force. Second, union strength is ebbing, the reduction of union victories in National Labor Relations Board (NLRB) elections suggests. NLRB elections decide whether a company should unionize. Usually, union organizers petition to hold an election, and employees vote by secret ballot. In recent years, when company employees vote in NLRB elections, labor unions have lost more often than they have won.

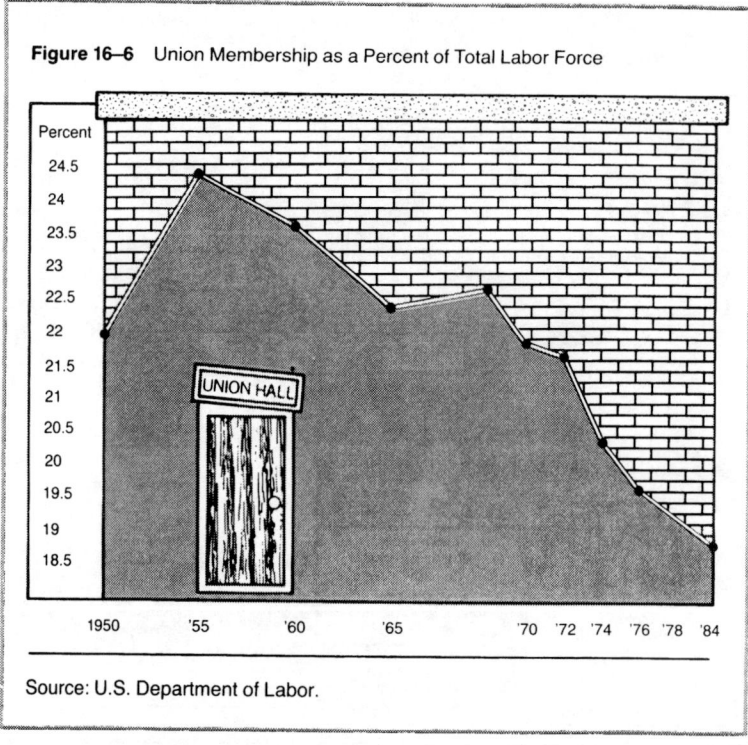

Figure 16–6 Union Membership as a Percent of Total Labor Force

Source: U.S. Department of Labor.

Union membership and union power are on the decline for four main reasons. The first is union leaders' bad image. When TV cameras show labor leaders getting in and out of limousines, like presidents of large corporations and political leaders, union members cannot see how this represents the underdog philosophy these leaders preach. Members rightly ask who is paying for the good life union professionals live. Scandals relating to pension fund abuse by some union officials also tarnish the image of unions.

Second, female employees frustrate union organizers because women tend to resist unionization. Historically, unions have not sought to organize women and so women have no reason to look kindly on them.

Third, young workers are not as pro-union as their parents were. A B. F. Goodrich Company spokesperson said, "The new worker comes from greater affluence, is better educated, and does easier work for shorter periods. His isn't a class struggle. More likely, his is a struggle for recognition, for independence, for individuality. Unions can't help toward achieving these aims."[3]

---
[3]*Business Week*, December 4, 1978, 57.

Finally, unions are less attractive than before because management is adopting a more participative style. "Sunrise" industries, with the greatest job growth, have young managements with up-to-date ideas about how to earn worker respect and cooperation. Management works increasingly hard to keep workers satisfied so that they have no need or desire to unionize.

Emphasis Is Shifting to Quality of Work Life

A movement called **quality-of-work-life programming (QWL)** is emerging to help end the traditional management-labor confrontation. QWL involves *installing programs to promote job satisfaction and productivity*. QWL programs are based on the ideas that most workers want to be productive and will eagerly involve themselves in their jobs if they are given the proper incentives and a climate of labor-management trust. Studies of worker attitudes about work show a "strong affirmation of the value of work."[4] Some of the largest companies (Polaroid, General Motors, and Procter & Gamble) and unions (United Auto Workers, United Steel Workers, and Communications Workers of America) now use QWL programs.

American managers are discarding the shortsighted concept that a company hires the hands of workers while using the brains only of management. Among the methods used to promote worker involvement are self-managed work teams, labor-management steering committees, problem-solving groups, and committees that combine social and technical ideas to redesign work.

Would Co-determination Help Improve QWL?

The West Germans have a law requiring **co-determination,** *a practice that gives workers equal representation with stockholders on the board of directors in making company policy.* The chairman of the board always represents the stockholders, however, and has a double vote in case of a tie on an issue.

Co-determination works well not only in West Germany but also in Austria, the Netherlands, Denmark, Norway, and Sweden. Neither U.S. management nor union leaders have yet shown much interest in co-determination. It does hold promise, though, because giving workers input into the decision-making process has many advantages: (1) workers can make practical recommendations because they know day-to-day operations; (2) better cooperation between management and workers results; (3) workers gain a better understanding of the company's basic goals and problems; and (4) workers can see that their interests are represented.

---

[4]*Business Week,* May 11, 1981, 87.

SUMMARY

- Noteworthy trends in the work force are the growing number of women who work outside the home and the increasing number of part-time employees.
- Principal causes of unemployment are imports exceeding exports, recession, technological development, and government cutbacks. Unemployment tends to be highest among teenagers, nonwhites, and blue-collar workers.
- The American Federation of Labor (AFL) was formed in 1886. In 1938, several unions left the AFL to form the Congress of Industrial Organizations (CIO). In 1955, the AFL and CIO merged.
- Current labor policy is based primarily on four laws: the Wagner Act, the Fair Labor Standards Act, the Taft-Hartley Act, and the Landrum-Griffin Act.
- Labor attempts to further its interests through lobbies, boycotts, and strikes.
- Management attempts to restrain labor through management consultants, employers' associations, lobbies, use of strikebreakers, and injunctions.
- Collective bargaining settles the majority of labor-management disputes. Successful collective bargaining results in a union contract covering wages, employee benefits, grievance procedures, and a variety of other matters.
- Unions are declining in membership and power. Quality-of-work-life programming and co-determination are two new approaches to solving labor-management problems.

KEY TERMS YOU SHOULD KNOW

American Federation of Labor (AFL)
arbitration
area-wide collective bargaining
boycott
closed shop
co-determination
collective bargaining
Congress of Industrial Organizations (CIO)
craft union
employers' association
Fair Labor Standards Act
featherbedding
grievance procedure
industry-wide collective bargaining
injunction
labor
labor force
labor union
Landrum-Griffin Act
lobby
mediation
National Labor Relations Board (NLRB)
primary boycott
quality-of-work-life programming
recession
right-to-work law
secondary boycott
social costs of unemployment
strike
strikebreaker
Taft-Hartley Act
union contract
union shop
Wagner Act

QUESTIONS FOR REVIEW

1. Labor is important both as an expense and as income. Explain.
2. Why are more women joining the labor force? More part-time workers?
3. What are unemployment's main causes?
4. What solutions are suggested to reduce unemployment?
5. Why is unemployment higher in some states than in others?
6. How do the goals of management and labor differ?
7. Trace the history of the AFL–CIO.
8. What are the AFL–CIO's goals?
9. What is the Wagner Act? The Fair Labor Standards Act? The Taft–Hartley Act? The Landrum–Griffin Act?
10. How does labor try to advance its interests? How does management?
11. Describe the steps in the collective bargaining process.
12. What is the difference between mediation and arbitration?
13. What does a union contract cover?
14. Why are labor unions declining in importance?

QUESTIONS FOR DISCUSSION

1. Do you think that, in some areas, labor has gone too far already? If so, describe new labor legislation that you would propose to correct the situation.
2. Some union wage agreements contain an automatic cost-of-living-increase clause that ties employees' wages to rises in the Consumer Price Index. Do you think such clauses are a good idea? Explain.
3. One Reagan administration goal was to slice about $1 billion from the costs of federal welfare in fiscal year 1982 by ending welfare rights for families of workers who go out on strike and then become eligible for public assistance. The administration said the proposal was justified because a striker's "decision to be unemployed is voluntary" and that it is not fair "to place the government on one side of the bargaining table," that is, on the side of the strikers. An AFL–CIO spokesperson says, "Strikers' children shouldn't be starved to force strikers back to work." What are the pros and cons of this issue? What is your position? Explain.
4. Keith Stanton, a junior in a liberal arts college, argued in a debate that labor unions are monopolies just like electric power companies. Therefore the rates they set for wages, fringe benefits, and worker privileges should be regulated by the state as utilities are. What do you think would be the probable impact of this proposal?

CASE STUDY

What Prompts Workers to Unionize?

The Delux Snacks Company makes potato chips, cookies, and other snack foods. The company employs 500 workers and is nonunion. For the past three years, the union has been trying to organize the workers. In an election last week, the union came within 20 votes of winning.

This narrow victory worries George Wren, company president. Delux is owned by a conglomerate, and Wren knows his job is on the line if the workers unionize. He discusses the problem with Phil Harris, plant superintendent, and Dorothy Hendricks, personnel director.

George: The election last week shocked me. For the past three years the union has been gaining on us. Last week they almost won. Why?

Phil: Well, as I see it, the problem is beyond our control. This year the union simply worked harder. I hear they spent 50 percent more time and money trying to get the employees to join.

G: If I follow your thinking, next year they will spend even more and will win the election. Now, we don't want that to happen. We've got enough problems already. A union would only complicate our operations even more. Dorothy, what do you think is wrong?

Dorothy: I've been here three years, and I've seen a sharp decline in employees' attitudes. Every day at least 10 employees come to see me with complaints about their superiors.

P: They have no business doing that. Job complaints are to be made directly to their supervisors. You're a staff manager, and your job is to deal with employees' pension plans, withholding tax, health—that sort of thing.

G: Phil's right. It's not your concern how employees' work is scheduled and how managers treat the employees.

D: I know that. But what am I to do if they bring it up? I get far more complaints about unfair, even humiliating, treatment of employees by supervisors than anything else. For some time I've been thinking the problem is with supervisors. Three supervisors in particular just don't know how to handle people.

G: Who specifically?

D: Chuck Brown, Gwen Wesson, and Claude Smith.

P: Look, I appointed each of those people. They are good supervisors and believe in getting the job done.

D: I don't know about that. All I do know is that their departments have by far the highest absenteeism and turnover. And I'm certain that their employees voted overwhelmingly for the union.

P: The union elections are secret, so you'll never know how any department voted. I resent your pointing a finger at those three. They are good people—that's why I brought them with me when I joined the company.

G: Dorothy, do you have documentation that people reporting to Chuck, Gwen, and Claude complain more than personnel reporting to the other supervisors?

D: Not with me, but I've got plenty of evidence in my office. My estimate is that 75 to 80 percent of all complaints come from people who report to them.

G: We'll meet early next week to discuss this again. And Dorothy, I'd like to see the files of those three supervisors who seem to be problems.

Questions

1. The statement is sometimes made that "unions are the result of management's mistakes." What does this mean?
2. Assume that the three supervisors in question do cause most of the employee dissatisfaction. What action would you take to correct the problem? Explain.
3. What can management do to avoid a pro-union vote in the next election?

EVOLUTION OF A BUSINESS

The Labor Movement and Employee Morale

Ray and Sara were continuing to discuss their employees and how to handle them. Their goal was to provide an environment where morale would run high and where work would be pleasant instead of a chore.

Ray: I've been hearing a lot lately about the so-called erosion of the work ethic. That's just a fancy way of saying that people don't work as hard as they used to.

Sara: I think the labor movement brought that about. Labor leaders have been telling their members for years now that they're being exploited. Certainly the conditions that gave rise to the labor movement were awful. But now I'm wondering if things haven't gone too far. Nowadays, employees seem to always be thinking of what they're *getting*—employee benefits, time off, and so on—and not thinking much about what they're *giving* in terms of productivity.

Ray: Well, don't you think we could make our office a place where employees would want to be productive?

Sara: I think we could. If we treat our employees right and create a good working relationship and pay adequately, I doubt they would ever feel they needed a union. Unions are the result of poor personnel policies.

Ray: Do you think we should have such things as weekly meetings where employees can offer suggestions and raise any complaints they have? What about company picnics and so on?

Questions

1. Do you think there has been an erosion of the work ethic? Are unions in part responsible for people's changing attitudes toward work?
2. How can a work environment be created in which people will be productive and enjoy working?
3. What about the effectiveness of Ray's proposals—weekly employee meetings, picnics, and so on?
4. Are unions the result of poor personnel policies?

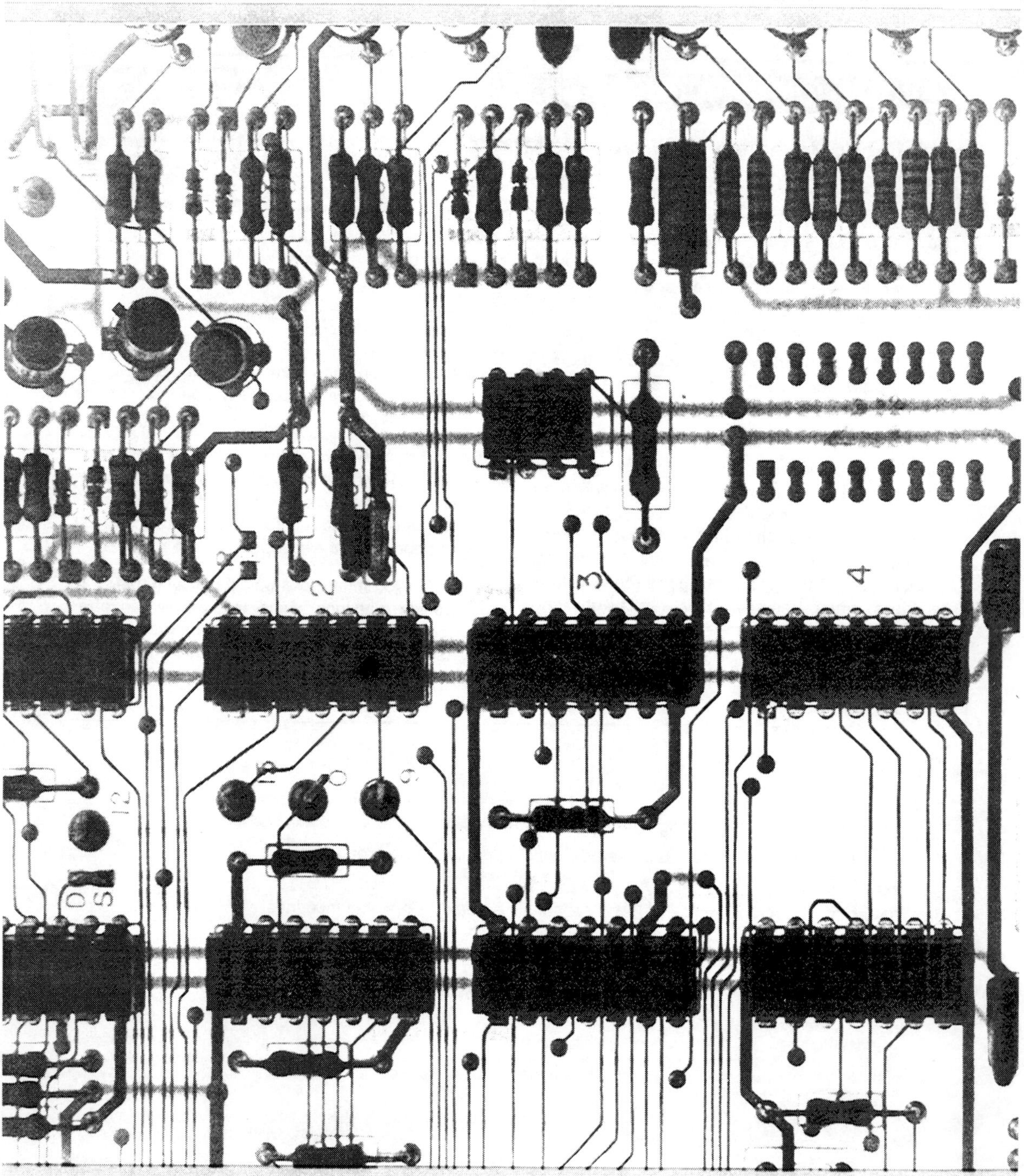

V

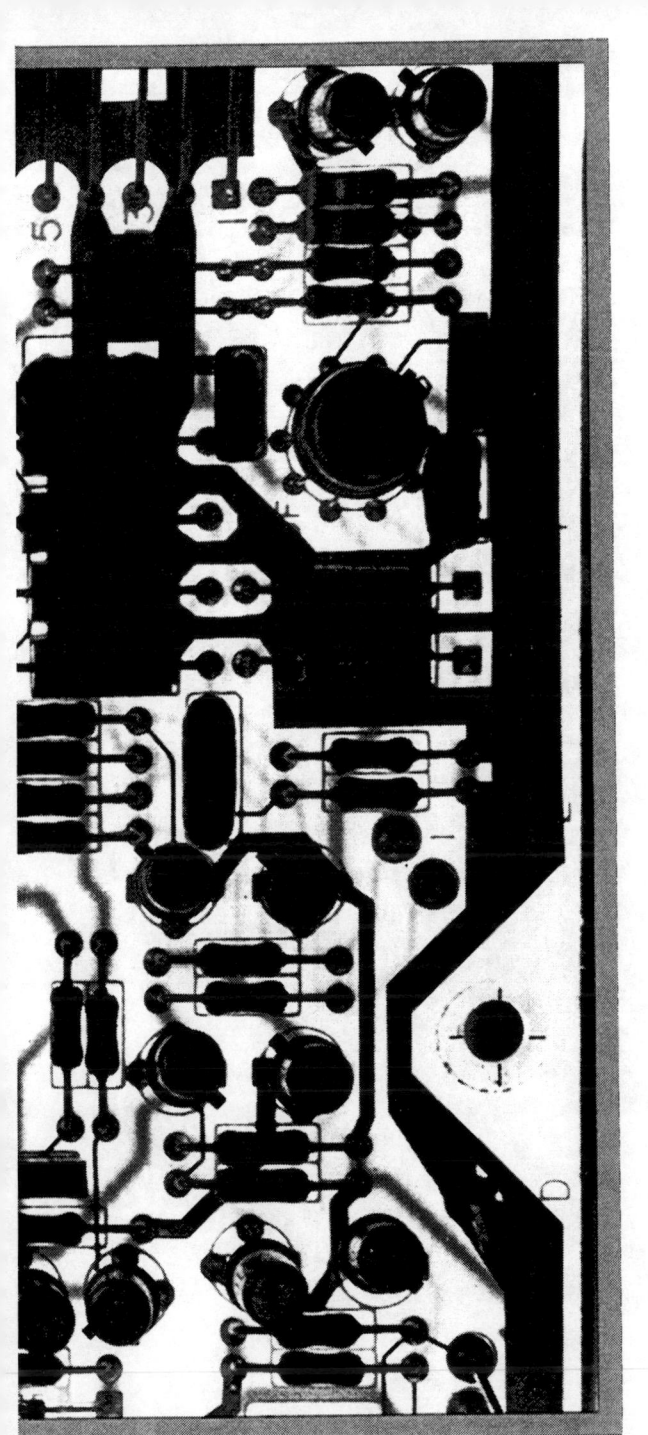

USING INFORMATION IN BUSINESS

17 ACCOUNTING AND FINANCIAL STATEMENTS

18 BUSINESS INFORMATION AND RESEARCH

19 COMPUTERS: THE ELECTRONIC SIDE OF BUSINESS

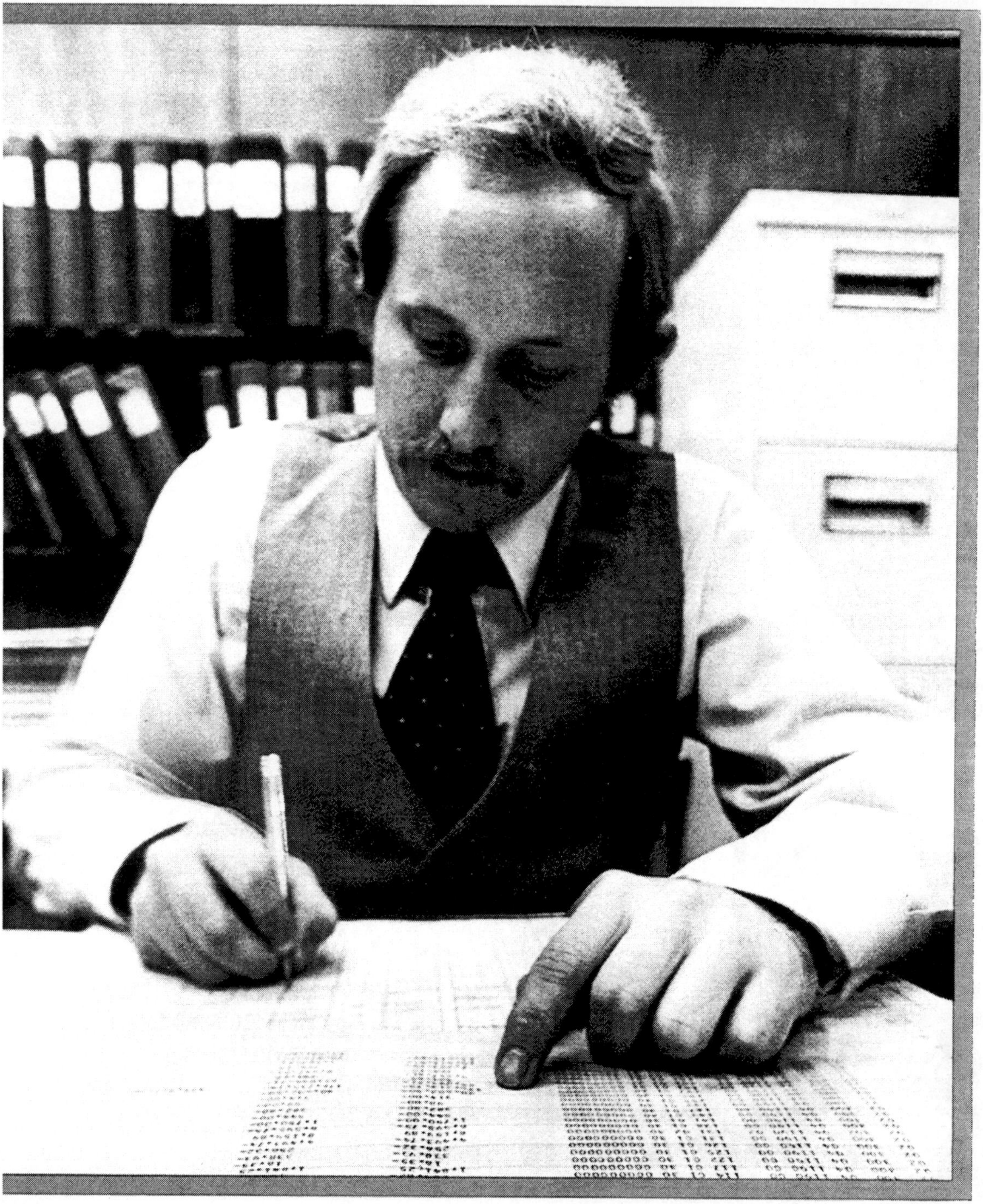

17

ACCOUNTING AND FINANCIAL STATEMENTS
Does It All Add Up—and Balance?

READ THIS CHAPTER SO YOU CAN:

Define accounting, and discuss its role in operating a business.

Explain the functions of accounting, and discuss it as a profession.

Detail the steps in the accounting process.

Explain how balance sheets and income statements are used.

Discuss the most important ratios used by management.

Describe cost accounting and standard costs.

Explain the role of the annual report in a business.

Define auditing and budgeting, and explain their purposes.

Explain why accounting is becoming more important.

Describe how accountants help minimize taxes.

WHAT IS ACCOUNTING?

Accounting is *the recording, classifying, summarizing, and interpreting of the financial transactions of a business.* Its purpose is to provide an up-to-the-minute picture of the company's financial position to help management make decisions and control the business.

Accounting is the fastest growing business major. In 1975, 31,100 degrees were granted in accounting. By 1984, the number had increased to 46,831—a gain of 50 percent. During this period, total employment in accounting grew from 720,000 to 1,362,000—a gain of 89 percent.

Three reasons account for the rapid growth of accounting careers:

INCREASED INCOME

Taxes were once of secondary significance to millions of people and many businesses because incomes were lower than they are now. But as incomes increase, so do taxes. Accountants can help taxpayers minimize or defer tax payments.

EMERGENCE OF FINANCIAL PLANNING PROFESSION

Financial planners are professionals who specialize in helping individuals and businesses select investments for long-term growth of capital. Accountants play a key role in financial planning because they can give advice on the tax consequences of different investments. How much net worth an individual or business accumulates is no longer based only on income or earnings; it depends also on how surplus money is invested. Ted and Paul make identical incomes, but 10 years from now Ted may have a much larger net worth than Paul because of wiser financial planning and careful accounting.

COMPLEXITY OF TAX LAWS

In the past decade, each Congress passed a tax law containing new provisions for dealing with income and expenses for tax purposes. As tax consequences of financial decisions become more complex, we can expect the accounting profession to become more important.

Accountants Are Business Scorekeepers

Accountants keep track of income and expenses in the business and report it numerically to management, owners, potential investors, and local, state, and federal governments. In keeping score, accountants provide answers to such questions as

- How much profit or loss resulted from last year's (or last month or quarter's) operations?

- What is the value of the owner's equity or net worth?
- What were the sources of income from product sales, sales of real estate, securities, rents, etc.?
- How did the business spend its income—raw materials, wages, salaries, utilities, taxes, interest, etc.?
- How much does the company owe?

Accountants Are Business Game Planners

Accountants do much more than keep score of how well businesses play the game. They also help decide how a firm should conduct business in the future. Accountants suggest answers to future related questions such as

- Should a firm purchase or lease equipment and real estate?
- Should a business increase, maintain, or decrease pension plan contributions?
- How can the firm minimize the cost of borrowed capital?
- How can the business take advantage of changes in tax regulations?

Accounting Is Much More than Bookkeeping

Experts sometimes use the terms "accounting" and "bookkeeping" interchangeably. However, **bookkeeping** is *just one phase of accounting*. Bookkeepers are *concerned mainly with the systematic recording of financial transactions.* They provide the data the accountant uses.

Accountants have broader responsibilities. They devise systems and forms for recording transactions, determine how these transactions should be classified, establish the procedures for making summaries of transactions, and consolidate and interpret various financial statements. Accountants often participate in making company policy.

Accountants Help Minimize Taxes

No business or individual wants to pay more taxes than the law requires. Accountants help businesses and individuals to meet their tax requirements, to defer taxes, and, in some cases, to eliminate tax liabilities altogether.

Table 17-1 shows how taxes increase in both dollar amounts and percentage as individual income increases. Note that a single person with no dependents who earns $20,000 per year pays well over three times as much in taxes as an individual who earns $10,000 per year. And a single person who earns $50,000 per year will have a tax liability of more than four times that of a person who earns $20,000.

TABLE 17-1 Federal Individual Income Tax
Effective or Average Rates and Marginal Tax Rates For Selected Income Groups 1983

SINGLE PERSON, NO DEPENDENTS	TAX PAID	1983 EFFECTIVE TAX RATE*	MARGINAL TAX RATE[†]
$10,000	$ 951	9.5	17.0
20,000	3,089	15.4	28.0
25,000	7,485	17.8	32.0
50,000	13,073	26.1	45.0
75,000	23,873	31.8	50.0
MARRIED COUPLE, TWO DEPENDENTS			
$10,000	$ 296	3.2	13.0
20,000	1,846	9.2	19.0
25,000	2,828	11.3	23.0
50,000	9,844	21.8	35.0
75,000	19,050	25.4	44.0

SOURCE: *Statistical Abstract of the United States, 1984,* 329.

*Effective tax rate represents the tax liability divided by stated income.
[†]Marginal tax rate is the percentage of the first additional dollar of income which would be paid in income tax. For example, a single person with a taxable income of $10,001 would have an effective tax rate of 17 percent on each dollar in excess of $10,000.

Increasing the tax penalty on people who earn more—presumably because they produce more—is one reason some feel a flat tax is important.

Is There Any Logic in Tax Policy?

Despite high tax rates, the federal government does not collect as much in taxes as it spends, which results in deficit spending or debt financing.

Federal tax policies stem from tax laws which voters develop through their elected members of Congress. Elected representatives also set state and local taxes and tax policies.

Critics often claim taxes are unfair. News items about wealthy people who pay little if any tax make popular conversation. Analysis shows, however, that considerable rationality determines tax policy. Consider these examples:

Tax credits or deductions encourage people to

- Conserve energy through home improvements and modernization of factories and office buildings.

- Gain more education. Deductions may be available for parents of college students and employers who pay the cost of education for employees.

- Invest in high-risk business ventures to create jobs.
- Donate property to foundations, colleges, and charitable organizations.
- Contribute to political campaigns.
- Improve the land through such measures as investing in soil conservation, planting trees, and creating lakes.
- Provide for their own retirement through Individual Retirement Accounts (IRAs) and corporate pension plans.
- Hire the handicapped and hard-core unemployed.

What some call tax loopholes, others consider incentives for advancing social welfare. Those who make our tax laws have enormous power to give direction to the way people and businesses invest their money. Congress can raise or lower taxes to increase or decrease revenue. It can increase or decrease spending, thereby raising or lowering taxes. In either case, the choice is political.

CONTEMPORARY ISSUE

"IRS Roulette" Helps Cause Deficit

One way to increase tax revenues without new taxes is by tightening collection procedures. Taxpayers are supposed to report their own tax liabilities and to remit whatever their computations indicate they owe. But, goaded perhaps by reports of a vast, untaxed underground economy, many have been playing "IRS roulette." They neglect to report all their income, or overstate their deductions or just plain cheat in some other way, gambling that an IRS buried in an avalanche of paperwork will never catch up with them. The Deficit Reduction Act of 1984 includes provisions to make tax evasion less popular. These provisions include:

- ☐ The requirement that all cash transactions involving $10,000 or more be reported to Uncle Sam.
- ☐ Information returns to be filed by recipients of mortgage interest.
- ☐ The need to log utilization of equipment with both business and personal applications.
- ☐ Reporting requirements imposed on tax shelter promoters.
- ☐ The call for names and Social Security numbers of alimony recipients.
- ☐ The demand for independent appraisal of non-cash charitable contributions.

In addition, the IRS is enlarging its computer industry capacity dramatically to match taxable transactions with taxpayers.

Other Ways Accountants Help Business

SUPPLY INFORMATION FOR DECISIONS

Accounting helps managers make decisions by supplying and interpreting financial information. Accounting can reveal, for example, whether (1) the costs of doing business are excessive, (2) the firm is investing money properly, (3) company property is correctly valued, (4) the various operations are contributing to company profits, (5) the firm should borrow additional funds, and (6) earnings of the business are satisfactory.

Accounting provides a continuous record of all financial transactions. Every dollar received, spent, invested, paid as dividends, or otherwise handled is accounted for. Since records accrue over a period of years, management can compare current performance and financial status with that of previous years. In short, accounting gives management objective measures of progress and efficiency. Also, by establishing checks and balances, accounting can control things like embezzlement and theft of company assets.

HELP IN BORROWING CAPITAL

When a business wants to borrow money, the bank or other lender wants to know about its financial status. The balance sheet and the income statement (discussed later) indicate whether the business is a good financial risk. A business that keeps poor records has less chance of getting the money it wants than the firm that keeps good records. Information demands for business loans can be so extensive that one nettled business person joked, "You can get a loan if you can prove you don't need it."

KEEP OWNERS AND INVESTORS INFORMED

Company annual reports and interim statements that accountants prepare help stockholders to keep track of what their company is doing. Potential investors read them to decide whether to buy stock.

REPORT TO THE GOVERNMENT

Certain laws, regulations, and taxes make demands on the recordkeeping and financial reporting of a business. Laws that regulate employee wages and hours, the Social Security program, federal and state income and withholding taxes, sales taxes, and other taxes make it mandatory that companies keep careful records.

ACCOUNTING AS A PROFESSIONAL FIELD

To achieve a high degree of proficiency in accounting requires years of study and experience. The earliest recognition of accountancy as a

AMERICA'S REEMERGING CREATIVITY

The Accounting Profession's Challenge: Reduce Paperwork and Manipulation

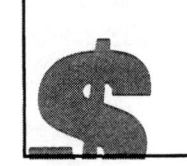

Experts throughout the world have always highly respected the American accounting profession. However, in recent years experts have challenged the role of accounting in the U.S. economy in two significant ways. First, they argue that the large growth in the number of accountants and lawyers indicates that the country is becoming bureaucratized—a sign of an aging and stagnating economy.

A representative critic who holds this view is Robert Reich, Director of the Office of Policy and Planning at the Federal Trade Commission. He maintains that we are becoming a nation of "paper entrepreneurs." People "who invent, produce, and sell products gradually give way to those who manipulate and rearrange laws, assets, processes, and ideas."* He claims that our society gives paper entrepreneurs the best financial rewards, greatest employment security, and highest social status. The result is a "brain drain" from product entrepreneurism. Paper entrepreneurs, he admits, "provide the necessary grease for the wheels of the capitalistic system, but do not themselves add to production."

Secondly, experts charge that our accounting practices make management shortsighted. Senator Lloyd Bentsen at a 1980 Harvard conference on competitiveness said, "Today's financial measurements are biased against the long term. When you want to make this year's annual report look as good as possible, why engage in **entry pricing**† in East Asia? Why accept losses for two or three years to build volume and brand recognition? I can assure you that our competitors in the world of trade are more than ready to make market investments that may not pay off for a decade."

Experts also charge that American management's "measurement of achievement and the goals to be reached are as short-term as a politician's next election. Bonuses, salaries, and promotions are too often dependent on this year's increase over last year."

Julian Scheer, a senior vice president of LTV Corporation had this to say. "In a number of our biggest companies, you have men who have risen for years through the ranks, and then have a very short stewardship as chief executive officers [CEOs]. They try to deal with long-range problems in the short term. They want to demonstrate to their directors, their stockholders, and the financial community that this year's rate of growth is as projected, that they'll meet this year's targets this year. What gets lost is the strategy that will take the company over 25 or 30 years."

In the long run it is probably good that experts are challenging the accounting profession. Such criticism serves as a revitalization stimulator.

Questions for Discussion

1. Do you agree that we have become a nation of "paper pushers"? If so, what can we do to reverse the trend? If you don't agree, explain why.

2. What can we do to funnel the nation's brains into more productive channels?

3. How can we change accounting practices to encourage management to become more long-range minded? (This question is excellent for posing to professional accountants!)

4. Evaluate the short-stewardship phenomenon of CEOs.

---

*All quotes from James Fallows, "American Industry," The Atlantic, October 1980.
†Pricing that doesn't bring in a profit until after a strong foothold is gained in the market.

profession was in 1896, when the State of New York passed a law providing for the certification of public accountants. By 1925 all states had enacted similar laws.

Today, approximately 265,000 accountants in professional practice have earned the designation of **certified public accountant (CPA)**. *A CPA has passed the Uniform CPA examination, satisfied other educational and professional requirements, and been licensed to practice public accounting.*

The CPA certificate is issued by the State Board of Accountancy found in each state. Specific requirements for becoming a CPA vary. Most states require CPAs to be college graduates, and have at least two years of accounting experience. All states require that the CPA applicant pass an examination administered by the American Institute of Certified Public Accountants.[1] Subjects covered in the examination include theory of accounting, practical accounting, auditing, and commercial law.

A growing number of states require CPAs to complete a certain number of hours in continuing-education courses related to their profession before they can renew their licenses.

Accounting has many facets. Some accountants concentrate on highly specialized tax preparation; others serve as bank examiners; still others work for only one industry segment, such as retail trade or heavy industry.

Accounting Is Specialized by Function and Industry

Accounting is highly specialized by function and industry. Taxes are so complex and varied that some accounting firms do only tax work, such as the approximately 8,000 franchises of widely known H & R Block.

Industry differences can be as great as functional differences. Retail accounting differs markedly from manufacturing accounting. For instance, different regulations, taxes, and methods of calculating apply in accounting for chain store inventories compared to manufacturing inventories. Consequently, if a steel company planned to employ an accountant, it would look for someone with accounting experience in steel or a related industry. Likewise, a department store would look for an accountant with substantial experience in retail accounting.

Federal, state, and city governments employ many accountants who are part of a civil service system. They audit tax returns, act as bank examiners, and handle government payrolls and expenses.

What Are Public Accountants?

Public accountants are *independent organizations or individuals that specialize in selling accounting services to businesses.* They are

---

[1]Specific information about becoming a CPA can be obtained from the American Institute of Certified Public Accountants, 1211 Avenue of the Americas, New York, N.Y. 10036.

commonly retained by businesses to help with the more difficult phases of accounting, especially with the preparation of tax returns, which the IRS may audit (see Table 17-2), and with company audits.

TABLE 17-2 What Are the Chances that the IRS Will Audit a Corporate Tax Return?

SIZE OF CORPORATION (ASSETS)	PERCENT OF RETURNS EXAMINED 1984	1979
Under $100,000	4.68%	4.19%
$100,000 to $1M	8.31	7.94
$1M to $10M	20.62	21.41
$10M to $100M	33.17	34.29
$100M or more	86.66	83.59

SOURCE: Internal Revenue Service.

Public accounting firms are increasingly expanding their services into other areas. For example, Touche Ross & Company, a leading accounting firm, performs the following management consulting functions for its clients:

- Management information systems
- Design and planning of computer systems
- Corporate strategic planning
- Manufacturing analysis and control
- Financial and budgetary control
- Marketing analysis and control
- Profit improvement through cost reduction[2]

These nonaccounting services are one of the fastest-growing activities of the profession. The Securities and Exchange Commission estimates that these functions amount to 10 to 20 percent of a major accounting firm's business.

Criticism of Accountants in Top Management

Accountants are becoming increasingly important in top management, but harsh critics charge that managers with accounting backgrounds offer negative leadership and base decisions on past performance. One critic goes so far as to blame the accounting mentality

---

[2]*Touche Ross and Its People* (a company recruiting brochure), 11.

(often called "bottom-line thinking," referring to the profit line found at the bottom of the income statement) for loss of the country's competitive leadership. He said, "The idea of protecting success has got to go. It makes managers into custodians of the past instead of midwives to the future. To get back on the right path, the country's corporations are going to have to scrap some assumptions... such as... the idea that accountants can guide companies to the future. Every venture throughout history that succeeded in raising us another notch over the animals involved the kind of risk no self-respecting accountant would ever approve."[3]

THE ACCOUNTING PROCESS

The **accounting process** is *the progression of financial data through the following steps:*

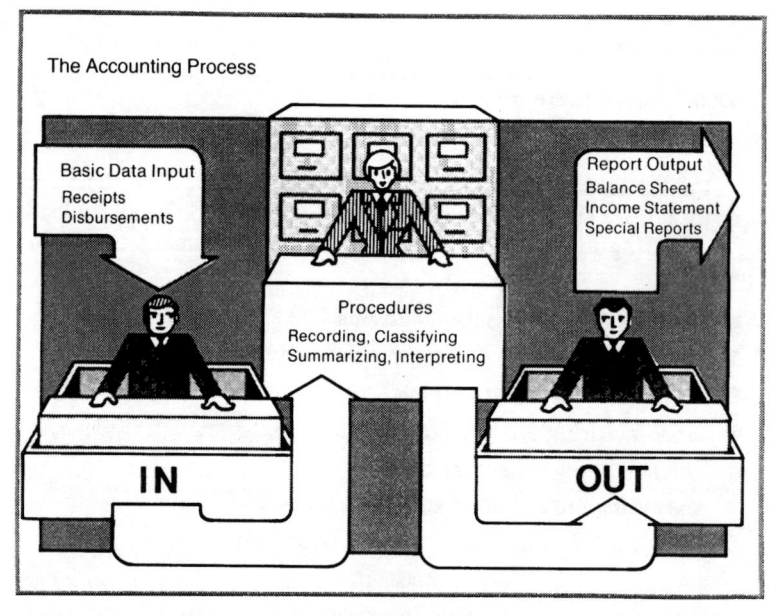

The Accounting Process

Basic Data Input
Receipts
Disbursements

Procedures
Recording, Classifying
Summarizing, Interpreting

Report Output
Balance Sheet
Income Statement
Special Reports

IN   OUT

Receipts are *monies paid into the company;* **disbursements** are *what is paid out. All transactions are recorded in chronological order* in **journals.** Entries into journals are made by hand or recorded in computers.

Increasingly, computers record, classify, and summarize transactions (see Chapter 19). For example, in mechanized banking, when a customer makes a deposit at a branch bank, the teller who uses a machine to record the new balance in the customer's bankbook is

---

[3]Murray Hillman, president of strategy workshop, Interpublic Group of Companies; quoted in the *New York Times,* October 30, 1980.

recording the deposit simultaneously on the customer's account ledger at the branch bank and at the bank's central office. Thus, at the close of each day, a bank with 37 branches will have a summary of deposits and withdrawals for each branch bank, as well as for the bank as a whole.

ACCOUNTING STATEMENTS

Accounting is sometimes called the language of business. Accountants communicate key accounting information to management, investors, and government agencies in the form of accounting statements and reports. The most important of these are the balance sheet and the income statement, which provide the overall financial picture of the business.

What Is a Balance Sheet?

A **balance sheet** *shows the financial status of a business at a specific time,* and it changes with each day's business activity. Accountants, therefore, prepare it as of a specific date, usually the last day of the year. The balance sheet *indicates the assets, liabilities, and equity of the owners of the business*—what the business owns and what it owes. A sample balance sheet appears in Figure 17-1.

ASSETS

Assets are *the various items of value—property or resources—the business has:* cash, merchandise, land, equipment, patent rights, and so on. On the balance sheet, assets are ordinarily classified into current, fixed, and investment assets.

Assets of The Sofa Factory include not only this truck and others, but the contents of the trucks and all the items listed.

Current assets. **Current assets** include *cash and items such as inventories and merchandise on hand that the business will convert into cash in less than one year.* Money that customers and others (called **accounts receivable** or **notes receivable**) owe the company, less allowances for doubtful accounts, is also a current asset. In Figure 17-1, total current assets are $238,600.

Fixed assets. **Fixed assets** are *items used for long periods of time.* Examples are land, buildings, equipment, and machinery. Fixed assets ordinarily decrease in value (depreciate) each year. A typewriter valued at $1,000 when new may depreciate at a rate of 10 percent, or $100, each year. When three years old, the machine would appear on the balance sheet as a fixed asset worth $700. In Figure 17-1, total fixed assets are $188,400.

Investment assets. **Investment assets** are *funds invested in the securities of other businesses for income or to control the second company.* Investment assets usually appear separately on the balance sheet. In Figure 17-1, investment assets are $6,000.

Figure 17-1 A Sample Balance Sheet

ASSETS

Current assets
Cash		$ 30,000
Accounts receivable	$ 42,000	
Less allowance for doubtful accounts	1,600	40,400
Notes receivable		6,000
Merchandise inventory		152,400
Prepaid insurance		3,400
Prepaid rent		6,400
Total current assets		$238,600

Fixed assets
Equipment	$ 37,200		
Less accumulated depreciation	6,800	$ 30,400	
Buildings	$176,000		
Less accumulated depreciation	42,000	134,000	
Land		24,000	
Total fixed assets			188,400

Investments (permanent)
Stock in American Supply Company	6,000

Intangible assets
Good will	20,000
Total assets	$453,000

LIABILITIES AND STOCKHOLDERS' EQUITY

Liabilities

Current liabilities
Accounts payable	$ 54,000	
Notes payable	6,200	
Accrued wages payable	5,200	
Accrued taxes payable	3,400	
Accrued interest payable	1,640	
Other expenses now payable	2,200	
Total current liabilities		$ 72,640

Long-term liabilities
Mortgage payable		80,000
Total liabilities		$152,640

Owners' equity

Common stock
(2,000 shares at $100 par value each)	$200,000	
Retained income	100,360	300,360
Total liabilities and stockholders' equity		$453,000

Intangible assets. *Assets that do not have tangible form but are of value to the business are* **intangible assets.** Examples include patents, franchises, copyrights, trademarks, and goodwill. **Goodwill** refers to *the valuation the company puts on its public acceptance, established brand names, and similar factors.*

LIABILITIES

Liabilities are *the money a company owes to bankers, employees, suppliers, holders of bonds, and other creditors.* Liabilities are either current or long-term.

Current liabilities. **Current liabilities** are *short-term debts that a company must pay in less than one year.* Short-term bank loans, employees' wages earned but not yet paid, interest on debts, and taxes are examples of current liabilities. *Money owed to suppliers,* called **accounts payable** on the balance sheet, is a current liability. In Figure 17-1, current liabilities are $72,640.

Long-term liabilities. **Long-term liabilities,** often called **fixed liabilities,** are *debts that extend over more than one year.* Examples are mortgages, bonds, and long-term notes. In Figure 17-1, long-term liabilities are $80,000 and total liabilities are $152,640.

Equity and the Meaning of "Balance"

The equity section of the balance sheet shows the **owners' equity** (*right to share in the assets of the business*). Basic to accounting is an understanding of the equation:

$$\text{Assets} - \text{liabilities} = \text{owners' equity}$$

In Figure 17-1, owners' equity is $300,360 (assets of $453,000 − liabilities of $152,640).

The equation can also be stated as follows:

$$\text{Assets} = \text{liabilities} + \text{owners' equity}$$

In conventional accounting, assets appear on the left-hand side of the balance sheet and liabilities and equity on the right. The totals of each column are always equal. Any change in an asset is always reflected in a corresponding change in either a liability account or in the equity section—hence the term "balance."

What Is an Income Statement?

An **income statement,** also called a **profit-and-loss statement,** is a second essential financial summary. It is *a detailed summary of business operations over a specific period of time.* Accountants prepare such statements monthly or quarterly, in contrast to the yearly preparation of the balance sheet.

The income statement is important to a business, since it indicates specific operating expenses and reveals reasons for a profit or loss. The formula for determining profit or loss is:

$$\text{Net sales} - \text{cost of goods sold} - \text{operating and administrative expenses} = \text{profit or loss}$$

A sample income statement is shown in Figure 17-2.

Operating Income

The income section shows *money the company received for goods sold minus returns and allowances and discounts given to purchas-*

Figure 17-2 A Sample Income Statement

```
BROWN WHOLESALE HARDWARE COMPANY
            Income Statement
           December 31, 19——
```

Income from sales			
Gross sales		$769,200	
Less returns and allowances		7,600	
Net sales			$761,600
Cost of goods sold			
Less merchandise inventory, January 1, 19——		$276,000	
Purchases	$385,640		
Less purchase returns and allowances	5,200		
Net purchases		380,440	
Cost of merchandise available for sale		$656,440	
Less merchandise inventory, December 31, 19——		192,400	
Cost of goods sold			464,040
Gross profit on sales			$297,560
Operating expenses			
Selling expenses			
Salaries and commissions	$105,220		
Advertising	9,000		
Delivery expense	18,400		
Total selling expenses		$132,620	
Administrative expenses			
Salaries and wages	$42,000		
Bad debts	2,200		
Depreciation on building	5,600		
Depreciation on equipment	1,580		
Supplies used	3,800		
Utilities	4,200		
Total administrative expenses		59,380	
Total operating and administrative expenses			192,000
Net profit from operations			$105,560

ers. The result is called **net sales** or **net income,** and is the **operating income** of the business. In Figure 17-2, net sales are $761,600.

COST OF GOODS SOLD

We compute the cost of goods sold *by adding the cost of inventory at the beginning of the period and the net cost of goods manufactured or purchased during the period; then we subtract from this the total cost of inventory at the end of the period.* We then subtract the cost of goods sold from the net sales figure. The result is the **gross**

profit on sales. In Figure 17–2, the cost of goods sold is $464,040. This figure subtracted from net sales equals $297,560.

OPERATING AND ADMINISTRATIVE EXPENSES
The income statement shows all expenses incurred in the operation of a business. This is the sum of **operating expenses** (*expenses incurred in the course of specific business activities;* here, expenses for selling) and **administrative,** or **general, expenses** (*expenses related to the enterprise as a whole*).

The advantage of breaking down operating expenses is that the firm can make a comparison between items of expense. The purpose is to measure efficiency. Thus, the company can compare its results with those of other companies.

In Figure 17–2, operating expenses ($132,620) and administrative expenses ($59,380) total $192,000.

NET PROFIT OR LOSS
To arrive at **net profit** or **loss** (called the "bottom line" in accounting jargon), we simply apply the formula shown earlier. In this case: net sales − cost = profits.

Net		$761,600
Cost of goods sold	464,040	
Operating expenses	132,620	
Administrative expenses	59,380	
	656,040	
Gross Operating Profit		$105,560

If costs had been greater than net sales, the income statement would have shown a loss instead of a profit.

WHAT IS RATIO ANALYSIS?
Ratio analysis is *the use of ratios or percentages to compare operating results with previous periods and similar companies.* Five important ratios follow.

1. *Pretax profit margin* is the ratio of profit, before interest and taxes, to sales. We express it as a percentage of sales and find it dividing the operating profit by sales.
2. *Current (working-capital) ratio* is the ratio of current assets to current liabilities. A two-for-one ratio is the standard. A gradual increase in the current ratio usually is a sign of improved financial strength.
3. *Liquidity ratio,* also called *acid-test ratio,* is the ratio of cash to total current liabilities. It results from dividing cash and equivalent by total current liabilities. This ratio is important as a supplement to the current ratio because it indicates the ability of a company to meet current obligations.

4. *Sales to fixed assets* is computed by dividing the annual sales by the value before depreciation and amortization of plant, equipment, and land at the end of the year. The ratio helps indicate whether funds used to enlarge productive facilities are being spent wisely.

5. *Net income to net worth,* one of the most significant of all financial ratios, is derived by dividing net income by the total of stock and surplus accounts (that is, money held in reserve). It answers the question, "How much is the company earning on the stockholders' investment?" Naturally, a large and increasing ratio is favorable.

COST ACCOUNTING AND STANDARD COSTS

Emphasis on business efficiency has led to wide use of **cost accounting,** or **cost analysis,** which *determines what it costs to handle an average order, produce a single unit of a product, sell a single unit, or even write a business letter by prorating all fixed and variable expenses to the single activities being studied.* Thus, if a firm wants to know how much it costs to produce a pair of shoes, it allocates the costs incurred for labor, materials, supplies, wear and tear on machinery, tools, rent, interest on borrowed money, and other expenses to the type of shoe produced. The total amount, divided by the number of shoes produced, gives the cost of a single pair of shoes. A manufacturer must know production costs in order to set the selling price high enough to cover costs and provide a profit.

To make cost accounting particularly valuable, accountants compute **standard costs** for activities studied. Standard costs *indicate what the cost of an activity should be:* cost accounting reveals what it *actually* costs to perform the operation. If actual costs exceed the standard costs, the firm should investigate in order to determine if workers are inefficient, materials are wasted, and so on. By using standard costing, management has a yardstick for controlling expenses.

AUDITING

Auditing is *a specialized branch of accounting concerned with verifying accounting records and practices and reviewing the validity of accounting decisions.* For example, if an auditor, on examining depreciation procedures, feels that the company is not depreciating certain assets at the proper rate, he or she may refuse to certify the accuracy of the company accounts.

Any of three groups may make audits: *internal auditors,* who are employees of the company; *independent public accountants,* who are retained to audit the firm's accounts; and *government auditors.*

The public accountant verifies business records that involve the actual counting of cash, determination of the value of assets, and verification of inventories. The public accountant certifies that in his or her opinion the accounting statements fairly present the financial position of the company as of a certain date.

Government auditors include bank examiners, who audit the accounts of banks; auditors of the Interstate Commerce Commission, who examine the books of public transportation agencies; and auditors of the Internal Revenue Service, who audit business records to verify tax reports. The General Accounting Office (GAO) is the official auditing branch of the government. The feature "How the nation's largest auditing agency operates," page 517, explains how the GAO works.

> **One accurate measurement is worth a thousand expert opinions.**
>
> UTVICH'S OBSERVATION

THE ANNUAL REPORT

The Securities and Exchange Commission requires publicly held companies in the United States to issue an **annual report**.[4] The annual report, *prepared as of the close of each fiscal year, includes a balance sheet, income statement, and verification from an independent auditor that it is accurate.* It usually also includes a president's letter, a list of directors and officers, plus other information.

A great deal of effort goes into the report because of (1) stringent SEC regulations, (2) guidelines laid down by the **Financial Accounting Standards Board** (the **FASB** is *the accounting profession's private sector standard-setting and rule-making body*), and (3) stock exchange requirements, if company stock is listed. Annual reports are important public relations tools that build image and provide product and financial data for shareholders, analysts, customers, and investors. Annual reports spring to life when we study them to see how readers can profit from them (see Table 17–3).

Social Auditing

Since the early 1970s, experts have discussed the notion that companies should include some kind of a social audit in annual reports. As a result, reports of about half of 120 corporations *Business Week*

---

[4]A word of caution is in order when reading financial and other numerical statements from non-American sources. Internationally, the meaning of words used for large numbers differs widely. The terms "billion" and "trillion," which are becoming increasingly relevant in these days of high inflation and the Space Age, have markedly different meanings. In the United States, one billion is a thousand million. This meaning differs in Great Britain and many other countries. The British and French, for example, use the term "milliard" for our "billion." "Billion" is a term the British use to mean a million million. To avoid misunderstandings, when terms such as "billion" and "trillion" are used with non-Americans, it is prudent to have all figures above 1 million written out as numbers. We suggest consulting numbers tables, sometimes included in large dictionaries, for clarifications of this easily complicated subject.

TABLE 17-3 How to Benefit from Reading Annual Reports

- *If you are an investor*—Review the report to decide whether the company is a good one in which to invest, in terms of your investment goals. Will an investment in company stock yield steady dividends? Or is the company geared to growth in stock value?
- *If you are a supplier*—Note how it can help members of your sales staff who call on the company to adjust their sales pitch to this potential customer's plans and activities.
- *If you are a business student*—You can realistically learn a great deal by following the fortunes of favorite companies by means of their annual reports.
- *If you are a job seeker*—You can decide whether a company has a bright future. If so, you can apply for a job and have confidence that you'll do well in the interview, since you'll know something about the company.
- *If you are a competitor*—It would be foolhardy if you failed to carefully follow the fortunes of your competitors by this readily available means.
- *If you are a banker*—Studying annual reports of companies in the area your bank serves alerts you to business opportunities and enables you to make forecasts helpful to both your management and your customers.
- *If you are a shareholder*—You'll want to follow the course of the company in which you share ownership—to decide whether to hold, sell, or expand your holdings.
- *If you are an employee*—You'll want to be informed about your employer. Morale is higher when employees are well informed about their company.
- *If you are a government official*—It will be refreshing for you and citizens you deal with if you know something about the business in the area of your jurisdiction. You can facilitate the idea that government and business working together will build a stronger economic base for the country.

surveyed in 1979 carried corporate social responsibility sections. **Social auditing** *tends to cover such things as social goals, energy conservation, ethics, safety, minority employment, and community activities.*

Most social responsibility reporting so far has been descriptive. Experts have attempted to measure, or quantify, social costs and benefits. After a four-year study, the American Institute of Certified

Public Accountants published suggestions on quantification. The Department of Commerce also expressed an interest in developing "procedures that would enable a corporation to judge its own social performance" on a voluntary basis.

Social auditing has gotten off to a slow start in the United States; in Europe, especially in Germany, social auditing is more advanced. The process should be viewed as something more than a public-relations exercise. Done conscientiously, and not just as a public-relations exercise, social auditing can help counteract antibusiness sentiment. Further, it can defuse pressures that lead to government control and restrictive legislation.

Some Criticize Auditing by Public Accountants

Typically, public accountants who serve the company in a tax preparation capacity and in other ways as well prepare financial statements included in the company annual report and supplied to the Securities and Exchange Commission and the IRS.

Critics claim this practice may result in financial statements

---

AMERICA'S REEMERGING CREATIVITY

How the Nation's Largest Auditing Agency Operates

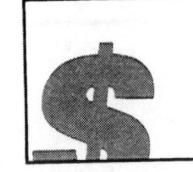

The GAO is by far the largest auditing organization in the nation and employs approximately 6,000 people, 4,200 of whom are professional staffers. About 70 percent of the professional staff members were trained in accounting or auditing. The other 30 percent are engineers, economists, mathematicians, statisticians, and computer specialists.

The General Accounting Office has the following basic purposes: to assist the Congress, its committees, and its Members in carrying out their legislative and oversight responsibilities, consistent with its role as an independent nonpolitical agency in the legislative branch; to carry out legal, accounting, auditing, and claims settlement function with respect to Federal Government programs and operations as assigned by the Congress; and to make recommendations designed to provide for more efficient and effective Government operations.

In general, the audit authority of the General Accounting Office extends to all departments and agencies of the Federal Government. Exceptions to this audit authority relate principally to funds relating to certain intelligence activities.

Where audit authority exists the General Accounting Office has the right of access to, and examination of, any books, documents, papers, or records of the departments and agencies.

The General Accounting Office has statutory authority to investigate all matters relating to the receipt, disbursement, and application of public funds. Additionally, GAO's audit authority covers wholly and partially owned Government corporations and certain nonappropriated fund activities. By law, it is authorized and directed to make expenditure analyses of executive agencies to enable the Congress to determine whether public funds are efficiently and economically administered and expended; and to review and evaluate the results of existing Government programs and activities.

The scope of the audit work of the General Accounting Office extends not only to the programs and activities which the Federal Government itself conducts but also to the activities of State and local governments, quasi-governmental bodies, and private organizations in their capacity as recipients under, or administrators for Federal aid programs financed by loans, advances, grants, and contributions.

GAO's audit activities also include examining and settling accounts of the Federal Government's certifying, disbursing, and collection officers, including determinations involving accountability for improper or illegal expenditures of public funds.

Within this audit authority is a responsibility to report significant matters to the Congress for information and use in carrying out its legislative and executive branch surveillance functions.*

Questions

1. The GAO is the official auditing agency of the federal government. Intentionally the agency maintains a low profile and its activities are not widely publicized. In your opinion is this good or bad? Why?

2. In virtually every political campaign the public hears charges of government inefficiency, corruption, and waste. Considering the size and power of the GAO, are these accusations likely to be valid or not? Explain.

3. To help control fraud and abuse in federal programs the GAO maintains a nationwide hotline which permits any taxpayer to call GAO auditors with information concerning misuse of federal funds. Do you think this is a good idea?

*The United States Government Manual 1982/83, Office of the Registrar, National Archives and Records Services, Washington, D.C., 1983, 41–44.

SOURCE: David Schwartz, Introduction to Management, 2nd ed., Harcourt Brace Jovanovich, 1983, 526.

---

that are not objective because the company-paid auditor may render an ostensibly independent judgment on procedures he or she previously recommended to the company. For example, questionable payments by Exxon, Lockheed, Boeing, and other companies to officials in foreign countries went "undetected" by public accountants who served as auditors for these companies.

One recommendation is that auditors should not serve the same firm they are auditing in any other capacity—such as providing tax or other advice. This solution would be expensive. However, preservation of the integrity of public accountants is to the advantage of business, the investing public, and the accounting profession.

WHAT IS BUDGETING?

A **budget** is *a financial forecast or plan that shows expected income and expenditures over a given period of time.* Expressed another way, the budget is the quantification of future plans. Usually prepared one year in advance, it shows details of both anticipated income and anticipated expenditures. If income equals expenditures, we say that the budget is balanced. If receipts are more than expenditures, a surplus results; if receipts are less than expenditures, a deficit results. Since the early 1980s, the U.S. Congress has been debating the merits of a constitutional amendment that would require a balanced federal budget. The Issue for Debate on pages 520–521 discusses the pros and cons of such an amendment.

What Does a Budget Accomplish?

Budgets help managers in three ways. First, they guide managers in planning business operations. When a budget forecasts expected revenue or estimates for a given period, the managers can plan expenditures.

Second, a budget sets goals and limits for outlays for raw materials, advertising, labor, and so forth. When sales managers know they have a fixed amount for traveling and entertainment expenses during a period of time, they plan to stay within those limits. Without the budget, management would never know whether the departments within the business were overspending or underspending.

Third, preparing a budget requires company executives to review their operations critically to eliminate waste and inefficiency. When they present their case for a new budget, they must justify their requests—a soul-searching experience.

Key People Should Help Prepare the Budget

Key people from each department, often members of a formally established budget committee, participate in budget preparation. Of course, the chief executive ultimately must approve the budget.

"Now, this over here, this is why you're going to have to go to jail."

The overall budget is actually a group of subbudgets, one for each department or functional activity within the business. The sales budget shows the total expected sales volume, which may be broken down by commodities sold, territories covered, or similar factors. This budget is generally the most important of the subbudgets, for all other plans relate to the revenue sales receives.

Other budgets include the advertising budget, which specifies the amount to be spent for advertising, and the production budget, which shows the number of units expected to be produced. Often companies also make a cash flow budget, a forecast of expected cash intakes and outlays.

When the overall budget is complete, each department receives a performance goal, sometimes called a "quota." Then funds are allocated to accomplish the various tasks.

A Budget Should Be Flexible

A budget is a guide, not a hard and fast rule. Business is dynamic, and frequently conditions change before the budget period expires. A rise in the price of raw materials, for example, will necessitate a budgetary adjustment. New competition may make it desirable to spend additional funds for advertising. Wisdom dictates that companies reconsider their budgets as conditions change.

ISSUE FOR DEBATE

Is a Balanced Federal Budget Amendment Needed?

In 1982 the Senate passed a hotly debated and proposed constitutional amendment requiring Congress to adopt a balanced budget. However, it fell short of the required two-thirds vote in the House. The amendment's major provisions called for:

- Congress to adopt a balanced budget before the beginning of each fiscal year. Expenditures could exceed revenue only if both houses of Congress so authorized by three-fifth majorities of the full membership;
- Limits in tax increases by the amount of economic growth; and
- A waiver of these provisions by a simple majority vote in both houses for any year in which a declaration of war is in effect.

Even though Congress defeated the amendment, the debate is not over. Thirty-one of the required 34 states have called for a constitutional convention to consider a balanced budget amendment. Following are some of the pros and cons of this issue.

PROS

The federal budget has been balanced only once in the past 25 years. The resulting deficits have resulted in a national debt of more than $2 trillion in 1985. A balanced budget amendment is needed to stop the growth of the national debt.

When government spending exceeds government revenues, Congress is simply passing on debts to the next generation. This action is unfair.

Huge budget deficits are the primary cause of inflation, high interest rates, and unemployment. We cannot spend our way to solid prosperity.

In the short run, excessive spending (spending more than the government takes in) for social programs may win elections, but, in the long run, it creates economic problems.

Unless we make efforts to balance the budget, the economy will go bankrupt, a deep and prolonged depression will result, and the private enterprise system may collapse. Proponents of a balanced budget amendment argue that the amendment would force Congress to be more disciplined, would pinpoint accountability, and would facilitate a focus on a few critical spending measures rather than on the hundreds now considered each year.

CONS

A balanced budget amendment would represent an abdication of responsibility by the supporters of the amendment. It would demean the authority and respect of the Constitution. Congress should not have its hands tied in deciding budgeting matters.

The best way to achieve a balanced budget is through a vigorous and growing economy. High profits and high incomes that result from a prosperous economy will generate the money needed to balance the budget. But if we are in a recession, Congress needs authority to borrow money to stimulate economic activity.

When the economy is weak, higher expenditures are needed for unemployment compensation and public assistance for those in need. This means deficit financing is necessary.

Efforts by Congress to balance the budget during severe recessions either by cutting expenses or raising taxes would only deepen the recession.

A balanced budget amendment would be a straightjacket. What is needed is a disciplined Congress which pursues policies to (a) stimulate the economy and (b) reduce deficits. The proposed constitutional amendment would take away the flexibility Congress needs to make the economy attain positive goals.

Questions

1. In principle, do you favor a balanced budget amendment? Why or why not?
2. Do you believe ratification of a balanced budget amendment is likely in the next decade? Why or why not?

SUMMARY

- Accounting tells managers how well a business is doing in terms of dollars. Accounting is much broader than bookkeeping.
- Properly performed, accounting helps management to make decisions. It also aids business in borrowing capital, informing owners of how well the business is doing, and meeting government requirements.
- Accounting is a professional field. To earn the designation CPA (certified public accountant), an accountant must pass an extensive examination and meet other requirements.
- Public accounting firms are increasingly expanding their services to include management consulting, market research, and computer system design.
- The accounting process is the progression of financial data through the following steps: basic data input, procedures, and record output.
- Two key accounting statements are the balance sheet and the income statement. Together they provide an overall financial picture of the business.
- Ratio analysis is the use of percentages to compare the operating results with previous periods and with similar companies.
- Cost accounting and standard costs are two tools that accountants use to study business efficiency.
- Auditing is a specialized branch of accounting concerned with verifying accounting records and practices.
- The annual report of a company gives valuable information about the company's operations.
- Accountants help set budgets for the business. A budget serves as a guide in planning business operations; sets limits for the purchase of materials, supplies, and services; and causes managers to think more critically about the business.

KEY TERMS YOU SHOULD KNOW

accounting
accounting process
accounts payable
accounts receivable
administrative expense
annual report
asset
auditing
balance sheet
bookkeeping
budget
certified public accountant
cost accounting
current asset
current liability
disbursement
Financial Accounting Standards Board
fixed asset
goodwill
gross profit on sales
income statement
intangible asset
investment asset
journal
liability
long-term liability
net profit or loss
net sales
operating expense
operating income
owners' equity
public accountant
ratio analysis
receipt
social auditing
standard cost

QUESTIONS FOR REVIEW

1. Why is accounting, as a profession, increasing in importance?
2. Accountants are business scorekeepers and game planners as well. Explain.
3. How can accountants help minimize taxes?
4. How does tax legislation relate to planning for social welfare?
5. What is "IRS Roulette"? What is the IRS doing to stop it?
6. Besides giving advice on how to minimize taxes, how does accounting serve business?
7. Why is accounting considered a professional field?
8. What steps are involved in the accounting process?
9. What are the basic elements of a balance sheet?
10. What is an income statement? What is its purpose?
11. Explain ratio analysis. What are the five most important accounting ratios?
12. What is cost accounting? How do cost accounting and standard costs relate?
13. Explain auditing. Who does auditing? What does the GAO do?
14. What is an annual report? Why do businesses prepare them?
15. What is budgeting? What goals does setting a budget accomplish?

QUESTIONS FOR DISCUSSION

1. Are tax laws likely to be more complex in the future? Why or why not?
2. Both the tax paid and the tax rate increase as one's income increases. Do you think this is fair?
3. For a generation, politicians have promised "tax simplification." Yet each new tax law is more complicated than the law it replaces. How do you explain this gap between political promises and political action?
4. Are accountants likely to have a larger voice in top management in the future? Why or why not?
5. Do you think corporations should pay higher income taxes? Why or why not?
6. Large companies employ more accountants than small companies do. Yet, the more assets a corporation has, the more likely the IRS will audit the company's tax returns. How do you account for this?
7. There are two ways the government can balance the budget: reduce spending or increase taxes. Which method do you prefer?

CASE STUDY

How to Increase Your Net Worth

Pete and Sheila Johnson, in their mid-20s, have been married three years. Both have full-time jobs and earn a "good" joint income. They have a common problem: They can't save money. Like many people, they live from paycheck to paycheck. Sheila decides to attend a Saturday seminar on money management sponsored by a local college.

On Sunday, the following discussion takes place between Pete and Sheila.

Sheila: The instructor showed us how to compute our net worth. I was shocked to discover how little we own. Aside from some equity in the cars and some furniture, we're broke.

Pete: But we live well. We've got nice clothes, we eat out a lot, and we take a short holiday every month or two.

S: I know. But suppose you or I had an accident or for some other reason couldn't work.

P: That's pretty unlikely. We're young, healthy, and well educated.

S: That's true. But there are other reasons we should save money and put it to work making more money. Someday we'll need money for a down payment on a home. And if we go ahead with our plan to have a couple of children, we'll need even more money.

P: But our incomes will increase. That's how we'll get the money to buy a house and afford the kids.

S: I disagree. Each of us has had two pay increases in the past two years, and we have nothing to show for them.

P: Well, you're the one who attended the money management seminar. Did you pick up any ideas?

S: One strong recommendation the instructor made is so simple that it might work for us. He said pay yourself first. Before you pay the landlord or the car note or the credit-card company, put some money aside for your future.

P: How much did he recommend paying oneself?

S: At least 15 percent of your take-home pay, ideally 20 percent.

P: That's a lot. In our case, I don't see how we could do it and not cut way back on our standard of living.

S: The instructor used an example that makes sense to me. He said if the government raised taxes by 15 percent, we'd figure out a way to spend less because we simply would have less to spend. The same point applies to the pay-yourself-first formula. We would force ourselves to spend less. And we would increase our net worth every month.

P: I'm willing to give the pay-yourself-first plan a try. Who knows, a personal austerity program might even be fun!

Questions

1. Do you think that it is practical for the average American family or individual to save 15 percent of take-home pay? Why or why not?

2. What are five specific actions that Pete and Sheila could take to get by on a 15-percent-less spendable income?

EVOLUTION OF A BUSINESS

Analyzing Figures to Produce Efficiencies

Travel agency income is derived from commissions. Airlines pay agencies 7 percent of the ticket price on domestic flights and about 10 percent on overseas flights. Hotels pay anywhere from 5 to 20 percent, with the average at about 10 percent. Other commissions are derived, of course, from almost everything else the agency books for clients—car rentals, boat trips, admissions, and so on. Fees to governments for visas and passports earn no commissions.

Sara: I've started to analyze the profitability figures for individual clients. It's about as we expected so far. Travelers going overseas usually produce more income for us than those traveling domestically. And travelers who buy packages—hotels, car rentals, and so on along with their transportation—are the most profitable.

Ray: Have you figured out specifically which packages are most profitable?

Sara: I'm working on it. I thought I'd develop a list of the things that are most profitable to sell and discuss them at our next staff meeting. We should be pushing those things and maybe consider eliminating some of the others.

Ray: Change our product mix, in marketing terms.

Sara: Right. Also, I've been keeping a record of the number of phone calls the company gets and makes each hour. And I've tallied the number of people who visit our office each hour. You know we've been staying open until 9:00 P.M. on Thursdays and Fridays. So far, from the records of phone calls and office visits, I don't think the expense of keeping open those extra late hours is justified. I've noticed only a slight increasing trend in business during those hours as the weeks go by.

Questions

1. What can be done to improve the product mix that customers buy?
2. What might be the negative repercussions if Excel tried to change the product mix it offers to its clients?
3. What are your feelings about a travel agency staying open after 6:00 P.M.? Should statistics alone be the basis for deciding whether to stay open or not?
4. What other kinds of figures might it be worthwhile to analyze?

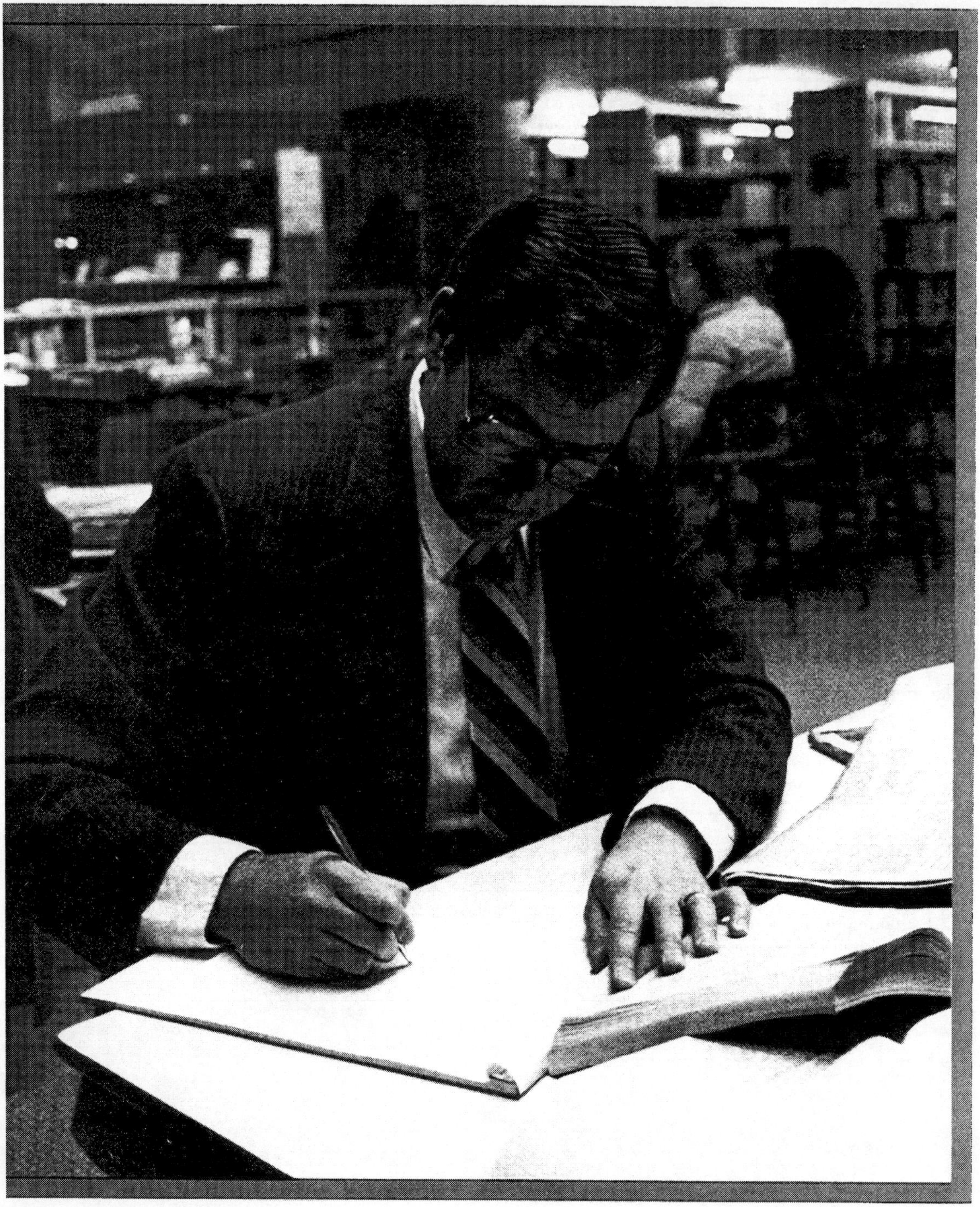

18

BUSINESS INFORMATION AND RESEARCH
Who? What? Where? When? Why? How?

READ THIS CHAPTER SO YOU CAN:

Define business research and explain why it is important.

Detail the steps in the research procedure, and explain the three main methods for collecting data.

Discuss the main sources of business information.

Describe the three most important types of averages, price indexes, and sampling.

Explain how tables and graphic devices are used in the presentation of statistics.

Understand the basic principles of report writing.

Research is the fact-finding arm of business. As a businessman, Norton Simon parlayed a $7,000 investment in a bankrupt orange juice plant into a $1 billion conglomerate that produces everything from catsup (Hunt-Wesson) to soft drinks (Canada Dry) to designer clothing (Halston). Simon, now retired, has also assembled one of the world's greatest private art collections. People who have worked with him often remark on one of his outstanding characteristics: *"He always gets all the facts before making a move."*

WHAT IS BUSINESS RESEARCH?

Business research is *the orderly gathering and interpretation of information that people need to make successful business decisions.* We can also think of it as a planned procedure for discovering solutions to business problems.

Figure 18–1 shows trends in total research and development expenditures between 1960 and 1980. Although engineering and technical research for product and production improvement do play an important role in business, in this chapter we will consider only research business people, economists, and business-oriented social scientists perform.

Research can be formal or informal. Gene Street is a proponent of informal research. A 39-year-old Texan, he has a $16-million restaurant business with about 700 employees, a 24 percent pretax profit, and an average growth rate for 1977–80 of about 100 percent.[1] He started his business when he couldn't get a job after graduating from college. He explains his success by saying that any business must satisfy the masses and ride trends. And the only way to discover what trends are popular is through market research. How does he do research? "I drive around town and look at the lines in front of places. I find out a lot talking to vendors. I ask the bread guy how many boxes of buns the drive-in down the street is buying. That's the way I research my market." Although informal research can provide helpful input for the alert manager, it is inclined to be haphazard. In this chapter we'll discuss formal research based on the scientific method.

How Does Intelligence Fit In?

Intelligence is the capacity to learn, to understand, to deal with new situations, and to think abstractly. Intelligence is important in generating ideas and making decisions, but being a genius is not. Ray Kroc sold milkshake mixing machines before buying the six-store McDonald's fast food chain and developing it into the international success

---

[1]*INC.*, November 1980.

Figure 18–1 Research and Development Funds: 1970 to 1984

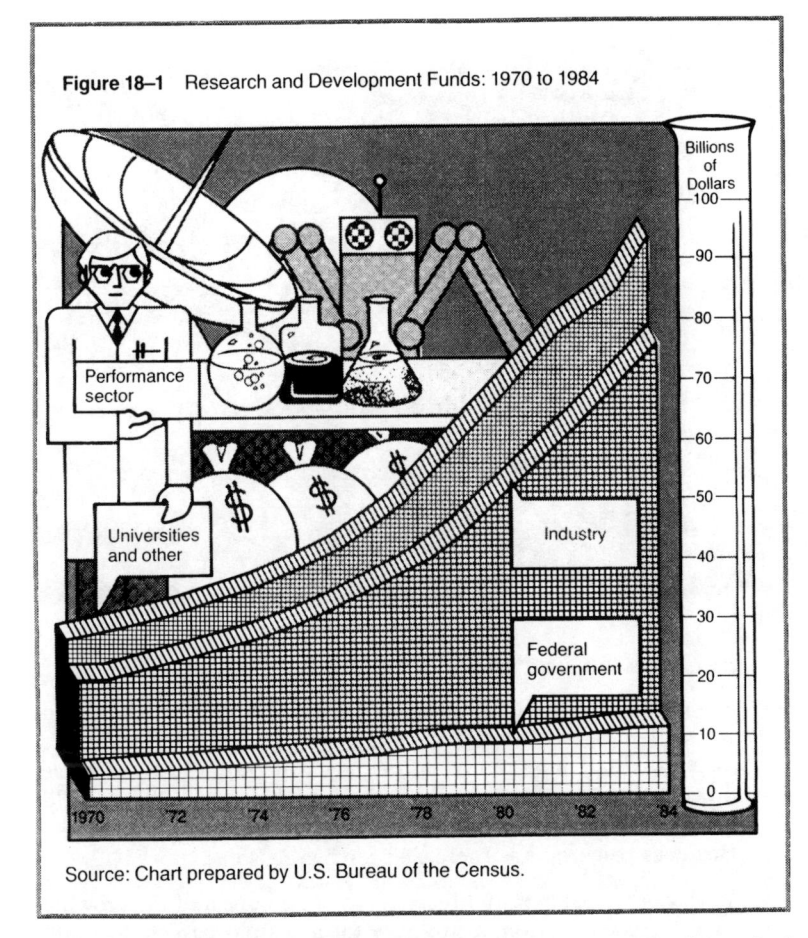

Billions of Dollars

Performance sector

Universities and other

Industry

Federal government

Source: Chart prepared by U.S. Bureau of the Census.

it is today. Debbi Fields, after baking cookies for six months to find the best cookie recipes, opened the first Mrs. Fields Cookies store in 1977. By 1984 she operated 150 stores in western states with annual sales estimated at $30 million. In 1976 Steven Jobs and Stephen Wozniak, both college dropouts, made the first Apple I personal computer in Jobs' garage. Apple Computer Company now has sales well over $150 million annually.

The history of great business personalities suggests that most successful people do not have extraordinary intelligence. What they do seem to have in common are (a) an unusual curiosity (They ask "Why?" "What if?" "Suppose . . ."), (b) a desire to find new solutions to problems (They think "Let's try a different approach." "Let's give it a try."), and (c) the strength of their convictions ("There must be a way to achieve our goal. Let's try again using a different method.").

Contemporary cattle ranchers use computers to do research on herds, markets, and prices for livestock.

Reasons for Increased Interest in Research

Business people can no longer rely on rule-of-thumb procedures and guesswork in making decisions. To guess what features customers want in a product, how many units they will buy, what the price should be, how the product should be transported, and how it should be advertised is asking for failure.

Business research has increased for five reasons:

- With drastic changes in lifestyles, the economy, and the growing need for conservation, a sure way for a company to go downhill is to be content to produce a regular product line without further development and to be satisfied to serve present markets.

- Growth and profit possibilities are most promising in new product and industry areas, such as biotechnology, cable TV, information processing, robots, holography, and semiconductors.

- Analyses show that the most profitable companies are those that lead in launching new products successfully.

- Consumer groups' actions and government concern about product dependability and a desire to reduce product recalls cause companies to focus on research. When General Motors in 1980 heralded the appointment for the first time of a vice president in charge of quality and reliability, it was a dramatic sign of the times.

- With the country lagging in international markets, export-oriented industries are recognizing the value of research that enhances their competitive capabilities.

Questions That Research Can Help Answer

Following are examples of the wide variety of questions that research can help answer:

- *Product and technological research*—What new products should we develop? How should we revise our product line? How can we make our products more energy-efficient? Should we lease or own our new production equipment?
- *Personnel research*—How can we reduce absenteeism? How can we design a more equitable wage and salary plan? How can we reverse the erosion of the work ethic? What must we do to conform with amendments to the labor laws?

AMERICA'S REEMERGING CREATIVITY

Using Information Technology for Better Business

The Information Age is here. Never before has so much information been available for use or misuse. Observers have estimated that the total volume of information has been increasing at 10 percent per year. Innovations in computer technology spur on the flood of information, which will continue to grow. And with it will grow the portion of the labor force that is dependent on information—both its generation and its use. Even more in coming years than now, those who control business information resources will be key to a business' success.

From the Industrial Revolution of the eighteenth century to the present age, information has changed the business environment; that, in turn, has changed society. Figure 18-2 shows how the work force has changed as information about technological developments began to accelerate with the Industrial Revolution. The first group to control the business organization was the manufacturing experts who could use and further develop the new production methods, machines, and power sources. These powerful people controlled the information related to the success of the business.

As the Industrial Revolution matured, business required greater capital investments, and control shifted to financial experts who knew how to use the financial information needed for business success. Even today many companies such as General Motors have traditionally had their chief executive officers come from this group of financial experts. As competition has increased between businesses, both domestic and foreign, marketing information has become the key to success. Those who control the information about market share, selling, and advertising become powerful business leaders.

Now, information technology drives the manufacturing, financial, and marketing control of business. Currently 54% of the U.S. labor force produces goods and services dependent on information. By 1990, it is estimated, 67% of the labor force will be information-dependent. The future success of business will depend on having chief executive officers who can understand information and its management and can use information to enhance the competitive advantage of their companies. Already Bank of America, Citicorp, and American Airlines have such leadership.

Information management has even changed the small business environment. The small business entrepreneur has discovered that a personal computer is a great asset. It can help with accounting, inventories, mailing lists, and most other business-related record-keeping duties. It can help, too, with planning and forecasting sales revenues. The small business person, like the corporate chief executive, must understand the management of information and its use. The Information Age is dramatically changing the way we do business from the large corporations to the small businesses.

Questions for Discussion

1. What is the Information Age?
2. How has the Information Age affected your life? Has it changed your career objectives?
3. What changes has the Information Age made in the business environment? Give specific details and examples.

SOURCES: David Vincent, "In Depth: Corporate Culture," *Computerworld*, Nov. 5, 1984, 21–30; "Readers' Forum," *Datamation*, Oct. 1, 1984, 175–76.

- *Economic research*—What will the inflation rate be for the next five years? What will economic conditions be like in six months? How will shortages of raw materials affect our purchasing requirements? How will uneven regional economic development affect our markets?
- *Marketing research*—Should we change our package or advertising appeals? In which shopping centers should we open stores? To what market segment should we direct our promotion campaigns? How would a price increase affect sales?
- *Financial research*—How can we increase the return on investment? Should we merge with the XYZ Corporation? What is the best way to acquire long-term capital? How can we reduce our tax liabilities?
- *International research*—What changes should we make in our products to better suit foreign needs? What government trade

barriers would we face if we export to Brazil? In which "down under" city should we set up a branch office to serve Australia and New Zealand? What languages and weight systems should we use on labels for products distributed in Southeast Asia?

THE THREE STEPS IN RESEARCHING

A characteristic that all researchers should have is an inquiring mind. Research works only when researchers ask questions, and works best when they follow three key steps or procedures.

Step 1: Recognize the Problem

The first step for the researcher is to recognize that a problem exists and that he or she must find a way to solve it. The personnel director may observe an increased turnover of employees and undertake research to determine the reason. Or, if the sales manager notes that rural sales are declining, he or she may need to do some research to find out why.

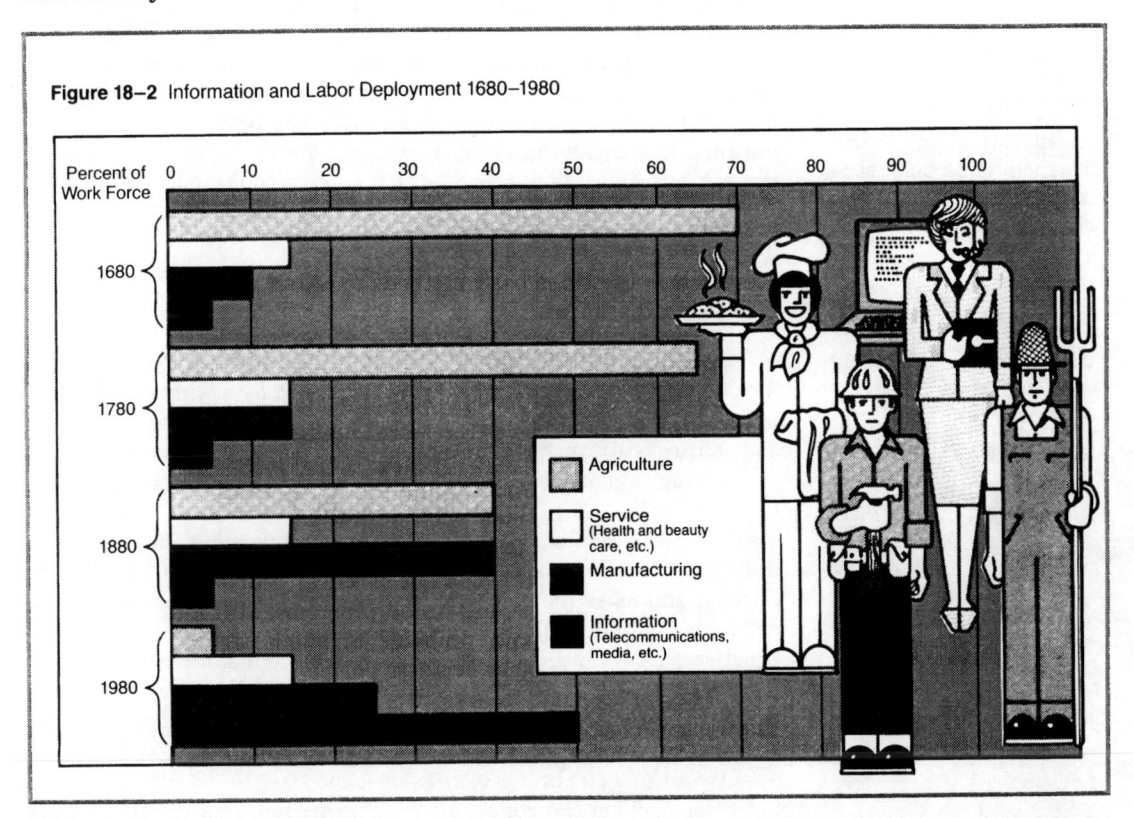

Figure 18–2 Information and Labor Deployment 1680–1980

Management becomes aware of problems in many ways. One research project often leads to the discovery of other problem areas. For example, a study to determine why sales representatives aren't selling more may suggest a study of personnel selection procedures, or it may call for a review of the sales potential in different territories. It is the responsibility of researchers to discover and recognize problems, as well as to encourage others within the company to do so. Only after a problem becomes apparent can employees take steps to solve it.

Step 2: Conduct an Informal Investigation

The second step is to define the problem as clearly as possible. This involves gathering all available information. The researcher will discuss the problem with company executives, employees, wholesalers, retailers, consumers, or anyone else who may be able to provide facts or informed opinions on the subject. During the informal investigation, the researcher should make a special effort to check pertinent company records and published information.

The **informal investigation** should *result in a concise definition of the problem and determination of the most logical method for collecting the data needed to solve it.* Researchers often do not make the decision whether to undertake the project until after an informal investigation, which may reveal, for example, that costs for the project would be too high or that profits would not result.

Personal interviews enable researchers to pinpoint specific consumer groups and guarantee responses.

Step 3: Collect Data

Researchers use three basic methods to collect data: survey, observation, and experiment.

SURVEY

The **survey**—*a procedure for collecting data by asking questions*—is the most common business research method. Sometimes referred to as the **questionnaire technique,** since researchers usually record the information on questionnaires, the survey serves a variety of purposes. Questionnaires may ask consumers about their taste preferences, buying habits, living standards, and personal interests and opinions. Questionnaires may ask business people about their production and sales plans, expansion programs, attitudes toward new products, opinions about probable economic trends, employment practices, credit and other business policies, and similar topics.

The survey method asks two basic kinds of questions: factual questions (What kind of car do you drive? What brand of soap did you last purchase?) and opinion questions (What do you like most about your present brand of breakfast food?).

Researchers can collect survey information in a variety of ways including:

Mail questionnaires. The **mail questionnaire** is *a set of questions sent to a selected group of people.* This technique collects information from a wide area. If a large number of people return questionnaires, it is a low-cost way to collect information. The chief disadvantage is that often only a small percentage of people return the questionnaires. Also, the people who respond may not be typical.

Personal interviews. In **personal interviews,** *trained interviewers ask questions of selected people.* While interviews generally are held in homes, offices, or stores, researchers occasionally interview people at athletic events, on streets, in buses, outside theaters, and so on. The personal-interview technique usually results in a high percentage of interviews in relation to people approached, thus overcoming a disadvantage of the mail questionnaire. On the negative side, personal interviews are expensive. The "human element," which can cause bias in the answers given by the respondent, may make answers more subjective.

Telephone interviews. Researchers use the telephone extensively for collecting information, especially about radio and television listening habits. One organization specializes in calling a number of people daily and asking, "Is your radio or television set turned on? If so, to what program are you listening?" Telephone interviewing is the quickest way to obtain data, and the cost per interview is low. Interviews, however, must be brief, and questions ordinarily cannot be of a personal nature because of the reluctance of people to talk about personal matters to strangers.

One fast, inexpensive way to obtain information is through telephone interviews.

Panel interviews. A fourth method for securing information is the **panel,** or **consumer-jury, interview,** *in which the carefully selected people who form the panel represent a group typical of those to whom the business wants its product to appeal.* Panels range in size from a dozen people to a hundred or more. Members of the panel may answer questions about anything from their shoe-buying habits to their favorite household pets. They may or may not receive compensation for their cooperation.

The main advantage of the panel is that information on many topics is readily available. However, the method has its limitations. Its members may answer questions as "experts" rather than as ordinary shoppers. Moreover, panels are hard to maintain. People drop out, fail to cooperate, or otherwise make it difficult to keep the group a representative one.

OBSERVATION

The **observation** method is *a procedure for collecting data by actually watching certain events take place.* Unlike the survey, the

> *Good as it is to inherit a library, it is better to collect one.*
>
> AUGUSTINE BIRRELL

researcher asks no questions. Observation is useful in a variety of studies—for example:

- *Workers and their jobs*—A trained observer can watch workers perform their tasks and record the exact movements they make and the time they take to complete each movement. Motion picture cameras and videotape machines facilitate studies of this kind. Findings may lead to work simplification and time savings.
- *Locations for business establishments*—Observation helps businesses find suitable locations for stores and other businesses. The number of cars passing a location, for example, is of value in site selection for service stations. Much observation takes the form of traffic counts, which may be of either foot or vehicle traffic.

The chief advantage of observation is that it is objective and can be quite accurate. It reveals what actually takes place rather than what people say takes place. The major disadvantage is expense. One researcher can observe relatively little at any one time.

EXPERIMENT

With the **experiment,** *researchers collect information through controlled tests.* Examples include experiments that test:

- *The effectiveness of advertising*—Firms selling goods by mail frequently test the strength, or "pull," of sales letters by the experiment. One sales letter is sent to a mailing list of, say, 10,000 people, while a second letter describing the same product in a different manner is sent to a second group of 10,000. The letter that draws the larger number of orders forms the basis for later sales campaigns.
- *The effectiveness of training*—A firm may give training to one group of employees but not to a second, comparable group. Then researchers compare the production records of the two groups to determine whether training increased production and, if so, by how much.

Use of the experiment is limited for several reasons: Controlled experiments are difficult to construct; they take a good deal of time and money; and results are often inconclusive.

SOURCES OF BUSINESS INFORMATION

Information useful in solving business problems and making business decisions comes from both primary and secondary sources. **Primary sources** of information are *those that supply original data.* The research methods described in the preceding section were all ways of collecting primary information. **Secondary sources** are *those that supply information already collected from primary sources.* They are generally publications and reports.

For example, a marketing manager who wants to find out occupational information about consumers in a given area may either survey them directly (primary source) or use data already gathered by the Census Bureau (secondary source).

An enormous amount of secondary-source data is available. Many people do not realize this fact. They may undertake expensive, time-consuming projects to obtain primary-source data when the same data could be obtained through a visit to a reference library. A primary objective of any potential business executive should be *to learn where to find information that already exists.*

Government Publications

The largest single source of published business information is the federal government. Various federal agencies publish research reports and statistics on almost every conceivable business problem. For most business people, the Department of Commerce publishes the most useful information.

THE STATISTICAL ABSTRACT OF THE UNITED STATES

This annual publication compiled by the Bureau of the Census is the most comprehensive and accurate source of statistical information. *The Statistical Abstract of the United States,* published since 1878, is the standard summary of statistics on the social, political, and economic organization of the United States. It serves as a convenient volume for statistical reference and as a guide to other statistical publications and sources. The Abstract includes data from many statistical publications, both governmental and private.

Information presented in the Abstract covers population, health, income, education, law enforcement, government spending, national defense, the labor force, prices, banking and finance, communications and much more. The publication is for sale at a nominal fee from the Superintendent of Documents, U.S. Government Printing Office, Washington, D.C. 20402.

The Business Press Boom

Reading business publications is one of the best and most pleasant ways to learn about business. A remarkable boom in the popularity of business publications (see Table 18–1) has made reading them one of America's fastest-growing productive pastimes.

The boom came about for a variety of reasons. Accelerating change quickly makes the nonreading business person obsolete. Also,

TABLE 18-1 Growth in Circulation of Business Periodicals

	CIRCULATION		
PERIODICAL (STARTED)	**1970**	**1983**	**GROWTH (PERCENT)**
Advertising Age (1930)	65,465	79,350	21.2
Barron's (1921)	224,622	300,251	33.7
Black Enterprise (1970)	100,000	244,566	14.4
BusinessWeek (1929)	677,989	855,391	26.2
Forbes (1917)	627,703	718,970	14.5
Fortune (1930)	568,365	700,360	23.2
INC. (1979)	—	450,622	—
Money (1972)	—	1,374,101	—
Wall Street Journal (1889)	1,215,750	2,081,995	71.2

in recent years business publications have become lively and interesting. As a consequence, the general public is increasingly turning to them for information and mental stimulation. Younger generations are better educated, and they tend to invest in stocks and bonds and real estate. They enjoy following economic and business news for investment-related reasons.

Subscribing to general business publications such as the *Wall Street Journal, Forbes,* and *BusinessWeek* is sensible for serious business students. Other sources of business information follow.

STANDARD AND POOR'S STOCK GUIDE
The S&P Stock Guide, published monthly, gives 48 financial particulars for 5,100 common and preferred stocks and over 400 mutual funds. It is the most widely read and easiest to understand statistical analysis of securities.

TRADE ASSOCIATION PUBLICATIONS
Trade associations are idea exchanges. Most businesses belong to trade associations which conduct periodic membership studies. They collect information on sales volume, industry problems, employment practices, growth opportunities, profit ratios, price levels, and similar matters. Information from trade associations is usually highly relevant and factual. Some trade association reports reach the media, but most information goes only to members. Some trade associations also publish monthly magazines such as *Publishers Week, Journal of Marketing, Journal of Retailing,* and many more.

Other Sources of Business Information

Many other sources of business information exist besides the published data. Some such sources follow.

PROFESSIONAL SEMINARS

Professional seminars market ideas. Colleges, universities, associations, and specialized educational businesses present seminars on a wide variety of business topics ranging from the most basic principles to advanced theory. Many business people attend seminars to learn about new methods and techniques, new opportunities, investing capital, training employees, reducing taxes, and similar concerns. Participants receive much valuable information at seminars in handouts or handbooks. Although some seminars may be free, most require a registration fee.

MEMBERS OF CONGRESS

Members of Congress help supply information, too. Supplying constituents with information about government-related matters is an important function of congressional representatives. Our elected representatives have direct and respected access to all government agencies, maintain a professional staff, and have a desire to serve voters. Members of Congress are especially good sources of information about government contract awards (remember, the government is by far the biggest customer of business) and sources of financial aid.

INFORMAL DISCUSSIONS

Informal discussions and conversations can be very valuable. Business people like to talk business. A prime source of ideas, which researchers may later study, are conversations with informed people, such as executives in other companies, professors, sales people, and other knowledgeable people.

Consider this example: a small law firm decided to make its operations more efficient by buying a word processing system. The lawyers narrowed their choices to two possible systems, one from a large well-known company and the other from a small regional company. The second system suited better the firm's needs and was $2,000 less expensive than the first. The responsible attorney decided to buy the second system, until another lawyer who was using the system happened to mention in conversation that she was afraid the company would soon go out of business. Further research indicated that the company was having serious financial problems. The risk of buying a word processing system from a company that could possibly fail was too great for the law firm. The law firm bought the larger company's system.

EXPERIENCE IS A GOOD TEACHER, BUT...

Experience is the knowledge and skill derived from direct observation or participation in a specific activity. Successful businesses place a premium on people with experience; and often, the more varied the experience, the better. An airline wants applicants for pilot positions to have flying experience; a business seeks a marketing manager with related experience; and a bank looking for a loan officer specifies what kind and how much experience it requires.

As a source of business ideas, however, experience, while desirable, has three limitations. First, *each business problem is unique.* It differs in some ways from all business problems previously encountered. Past experience is never completely relevant to the current problem.

Second, *experience is always limited.* No manager or group of managers has had exposure to every kind of situation, problem, or question. Third, *experience is perishable.* Conditions in business are dynamic. Unless past experience is recent, it may not have value. People who had a good understanding of computers in the 1960s are almost helpless in using computers in the 1980s unless they have kept up with changes in technology and methodology.

Experience is indeed a good school for knowledge; however, the tuition is high. It is so high, in fact, that Bismarck was led to observe, "Fools say they learn by experience. I prefer to profit by others' experience."

People interested in becoming effective decision-makers will (1) devise ways to keep their experience current, and (2) learn to gather and draw on the experience of others.

Research for Truth

Research should discover truth, not "prove" something. Sometimes an executive tells an assistant that he wants to do some research to prove a specific idea. For example, a manager instructs an assistant to "put together some facts to prove that low-income people don't buy our product, so I can convince the ad people to stop selecting media reaching that segment."

This approach is a cardinal sin in research for it is subjective. A better procedure is to be objective and ask the assistant to "find out how our product is selling to different income classes." If the researcher receives prejudiced instructions, then the results will probably reinforce biased opinion.

Use Information Wisely

Business people must be selective in using information. The amount of business information available is almost beyond comprehension.

More than 1,000 business periodicals, thousands of private and government reports, and a large and varied number of books about business are available. Every week, managers review brochures and catalogs describing informational seminars about business topics.

How then can a manager keep up with what is happening? Selectivity is essential in choosing information. Wise business people often allocate a certain period each day for reading and idea generation. The "Application to Personal Affairs" on page 553 suggests that we can almost always find some time for reading and digesting information if we recognize how important acquiring the information is.

STATISTICS: THE BASIC TOOL OF RESEARCH

Statistics is *a collection of numerical data.* The field of statistics, however, has a much broader scope than the mere compilation of numbers. It embraces *the collection, analysis, interpretation, and presentation of numerical data.*

Those who specialize in statistics are called statisticians. Statisticians are trained in quantitative methods and in the use of computers. Business statisticians, in addition, are usually trained in both business administration and economics.

The purpose of statistical analysis in business is to supply information helpful in making management decisions. The more important ways statistics benefit management are:

- *Statistics give meaning to masses of data*—Numerical data have no value until experts have organized and interpreted them well. The results of careful statistical analysis present a picture in which essentials stand out from the mass of detail.
- *Statistics help eliminate guesswork*—Statistics substitute facts for guesses and hunches.
- *Statistics facilitate measurement of business efficiency*—Through the orderly collection, analysis, and interpretation of numerical data, business people can develop yardsticks for measuring how well their firm is doing in comparison with similar firms or with previous time periods.

"Average" Means Different Things

A function of statistics is to make numbers understandable and manageable. A valuable statistical device for this purpose is the **average,** defined as *a single numerical value descriptive of a group of values.*

The word "average" is a common one: We often hear terms such as "average rainfall," "average temperature," "average height," "grade point average," and "batting average." Business people also think in averages. They may speak of "average income," "average profits," "average costs," "average daily output," "average markup," or "average sales per month."

There are several kinds of measures referred to as averages. Each gives a different picture of the figures it represents. The most commonly used averages are the arithmetic mean, the median, and the mode.

THE ARITHMETIC MEAN

The **arithmetic mean**—or, the **arithmetic average**—is the simplest and most frequently used average. When we use the word "average" in everyday conversation we mean the arithmetic average.

The arithmetic mean is computed easily—just *add all the items in a series and divide by the total number of items.* The arithmetic mean of examination scores appears in Figure 18–3.

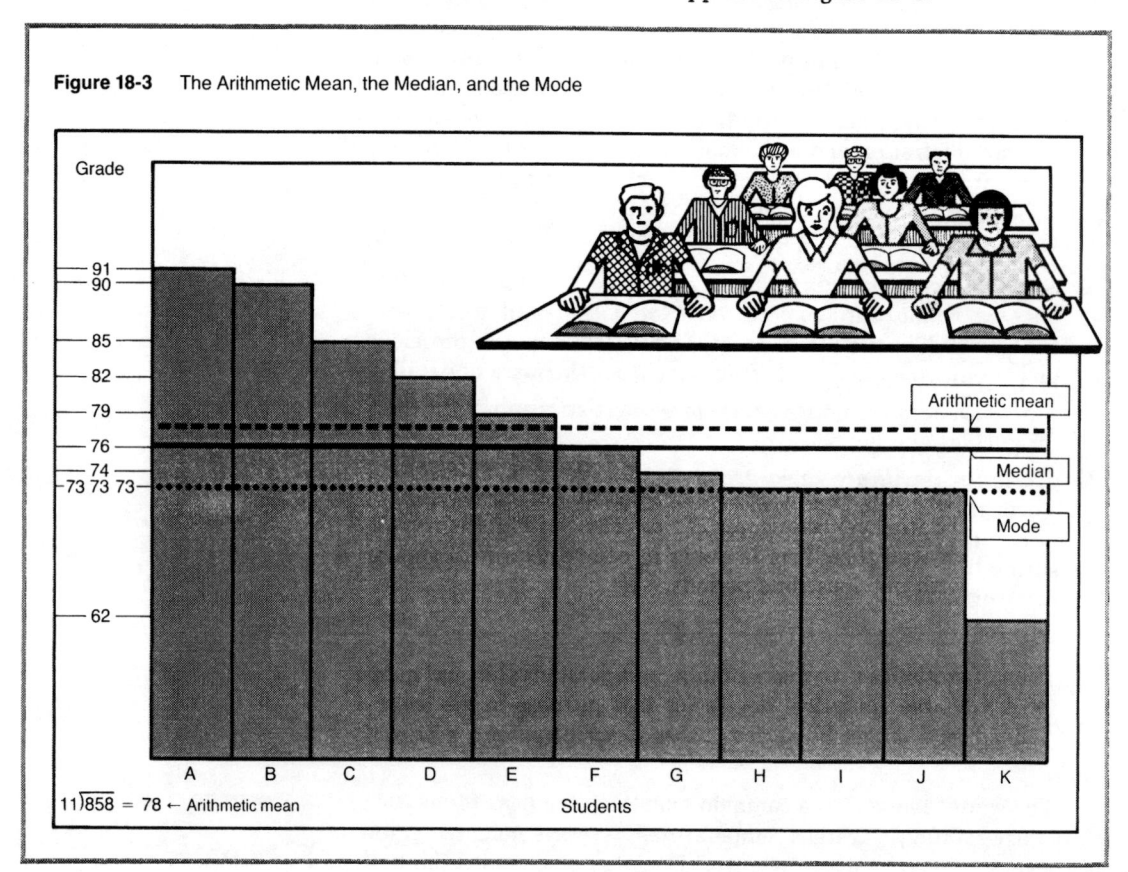

Figure 18-3 The Arithmetic Mean, the Median, and the Mode

$11\overline{)858} = 78 \leftarrow$ Arithmetic mean

THE MEDIAN

The **median** is the **position average:** We compute it *by arranging items in order from smallest to largest. The midpoint number is the median.* In Figure 18-3, the median is 76, because five numbers appear above and five below that number.

THE MODE

The **mode,** or **modal average,** is *the number that occurs most frequently in a series of data.* Thus, in Figure 18-3, 73 is the mode. We compute the mode most easily by arranging all numbers in sequence. On occasion we may find two or three modes. When this occurs, reference is made to bimodal, trimodal, or even multimodal averages.

WHICH "AVERAGE" TO USE?

Obviously, the average for a large series of numbers differs, depending on the choice of averaging methods. For example, suppose the average income per household in one county using different kinds of averages was as follows:

Arithmetic mean	$29,103
Median	24,930
Mode	22,874

For a sales executive evaluating the size of a market on the basis of average income per household, the type of average makes a considerable difference. The arithmetic mean is larger in this example because high incomes, some over $100,000, are included in the averaging process. Insofar as income analysis is concerned, the mode is the most meaningful, since it represents the income received by more people than any other.

Means, medians, and modes are valuable statistical tools, but we should always be cautious of "averages." When an average is referred to, find out which average it is. A statistician with his head in a deep freeze and his feet in an oven might be described as feeling normal, on the average.

Index Numbers: Yardsticks of Progress or Gloom?

Another widely used statistical device, much in the news, is the **index number,** *which compares business activity during one time* *period with similar activity during another time period.* Through the use of index numbers, one can answer the questions: "How do wholesale prices today compare with those last year?" "How does the cost of living now compare with the cost five years ago?" While the construction of an index number can be quite complicated, the theory behind it is simple and involves the following two points:

- A certain figure of one time period serves as a base and receives a weight of 100 percent. This "certain figure" can represent any type of statistical data—carloadings, miles traveled, number of persons employed, prices paid, tons produced, dollar sales volume.
- Corresponding data for a later time are then expressed as a percentage of the base period.

Study this sample illustration. Assume you wish to construct an index number for domestic automobile sales. You select a certain year, say 1973, as the base period. American-made passenger automobile sales in that year were 9.7 million. Therefore, since this is the base period, 9.7 million = 100 percent. In 1984, sales of American cars were 6.9 million. You now ask, what percentage increase or decrease of the base year does this represent? In this example, you calculate the percentage as follows:

$$\frac{9.7 \text{ million}}{6.9 \text{ million}} = \frac{100}{x}$$
$$x = 71.1\%$$

Thus, sales in 1984 were 71.1 percent of what they were in 1973. In other words, they fell 28.9 percent.

Comparing data in percentage form like this is much simpler and more understandable than comparing absolute numbers. Of the various indexes, price indexes are the most widely used and debated.

CONSUMER PRICE INDEX

The U.S. Bureau of Labor Statistics publishes the most widely used data in the **Consumer Price Index (CPI).** It is *based on nationally averaged prices in the marketplace* and not on individual living costs. Wages of millions of workers are tied to it, as are Social Security benefits, many pension plans, and eligibility for programs such as food stamps.

Table 18–2 shows what has happened to consumer prices since 1940 using 1967 as the base year of 100. The dollar bought 238 percent as much in 1940 as in 1967. Going forward in time, the dollar in 1984 bought only one-third as much as in 1967, and it took $7 in 1984 to purchase as much as $1 did in 1940. (2.381 ÷ .332)

TABLE 18-2 Consumer Price Index 1940–1983
1967 = 100

1940	2.381	1975	.621
1950	1.387	1978	.512
1960	1.127	1980	.406
1967	1.000	1983	.337
1970	.860	1984	.332

During the 43-year period 1940–1983, two periods of rapid inflation occurred between 1940–1950 and 1970–1980. World War II caused the first, and the energy crisis the second. If inflation is as great over the next 43 years as it was over the past 43, when the 20-year-old of today reaches age 63 he or she will see $2 hamburgers selling for $14; $10,000 cars priced at $70,000; and $80,000 houses going for more than half a million.

Indexing means that, as the Consumer Price Index goes up, wages and other cost items are adjusted proportionately. For example, if the Consumer Price Index increases by 8 percent a year and a person earning $20,000 has his or her salary indexed, the person would receive a pay increase of $1,600. Unfortunately, the more indexing is used, the more inflation is built into the economy, and already more indexing is built into the economy than most people realize. For example:

- Many suppliers of basics, such as coal and newsprint, tie prices in long-term contracts to indexes.

- Sales contracts of providers of long-lead-time industrial products, such as turbines and commercial aircraft, include indexing clauses. Boeing uses them when it sells fleets to airlines.

- Social Security payments and military retirement pensions are tied to the Consumer Price Index.

The solution to the inflation-fueled indexing is not easy because it is politically popular. A person who retired in 1984 with $800 a month in Social Security benefits expects to be able to buy as much in 1994 as in 1984. Thus the demand for indexing is great.

The only thing certain about indexing is that it is becoming a permanent part of the economy and that the business community will be increasingly involved.

Sampling

A basic statistical technique is the **sample,** or *a relatively small number of a group that has the same characteristics as the larger group from which it is taken.* The larger group, called the **universe** or **population,** *includes all things or entities that might have been selected.*

There are limitless varieties of universes. All Cincinnati homeowners combined constitute a universe. A jar of wheat taken from an entire carload is a sample; the carload is the universe.

WHY DO WE USE SAMPLES?

We use samples mainly for economy. To study an entire universe would be too time-consuming and expensive. For example, to obtain attitudes of Porsche owners about the current model, one would question only a small fraction of the owners. If the sample is properly constructed, interviews with only a relatively few owners will yield results as valid as if every owner had been surveyed.

CONSTRUCTION OF SAMPLES

While sample construction looks easy, in practice it is complex. How large the sample should be, what characteristics it must possess, when the sample should be taken, and similar decisions are best made by qualified statisticians. The important point is that the sample should reflect the characteristics of the total universe or the results are likely to be misleading.

A sample can be either controlled or random. A **controlled sample** is *chosen deliberately*—for example, couples with two or more children under 15 years of age will be interviewed. A **random sample** is *chosen so the selection of any member of the universe does not affect the selection of any other member. That is, each unit has the same chance of being included in the sample.*

Experts often do sampling so precisely that a very small number of people selected for study represents the whole population. Experts have forecast national elections accurately and based their results on a sample size of only 1,800 voters or about one voter per 55,000 people who cast ballots. National TV program ratings rely on research using only one in 10,000 viewers. Taste tests to determine consumer preferences for food and beverages for a national market may use only 100 subjects for study.

RESEARCH INCLUDES FORECASTING EVENTS

People trained in research, quantitative methods, and economics often receive forecasting assignments. To a business, the most important forecast deals with projected sales or revenue. To the overall economy, key forecasts project inflation, employment, interest rates, and stock prices. Individuals in the private sector, such as consultants, analysts and university economists make most such economic forecasts.

Forecasting techniques include:

- *Trend Analysis* or simply extending past trends into the future. If sales increased an average of 12 percent over the past three years, simple trend projection would forecast a 12 percent gain next year.
- *Executive Judgment* or the pooled views of key personnel regarding future events is common.
- *Customer Surveys* which ask consumers their buying plans for a coming period, is a popular way of forecasting sales.

PEOPLE WHO MAKE THINGS HAPPEN

A PROFILE OF
WOLFBERG, ALVAREZ, TARACIDO & ASSOCIATES

People who make things happen are not always rugged individuals who go into business on their own. They often start out and work best as partners. Wolfberg, Alvarez, Taracido & Associates (WAT), one of Florida's fastest-growing architectural firms, is an example. Started in 1976 by three ambitious professionals in their late twenties, the company had over $4 million in revenues in 1981 and will have over $10 million in 1982.

Two of the partners—Julio Alvarez and Manuel Taracido—are exiles from Cuba who have degrees in engineering. David Wolfberg studied architecture. They joined and added to the name of a small architectural firm that had revenues of only $176,000 and set their sights on the future. In reflecting on how the company developed, Wolfberg says, "We couldn't afford to hire enough people to do the work. So we just rolled up our sleeves and did it ourselves."* He feels that doing so is a great advantage that a company tends to lose as it expands. As Taracido explains:

As the organization grows, it starts developing all the lethargic characteristics of the large office. The business begins to generate an impressive but often unnecessary quantity of statistical studies and reports. Partners who had been actively involved in practical work find themselves spending more and more time in managerial work. Veteran employees begin to feel unappreciated, and turnover rates soar. New, inexperienced employees, who do not always share the enthusiasm of those who were present from the start, put in a less-than-productive 40 hours. Critical mistakes occur. Things begin to fall apart.

This happened at WAT. The partners concluded that "employees no longer had a tangible

> stake in the way the company was managed, and management was out of touch with day-to-day operations. The 'working partnership' had broken down." In seeking a solution, the partners created a series of "organizational cells," which are self-sufficient teams. Each team is assigned its own projects and has easy access to the owners. The team idea has helped restore the partnership spirit that WAT had once enjoyed because employees now determine how they organize their work.
>
> Then the partners went one step further, asking themselves, "If WAT's employees were being asked to think of themselves as partners in the business, why not offer them some of the traditional rewards of management?"
>
> Thus, the partners gradually eliminated company rules and petty administrative procedures. Employees no longer punch time clocks; formal sick leaves and late-arrival policies have been relaxed. Formal job descriptions no longer limit employee ingenuity.
>
> The partners are aware that employees can abuse these freedoms. WAT tries to overcome this by hiring people who "care about what they are doing. A big mistake in any business is hiring people who just come to work, put in their eight hours, and go home again. We care a lot and put in a lot of energy and we expect our people to do the same." One measure of the success of these policies, according to Alvarez, is that WAT's employees have achieved nearly twice the industry norm level for productivity and billings.
>
> Wolfberg's views on creativity are inspiring. "There are static manufacturers and creative manufacturers. There are static service businesses and creative service businesses. To me, it all depends on the dynamics of the people who are running the show.... The mass of this country is running on an average keel because they're being told what to do by average people.... You do your homework, you think creatively, and you don't bog yourself down in doing things by the book. You'd be surprised how easy it is to be successful if you follow that route."
>
> *Based on research for INC.

- *Correlation Analysis* is a forecasting method that involves finding a relationship between past sales and some other factor(s). For example, the sale of steel relates closely (correlates) with sales of automobiles and construction.
- *Composite Forecasting Method* is the most widely used forecasting technique. Firms use all of the methods above and also give consideration to changes in a company's product line, competition, promotion, and other factors that affect demand.

Many forecasts prove to be incorrect. But business relies on them to some extent because they are an aid to planning.

HOW TO PRESENT STATISTICAL DATA

Presentation of statistical data means more than just passing along numerical facts. It means preparing the data so that people can quickly grasp their significance. Statisticians should present data in the clearest, most concise, and most easily understood manner.

Tables

Statistical data often appear in tabular form. A title at the top of each table tells what the table shows. Data are arranged vertically in columns and horizontally in rows. At the top of each vertical column is a heading that tells briefly what the data in the column represent (In Table 18-1 the headings are "periodical," "circulation," and "growth.") At the left of horizontal rows of data is information, called the **stub**, *which tells what the horizontal rows represent.* (In Table 18-1 the stub is the information at the left-hand side of the table.)

A table is useful when showing actual figures is important. Tables take more time to read and understand than graphic presentations, which we discuss next.

Graphic Devices

Graphic methods of presenting data are often superior to tabular arrangements in several important respects:

- Relationships can be seen more readily.
- Comparisons are easier to make. In tables, the reader makes comparisons of data; with graphic devices the artist has already drawn the comparisons and they are usually apparent.
- Graphic devices are time-saving. They are a form of "statistical shorthand."
- Visual impact is greater. Most people would rather look at pictures than rows of numbers.
- Presentation to groups is easier.

Tables organize complex material in a form that is easy to understand and remember. Here, an executive explains a table to his colleagues.

On the negative side, graphic devices are more difficult to prepare than tables; the amount of training and imagination needed to construct graphs and the expense are generally greater. Also, graphs ordinarily cannot show exact figures, as tables can. Computers can now be programmed, however, to convert statistical data into graphs and charts. This development has begun to and will continue to improve business forecasting dramatically.

The most popular graphic devices include:

LINE GRAPH

The **line,** or **curve, graph** is probably the most widely used of all graphic devices. It is *used primarily to indicate trends,* as shown in Figure 18–1 on page 529. The time factor is plotted along the horizontal scale, with the data series plotted on the vertical scale and connected with lines.

BAR CHART

The **bar chart** is *useful for comparing statistics.* The bars can run vertically or horizontally, depending on need. See Figure 18–2 on page 533. Bar charts are convenient for comparing data of different time periods. Because the length of the bar represents the quantity, comparisons are especially easy to grasp. **Pictograms,** a variation of the bar chart, bring statistics to life by *using symbols to indicate quantities.* See Figure 18–4(a).

PIE CHART

A **pie chart** is *a graphic device in which the pie equals 100 percent and the items being compared appear as slices of the pie in proportion to their sizes.* See Figure 18–4(b). We often use pie charts to show how the sales dollar is divided among cost of production, profit, expenses, and other factors.

THE BUSINESS REPORT

The culmination of any formal investigation is the all-important preparation of the report. The researcher puts statistics, explanations, and results together for management—assuming the results are worth reporting. For as George Eliot wrote, "Blessed is the man who, having nothing to say, abstains from giving in words evidence of the fact."

Basic Principles of Report Writing

Whether a company takes action on a report depends in part on how well the researcher has written the report. Management is likely to pass over poorly prepared reports. Certain rules, if followed, are sure to improve the effectiveness of a report. This excerpt from Rudyard

Figure 18-4 Graphic Devices

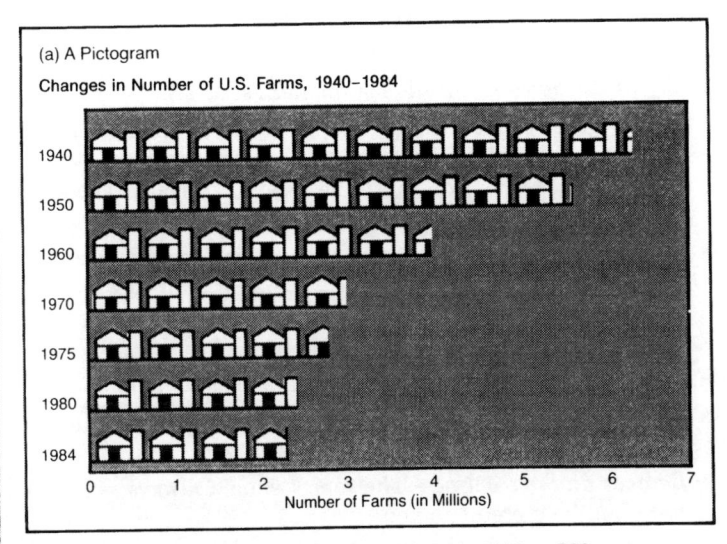

(a) A Pictogram
Changes in Number of U.S. Farms, 1940–1984

Source: *Statistical Abstract of the United States, 1985*, p. 686.

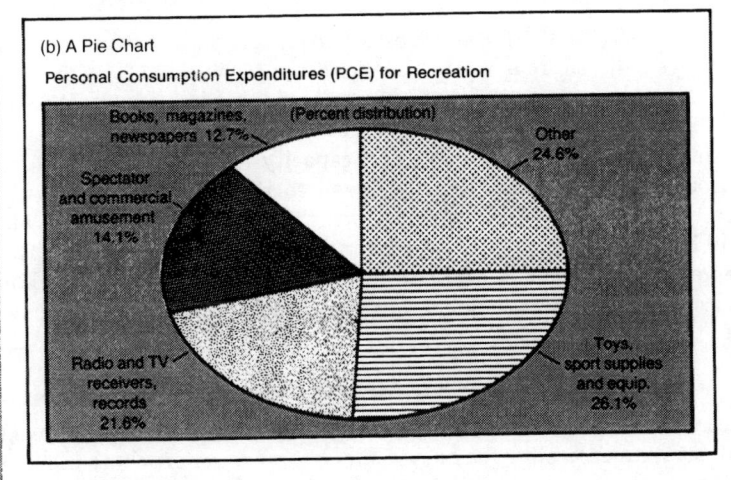

(b) A Pie Chart
Personal Consumption Expenditures (PCE) for Recreation
(Percent distribution)

- Books, magazines, newspapers 12.7%
- Spectator and commercial amusement 14.1%
- Radio and TV receivers, records 21.6%
- Toys, sport supplies and equip. 26.1%
- Other 24.6%

Source: Chart prepared by U.S. Bureau of the Census.

Kipling's poem "The Elephant's Child" covers the basic points a business report should include:

I keep six honest serving men,
They taught me all I knew.

Their names are what and where,
And when, and how and why and who.[2]

It would be worthwhile, in fact, for you to memorize those four lines and refer to them when preparing reports.

Here are some specific report-writing suggestions. You should

- *Organize the report well* (see the next section).
- *Prepare the report with the reader in mind*—If the reader has little technical background, you should keep technical terms to a minimum. Good writers can be most effective if they assume the reader knows nothing about the subject.
- *Develop the report so that your reader can read it rapidly and easily*—You can accomplish this with clear subtitles for all sections; topic sentences at the beginning of each paragraph; clear, crisp paragraphs; and short sentences.
- *Write clearly*—Avoid vague, unintelligible statements.
- *Be objective*—You should refrain from allowing your personal feelings to intrude and avoid exaggeration.
- *Be neat and attractive*—The report should always reflect good taste and be a credit to you.
- *Be concise*—Your objective should not be to include all you know but should include all the reader needs to know.

Well-written reports require hard work and careful thought. However, the effort is worthwhile, and the technique of report writing is worth mastering. For the person beginning in business, it is one of the best ways to demonstrate a grasp of business problems, organizational abilities, intelligence, and capacity for analysis. Reports go through doors that are usually closed to beginners. Managers who read reports will inquire about the writer of an impressive report and will keep an eye on such a person for future promotions. Well written reports can also be helpful to businesses in applying for loans, making sales, informing stockholders, and performing other important communications objectives.

How Reports Should Be Organized

Researchers should organize reports in a logical sequence. To make information accessible for busy readers, arrange reports in the following sequence:

---

[2]Excerpt from "The Elephant's Child" from *Rudyard Kipling's Verse: Definitive Edition*. Used by permission of The National Trust, The Macmillan Co. of London & Bastingstoke, and Doubleday & Co., Inc.

APPLICATION TO PERSONAL AFFAIRS

The Importance of Time Management

Just as business people must manage information, so must they manage time. Time management is a problem for many people, both inside and outside of business. How often have you heard these remarks: "Time just gets away from me"; "I never have time to get everything done"; "I've been wanting to do that, but there never seems to be time"? Two things are key to good time management: awareness and organization.

Be aware of the value of time—Effective business people invariably are very time conscious. They recognize time as the raw material of life. To appreciate the value of time, consider these observations:

- Even a full life is short. A person who lives to age 73 will have lived only 26,663 days, or 639,912 hours.

- Various studies show that the average American watches television in excess of six hours each day. Six hours per day over a lifetime equals 79,990 hours, or eighteen full years.

- Reading is something that people commonly complain they have no time for. Yet if a person spends only 30 minutes per day reading (at the rate of 400 words per minute), he or she can read approximately 50 average-sized books per year.

- Many people also say they can't find time to obtain a degree. Yet only about 6,000 hours (in class and study time) are required to earn a bachelor's degree. That's about 1 percent of a total lifetime, and about 6 percent of the time that the person will spend working over a lifetime.*

- Your time is worth money. Consider these examples.

IF YOU EARN...	YOUR APPROXIMATE VALUE PER HOUR IS...	YOUR APPROXIMATE VALUE PER MINUTE IS...
$12,000 per year	$ 6	10¢
24,000 per year	12	20¢
48,000 per year	24	40¢

Keeping these figures in mind can help you evaluate whether some tasks are worthwhile. For example, is it worth spending an hour driving to and from a discount store in another neighborhood where you'll be able to save $2 on a purchase?

- We cannot really "make up for lost time"—there is no way to bring back yesterday or the past hour.

Organize your activities—Individuals waste a lot of time because they do not organize their activities efficiently. Many people could "find" 10 to 20 additional hours per week if they:

- Organized their shopping so repeat trips to stores were unnecessary

- Set aside definite time periods each day for studying

- Restricted television watching to one hour per day

- Scheduled their work or college classes to avoid rush-hour traffic

- Cut gossiping and small-talk conversations in half

*Assuming a work life of 50 years, 2,000 hours per year.

- *Introduction*—The introduction answers the first question in the mind of the executive: "What is this report about?" This section tells the reader the purpose of the report, the background leading up to its preparation, and the methods employed in making the study. Included in this section are a title page, statement of the problem, the name of the person preparing the report, and its date.

- *Conclusions*—At first glance it may seem odd to have the conclusions immediately after the introduction, since a conclusion is a summation or final statement. Here again, however, the writer must consider the interest of the person for whom the writer prepares the report. The first question in the executive's mind after reading the introduction is: "What did the researcher find out in the investigation?"

- *Recommendations*—This section answers the executive's next question: "What should we do about the findings?" The writer presents a recommended course of action in condensed form.

- *Discussion or body of the report*—This section contains the bulk of the report, because the first three sections—the introduction, conclusions, and recommendations—to be most effective, should be concise. The discussion section provides detailed information concerning the findings and the factual information on which the researcher has based conclusions and recommendations.

- *Appendix*—The appendix, if one is necessary, contains tables, charts, bibliographies, and other detailed data that would hinder easy reading of the report itself but give essential substance to findings and present valuable reference materials.

Interpret Statistics and Research Findings Carefully

Perhaps you have heard such statements as "You can prove anything with statistics" or, to quote a humorous definition, "A statistician is a person who draws a mathematically precise line from an unwarranted assumption to a foregone conclusion." There is a basis for wisecracks related to statistics, so it is prudent to train oneself to watch for possible shortcomings when reviewing statistics.

General Georges F. Poriot once said, "An auditor is like a tailor; he can make a fat man look thinner or taller or younger." The same may be said of statisticians. For example, in wage negotiations, statistics were presented that showed that municipal wages had fallen behind private-sector wages by 25 percent since the 1970s. A skeptic asked for actual figures rather than just percentages alone for the 1970s and the 1980s. When they were produced, they showed that

CONTEMPORARY ISSUE

How Will Business Information Be Managed?

The Information Age has brought a crisis to the business world and to society as a whole: Will we be able to manage and use the great abundance of information available to us or will the flood overwhelm us? It is a question of great importance, for the key to making successful business decisions is having relevant data that is timely and accurate. When the necessary data cannot be separated from the total mass of information, decisions may be inadequate to solve a given problem. How can business cope with the rising tide of information?

One way business manages information is to fit it into the existing structure of the departmentalized company. Information becomes financial data, or public relations data, or management data. Compartmentalizing information in this way could lead to narrow analyses of data that lack company-wide significance. It could also lead to jealousy between departments that prohibit one department from sharing data with another "rival" within the company.

Another approach to solving the information problem is to give the chief executive officer direct access to all available data through a computer terminal. Because it would probably be raw data, the CEO would need the time to research and analyze the data before reaching a decision. Such a method of information management could prevent the CEO from benefitting from others' perspectives and advice in interpreting the data.

Another approach is to centralize all information management in a single position or department. Every corporation has a senior executive in charge of manufacturing, one in charge of finance, another in charge of marketing. Why not have one in charge of information? Information management is at least as important as those other positions, and possibly more so. A corporate director of information could combine separate strands of information from different sources, both from inside and outside the company—economic data, survey results, demographic data, production figures, and other data—into a total picture of the business environment. Such information could easily be disbursed for use throughout the company in any department.

Information has become the most abundant commodity we have. How we manage it and how we use it may well change the environment of business.

Questions

1. How does information management affect our daily lives?
2. How do you think information management will change business in the next decade?

SOURCES: David Vincent, "In Depth: Corporate Culture," *Computerworld*, Nov. 5, 1984, 21–30; "Readers' Forum," *Datamation*, Oct. 1, 1984, 175–76.

municipal wages were considerably higher than private-sector wages in the 1970s. Figures for the 1980s showed that municipal and private-sector wages had evened out, and so there was no longer a discrepancy. Percentages alone produced a picture of municipal wages falling behind, whereas in reality the private sector had caught up!

Opinion polls should also be considered skeptically. One public-opinion poll found that 55 percent of the population bought less beef, while only 14 percent bought more beef. Yet statistics on aggregate beef consumption for the country showed a rise in per-capita consumption from 117 to 120 pounds during that year. It is a quirk of marketing research that there frequently are discrepancies between what people say they do as compared with what they actually do. An interesting question is why people subjectively thought they were eating less beef when actually they were eating more.

Remember that statistics can be dangerous in the hands of people who lack proper qualifications to collect and analyze them or have a vested interest in proving a predetermined conclusion.

SUMMARY

- Business research can be used to answer questions about products, personnel, the economy, marketing, finance, and management.
- Research procedure steps are to recognize the problem; conduct informal investigation; collect data by survey, observation, or experiment.
- Information useful in solving business problems comes from both primary and secondary sources. The largest single source of published business information is the federal government. A wide variety of nongovernmental publications is also available.
- Statistics is the basic tool of research. Statistics give meaning to masses of data, help eliminate guesswork, and measure business efficiency.
- Statisticians work with averages, index numbers, and samples. They present statistical data tables and graphic devices such as line graphs, bar graphs, pie charts, and pictograms.
- Written reports should be well organized; prepared with the reader in mind; readable; written clearly; objective; neat; attractive; concise.
- Statistics and research findings should be interpreted carefully.

KEY TERMS YOU SHOULD KNOW

arithmetic mean	line graph	primary source
average	mail questionnaire	random sample
bar chart	median	sample
business research	mode	secondary source
Consumer Price Index	observation	statistics
controlled sample	panel interview	stub
experiment	personal interview	survey
index number	pictogram	universe
informal investigation	pie chart	

QUESTIONS FOR REVIEW

1. What is the difference between formal and informal research?
2. What factors account for the increased interest in research?
3. What questions can research help answer?
4. Explain the three steps involved in conducting research.
5. What are the four main methods of collecting data? Explain the advantages of each.
6. Contrast the observation method and the experiment method for collecting information.
7. What are primary sources of business information? Secondary sources?
8. What factors account for the boom in business publications?
9. Explain the limitations of experience in making business decisions.
10. Explain the three kinds of averages.
11. What is the consumer price index?
12. Explain sampling. What is the difference between a controlled sample and a random sample?
13. Explain the five forecasting techniques.
14. What are the basic principles for writing a good report?

QUESTIONS FOR DISCUSSION

1. "The first step in the research procedure is recognition of a problem." Is this easy? Discuss.
2. Assume you are asked to find out which of the states in the table has, on average, the most reckless drivers. The table gives this information about death rates caused by automobile accidents for selected states for 1980.
   a. Why are death rates not enough to determine which state has the most reckless drivers?
   b. What additional data is needed to find out which state has the most reckless drivers?
3. There are criticisms that American business managers operate too much "by the numbers" and that business schools have gone overboard in stressing quantitative techniques. The argument holds that this dampens creativity and fosters short-range, bottom-line decision making (concern with current profits to the exclusion of long-term consequences). Is this argument valid? Explain.

STATE	DEATH RATE PER 100 MILLION VEHICLE MILES
Alabama	3.6
California	3.2
Florida	3.2
Illinois	3.5
Massachusetts	2.4
Michigan	3.3
Nebraska	2.9
New York	3.7
Ohio	2.8
Pennsylvania	2.9
Texas	3.9
West Virginia	4.0

SOURCE: *Accident Facts*, Chicago National Safety Council, 1984.

CASE STUDY

Predicting the Birth Rate for the Next 20 Years

The birth rate affects future demand for all products, ranging from housing to education to medicine. All businesses and nonprofit organizations, therefore, are interested in what future birth rates will be.

The Future Foundation is a nonprofit research organization funded by contributions from businesses. Its purpose is to make studies that will indicate trends in social and economic affairs.

The foundation has contracted with Dan Robinson, a business professor, Abby Sauder, a statistics professor, and Juanita Raphael, a sociology professor, to conduct a study to forecast the birth rates for each of the next 20 years. The following discussion takes place at the first planning session.

Dan: Our mission is not an easy one. But it is important, since mistakes made in birth rate predictions translate into planning mistakes by all kinds of organizations.

Abby: I think we appreciate the importance of a reliable forecast of future birth rates. The official birth rate predictions the government made in the late 1950s helped create some of our economic problems of today. Back then, the experts claimed we would have a population of about 300 million by 1980. They missed it by about 75 million. Their erroneous forecasts resulted in overbuilding of schools and hospitals in many areas.

Juanita: That's because the statisticians assumed the birth rate of about 25 live births per 1,000 population would hold up. But it dropped dramatically.

D: I want us to look not just at past birth rates to project the future. We need to examine possible trends that will affect how many children people have. Some of these trends are economic and some are social.

A: One economic trend I see that will have a major impact is the increasing cost of rearing children. I keep hearing people say that they simply can't afford to have children.

J: I think we should be careful in making that assumption. Around the world and here in the United States people with low incomes have more children than people with high incomes. Should we have a severe and prolonged depression, birth rates may rise.

D: That's a possibility. And that is one of the questions on which we'll need to focus. But our forecasting assignment takes us into other areas.

A: I think we should look closely at attitudes and laws relating to abortion. In 1981, there were 1.5 million abortions—that was equal to about one-third of all pregnancies. If a strong anti-abortion sentiment develops, we would see a dramatic increase in the birth rate.

J: We should also consider women's attitudes toward careers versus families. Can they be better combined in the future? If so, that could mean an increase in the birth rate.

A: Especially if we have better day-care centers.

D: We've already identified some of the areas to examine. What I would like us to do now is to make a comprehensive analysis of all the economic and social factors that may affect the birth rate. Then we'll decide how to divide and coordinate the work.

But we must also consider the fact that there will be a declining number of women of childbearing age over the next two decades because of the birth rate decline in the post-1960 era.

Questions

1. In your opinion, will the birth rate decline, remain the same, or increase over the next 20 years? Why?
2. Would a higher birth rate be beneficial to the overall economy? Why or why not?
3. Changes in birth rates cause shifts in income expenditures. How are the following products and services affected as birth rates rise or fall: tourism, restaurants, television, construction, agriculture, and health care?

EVOLUTION OF A BUSINESS

Whither Changing Lifestyles?

Ray and Sara were taking stock of their current marketing strategies and of the future of the travel agency business in general. Ray, who had studied the latest census figures, was pleased to find that the singles market, on which he had been concentrating, was continuing to grow in importance. More and more households consisted of one person or of persons who were living together who were nonrelatives or unmarried. Changing lifestyles, higher divorce rates, lower birth rates, more living in multiple rather than single dwellings, and other factors all contributed to this phenomenon.

Sara: American lifestyles are changing in so many other ways, too. The things I keep noticing are increased mobility and reduced emphasis on home life. More and more people are living in mobile homes, people are eating out more often, and they're moving more often.

Ray: Our society is certainly much freer and less bound to possessions and family than it used to be.

Sara: Some of these changes in social values should be good for the travel business, right?

Ray: Definitely. Since people attach less importance to owning a house and buying furniture and appliances and a large car, they have more discretionary income available for leisure-time pursuits—including travel. And total household incomes are rising.

Questions

1. What evidence do you see that supports or refutes what Ray and Sara have been talking about?
2. Do you feel that the trends they identify will become further entrenched?
3. What opportunities, exactly, do these trends present for the travel industry?
4. How can the marketer best communicate with the singles population segment?

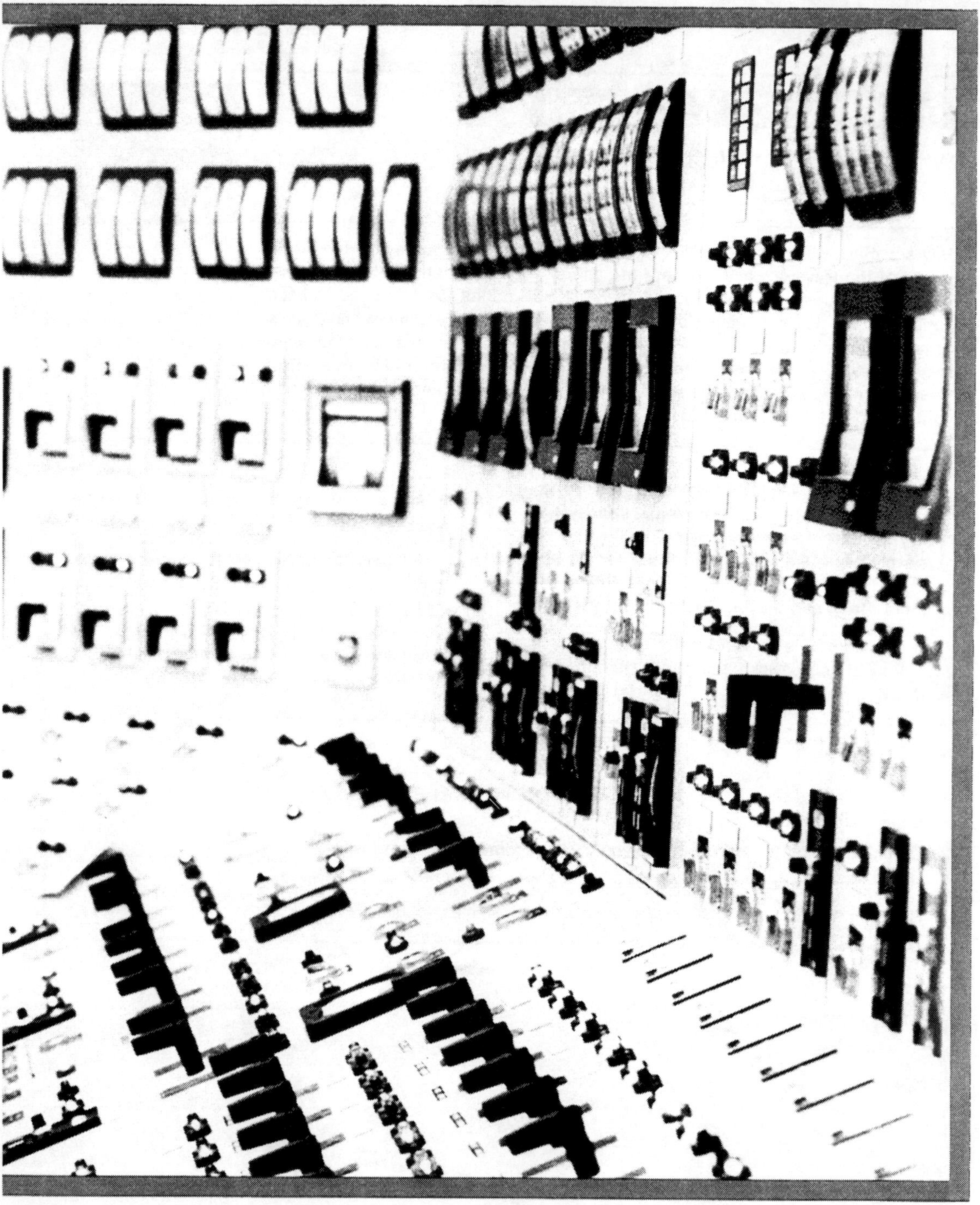

19

COMPUTERS: THE ELECTRONIC SIDE OF BUSINESS
Multiplying Efficiency

READ THIS CHAPTER SO YOU CAN:

Trace the history of data processing.

Explain the advantages of computerization.

Describe the common business applications of the computer.

Describe basic computer hardware—the central processing unit and the various input/output devices.

Discuss computer software.

Explain the roles of systems analysts and computer programmers.

Explain how word processing systems work.

Computers have already ushered in the world of tomorrow. Much of the science fiction that you and your classmates read when you were children is now reality. Computers dominate our lives; we take them so much for granted that we often do not even realize a computer is at work. For example, every time we use a telephone, turn on a TV, make a bank deposit or withdraw money, read a regional edition of *USA Today* or the *Wall Street Journal,* make an airline reservation, or play a video game, we depend on computers.

We become more conscious of computers when, for example, we ask an operator to furnish us with a telephone number and then hear a computerized recording—that eerie staccato voice that supplies the number digit by digit. Touch tones also allow us to dial a telephone number and then talk to a computer by pressing certain buttons on our telephone. People have already used this system in experiments for catalog ordering and for obtaining consumer information (you could use it to find out which restaurants in your area serve pizza).

Perhaps you have enjoyed the convenience of automated tellers. By pushing buttons in response to lighted questions or instructions on a computer display, you can withdraw cash from your account in the middle of the night without disturbing a single human being. These transactions are possible, of course, because of computers.

The next time you file an income tax return, the IRS will rely more on computers than on tax collectors to determine whether or not you have "overlooked" any taxes due. If the computer suspects an inaccuracy, it—not he or she—will notify you.

The stock market has become so computerized that it no longer generates large amounts of ticker tape. In fact, in 1984, when a New York "ticker-tape" parade honored the American Olympic participants, a paper company—not Wall Street—supplied the paper.

WHAT IS A COMPUTER?

The computer is an amazingly efficient tool that increases our capacity to do intelligent work and to handle masses of data. Specifically, a **computer** is *a programmable electronic device that can store, retrieve, and process data.* The computer industry has become the world's fastest growing industry, and experts predict that computers may well surpass the automobile and petroleum industries and become the world's largest industry—all before the year 2000!

The first industrial revolution, which started in England in the mid-eighteenth century, used machines to generate additional physical power. The "second industrial revolution," of the mid-twentieth century, owed most of its impetus to the computer—which generates a sort of "mental" power. Herbert Simon described the significance of these technical developments in this way: "In recorded history there have perhaps been three pulses of change powerful enough to alter [society] in basic ways. The introduction of agriculture ... the Industrial Revolution ... [and] the revolution in information processing technology of the computer."[1]

Computers Do Not Think

Computers are tools of people. They are only as accurate and reliable as the people who control them. Computers do not possess mystical powers as science fiction often depicts. Computers cannot "think" any more than telephones can "talk." Information and insight about computers help people overcome their fears of them.

Is Knowledge of Computers Really Important?

The work place of the future is intimately tied to computers. Consider this observation:

In 1980 there was one electronic work station for every 23 white collar employees in the economy; by 1989 there will be one for every two. This growth portends enormous changes in the way managers obtain information, make decisions, and perform their work. It is clear you won't be able to avoid the computer if you are just starting your career. The Pac-Man generation is coming up and gaining fast. You have no choice but to become computer proficient, at least as a user. If you don't, you will inevitably be left behind.[2]

Anyone contemplating a business career today must have a positive attitude toward computers since business increasingly depends on them. Although such automation may, in certain instances, lead to redefinitions of jobs and duties, strong evidence indicates that the result will be more, rather than fewer, jobs. (See "Issue for Debate," page 564.)

THE EXECUTIVE IN TOMORROW'S BUSINESS WORLD

Experts debate the future roles of the office secretary and the executive. Some futurologists believe that the secretary's role will change and that the executive will take on or share the typing chore. One consulting-firm spokesperson is convinced that "far from being reduced to mindless, repetitive processors, [secretaries] will become 'para-principles,' sharing in some of the professional work and decision making from which they have been largely excluded until now."[3]

---

[1]Herbert A. Simon, quoted in Yoneji Masuda, *The Information Society as Post-Industrial Society.*

[2]Paul Gray, "New Information Careers," *BusinessWeek's Guide to Careers,* Spring-Summer, 1984, 39.

[3]Quoted in Alvin Toffler, *The Third World* (New York: Bantam, 1980), 192.

ISSUE FOR DEBATE

Will the New Technology Create Massive Unemployment?

The following discussion between Bob, age 20, and his grandfather, age 70, took place one weekend.

Bob: Hey, Granddad, you would have loved to hear this man that gave a lecture in our business class today. He calls himself a futurist, and he predicted where our economy will be 20 years from now.

Granddad: Was he very optimistic?

B: Well, you might say yes and no. He was bullish on the emerging technology—especially in the fields of automation and robots and communications. Oh, also pharmaceuticals. And, well, computerization in general.

G: Sounds like he's predicting a good start for the next century. What was he pessimistic about, Bob?

B: Oh, he's afraid there won't be enough jobs to go around. He thinks that the new technology will result in massive unemployment. He says the number of workers in the basic industries—you know, mining, automobiles, steel, construction—will greatly decrease.

G: Well, in 20 years, probably fewer people *will* work in those industries. But think of the new industries that will sprout up. I think they will take up the slack. Technology has solved a lot of problems we never dreamed it could, and I think it will find a way to produce jobs for everyone.

B: Granddad, it's not that simple. This guy says the industries will require fewer but more intelligent and better-educated people. Just a small segment of the work force will be qualified for these jobs, because he says for every person with an IQ of 130, there is another person with an IQ of only 70. And he also said something else that frightened me. He claims that if unemployment goes up to 20 percent and stays that high for several years, we will have a political revolution. He says we would become socialistic or something worse.

G: Well, I remember how bad things were back in the depression of the thirties. And if things had continued that way, we might have had a revolution. I remember my dad saying something like that when I was a teenager. But what solutions did your lecturer propose?

B: Hah! None! But he says technological progress is inevitable. He says we shouldn't even try to stop it.

G: Well, Bob, you've told me what this futurist of yours thinks. Now let me tell you what your old granddad believes. We've adjusted pretty well to new technologies for the past two centuries. Railroads put canals out of business, and then trucks and planes hurt the railroads. And tractors did away with horses. When I was a child, not every family had a car, not by a long shot. And my dad could remember the real horse-and-buggy days. And my high school science teacher told us it was impossible for man to go to the moon. We've come a long way, and we've found answers. In the years ahead people will travel even more and have more complex lives, but I believe that technology will provide the answers. On the other hand, you ought to buy yourself a good life insurance policy.

B: Life insurance policy? Then you think we might have a nuclear war.

G: I didn't say *death* insurance policy. I call a good education a life insurance policy. It helps to ensure a good life for you and your future family. Get the best education you can, and choose your career very carefully.

Questions

1. Do you believe that the emerging new technology will cause large-scale unemployment in the future? Why or why not?
2. What kinds of jobs will be least affected by technology?
3. Do you agree that a 20 percent unemployment rate for, say, five years would cause a political revolution? Why or why not?
4. Do you think Granddad's advice about buying an "insurance policy" is good? If yes, why are so many people not preparing for a major change in the types of jobs that will be available in the future? If no, explain.

Other futurologists think the opposite, and suggest that the secretary's job as such will disappear because the electronic office of tomorrow will eliminate many of the secretary's functions. The goal of electronic word processing is the paperless office, which is close at hand. When computer memories can store all communications and when operators can change and correct information on desk-top screens and instantly retrieve information without shuffling papers in files, the need for the secretary as presently known will disappear.

The hitch in this scenario is that until voice or electronic ray techniques that can type and make changes in communications that appear on screens are available, executives will have to know how to type. Alvin Toffler predicts that in the changeover period (which is not too far off), help-wanted ads for vice-presidents will include the phrase. "Must be able to type."[4] While electronic equipment manufacturers already would like to promote the idea that all executives should be able to type, they are understandably cautious about offering a product that would actually require an executive to set fingers to a keyboard. As one observer quipped, "It is funny how a professional views a pencil as a professional tool and a keyboard as a clerical tool."

The changeover will not be easy, for as Toffler points out, "New systems challenge old executive turfs, the hierarchies, the sexual role divisions, [and] the departmental barriers of the past."[5]

HOW OLD IS DATA PROCESSING?

Data processing—*the classifying, sorting, calculating, summarizing, recording, and reporting of factual information*—is not a new function. Early calculating was done by placing pebbles in rows—the forerunner of the abacus, still used in some parts of the world.

[4]Ibid.
[5]Ibid.

For hundreds of years mathematicians recognized a need for a mechanical device to expedite data processing. At first progress was slow. In 1642, Blaise Pascal, a French mathematician and philosopher, built a simple, manually operated adding machine. In 1692, Gottfried Leibnitz, a German mathematician, demonstrated a calculating machine that could add, multiply, and divide. Years later, an English mathematician, Charles Babbage (1791–1871), developed a forerunner of the modern computer. While Babbage's basic ideas were sound, the limited technology of the day made it impossible for him to complete what he had envisioned.

In the latter part of the nineteenth century, people made definite strides toward the development of the modern computer. Around 1880, W. H. Odhner invented the pinset calculator, which performed arithmetic operations by mechanical devices. In 1885, William Burroughs produced the first commercial adding machine, and in the same year Herman Hollerith introduced the first punch-card calculating system. Hollerith's punch-card technique was used to process census data in 1890. This task "was completed in two and one-half years, less than one-third the time required for the 1880 census, despite the fact that the population of the United States had increased from 50 million to 63 million during the decade."[6]

The Three Generations of Electronic Computers

World War II brought about a new and urgent need for more effective data-processing methods. The first truly electronic computer, called ENIAC (Electronic Numerical Integrator and Calculator), was built between 1939 and 1946 at the University of Pennsylvania. In 1951, UNIVAC I, the first computer designed for commercial purposes, was delivered to the U.S. Department of Commerce for use by the Bureau of the Census.

Since then, progress in computer engineering has been phenomenal and has resulted in three "generations" of computers. The first generation, which appeared in the early 1950s, used vacuum tubes for circuitry. These bulky computers generated so much heat that they required massive air conditioning. By today's standards they were slow, doing fewer than 2,000 additions per second. Nevertheless, in one day they performed calculations that would take 300 days to do manually.

The second computer generation, introduced in the late 1950s, used transistors instead of vacuum tubes, an innovation that reduced the size of the computer and speeded up its operations tenfold.

In the mid-1960s, the third generation of computers appeared. These computers, which used integrated circuits instead of tran-

---

[6]Marilyn Bohl, *Information Processing*, 3rd ed. (Science Research Associates, 1977), 4.

sistors, provided increased speed and data-storage capacity. Third-generation computers could multiply two 10-digit numbers at a rate of more than 2 million complete calculations per second—a task that would take a person using a pencil and paper 38 years of nonstop work!

The most recently developed computers (sometimes referred to as the fourth generation, although they are essentially a continuation of the third) use a technology called **large-scale integration (LSI).** These computers *use chips of silicon the size of pinheads as electronic circuits.*

The Microprocessor

The development of large-scale integrated circuits led, in the early 1970s, to another major breakthrough in computer technology: the microprocessor. A **microprocessor** is *a core of a computer consisting of one silicon chip.*

The new technology also brought about the development of minicomputer and microcomputer systems, which have become important and dynamic growth industries. **Minicomputers** are *small general-purpose computers that can perform many of the functions of large computers.* They are also used in word processors, cash registers, and other business machines.

Microcomputers, sometimes referred to as **computers on a chip,** are *small minicomputers capable of performing a broad range of memory and control functions.* Minicomputers have made it possible for even very small enterprises to own a computer to handle transactions such as payroll, inventory, order entry, accounts receivable, accounts payable, and so on.

The home, or so-called personal, computer is one of the most popular applications of microprocessor technology. Expectations are that by the mid-1980s the number will soar to 3 million.

The lowest-priced personal computers are for such home uses as playing video games, maintaining household expense accounts, balancing checkbooks, and so forth. Home computers have become an essential tool in the so-called cottage industry, which enables a professional person to conduct work in the home, sometimes by using a telephone connection to an outside computer system.

So rapid is progress in the computer field that the differences between today's most advanced model and UNIVAC I are more pronounced than those between the modern jet airliner and the Wright brothers' first aircraft. When we consider that the first computer weighed 30 tons, it seems incredible that many computers are now light and compact enough to be carried in a matchbox. Actually, the memory of the 30-ton ENIAC was about the same as that of a microcomputer memory, which is smaller than the size of a cube of sugar.

WHAT ARE THE BASIC ADVANTAGES OF COMPUTERS?

Computers owe their great popularity to their ability to increase business efficiency. In a very real sense, the computer was invented out of necessity—in response to a great paperwork explosion. Without the computer, many large enterprises and communication systems, such as the space program, the banking industry, and airline reservation facilities, would now be drowning in paperwork or would not exist.

For example, average daily transactions on the New York Stock Exchange climbed from less than 2 million shares in 1950 to about 73 million in 1983. Specific advantages of computers are cost reduction, increased accuracy and manageability, and opportunity for people to think creatively.

COST REDUCTION

While computers represent a substantial initial investment, the savings that result from speed and other advantages lower overall costs.

Figure 19-1 contrasts the cost of handling records manually with the cost of handling them by computer. It illustrates the fact that manual processing costs will continue to grow indefinitely at approximately the same rate, regardless of how much the workload expands, whereas with computer processing, the rate declines dramatically with an increase in workload.

Let's expand this illustration by using some exaggerated figures. Assume that you have been employed by a small company to process

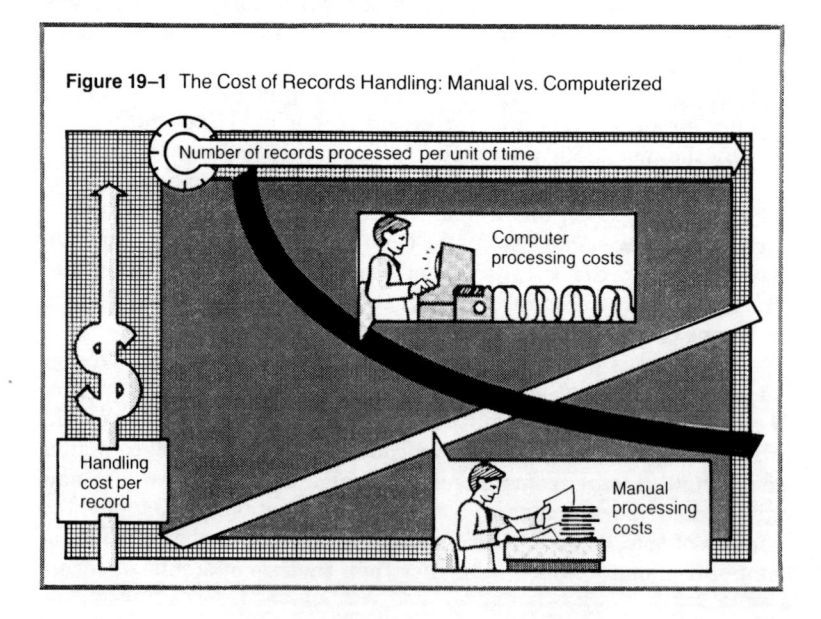

Figure 19-1 The Cost of Records Handling: Manual vs. Computerized

its five accounts manually. As new accounts are acquired, you discover that your maximum capacity will probably be ten accounts. Therefore, each time that the company acquires ten additional accounts, it will have to hire an additional processor and provide the necessary work space, desk, and telephone. Processing Account Number 3003 would be as time consuming and expensive as processing Account Number 3. But let's assume that when the company has a total of ten accounts, it decides to buy a computer that allows one person (you) to process 5,000 accounts. The initial investment (the cost of the computer) will be high, and immediately the cost of processing each account will skyrocket. Nevertheless, as the company grows and approaches Account Number 5000, the processing cost per account will drop drastically. Instead of hiring 500 employees, renting an additional office building, buying 500 desks, installing 500 telephones, and employing additional personnel required for such a large staff, the company would keep you as the only account processor, and the only additional expenses would be those associated with the computer. Although the statistics in this illustration are imaginary, you can easily see how advantageous computers can be under certain circumstances.

Record handling costs are going down even further due to the rapid advances in electronic technology. Costs relative to computation power will probably continue to decline, partly because of competitive forces and partly because of trends in the electronic industry.

GREATER ACCURACY AND MANAGEABILITY

As a business grows, the number of transactions involving records also grows—and the sheer physical handling of records becomes more and more difficult. Without computers, physical storage of records, summarization of data, retrieval of information, and arithmetic calculations could quickly get out of hand.

Furthermore, the accuracy of manual systems tends to decline with the addition of more clerks, who are required to do repetitive, boring tasks. While mistakes certainly occur with computerized systems, they are generally less frequent than with manual systems.

FREEDOM FOR MORE CREATIVE THINKING

The computer frees human beings for more creative and challenging work. By freeing business people from routine chores, the computer enables them to devote more time to analysis, planning, and creative effort.

The computer, which some people say symbolizes the growing impersonality of our society, may, ironically, result in *more* personal service. As one airline manager put it, "Freeing employees from routine work means that more courteous employees are out front dealing with the public and personalizing their service."

HOW ARE COMPUTERS USED?

Computers are now commonplace for preparing payrolls, billing customers, processing payments, keeping track of inventory, and providing a variety of production and sales reports; and people find new uses for computers each year. Below we discuss some applications that are growing in importance: word processors, robots, electronic mail sorters, mobile telephones, checkout scanners, health care computers, and process control devices.

Word Processors Increase Office Productivity

A **word processor** is *a computer designed to type, edit, and print letters, reports, manuscripts and other forms of text materials.* The operator facilitates these functions by giving the computer a set of instructions called a word processing program.

Word processors replace typewriters. The main difference is that a word processor stores the copy as electronic or magnetic impulses instead of as printing on paper. The typist uses a keyboard similar to a typewriter keyboard, but the text appears on a screen and the typist can obtain a printout or hard copy at any time without erasing the stored material.

The flexibility of word processors increases the amount of work that office personnel, writers, editors, and journalists can accomplish.

Word processors make revising material without extensive retyping easy. The operator can change a word or a sentence in a matter of seconds. The writer can move whole sections from one part of the text to another or change a particular word throughout the text (as in mass-produced direct mail in which the receiver's name is inserted in the letter to personalize the message). Word processors can greatly boost productivity in an office. One authority says, "One person on a word processor can do the work of three on an electric typewriter and do it better."[7]

Some of the major applications of word processors are:

- Repeating letters and standard paragraphs
- Correcting typing mistakes, including the use of "computer dictionaries" for checking spelling, hyphenation, and so on
- Restyling documents, inserting portions of other documents, and similar editing procedures
- Storing documents on magnetic tapes, floppy disks, and similar media
- Transmitting documents from one location to another and then reproducing them (electronic mail)

The major attraction of word processing is efficiency. In the case of manual typing, major revisions often require complete retyping and associated proofreading. This is not only extremely time-consuming but also expensive. Manual retyping also often leads to new typographical errors, further retyping efforts, or the use of pasteup procedures. Word processing reduces these problems. However, some feel that its impersonal nature is a limitation.

SOME COMPLAINTS IN USING WORD PROCESSORS

Widespread use of word processors and other visual display terminals (VDTs) has resulted in complaints from some of the employees who operate the keyboards and watch the screens several hours a day. Main complaints focus on eye strain, aches and pains, excessive fatigue, and stress. To help combat these problems, ergonomics, or the science of adapting machines to people, is becoming important. Ergonomists are playing a leading role in designing VDTs and the office environments where employees use them.

WORD PROCESSORS WON'T TAKE OVER COMPLETELY

Although word processing is a major breakthrough in office productivity, it has not completely replaced conventional methods of converting ideas and messages to readable copy. In 1983 IBM, for example, sold two million personal computers, but it also shipped 600,000

---

[7]Arthur Naiman, "Word Processing Buyer's Guide," *BYTE*, 1983, 4.

Selectric typewriters. There are eight million Selectrics and 24 million other noncomputerized typewriters in use in the USA.[8] Conventional methods of handling words will be in use for some time.

Robots: Computerization of the Assembly Line

Fifty years ago people considered the assembly line an enormous breakthrough in production. Workers, each of whom did only a small part of the assembly operation, were, collectively, more productive because specialization eliminated wasted motion and time. The tasks they did were extremely repetitive, and the pay (thanks in large part to unionization) was good. In the past decade, mass assembly work has become less attractive as a job choice because it is boring, provides little opportunity for promotion, and—compared to service sector jobs—is much more disciplined and confining.

A technological breakthrough in the 1970s, the industrial robot, may prove as revolutionary as the assembly line half a century ago. A "robot" need not look like the little mechanical man who is often pictured in cartoons. In fact, the Robot Institute of America defines an **industrial robot** as *"a reprogrammable multifunctional manipulator designed to move materials, parts, tools or specialized devices through variable programmed motions for the performance of a variety of tasks."* Therefore, a robot's ability—not its appearance—is the definitive factor, and industrial robots are being designed to replace human beings in assembly-line tasks. Robots will also dig minerals from the ocean floor, repair satellites in space, and perform other programmable work.

Experts predict that as the use of computerized robots increases, numerous controversies will occur between labor and management. Production management will welcome the coming of robots because robots are never late for work, do not call in sick, are not part of a union, work three shifts if needed, and do not require overtime pay. Labor will contend that robots rob jobs from human beings; management will counter that their companies need lower costs of production to compete domestically and internationally.

Electronic mail, transmitted from computer to computer, has great potential for streamlining written communication.

Electronic Mail Is on the Way

The United States Postal Service is a large industry. It operates 30,000 post offices, delivers 500 pieces of mail (55 percent first class) per capita per year, spends $26 billion annually, and employs over 600,000 people. Since the early 1970s, computer companies and the postal service have been experimenting with sending messages by electronic mail. Although computerized mail delivery has not become commonplace yet, it has great promise for the future.

[8]"The Computer For Your Future," *BusinessWeek's Guide to Careers*, Spring-Summer, 1984, 66.

Sending messages from one computer to another is easy, but not everyone has a computer to accept messages. Also many people still want hard copy or text material, so the letter as people know it today will not disappear for a while. Therefore, the MCI Communications Corporation has been successful in combining electronic mail with overnight package express service. A computerized message can be sent to one of 15 MCI post offices, printed, placed in an envelope, and delivered by courier service or, for less money, by the U.S. Postal Service.

In 1982 the U.S. Postal Service launched its own form of electronic mail, called E-COM but does not plan to enter the computer-to-computer mail business. E-COM is designed to service volume mailers. It requires sending a letter to 200 recipients and guarantees two-day delivery.

Other companies are planning to transmit letters and other documents electronically by using facsimile machines. The electronic mailer transmits a document by machine to an office near the addressee, where it is printed and delivered by a messenger. This system has the advantages of speed—as little as two hours elapse from pickup to delivery; the addressee receives exact copy or artwork and does not need a computer compatible with that of the message sender.

Computers Expand Mobile Telephone Service

For a generation telephones have been available for use in automobiles. However, the few available frequencies have restricted the number of mobile telephones. But now Bell Laboratories has developed computerized mobile telephone service, based on cellular technology. Instead of one high-power transmitter for a large area, the cellular system divides transmission into smaller regions called cells, each served by its own low-power radio transmitter.

Customers of cellular telephone service do not need to talk to an operator or make or receive a call. Users can dial local, long-distance, and international calls directly, as easily as from an office phone. Cellular service can help boost productivity of salespeople, physicians, executives, and others who need frequent access to a phone and spend considerable time in an automobile. Bell expects to sell millions of units in the next decade as familiarity with the system increases and costs come down.

Computers have made mobile telephone services, based on cellular technology, possible. Dialing from your car is now as easy as calling from your easy chair.

How Checkout Scanners Increase Retailing Efficiency

A **checkout scanner** is *an electronic device which uses laser beams to read and interpret the ten-digit universal product code (UPC) printed on more than 85% of food-store merchandise.* The product, price, size, quantity, and even the time of day are recorded by a computer as the product is scanned. Many scanners can read codes in a 180-degree field.

Checkout scanners date back to the early 1970s, but their widespread acceptance did not occur until the 1980s. Scanners increase retailing efficiency in three ways: (a) the checkout function is faster and more accurate, (b) inventory control is automatic, and (c) marketing strategy is improved.

CHECKOUT FUNCTION IS FASTER AND MORE ACCURATE

The scanner reads key information on the UPC, calls out the price of each item for the customer, and makes a continuous tally. Scanners are considered the most important innovation in food retailing since the introduction of the self-service concept half a century ago. Cashiers can now handle twice as many customers as before.

INVENTORY CONTROL IS AIDED

The scanner is connected to a computer that keeps a running inventory on each item sold. When programmed properly, the computer tells management when to reorder specific items, what products are *not* selling well, and similar information.

MARKETING STRATEGY IS IMPROVED

Instantaneous information on how well a product is selling helps management decide whether a new package is needed, a price change is called for, or a different shelf or store location is needed; and it even indicates how effective advertising is in selling a product.

For some food retailers, scanners have doubled profits. Scanners will find wide use by discount stores and other mass-merchandising outlets in the near future.

How Computers Aid Health Care

The health care industry, which accounts for 10 percent of our gross national product, is making extensive use of computers for diagnosis, treatment, and administration. Computerized devices evaluate blood and tissue samples, monitor electrocardiograms, and record changes in postoperative conditions. Computers now administer blood, intravenous fluids, and drugs with much greater precision than is possible by human beings. Cost control in the health industry is also aided by computers.

Process Control

A **process-control computer** is *one that controls a physical process.* For example, the computer might control a valve that regulates the flow of material in a chemical process or the flow of electricity in

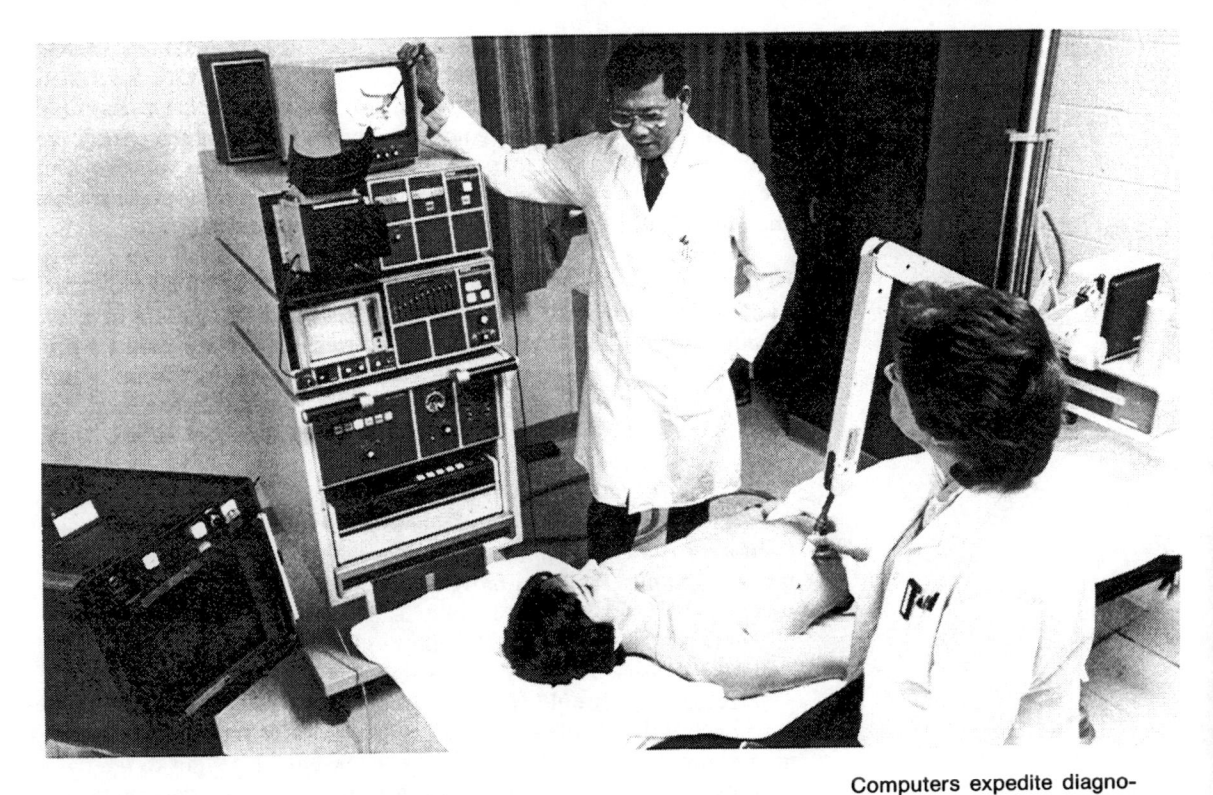

Computers expedite diagnoses, treatment, and administration at hospitals and clinics.

a power system. It senses conditions in the device being controlled through attached sensors. It then reacts by sending pulses to devices (called servomotors) that change the position of the valve or change the sequence of steps being executed.

Process-control computers relieve people of many tedious chores required in monitoring measurement devices, determining appropriate settings, and supervising various processes. They are also faster and more reliable than human supervisors.

ANALOG AND DIGITAL FUNCTIONS

A process-oriented computer may perform either an analog or a digital function, or both. An **analog function** is *the continuous measurement by a computer of some physical quantity, such as temperature, speed of motion, electrical current, pressure, or flow.* A **digital function** is *the computer's reading of discrete numbers (for example, 1, 2, 3) rather than sensing of continuous amounts.* The computer then produces an output based on the value of the quantity being measured.

Process-control computers have found applications in many industries that involve continuous flow, such as petroleum, chemicals, utilities, metals, aerospace, and transportation. They have been used for patient monitoring in hospitals, for traffic control, on assembly lines (where the computer guides machines that produce parts), for automated testing and inspection, for control of space vehicles, and for materials movement in warehousing (where the computer controls the movement of vehicles that transport merchandise).

A computer that operates so that output is available so quickly that it can be used to control real-life activity is called a **real-time system.** The response time may vary from near immediate to a few seconds. Systems that respond almost immediately are used for airplane flight progress information and aboard spacecraft for monitoring the activities of astronauts. The "slower" systems are used, for example, by an insurance company in serving customer needs.

THE CALIFORNIA AQUEDUCT SYSTEM

An excellent example of large-scale process control is provided by the California Aqueduct System (see photo on page 577). This huge system is 450 miles long and moves water from the northern half to the southern half of the state. It includes 27 pumping and power plants, 66 check structures with 213 separate gates, and a minimum of 49 major turnout structures where water is delivered to customers.

Normally it would take a particle of water eight to ten days to travel 450 miles. Without special controls, water input at the beginning of the system would have to be forecast at least eight to ten days in advance to provide service to the terminal end. Under controlled volume arrangements that regulate the speed of flow at many points, the system can respond quickly to changes in demand.

Area control centers monitor and/or control events at the check structures, pumping plants, flow measurement stations, and turnouts. Each area control center contains a digital computer, which operates through a console that is the primary person/machine interface for the system. The area control centers also have high-speed paper tape equipment, information storage devices, input/output devices, and other essential peripheral equipment.

In the California Aqueduct System, computers again aid in cost control. For example, the 14 pumps at the A. D. Edmonston pumping plant, where the aqueduct passes over the Tehachapi Mountains, require a power capacity of 896,000 kilowatts. In one year of full operation, this plant alone consumes 6.4 billion kilowatt hours of energy. Because of billing rules of electric utility companies, power must be paid for evenly over 12 months of a year, based on one peak value. The objective sought by the computer was to find a total system operating over a five-year period that would reduce peaks and produce a uniformly low set of monthly power requirements.

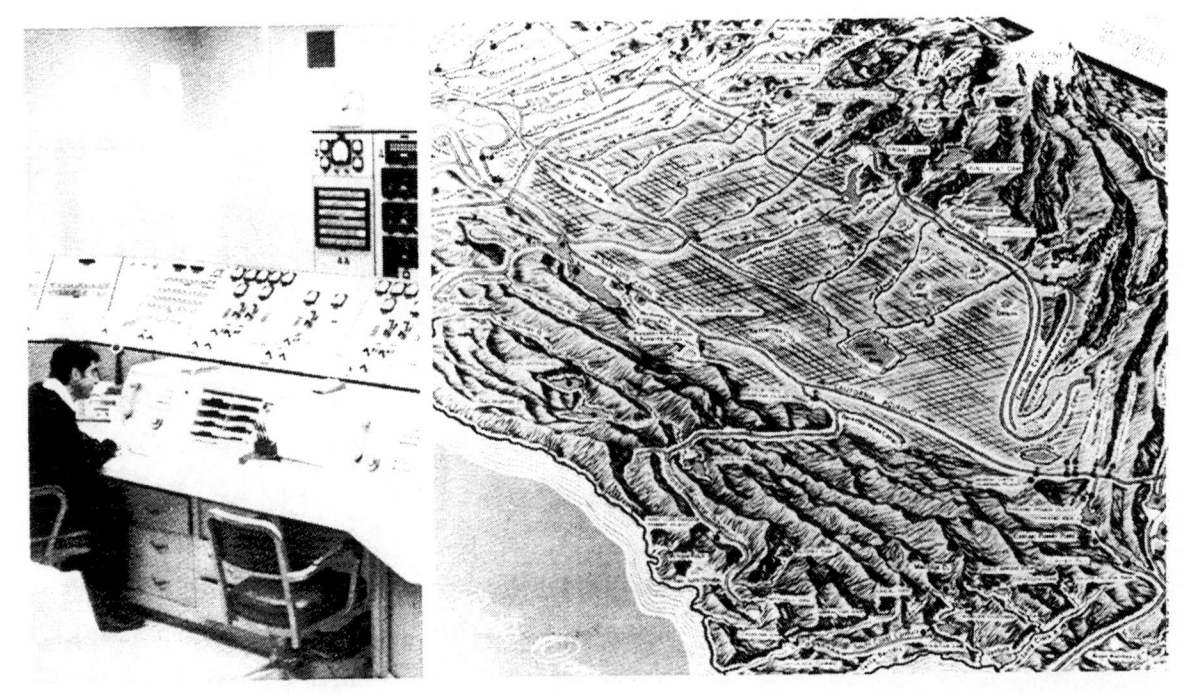

WHAT IS COMPUTER HARDWARE?

Hardware refers to *the physical components that make up a computer installation.* Figure 19–2 illustrates the way a computer works.

The Central Processing Unit

The core of the computer is the **central processing unit (CPU)**, which performs the following functions:

- *Memory*—Data and programs put into the computer must be stored until needed. The computer must hold, or memorize, information. Each storage location has an "address" so that the computer knows where to find that information when it wants it. In addition to holding the data needed to solve a problem, the computer also stores instructions on how to use the data.
- *Calculation*—The calculation section of the computer adds, subtracts, multiplies, divides, and compares numbers.
- *Control*—The control unit is the central nervous system of the whole computer installation. It guides the computer along each step of the operation to see that everything is done in proper sequence. By selecting, interpreting, and executing the instruc-

Computers are a key element in the vast California Aqueduct System. At each area control center, a digital computer monitors and controls events at the installations.
SOURCE: California Department of Water Resources. F & M Systems Company, a Division of Fischbach and Moore, Inc., Dallas, Texas: John Matucha, "Don't Reject Dynamic Programming for Complex Systems." *Computer Decisions* (April 1972), pp. 18–19.

Figure 19-2 Anatomy of a Computer

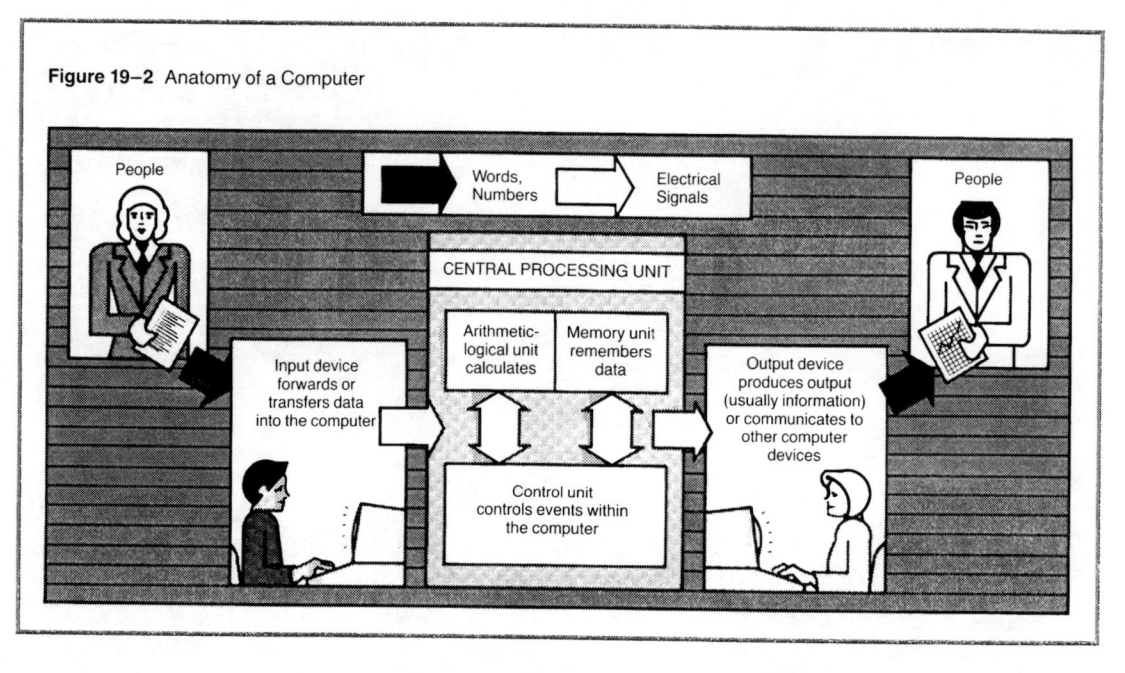

tions programmed into it, the control unit directs and coordinates the entire operation of the computer.

Input/Output Devices

In order to use a computer, there must be devices for input and output as well as a CPU. Just as a person needs information to solve a problem, so does a computer. *The process of feeding data or instructions to the computer* is called **input**. **Output** is *the result of the data-processing operation.*

Output may take the form of information, such as a computer printout. It may alternatively take the form of an action. For example, assume that a computer controls a certain valve in a pipeline. If certain events occur, the computer may direct that the valve be partially closed. In this case, the closing of the valve is the output.

MAGNETIC INK AND OPTICAL SCANNERS

Magnetic ink and optical scanners are often **off-line devices**—that is, they are *separate devices not part of the main computer installation. These input/output devices consist of printing in magnetic ink characters that can be read by both people and computers. An optical scanner has a set of electronic patterns stored in its memory. A photoelectric cell scans the material to be read and then converts characters into electric impulses. The scanner reads any character that matches the patterns stored in its memory.*

U.S. banks, which are involved in the clearance of millions upon millions of checks each day, issue their checking-account customers individually prepared books of blank checks. The numbers on these checks, which are printed with magnetic ink, give the customer's account number and other information needed for check clearance. After a check is written and presented for clearance, further magnetic numbers are added to it. The numbers permit computers at various steps in the clearing process to credit and debit accounts for the amount for which the check was written (see Figure 19-3).

Optical scanners are also commonly used in the analysis of test-score sheets, survey instruments, questionnaires, payrolls, and inventories, as well as in the preparation of utility bills.

KEYBOARDS AND PRINTERS

The computer **keyboard,** or **terminal,** *looks essentially like a modified typewriter keyboard with additional function keys to control the computer.* Using the keyboard, a computer operator can enter information into the computer and activate the printer. The **printer** is *often a separate unit, which may vary in regard to functions and printing speeds.* **Line printers** *print one line at a time,* and **character printers** *print one character at a time.*

Some character printers may be connected to a computer by direct wire or over telephone lines. The most common is the Teletype

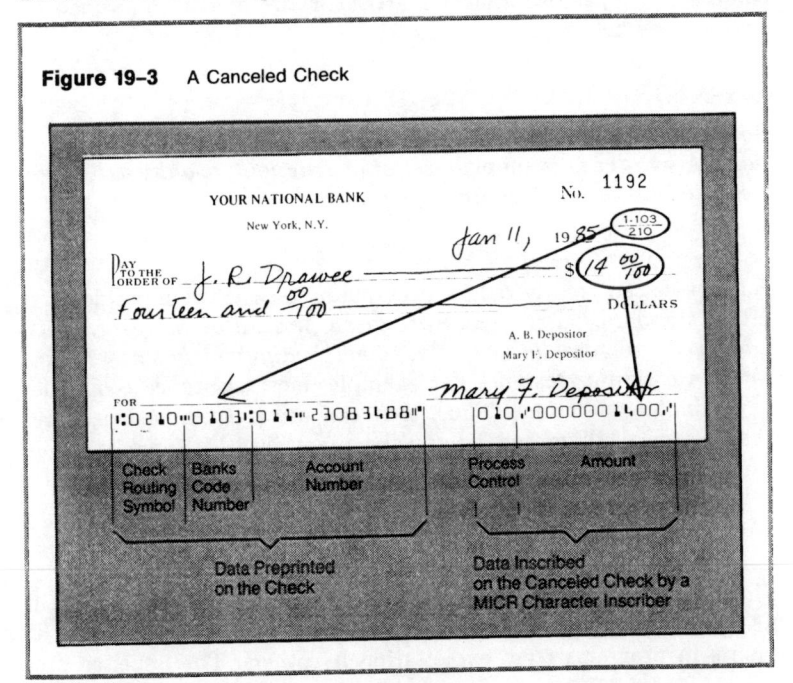

Figure 19-3 A Canceled Check

printer, manufactured by the Teletype Corporation. Character printers have the advantage of being able to serve as remote terminals located far from a central computer.

There is a variety of low-cost terminals, which are often portable. Using a telephone and regular telephone lines, they may be connected to various main computer systems. Some of these systems are discussed later in this chapter.

THE VIDEO TERMINAL

A **video terminal** is *an output device that operates electronically rather than mechanically.* Images are thus displayed more rapidly than with character or line printers. The most common type contains a cathode-ray tube (CRT), which resembles a small television set placed on top of a typewriter keyboard. A personnel director, for example, may enter an employee's code on the keyboard, and the person's records will immediately by flashed on the screen. A record can be altered or deleted simply by typing in the change, a procedure that cuts down on file searching and paper shuffling. Because of their speed, these devices are popular as remote terminals for use in banking, airline ticket reservations centers, and so on (see "Evolution of a Business," page 589).

In addition to displaying printlike characters, some video terminals can produce line drawings and graphic images. Others can "read" from a light pen, so that an artist or draftsman can construct drawings by holding a "conversation" with the computer.

WHAT IS COMPUTER SOFTWARE?

Software refers to *the programs that give the computer its instructions.* A **program** is simply *a set of instructions, usually written by a specially trained computer programmer.*

Software Packages

Businesses can greatly reduce programming costs when problems fit into a standardized scheme. **Software packages** are *generalized packaged programs used for tasks many different businesses perform in a similar fashion.* For example, most insurance companies have similar operations. Thus, they can use programmed packages that perform billing and accounting tasks with little modification. Companies can often purchase packages less expensively than develop the programs themselves.

Patents for Computer Programs?

Since many man-hours of highly skilled labor go into the design of programs, companies have searched for a legal way to protect investments in programs from exploitation by others. The issue, as presented in cases before the Supreme Court, is "whether a machine system implemented in software (a computer program) is equally as patentable as the same machine system implemented in hardware (a series of hard-wired circuits)."[9]

After years of debate, Congress enacted new Patent and Trademark Laws to make explicit that computer programs are copyrightable.[10] The issue of patentability advanced when the Supreme Court affirmed the decision of the Court of Customs and Patent Appeals that a computer-related invention—a machine that included hardware elements containing microprogrammed information, termed "firmware"—may be patentable.[11] The new legislation provides definitions of both "computer program" and the rights to make copies of such programs for "archival purposes."

The Rising Cost of Software

One could easily assume that the hardware elements of the computer are the more costly, since they are tangible, complicated equipment. Actually, over a period of time, software costs usually exceed those of hardware. Two reasons account for this. First, hardware is becoming more standardized, resulting in production economies. Second, computer programs are meanwhile becoming more complex. It costs relatively less today to build computers but relatively more to tell them what to do. In 1955, software costs were less than 20 percent of total computer costs; by 1977, they were over 60 percent; and by 1987, they are expected to rise to over 80 percent.[12]

WHAT DO SYSTEMS ANALYSTS AND COMPUTER PROGRAMMERS DO?

The Systems Analyst

The **systems analyst** is *the person who decides what a computer will do and how it will be done.* These can be intricate processes, since systems analysis deals with problems as a whole, not just with their separate parts. The analyst may be concerned, for example, with using the computer to schedule production, monitor inventory, record sales, and perform cost accounting.

The Programmer

The **programmer** is *the person who develops the actual instructions (programs) for a computer based on the systems analyst's*

---

[9]Prater-Wei (1969), Benson (1972), Johnson (1975), Knoll (1976), Chatfield (1976), and others.
[10]Public Law 96-517, December 12, 1980.
[11]Diamond v. Bradley, No. 79-855, March 9, 1981.
[12]*Computerworld,* May 2, 1977, 13.

specifications. (There is not always a clear line between the systems analyst and the programmer. In some companies, the same people perform both functions.) To write a program, the programmer must first develop a clear picture of the problem and the logical steps required to solve it. Usually he or she draws a **flow chart**—that is, *a sketch that shows the breakdown of a problem into its component parts and the relation of the parts to each other.*

A flow chart is something like a road map. However, instead of tracing a sequence of routes, towns, and stopover places, it traces a logical sequence. A computer can make only simple yes-no decisions. Basically the programmer prepares a series of instructions that state "If X, do this...." "If Y, do this...." and so on. While each individual decision is simple, the entire logical flow in a program is usually very complex and requires days or weeks of thought and preparation.

COMPUTER LANGUAGES

After developing a flow chart, the programmer must write up the instructions in a form that the computer can understand. **Binary code** is *a numerical system made up of just two elements—0 and 1—that is used in the internal operations of computers.* (The decimal system, in contrast, involves ten elements—0 through 9.) A binary number is any string of zeros and ones, such as 101101001. To communicate most directly with the computer, a programmer would write instructions in this form.

This system, however, is extremely cumbersome and tends to encourage human errors. Therefore, computer communications are generally translated into a shorthand language. *The most common language for business applications is* **COBOL (COmmon Business Oriented Language),** which *closely resembles English* (see Figure 19–4). Another language, **RPG (Report Program Generator),** is *also specifically designed for business applications.*

The Relation Between Analyst, Programmer, and User

In tackling a computerization problem, a systems analyst begins by conferring with users—that is, the people who wish to make use of a computer. For example, several members of a marketing department may come to the systems analyst to inquire about the possibility of computerizing the order-processing system. The systems analyst then studies the present procedures and flows of information used in processing orders. By analyzing the system—breaking it down into its parts and examining each one in detail—he or she is able to identify current problems and decide how to use the computer. This may involve revising the user's procedures, redefining the way the procedures fit together, or replacing manual with automated procedures where appropriate. Systems analysis need not involve computerization: It is simply a close look at the way an organization is carrying out a task or group of tasks.

Figure 19-4 Telling a Computer What to Do

Imagine trying to instruct a visitor from another planet on how to boil an egg. To begin, a common language has to be learned. But even after that is accomplished, the visitor has to be given explicit, step-by-step directions, since he does not know an egg from an orange. For example: 1. Walk to the cupboard. 2. Open the doors. 3. Take out the big pot. 4. Go to the sink. 5. Turn on the cold water tap. 6. Fill the pot half-full of water. And so on. If he misses just one of the dozens of steps, the visitor will be confused and unable to complete his task.

That scenario is not unlike what a programmer goes through in writing the software, a set of instructions to perform a job on a computer. Writing a computer program is a most rigorous and exacting job that requires the utmost attention to detail. Even a misplaced comma can cause the computer to forget what it is doing and begin turning out garbage.

With the most basic computer languages—such as Assembler—programmers have to write one line of instruction, or computer code, for each tiny chore that the computer is to execute. The so-called higher-level languages such as FORTRAN and COBOL incorporate instruction subsets in the language so that one line of code can contain about six instructions. Even easier to write—because the language itself is more complex—are the software programs in the new query languages that understand English-like commands. Unlike COBOL or FORTRAN, however, which can be used to program the computer to do a wide variety of functions, query languages will instruct the computer only in how to file or retrieve information.

Shown below are portions of three programs—one in Assembler, one in COBOL, and one in a query language. Each is designed to generate the same report showing the account balances for a list of customers. But to do the job, the Assembler program takes more than 3,000 lines. The COBOL program runs more than 600 lines. But the one sentence in query language is all that is needed.

Assembler

```
215   LA   R2, @ IDTWO (,R9)
216   LA   R1, @ PTENDL + @ PTNEXT (,R1)
217   B    PTM1
```

COBOL

```
330820   IF PRIORBAL   NOT NUMERIC MOVE 'Y' TO YES-NON MOVE
330822   'PRIORBAL    'TO MVLAB PERFORM NONNUM-1 THRU NONNUM-1-EX
330824   MOVE ZEROES TO PRIORBAL
```

Query language

I WANT A REPORT FOR BUSINESS TYPE 17 IN ORDER BY BRANCH, SHOWING ACCOUNT NUMBER, NAME, AND BOTH CURRENT AND PRIOR BALANCES.

SOURCE: *BusinessWeek*, September 1, 1980, data from Cullinane Corp.

The analyst next meets with the users to discuss the findings and proposed changes. After the analyst and the users agree on what is to be done, the analyst prepares specifications for programming (or decides on a software package to be purchased). **Programming specifications** are *fairly detailed descriptions of tasks the computer will perform and how each task or process will work in conjunction with all other tasks and processes in the new system.*

While designing and implementing the system, the analyst confers frequently with users and programmers. In this way the systems analyst resolves final questions and refines the system so that it meets the needs of users and fits well with their ongoing operations.

Job Outlook for Computer Specialists Is Excellent

The demand for programmers is rising. Two observers note, "The demand for computer programmers already outstrips the supply by 50,000 to 100,000. We think that by 2000, there will be almost 1 million new jobs generated for computer programmers."[13] Lawrence A. Welke, president of International Computer Programs, Inc., stated, "If you give me names of 600 good programmers, I could place them all by 5 P.M. today."[14]

Demand for other computer specialists will also grow. Businesses will need managers: (a) for overall systems development and implementation; (b) to direct operations of the mainframe, data entry, and data control; and (c) to direct the organization's overall data processing activities. Demand will also increase for marketing representatives, marketing technical support personnel, and senior marketing managers.

WHERE IS THE COMPUTER INDUSTRY HEADED?

The computer industry has evolved faster and in more directions than any other industry in history, including automobiles, aircraft, electricity and telephones. In only 30 years, it grew from a single bulky, clumsy, complicated, and expensive machine into tens of millions of small, inexpensive, and powerful devices simple enough in some cases for children to operate.

Seven trends in computerization seem likely:

1. Evolution of the industry depends on new needs to analyze and communicate data. Advances in the emerging fields of microsur-

---

[13]Marian Cetron and Thomas O'Toole, authors of *Encounters with the Future: A Forecast of Life in the 21st Century* (McGraw-Hill) as reported in "Careers 1984," *Atlanta Journal-Constitution,* April 29, 1984, 34–35.

[14]Fredrick G. Withington, quoted in *BusinessWeek,* September 1, 1980, 49.

gery, animal and plant genetics, engineering, and space exploration will lead to advances in computer state of the art.

2. New applications will develop for computers as a teaching and learning tool. Whereas less than one-fifth of today's high-school graduates can type, virtually every graduate in the future will have some knowledge of computer operation.

3. The integration of computers with other electronic devices—such as the telephone, television, and metering systems—will continue.

4. Word processing will be necessary for virtually all offices in the next decade.

5. Voice-activated reproduction devices capable of converting spoken words into printed words will be available.

6. Robots, conveyor systems, and other computer controlled devices will handle simple, routine operations—such as assembly line work and movement of products inside warehouses.

7. The number of jobs for people working exclusively with computers will increase; and nearly all jobs in the future will require some use of computers, just as many jobs today require some use of the telephone.

Ben Bova summed up the overall positive social impact of computers when he said:

With technology, we are producing a true revolution in our ability to communicate. Modern computers and electronics are producing a new human freedom: the freedom from repetitive tasks. This is merely the beginning of the so-called second industrial revolution. The day will come when people will be hard pressed to believe that humankind ever existed without automated machinery and computer-powered information systems.[15]

The computer industry will continue to grow. Its rate of evolution, in terms of new applications and sophistication is limited only by our imagination and by the industry's ability to increase efficiency and lower costs (see "America's Reemerging Creativity," page 586). Computer products and software are still in the growth phase of the product life cycle. Like all industries, the period of enormous growth will eventually reach maturation. But, for the foreseeable future, rapid growth is assured.

One of the industry's leading visionaries, Alan Kay, a chief scientist at Atari, said, "The best way to predict the future is to invent it."[16]

---

[15]Ben Bova, "The Revolutionaries," *Computer Decisions*, January 1975, 23–26.

[16]Joel Dreyfuss, "What Will Send Computers Home?" *Fortune*, April 2, 1984, 74.

AMERICA'S REEMERGING CREATIVITY

The Space Shuttle

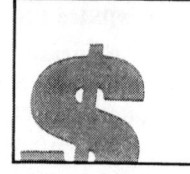

The successful launch of the first space shuttle, *Columbia,* in 1981 ushered in a new age in space technology and exploration. The launch and the 54½-hour trip went exactly as planned—a credit to the enormously complex engineering that went into the project.

The space shuttle takes off like a rocket, circles the earth like a spaceship, reenters the atmosphere like a capsule, and flies back to earth like an airplane. Thirty seconds after launch the space shuttle flies faster than the supersonic Concorde.

Although some criticized the development and launch of the *Columbia* because of the cost of $9½ billion, others believe that the space shuttle will prove to be one of the best investments any nation has ever made.

One of the first beneficiaries of the shuttle was the communications industry. Increasingly, communications companies are using satellites to transmit radio and television messages, but satellites are very expensive to launch by means of rockets. With the space shuttle, a number of satellites are placed on board and then put into space when the shuttle is in orbit. Satellites already in orbit have also been retrieved and taken aboard the shuttle in space.

In addition to helping make the communications industry more efficient, high-technology manufacturing will also use the space shuttle. Products such as high-purity electronic crystals needed to improve the performance of electronic components can only be made in a gravity-free environment. Other products that will likely be produced in space are pure vaccines and hormones.

Experts estimate that by the year 2,000, business conducted in space could generate revenues of $30 billion. Both the public and private sectors are already benefiting. Solar power generating, manufacturing in space (for making things that require weightlessness, like the perfect ball bearing, which cannot be made in the presence of gravity), and space hospitals are all very much in the picture. Severe burn victims heal much better when suspended weightlessly in space. Geologists can add to their effectiveness from space by scouring the earth's land and seas for mineral resources.

The space shuttle can carry a payload of 65,000 pounds. A number of foreign countries, including China, Australia, Canada, Japan, and Great Britain, have rented payloads for various purposes.

One of the planned scientific projects for the shuttle is the placement in space of a telescope that can see 14 billion light years into space—seven times the distance earth telescopes can see. Since the earth is estimated to be four to five billion years old, some science fiction writers believe that someday we may be able to see our solar system being created!

Who knows?

Questions for Discussion

1. Resources are always limited, whether we think of individuals, businesses, or governments. Do you think that the space shuttle program is worth the money allocated to it? Why or why not?

2. To this point, the chief benefit of space research and exploration has been in communications via satellite. What other uses of space technology seem likely to occur over the next 25 to 50 years?

SUMMARY

- The computer industry is growing rapidly because of technological innovations. Hardware is increasingly sophisticated, but costs compared to software are decreasing.
- Computer advantages: reduced cost, increased accuracy, manageability, and creative thinking.
- Hardware includes the central processing unit, input/output devices, magnetic ink, optical scanners, keyboards, printers, video terminals.
- Software consists of programs and programming aids to give the computer instructions.
- Systems analysts and programmers instruct the computer. Their close cooperation is essential in efficient computer use.
- Businesses have found many computer applications such as payroll, billing, inventory, process control, and integrated information systems.
- New uses are word processors, robots, electronic mail, mobile telephones, checkout scanners, health care, and process control.
- The outlook for computers is excellent: new industries will require computers, educators will use them more widely, new technology will permit merging computers with other electronic devices, word processing will become more important, voice-activated reproduction devices will be developed, robot development will expand, and virtually all jobs in the future will be computer-related.

KEY TERMS YOU SHOULD KNOW

analog function	input	process-control computer
binary code	keyboard	program
central processing unit	large-scale integration	programmer
character printer	line printer	programming specifications
checkout scanner	magnetic ink and optical scanner	real-time system
COBOL		RPG
computer	microcomputer	software
data processing	microprocessor	software package
digital function	minicomputer	systems analyst
flow chart	off-line device	video terminal
hardware	output	word processor
industrial robot	printer	

QUESTIONS FOR REVIEW

1. Why have computers developed so rapidly since 1946?
2. What is data processing? Explain the three generations of electronic computers.
3. What are the computer's main advantages?
4. Why does software cost more than hardware?
5. Why is systems analysis so important to the effective use of a computer?
6. What is a binary code? Why is it used instead of the decimal system in computer operations?
7. Differentiate between analog and digital functions of computers.
8. Explain word processing. How can it change office procedures and secretarial duties?
9. What do you think future developments in computer technology will be? Why?

QUESTIONS FOR DISCUSSION

1. Many new jobs in the next decade will be for fast-food workers, waiters, sales clerks, and janitors. Such jobs pay relatively low wages to low-skilled employees. Can they be computerized? Will such workers require substantial pay subsidies to maintain purchasing power even with technology workers?
2. How will more computerization affect education and leisure-time pursuits?
3. Because of computerization, what controls may be necessary to protect individual privacy?
4. How will the projected gains in technology affect (a) the arms race, (b) international trade, and (c) exploration of outer space?
5. Do you believe computerization will lead to greater happiness among people? Why?

CASE STUDY

Can a Computerize-the-Phone-Book Venture Succeed?

Superstar Electronics, a successful firm, specializes in marketing, installing, and servicing cable television systems. Herb, the president, wants to market a computerized phone directory. Herb, Phil, director of marketing, and Alice, head of research, discuss it.

Herb: The volume of home computers and predictions for sales are phenomenal.
Alice: Years ago the so-called experts were predicting that by now most homes would have video telephones. At the end of World War II experts said that 5 million people would own airplanes within 10 years. But how do sales of home computers affect us?
H: You're right. Experts are sometimes off target. Let me explain how home computer sales may relate to us. Urban phone books have gotten too big.
Phil: I agree. I call information too often. It saves time—and time is money.
A: And I have trouble reading the small print.
H: My idea will solve that problem. Let's make a deal with the telephone company to lease their computerized white pages which we put into our central computer. We sell home computer owners a number service. They type in the name and address: The number appears in big type on the screen.
P: Will the phone company go for that?
H: It will have to print fewer directories—and printing is expensive.
A: I see a major problem. How are most people, who are bad spellers, going to get the right number if they can't type in the exact spelling?
P: We can find a way around that. But can we find enough people to make the project worthwhile? Most people may prefer the free phone book.
H: From your marketing experience you know that people pay for movie channels even if they get similar entertainment free on commercial TV. Many pay to avoid commercials. Our market is affluent, since it owns home computers. Besides, many people want speed, convenience, and accuracy.
A: That's right. Maybe we can figure out how to press one button to dial the number on the screen?
H: Alice, before we consider that, I want you to study people who own home computers: their interest level, and what they would pay for the service. Phil, think out a marketing plan to convince people to buy.
P: Ok, Chief, I'm on it.
H: I'll bet telephone directories as we know them won't be around two decades from now.

Questions

1. Do you agree with Herb's parting comment? Why?
2. What other pro and con arguments can you make for Herb's idea?

EVOLUTION OF A BUSINESS

Using Computer Output in the Marketing Effort

The computer has revolutionized the making of reservations. Transportation carriers and many of the large hotel/motel chains have impressive reservations networks. They provide immediate on-line computer reservation information—that is, confirmations are available as quickly as reservations clerks can punch keyboards. Such service has facilitated the travel agent's job immeasurably. Most reservations can be confirmed or, if not available, discussed while the customer is in the TA's office or on the telephone.

There is also a vast amount of computer printout information potentially available to travel agents.

Sara: You know, there's so much data and it's come so fast that we haven't learned how to use it imaginatively in our operations. I've been examining data that's available about airlines, and I think some of it could be of value in serving our clients.

Ray: How so?

Sara: Well, customers often ask which airline is best when there's a choice of more than one. What if we gave them comparative data? For example, in a recent year TWA's on-time performance on domestic flights was 87.2 percent (within 15 minutes of schedule) and for international flights 80 percent (within 30 minutes of schedule). We could gather similar data about other airlines.

Ray: That's an interesting idea. If clients liked it, it would be another way of distinguishing ourselves and increasing word-of-mouth references.

Sara: Also, I think we should collect some background information about our clients, such as age, marital status, profession, education, and so on. We could have a computer correlate that information with the amount and kinds of business each client produces. It would tell us a lot about what kind of people we should pitch our promotional efforts toward. I think a statistical profile of our best potential customers would be very helpful.

Questions

1. Would it be worthwhile to assemble comparative statistical data on airlines for clients?
2. What problems could arise if such a service were provided?
3. What are the pros and cons of Sara's idea for collecting and processing background data on clients?
4. How else could the computer be used to increase the efficiency of a travel agency?

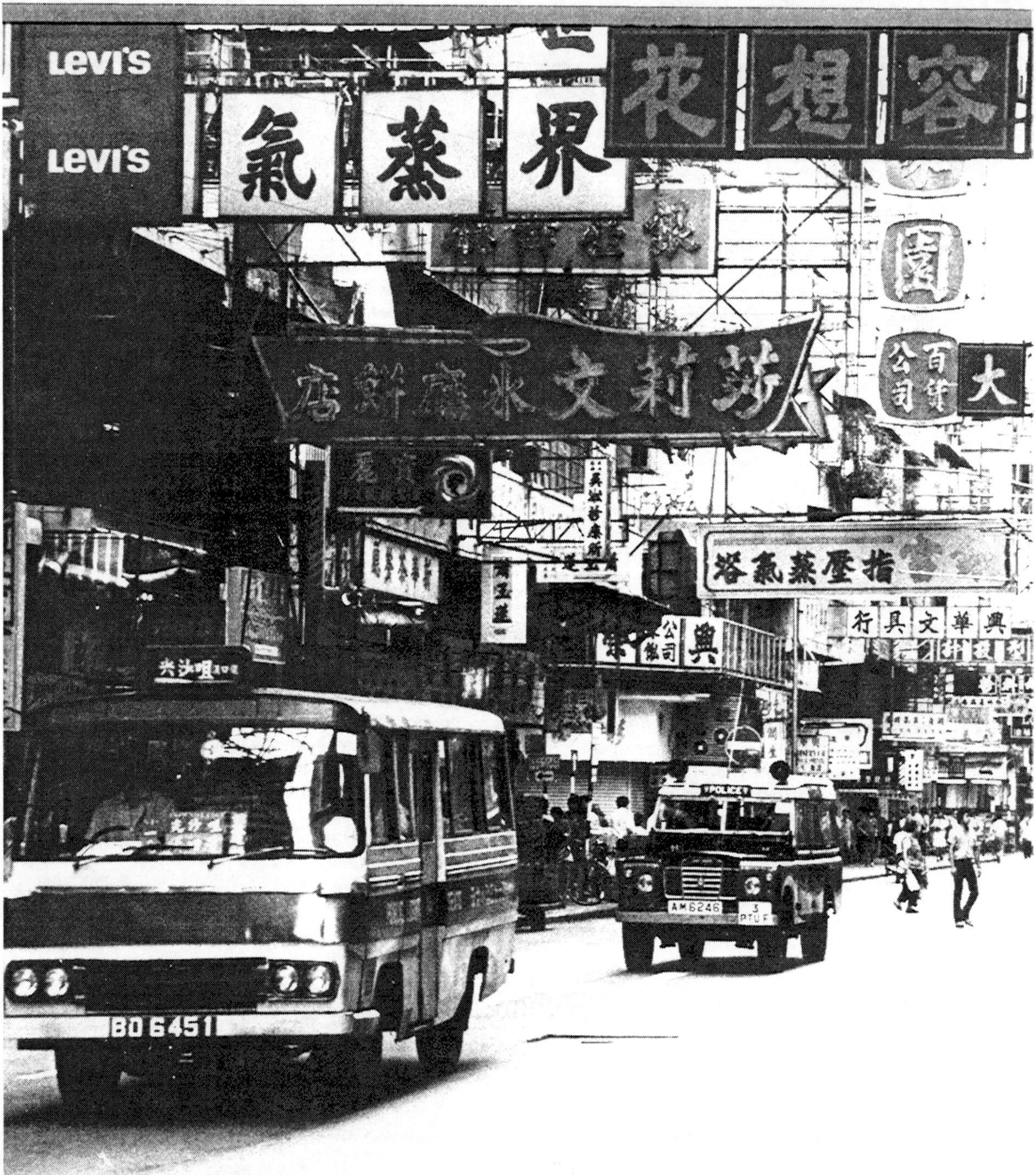
Levi's
Levi's
界蒸氣
指壓蒸氣浴
興華文具行
POLICE
AM 6246
BD 6451

VI

SPECIAL BUSINESS SITUATIONS

20 BUSINESS LAW AND LEGAL SERVICES

21 INTERNATIONAL BUSINESS

22 NONPROFIT ORGANIZATIONS

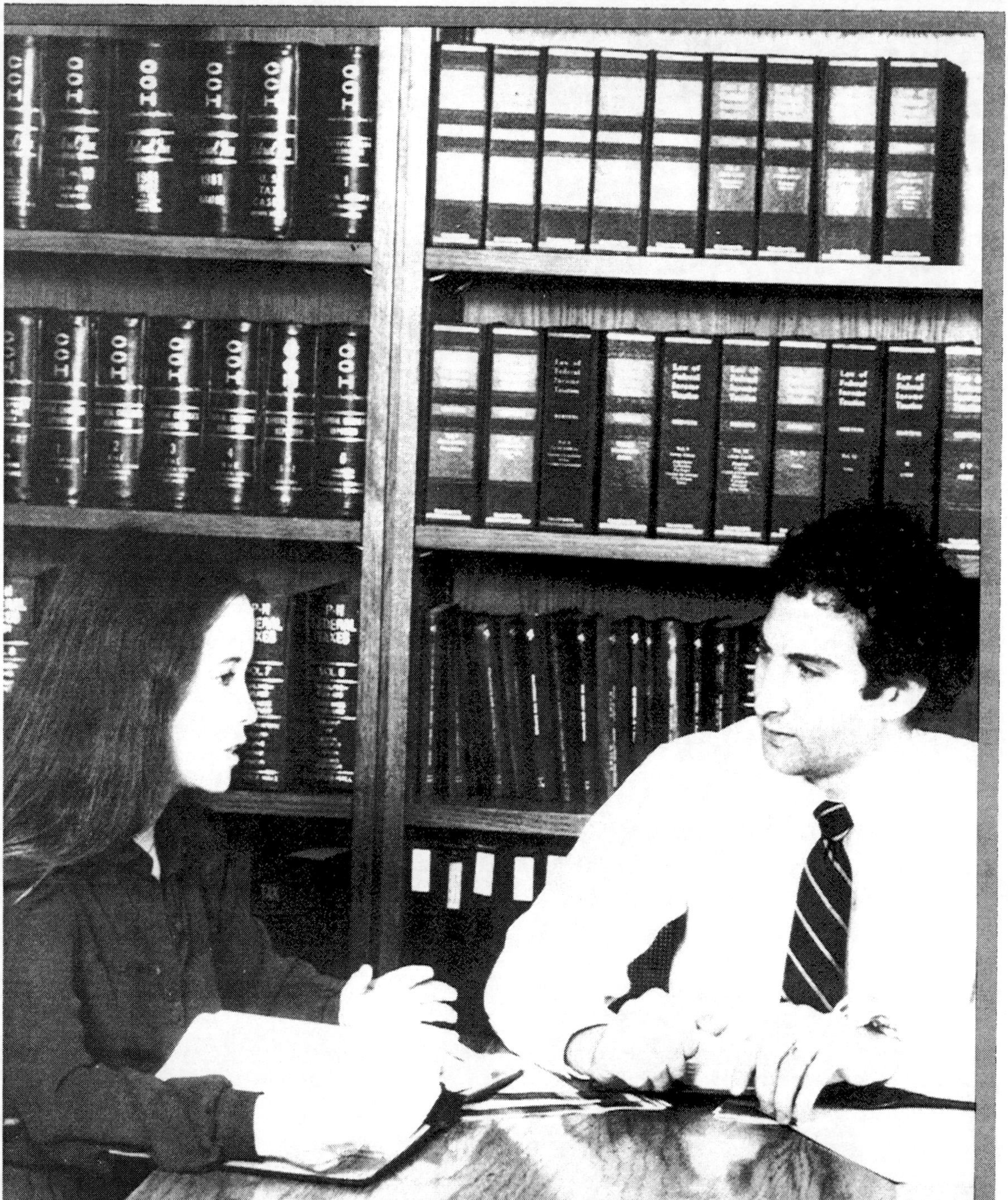
CCH

20

BUSINESS LAW AND LEGAL SERVICES
Playing by the Rules

READ THIS CHAPTER SO YOU CAN:

Explain why the demand for lawyers is increasing.

Define business law, and explain why a basic familiarity with its principles is essential.

Detail the conditions that ensure a contract is valid and enforceable.

Discuss assignment of contractual rights/obligations and breach of contract.

Explain the legal principle of agency and the law governing employer-employee.

Discuss the legal provisions affecting the sale of personal property.

List the requirements for negotiability, and explain the five forms of endorsement.

Describe the process of negotiation.

Discuss bankruptcy and the laws that control it.

Explain how trademarks, patents, and copyrights protect the intangible assets of businesses.

Explain the proposals suggested for reducing dependency on lawyers.

Explain how crime affects business.

Law—like accounting—is one of the fastest growing professions. In the United States there are more than 630,000 lawyers or one for every 384 people. For every 1000 persons, we have three times as many attorneys as Germany, ten times the number in Sweden, and 20 times as many as Japan. There are more lawyers than college teachers; they outnumber physicians almost two to one, and their numbers continue to swell the executive suites of the *"Fortune* 500" (see Table 20–1).

Some argue that we have too many lawyers. Others contend we do not because demand for legal services is growing faster than the population.

WHY DEMAND FOR LAWYERS CONTINUES TO GROW

Six reasons are clear. *First:* American culture stresses individualism, competition, and success. In commenting on the vast number of lawyers, one observer notes:

... ours is a society built on individualism, competition, and success. These values bring great personal freedom and mobilize powerful energies. At the same time, they arouse great temptations to shoulder aside one's competitors, to cut corners, to ignore the interests of others in the struggle to succeed. In such a world, much responsibility rests on those who umpire the contest. As society demands higher standards of fairness and decency, the rules of the game tend to multiply and the umpire's burden grows constantly heavier.[1]

Second: People have more rights guaranteed by law. A free society necessarily has more legal activity than a totalitarian nation because people enjoy more rights. For example, enforcement of civil rights legislation often results in litigation to remedy discrimination in employment, promotion, and wages—as well as discriminatory practices based on sex, race, age, and alienage. In many communities private lawyers and public agencies provide legal aid to those in need but without means. In addition, each new law contains adequate means to enforce its provisions through legal action. And our judicial system encourages the appeal of unfavorable decisions, another factor contributing to the increased demand for legal services.

Third: Promotion sells legal services, too. In Chapter 12 we learned that advertising creates greater demand for products and services. Now that lawyers are permitted to advertise ("Issue for Debate," page 320), demand for legal service is increasing—especially in

---
[1]Derek Bok, "The Ballooning Waste of Legal Hot Air," *Business and Society Review,* Fall 1983, 79.

TABLE 20-1 The Company Bar—The Largest Corporate Legal Departments

CORPORATION	NUMBER OF CORPORATE ATTORNEYS
ATT	905
Exxon	551
General Electric	415
Ford	210
Prudential	203
Mobil	188
Hartford Insurance	183
Standard Oil (Indiana)	181
Gulf	151
BankAmerica	151
General Motors	145
Atlantic Richfield	138
IBM	138
Western Electric	137
Citicorp	124
RCA	124
Union Carbide	117
United Technologies	114
Texaco	107

—Paul Hoffman
Lions of the Eighties
(New York: Doubleday, 1982)

SOURCE: As reported in *Business and Society Review*, Fall 1982, no. 43, 70.

the areas of divorce, bankruptcy, drunken driving, and negligence.

Publicity also creates demand for legal services. Substantial awards to victims of discrimination, unsafe products, and professional malpractice encourage others to take legal action. "Why not sue your doctor, big business, or your employer for a bundle?" is an all too common thought.

Fourth: Little stigma is attached to legal action. A generation ago many people were embarrassed to "go to court." In today's more impersonal and liberal society, this fear has largely disappeared.

Fifth: The complexity of business is continually increasing. Many aspects of business—taxes, patents, pensions, employment practices, investments, zoning regulations, competitive practices—are increasingly complex. Lawyers become indispensable for dealing with the legal technicalities that enable business to pursue its goals.

Sixth: More crime means more prosecution and more defense. The long-term trends suggest that violent crimes such as murder and rape and nonviolent crimes such as shoplifting, fraud, and embezzlement are increasing. As discussed on pages 614–16, crime is a major cost to society; only lawyers may prosecute or defend the accused.

With the six reasons just mentioned it is easy to see why the lawyer population has grown so large, so quickly. Figure 20–1 shows that the number of lawyers in the United States grew from 285,933 in 1960 to 542,205 in 1983—by 89.6%, whereas the total population grew by only 37.4% in comparison.

HOW ARE LEGAL DISPUTES RESOLVED?

Most Legal Disputes Never Reach the Courts

The enormous publicity given lawsuits and trials by the media leads us to believe that lawyers spend most of their time in court. This is

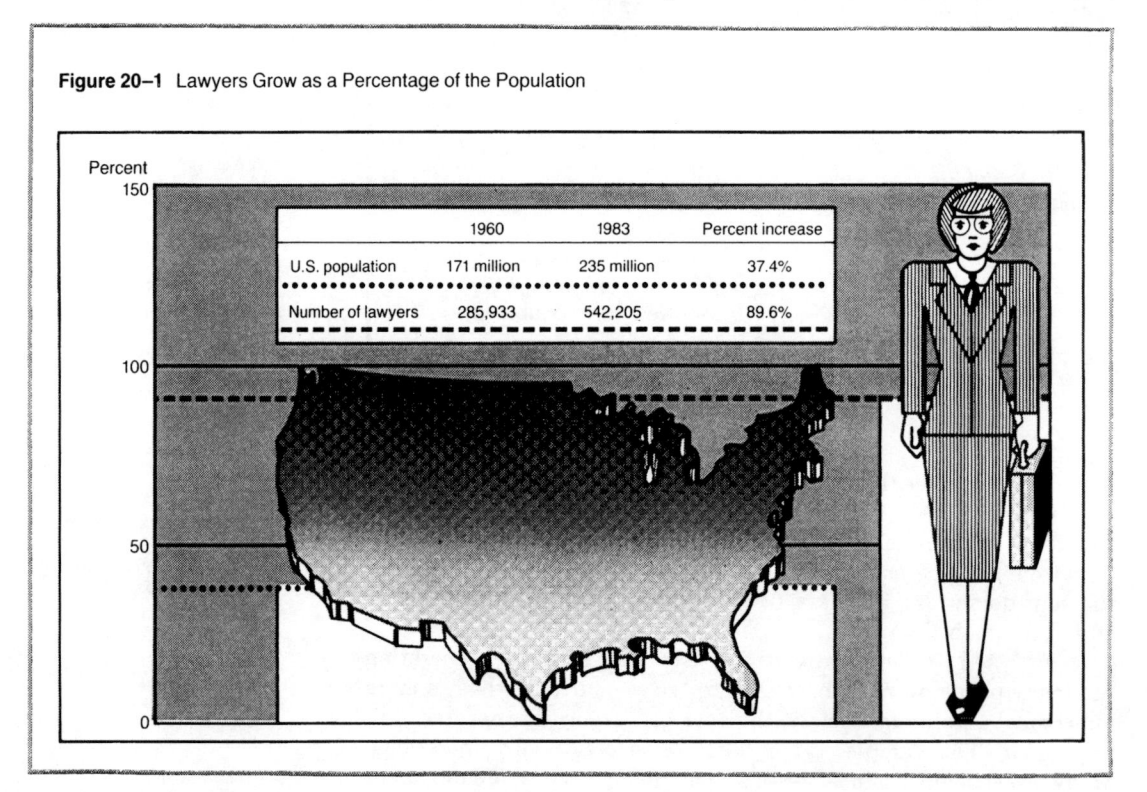

Figure 20–1 Lawyers Grow as a Percentage of the Population

	1960	1983	Percent increase
U.S. population	171 million	235 million	37.4%
Number of lawyers	285,933	542,205	89.6%

not the case. Greater than 95 percent of all legal service is designed specifically to avoid court action by preventing legal disputes and negotiating them when they arise.

Prevention of Legal Problems

Making a will is an example of preventive "legal medicine." A will that clearly states how one's property is to be distributed helps prevent lawsuits brought by heirs and minimizes estate taxes. Tightly drawn articles of incorporation help prevent future lawsuits by shareholders and the government. Skillfully written employment contracts can prevent future legal action by discontented employees. A close review of employment practices may prevent lawsuits charging discrimination. And a carefully structured contract for the lease or purchase of real estate often avoids future disputes.

Negotiation of Disputes

Lawyers can help avoid court action by negotiating disputes between the parties. (The art of negotiation is discussed on page 607). Even in relatively simple yet emotional disputes involving divorce, lawyers often are able to negotiate an agreement and avoid a court-dictated decision. Through legal representatives, businesses negotiate most disputes concerning competitive practices, tax questions, pension problems, employment practices, shareholder complaints, consumer dissatisfaction, and other conflicts of interest.

Although some lawyers undoubtedly enjoy the drama and competition of trials—just as some doctors insist on surgery to cure what ails you—the majority of lawyers regard court action as indicative of failure to prevent a problem or to negotiate it satisfactorily.

WHAT IS BUSINESS LAW?

Business law refers to *rules, statutes, codes, precepts, and regulations established to provide a legal framework within which business may be conducted and that is enforceable by court action.*

Business law is of three types: mandatory, permissive, and prohibitive. **Mandatory laws** *require a business to do something.* Examples are environmental protection laws and building safety codes. **Permissive laws** are *available to a business for self-protection.* Examples are patent, trademark, and copyright laws. **Prohibitive laws** *forbid certain practices by a business.* They include, among others, licensing laws that allow only a licensed business (like a health store, liquor store, or beauty salon) to operate.

WHY BE FAMILIAR WITH BUSINESS LAW?

First, a familiarity with business law helps to avoid legal blunders. Lawyers report that lawsuits might frequently have been avoided

"Go home! The world has enough stuff! We don't need any more!"

if legal questions had been considered prior to taking the action that led to the problem. Yet those ignorant of law may not recognize when legal issues are involved.

Second, a knowledge of business law leads to an appreciation of the rights and privileges of individuals and business people. Some years ago an important patent was granted to the Marks Polarized Corporation of Whitestone, New York, for a device that transforms glass panels from clear to opaque and back. The invention grew out of a Navy and Air Force contract for development of a protective shutter for nuclear flashes. If the company had not drawn the contract in advance—specifying that it would retain all commercial rights to military research—it would not now own this important patent.

Third, a grasp of business law can help to protect individuals and business people against unscrupulous practices. For example, many people believe that once they have signed a contract they must adhere to its provisions regardless of circumstances. However, a number of conditions (such as misrepresentation of property being sold) may make the contract invalid and unenforceable.

CONTRACTS

Basic to almost every business transaction is the **contract**—*an agreement between two or more persons or businesses that is valid and enforceable in a court of law.*

What Constitutes a Contract?

Six conditions must be met for a contract to be valid and enforceable.

There Must Be an Offer

An **offer** is simply *a proposal by one party, called the offeror, to enter into a contract with a second party, called the offeree.* The offer may be communicated in words (either in person or over the telephone) or in writing (by letter or telegram). Sometimes offers take the form of conduct. For example, the presence of a public transit vehicle on a city street is an offer to carry passengers.

The offer must be sufficiently specific so that a court of law can reasonably determine the intention of the parties. In this connection, we must differentiate between *offers* and *invitations for offers.* An advertisement that simply states prices and qualities of merchandise is not an offer. Rather, it is an invitation to consumers to enter the store and buy the merchandise.

There Must Be Voluntary Acceptance

A second essential element of the contract is **voluntary acceptance;** that is, *the offer must be voluntarily accepted by the party to whom it is made.* If, for example, Jones makes an offer to sell a house to Brown, someone else—say, Smith—cannot accept on Brown's behalf.

Acceptance must conform to the terms of the offer to be legally enforceable. If a party receiving an offer modifies its terms, he or she is in effect rejecting the offer by making a counteroffer. Acceptance of the counteroffer must then come from the party who made the original offer.

There Must Be Genuineness of Assent

The principle that a party cannot be held to a contract if some fact was misrepresented is called **genuineness of assent.** Some types of mistakes that can invalidate assent are mistakes as to fact, such as whether a house has gas or electric heat; mistakes as to the existence of the subject matter, as when one party purchases a stallion which is in reality a gelding; and mistakes as to the identity of the parties. To illustrate the latter mistake, say a young man named Smith obtains goods on credit when he says he is Mr. Smith's son. The merchant thinks he is the wealthy John Smith's son; actually he is the son of Thomas Smith, a poor man.

The law does not treat all mistakes equally. Some mistakes do not materially affect the contract; others relate to the essence of the bargain.

Something of Value Must Change Hands

Consideration is an essential element of every enforceable contract. *A promise is binding on a party only when he or she has*

APPLICATION TO PERSONAL AFFAIRS

Nine Tips for Selecting and Working with a Lawyer

The chances are likely that you will require legal services several times during your professional career. Probably someone will sue or threaten you with legal action. Someone may default on a loan, fee, or rent owed you. You may make investments and need to know your potential liability. You may buy and sell real estate and file claims with insurance companies. If you go into business for yourself, you must deal with employees, consumers, government, suppliers, and others—each one increasing your exposure to legal involvement.

Carefully selecting a lawyer and developing an effective working relationship with him or her are good business practices. Here are some suggestions:

1. Select an attorney before you need one. If you wait until an emergency legal matter arises, you may make a hasty choice.
2. Don't act as your own legal counsel. The old adage that "a person who acts as his or her own lawyer has a fool for a client," is often true. For example, you can incorporate a business without legal assistance, and you can act as your own defense attorney in a criminal action—but to do so is extremely foolish.
3. Regard selection of legal counsel as a long-term decision. You will be better served if one law firm has an opportunity to know you, your business, your goals, your family, and your financial status.
4. Select an attorney you feel comfortable with. Always disclose fully to your counsel what you have done and what you plan to do. Try never to do business with anyone who attempts to intimidate you.
5. Ideally, your business counsel should be a "generalist" who can provide most of your legal needs—but who will secure a legal specialist if necessary.
6. Discuss legal fees up front. All professionals should want their clients to understand how they price their services. Investigate the limits, if any, to legal consultation advertised as "free."
7. Remember that in legal matters especially, an ounce of prevention is worth a pound of cure. Consult your lawyer before entering into important business relationships.
8. Keep in mind your goal is to avoid litigation if possible. Ethical lawyers seek to prevent issues that can be resolved only by jury trial.
9. Encourage your legal counsel to work closely with your accountant—particularly if you operate your own business. Most businesses require certain documents that an accountant *and* a lawyer should examine.

received something of value in exchange for his or her promise. Consideration may take the form of money, goods, services, or forbearance of a right. In a contract to purchase an automobile for $10,000, the $10,000 is consideration. The grandfather who agrees to pay his granddaughter $10,000 if she will not smoke until she is 21 receives the granddaughter's forbearance of a right (refraining from the right to smoke) as consideration. The amount of the consideration is generally not relevant to the validity and enforceability of the contract.

Parties to the Agreement Must Be Competent

Certain classes of persons possess only limited contractual capacity. Minors (in most states persons under 18 years of age), intoxicated people, and people who have been declared legally insane enjoy contractual capacity only for necessities—clothing, food, shelter, medical care—and can be held responsible only if a reasonable price was charged. In all other contracts made with such persons, the person or the person's relatives can reject the contract. Convicts, aliens, and corporations limited by their articles also have limited contractual capacity.

Contracts Must Be for Lawful Purposes

Any contract whose performance involves an act in violation of a law is illegal. In states where gambling is illegal, for example, promises to pay gambling debts are not enforceable. A contract let to a "hit man" is unenforceable in a court of law. A lender of money who attempts to collect interest on a loan in excess of the state's legal limit may lose all right to interest or to the illegal part thereof—though not, usually, to the principal. Contracts that restrain trade unduly or that are detrimental to the public welfare are illegal. A "wholesaler" of cocaine or other contraband substance cannot legally enforce a contract to purchase made with a "pusher."

Must Contracts Be Written?

Contracts may be either oral or written. The disadvantage of an oral contract is in proving the terms of the agreement. The law requires certain contracts to be in writing. These include contracts that cannot be fulfilled in less than one year, contracts for the transfer of real estate, and contracts for the sale of personal property in excess of a certain dollar amount—depending on the state. One common type of written contract is a lease.

In some cases the parties to a written contract may alter it orally by mutual consent, provided there is proof (for example, a witness) that the change is acceptable to both parties. It is always good business practice, however, to make changes in writing and for each party to initial each change made to a written agreement.

The language lawyers use is often notoriously obscure. Attempting to correct this, New York State has enacted a plain English law for use in contracts.

Some Contractual Rights/Obligations Can Be Assigned to Others

An **assignment of contract** occurs when *one party transfers his or her rights or obligations in a contract to another.* The party transferring the rights is the *assignor;* the party receiving them is the *assignee.*

A party who has payments due him or her (or to become due) under a contract can assign the right to these payments to another. The right to receive property also can be assigned. A merchant who has contracted to purchase a shipment of goods may transfer the right to these goods to some other party.

Important exceptions to the right of assignment concern those contracts involving personal services. An employer who has contracted with an employee cannot assign his or her rights in that contract to another. A building contractor cannot assign his or her right to erect a structure to another because the contractor was selected on the basis of his or her particular skills. Nor can a legal firm under contract to represent a company transfer this right to another legal firm; it must be assumed the firm was chosen because of its special abilities.

Performance and Discharge of Contracts

Performance of a contract involves fulfillment of its terms. Under certain conditions, performance by one or both parties may be excused and the contract terminated. Examples include the death or illness of a party who was to perform personal services, changes in laws that would make performance of the contract illegal, or destruction of the subject matter of the contract—death of *identified* animals under contract for sale, for instance.

What Is Breach of Contract?

Breach of contract is *failure to perform the terms of a contract.* Except in situations such as those discussed previously, a party who fails to perform according to the terms of the contract is in breach of contract. The party injured by the breach of contract is entitled to a remedy. He or she has the right to rescind the contract—to act as though no contract had ever been made. Or he or she may seek a court order requiring that the party in breach pay damages or fulfill the terms of the contract.

When a court orders that damages be paid, it issues a judgment against the defendant—the contract breaker. Property of the defendant may be sold. And if the defendant does not have sufficient property to satisfy the judgment, some states permit garnishment of wages. Under **garnishment,** *the defendant's employer is ordered to withhold a fixed amount of his or her usual earnings each payday until the judgment is satisfied (paid in full).*

LAW OF AGENCY

The **law of agency** *governs a relationship whereby one person is authorized to act for another in transactions with a third party.* The

principal is *the party granting the authority to act;* the **agent** is *the party given the authority to act.* The agent may be a person, a partnership, or a corporation.

Almost every legal transaction can be negotiated by an agent. Exceptions include voting, making a will, and executing an affidavit (statement under oath). Any person legally competent to act for himself or herself may appoint an agent.

An agent has the power to negotiate contracts; an employee does not. Agents are used in a wide variety of circumstances. The stockbroker acts as agent for a client, the realtor for a property owner, and so on. Agent intermediaries, discussed in Chapter 9, are also governed by the law of agency.

There is a useful legal instrument called the **power of attorney** that *can establish a principal-agent relationship: It can grant the authority to act on another person's behalf.* Sole proprietors or partners planning vacations find the device convenient. People may wish to be represented by an accountant at an Internal Revenue Service tax audit. This is permissible if the accountant has the taxpayer's power of attorney.

LAW OF EMPLOYER-EMPLOYEE

The **law of employer-employee** (master-servant as it was once termed) is extremely important in business. *The relationship between employer and employee is contractual even when no written agreement is executed.* An employer is legally obligated to provide:

- Reasonably safe machines and other equipment
- A reasonably suitable work environment
- Competent work companions (an employee is not legally obligated to work with reckless, intoxicated, or negligent associates)
- Necessary instruction in the use of dangerous equipment

In recent years many statutes have been enacted that greatly restrict the power of an employer to discharge an employee arbitrarily. In specific situations covered by certain regulatory legislation, however, an employee may be discharged for:

- Deliberate disobedience of any *reasonable* order, disloyalty, or insubordination
- Gross moral misconduct, such as defrauding the employer, or theft
- Unquestionable incompetence, prolonged illness, or permanent disability

Completion of a job—as in seasonal crop harvesting, or a cutback in production is sufficient legal justification for discharge.

Contracts negotiated between labor and management (see Chapter 16) define termination, layoff, overtime, and other job-related matters.

SALE OF PERSONAL PROPERTY

Because businesses sell goods and/or services, it is essential to understand the legal components of buying and selling. Personal property includes all property other than real estate—motor vehicles, clothing, securities, furniture, food, cattle, and so on. Each sale of such property involves a contractual relationship governed by certain legal provisions.

Transfer of Title

It is important to know *when* title (legal ownership) passes. Should goods be lost, damaged, or destroyed, the loss is suffered (incurred) by the party holding title. There are many situations that make it difficult to determine exactly when title passes.

Following are the essential rules concerning transfer of title:

- Under a contract to sell specific goods in which the seller agrees to put them in a deliverable condition, title does not pass until that act is done. Suppose the Brown Automobile Company sells Smith a used car, promising to replace all the tires with new ones. Before the tires are replaced, however, the car is destroyed through no fault of either party. The Brown Automobile Company must bear the loss because it failed to put the car in a deliverable condition.

- When goods are sold on a trial or approval basis, title passes when the buyer signifies acceptance or when he or she has kept the goods for longer than a reasonable length of time (usually 30 days).

- If the contract states that the seller is to deliver goods to a designated place, title does not pass until goods are so delivered.

- If the contract to sell states that goods are to be shipped F.O.B. (free on board) point of origin, title passes when the goods are delivered to the *point of shipment*. Thus, if a company in Chicago sells a piano to a buyer in St. Louis F.O.B. Chicago, title and the accompanying risk pass to the buyer when the piano is delivered to the carrier or put on the seller's truck—in Chicago.

- In C.O.D. (cash on delivery) shipments, title passes to the buyer when the goods are delivered by the seller to the carrier (truck, rail, and so on).

What Is an Unpaid Seller's Lien?

In some cases *a seller passes title to the buyer but retains either actual possession of the goods or the right to their possession.* The seller then has a **lien** on the goods until the money owed has been paid. This situation may exist regardless of whether the merchandise has been delivered to the buyer or retained by the seller (as with layaway plans). An auto repair shop may retain possession of a vehicle it has repaired (called a mechanics lien) until the automobile owner (who has title to the vehicle) pays the amount due.

Warranties

A **warranty** is *a legal promise by a seller that property is or will be as represented.* Warranties traditionally are made to induce the buyer to make a purchase. An **express warranty** is *a statement of fact regarding specific characteristics of the property sold.* For example, statements such as "This suit is 100 percent wool," "This house is four years old," and "This automobile has a new engine" are all express warranties. Should the purchaser determine that the statements were untrue, he or she is entitled to seek legal redress or demand that the seller remedy the defect.

An **implied warranty** differs from an express warranty in that it is *not stated in specific terms but is implied.* For example, the consumer always has an implied warranty that the retailer has the legal right to sell the goods offered in his or her store. Other implied warranties concern the goods being fit for the purpose indicated by the seller and that goods sold by sample will correspond to the sample. In mail-order purchases from a catalog, it is implied that the goods will be as described or pictured.

NEGOTIABLE INSTRUMENTS HELP TRANSFER PROPERTY

Negotiable instruments are *written contractual obligations used extensively in business transactions as substitutes for money:* such instruments as checks, promissory notes, and bills of exchange.

Negotiable instruments serve as credit instruments. They are convenient and indispensable in modern business.

Requirements for Negotiability

For an instrument to be fully negotiable, it must:

- Be in writing and be signed by the maker or drawer. Pen, pencil, typewriting, or print may constitute "writing" in the legal sense.
- Contain an unconditional promise or order to pay money. A promise that reads "on condition that" clearly is conditional, and the instrument is nonnegotiable.
- Be payable on demand or at a fixed future date.

Endorsement Transfers Ownership

The most common way to transfer a negotiable instrument is by **endorsement**—*writing one's name (or the business name) on the* back of the instrument. There are five forms of endorsement, each pictured in Figure 20–2.

A **blank endorsement** is the most familiar. *The payee or holder of the instrument simply writes his or her name on the reverse of the instrument.* Then the instrument can be negotiated by anyone. To illustrate, a payroll check endorsed in blank and lost can be cashed by any finder. Thus a blank endorsement should be made only when the instrument is cashed or actually given to another party.

A **full,** or **special, endorsement** *specifies a person or entity to whom the payee wishes to transfer title of the instrument.* The words "pay to the order of" precede the name of the transferee. The payee then signs his or her name below.

A **restrictive endorsement** *limits the negotiability of the instrument to a specific purpose.* Common forms of restrictive endorsement are "for deposit only" (signed), "for collection only" (signed), and "pay to First National Bank only" (signed).

A **conditional endorsement** is one in which *the payee transfers the instrument to someone else but retains title to it until some condition has been fulfilled.* The payee writes the words "pay to" followed by the name of the transferee *and* the condition that must be met.

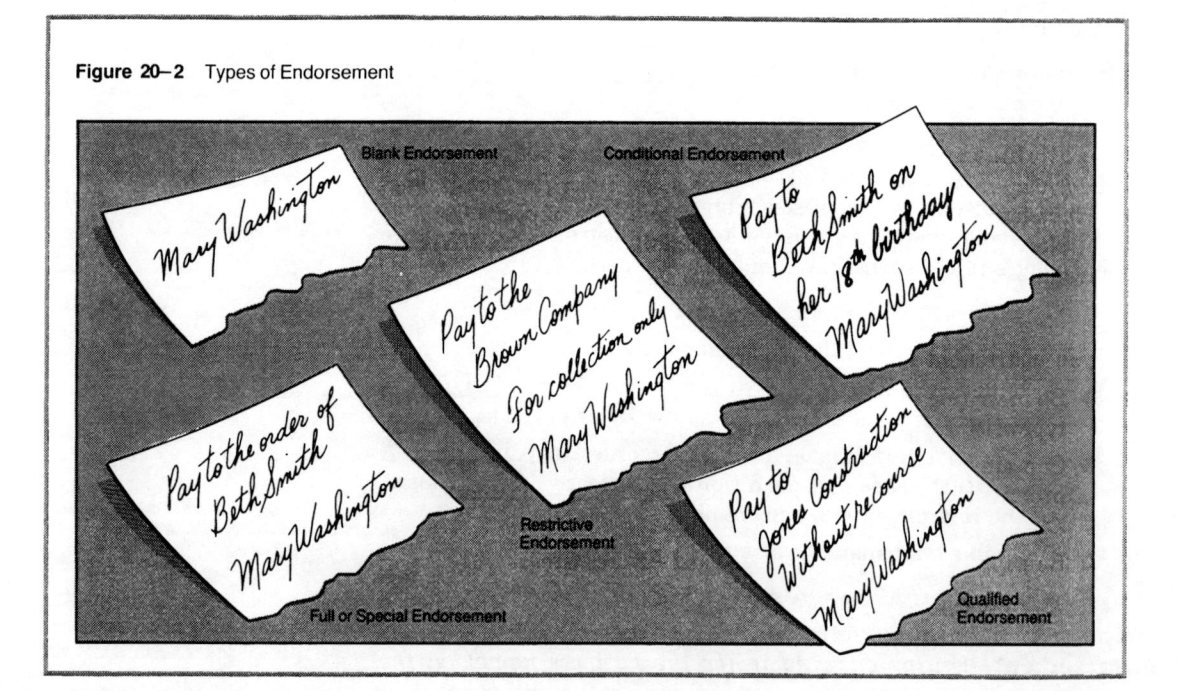

Figure 20–2 Types of Endorsement

A **qualified endorsement** is often important in business transactions. *A holder of a check or other negotiable instrument who wishes to be exempt from liability for the default of the party primarily responsible for the payment of the instrument can endorse the check by writing "without recourse" before his or her name.* This notation is important when a person cashes a check for someone else.

Consider a situation in which an unqualified endorsement is made. A retail merchant receives a check from a customer. The merchant endorses the check and gives it to a wholesaler. The wholesaler endorses it and takes it to a bank for collection. The bank finds that the check is worthless. The bank has recourse against the wholesaler, who has recourse against the retailer, who has recourse against the customer.

NEGOTIATING: AN ART WHOSE TIME HAS COME

When *people seek agreement through an objective exchange of views,* they are **negotiating;** when people subjectively state reasons for or against a position, they are arguing. Negotiation is positive and often leads to settlement; argument is negative and generally leads nowhere. Everyone profits from effective negotiating skills—individuals, managers, labor leaders, salespeople, marriage counselors, and government leaders. Often lawyers are retained to negotiate for us because they are professionally trained to plead causes and to design psychological strategy.

How to Improve Negotiating Skills

To learn the art of negotiating, we do not have to start from scratch because most of us have had "give and take" experiences in reaching agreements with employers, merchants, friends, and family. Knowledge, flexibility, analytical ability, patience, emotional control, and a sense of humor are the successful negotiator's essential virtues.

The goal of negotiating is an agreement that both parties accept as fair. Through good-faith negotiation, everybody wins; through good-faith litigation, the lawyers win. The steps in the negotiating process are:

- *Define your objectives*—What is it you want to achieve? What is the least you are willing to settle for?
- *Identify the issues*—Issues might be price, working conditions, selling rights in another country, commissions, and so on. Each issue that is identified should be negotiated.
- *Know your opponent*—This is essential to predicting responses. Does he or she react more to logical or emotional appeals? Is his or her background in law, accounting, or what? How much authority does the person have?

- *Plan your strategy*—What arguments should you use to set the stage? Which points should you withhold until later? How can you time concessions for greatest impact?

Negotiating is an art, not a science. It can be learned and perfected through practice. And as the art is mastered, it provides enormous satisfaction.

BANKRUPTCY IS A POPULAR LEGAL REMEDY FOR DEBT

Bankruptcy is *the legal process by which specific assets of the debtor are liquidated as quickly as possible to satisfy creditors' claims and to free the debtor to begin anew*. **Voluntary bankruptcy** is *a process initiated by the person or organization seeking to be declared bankrupt*. **Involuntary bankruptcy** is *a process initiated by the creditors of a person or business*.

The Bankruptcy Act

The Constitution of the United States provides that Congress shall have the power to establish uniform laws on bankruptcy throughout the nation. Congress originally enacted the Bankruptcy Act in the 1890s and has revised it periodically.

The legislation under which bankruptcy petitions are administered today is the Bankruptcy Code as Amended by the Bankruptcy Amendments and Federal Judgeship Act of 1984, which allows the bankrupt to retain $40,000 of equity in a house ($80,000 if a spouse files jointly), $1,200 in a car, and a generous share of other personal property. States have their own sets of exemptions.

News concerning major corporations that contemplate or go bankrupt makes headlines. But bankruptcy primarily concerns individuals and is largely voluntary—the debtor initiates the court action, not the creditors. Consider these facts:

In 1984, 99.7 percent of all bankruptcies were voluntary actions initiated by individuals and businesses. Eighty-two percent of bankruptcies involved individuals, not businesses. And most of the businesses that went bankrupt were small.

Chapters in Bankruptcy Law Explain Legal Procedures

Most bankruptcies are processed under three sections (called chapters) of the Bankruptcy Act. **Chapter 7** *provides for "straight bankruptcy," requiring the liquidation of nonexempt assets of individuals and corporations*. When liquidation is complete, the remaining assets are divided among the creditors—including the government, for unpaid taxes. In 1984, 67 percent of all bankruptcies were filed under Chapter 7.

Another provision of the Bankruptcy Act, **Chapter 11,** relates specifically to business bankruptcies. It *allows a company to reorganize and continue operations while it retires a limited portion of its debts.* Chapter 11 bankruptcies, which account for about 3 percent of all bankruptcies, can be initiated only by the debtor. Under some circumstances the entity seeking bankruptcy relief may borrow additional capital, sell certain assets, and change its management team. The court conducts hearings on proposals submitted by the debtor company and ordinarily appoints a trustee to protect the interests of creditors. The goal of Chapter 11 is to help debtors and creditors work out the best possible long-term solution. If Chapter 11 proceedings fail, what assets remain are liquidated and the proceeds are divided among the creditors. Liquidation of small businesses is routine; major concerns are typically absorbed by or merge into another company.

Chapter 13 is the Act's second-most popular provision and accounts for 27 percent of bankruptcy actions. This means of being freed from debt was once available only to wage earners. Now Chapter 13 is available to all individuals with regular income—including people who operate small businesses, who receive pensions, and who draw unemployment compensation. **Chapter 13** *permits the debtor to repay debts over a three- to five-year period. It is less complicated and less expensive than Chapter 7, and is considered by lawyers to work to the advantage of debtors—not creditors.*

Table 20–2 shows bankruptcies for the years 1977 and 1984. During this period bankruptcies increased two and one-half times, the greatest increase in more than 50 years. Yet the number of bankruptcies understates the extent of financial difficulties because so many debts are secured by mortgages that, in most cases, make bankruptcy unnecessary as a means for securing financial relief.

Bankruptcy Understates Debtor–Creditor Problems

Debt is either secured or unsecured. When a person purchases real estate, he or she makes a down payment and receives a mortgage or trust deed for the unpaid balance. The real estate itself is the security. And if the buyer does not make mortgage or trust deed payments on time as agreed, the lender can foreclose the mortgage or trust deed and take physical possession of the property.

When a person finances the purchase of an automobile, a boat, a motorcycle, or other movable property, the buyer and lender execute a chattel mortgage. If the buyer fails to make payments as promised, the lender may repossess the personal property.

When a buyer secures a debt with property, bankruptcy is usually not necessary; the lender may simply take back the real estate or movable item. Bankruptcy is much more common when a buyer bor-

TABLE 20-2 Bankruptcy or Debt Freedom Doubles in 5 Years

	1977	PERCENT	1984	PERCENT
Business bankruptcies	32,189	15.0	95,572	17.8
Personal bankruptcies	182,210	85.0	440,025	82.2
Totals	214,399	100.0	535,597	100.0

SOURCE: *Statistical Abstract of the United States 1985*, 520.

rows money without the pledge of tangible property—as in the case of credit cards. Sellers of services provide consumers with no tangible property that the sellers can repossess. For example, a surgeon cannot retrieve an operation any more than a consultant can regain the labor of his or her profession.

Railroads, banks, insurance companies, building and loan associations, and incorporated cities do not come under the Bankruptcy Act.

ISSUE FOR DEBATE

Who Is Primarily Responsible for Bankruptcies: Business or Consumers?

More than a half million bankruptcies occur each year. This constitutes a major cost to businesses, individuals, and society in dollars, in personal and professional misfortune, in lost investments, in bitter feelings, and in dashed hopes. Some blame business for the insolvency problem; others say consumers are at fault. Below are two sides to this complicated issue.

PROS

CONSUMERS ARE RESPONSIBLE
No one is actually forced to buy on credit or to borrow money. People who build up high debts are responsible for their condition and should not receive lenient treatment when they go bankrupt.

Debts are serious obligations. People understand that they must repay debts of every kind, or they must suffer the legal consequences—including bankruptcy.

CONS

BUSINESS IS RESPONSIBLE
A person has limited control over his or her economic destiny. Workers and their dependents become ill, suffer injuries, and lose their jobs. If anything, courts should interpret bankruptcy laws affecting consumers more leniently.

Businesses don't have to sell on credit or loan money. Many businesses take advantage of consumers as drug pushers take advantage of children.

PROS	CONS
Lack of education is no excuse for bankruptcy. Adequate information about money management is available, and much of it is free. In addition, credit counseling services—also free—are available in most cities.	Most people have little knowledge of how to manage money. The educational system has adequate time for sports, music, and sex programs—but ignores the subject of using money wisely. Blame education for bankruptcies, not consumers.
The adage "there is no free lunch" applies neatly to the bankruptcy issue. People who go bankrupt in affect say to their neighbors, friends, relatives, and other members of society—"You pay my debts. I enjoyed spending more than I earned but I cannot (or will not) pay what I owe." Someone else always pays directly or indirectly what the bankrupt can't or won't pay.	Bankruptcy affects business and society only indirectly. The price of every product contains an allowance for bad debts, some of which business can collect only through bankruptcy proceedings.
99.7 percent of all bankruptcies are voluntary, meaning the debtor chooses to go bankrupt and is not forced to do so by creditors. Some voluntary bankrupts see it as an easy way to avoid paying their debts.	Businesses promote credit aggressively. Consumers are advised: "Don't leave home without your credit card," "No payment for 90 days," and "easy, easy credit." Yet easy credit leads to money problems—many of which people can remedy only through bankruptcy.

Questions

1. Which group do you feel is primarily responsible for bankruptcies, business or consumers? Why?
2. What steps do you recommend to ease the bankruptcy problem?

TRADEMARKS, PATENTS, AND COPYRIGHTS

An important area of law seeks to provide protection for intangible assets such as trademarks (which, as in the case of Coca-Cola, might well be a company's single most valuable asset), patents, and copyrights. Businesses spend large amounts of time and money ensuring that everything possible is done to provide these essential legal protections.

Trademarks Protect Names and Symbols

A **trademark** is *a name, symbol, or other device used to identify a product and officially registered by the owner or manufacturer.* "Coca-Cola" and "Coke" are registered trademarks that identify the Coca-Cola Company product—as are the shape, contour, and design of the bottle. A trademark, if used properly, remains the exclusive property of its owner forever.

The symbol ® indicates that a trademark has been issued. To date, over one million trademarks have been granted by the United States Patent and Trademark Office.

Trademarks must be handled with utmost caution; careless usage of them can destroy their protection. Federal law provides that the right to a registered trademark is forfeited "when any course of conduct of the registrant, including acts of omission or commission, causes the mark to lose its significance as an indication of origin."

Business history is replete with examples of trademarks lost because they have become generic terms. Cellophane, escalator, aspirin, linoleum, kerosene, and celluloid are well-known examples.

Once it is proved that the meaning of a trademark has changed in the public mind, there is danger that the trademark will fall into public domain—unless it is proved that the owner regularly took steps to identify its trademark. A key principle is that the trademark must always be identified *as* a trademark when a company uses it.

Another rule is that a trademark should *never* be used as a noun—but always as an adjective. The Supreme Court has allowed few exceptions to this rule—Coca-Cola is one. In the courts it was shown that the Otis Elevator Company used "Escalator" as a noun in its own advertising. The trademark should have been used as "an Escalator moving staircase" instead of merely "Escalator." Because such careless usage is deemed to confuse the public, the word is now generic, included in the dictionary, and used by all.

Levi Strauss—whose copper colored, five-eighths inch by quarter-inch tab trademark is found on the pockets of the pants it manufactures—has instituted over 200 infringement lawsuits. Dungarees, denims, and jeans are extensively trademarked. However, the words themselves are not trademarks—as is Levis—because they define where the cloth was originally made. The word "dungaree" comes from Dungri, a section of Bombay, India; "denim" is from ("de") Nîmes, a city in southern France; and "jeans" is from Gênes, the French spelling of Genoa, a city in Italy.

Patents Protect New Inventions

A **patent** is *an exclusive legal right to a product, granted by the U.S. Patent and Trademark Office for 17 years and not renewable.* Businesses closely watch the expiration dates of their patents and of those owned by their competitors. When a patent expires, the product falls into public domain for anyone to use.

The Patent Office receives more than 100,000 patent applications and issues more than 70,000 patents each year. More than four million patents have been issued since 1790. Many of the nation's leading companies as well as entirely new industries have been based on patented inventions—from the lead pencil to the word processor, from the wood-fueled stove to the microwave oven.

What the world needed. An ad written by lawyers.

Ahem.
We hate to be stuffy; but legally speaking, please remember that Xerox is a registered trademark. It identifies our products. It should never be used for anything anybody else makes.
You remember that, and we won't write any more ads.

XEROX

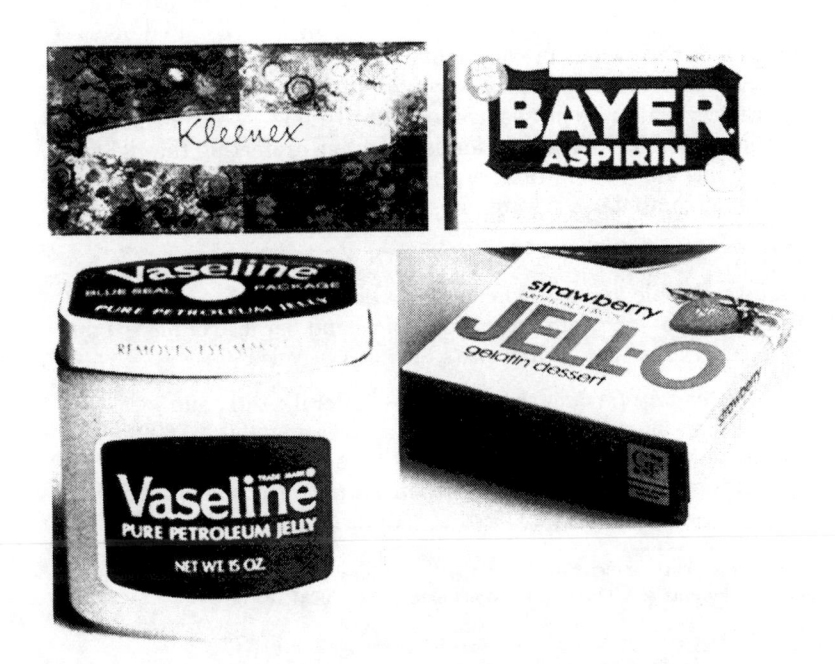

The names Jell-O, Vaseline, and Kleenex—registered trademarks—are often incorrectly used to indicate generic products (gelatin dessert, petroleum jelly, and facial tissue). Some terms have lost their protection as trademarks and can now be used by all. For example, the name Aspirin was originally a registered trademark for a brand of analgesic. Today it is a generic term used by many manufacturers.

Companies frequently take extensive precautions to protect their trademarks. See the above advertisement prepared by the Xerox Corporation.

Large libraries carry the weekly *Official Gazette* of the United States Patent and Trademark Office, which features abstracts of all the patents granted that week. There is also an annual index of patents published in two parts: an alphabetical index of patentees and a subject matter index. In addition, a copy of an individual patent can be obtained from the government for a nominal charge.[2]

Copyrights Protect Creative Works

A **copyright** is *the sole legal right to control the reproduction and dissemination of creative works.* The primary purpose of copyright laws is to encourage creativity by ensuring that those who create will be properly rewarded.

Copyrights are granted without a prior search to determine whether anything similar has been copyrighted and may be used to register artistic package and label designs, as well as anything else that is printed or illustrated. Registration applications are available free from the Copyright Office, The Library of Congress, Washington, D.C. 20559.

After many decades of debate by congressional committees, a new copyright law was enacted in 1976—superseding the outdated law of 1909. In general, copyrights now expire 50 years after the death of the author, artist, or composer who created the work. The new law contains a complex set of provisions designed to reward more fairly those who create. For example, one of the provisions requires that jukebox owners pay $8 a year for each machine for the privilege of playing records on their machines. The money is distributed under a formula to the owners of copyrights on phonograph records.

Three years after the new copyright law took effect, Congress enacted legislation to protect computer programs—which had resided in a legal limbo. This legislation is aimed at protecting the rights of individuals and corporations engaged in the development, sales, and leasing of computer-software programs.

HOW CRIME AFFECTS BUSINESS

Business people are acutely concerned about crime because—like all other citizens—they are potential victims and because crime is a major business expense. Crime costs business because:

1. *Taxes pay for law enforcement*—Federal, state, and local law-enforcement agencies employed approximately 606,000 people in 1984. Another 296,000 persons were employed by correctional institutions. Direct public expenditures for criminal justice exceeded $41 billion in 1984 (see Table 20-3).

---

[2]Send the patent number and 50 cents (20 cents for a design patent) to the Commissioner of Patents and Trademarks, Washington, D.C. 20231.

TABLE 20-3 Public Expenditures for Criminal Justice (in millions)

	1970	1984
Police	$5,080	$18,381
Judicial	1,190	10,240
Legal services	442	3,167
Public defense	102	902
Corrections	1,706	8,931
Total	$8,520	$41,621

SOURCE: *Statistical Abstract of the United States 1985,* 197.

2. *Some employees are under correctional supervision*—Over 1.4 million people age 18 and over are not in prison but are under court ordered correctional supervision. Some are on probation, have jobs, and their employers are required to exercise special control over them and file progress reports with appropriate agencies.
3. *Insurance rates are higher because of crime*—Robbery, arson, burglary, and other crimes result in increased insurance costs. Arson accounted for 16,900 arrests in 1982, yet this is believed to represent only a small fraction of fires deliberately set. Crime is so high in certain sections of some cities that business property is simply uninsurable.
4. *Police protection is often inadequate, making employment of private security necessary*—Protection services is a growth industry because law enforcement is increasingly unable to provide effective crime prevention. Many businesses also install elaborate detection equipment designed to deter crime and aid in the apprehension of criminals.

When measured by tax dollars, numbers of enforcement and correctional personnel, increased insurance rates, lost productivity of prisoners, stolen property, and arson—the cost of crime is extremely high. When measured by lives lost as a result of murder (19,000 in 1982), rape, batteries, assaults, and crime-related injuries—the cost of crime is beyond comprehension.

Crime Rates Are Highest in Large Cities

Table 20–4 shows that cities with a population of 250,000 and over—when compared with cities of a population of 10,000 or less—have a much higher violent crime rate. Large cities—when compared with

TABLE 20-4 Crime Rates by Type—Population-Size Groups and Selected Cities: 1983

CITY-SIZE GROUP AND CITY	Crime total	VIOLENT CRIME (per 100,000 population)						PROPERTY CRIME (per 100,000 population)			
		Total	Murder	Forcible rape	Robbery	Aggravated assault	Total	Burglary—breaking or entering	Larceny—theft	Motor vehicle theft
Cities with population of—										
250,000 or more	8,639	1,294	20.2	71	713	490	7,345	2,190	4,112	1,043
100,000—249,999	7,694	736	10.1	49	294	382	6,958	1,989	4,437	531
50,000—99,999	5,999	511	6.3	35	184	285	5,488	1,519	3,501	467
25,000—49,999	5,534	403	4.9	26	126	246	5,131	1,327	3,440	364
10,000—24,999	4,510	297	3.9	18	72	203	4,213	1,043	2,909	261
Fewer than 10,000	4,180	260	3.6	16	42	198	3,921	912	2,808	201
Selected cities—										
Baltimore, MD	8,524	2,003	25.0	62	1,138	778	6,522	1,806	4,162	554
Chicago, IL	7,997	1,317	24.1	74	777	441	6,680	1,620	3,767	1,293
Dallas, TX	10,793	1,149	26.8	89	492	541	9,644	2,961	5,966	717
Detroit, MI	12,900	2,169	49.3	129	1,438	553	10,731	3,874	3,859	2,998
Indianapolis, IN	6,754	893	12.1	81	393	407	5,861	1,993	3,263	605
Los Angeles, CA	9,735	1,692	26.0	79	926	661	8,044	2,523	3,966	1,555
Memphis, TN	8,306	1,138	19.1	115	676	328	7,168	2,741	3,586	841
New York, NY	8,773	1,868	22.8	52	1,184	610	6,905	2,024	3,575	1,306
Philadelphia, PA	5,304	1,003	18.4	49	635	301	4,301	1,256	2,222	823
Phoenix, AZ	8,145	625	9.8	59	234	322	7,520	2,226	4,735	559
San Antonio, TX	8,050	609	18.9	59	275	256	7,441	2,546	4,239	656
San Diego, CA	6,811	582	8.2	42	272	260	6,228	1,726	3,697	805
San Francisco, CA	8,687	1,403	11.5	75	824	492	7,284	1,718	4,781	785
Washington, DC	9,294	1,915	29.4	65	1,236	585	7,358	2,004	4,720	635

SOURCE: U.S. Federal Bureau of Investigation, *Crime in the United States*, annual.

small cities—have 5 times the murder rate, 4 times the forcible rape rate, 15 times the robbery rate, and double the aggravated assault rate.

The high crime rates prevalent in large metropolitan cities are a major reason why many manufacturing, retail, and service businesses relocate in suburban communities and in smaller cities.

Crime Rates Vary by City

Table 20-4 also shows that certain cities report significantly more violent crimes than others. Detroit has a murder rate more than five times that of Phoenix; Dallas has a forcible rape rate three times that of Chicago; robbery is five times as common in Detroit as in San

Antonio; and aggravated assault is three times as prevalent in Baltimore as in San Diego.

For all violent and property crimes, the five safest large cities are Philadelphia, Chicago, San Diego, Indianapolis, and San Antonio. The five cities with the highest crime rates per 100,000 population are Detroit, Dallas, Washington, Los Angeles, and New York.

Most White-Collar Crime Is Both Increasing and Underreported

White-collar crime, sometimes called "crime in the executive suites"—such as embezzlement, false insurance claims, stealing competitors' secrets, bid rigging, buying and selling company stock based on insider knowledge, and outright theft of company property—costs an estimated 9 percent of our GNP.[3]

Most white-collar criminals are never caught. Of those who are, only an estimated 20 percent are ever prosecuted.[4] Companies who discover their employees stealing rarely prosecute them because of the negative publicity. For example, depositors frequently withdraw their savings when they learn of employee theft from a bank.

Besides the negative public relations, much white-collar crime goes undetected and unreported because few executives are trained to deal with business crimes (few business curricula include courses on white-collar crime detection), attorneys and accountants are not legally required to inform public authorities when they uncover private white-collar crime, upper-level management may be involved, and government has the personnel and funds with which to investigate and prosecute but a fraction of white-collar crime.

Who Pays for Business Crime?

We all share the cost of business crime. For example:

In 1982, authorities in New York uncovered a tremendously sophisticated insurance fraud ring that ran with the complicity of hundreds of insurance adjusters, bank officers and even some doctors. That operation, all by itself, was responsible for adding nearly 15 percent to every premium paid by insured motorists in the state of New York.[5]

In addition to the direct cost to consumers in the form of higher prices for products and services, white-collar crime drives honest competitors from the marketplace, incomes from criminal activity go untaxed, and shareholders receive lower returns on their investments. It is an unpleasant and accurate observation that white-collar criminals have written an eleventh commandment: "Thou shalt not get caught breaking the other ten."

---

[3]William McGowan, "The Great White Collar Crime Cover-Up," *Business and Society Review,* Spring 1983, 26.

[4]Ibid., 28.

[5]Ibid., 27.

How Can We Make Sure Our Legal System Works?

Despite the increasing numbers of lawyers and judges, legal remedies to guarantee people's rights, to deal with the complexities of business, to administer bankruptcies, and to deal with crime increase even faster. The major recommendations emerging from concerned citizens, business people, legislatures, lawyers, and victims include:

1. Use the no-fault concept of automobile insurance (Chapter 8) in other areas where "who-is-legally-*liable*?" is often costly.
2. Remove incentives to sue—such as awarding triple damages to "winners" of specific types of lawsuits.
3. Require convicted persons to serve longer prison terms. For most offenses, convicted persons serve only about half their sentence.
4. Eliminate regulations that serve no useful purpose.
5. Increase the use of paralegals to handle routine legal matters.
6. Place emphasis on mediation and negotiation in law school. Courses in these areas are traditionally elective.

SUMMARY

- Demand for legal services grows because we emphasize individualism, competition, success; we enjoy more guaranteed rights; legal services are promoted; little stigma is attached to legal action; business complexity grows daily; crime continues to rise.
- There are three types of business law: mandatory, permissive, and prohibitive.
- Contracts are essential to most transactions. For an agreement to be valid and enforceable, an offer, voluntary acceptance, genuineness of assent, consideration, competent parties, lawful purposes must exist.
- The person assigning the contract is the assignor; the one receiving the rights is the assignee.
- A party injured by breach of contract may elect to rescind the contract or seek damages through court action or mediation.
- Under the law of agency, one person can act for another in transactions involving a third party.
- The relationship of employer and employee is contractual even without a written agreement. An employer must provide a safe work environment, suitable workplace, competent colleagues, and appropriate instruction. The employee must obey reasonable orders, not steal or behave immorally, and perform competently.
- Personal property sales create contractual relationships governed by legal provisions involving transfer of title, liens, and warranties.
- Negotiable instruments are substitutes for money and must be in writing, signed by the maker, unconditionally promise to pay a certain sum, be payable on demand or at a fixed time, and be payable to the order of or to the bearer.
- The process of exchanging viewpoints to reach an agreement is called negotiating.
- Bankruptcy law lets debtors be relieved of indebtedness by distribution of assets among creditors.
- One area of business law protects intangible assets such as trademarks, patents, and copyrights.
- Crime affects business because taxes pay for law enforcement, insurance rates increase, and private security is needed.

KEY TERMS YOU SHOULD KNOW

acceptance	copyright	negotiating
agent	endorsement	offer
assignment of contract	express warranty	patent
bankruptcy	full endorsement	permissive law
blank endorsement	garnishment	power of attorney
breach of contract	genuineness of assent	principal
business law	implied warranty	prohibitive law
Chapter 7	involuntary bankruptcy	qualified endorsement
Chapter 11	law of agency	restrictive endorsement
Chapter 13	law of employer-employee	trademark
conditional endorsement	lien	voluntary bankruptcy
consideration	mandatory law	warranty
contract	negotiable instrument	

QUESTIONS FOR REVIEW

1. Cite six reasons why demand for lawyers is growing.
2. Why do most legal disputes never reach the courts?
3. How can a lawyer help to avoid legal problems?
4. What are the three types of business law?
5. For a valid and enforceable contract to exist, what six conditions must be met?
6. Must a contract be in writing to be valid and enforceable?
7. Explain the law of agency and the law of employer–employee.
8. What is an unpaid seller's lien? A warranty?
9. For an instrument to be fully negotiable, what requirements must be met?
10. Explain the five kinds of endorsement.
11. Define bankruptcy. Explain what each of the three major chapters of bankruptcy law seeks to accomplish.
12. "Bankruptcies understate creditor–debtor problems." Explain.
13. What is a trademark? A patent? A copyright?
14. List four reasons why crime affects business.
15. Why does so much white-collar crime go undetected and unreported?
16. What specific steps should be taken to improve the efficiency of our legal system?

QUESTIONS FOR DISCUSSION

1. An observer stated that lawyers simply help divide the economic pie by using legal guidelines and techniques, whereas engineers make the pie grow larger by designing and building for the future. What is your understanding of this observation? Do you agree?
2. List ten circumstances in your personal and professional life that indicate a potential need for legal services. (Think of your job, home life, car, property, and so forth.) Does your list suggest that you may need a permanent professional relationship with a lawyer? Why? Why not?
3. Have students identify white-collar crime in an industry that they are familiar with. Discuss the implications.

CASE STUDY

Should Williams Printing Company Employ a Staff Lawyer?

Henry Williams founded Williams Printing Company 15 years ago. The company employs 40 people and has annual sales of $3 million. Since its incorporation, Williams has retained the services of Wilder and Wiseman, a prestigious law firm of 28 lawyers. Williams Printing has no lawyer in its employ.

The following discussion takes place at Williams' regular Monday morning staff meeting. Present are Harry Williams, president; Jane Heath, vice president for accounting, Norm Fedder, vice president for operations; and Mildred Wilson, vice president for marketing.

Harry: I've been going over our expenditures for last year and I notice we paid Wilder and Wiseman $52,000 for legal services. I'm thinking we're big enough now to hire a staff lawyer.

Jane: Actually, in my opinion, $52,000 in legal fees was not all that much—it's less than two percent of sales.

Norm: Before we employ a staff lawyer, I think we should review the performance of Wilder and Wiseman. As I see it, they've done exceptional work for us.

Mildred: I agree with Norm. Last year, for example, they helped us collect over $100,000 from an account that went bankrupt. And they sure did a good job representing us before the IRS.

H: I know they have done a fine job protecting our interests. But let's face it: They bill us at $150 per hour. That means they only delivered about 350 hours of service for all of last year. If we had a staff lawyer, we could get over 2,000 hours of legal service a year for less money.

J: I won't argue with your arithmetic, Harry. For $52,000 we probably could have a beginning lawyer and provide the needed clerical services. But we're overlooking the fact that law is not just law. Law is like medicine—it's highly specialized.

N: Jane has a good point. Wilder and Wiseman have specialists in tax, real estate, contracts, labor, pension plans—you name it. For just about every conceivable problem we might face, they have an expert who can handle it.

M: I agree. No one lawyer has all the knowledge and skills needed to deal effectively with all legal problems. We all agree that Wilder and Wiseman have served us well, so why add a lawyer to our staff?

H: I realize I've based my argument for an in-company lawyer on the fact that we paid $52,000 in legal fees last year. But there's another big reason I think we need a lawyer on our staff. We need someone around here who can spot legal problems before they develop—someone who practices preventive law like wise physicians practice preventive medicine.

Think about my idea and we'll discuss it again next week.

Questions

1. If an in-company lawyer is employed, is it likely that Wilder and Wiseman (or another large firm) will still be retained from time to time? Why? Why not?

2. What are some examples of "preventive law" that an in-company lawyer might practice?

3. If you were Williams, would you employ an in-company lawyer? Why? Why not?

EVOLUTION OF A BUSINESS

Establishing Credibility and Trust

Ray was somewhat shaken one day when he had lunch with an old friend, Craig Spense. The two men had worked for the same company when Ray was in public relations.

Craig: I'd say one of your biggest problems is credibility.

Ray: What do you mean?

Craig: You should be concentrating on getting the public to believe in you. Aren't you aware of all the bad press travel agencies have been getting in recent years? You know there are crooks in your field. And you suffer from that because they make front-page headlines. Papers write stories about charter groups that get stranded in London because a travel agent goes bankrupt. And there was a story about tour operators in California who got hundreds of people out there to pay $985 for a 15-day magic cure trip to the Philippines. The doctor made those people's dollars disappear, not their illnesses.

Ray: Yes, I think I read about that. You know, Sara and I first got the idea for Excel Travel because we were unhappy with TA ripoffs. Since then, we've gotten so involved in our business that we've practically forgotten about the bad reputation many TAs have. We've certainly kept all our operations above board. But I wonder if we should do something more. It might be a good idea to promote the fact that we belong to ASTA. That's the American Society of Travel Agents. We could point to the certificate on our wall when people came in and explain that we're a member.

Questions

1. Do you think the reputation of TAs is as bad as Craig makes it out to be?
2. How can Ray find out what people think of TAs?
3. Would Ray's proposed approach serve a useful purpose, or would it merely be looked upon as eyewash? (ASTA has over 14,000 members in 120 countries; its members must be bonded and demonstrate that they are financially sound.)
4. What other steps could Excel take to establish credibility and trust?

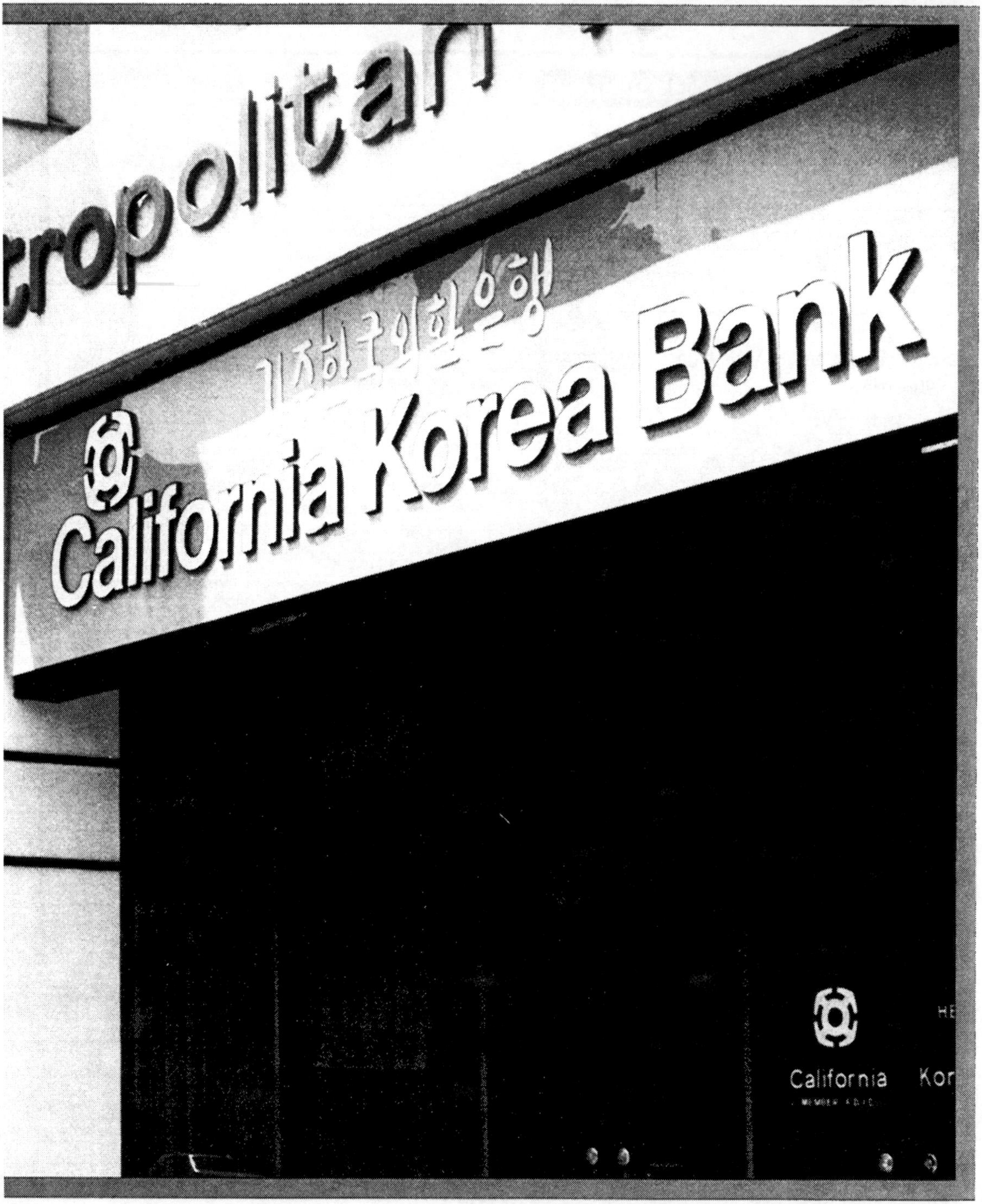
tropolitan
California Korea Bank
California

21

INTERNATIONAL BUSINESS
Winning the Global Challenge

READ THIS CHAPTER SO YOU CAN:

Define international business and the exchanges it involves.

Define international trade and explain its rationale.

List the main reasons we import and export.

Discuss the obstacles to international trade.

Explain the channels for exporting and importing.

Discuss key international economic systems and institutions—current account and balance of trade, BIC, and the Export-Import Bank.

Discuss the growing impact of multinationals.

Describe OPEC, OECD, LAFTA, and CACM as world economic organizations.

Discuss trends in international trade.

We can divide international business into two segments: importing and exporting. Those items that international business exchanges consist of products, investments, and ideas.

INTERNATIONAL BUSINESS: PRODUCTS, INVESTMENTS, AND IDEAS

We see the import side of international trade every day. Foreign-made cars are everywhere, and much of the gas we use to run them comes from foreign nations. The TV sets we watch may have an American name, but most of their components are imported. Much clothing and many shoes Americans wear come from Taiwan, Italy, and other nations. Many Americans prefer beer from Germany, distilled beverages from Great Britain or Poland, and wine from France or Italy.

The export side of international trade is less apparent but nonetheless real. Two-thirds of our wheat and over half our soybeans are sold to overseas buyers. Most of the airlines in other free world coun-

We sell two-thirds of our wheat overseas. Here grain is loaded aboard a ship bound for Russia.

tries use airplanes built by Boeing, Lockheed, or Douglas. Other nations build most of the television components, but Americans made and launched the satellites that transmit TV programs, information, and telephone calls.

The investment side of international trade is important, too. For generations, Americans have exported great amounts of capital. Some investments are in manufacturing and distribution facilities in other nations. Americans also export much capital as loans to other nations, particularly to less developed countries. And we buy securities in foreign companies almost as easily as in our own country.

America also imports capital. Japan and Germany own automobile plants here. Many foreigners invest capital in office complexes, shopping centers, and land. And many foreign investors buy securities in American companies as well as government-backed notes.

The exchange of products and investments is tangible: Careful accounting tracks such transactions. Although accounting techniques do not tally idea exchanges, such exchanges are real and powerful.

We export American ideas, methods, and attitudes in many

Along with goods, we export our culture. People around the world now drink American soft drinks.

ways. Over 800,000 American military personnel and their dependents live in other nations and influence foreign cultures. Other Americans reside in foreign nations as managers of American-owned companies and branch offices. Students attending colleges in other countries and tourists who travel overseas also export American ideas. And foreigners enjoy many American television programs and movies.

On the other hand, we import many ideas and attitudes from other nations. Increasingly, foreign companies with American branches transmit their ideas on management methods to us. For example, American companies are looking carefully at Japanese management techniques. Immigrants to the United States bring with them their ideas about such varied matters as food preparation, music, art, religion, and work. Most colleges have students from other nations. And foreign tourists influence our society just as American tourists affect the societies of other nations.

INTERNATIONAL TRADE AND AMERICAN BUSINESS

International trade is very much interwoven with American business. From our beginning as a nation, we have traded with other nations. International economic differences have sometimes caused even the most tragic side of our history, our wars—beginning with the Boston Tea Party conflict with England over two centuries ago.

International trade is increasingly important to our economic well-being. Profits and jobs at home are related to economic conditions abroad. Reduction of foreign trade reduces our standard of living and invites economic stagnation. Trading with other nations is mutually beneficial. And the future points to more, not less, foreign trade.

Most international trade products are transported by ship, so many import and export centers are seaports. Figure 21-1 shows the projected ten largest urban areas in the world in the year 2000. Most of these giant metropolitan areas are either seaports or, like Chicago, have easy access to the oceans.

WHAT IS INTERNATIONAL TRADE?

International trade is *the management of business between countries. It is the application of efficiency and good business judgment to the conduct of business between domestic and foreign organizations.*

International trade involves more than moving merchandise. A firm also engages in international trade when it builds a factory overseas; enters into joint business ventures abroad; or exports or imports

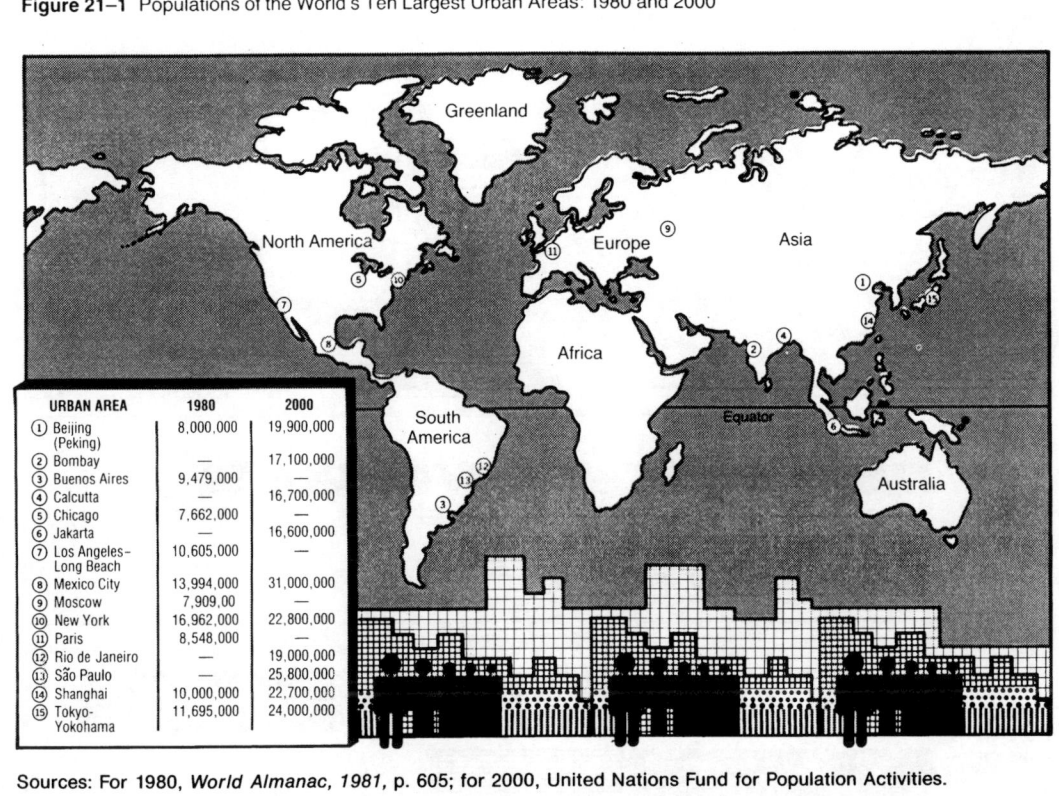

Figure 21-1 Populations of the World's Ten Largest Urban Areas: 1980 and 2000

URBAN AREA	1980	2000
① Beijing (Peking)	8,000,000	19,900,000
② Bombay	—	17,100,000
③ Buenos Aires	9,479,000	—
④ Calcutta	—	16,700,000
⑤ Chicago	7,662,000	—
⑥ Jakarta	—	16,600,000
⑦ Los Angeles–Long Beach	10,605,000	—
⑧ Mexico City	13,994,000	31,000,000
⑨ Moscow	7,909,00	—
⑩ New York	16,962,000	22,800,000
⑪ Paris	8,548,000	—
⑫ Rio de Janeiro	—	19,000,000
⑬ São Paulo	—	25,800,000
⑭ Shanghai	10,000,000	22,700,000
⑮ Tokyo-Yokohama	11,695,000	24,000,000

Sources: For 1980, *World Almanac, 1981*, p. 605; for 2000, United Nations Fund for Population Activities.

capital, know-how, patents, or trademarks.

We export talent to England, for example, when an American rock group appears there. The converse is also true: When English actors appear in our country, we are importing talent.

The Law of Comparative Advantage Explains International Trade

The **law of comparative advantage** means that *a nation has some advantages—technology, wage, climate, resources, land—over other nations in producing certain products and services.* For example, we have a comparative advantage over other nations in producing wheat, soybeans, and aircraft. South Africa enjoys a comparative advantage over other countries in producing gold because that is where

628 CHAPTER 21/INTERNATIONAL BUSINESS

Figure 21-2 The Law of Comparative Advantage at Work

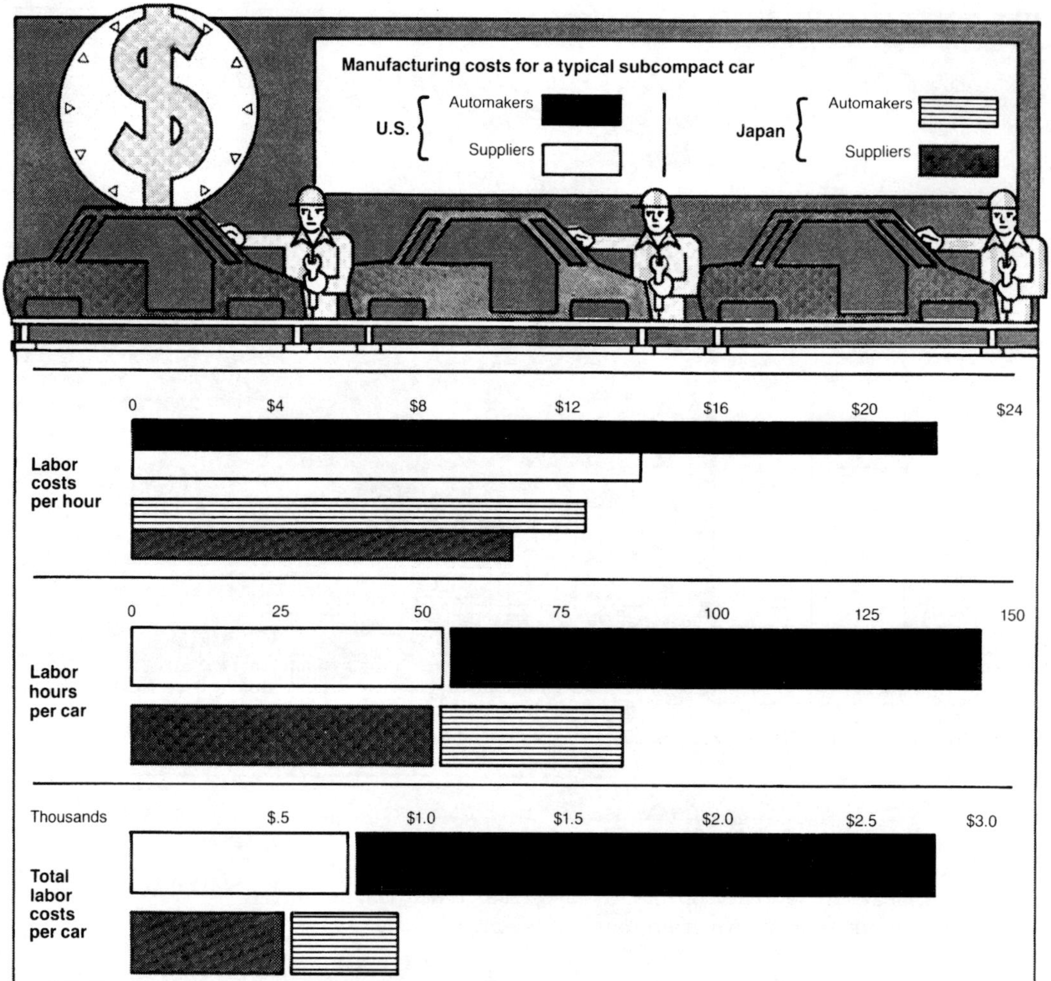

Manufacturing costs for a typical subcompact car

U.S. { Automakers / Suppliers }   Japan { Automakers / Suppliers }

Labor costs per hour: 0 — $4 — $8 — $12 — $16 — $20 — $24

Labor hours per car: 0 — 25 — 50 — 75 — 100 — 125 — 150

Total labor costs per car (Thousands): $.5 — $1.0 — $1.5 — $2.0 — $2.5 — $3.0

Detroit still has a long row to hoe
Despite record capital expenditures and newfangled production methods, productivity at U.S. auto companies trails Japanese productivity by a country mile. And a relatively austere UAW contract hasn't kept labor costs from growing 10% a year—twice the rate of increase for Japanese automakers.

Source: Anne B. Fisher, "Can Detroit Live without Quotas?" *Fortune*, June 25, 1984, p. 23.

most deposits are. The Middle East has a comparative advantage in oil production and the Japanese in auto production. Figure 21-2 shows the advantages Japan has in producing automobiles.

Countries engage in international trade because it enables them to specialize in producing products for which they have economic advantages and to import products for which they have economic disadvantages. No two nations are alike—they differ in climate, natural resources, scientific know-how, and production capability. The idea behind international trade is that nations should export what they produce well and import what they do not produce so efficiently.

For example, Central America has a climatic advantage in growing bananas. While it is conceivable that we could create an artificial climate to grow bananas, doing so would be foolish because the cost would be excessive. The Arab nations have an economic advantage in a mineral resource—oil. They are at an economic disadvantage in scientific know-how and products. Obviously, it is to their advantage to export oil and import computers and appliances. Meanwhile, it is to our advantage to import oil, which we do not produce enough of, and to export technical products, which we readily produce.

In a perfectly structured world community, all nations would sell their products at reasonable prices, and no resources would be wasted. The net result of this ideal condition would be a higher standard of living for everyone. Unfortunately, political differences, economic inefficiencies, and surpluses and shortages in what nations produce thwart this perfect economic model. Periodic shortages of oil and coffee give nations that produce those commodities an advantage, and other nations have surpluses of bananas and automobiles, which creates trading problems for nations that produce them.

Table 21-1 gives the reasons we import and export in more detail.

> Despite record capital expenditures and new-fangled production methods, productivity at U.S. auto companies trails Japanese productivity by a country mile. And a relatively austere UAW contract hasn't kept labor costs from growing 10% a year—twice the rate of increase for Japanese automakers.

WORLD TRADE AND THE U.S. ECONOMY

Because relatively few people or businesses participate directly in international trade, many people underestimate its importance to the national economy. The oil shortages of the 1970s called attention to the interdependency of nations in this respect.

Exports account for one of every eight U.S. factory jobs and one of every four farm jobs, yet the Department of Commerce estimates that only some 30,000 of our 252,000 manufacturing firms export goods, indicating enormous expansion possibilities. Professor Warren J. Bilkey of the University of Wisconsin's business school found that the majority of "our overseas sales originate not with a salesman's call but with a request from a foreign buyer."

TABLE 21-1   Main Reasons We Import and Export

WHY WE IMPORT
- To obtain products we need but do not produce. Examples include bananas, coffee, cocoa, natural rubber, and some minerals, such as tin, nickel, and lead.
- To obtain products we produce but not in sufficient quantity. Oil is the principal example. Others include newsprint, hides, and sugar.
- To obtain products that we can purchase at lower prices than similar products made domestically. Television sets, some automobiles, textiles, and paper products are examples.
- To satisfy American preferences for qualities not found in American-made products. Examples are certain gourmet foods, wines, apparel, artwork, and shoes.
- To keep abreast of latest techniques. Often, for example, the Germans or Japanese produce superior machinery that U.S. firms buy to increase their production efficiency.

WHY WE EXPORT
- To sell agricultural products of which we produce a surplus, such as wheat, rice, cotton, tobacco, pineapples, and citrus fruits.
- To sell products for which we have a technological advantage over other nations. Examples are computers, aircraft, some types of scientific instruments, and some medicines.
- To utilize more fully our production capacity and thereby lower per-unit production costs. By selling to foreign customers, a firm can produce in greater volume and thus take advantage of economies of scale.
- To satisfy foreign customers' preferences for certain American-made products, such as movies, television plays, airplanes, and cigarettes.
- To make it easier to introduce new models domestically. Trade-ins and older models of some products (for example, aircraft and computers) are often sold overseas.

U.S. Exports

EXPORTING GOODS

The United States is the largest seller of merchandise in the world market. Figure 21-3 shows the percent distribution of our exports and imports by commodity class for 1984. Sales of machinery and transportation equipment, mainly power generating equipment, computers, tractors, and aircraft, account for 41.2 percent of our exports. Other manufactured products, particularly scientific instruments, metal products, power machinery, paper and textiles, are important exports. In the food category, grains are the most important commodity sold to other countries.

On the import side, machinery and transportation equipment, mainly automobiles, are the largest category, followed by fuels and manufactured products, principally metals, clothing, and manufactured paper products.

In historical perspective, we see some dramatic changes in the relative importance of the products we export. In 1960, exports of machinery and transportation equipment accounted for 34.3 percent

Figure 21-3 Percent Distribution of U.S. Exports and Imports by Product Category 1984

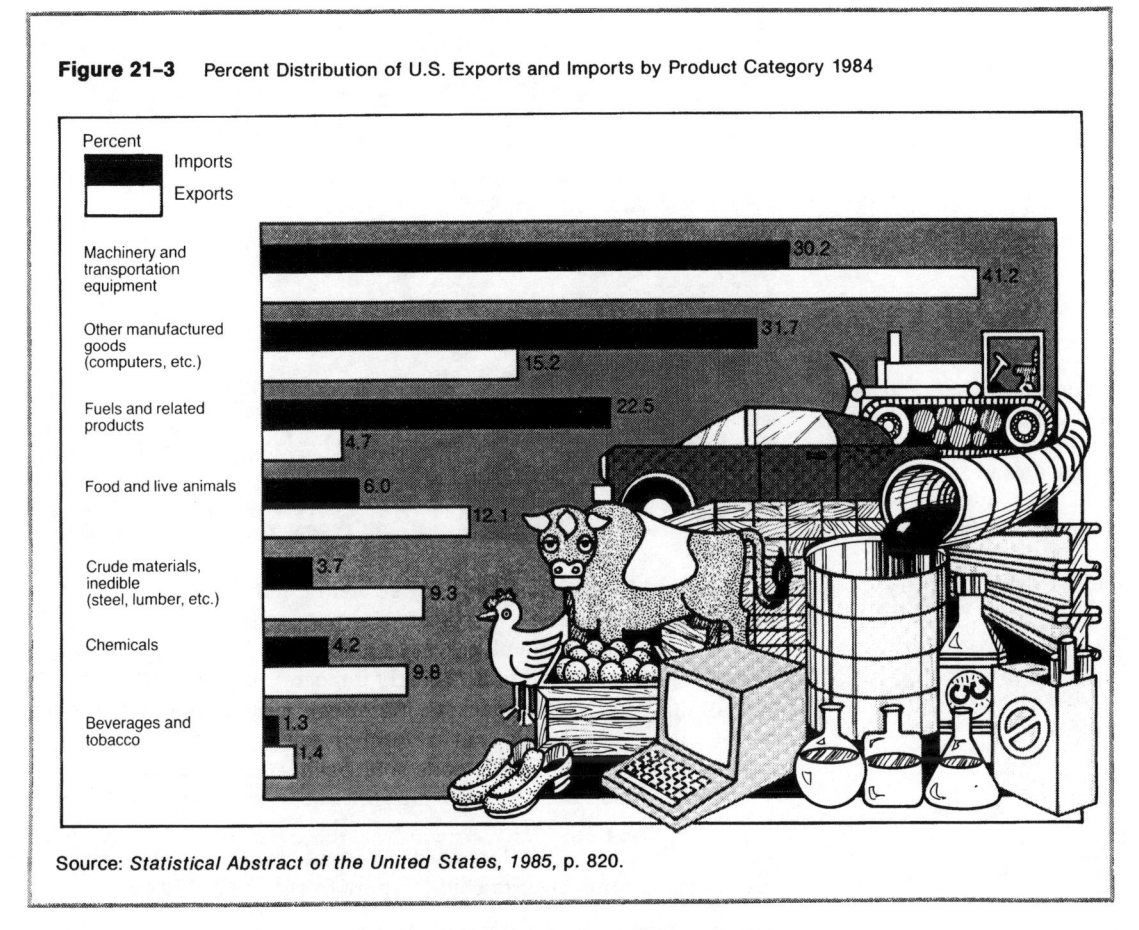

Category	Imports	Exports
Machinery and transportation equipment	30.2	41.2
Other manufactured goods (computers, etc.)	31.7	15.2
Fuels and related products	22.5	4.7
Food and live animals	6.0	12.1
Crude materials, inedible (steel, lumber, etc.)	3.7	9.3
Chemicals	4.2	9.8
Beverages and tobacco	1.3	1.4

Source: *Statistical Abstract of the United States, 1985*, p. 820.

of exports, and in 1984, 41.2 percent. On the import side, only 9.7 percent of machinery and transportation equipment in 1960 came from foreign nations. By 1984, the percentage was 30.2. Oil accounted for only 10.5 percent of imports in 1960, but increased to 22.5 percent in 1984.

U.S. Imports

If any nation could be economically self-sufficient, it would be the United States. We have a varied climate, fertile land, vast mineral resources, advanced technology, and great mass-production capabilities. Yet, despite these assets, the United States is the world's leading importer. The import side of our international trade clearly shows the law of comparative advantage at work. We could make all of the automobiles we can use, but Japan now has a comparative advantage: It can make cars with less input of time and labor. And the United

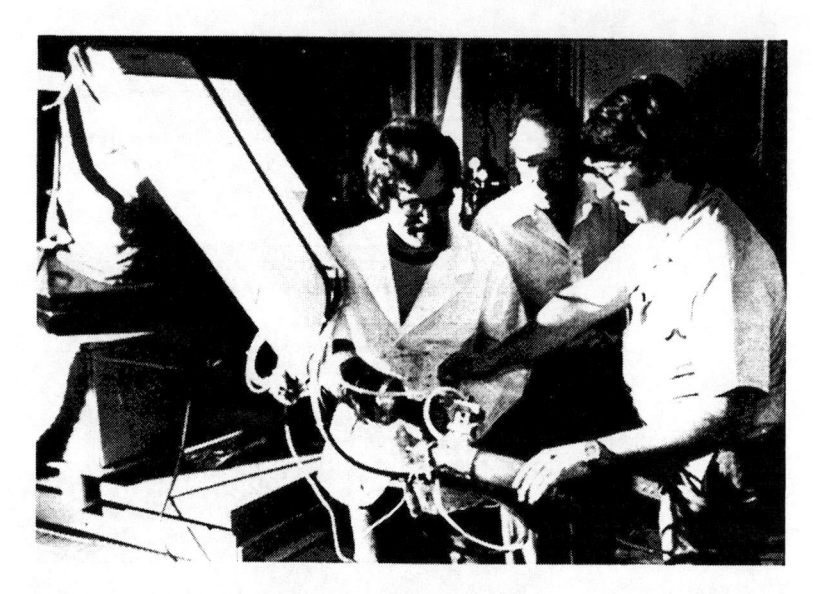

Not only do we import goods from Japan, we also import know-how and capital. This Nissan plant in Smyrna, Tenn., has Japanese owners and American managers.

States could be self-sufficient in petroleum, but the costs of producing additional oil here are still more expensive than importing oil.

The U.S. government serves as a watchdog for imports. Through controls, it tries to maintain "orderly imports" so that imports do not unduly upset domestic markets. American manufacturers can lodge complaints by charging that a foreign country is **dumping,** that is, *flooding a market with goods sold below cost.* Also, the U.S government's diplomatic arm can put pressures on the government of another country to restrict exports to the United States. This happened in 1981 when the Japanese government set quotas for what its automobile manufacturers could export to the United States.

With Whom Do We Trade?

Table 21–2 shows percentages of total exports and imports with our 14 leading trade partners. These 14 nations account for over 67 percent of all American exports and 70 percent of our imports.

We trade little with the Communist nations in Europe. In 1984 only 1.4 percent of our exports and less than one-half of one percent of our imports were with the Soviet Union, Poland, Hungary, East Germany, and other Communist nations. Communist countries in Asia, principally China, accounted for 1.1 percent of the products we exported and only .9 percent of our imports.

Another example of ideology interfering with world trade is the Arab nations' practice of not buying from firms that do business with Israel. Arab nations, for example, will not purchase Ford automobiles because Ford makes cars in Israel.

TABLE 21-2 Sales and Purchases with Our Fourteen Leading Trade Partners 1984

NATION	AMOUNT WE SOLD	AMOUNT WE BOUGHT
Canada	$ 38.2	$ 52.1
Japan	21.9	41.2
Mexico	9.1	16.8
United Kingdom	10.6	12.5
West Germany	8.7	12.7
Saudi Arabia	7.9	3.6
Netherlands	7.7	2.9
France	5.9	6.0
Korea	5.9	7.1
Belgium	5.0	2.4
Venezuela	2.8	4.9
Italy	3.9	5.4
Australia	3.9	2.2
Taiwan	4.6	11.2
Total	$136.1	$181.0
Percent of Total Exports	67.9	70.1

SOURCE: *Statistical Abstract of the United States 1985*, 819.

WHAT OBSTACLES RESTRICT INTERNATIONAL TRADE?

Differences in political ideologies, income, trade restrictions, laws, currencies, languages, and social customs complicate doing business with other nations.

Politics Interferes with Trade

Approximately 2 billion or 40 percent of the world's population live in the Soviet Union, China, and their satellite Communist nations. The need for trade exists, but official government policies stand in the way.

Some Nations Lack Income

As we saw in Chapter 9, to have a market, people must have money to buy goods. Many nations, especially in Africa, South America, and parts of Asia, have economic needs but lack the money to satisfy them. To acquire the money to engage in substantial foreign trade, nations must devise ways for such countries to be more productive.

AMERICA'S REEMERGING CREATIVITY

How U.S. and Global Revitalization Relate

The revitalization of the American economy depends to a large extent on the revitalization of other industrialized nations. Our revival also depends on expanding the capabilities of the so-called Third World economies, nations that are just entering the industrial age.

In energizing and expanding our economic efforts, we depend on similar efforts in other nations. Because of the growing interdependency of all nations, poverty in one nation and prosperity in another is becoming incompatible in our modern world. The United States wants other nations to become more productive and prosperous because their success stimulates a higher standard of living for us.

For example, great progress has been made in relaxing trade restrictions with the People's Republic of China. But our trade with China is still at a low level, mainly because China still lacks the wealth to produce products we want and to buy products we make. As its economy gains new vitality, more trade benefiting both nations is certain to result.

Revitalization of other nations affects the United States' economy in another important way. As economies become increasingly interdependent, the danger of international conflict decreases. To use an extreme example, chances of an armed conflict with Canada are virtually none. Similarities in cultural and historical backgrounds are factors preventing a severe strain on our relationship. But another key factor is our economic interdependence. We are each other's biggest customer in international trade.

Investment in the economic development of other nations is another important element in global revitalization. Many people object to the high prices of petroleum products OPEC nations charge. But we may not recognize that many of the dollars we send to other nations for energy return to the United States as investments in American industry.

Sharing knowledge is also an important approach to American and global economic revitalization. Never before have so many international societies of experts in medicine, science, engineering, nutrition, agriculture, and other basic pursuits worked together to advance knowledge for the welfare of all.

We can paraphrase a famous statement from Hemingway: "When one nation is poor and economically diminished, all nations are made somewhat poorer and economically impoverished." The revitalization of the U.S. economy relates to and depends on the revitalization of other nations to a greater extent than many realize.

Questions for Discussion

1. Assuming that our long-run economic success depends on the success of other nations, do you support foreign aid to underdeveloped nations? Why or why not? If you feel that foreign aid is worthwhile, what restrictions would you place on it?

2. Suppose the United States makes a great breakthrough in production of cereal grains (wheat, corn, and so on). Should we keep such a discovery a secret from other nations? Why or why not?

Trade Restrictions

All nations have different regulations on imports and exports. American firms must be familiar with the regulations of each country with which they do business. Getting goods into another country often involves considerable red tape and risk of loss.

TARIFFS

A **tariff** is *a tax or customs duty levied on imported goods.* Tariffs generally range from 10 to 18 percent of the value of goods. Three types of tariffs may be imposed: *ad valorem* (according to value) taxes, such as "15 percent of value"; specific taxes, such as "6 cents per pound"; and a combination of the two, such as "6 cents per pound plus 15 percent of value."

OTHER GOVERNMENT CONTROLS

Controls governments use to limit imports or increase exports include (1) **import licenses,** which *limit the volume or value of imports permitted;* (2) quotas on amounts to be imported; (3) *licenses* (called **exchange licenses**) *for obtaining foreign currencies with which to buy goods abroad;* and (4) **subsidized exports** *to increase foreign sales.*

Domestic industries, when faced with extreme foreign competition, commonly ask Congress to raise tariffs or set import quotas. This, in effect, limits competition from abroad. In the past, manufacturers of television sets, textiles, and shoes sought such relief. Both labor and management have asked for protection from foreign competitors: Over the years both have often told the public to "buy American" and save jobs. But what they have not told the public is that if we don't import we can't export, a situation that also costs Americans jobs. We cannot sell our products abroad if we do not also buy from abroad.

Differences in Laws

The laws of a foreign country govern transactions within that country. Laws pertaining to shipping, taxation, employment, selling, and other phases of business differ widely and can bewilder Americans doing business in foreign nations unless they have competent assistance from people who have experience in the country.

Foreign companies doing business in the United States may have difficulties with our laws, just as we have with theirs. In recent years, several Japanese companies have been sued in the United States for alleged violation of our Civil Rights laws. Specific charges are that the Japanese show preference to their nationals working in the United States.

Many Americans working in Third World countries are coming home because these nations discriminate against Americans. Two qualified observers raise these questions about this issue:

- Should a foreign multinational have a right to bring its own people into the United States for specific management jobs or must it hire local American citizens if similarly qualified people are available?

- A foreign multinational may have a psychological predisposition to hire its own people for certain top management jobs in the United States. Should this be considered a prerogative of the owners, or should it be considered a job restriction based on national origin?

- The comparative similarity of candidate qualifications and the job functions may be more apparent than real. A foreign multinational may have a different managerial philosophy and operational style that is the product of the particular sociocultural milieu of its home country and people. This difference may make it difficult, if not impossible, for any direct comparisons of job specifications or individual qualifications as to suitability for certain positions. What criteria can be used for comparing job performance and individual qualifications under those circumstances?[1]

---

[1] S. Prakash and Carl Swanson, "How Japanese Multinationals Skirt Our Civil Rights Laws," *Business and Society Review,* Winter 1983, 47–48.

ISSUE FOR DEBATE

Should the U.S. Trade with Nations That Practice Discrimination?

In 1977, the Reverend Leon Sullivan of Philadelphia drew up a list of principles to eliminate the inequalities that existed between white and black workers in South Africa. Specifically, the Sullivan Principles called for:

- Nonsegregation of the races in all eating, comfort, and work facilities.
- Equal and fair employment policies for all workers.
- Initiation of training programs to bring blacks into supervisory, administrative, clerical, and technical employment.
- Recruitment and training of minorities for management and supervisory positions.
- Improving the quality of life for minorities in housing, health, transportation, schooling, and recreation.

About 400 American companies that do business in South Africa were asked to sign the Sullivan Principles. As of 1984 only about 50 percent have done so. And, of the signing companies, many are not living up to the stipulated requirements. A continuing debate concerns whether American businesses in South Africa and other nations should practice discrimination.

PROS	CONS
An old adage says, "When in Rome, do as the Romans." The United States has no right to violate business standards in other societies. The way another nation treats its people is its concern, not ours.	It is hypocritical for American companies not to discriminate in the United States but do so in other nations. If equal treatment is a good idea here, it is a good idea in South Africa too.
Many American firms doing business in South Africa are small with less than 20 employees. They must select employees from the pool of qualified people, regardless of their race, religion, national origin or other factors. Skilled black workers are in short supply.	Other nations regard the United States as the leader in international commerce. Our example is important. If American firms adhere to the Sullivan Principles in South Africa, other nations will follow and discrimination will end.
Even if American companies followed the Sullivan principles completely, their example would not change the way South African businesses treat employees.	Moral values such as equal opportunity and fair play for everyone are more important than economic values or profits.
Local authorities may discriminate against an American business that goes against local traditions and customs. South African officials may make it more difficult for such an American firm to obtain business licenses, find desirable locations, and secure favorable treatment.	It is insulting to minorities in the United States to see the firms they work for here practice discrimination in other parts of the world.
Economic principles, not moral values, must guide business, wherever practiced. The role of governments, religious bodies, and private organizations is to change attitudes in other nations. This is not the role of business.	All American companies should follow the lead of many banks and brokerage houses which refuse to market Kruggerand coins, one of South Africa's leading exports.
	Treatment and living conditions of black, colored, and Asian miners is deplorable. Wages for non-Whites are only about one-third the wages of Whites.

Questions

1. Do you feel U.S. companies should do business in or with countries that practice discrimination? Why or why not?
2. Should the Federal Government force American firms to trade only with nations that do not engage in discrimination? Why or why not?

Differences in Currencies

Currencies differ widely throughout the world. The United States and its possessions use the American dollar, but other nations have different currencies that vary in value in relation to the dollar. The currency unit in Great Britain is the pound; in West Germany, the mark; in France, the franc; in the Philippines, the peso; and so on.

A retailer in Paris who buys a shipment of American computers sells them in his store for French francs. The American computer manufacturer wishes to be paid in American dollars, since he cannot use French francs to defray business expenses. Large commercial banks, American or foreign, arrange for the conversion of currencies. The **exchange rate** is *the value of one currency in relation to another.*

Exchange rates vary daily, are broadcast on many radio stations daily and appear in some financial publications. When the dollar is "strong" relative to a foreign currency, it buys more than when it is "weak." In recent years, American tourists have found the dollar has more purchasing power in South America and Europe.

Because exchange rates fluctuate freely, often daily, and since each nation's currency restrictions also vary, business people should have expert banking advice and assistance in all foreign dealings.

Differences in Languages

Relatively few Americans are able to converse in more than one of the world's almost 3,000 languages. Although English is the third most widely spoken language in the world, the volume of written information in English makes it the most valuable. A good indication is the number of newspapers in English (2,400) compared with the next biggest newspaper language, Spanish (1,000).

What Happens When Translations Are Careless?

Businesses that promote products in foreign nations should make sure experts—people who understand fluently the language, including the jargon, slang, idioms and mores of the foreign target market—translate advertisements. Examples of American messages that failed to achieve their objective include:

- General Motor's slogan, "Body By Fisher," was translated into Flemish as "Corpse by Fisher."

- Pepsodent's slogan, "Wonder Where the Yellow Went," was viewed as a racial slur in Southeast Asia, where darkly stained teeth convey prestige.

- A detergent maker overlooked the fact that people in the Middle East generally read from right to left. Its TV commercial showed dirty clothes on the left, the soap in the middle and the clean clothes on the right. But the people watching the commercial from right to left got the idea that the detergent made their clothes dirty.

- An ad for refrigerators failed in the Middle East because a ham was featured inside the refrigerator. Muslims do not eat ham and considered the ad offensive.[2]

Differences in Social and Business Customs

Each nation has customs and ways of looking at things that are unique. To deal effectively with foreign nations, American business must understand foreign customs. For example, in Islamic countries, charging interest is a religious taboo, whereas making profits is allowed, since "Allah hath permitted trading and forbidden usury." Thus they charge no interest in commercial arrangements, but they have a profit-sharing provision that makes financing possible.

Differing moral standards are troublesome. Bribery, for example, is acceptable in certain countries. Some American companies would not pay bribes at home but accept the practice in countries where bribery is customary. They believe that moral codes are not exportable and that mores of host countries should prevail within their borders. When competitors pay bribes, how can American companies compete without doing so?

HOW TO ORGANIZE FOR EXPORTING

American manufacturers choose one of two methods to sell to foreign markets. They either sell indirectly through domestic export channels, or sell directly through their own export departments.

Indirect Export Channels

An **indirect export channel** is *a marketing channel through which an American manufacturer sells to foreign markets using a third party.* Following are the major indirect export channels.

Differences in language and social and business customs make educational and cultural exchanges essential in our contemporary world. Hence, an African student at Boston University has a discussion with American friends.

EXPORT MERCHANTS

Wholesalers who specialize in buying merchandise from various domestic manufacturers and reselling it in foreign markets are called **export merchants.** Selling to export merchants is usually no more complicated than selling to domestic intermediaries.

A disadvantage of this export channel is that the exporter makes no personal contact with foreign customers and therefore limits business expansion possibilities. The manufacturer has little opportunity to adapt to the market, create demand, or build goodwill.

BUYERS FOR EXPORT

Foreign buyers who canvass American markets in search of goods foreign consumers need are **buyers for export.** They represent

---

[2]David A. Ricks, "How to Avoid Business Blunders Abroad," *Business*, April 1984, 12–15—provides specific suggestions for improving communication in other nations.

foreign clients from whom they receive a commission for their purchases. Their method is more complicated than marketing through export merchants because the manufacturer must assume shipping responsibilities.

EXPORT AGENTS

Export agents function in world trade much as manufacturers' agents do in domestic trade. They usually *represent several noncompeting American manufacturers in a foreign market.* The export agent makes sales in the name of the manufacturing firm, which does the financing and shipping. Export agents can be effective when the need to create a demand for American products requires aggressive selling efforts. Export agents provide feedback of information about the foreign markets, because they deal regularly with the same overseas customers.

> *"The merchant has no country."*
>
> THOMAS JEFFERSON

Direct Export Channels

A **direct export channel** is *a marketing channel through which an American manufacturer sells directly to foreign consumers.* In this case, the firm establishes its own export department, which either sells directly to foreign intermediaries or supervises the company's own representatives overseas. Or a manufacturer may wish to establish a foreign branch, a foreign subsidiary, a licensing agreement, a contract manufacturing arrangement, or a joint venture.

FOREIGN BRANCHES

A **foreign branch** is *an actual division of the domestic company that functions very much like a foreign wholesaler except that it is owned by Americans.* Branches usually employ citizens of the country in which they are located if possible. Foreign branches are important when a company sells technical products that require service and parts.

FOREIGN SUBSIDIARIES

Foreign subsidiaries are *separate companies that parent American corporations own, but that are subject to the laws of the foreign country.* Companies establish them to obtain favorable tax considerations or to comply with requirements of foreign governments. Companies use them to maintain maximum control over overseas investment.

Many foreign countries have laws that make building manufacturing facilities attractive. Overseas manufacturing has several advantages. First, it avoids most foreign tariff and import restrictions. Second, companies can use local labor. Third, transportation of parts to the foreign country is much less costly than transportation of the finished product within the country. Fourth, manufacturing in the country promotes good will.

For example, a General Motors plant in Germany is able to sell its output in all the other Common Market countries without paying tariff. If GM shipped the cars from the United States, the company would have to pay both transportation and tariff.

Increasingly American manufacturers are becoming major international producers. An IBM spokesperson has said, "The trend is such a reality that American big business is no longer national, but rather world in character."

LICENSING AGREEMENTS

An agreement made between a manufacturer in this country and a manufacturer abroad (the licensee) whereby the licensee obtains rights to sell the product in a specified market on a royalty basis is known as a **licensing agreement.** Licensing agreements encourage companies to invest in the manufacture of American products. For example, in addition to establishing its own assembly plants in several countries, General Motors has licensing agreements for assembling and manufacturing in more than 20 other countries.

CONTRACT MANUFACTURING

In **contract manufacturing** *a foreign producer manufactures the U.S. company's product abroad.* Local producers make the American product, usually on a **cost-plus basis.** That is, after the work on the product is completed, *the American company pays the foreign producer its costs plus an agreed-on percentage.*

JOINT VENTURES

When a U.S. firm and a foreign firm combine interests, usually to finance a new, third company in the foreign country, it is called a **joint venture.** This arrangement is growing in popularity, especially in developed countries where experienced partners are available. A joint venture assures that the American company has an experienced foreign company with a vested interest in looking out for the welfare of the American company. Joint ventures are often owned on a 50-50 basis. However, the percentages vary greatly.

HOW TO ORGANIZE FOR IMPORTING

Importing channels, like those of exporting, can be either indirect or direct.

Indirect Import Channels

An **indirect import channel** is *a marketing channel in which an intermediary in this country purchases goods from a foreign firm.* Indirect import channels are popular with American firms because using them is as convenient as buying goods from domestic sources. Most American businesses prefer buying indirectly through import merchants, import commission houses, or import brokers.

Figure 21-4 U.S. International Transaction Balances: 1970 to 1983

Source: Chart prepared by U.S. Bureau of the Census.

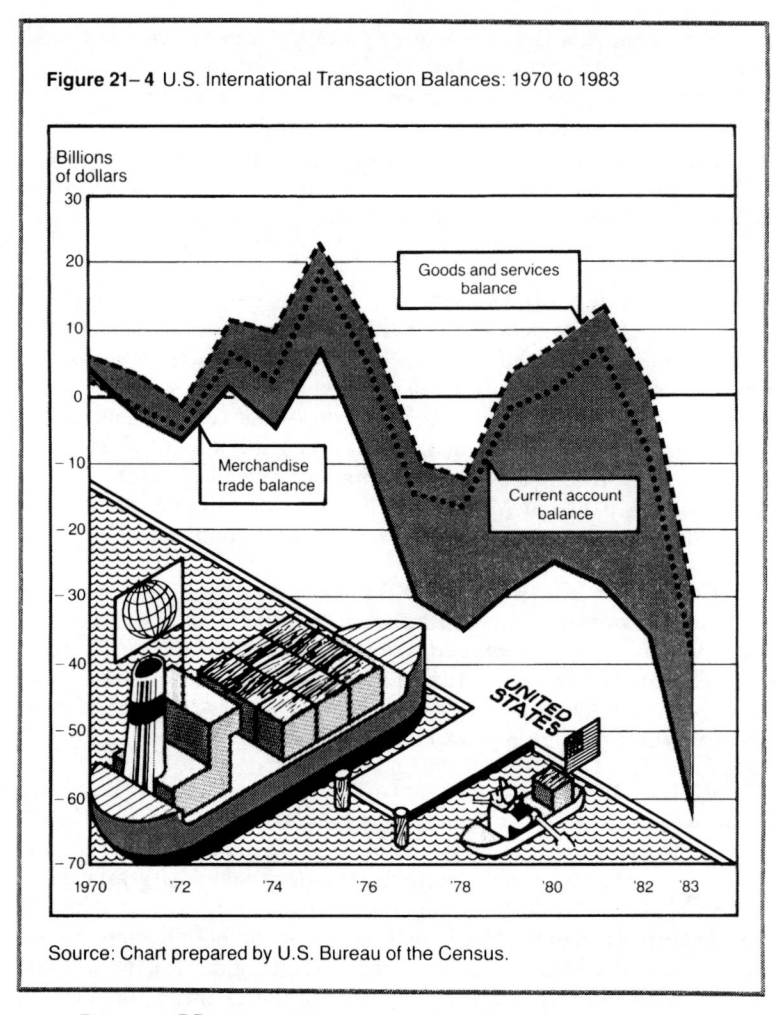

IMPORT MERCHANTS

A company that buys from foreign firms on its own account and assumes all risks is an **import merchant.** Import merchants may specialize in one or a few products or may import a wide variety of merchandise. They maintain sales forces that call on American businesses.

IMPORT COMMISSION HOUSES

An intermediary that receives goods on consignment from foreign businesses and sells to American buyers is an **import commission house.** The import commission house does not take title to goods but in other respects functions much like the import merchant.

IMPORT BROKERS

An **import broker** is *an intermediary who brings a foreign seller and an American buyer together.* The broker does not take title to merchandise and seldom handles it.

Direct Import Channels

A **direct import channel** is *a marketing channel in which an American firm buys directly from a foreign business.* Most domestic organizations that import directly have an import department and either send buyers to foreign countries or maintain resident buying offices abroad. Resident buying offices may buy for one firm or for a group of noncompeting American firms that share the costs of maintaining the overseas offices.

Importing directly has the advantage of having company representatives in a foreign market. They closely study sources in order to get the most suitable merchandise available at the best prices. Since they know foreign capabilities, they often order goods made especially for American tastes. This is a big plus for department and specialty stores featuring exclusive merchandise.

WHAT DO CURRENT ACCOUNT AND BALANCE OF TRADE MEAN?

All but the smallest countries of the world are part of the international system that calls for keeping current account and balance-of-trade accounts with every other country, just as a firm keeps accounts with those with whom it does business.

The **current account,** or **balance of payments,** is *a summary of a country's financial transactions with other nations.* It includes tourist spending, foreign assistance, loan repayments, foreign business investments, expenditures for shipping and transportation, exports and imports of goods and services, and, in some cases, the support of troops overseas. Figure 21–4 charts the international transaction balances for the United States from 1970 to 1983.

Balance of trade is a narrower concept. It is *the record of a country's merchandise transactions only.*

If exports of goods exceed imports of goods, we say there is a favorable balance of trade; if imports exceed exports, the trade balance is unfavorable. Similarly, if there is an overall financial surplus, a country has a favorable current account; if there is a financial deficit, the current account is unfavorable.

For many years the United States was relatively unconcerned about its trade balance and its current account, since they were usually favorable. However, after World War II the picture changed. Not only were there chronic trade deficits, but the current account deteriorated because of the need to maintain a large military establishment

Each country is concerned about its balance of trade. The United States, Australia, and Canada all use flour and grain exports to help balance their imports. By exporting wheat, they establish credit to buy other goods they need.

overseas, to provide foreign aid, and particularly to pay for our growing reliance on oil imported from other countries.

To improve this situation, we now attempt to stimulate exports and foreign business investments in the United States. **Free trade zones**—areas in seaports, airports, or other inland points where producers may bring in goods of foreign origin without paying customs duty—offer advantages to many firms involved in international trade. We encourage American firms to finance their foreign operations with foreign funds. If American companies raise the capital they need in overseas money markets, U.S. dollars do not have to be sent abroad for such purposes. This practice has caused negative reactions in underdeveloped countries, where there is resentment that the countries' own capital is being used by American companies to operate within their boundaries.

U.S. BUREAU OF INTERNATIONAL COMMERCE

An institution responsible for stimulating exports and foreign investments in the United States is the Department of Commerce's **Bureau of International Commerce (BIC)**. BIC has *a program for providing U.S. business people who wish to venture abroad with business and economic information gathered by American embassies and consulates throughout the world.*

BIC operates an international trade information system that provides U.S. exporters with access to export information. The service, for a nominal charge, provides:

- Leads to thousands of potential business contacts in the U.S. and abroad
- Actual offers to export or import specific products
- Statistics and information on market conditions and potential abroad, product by product and market by market
- Schedules of upcoming international and domestic events for promoting products
- Guidance on how to begin exporting and where to go for assistance
- Financial, trade, and product information on thousands of foreign companies and U.S. product information from firms that want their products exposed to foreign customers

In connection with BIC, we should mention foreign aid here. Although the very phrase implies that the U.S. is giving money away, actually, most aid is in the form of loans, most of which foreign countries spend on American goods and services. And foreign nations repaid half of the principal and interest on the $44 billion in such loans made over the past 35 years by 1978. Foreign aid contributes generously to maintaining the estimated 1.2 million American jobs that now depend directly on exports. As the *New York Times* once editorialized, "Americans pay the equivalent of a weekly pack of cigarettes for our foreign aid."

The Export-Import Bank

The purpose of the government-sponsored **Export-Import Bank** of the United States, sometimes referred to as **Eximbank,** is *to facilitate the export of U.S. products and services.* Eximbank offers both credit and insurance assistance.

Most U.S. exporters arrange their own financing, either by selling for cash or by obtaining funding through a private financial institution. Eximbank offers financing to U.S. exporters who cannot meet competition from exporters of other nations which receive government help. Eximbank also helps U.S. firms obtain insurance they are unable to obtain through private firms.

Eximbank also helps foreign firms raise money to buy U.S. exports. Such firms, when they wish to buy high-technology products, often cannot raise the funds necessary to finance their imports in their own countries.

Finally, Eximbank has a small-business advisory service. This service is available to both U.S. exporters and foreign importers of U.S. goods.

WHAT ARE MULTINATIONALS?

During the past three decades, the world has witnessed the growth of an economic phenomenon—the multinational corporation. **Multinationals,** commonly referred to as **MNCs,** are *companies that have major operating facilities in five or more countries.* Such corporations have become formidable powers.

The number of foreign multinationals has been growing faster than the number of American multinationals in recent years. Despite the slippage, the United States still has a lead over all other countries. Japan is second with 71 firms in the top 500, followed by the United Kingdom with 51, West Germany with 37, France with 27, and Canada with 19.

American multinationals overseas employ surprisingly few Americans. One interesting result of many foreign nationals managing overseas operations is that increasing numbers of them are rising into top-management positions of U.S. parent companies.

Not all economic observers applaud the burgeoning of multinationals. While many see the multinational as a positive force because it can provide the base for a true world political community, others condemn it as an exporter of jobs and as an exploiter of host countries. Numerous proposals exist for bringing multinationals under some form of international control. Undoubtedly debate will continue on this topic.

WORLD ECONOMIC ORGANIZATIONS

A characteristic of post–World War II international business has been the formation of blocs of nations whose goal is to organize their economic activities. Prior to World War II, world markets were chaotic. Commodity prices and supply availabilities fluctuated widely. Since then nations producing major commodities such as oil, coffee, cocoa, sugar, and so on have organized to control supplies and stabilize prices.

Many nations have formed organizations to improve trading with each other and with nonmember countries. Specific goals of these combinations of nations are:

- To simplify, reduce and eliminate tariffs, quotas and other trade restrictions
- To increase exports of member nations
- To exchange technology, and
- In some cases, to fix prices of exported products

Four international economic organizations are OPEC, OECD, LAFTA, and CACM.

OPEC

In 1960 Middle East oil-producing nations formed the Organization of Petroleum Exporting Countries (OPEC) to control the price and supply of petroleum. OPEC functions as a cartel. A **cartel** is *a combination of countries designed to limit competition, set prices, manage supplies, and allocate markets among its members.*

Member nations of OPEC are:

- Iran
- Iraq
- Libya
- Algeria
- Venezuela
- Kuwait
- Gabon

- United Arab Emirates
- Ecuador
- Nigeria
- Saudi Arabia
- Qator
- Indonesia

While the group appears to the outside world to be strongly united and solidly established, it is actually a grab bag of nations, some of them openly warring with each other (Iran and Iraq), who have little in common except oil. They range from politically radical (Libya) to conservative (Saudi Arabia). However, in spite of internal squabbles, they have succeeded in controlling the price of oil.

OECD

The Organization for Economic Cooperation and Development (OECD) founded in 1960 consists of:

- Belgium
- Luxembourg
- Denmark
- France
- West Germany
- Greece
- Ireland
- Italy
- Netherlands
- United Kingdom
- Austria
- Finland
- Iceland
- Norway
- Portugal
- Spain
- Sweden
- Switzerland
- Turkey

OECD is the most important organization of nations for trade purposes.

LAFTA

Latin American Free Trade Association (LAFTA) consists of eleven South American nations:

- Argentina
- Bolivia
- Brazil
- Chile
- Colombia
- Ecuador
- Mexico
- Paraguay
- Peru
- Uruguay
- Venezuela

LAFTA is still a relatively weak economic association.

CACM

Central American Common Market (CACM) consists of:

- Costa Rica
- El Salvador
- Guatemala
- Honduras
- Nicaragua

Members of the Central American Common Market have been engaged in severe political conflict, which restricts economic development and their ability to act jointly in international trade.

APPLICATION TO PERSONAL AFFAIRS

Should You Seek Employment Overseas?

Since many people would welcome the opportunity to live and work in a foreign country, at least temporarily, a list of some potential advantages and disadvantages follows. Note that opportunities, freedoms, and restrictions vary widely from country to country. If you are contemplating work overseas, you should do some reseach on the country you are considering to find out which items apply.

POTENTIAL ADVANTAGES

- Overseas travel affords exposure to people, art, and other elements of culture little known in the United States.

- Income earned over a continuous 18-month period in foreign countries may not be taxable in the United States. While Americans must pay income taxes in the host country, they are sometimes considerably lower than they would be in the United States. Further, people with certain technical skills can sometimes earn salaries equal to or greater than their salaries in this country.

- The cost of living is sometimes lower in foreign countries. (Contrary to popular belief, however, the cost of living—as Americans are usually accustomed to living—is higher in some nations.)

- Rail transportation in some areas, such as northern Europe, is inexpensive and convenient.

- Some foreign countries—notably the Scandinavian ones—have less crime, pollution, urban blight, and other social ills.

- Some foreign countries have educational opportunities unavailable in the United States.

POTENTIAL DISADVANTAGES

- Unless you are bilingual or multilingual, communication may be problematic. Further, Americans working abroad often feel relatively isolated socially.

- Crime, poverty, disease, urban blight, and so on are more prevalent in some foreign countries. Political violence is a fact of life in some Middle Eastern, African, and South American countries.

- Many of the rights and liberties guaranteed Americans are unknown in some foreign countries. For example, a country may actively promote job discrimination on the basis of sex, religion, and/or race.

- Taxes and the cost of living are higher in some foreign countries.

- Work visas are usually difficult to get, since most countries want to preserve jobs for their own nationals. Once acquired, a work visa may be difficult to renew.

- Children may acquire cultural values of the host country. Parents may not want their children to hold these values.

WHERE IS INTERNATIONAL TRADE HEADED?

The perfect economic model calls for each nation to produce those products for which it has comparative advantages and to import products which it produces less efficiently than other nations. Such a model will not become a reality soon. Political, economic, social, and religious differences, often more important to people than the highest possible standard of living, thwart international trade. But progress toward greater exchange among nations seems likely.

From the American perspective, four trends are evident.

1. *Foreign investors are making more direct investments in the United States*—Direct investment means ownership or control by a foreign business of ten percent or more of a U.S. enterprise. The United States still has more than twice as much invested in other nations as foreign countries have invested in the United States. But the gap is narrowing. Note these figures.

	1975	1982	PERCENT INCREASE
	(In Billions)		
Foreign investment in the U.S.	$ 27	$101	374
U.S. investment in foreign nations	124	221	178

The United States attracts foreign investors because of (a) low inflation compared to most of the world, (b) government stability, and (c) profit potential of American companies. Foreigners are establishing or buying interests in all kinds of enterprises ranging from real estate to manufacturing to retailing.

2. *Trading of services is increasing*—Increased use of satellites for communication and expanded air travel make trading services easier than ever before. In the future, we can expect to see expansion in both the exporting and importing of money, engineering, medical care, education, travel, consulting, and recreation.

3. *Importing of manufactured products is increasing*—Most new jobs in the United States are in services not manufacturing. Meanwhile, most jobs in foreign countries, especially in developing nations, are in manufacturing. Probably other nations with comparative production advantages—mainly lower-cost labor—will expand sales in the United States.

> *"There are limitless opportunities in every industry. Where there is an open mind, there will always be a frontier."*
>
> CHARLES F. KETTERING

4. *Exporting of high technology is increasing*—The United States has acquired leadership in technology principally because of advances in genetic engineering, space, computerization, and nuclear energy. Developments in these areas will be important exports in the decades ahead.

SUMMARY

- International trade is important to our economic well-being. The idea behind international trade is that nations should export what they produce most efficiently and import what they produce least efficiently.
- We are the world's largest exporter, and most of our trade is with North America, Europe, and Asia.
- Main obstacles to international trade are trade restrictions and differences in political ideologies, laws, currencies, language, social and business customs, and climate.
- American businesses export to other nations indirectly through export merchants, buyers for export, or export agents—and directly through foreign branches, foreign subsidiaries, licensing agreements, contract manufacturing, or joint ventures.
- American businesses import from other nations indirectly through import merchants, import commission houses, or import brokers—and directly by sending buyers to foreign countries or by maintaining resident buying offices in other nations.
- Key international economic systems and institutions are the current account, the balance of trade account, the U.S. Bureau of International Commerce, and the Export-Import Bank.
- Foreign investments in our country are growing rapidly. The growth of multinationals is another notable trend.
- Four key world organizations are OPEC, OECD, LAFTA, and CACM, which further their member nations' economic interests.
- Trends affecting the U.S. in international trade are (a) more direct investment in the U.S. by foreign nations, (b) more trade in services, (c) more importing of manufactured goods, and (d) more exporting of high technology.

KEY TERMS YOU SHOULD KNOW

balance of trade	export agent	law of comparative advantage
Bureau of International Commerce	Export-Import Bank	licensing agreement
buyer for export	export merchant	multinational
cartel	foreign branch	Organization for Economic Cooperation and Development (OECD)
contract manufacturing	foreign subsidiary	
cost-plus basis	import broker	
current account	import commission house	Organization of Petroleum Exporting Countries (OPEC)
direct export channel	import license	
direct import channel	import merchant	tariff
dumping	indirect export channel	
exchange license	indirect import channel	
exchange rate	international trade	
	joint venture	

QUESTIONS FOR REVIEW

1. Explain how international trade relates to the products we buy, American jobs, and exchange of ideas.
2. Define international trade.
3. Explain the law of comparative advantage.
4. What are our major exports? Our major imports?
5. What are the specific reasons we import? The specific reasons we export?
6. We trade little with communist nations. Why?
7. What are the obstacles to foreign trade?
8. What is a tariff? An import license?
9. What are the Sullivan Principles?
10. Define export merchants, buyers for export, and export agents.
11. Explain each of the following as they relate to exporting: foreign branch, foreign subsidiary, licensing agreement, contract manufacturing, and joint venture.
12. What are indirect import channels? Direct import channels?
13. Explain the difference between current account and balance of trade.
14. What is BIC? How does it help in international trade?
15. What does the Export–Import Bank do?
16. Define multinational.
17. What are OPEC, OECD, LAFTA, and CACM?
18. What four trends are now at work in international commerce?

QUESTIONS FOR DISCUSSION

1. What is the basic rationale for international trade? Explain how world trade promotes a higher international standard of living.
2. Singapore, which lies on the equator about 3,300 miles south of Tokyo and 4,000 miles north of Sydney, has one of the most impressive growth records of any of the developing nations, with a thriving private enterprise economy. The following statement is typical of those the Singapore Broadcasting System airs: "While due respect must be given to personal rights, we should strive to get rid of the influence of ultraindividualism and carefree liberalism currently so rampant in the West. In case of conflict, personal convenience and enjoyment must give way to group interest" (quoted in *Asiaweek*, April 17, 1981). How do you evaluate this government indoctrination effort and the ideas expressed?
3. Would tariff reduction be harmful to the American economy in the short run? In the long run? Explain why or why not.
4. What is a multinational corporation? Do you think the growth of multinationals is good or bad for the United States? For the world?
5. Adam Smith advocated free trade between nations (no tariffs or other restrictions). Why has this idea not been adopted? In your opinion, will it ever be adopted? Why or why not?
6. A survey of 3,000 students at 185 schools concluded that college students today have little knowledge or understanding of world affairs. Why should students be interested in other countries and international affairs? What, if anything, should be done to encourage their interest?

CASE STUDY

Should J. T. Borders Sell Land to Foreigners?

J. T. Borders, Inc., is a timber management and sales company, which sells management services to owners of woodlands. These services include advice on what kinds of trees to grow, how to control insect and fire damage, and when to sell the trees.

Most of the company's income comes from selling timber and timberland for its 41,000 clients. When a client wants to sell wood or woodland, J. T. Borders prepares a detailed description and sends it to as many as 500 wood-processing companies. Interested buyers then submit a sealed bid. For this service, J. T. Borders charges the seller a commission of ten percent.

Mr. Borders founded the company in 1950. The company maintains offices in 11 southern states, and profits are excellent. But Mr. Borders, now age 68 and still head of the company, is eager to increase them. The following discussion takes place between J. T. and his sons, Bill and Howard, who serve as the two vice presidents.

J. T.: I think we should aggressively promote timberland as an investment in foreign nations, especially the OPEC nations. Investors there are putting money into all kinds of projects—why not sell them land?

Bill: But J. T., from what I know, OPEC people aren't particularly turned on by land. When they do invest, they buy cropland, not woodland.

J. T.: That's because they don't understand the enormous potential in forest land. All over the world people are using timber faster than it's growing. Once they see this, we'll attract investors.

Howard: I see a public-relations problem. A lot of our clients don't like the idea of selling land to foreigners. One client told me that he'd burn a neighboring tract if someone from the Middle East bought it.

J. T.: That wouldn't happen. People get emotional over differences in political philosophies, but when economics comes up, they get very rational. You see, we serve clients by getting them the highest possible price for their wood or land. The net effect of selling to foreign investors will be increased demand and higher prices for our sellers. That's good business.

B: But J. T., we have no experience in dealing with foreigners. We could really foul up.

J. T.: I know. We've got to have a good plan. Here's what I want you to do. Think for the next week of how to approach the foreign market, and then we'll discuss it.

One week later.

J. T.: Well, what have you come up with?

B: We're going to have a lot of problems with differences in language, culture, and business tactics. I recommend we first decide in which countries we want to seek investors. Then I'll find two or three university students from each country. They can help translate our ads, tell us dos and don'ts—that sort of thing.

H: My idea is to contact the Department of Commerce. They've got guidelines on doing business in just about all countries. Next, I want to contact our governor's office—he just got back from a trade mission in the Middle East. Another step I recommend is contacting the appropriate officers in the American Bank. They could help us handle fund transfers.

J. T.: You're off to a good start. How about discussing the specifics of your ideas at our next weekly meeting?

Questions

1. Is the logic behind J. T.'s idea sound? Why or why not?
2. Is adverse public relations more of a threat than J. T. perceives? Why or why not?
3. Is the idea of using foreign students as advisers sound? Why or why not?

EVOLUTION OF A BUSINESS

The International Side of the Travel Business

Sara and Ray ended their first year as owners of what turned out to be a successful partnership, the Excel Travel Agency. During the last three months of the year they turned in a small profit, which indicated that they were becoming solidly established. In conclusion, we again find them talking about their favorite subject—plans for the future of their company.

Sara: The overseas side of our operation holds a lot of promise. What do you think we could do to develop it more?

Ray: Well, for one thing, I think we've been handicapped in talking to our customers this past year, since we haven't visited many of the countries we were advising about. Now that we're established, one of us can afford to be away while the other runs the office.

Sara: I agree. With TAs having the privilege of flying for one-quarter of what other people pay, and with hotels and restaurants picking up the tabs at the other end, I don't see any reason why we shouldn't be able to become experts on the overseas locales we sell.

Ray: Do you think we should try eventually to recommend only places and accommodations we know about personally?

Sara: I think that's too ambitious and unrealistic a goal. I'd rather find a good local agent in each country and work through that person. After all, it takes someone on the spot to keep up with the changes. Otherwise we might end up recommending a restaurant that's been closed for three months or has changed hands and is no longer any good.

Questions

1. What do you think about Sara's idea of establishing a working relationship with someone on the spot rather than trying to check things out personally?
2. Would it be in the best interests of the company for Sara and Ray to spend so much time traveling?
3. What should they look for when overseas?
4. How could U.S. travel agents contribute to the building of better international understanding?

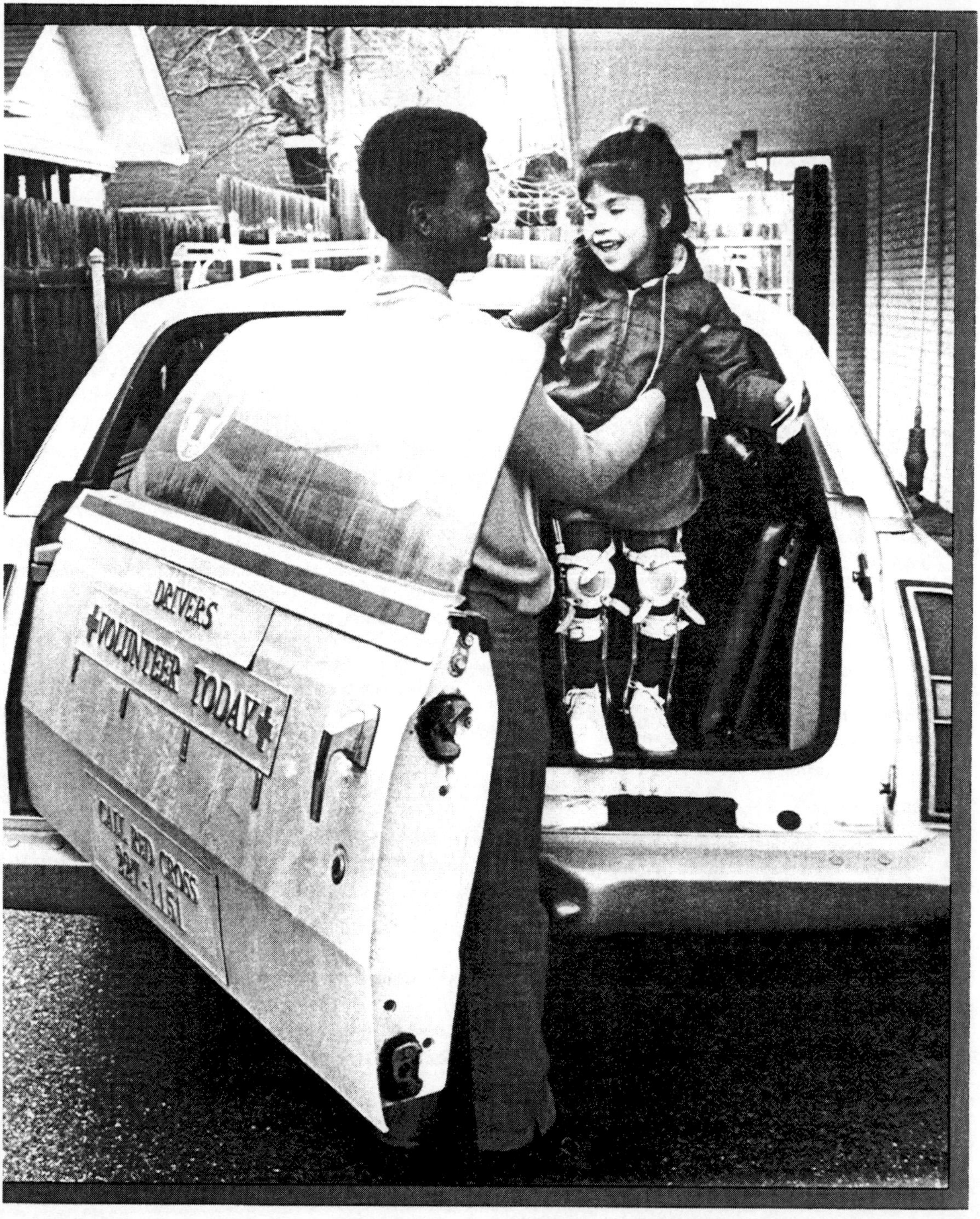
DRIVERS
VOLUNTEER TODAY
CALL RED CROSS

NONPROFIT ORGANIZATIONS
Managing with a Different Goal

READ THIS CHAPTER SO YOU CAN:

Define nonprofit organizations and explain how nonprofits differ from profit-seeking enterprises.

Explain how governments differ from other nonprofit organizations.

Describe the type of products nonprofits provide, how nonprofits get financing, employ marketing tactics, and why public relations and communications are especially important for them.

Understand how nonprofits are managed.

Explain how nonprofits compete with other nonprofits and with profit-seeking enterprises.

Discuss how nonprofits market social causes, generate profits for profit-seeking businesses, promote philanthropy, and function as cooperatives.

So far, we have looked at financing, marketing, management, and other activities as they relate to profit-seeking enterprises. We have stressed the role of private businesses with a strong profit goal. Now we'll look at the many enterprises in our society which have other goals: the nonprofit organizations or simply "nonprofits."

We all deal with nonprofit organizations daily. Most schools, colleges, and universities are nonprofit. So are most hospitals, police and fire departments, and welfare agencies. Local, state, and federal governments are nonprofit, as are religious groups, charitable institutions, trade associations, chambers of commerce, labor unions, museums, foundations, and political parties.

What Are Nonprofit Organizations?

The primary goal of **nonprofit organizations** is *providing public or social services—not earning profits for investors.* These organizations have two common characteristics:

1. They do not seek profits in the accounting sense.
2. They have tax-exempt status: They do not pay property and income taxes.

See Table 22-1 for a listing of nonprofit organizations.

TABLE 22-1   Some Nonprofit Organizations

Federal, state, and local governments
Political parties
Labor unions
Trade associations
Civic organizations (Lions, Rotary)
Charitable organizations (Red Cross, American Cancer Society)
Social movements (Planned Parenthood)
Social causes (antismoking, antinuclear energy)
Foundations
Religious organizations
Private and taxpayer supported colleges
College alumni associations
Most hospitals

SOURCE: Adapted from David J. Schwartz, *Marketing Today,* 3rd ed. (New York: Harcourt Brace Jovanovich, 1981), 257.

In this chapter, initially we focus on governments as nonprofit organizations. Then we examine key characteristics of charitable, civic, and other nonprofits.

GOVERNMENTS ARE THE MOST IMPORTANT NONPROFITS

About 16 percent of all employed Americans work for the federal, state, and local governments. Governments at all levels employ more people than the 300 largest businesses. Figure 22-1 shows that over a 14-year period, 1970-1984, the number of federal employees remained almost the same, but the percentage of all government employees working in the federal sector dropped significantly from 22.1 to 17.9 percent. Meanwhile, the states increased employment by over one million and local governments by almost two million.

The bulk of federal employees in 1984 were employed in (a) national defense—1,042 million, or 36 percent; (b) the postal service—669,000, or 23 percent; (c) natural resources—244,000, or 8.5

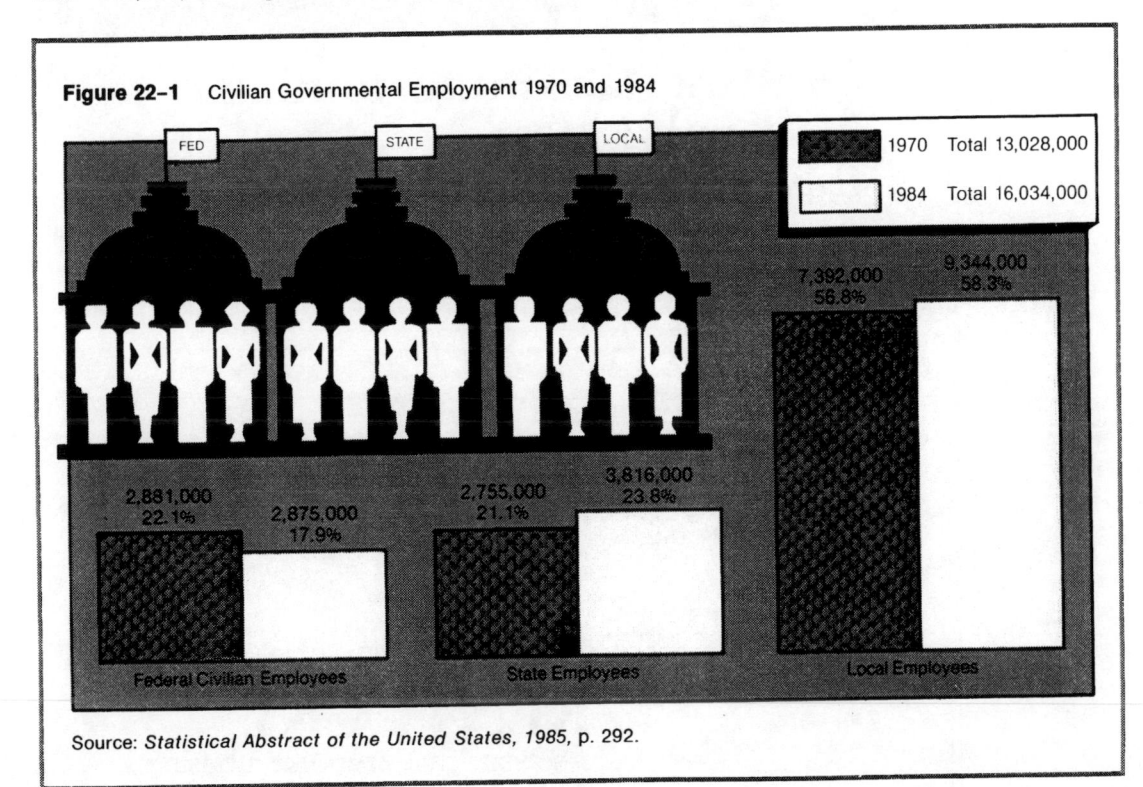

Figure 22-1 Civilian Governmental Employment 1970 and 1984

1970 Total 13,028,000
1984 Total 16,034,000

Federal Civilian Employees: 2,881,000 (22.1%) / 2,875,000 (17.9%)
State Employees: 2,755,000 (21.1%) / 3,816,000 (23.8%)
Local Employees: 7,392,000 (56.8%) / 9,344,000 (58.3%)

Source: *Statistical Abstract of the United States, 1985*, p. 292.

658 CHAPTER 22/NONPROFIT ORGANIZATIONS

Some Nonprofit Organizations Pride Themselves on Being Businesslike

Of all the states in the running for your business, this one is run like a business.

Any state reflects the goals, priorities and skills of its chief executive. In John Y. Brown, Jr., Kentucky has a Governor who believes the best place to locate a business is in a state that's run in a businesslike fashion.

To help build the positive environment your business needs to succeed, Brown has selected businessmen to head the key government departments of development, commerce, energy and transportation. He's worked with the Kentucky General Assembly to pass important pro-business legislation such as the new "Workers' Compensation Bill." And he's cut through red tape to open communications and opportunities for business.

After all, with his successful business background, Brown understands what it takes to build a business. And as Governor, he and his staff are making sure Kentucky has the right climate for you to build a successful business.

To find out more about what the state that's run like a business could mean to you, write: Jack H. Segell, Commissioner, The Department of Commerce, Commonwealth of Kentucky, Frankfort, Kentucky 40601. Or better yet, call him businessman-to-businessman at 502/564-4270.

KENTUCKY
The state that's run like a business.

percent; and (d) health and hospitals—269,000, or 9.3 percent. Military personnel are not included in these statistics.

Most state employees—1,666,000, or 43.6 percent—work in education. Employment in health care accounts for 670,000 employees or 17.5 percent, and there were 243,000 highway employees—6.3 percent of the total.

The three main types of employment in local government were education—5,125,000, or 55 percent; health and hospitals—730,000, or 7.8 percent; and police and fire protection—905,000, or 9.6 percent.

HOW GOVERNMENTS DIFFER FROM OTHER NONPROFITS

Governments differ from other nonprofit organizations in four ways: (a) they have power to tax, (b) they have special enforcement procedures, (c) civil service rules govern employment practices, and (d) citizens elect top managers.

Power to Tax

Taxes are compulsory. Local, state, and federal government have the power to determine how much they will be. Other nonprofits must rely on voluntary contributions for operational revenue.

Power to Enforce Decisions

Governments have the power to force or demand payment of taxes and obedience to laws. While appeal processes may be lengthy, ultimate refusal to pay taxes can result in confiscation of property and/or prison sentences.

Civil Service Practices Dominate Employment

Under civil service, merit and examination determine appointments, promotions, and status. This prevents a newly elected political official from firing employees and replacing them with his or her supporters. In other nonprofit organizations, employment practices are more subjective.

All organizations must obey civil rights legislation, but other nonprofits do not have to follow the stringent provisions of civil service.

Top Management in Governments Is Political

While operational employees are selected under civil service, top managers in governments are either elected or appointed by elected officials. A change in political leadership does not usually affect rank and file government employees, but the *direction* of the governmental unit often does. In other nonprofit organizations, a board of directors—not the voting population—selects top management.

HOW NONPROFITS OPERATE

In this section, we look at nongovernment nonprofits: What products do they offer, how do they finance their activities, what marketing tactics do they employ, and how do they approach the management of their organizations?

Nonprofits Provide Services or Intangible Products

Nonprofits concentrate on providing services. Religious groups, for example, provide morality, charity, and fellowship. An educational institution produces education, research, and community service. A foundation may sponsor cultural events. And a civic organization may support aid to crippled children. The variety of social services the nonprofit sector provides is as diverse as human needs.

Nonprofit organizations like the American Cancer Society use volunteers extensively, here in a patient transportation program. Such use of nonsalaried people saves nonprofits much money, which they can budget for other services.

Financing Is Through Voluntary Contributions

Businesses finance operations through the investments of owners, including stockholders, and by borrowing. Governments raise funds through taxation and borrowing. Other nonprofits obtain capital from donations and contributions. The United Way, for example, solicits donations from a broad segment of the population as does the Salvation Army, the Cancer Society, and the Red Cross.

Some nonprofits are membership organizations, such as the Kiwanis, Lions, and Rotarians. Membership organizations charge dues. But the dues are voluntary because no one is forced to be a member. Some of the dues go for education, health care, and other worthy projects to help people with specific problems. Labor unions and trade associations also charge dues as a condition of membership.

Usually an individual or small group of people funds foundations. Typically, the person or persons establishing a foundation donate a substantial sum to the foundation and specify how they want the money spent. The foundation invests the donated money in real estate and/or securities, and the foundation uses the income to finance the designated project, such as to conduct a specific kind of research or to help orphans receive an education. Figure 22-2 shows the assets and grant payments of the 25 largest foundations.

Colleges and universities fund many scholarships in a way similar to foundations. Contributions to nonprofit organizations are tax deductible and provide a special incentive to individuals and businesses to contribute.

The IRS sets guidelines which nonprofit organizations must meet to qualify as tax-exempt. These guidelines affect both the people donating funds or other property and the income the organization earns.

HOW NONPROFITS MARKET THEIR SERVICES

Marketing is important to nonprofits because (a) they obtain funds through voluntary contributions, and (b) volunteers contribute much of the labor. Gaining widespread public acceptance through marketing makes it easier for a nonprofit to both raise funds and obtain willing supporters who donate time and talent.

EFFECTIVE PUBLIC RELATIONS IS A MUST FOR NONPROFITS

In Chapter 12, we discussed why good relations with the public are important to business. But projecting a positive, worthwhile image to the public is even more important for nonprofits for three reasons.

Figure 22-2 Assets and Grant Payments of 25 Largest Foundations (Millions of Dollars)

Foundation	Assets	Grant payments
Ford Foundation		
Robert Wood Johnson Foundation	$2,782,942	$103,370
Andrew W. Mellon Foundation		
John D. and Catherine T. MacArthur Foundation		
Pew Memorial Trust		
Lilly Endowment, Inc.		
Rockefeller Foundation		
W.K. Kellogg Foundation		
Kresge Foundation		
Charles Stewart Mott Foundation		
Duke Endowment		
San Francisco Foundation		
Carnegie Corporation of New York		
Richard King Mellon Foundation		
Houston Endowment Inc.		
Alfred P. Sloan Foundation		
New York Community Trust		
J.E. and L.E. Mabee Foundation, Inc.		
Bush Foundation		
Edna McConnell Clark Foundation		
Moody Foundation		
James Irvine Foundation		
Cleveland Foundation		
Gannett Foundation, Inc.		
Samuel Roberts Noble Foundation, Inc.		

Purpose of Grants, 1980
Total $1,191 Million

- 27% Welfare
- 13% Culture
- 2% Religion
- 10% Sciences
- 22% Health
- 26% Education

Source: *The Foundation Directory*, 8th ed. (New York: The Foundation Center, 1981), pp. xi, xix. The year in the chart on the right is the latest fiscal year reported by the foundation, generally 1979 or 1980.

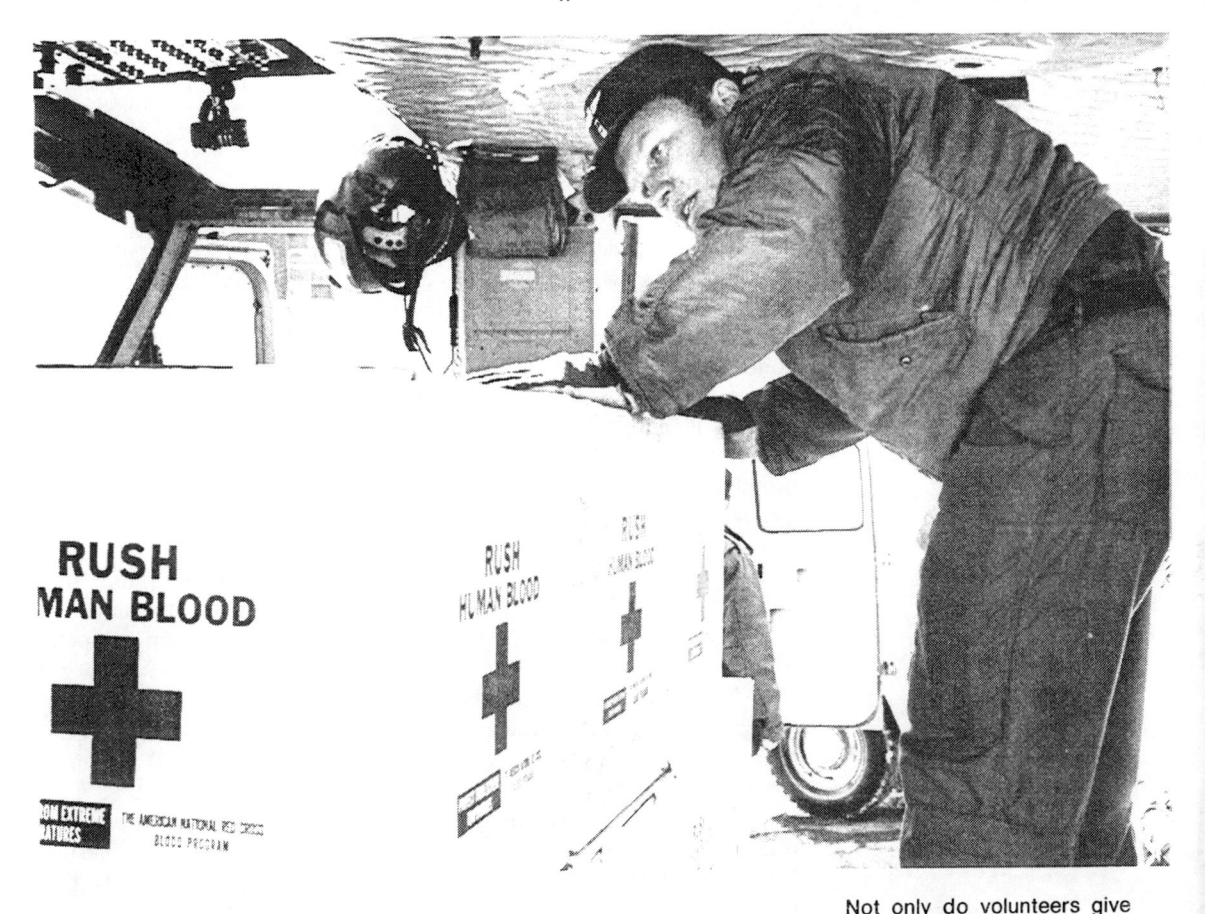

Not only do volunteers give their money and time, they literally give their life blood.

First, *publicity is the main promotional tool of nonprofits.* Most nonprofits have small budgets for advertising, personal selling, and sales promotion. Therefore, they rely on favorable news items in the media to generate public interest and support.

Second, *nonprofits depend on voluntary contributions for financial support.* All of us must buy necessities such as food, shelter, clothing, medical care, and transportation. But we do not have to support nonprofit causes, such as research, charity, and scholarships. If the public image of a nonprofit enterprise is positive—if people approve of its goals, services, and methods, it will receive financial support more easily than if the public disapproves of what it stands for.

Third, *nonprofits' status as tax-exempt enterprises depends on public acceptance.* Directly and indirectly the public as voters decides what kind of laws and regulations the government imposes on the people. Bad public relations may result in a nonprofit organization losing its tax-exempt status.

Nonprofits Depend on Publicity and Free Promotion

Profit-seeking organizations pay for their advertising and sales promotion. Businesses often receive much unpaid publicity, but it is largely out of their control and may be negative or positive.

Nonprofits, on the other hand, receive free radio and television commercials (public service announcements) and print advertisements. (See the example of a public service advertisement on page 665.) The advertising counsel, also a nonprofit organization, and actors donate their time and talents to produce public service announcements and free advertisements. The radio, television, newspapers, and magazine media typically do not charge for time and space used to promote the message of the nonprofits.

The media, however, are selective in deciding which public service announcements and free advertisements they broadcast or print. Obviously, they can only present a few messages from the many nonprofit organizations which offer them information.

Table 22-2 lists examples of marketing activities nonprofit organizations perform. Nonprofits need to use market research techniques to determine the target markets for their services. To promote these services, organizations advertise—in print, on radio or TV, or through personal solicitation. And finally, they must ensure that they can readily deliver their services to their target markets. Delivering the service involves ensuring that it will be readily available to the intended markets.

Communication with the Public Is Important

Effective nonprofit organizations place strong emphasis on communicating with their publics through a three-step process:

Step One: *Identify each public that has a relationship to the nonprofit organization.* The American Heart Association's publics include physicians, victims, and hospitals. And the Girl Scouts' publics may consist of parents, teachers, the clergy, and others. The identified publics will differ depending on the goals of the nonprofit, but they always include supporters who contribute money, time, and talent and beneficiaries of the nonprofit activities.

Step Two: *Determine the special interests and needs of each public as they relate to the nonprofit.* The alumni public of a college may be interested in providing scholarships, assisting new academic programs, and supporting the athletic program. Meanwhile, the parents of students may focus attention on the quality of the faculty,

Have you got arthritis yet?

Your chances of getting arthritis, the nation's number one crippling disease, are one in seven. Arthritis strikes the young as well as the old; a new case occurs every 33 seconds. And right now, seven million Americans are disabled by it. Here are just a few of the effects of the many forms of arthritis.

(a) back pain, stiffness

(b) inflammation of the shoulders

(c) inflammation of the hips

(d) swollen wrists or thumbs

(e) heart damage

(f) acute pain in toes

(g) inflammation of the elbows

(h) severe pain in ankles

(i) liver damage

(j) stiff, inflamed knees

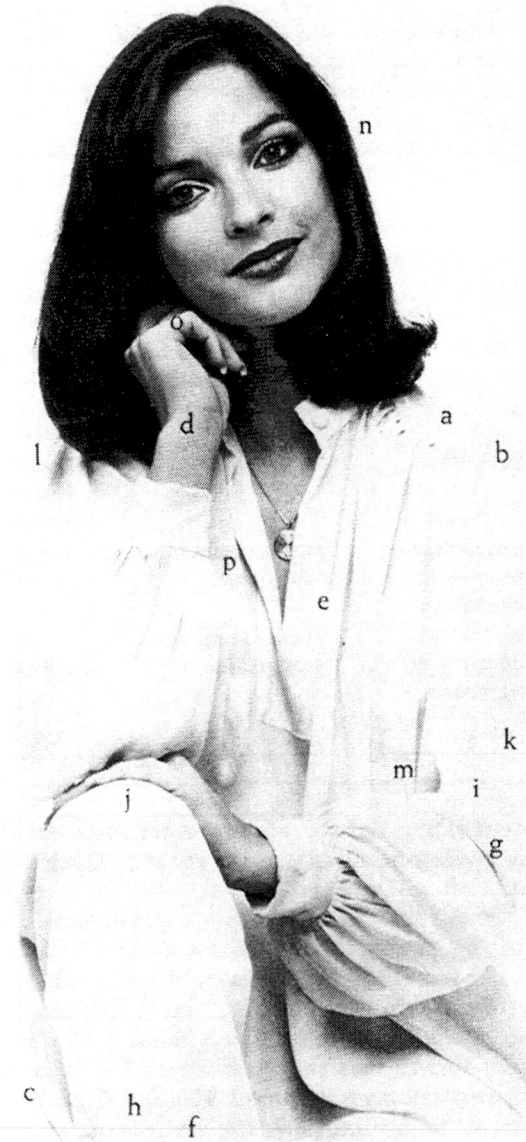

(k) kidney disease

(l) damaged connective tissue

(m) spleen damage

(n) cataracts

(o) enlarged joints in fingers

(p) lung damage

If you have any symptoms of arthritis or any suspicions that you might have the disease, don't ignore them for a moment. Arthritis can be controlled. In some cases, with early detection, disability can be prevented. But proper medical diagnosis and care are absolutely essential. Find out what you need to know about arthritis. Now. Whether you've got it or not. Ask your local Arthritis Foundation chapter for your copy of "Arthritis—The Basic Facts."

ARTHRITIS FOUNDATION

A public service of this magazine.

A Public Service Advertisement

TABLE 22-2 Marketing Activities by Nonprofit Organizations

ORGANIZATION	EXAMPLES OF "PRODUCTS"	THE MARKET	EXAMPLES OF MARKETING ACTIVITIES
A political party	Promises of better government, reform, new laws	People with no political affiliation; members of the other party; uncommitted voters	Advertising; speeches; rallies; personal visits
The military services	A satisfying career for enlistees; more appropriations from government	The public; lawmakers	Advertising; personal solicitation of high school and college graduates.
College alumni association	Financial support of the school; fellowship; good times	Alumni and professional and business leaders	Advertising; homecoming parties; special events
A church or other religious organization	Morality; charity; fellowship	The public, particularly those people unaffiliated with a religious institution	Some advertising; personal solicitation for membership; revival meetings
Symphony orchestra	Aesthetic enjoyment	General public	Fund-raising campaigns; printed programs; advertising
Charitable organizations	More and better services to people who cannot afford them	Citizens; businesses; foundations	Personal solicitation; advertising
Continuing education division of a college	Special seminars in latest techniques for performing various activities	Interested segments of the population	Advertising; personal solicitation

student safety, and tuition, and other costs. Another college public, state legislators, wants to know about total costs per student, overall reputation, and competition with other state supported institutions.

Step Three: *Engage in two-way communication with each public to:* (a) learn of special services the public wants the nonprofit to provide, and (b) report to the public what the nonprofit is doing to meet the needs of the public. The Red Cross, for example, learns about needs for blood, disaster relief, and other assistance from community leaders, media representatives, health authorities, on-location staff, and volunteer personnel. The Red Cross reports to the publics it serves through public service announcements, activity summaries, and public meetings.

PEOPLE WHO MAKE THINGS HAPPEN

A PROFILE OF **NATHANIEL R. WOODS**

Mr. Nathaniel Woods was born in 1944 but did not begin college until he was 29. Now he holds an Associates degree in Business Management, a Bachelor of Science degree in Business Administration, and a Master of Education degree in Higher Education. He plans to seek a Ph.D. in education so that he can be of greater value to students.

Nathaniel Woods is a U.S. Marine Corps. veteran. He worked in private industry for eleven years for White Westinghouse Corp. Nathaniel is the only member of a family of nine who has pursued a college degree. He is proud to be an instructor in the college he attended. He also is coordinator of business management at Columbus Technical Institute.

He advises students, "Education never ceases; it just goes deeper and keeps getting broader. Discipline and motivation are the keys to success. Education is a resource that we must pursue."

Mr. Woods enjoys his work tremendously. He has not missed a day of work since appointed a college instructor in 1979. If private enterprise system is to flourish, he feels it must concentrate and rely upon those who are presently being educated and those who will be educated. Without educators helping to motivate and advise students in this highly technical, competitive market, private enterprise will suffer.

How Nonprofits Are Managed

A BOARD OF DIRECTORS DECIDES POLICIES

In nonprofits a membership-elected or appointed Board of Directors typically decides goals and strategies for reaching the goals. The Board of Directors is usually concerned only with matters of broad direction.

IMPLEMENTATION OF GOALS AND STRATEGIES IS THE RESPONSIBILITY OF A PROFESSIONAL STAFF

Usually a paid professional staff handles day-to-day management of nonprofits. Members of the professional staff include an executive director or president and department heads in charge of membership, fund raising, publications, and other key activity areas. The professional staff directs the activities of local chapters, units, divisions, or clubs.

VOLUNTEERS DO MOST OF THE WORK

Unpaid volunteers, responsible to the professional staff, do most of the work of nonprofits. Credit unions, labor organizations, civic clubs, cultural societies, and most other nonprofits depend on people who volunteer their talents and time to accomplish the goals of the organization.

HOW NONPROFITS MEASURE RESULTS

In business, profits earned is a convenient test to measure performance. If profits are greater than last year or exceed those earned by competitors, we conclude the business is performing well. In nonprofits, the performance test is not profits in the accounting sense. Nonprofits measure results in services provided, people helped, or some other form of intangible "gains."

Table 22–3 shows gains and losses for different kinds of nonprofit seeking organizations. Note that gains and losses in some cases are quantifiable, or can be measured in numbers.

TABLE 22–3 Examples of Gains and Losses in Noncommercial Enterprises

ENTERPRISE	EXAMPLES OF GAINS	EXAMPLES OF LOSSES
University	● Establishment of new degree programs ● Hiring of expert scholars ● Well-received public-service programs	● Resignation of key faculty members ● Decrease in enrollment ● Decline in quality of students
Political party	● Increase in contributions and membership ● Winning of elections ● Growth of public respect	● Decrease in contributions and membership ● Loss of elections ● Scandals
Research foundation	● Funding of worthwhile projects ● Employment of respected scientist	● Decline in funding ● Resignation of key employees
Religious organization	● Increase in contributions and membership ● Improvement in attendance	● Decrease in membership ● Decline in contributions
Professional business fraternity	● Well-received community projects ● Awards for creative effort ● Growth in membership	● Decline in membership ● Poor attendance at meetings ● General disinterest by members

SOURCE: *Introduction to Management*, David Schwartz, Harcourt Brace Jovanovich, 1983, 85.

Nonprofits Compete with Other Nonprofits

We have made many references in this text showing how businesses compete for consumers' dollars, a larger market share for their products, the best qualified personnel, and capital. Competition is a foundation of the private enterprise system.

Competition carries over into the nonprofit sector as well. Nonprofits such as the Red Cross and the United Way compete for contributions; civic clubs such as Lions and Kiwanians compete for members; and colleges compete for academically talented students and football players. Regardless of what a nonprofit offers society, it encounters other nonprofits who offer similar services to the same target market.

Nonprofits May Compete with Profit-seeking Organizations, Too

Besides competing with each other, nonprofits sometimes compete with profit-making businesses as well. The YMCA, for example, offers a variety of body-building programs, such as weight-lifting, running, and swimming—but so do many fitness centers operated as profit-seeking enterprises. Research foundations compete with private companies for research grants from the federal government.

The most dramatic evidence of nonprofits competing with profit-seeking enterprises occurs in health care. Historically, the public owned virtually all hospitals and supported them with tax dollars, or religious groups and foundations owned them and supported them with contributions. In the past two decades, however, profit-seeking businesses have entered the health care industry and now compete vigorously with nonprofit hospitals for patients, physicians, other personnel, and money.

MANAGEMENT OF NONPROFIT ORGANIZATIONS: A VIABLE CAREER ALTERNATIVE

The nonprofit sector is fast becoming a major factor in our economy. As this happens, certain consequences become apparent.

As the nonprofit sector assumes greater significance in our economic life, it must operate productively and responsibly. Management has always played a significant role in the success of profit-oriented concerns. There is a growing awareness on the part of nonprofit organizations that if they are to be successful, they must recognize the importance of management in their operations. Nonprofit organizations are becoming more management-conscious. They are turning increasingly to business to learn the techniques of man-

> *"You cannot push anyone up the ladder unless he is willing to climb himself."*
>
> ANDREW CARNEGIE

agement—management training, systems analysis, and management by objectives, for example.

Thus, it is reassuring to students to know that most of what they are learning in their business courses about management concepts and methods can be applied to the nonprofit sector. To some students, a further attraction of working in the nonprofit sector is the satisfaction of being involved in areas other than business-for-profit. Some people find greater fulfillment of their ambitions and ideas in humanistic, cultural, or environmental activities.

Management Training for Nonprofit Organizations

For centuries the military has placed great emphasis on officer training. Today, career officers can expect to spend approximately 25 percent or more of their service time in school, where they study such management-oriented subjects as leadership, budgeting, efficiency, and personnel selection.

Until recently, most nonprofit organizations, with the exception of the military, paid little attention to mastering business administration. In the 1960s, Blue Cross/Blue Shield, faced with rising medical costs, asked universities with medical schools to develop management-oriented hospital administration programs. Today, many nonmedical colleges also offer hospital administration education.

Professional management education is now offered widely in governmental management and administration programs. Formal management training is also given to executives of charitable organizations, trade associations, and other nonprofit organizations.

ACTIVITY AREAS FOR NONPROFIT ORGANIZATIONS

A wide spectrum of nonprofit organizations are using management and marketing techniques successfully. Following is a discussion of four important areas of the nonprofit sector, which is feeling their impact: marketing of social causes, nonprofit organizations that generate profit for others, administration of philanthropy, and nonprofit cooperatives.

Marketing of Social Causes

A specific kind of marketing in nonprofit organizations is called **social marketing,** or **nonbusiness marketing.** This is *the application of marketing concepts and techniques to promote worthwhile social goals.* Public service organizations and government agencies use it to further causes such as forest fire prevention, safe driving,

AMERICA'S REEMERGING CREATIVITY

Growth in Continuing Education for Business

In the past decade, colleges and universities—nonproft organizations—have greatly expanded their efforts to help individuals in the private sector acquire nondegree related education. Today hundreds of educational institutions provide a wide variety of specialized courses, in subjects ranging from how to appraise real estate to using the computer in small business to essentials of marketing.

Several factors have contributed to the growth in continuing education for business practitioners. First is the expansion of knowledge in the many fields that make up business management. Just as the knowledge of the physician who stopped learning upon completion of formal medical training a few years ago falls behind that of his colleagues, the business practitioner who doesn't keep up with new concepts and techniques falls behind in the practice of business administration.

Furthermore, as managers are promoted, they often find themselves directing activities in which their knowledge is limited. Persons who specialized in marketing, for example, may move up to senior positions in which they need knowledge of finance or information systems. They may take short courses in these areas to help fill their informational deficiency.

Second, enrollments of degree-seeking students in many colleges and universities have stabilized, making more resources available to provide instruction to business practitioners.

Besides being exposed to expert instruction, people attending continuing education programs share experiences with individuals from other organizations. This, too, facilitates learning.

Typically, courses taken in a continuing education program do not count toward a degree. However, most colleges and universities award a certificate upon completion of a course and keep a record of the individual's participation in the program on file. Usually, continuing education programs do not require students to take examinations to complete continuing education programs satisfactorily.

Usually, continuing education courses are short—only a few days in length. Highly advanced programs for senior executives, however, may extend over several weeks.

Normally the sponsoring college or university provides the instructional staff. However, if the program deals with an exceptionally specialized area, the sponsoring institution may retain professors from other colleges and universities.

Today's business school graduates will likely attend numerous college- and university-sponsored specialized clinics, seminars, and programs in their careers. Education in business is now recognized as a never-ending process. And organizations in the nonprofit sector—colleges and universities—are doing much to facilitate this ongoing process.

Questions for Discussion

1. Will colleges and universities likely continue to expand their offerings of continuing education in business in the future? Why or why not?

2. If you had the opportunity, what specialized short business courses would you like to take? Explain your choices.

wildlife protection, and control of social diseases. It gained popularity when advocates of social causes realized that promotion and other business techniques were effective ways to change public attitudes and behavior.

How does marketing help in the effort to produce social change? The following passage on methods of inducing people to reduce their cigarette consumption illustrates how social marketing works:

The *legal* approach is to pass laws that make cigarette smoking either illegal ... or difficult (e.g., prohibiting smoking in public places). The *technological* approach is to develop an innovation that will help people reduce their smoking or the harm thereof (e.g., an antismoking pill, a harmless cigarette). The *economic* approach is to raise the price or cost of smoking (e.g., higher cigarette taxes, higher insurance rates for smokers). Finally, the *informational* approach is to direct persuasive information at smokers about the risks of smoking and the advantages of not smoking (e.g., "Warning: The Surgeon General Has Determined That Cigarette Smoking Is Dangerous to Your Health").[1]

Social marketing stresses the informational approach, using mass communication and publicity techniques to reach the intended audience. Its use is "clearly on the up-swing."[2]

Recognizing the importance of social causes, the government, through the operation of the IRS, encourages profit-seeking businesses to participate in public service activities. The IRS regulation reads: "A deduction will ordinarily be allowed for the cost of advertising which keeps the taxpayer's name before the public in connection with encouraging contributions to such organizations as the Red Cross, the purchase of U.S. Savings Bonds, or participating in similar causes."

Some Nonprofit Organizations Generate Profit for Business

The main function of many nonprofit organizations is to create a healthy economic environment for business. These organizations' energies are directed to activities that provide employment and help stimulate the economy. Tourism, for example, creates jobs not only in hotels and restaurants but also in agriculture, food processing, handicrafts, transportation, and many service industries. Table 22–4 shows examples of nonprofit organizations that support economic growth.

Because they work closely with business and usually have staff members trained and experienced in business, many of these organizations operate in a very businesslike manner (see the advertisement on page 658).

---

[1] Karen F. A. Fox and Philip Kotler, "The Marketing of Social Causes: The First Ten Years," *Journal of Marketing,* Fall 1980, 24–33.

[2] Ibid.

TABLE 22-4   Examples of Nonprofit Organizations That Generate Profit for Others

ORGANIZATION	ACTIVITY	PURPOSE
New York State Department of Commerce	Tourism promotion	To attract tourists to New York State
Connecticut Development Commission	Industry promotion	To attract industry to Connecticut
State of Illinois Center, Chicago	Convention promotion	To attract groups planning conventions, trade shows, and similar large gatherings
Pan-American Coffee Bureau	Advertising, lobbying, store promotions, and similar activities	To promote the coffee industry of countries that belong to the sponsoring association
A utilities lobby	Lobbying efforts at federal, state, and local government headquarters	To influence the various legislative bodies

Nonprofit Cooperatives

A cooperative functions in the fields of finance or marketing or in the production of goods or services. Cooperatives may be profit-facilitating or nonprofit organizations. Examples of profit-facilitating cooperatives include such farmers cooperatives as Sunkist, Diamond Walnut, Ocean Spray, and Land O' Lakes. Examples of nonprofit cooperatives include credit unions, apartment cooperatives, and consumer co-ops.

A **consumer co-op** is *a retail establishment established to save consumers money on the goods or services the co-op sells.* College bookstore co-ops are probably the most familiar to students. The Harvard Co-op is the nation's oldest university co-op. It was established in 1882 by students angry at the high prices of books and firewood. Nearly 100 years later, during the fiscal year that ended June 30, 1980, sales exceeded $37 million. Its 90,000 members shared patronage refunds totaling $2.1 million—9.5 percent of the co-op's sales. Although anyone can shop in the store, under tax laws for cooperative institutions, the co-op can rebate profits only to Harvard students who pay the $1 fee to join it. Rebated profits are tax exempt. Profits from nonmember sales go back into the business.

Profit-facilitating cooperatives have long employed management concepts and techniques to increase their profitability. And just as in other areas of the nonprofit sector, nonprofit cooperatives are beginning to apply these tools to improve the success of their own operations.

AMERICAN CANCER SOCIETY: AN EXAMPLE OF A LEADING NONPROFIT ORGANIZATION AT WORK

Founded in 1913, the American Cancer Society has become one of the leading organizations in the nonprofit sector. In 1980, 2.5 million people volunteered their time to help raise $162 million to carry on the society's service program.

How the Society Is Managed

The society has two primary goals:

1. To represent multiple interests at the community, state, and national levels
2. To coordinate useful activities in cancer control in the United States and cooperate with groups involved in similar activities throughout the world.

The 58 chartered, incorporated divisions of the society are represented in a national House of Delegates, which meets annually in the fall. Membership is composed of 116 division delegates (one professional and one lay delegate from each division), as well as 36 proportional delegates (selected on the basis of population) and 42 delegates at large, for a total of 194 voting members.

Among the duties and responsibilities of the House of Delegates are to act on amendments to the constitution and bylaws of the society; to review and determine basic fund-raising policies; and to recommend major policy changes. Perhaps its most important function, however, is to elect the members of the board of directors, half of whose two-year terms expire each year.

A national board of 116 volunteer directors, representing each of the 58 incorporated divisions formulates policies. The national board meets three times a year; between meetings, an executive committee of 25 board members exercises leadership. Volunteer experts in a variety of fields advise the board, and the board reaches decisions based on their recommendations. Among the committees serving the board are those on public information, public education, professional education, medical and scientific affairs, service and rehabilitation, field services, the April Crusade, and research.

Naturally, as part of the management process, the society must prepare a budget. Table 22–5 shows the budget for 1984.

Who Does the Work?

The real strength of the society lies in its approximately 2.5 million volunteers. These volunteers—neighborhood workers, members of clubs and civic organizations, business people, homemakers, profes-

TABLE 22-5 How the American Cancer Society Spent Its Budget in 1984

CATEGORY	AMOUNT	PERCENT OF TOTAL
Research	$ 54,720,000	23
Public education	35,943,000	15
Professional education	21,026,000	9
Patient services	27,060,000	12
Community service	14,331,000	6
Management and general	19,570,000	8
Fund raising	34,180,000	15
Others	28,371,000	12
Total	$235,201,000	

SOURCE: American Cancer Society, *Annual Report*, 1984, 17.

sionals, entertainers, retired people—a cross section of concerned Americans, translate policy into action. Motivated by a concern for the health and lives of others, they do much of the work of the society's service program designed to help the cancer patient and his or her family. During the April Crusade they canvass their neighbors—house-to-house, face-to-face—to solicit funds to advance the fight against cancer and, at the same time, to bring them lifesaving information.

Coordinating the entire organizational effort is a professional staff of approximately one paid member to 900 volunteers. The national staff, with headquarters in New York City, directs the society's ongoing volunteer programs and coordinates the work of the national volunteer board of directors and the committees with that of the divisions. It provides numerous technical and professional services, such as legal advice, accounting expertise, scientific information, medical policy planning, and counseling. The divisions create and produce materials to support programs for distribution. In fact, the professional staff advises and supports the volunteer effort at all levels—local, state, and national—and helps volunteers to carry out the policies of the board of directors. By providing an ongoing, day-to-day communications link, the staff not only assists the society's volunteers in implementing programs of cancer control but also maintains close working relationships with the staff of the National Cancer Institute and with cancer control organizations in other countries.

From this chapter you have learned that management techniques can be universally applied and that management opportunities are not limited to the profit-oriented business sector. We hope that this information has opened new doors for you to consider. Per-

Volunteers help with fund-raising, either by personal contact with neighbors and friends or, as here, through telephone solicitation.

haps one of them is marked "opportunities for management in nonprofit organizations." If so, open it and take a closer look. You may then want to continue your study of business with new and different objectives in mind. In speaking of her approach to opportunity, Norma J. Wisor, head of the Arkansas Community Foundation, said, "Doors are there in all our lives; when they open, we have to be prepared to step through them. If we sit around and wait for them to be opened for us, we'll sit a long time."[3]

[3]Quoted in *New York Times*, August 8, 1980, A18.

SUMMARY

- Nonprofit organizations have two common characteristics: They do not seek profits and they are tax-exempt.
- Local, state and federal governments are the most important forms of nonprofit organizations and employ about 16 percent of all working Americans.
- The federal government employs fewer people than either the state or local governments.
- Governments differ from other nonprofits in that (a) they have the power to tax, (b) they have power to enforce decisions, (c) civil service practices dominate employment, and (d) top managers are elected.
- Nonprofit organizations, other than governments, are distinguished in that (a) they only offer services, (b) voluntary contributions provide financing, (c) they depend greatly on publicity and public relations, and (d) communications are vital.
- A board of directors sets policies for nonprofits. A professional staff implements goals while volunteers do most of the work.
- Nonprofits compete with other nonprofits as well as profit-seeking enterprises.
- Nonprofits provide attractive career opportunities.
- Key activity areas for nonprofits are marketing of social concerns, administration of philanthropy, and operation of cooperatives.

KEY TERMS YOU SHOULD KNOW

consumer cooperative
nonprofit organization
social marketing
trade association

QUESTIONS FOR REVIEW

1. What characteristics do all nonprofits have in common?
2. Which level of government employs the most people? The least?
3. In what four ways do governments differ from other nonprofit organizations?
4. How do nonprofits other than governments finance activities?
5. Why is marketing especially important to nonprofits?
6. "Nonprofits depend on publicity and free promotion." Explain.
7. What three steps do nonprofits follow in communicating with the public?
8. What is the role of the board of directors in managing a nonprofit organization? The professional staff? The volunteers?
9. How do nonprofits measure performance results?
10. Explain how nonprofits compete.
11. Why may employment in a nonprofit enterprise be attractive?
12. Explain the following activity areas for nonprofits: marketing of social causes, administration of philanthropy, and operation of cooperatives.

QUESTIONS FOR DISCUSSION

1. Political parties, labor unions, and charitable organizations are examples of nonprofit organizations. Why do we consider them part of the nonprofit sector, and how do they differ from profit-oriented enterprises?
2. Consumer cooperatives are nonprofit organizations. Choose a consumer cooperative that you are familiar with and discuss how it functions and why it qualifies for nonprofit status.
3. Do you believe nonprofit organizations will become more or less important in the future? Why?
4. How do you account for the fact that employment by the Federal Government as a percentage of total employment is declining?

CASE STUDY

Developing a Plan for Financing a Trade Association

Trade associations are "big business" in the United States. **Trade associations** are *nonprofit organizations that represent the common interests of their members who belong to the same industry.* Typically, trade associations lobby for favorable legislation, provide educational programs, make group insurance available, and perform other activities that generally benefit members. Virtually all profit-seeking companies belong to one or more associations.

Trade associations are financed by dues collected from members. Dues are sometimes difficult to collect, since some benefits are intangible. In this case study, a trade association desperately needs to increase its dues if it is to continue its present level of membership services. The following discussion takes place between the executive director, Jack Brown; the finance manager, Fay Baker; and the promotion manager, Alan Hudson.

Jack: I don't like to say this, but we're going to have to ask our next convention for another dues increase. Membership didn't increase this year, but costs did.

Fay: And this will be the third year in a row we've asked the delegates to raise the dues. They won't be happy about still another increase.

J: I know! I've got a lot of flak from the lay leadership. You see, the typical member has only a vague idea of the good we do. They think most of their dues go to pay the professional staff big salaries and take care of expense accounts.

(Everyone at the table laughs.)

Alan: But if the members read our semimonthly paper, they would know they're getting a lot in return for their dues.

J: Alan, you still don't understand human nature. Some people want something for nothing. And our members are not exceptions.

F: I don't think our members really believe the dues are too high. But I think they resent being asked to pay higher dues every year.

J: You're right. And I feel like a fool having to ask the board of directors to pass a dues increase at every convention. We've got to figure out a way to assure us the money we need to provide first-rate service without having to hound the membership for more money every year.

A: I've got an idea. Why don't we do two things. First, develop a ten-year plan in which we focus on how great our association can be if we have adequate financing. Then, second, devise a formula for increasing the dues by a certain percentage, say, every other year. If we can get the delegates at the next convention to ratify the plan, then dues increases will be automatic and the members will complain less.

J: I like your idea. Go ahead and develop a ten-year plan. Capture the imagination of our members. Show them what the association can become if we have a solid financial plan. Point our new services that we can provide—that sort of thing.

F: I also think a ten-year plan is what we need. It sure would simplify my financial planning.

J: We've got four months until the next convention. Put the basics of your idea on paper. Then let's get back together.

Questions

1. What are some of the reasons trade association members would be reluctant to pay dues?
2. What can a trade association do to satisfy its members?
3. Are trade associations really necessary? Why or why not?

APPENDIX:
Tips on Selecting a Career and Finding a Job

For some, the word "work" has an unpleasant connotation—it means something people have to do rather than something they enjoy doing. In our complex and rapidly changing society, work should be an enjoyable activity, not drudgery. It should offer psychological rewards, not loss of individuality. As Sigmund Freud once noted, "No other technique for the conduct of life attaches the individual so firmly to reality as laying emphasis on work; for his work at least gives him a secure portion of reality in the human community."

Selecting a career—choosing the kind of work you want to do—is important for several reasons. First, chances are that you will spend more of your waking hours working than doing anything else (see Table A-1). Since work for most of us is the dominant aspect of living, it makes good sense to select a career we enjoy.

Second, people tend to earn more money doing what they enjoy. There are many square pegs in round holes and round pegs in square holes. Selecting the wrong career usually leads to job dissatisfaction, mediocre achievement, and limited financial gain.

TABLE A-1   A Career Represents a Lot of Time

PRESENT AGE	PLANNED RETIREMENT AGE	TOTAL YEARS WORKED	CAREER WORKING HOURS*
20	65	45	90,000 to 112,500
25	65	40	80,000 to 100,000
30	65	35	70,000 to 87,500
35	65	30	60,000 to 75,000
40	65	25	50,000 to 62,500
45	65	20	40,000 to 50,000
50	65	15	30,000 to 37,500

*Based on 2,000 to 2,500 hours per year (40 to 50 hours per week, 2 weeks' vacation per year).

Third, a career should be selected carefully because preparing for it often requires much time and effort. Also, while changing employers is a fairly simple process, changing careers can be very time-consuming and costly.

The purpose of this appendix is to give you some pointers on how you can choose a career, find a good job in the field you have selected, and make progress once you've started a job.

SELECTING A CAREER

If you wish to make a rational, careful career decision, you should (1) match your interests with the work, (2) evaluate the experiences of others, (3) consider employment trends, (4) visit the counseling center at your school, and (5) do further research on the subject.

Match Your Interests with the Work

Job satisfaction is of overriding importance. There is evidence that people in recent years enjoy their work less. One frequently hears about the erosion of the work ethic, job boredom, high turnover in some industries, and even accidents that relate to job dissatisfaction.

Job dissatisfaction arises most often because there is a poor "fit" between a person and his or her job. Before you select a career you should ask yourself the following questions:

- *Am I most interested in people, things, or ideas?* All human attention is directed toward people, things, and ideas. Before selecting a career, you should consider the degree of interest you have in each of these areas. Say, for example, you are interested primarily in people. You might be unhappy in a career in engineering or accounting, where you would be dealing primarily with things. A career in sales or management might be more to your liking.
- *How much responsibility do I want?* Not all of us want to manage other people. A key consideration, then, is whether you want to be responsible for the performance of others or simply want to be responsible for your own work.
- *How much money do I want to earn?* Careers vary widely in terms of monetary rewards. Significantly, salaries also vary with geographic location. And some people have a greater desire for money than other people.
- *Will my career enable me to make full use of my abilities?* You will be unhappy if you choose a career that is too limiting for you.
- *How important is it to me to feel that I am doing something useful?* Some people can feel fulfilled in a job only if they are directly or indirectly helping others. A career that does not give them this opportunity may leave them feeling frustrated.

Evaluate the Experiences of Others

Valuable insights can often be gained by talking with people in the fields you are considering. Drawbacks or advantages of a job may be revealed. An insider's view of the field is bound to be valuable.

An important study on college education and job satisfaction was published by the College Placement Council Foundation, a nonprofit corporation concerned with career counseling and placement of college graduates.[1] The study examined the levels of job and career satisfaction of 4,100 college graduates. Some of the graduates had been employed for as long as nine years.

The report found that most college graduates were satisfied with their careers (see Table A–2). The "very satisfied" ranged from 69 percent for administrators to 33 percent for office workers. The "not at all satisfied" ranged from only 2 percent for administrators and allied health workers to 11 percent for office workers.

Were business majors satisfied with their jobs? Table A–3 shows that administrators (70 percent), salespeople (65 percent), and accountants (53 percent) were very satisfied.

Significantly, the study compared those who had made their career choices early with those who had made their choices late. Interest-

---

[1] Ann Stouffer Bisconti and Lewis C. Solmon, *Job Satisfaction After College: The Graduate's Viewpoint.*

TABLE A-2 Overall Job Satisfaction, by Occupation (in percentages)

LEVEL OF SATISFACTION	ACCOUNTANT	OFFICE WORKER	ADMINISTRATOR	SALESPERSON	MATHEMATICIAN, SCIENTIST	ALLIED HEALTH WORKER
Very	54	33	69	63	49	56
Somewhat	43	56	28	34	48	42
Not at all	3	11	2	3	3	2

	ENGINEER	EDUCATOR	SOCIAL WORKER	OTHER PROFESSIONAL	OTHER NON-PROFESSIONAL
Very	47	56	45	64	46
Somewhat	50	41	48	33	45
Not at all	3	3	7	4	9

SOURCE: Ann Stouffer Bisconti and Lewis Solmon, *Job Satisfaction After College: The Graduate's Viewpoint* (Bethlehem, Pa.: CPC Foundation, 1977), p. 8.

ingly, the late-deciders were equally well satisfied with their eventual employment. This finding should comfort students who still have not decided on a career. Apparently it is the *care*

TABLE A-3 Job Satisfaction, by Occupation

OCCUPATION	NUMBER RESPONDING	PERCENTAGE RESPONDING "VERY SATISFIED"
Educator	36	81
Other professional	83	74
Administrator	249	70
Salesperson	83	65
Accountant	145	53
Other non-professional	51	45
Mathematician, scientist	23	44
Office worker	55	26

SOURCE: Ann Stouffer Bisconti and Lewis Solmon, *Job Satisfaction After College: The Graduate's Viewpoint* (Bethlehem, Pa.: CPC Foundation, 1977), p. 45.

that is taken in making the decision that determines the degree of satisfaction. This suggests that college students should be flexible in choosing courses rather than lock themselves into highly specialized career paths before they have even considered other fields.

Another significant finding concerned sex stereotyping of careers. Even though business occupations are often associated with men and teaching occupations with women, the study found that male teachers were as satisfied with their jobs as female teachers. Women business administrators, moreover, appeared to be substantially *more* satisfied with their work than men in the same occupation.

Consider Employment Trends

Another consideration in career selection is employment trends. Sometimes students begin preparing themselves for a career that has been enjoying rapid growth but find, by the time they graduate, that the number of jobs in the field has shrunk. They may then have difficulty finding an entrance-level job. Currently, for example, education majors in many fields are experiencing this problem.

An excellent source of job availabilities is the *College Placement Annual*.[2] It is available in most college placement offices.

The *College Placement Annual* lists by geographical location the names of hundreds of companies looking for business majors in many fields, including:

- Accounting
- Actuarial science
- Administration (Business)
- Administration (Public)
- Administration (Technical)
- Advertising
- Agricultural business
- Appraising and claim adjusting
- Banking and finance
- Computer science
- Economics
- Employee relations
- Financial analysis
- Hotel and restaurant management
- Instruction and training
- Management (Nontechnical)
- Management (Technical)
- Manufacturing Supervision
- Marketing and marketing research
- Merchandising
- Public relations
- Purchasing
- Retail and wholesale management
- Sales (Nontechnical)
- Sales (Technical)
- Secretarial science
- Statistics

- Traffic and transportation
- Underwriting

Visit the Counseling Center at Your School

Most colleges have a counseling center. People at the center can answer questions about different kinds of careers and their general advantages and disadvantages. Usually they can also give you a variety of tests to help you understand your aptitudes, interests, and other psychological factors that relate to career choice.

Do Further Research on the Subject

Many books that give guidance on career selection are available. Trade associations are also excellent sources of information about careers.

One important thing that you should research is the requirements for entering various careers. In some cases, specific conditions must be met before you can practice in a field—for example, you must establish state residency, get a certain amount of experience in the field, pass a certain test, and so on. It is a good idea to find out these requirements the very first time you begin thinking about a particular career. You may be able either to get a part-time job that will eventually enable you to meet the requirements or to take courses that will help you pass the test.

WHAT ABOUT THE SECOND CAREER?

Some of you taking the introduction to business course may have already completed one career—perhaps in the military, government service, or child rearing. You may ask, "How does choosing a second career differ from selecting the first?"

The answer is that choosing a second career is easier because a person has more experi-

---

[2]Published annually by the College Placement Council Foundation, P.O. Box 2263, Bethlehem, Pa. 18001.

ence and a clearer understanding of what he or she would like to do the second time around. The five steps discussed previously, however, are applicable to people of all ages and experiences.

JOB HUNTING

After you have decided on a career, your search for a job begins. The editors of the *College Placement Annual* make seven specific recommendations (besides contacting on-campus placement centers) for finding the right job:

- Obtain lists of suitable prospective employers from sources such as the *College Placement Annual,* Yellow Pages of telephone directories, chamber of commerce listings, directories from professional associations, and library references like *Standard & Poor's Register,* the various Moody manuals, and Dun & Bradstreet's directories.

- Talk to friends, faculty members, associates, relatives, and other personal contacts who may know of available openings or about prospective employers.

- Read newspapers (including the want ads), trade publications, business weeklies, journals, and books on the subject, such as Richard Bolles's *What Color Is Your Parachute? A Practical Manual for Job Hunters and Career Changers,* Robert Calvert and John Steele's *Planning Your Career,* Arthur Pell's *College Graduate Guide to Job Finding,* and Newell Brown's *After College What: A Career Exploration Handbook.*

- Prepare by learning all you can about any employer in whom you have a strong interest. Be able to describe clearly what you would like to do for that organization. Contact the person most likely to be in a position to hire you. If you have selected a city or a general locale and will be looking for a job there, subscribe in advance to the local newspapers and obtain lists of prospective employers in the area before you relocate.

- Contact the nearest office of the state employment service. Even if it primarily handles local listings, it should be able to refer you to employment services in other cities and states.

- Send your résumé with a covering letter to any potential employers and state that you will be contacting them regarding an interview upon your arrival. Exercise care in organizing and constructing your résumé; it is one of the most important documents you will ever write.

- Pursue all possible avenues, and don't become discouraged by a number of rejections. Follow up all leads in a businesslike manner. Don't press the panic button. The job you're seeking may turn up when you least expect it. But you can't wait for it to come to you. You must be aggressive and go after it.

Self-defeating Myths about Getting a Job

There are several myths that surround the subject of job hunting. If you believe in these myths, you will develop a negative attitude that is almost bound to be self-defeating:

- *Myth #1: When you apply for a job you play the role of a beggar*—Belief in this myth makes many people excessively timid. The truth is that when you apply for a job you are making an offer. View the employment process this way: "I, an important person, am going to meet with another important person, a representative of Company X, to discuss something of mutual importance—a job."

- **Myth #2: Getting a good job depends on pull**—A wide range of contacts is indeed helpful in getting a job. The more exposure you have in the job market, the better your chances of finding the right job. Contacts are the oil that lubricates the hinges of the door marked "opportunity." But many people exaggerate the importance of pull—defined as hiring people because of whom they know rather than what they can do. Placement directors will tell you that competition for the best qualified and most promising graduates is keen. The help-wanted sections of large newspapers tell a story of the painstaking effort used to find the "right people."

- **Myth #3: Everyone else is better qualified**—Many of us have inferiority complexes for various reasons. We stand in awe of a big company that has a lot of prestige. We may feel that the school we graduated from is second rate, that we come from too humble a background, and so on.

   There are some people who do set their goals too high, but their number is small compared with people who set their goals too low. Many of the individuals featured in "People Who Make Things Happen" came from very ordinary backgrounds. The important point is to set the size goal that you feel is right for you!

- **Myth #4: When job hunting, "know thyself"**—Self-understanding is a critical part of the job-seeking process. If your college has a psychological counseling center, take advantage of it. Often we think we know who we are, what we want, and where we want to go. But often, in fact, we don't really know ourselves, and as a result we pursue the wrong kinds of jobs. Take time to study the self-evaluation work sheet (Figure A–1) to understand better what kind of work you will find most satisfying.

Preparing an Effective Résumé

A **résumé,** or **personal data sheet,** is *a summary of who you are and of your qualifications.* It should describe briefly your academic and work experience. It may also include your personal interests, career objectives, and extracurricular activities. An effective résumé should be neatly typed, professionally reproduced, brief (one or two pages), and complete.

There are a number of different formats for preparing a résumé, depending on the kind of job you are looking for. A good source of information on how to prepare a résumé is the *College Placement Annual,* found in most college placement offices. Figure A–2 shows a sample résumé.

It should be remembered that qualifications set for a job are the employer's way of making sure the person hired will do well. A person who is insufficiently qualified may be unable to close the experience gap quickly enough to succeed. Applicants should ask themselves, "Is this the right job for me?" before they ask themselves, "Now, how can I manage to get this job?"

Preparing an Effective Letter of Application

In the course of your job hunting, you will often be writing letters to companies expressing interest in a job that you have heard about or simply inquiring whether the company might have a suitable position for you. Such letters of application are exceptionally important and should be carefully prepared. You are urged to consult the *College Placement Annual* or other sources for ideas and recommendations.

Conducting Yourself in the Personal Interview

In finding a job it is probable that you will be involved in a number of personal interviews. Keep in mind that the interview is the most important part of the job-getting process.

Figure A-1 Self-evaluation Work Sheet

One important aspect of choosing a position is understanding yourself. Self-evaluation can help you analyze what is important to you in the kind of work you will do and the kind of organization in which you will work.

The following are some of the things you should consider in your own self-evaluation. Your answers should be honest. They are meant to help you and should not represent a "good" or "bad" value judgment.

1. What are the things you do best? Are they related to people, data, things?
   _____ related to _____
   _____ related to _____
   _____ related to _____

2. Do you express yourself well and easily?
   Orally: Yes _____ No _____ In writing: Yes _____ No _____

3. Do you see yourself as a leader of a group or team? Yes _____ No _____
   Do you see yourself as an active participant of a group or a team? Yes _____ No _____
   Do you prefer to work on your own? Yes _____ No _____
   Do you like supervision? Yes _____ No _____

4. Do you work well under pressure? Yes _____ No _____
   Does pressure cause you anxiety; in fact, is it difficult for you to work well under pressure?
   Yes _____ No _____

5. Do you seek responsibility? Yes _____ No _____
   Do you prefer to follow directions? Yes _____ No _____

6. Do you enjoy new ideas and situations? Yes _____ No _____
   Are you more comfortable with known routines? Yes _____ No _____

7. In your future, which of the following things will be most important to you?
   a. Working for a regular salary _____ b. Working for a commission _____
   c. Working for a combination of both _____

8. Do you want to work a regular schedule (e.g., 9 A.M. to 5 P.M.)? Yes _____ No _____

9. Are you willing to travel more than 50 percent of your working time? Yes _____ No _____

10. What kind of environment is important to you?
    a. Do you prefer to work indoors? Yes _____ No _____
    b. Do you prefer to work outdoors? Yes _____ No _____
    c. Do you prefer an urban environment (population over 1 million)? Yes _____ No _____
       Population between 100,000 to 900,000? Yes _____ No _____
    d. Do you prefer a rural setting? Yes _____ No _____

11. Do you prefer to work for a large organization? Yes _____ No _____

12. Are you free to move? Yes _____ No _____
    Are there important "others" to be considered? Yes _____ No _____

SOURCE: *College Placement Annual* (Bethlehem, Pa.: College Placement Council, 1982).

Figure A-2 Sample Résumé

Angelo Novarro
999 Carson Drive
Sacramento, CA 95804

(916) 555-7584

EDUCATION

Institution	Dates	Diploma Degree
Central High School Buffalo, NY 14213	1980-1984	Commerical
Castleton Junior College Castleton, CA 95807	1984-1986	A.A.S.

<u>Major</u>: Accounting   <u>Scholastic Standing</u>: 3.2 (B+)

<u>Major Courses</u>   <u>Background Courses</u>
Elementary and Advanced   Business Communications
   Accounting I, II, III, IV   Business Law I, II
Auditing   Money and Banking
Income Tax Procedures   Economic Analysis
Cost Accounting   Marketing
Business Management

EXTRACURRICULAR ACTIVITIES AND HONORS

Accounting Club, President (elected office) 1985-1986
Collge Glee Club 1984
Phi Beta Lambda 1986 (honorary undergraduate business education
   association)
Future Business Leaders of America 1982-1984
High-school valedictorian 1984

EXPERIENCE

<u>Company</u>	<u>Dates</u>	<u>Job Duties</u>
Bullock's Department Store Sacramento, CA 95804	September to present (part-time)	Retail selling, men's funishings
Lane's Buffalo, NY 14213	Summers	Stock clerk

REFERENCES

Professor James Devine, Economics Department, Castleton Junior College,
   Castleton, CA 95807
Mr. John Knight, Manager, Shoe Department, Lane's, 111 Main Street,
   Buffalo, NY 14213
Mr. Frank Naber, Department Manager, Men's Furnishings, Bullock's
   Department Store, 18 State Street, Sacramento, CA 95804
Mrs. Hazel Hines, 184 West School Street, Sacramento, CA 95602

In Chapter 15 of the text we discussed some of the most important do's and don'ts for job interviews. In addition, the characteristics listed in the box to the right will make either a favorable or unfavorable impression.

Evaluating Potential Employers

Before going to work for any organization, business or nonbusiness, it is wise to examine it carefully. Following are five questions to consider:

- *What will I learn?* Most people work for more than one organization during their careers. It makes sense, then, to consider the experience and training an organization offers. A key question to contemplate is, "If I go to work for this company, will I be more salable in the job market in the future?"

- *With whom will I work?* Co-workers are the most important part of the working environment. In evaluating prospective co-workers one should consider questions such as, "Do they appear satisfied and enthusiastic?" "Do they appear courteous and helpful?" and "Would I like to be one of them?"

- *What will I earn?* Some organizations—like some careers—pay better than others. Two key questions to ask are, "Is the beginning pay consistent with my current requirements?" and "What level of income can I expect to earn two, five, or ten years from now?"

- *What about other benefits?* Fringe benefits are becoming more important as part of the job package. Bonus arrangements, medical and life insurance, profit sharing, pregnancy leave, day-care centers, and paid vacations are examples of possible benefits an applicant may want to consider.

FAVORABLE	UNFAVORABLE
Strong motivation toward success	Lackadaisical approach to life
Ability to speak clearly and correctly	Poor voice, grammar, and diction
Humility—the realization that there is much to be learned	A "know it all" attitude
Poise	Nervousness, uneasiness, apprehension
Willingness to start at the bottom	Too much concern about initial salary and employee benefits
Better-than-average academic record	Poor academic record
Evidence of constructive extracurricular activities	No record of active participation in campus life
Experience of having earned at least part of your expenses while in school	Complete financial support from others while in school
Definite career plans	No real consideration given to career plans
Good personal appearance	Poor personal appearance
Failure to smoke—even if the interviewer offers you a cigarette	Smoking
Interest in what the employer looks for in considering people for promotions	Apparent lack of interest in future advancement
Good body language—you should "sit up" and lean forward	Slumping back in the chair
A followup letter thanking the employer for talking with you	No followup

- *Is the organization financially sound?* As observation and reading will tell us, not all organizations succeed. As noted in Chapter 20, even some giant businesses fail. Businesses also differ greatly in their prospects for growth. Thus, consideration should be given to the overall long-run prospects for the business.

Sources of Information about Companies

Here are some ways you may obtain information about a company for which you might like to vork:

- *College placement office*—Many companies regularly visit campuses to recruit new employees. The placement office should have a general description of the company and the jobs it wants to fill. The office may also be able to steer you to individuals who joined a specific organization in earlier years, so that you can find out their impressions.
- *Company annual reports*—These can be obtained directly from the company. If the organization is large, a brokerage firm should be able to supply its most recent report.
- *Employees*—This is an excellent source, but finding representative employees to give their views is difficult if the company is located some distance away.
- *Business publications and financial news*—Major corporations are frequently featured in the news, especially in business publications such as the *Wall Street Journal*. Publications of Standard & Poor and Dun & Bradstreet, available in most reference libraries, carry extensive background information about larger companies.

AND ONCE YOU HAVE THE JOB...

In many ways, your first job can be the most important that you will ever have. Poor marks on the first job can plague you for years to come. While you should not stick with a job or a company that you feel is definitely wrong for you, you should try hard to make the most out of your first job. Bear in mind that many prospective employers are skeptical when they see a long record of job hopping. Their goal is to keep employee turnover low; it costs money to hire and fire.

The bases for success in a new job are not obscure. Those who do best are willing to learn, are willing to work hard, turn out quality work, gain the respect of fellow workers, and prove their integrity. The following suggestions can also improve your chances for advancement once you have the job.

Be Businesslike

We have all heard the term "businesslike"; it is the label for an overall quality that employers look for in people they hire. In many cases, this is an umbrella type of attribute that any individual must have before he or she is even considered for a job with responsibility. Being businesslike means acting in a fashion that wins the respect, confidence, and loyalty of others. One projects a businesslike attitude by:

- Being well-organized
- Finding out the facts before making judgments
- Listening attentively to what people say
- Being in control of one's emotions
- Not being a clock watcher
- Behaving confidently
- Keeping one's word
- Being prompt
- Avoiding office gossip, small talk, and interpersonal frictions

BUSINESSLIKE DRESS

The above factors are all intangible. There are also tangible factors involved—including dress and grooming. The press recently has been reporting on an awakening of fashion consciousness in America; people are dressing with more care. Some of this is due to young people's concern about finding jobs. As one woman (about to graduate from college) said, "If you are going to interview for a job, you are going to have to look serious about it. It's to sell an image of someone who is competent, who is going to be serious about the whole thing."

A placement director at Columbia University said, "If you are going to make a mistake, make a mistake on the side of being conservative." When it comes to the question of how to dress for a job interview, another placement director said that neatness counts and recommended "attire not distracting from the interview."

DOES BEING BUSINESSLIKE MEAN LIMITING YOUR FREEDOM?

This discussion about being businesslike may give you a feeling that you must give up your individuality once you leave the permissive environment of the college campus. Whether you feel this way depends on how you view the issue. One young woman graduate, discussing this subject, had this to say after she had worked at her new job for a few months: "Dressing and acting the part that was expected of me gave me a certain confidence I would otherwise not have had.... I don't feel it's a sacrifice, I feel I'm getting something and have matured. I can still live any life-style I like when I'm not working." A great deal depends on the particular department in which one works and on whether one's approach to the first job meshes with the environment there.

Be a Crew Member, Not a Passenger

Some people in organizations are like passengers in a plane—they are just going along for the ride and are not really helping the enterprise make progress. If you want to do well in your job, you should behave like a crew member—that is, make active efforts to help the organization attain its objectives rather than simply coast along.

In a given organization, "crew members" can often be distinguished from "passengers" by the way they refer to the organization. Crew members say "we"; passengers say "they."

Volunteer for Additional Responsibilities

Some people perform their jobs in an active, energetic manner—serving as crew members rather than passengers—but never consider stepping beyond the bounds of their job. If you want to advance, you should ask for additional work, make suggestions for improving departmental performance, and so on. When a higher-level position opens up, your supervisor is likely to fill it with someone who has already shown a desire for additional responsibility.

Is Advancement Always the Best Course?

In large part because of the competitive nature of our society, individuals often believe that they *must* move up the ladder in the company hierarchy in order to be successful. In other words, they feel that they should always be aiming for their boss's job.

Such a definition of success should be examined carefully and not blindly embraced. We each differ in the kind of work that makes us happy. It is possible to achieve great job satisfaction without being promoted in the conventional sense we have come to accept. There are sales representatives who make more money than a company vice-president and who turn down offers to go into management. College professors who go into administration often return to teaching. Some copywriters and computer programmers would be miserable in any other kind of job.

You owe it to yourself to define success in your own terms before you begin to set career goals. Society's conventional ideas of success may not be compatible with your nature. And only you can determine what will give you a happy and fulfilling life.

GOING INTO BUSINESS FOR YOURSELF

The pros and cons of going into business for oneself were discussed in Chapters 1 and 3. In considering the choice, you should keep in mind that the chances for limited success or even failure outnumber the chances for great success. However, you may be a person who will attain greatest job satisfaction and success by being your own boss rather than working for another. The self-analysis test on page 14 can help you judge whether you would be successful as an entrepreneur.

If you are contemplating having your own business, it is probably a good idea to first obtain experience as an employee in a business of the type you want to start. Many of the most successful retail stores, advertising agencies, manufacturing plants, and real estate firms were founded by people who, after completing their formal education, served as employees until they had obtained a sound grasp of the intricacies of business management.

The text gives specific advice on how to evaluate franchising opportunities (page 84) and how to get an SBA loan (pages 76–79).

QUESTIONS AND EXERCISES

1. Prepare a personal résumé for use in obtaining the kind of employment that interests you. Consider including information about your education, work experience, personal interests, employment goals, extracurricular activities, and other facts that will help a prospective employer evaluate you.
2. Would you hire yourself? Why or why not? Prepare a plan for making yourself a more desirable job candidate.
3. What are the benefits of a wise career choice? What are the consequences of failing to choose the right field?
4. Why, when career selection decisions are so important, do you think young people are often so casual about making them?
5. Many college graduates end up in fields for which they have not been formally trained. Why do you think this occurs?
6. In selecting a career, why is "knowing yourself" even more important than "knowing the company" or "knowing the job area"?
7. Why do you think part-time and summer jobs are considered important by employers even when they may not relate to the job they have in mind for the applicant?
8. What are the factors to consider in determining the "right company" to work for?
9. In view of the material in this appendix, what can a person do to improve his or her chances for promotion into jobs with responsibility?

GLOSSARY

acceptance An essential condition of a contract by which the offer must be accepted by the party to whom it is made.

accounting process The progression of financial data from basic data input (receipts, disbursements) through procedures (recording, classifying, summarizing, interpreting) and report output (balance sheet, income statement, special reports).

accounts payable Money that is owed to suppliers.

accounts receivable Money that is owed to a company by customers and others. Also called *notes receivable*.

achievement test A test that seeks to measure an individual's ability to perform specific tasks.

actuary A person who calculates insurance premiums by estimating expected claims, interest that the premiums will earn, and the like.

administrative expense An expense that is related to an enterprise as a whole. Also called *general expense*.

advertising Any form of paid, impersonal presentation of goods, services, or ideas for the purpose of inducing people to buy or to act favorably on what is called to their attention.

advertising agency A service organization composed of specialists who plan, prepare, and place advertising for companies.

advertising medium Any device used to carry an advertising message to the people it is intended to influence.

affirmative action Special efforts to increase the proportion of women and minority-group members who hold positions of responsibility in a company.

AFL See *American Federation of Labor*.

agent In law of agency, the party that is given authority to act.

agent intermediary An intermediary who does not take title to the goods in which he or she deals, who normally performs few services, and whose chief function is to negotiate a sale.

American Federation of Labor (AFL) An organization of craft and other unions that was established in 1886 and was merged with the CIO in 1955.

analog function The continuous measure by a computer of some physical quantity, such as temperature, speed of motion, electrical current, pressure, or flow.

annual report A business report that is prepared as of the close of each fiscal year and basically includes a balance sheet, income statement, and verification from an independent auditor that it is accurate.

aptitude test A test that identifies personal talents or capabilities, such as mechanical aptitude.

691

arbitration An attempt to settle labor disputes by which both parties agree in advance to abide by the decision.

area-wide collective bargaining Collective bargaining that is conducted between representatives of management and labor from several companies in the same industry and in the same geographical area.

arithmetic average See *arithmetic mean*.

arithmetic mean The simplest and most frequently used average, computed by adding all the items in a series and dividing the sum by the total number of items. Also called *arithmetic average*.

assessment center A place where managers can practice their job-related skills through simulations. Also called *evaluation center*.

asset An item of value—property or a resource—that a business has.

assignment of contract The transfer of one party's rights or obligations in a contract to another party.

associate See *franchisee*.

attribute evaluation See *trait evaluation*.

auditing The specialized branch of accounting that is concerned with verifying accounting records and practices and reviewing the validity of accounting decisions.

authorized stock The maximum number of shares of stock that can be issued, as specified in a company's corporate charter.

autocratic leader A dictatorial leader; one who makes the decisions and issues all orders.

automation The elimination of as much manual operation of machines as possible.

automobile insurance Insurance held by automobile owners to protect themselves from loss, generally collision, fire and theft, and liability.

automobile liability insurance Automobile insurance that covers bodily injury to another person or damage to the property of another person.

average A single numerical value that is descriptive of a group of values.

balance of payments See *current account*.

balance of trade The record of a country's merchandise transactions.

balance sheet A statement of the financial status of a business at a specific time, indicating the assets, liabilities, and equity of the owners of the business.

bankruptcy The legal process by which assets of a debtor are liquidated as quickly as possible to pay off creditors and to free the debtor to start with a clean slate.

bar chart A graphic device used when statistics are to be compared; the bars can run horizontally or vertically.

Better Business Bureau A voluntary organization composed of businesspeople in a community seeking to prevent unethical practices through self-regulation.

BIC See *Bureau of International Commerce*.

bill of lading A receipt issued by a transportation agency for merchandise to be transported from a named shipper (the consignor) either to a specified consignee or to the order of any person.

binary code A numerical system made up of just two elements—0 and 1—that is used in the internal operations of computers.

biodegradable packaging material A material that readily disintegrates when exposed to sun and rain and that enriches instead of contaminates the earth.

blank endorsement An endorsement in which the payee or holder of a negotiable instrument simply writes his or her name on the reverse side of the instrument.

board of directors The governing body of a corporation, elected by the stockholders.

bond A certificate indicating that a corporation owes money to a bondholder.

bond indenture A detailed statement describing the rights and privileges of bondholders and the rights, privileges, and responsibilities of the issuing corporation. Also called *trust indenture*.

bond trustee An individual or, more commonly, a bank or other financial institution specializing in bonds and appointed by the issuing corporation to represent the bondholders.

bonus A cash payment used as an incentive.

bookkeeping The phase of accounting that is concerned mainly with the systematic recording of financial transactions.

boycott A concerted effort to stop the purchase of goods or services from a company until it grants the boycotters' demands.

brand name A term chosen by a firm to identify its products.

breach of contract The failure to perform what is called for in a contract.

break-even analysis The process of determining the relation between cost and revenue at various levels of sales volumes, used to determine the point at which it becomes profitable to make and sell a product.

broker An agent intermediary who negotiates transactions for merchandise without having either title to or physical possession of the goods; also, a person who trades on a securities exchange for his or her clients.

budget A financial forecast or plan that shows expected income and expenditures over a given period of time.

building code A community's prescription about building materials that can be used, fire precautions, and the like.

Bureau of International Commerce (BIC) A division of the U.S. Department of Commerce that provides U.S. businesspeople who wish to venture abroad with business and economic information that is gathered by U.S. embassies and consulates throughout the world.

business Any establishment that serves the public through the production or distribution of goods or through the provision of services; collectively, the commercial life of a nation.

business law The rules, statutes, codes, precepts, and regulations, enforceable by court action, that have been established to provide a legal framework within which business may be conducted.

business research The orderly gathering and the interpretation of information about business problems.

business risk The chance that something will happen to cause a financial loss.

buyer for export A foreign buyer who canvasses U.S. markets in search of goods needed by foreign consumers.

buying cooperative A cooperative formed to sell supplies to its members at good prices.

buying motive A consumer's reason for purchasing.

call option A method of retiring bonds by which the issuing corporation has the right to do so at any time before the maturity date.

capital Wealth used to produce more wealth.

capital-investment good A product or facility used to manufacture.

capitalism See *private enterprise system*.

carrier A company that engages in transportation.

cartel A combination of independent enterprises designed to limit competition.

cash discount The amount that can be deducted from a bill if payment is made on or before the designated due date; an inducement to buyers to pay promptly.

cash rebate The payment of cash by the seller to the buyer of the seller's product.

catalog/showroom/warehouse operations A form of non-store retailing in which the customer preselects merchandise at home or at the showroom.

centralized organization Organization in which authority is retained by higher-level managers.

central processing unit (CPU) The core of a computer, which performs the functions of memory, calculation, and control.

certificate of incorporation See *corporation charter*.

certified check A check that is guaranteed by the bank that issues it.

certified public accountant (CPA) A person who has passed the Uniform CPA Examination, has satisfied other educational and professional requirements, and has been licensed to practice public accounting.

chain of command The route by which authority is delegated downward and employees report upward.

chain store A retail store that operates on the principle of mass (large-scale) merchandising.

channel of distribution The route taken in the transfer of ownership of a product as it passes from producer to consumer.

Chapter 7 A provision for "straight bankruptcy," requiring the liquidation of nonexempt assets of individuals and corporations.

Chapter 11 A provision in business law that allows companies to reorganize and continue to operate while they pay off a limited portion of their debts.

Chapter 13 A debt consolidation program with legal safeguards, whereby the debtor draws up a plan for repaying current debts over a period of up to three, or with special court permission, five years.

character printer A computer printer that prints one character at a time.

charge-account credit Credit that resembles the open-account credit extended by business firms in that at the end of a given period, usually 30 days, consumers are billed for purchases.

chattel mortgage A legal device by which movable property is pledged as collateral.

checking account A bank account from which the depositor can withdraw or transfer money at will by writing a check.

checkout scanner An electronic device that uses laser beams to read and interpret the ten-digit universal product code (UPC) printed on more than 85 percent of foodstore merchandise.

CIO See *Congress of Industrial Organizations*.

Civil Rights Act (1964) A federal law that prohibits discrimination in employment based on race, religion, national origin, or sex by any employer with 15 or more employees who engages in interstate commerce.

class action suit A lawsuit in which an award to a single consumer results in awards to all similarly injured parties.

Clayton Act (1914) A federal law that supplemented and strengthened the Sherman Antitrust Act with regard to monopolies; it declares unlawful certain practices whose effect will be to lessen competition substantially or to tend to create a monopoly.

closed shop A now-illegal situation in which managers hired only people who were already members of a union.

coaching A type of internal training consisting of informal person-to-person counseling about how to perform a job more effectively.

COBOL (COmmon Business Oriented Language) The most common computer language for business applications, which closely resembles English.

co-determination A practice that gives workers equal representation with stockholders on the board of directors in making company policy.

coinsurance clause A clause in an insurance policy that states, in effect, that if the insured person has insured the property for less than a certain percentage (usually 80 percent) of its value, the insurance company will not pay the full value of a partial loss.

collateral Assets that can be used to guarantee repayment of a loan.

collective bargaining A procedure in which representatives of management and labor meet to discuss and resolve their differences.

collision insurance Automobile insurance that protects against damages to one's automobile resulting from collision with other automobiles or with other objects, either moving or fixed.

commercial bank A public corporation that accepts demand deposits and specializes in making loans to businesses and individuals.

commercial loan A loan made to a business.

commission Compensation whereby a sales representative is paid a certain percentage of his or her sales volume.

commodity contract A commitment to buy or sell a commodity at a specified time and place in the future.

COmmon Business Oriented Language See *COBOL*.

common carrier A carrier that operates on regular schedules over definite routes.

common stock Equity shares in a corporation whose owners share in dividends after debts are paid.

communication The transmission of information.

communism An economic system in which all industries and resources are owned by the government, and individuals have little economic freedom.

companywide objective A general goal that an organization wants to achieve.

competition The independent effort of two or more businesses to secure the patronage of the same customers.

component A part that will be assembled with others to make up a finished product.

comprehensive coverage Automobile insurance that covers losses resulting from windstorm, riot, flood, fire, theft, and almost any other risk not covered under the collision policy.

computer A programmable electronic device that can store, retrieve, and process data.

computer on a chip See *microcomputer*.

conditional endorsement An endorsement by which the payee transfers a negotiable instrument to someone else but retains title to it until some condition has been fulfilled.

conglomerate A corporation made up of a number of previously independent companies (or subsidiaries) in different industries.

Congress of Industrial Organizations (CIO) An organization formed in 1938 to promote the organization of the workers in mass-production and unorganized industries and to encourage their affiliation with the AFL; in 1955 the CIO merged with the AFL.

consideration An essential condition of a contract by which something must be given in exchange for a promise.

consumer cooperative A cooperative organized for the benefit of consumers.

consumer finance company A company that specializes in making cash loans to consumers for almost any worthwhile purpose. Also called *small loan company.*

consumer good A good purchased by ultimate consumers for personal and household use.

consumerism A loosely organized movement of private individuals and citizens' groups formed to protect the public from various business malpractices.

consumer-jury interview See *panel interview.*

consumer loan A loan made by a commercial bank directly to a consumer for a variety of purposes.

Consumer Price Index (CPI) An index number that measures the national average change in prices over time in a fixed market basket of goods and services.

consumer product A product that an ultimate consumer buys.

containerization The loading of goods into a container at the point of origin, where a seal is placed on it that is not broken until it reaches its ultimate destination.

contest A kind of sales promotion in which prizes are offered to consumers as a reward for analytical or creative thinking.

contract An agreement between two or more persons or businesses that is enforceable by court action.

contract carrier A carrier that is engaged in "for hire" transportation and does not offer the same service or the same price to everyone.

contracted industrial service An industrial service that is performed on a contractual basis.

contract manufacturing An arrangement between a U.S. company and a foreign producer whereby the U.S. company's product is manufactured abroad.

controlled sample A sample that is chosen deliberately.

controlled shopping center See *planned shopping center.*

controlling The management function of setting standards for work, measuring actual performance against standards, and taking corrective action if performance does not meet the standards.

convenience-food store A retailer that carries a limited line of food products, gives fast service, and is open long hours.

convenience good A good purchased frequently, in small quantities, and with a minimum of effort.

convertible bond A bond that can be exchanged for other securities, usually common stocks.

cooperative A voluntary nonprofit enterprise owned by and operated for the benefit of those using its services.

copyright The right to control the reproduction and dissemination of creative works.

corporate entrepreneur A person with drive and initiative who wants to run a small business within the structure of a large business.

corporate income tax A federal tax on a corporation's profits.

corporation A legal entity that has certain characteristics, rights, and obligations as set forth in the charter that created it.

corporation charter A document granted by the state that spells out in some detail the rights and privileges of the corporation. Also called *certificate of incorporation.*

corrective action A plan to make performance meet standards.

cost accounting A determination of the cost of handling an average order, producing a single unit of a product, selling a single unit, or even writing a business letter by prorating all fixed and variable expenses to the single activity being studied. Also called *cost analysis.*

cost analysis See *cost accounting.*

cost-plus basis A manufacturing arrangement whereby a U.S. company pays a foreign producer its costs plus an agreed-on percentage after the work is completed.

coupon A certificate to be presented to a retailer for savings or a cash refund on an item.

CPA See *certified public accountant.*

CPI See *Consumer Price Index.*

CPU See *central processing unit.*

craft union A labor union that limits its membership to workers who practice one trade or a group of related trades, even though the workers may work for a number of different employers.

credit bureau An organization of various businesses that extend considerable consumer credit.

credit-card company An outside agency that supplies consumer credit.

credit life insurance Term life insurance that pays a debt if the borrower dies.

credit limit The fixed maximum amount of credit permitted to be outstanding at any given time. Also called *line of credit*.

credit management The process of minimizing bad debt losses and maximizing sales volume.

credit term A stipulation of the length of a credit period and the cash discount for prompt payment.

credit union A group of people who have a common bond and who agree to save their money together and to make loans to members at low rates of interest.

criminal loss protection Insurance against burglary, robbery, and theft.

cumulative discount A quantity discount based on the total amount a customer purchases over a given period.

cumulative dividend A means of paying dividends on preferred stock whereby there is a continuing obligation to pay a dividend in the future if it is skipped.

current account A summary record of a country's financial transactions with other nations. Also called *balance of payments*.

current asset Cash or an item such as inventory or merchandise on hand that will be converted into cash in less than one year.

current liability A short-term debt that must be paid in less than one year.

curve graph See *line graph*.

data processing The classifying, sorting, calculating, summarizing, recording, and reporting of factual information.

dealer See *franchisee*.

debenture bond An unsecured obligation of a corporation.

debt capital A bond, so called because it represents a debt owed by a corporation to a bondholder.

decentralized organization Organization in which authority is granted to subordinates in a relatively large measure.

decision making The process of defining a problem, developing alternative solutions, gathering information, evaluating the alternatives, and reaching a final decision.

decline stage The fourth stage in a product's life cycle, which occurs when the product's usefulness and profitability decrease.

deductible coverage insurance Collision insurance that provides liability (responsibility) only for losses over a specified sum.

delegation of authority The act of empowering subordinates to perform certain activities and make decisions in order to carry them out.

demand deposit A bank deposit that can be withdrawn by the depositor at any time, with no advance notice.

demand-side economics The theory that states that pouring government funds into the economy will stimulate demand.

demographics The statistical study of human populations with reference to their size, density, distribution, and vital characteristics.

dental expense insurance Health insurance that covers the insured for dental services.

departmentalization The arrangement of work into manageable parts.

departmental objective A goal that is set for each department and that should be related to—and lead directly to the achievement of—the general companywide objectives.

Department of Commerce The federal department that encourages, serves, and promotes the nation's economic development and technological advancement.

department store A retailer that carries an unusually wide variety of merchandise.

digital function A computer's reading of discrete numbers, for example, 1, 2, 3.

diminishing utility A principle that holds that the more units there are of something, the less valuable each additional unit is.

direct export channel A marketing channel by which a U.S. manufacturer sells directly to foreign consumers.

direct import channel A marketing channel by which a U.S. firm buys directly from a foreign business.

directing The management function of motivating, leading, and communicating with employees so that the goals of the organization can be more efficiently met.

direct-to-the-consumer retailer A person who specializes in soliciting, billing, and delivering merchandise to consumers in their homes.

disability benefits Benefits paid under the Social Security Act of 1935 to a person who is disabled.

disability income Health insurance that provides benefits to replace income when an insured person is unable to work as a result of illness, injury, or disease.

disbursement Money that is paid out by a company.

discharge Dismissal from a firm because of incompetence, intoxication on the job, insubordination, curtailed business, and so on.

discount broker A broker who executes buy or sell decisions made by a client.

discount rate The amount of money that the Federal Reserve charges member banks for what they borrow, deducted ahead of time.

discount store A retailer that sells a large selection of well-known merchandise at below list prices.

disposable personal income The income an individual receives after tax and other deductions have been made.

distribution business An enterprise that sells goods for others.

dividend A share in a corporation's profits.

dumping The practice of flooding a market with goods sold below cost.

EEOC See *Equal Employment Opportunity Commission*.

EFT See *electronic funds transfer*.

elastic demand Demand that changes if the price of a product changes.

electronic funds transfer (EFT) A transaction initiated through an electronic terminal, a telephone, a computer, or a magnetic tape for the purpose of ordering, instructing, or authorizing a financial institution to debit or credit an account.

emotional buying motive A buying motive that is subjective in nature, often impulsive, and not based on logical thinking.

employers' association A group of employers acting together to present a solid front in management's dealings with labor.

endorsement The writing of one's name (or the name of one's business) on the back of a negotiable instrument in order to transfer the instrument.

entrepreneur An individual who starts a business.

entrepreneurship The willingness to exercise initiative and take considerable risk to operate one's own business.

Environmental Protection Agency (EPA) A government agency empowered to develop and enforce standards for clean air and water; to regulate pollution from pesticides, noise, and radiation; and to approve state pollution abatement plans.

EPA See *Environmental Protection Agency*.

Equal Credit Opportunity Act (1975) A law that makes it illegal to discriminate in the granting of credit on the basis of an applicant's sex or marital status.

Equal Employment Opportunity Commission (EEOC) A federal agency that enforces the Civil Rights Act of 1964.

equity capital A common or preferred stock, so called because the owner has part ownership in the corporation.

evaluation center See *assessment center*.

exchange license A control used by a government to obtain foreign currencies with which to buy goods abroad.

exchange rate The value of one currency in relation to another.

excise tax A federal tax levied on commodities or services that are regarded as luxuries.

Eximbank See *Export-Import Bank*.

experiment A procedure for collecting data through controlled tests.

export agent An agent who represents several noncompeting U.S. manufacturers in a foreign market.

Export-Import Bank A bank sponsored by the U.S. government that facilitates the export of U.S. products and services. Also called *Eximbank*.

export merchant A wholesaler who specializes in buying merchandise from various domestic manufacturers and reselling it in foreign markets.

express warranty A warranty that contains statements of fact regarding the characteristics of property being sold.

external communication Communication with people outside a company.

Fair Credit Reporting Act (1970) A law that protects consumers from inaccurate or obsolete information in reports used to determine eligibility for credit or employment.

Fair Labor Standards Act (1938) A law that sets the minimum wage and prohibits employment of people under age 16 in most jobs. Also called *Federal Wage and Hour Law.*

Fair Packaging and Labeling Act (1966) A law that regulates all consumer commodities that are packaged, labeled but not packaged, or packaged and unlabeled.

FASB See *Financial Accounting Standards Board.*

fault law Law that involves determining who is legally responsible for losses suffered. Also called *tort law.*

FDIC See *Federal Deposit Insurance Corporation.*

featherbedding The practice of causing an employer to pay for services not performed.

Federal Deposit Insurance Corporation (FDIC) A federal organization for banks that insures depositors' accounts.

federal regulatory agency A government agency that maintains competition, protects the consumer, and provides advice and counsel to business.

Federal Reserve System A federally controlled system whose objective is to regulate the supply of money and credit so as to contribute to a high level of employment, economic growth, and price stability.

Federal Trade Commission Act (1914) An act that controls and makes illegal unfair trade practices.

Federal Wage and Hour Law See *Fair Labor Standards Act.*

fidelity bond Criminal loss protection that insures employers against theft, forgery, and embezzlement by employees.

Financial Accounting Standards Board (FASB) The accounting profession's private sector standard-setting and rule-making body.

financial management In a business, the responsibility for obtaining and using funds.

financial supercompanies (financial supermarkets) Companies that serve the consumer's total needs in banking, insurance, credit cards, security investments, and real estate.

fire-and-theft Automobile insurance that compensates for losses caused by fire or theft.

fire insurance Insurance against fire, for which policies are written for one to five years and rates vary according to the risks involved.

first-line supervisor A supervisor who is immediately responsible for directing the work of employees.

fixed asset An item that is used for a long period of time.

fixed cost A cost that does not vary with volume of business.

fixed liability See *long-term liability.*

flextime The process of letting workers decide when they will begin and end the workday within a required core period.

floor broker See *floor member.*

floor member A person who trades securities for a firm that is a member of a stock exchange. Also called *floor broker.*

floor planning A method of obtaining short-term financing under which the lending agency holds title to the car or appliance as collateral. Used on expensive or "big ticket" items such as automobiles and home appliances.

flow chart A sketch showing the breakdown of a problem into its parts and the relation of the parts to each other.

FOB pricing See *free-on-board pricing.*

foreign branch An actual division of a domestic company that functions very much like a foreign wholesaler, except that it is owned by Americans.

foreign subsidiary A separate company that is owned by a parent U.S. corporation but is organized under the laws of the foreign country.

form utility The physical structure and properties people want in a product.

franchise An arrangement binding two parties to do business in a particular way.

franchisee A private investor in a franchise operation. Also called *dealer, outlet, associate, licensee, member.*

franchising A method of distributing a product or a service through licensed dealers, who are provided with a trademark, a marketing strategy plan, operating manuals, quality control standards, and a communication system.

franchisor A manufacturer or operating company

that has systematized a method for producing or distributing a product or service. Also called *seller, licenser.*

free enterprise system See *private enterprise system.*

free market An economic system in which owners of products seek to sell them at the highest possible price, and bidders for products seek to buy them at the lowest possible price.

free-on-board (FOB) pricing A geographic policy by which the purchaser pays all shipping costs excluding loading charges.

fringe benefit Compensation for labor in a form other than wages, salary, or other monetary reward.

full-coverage insurance Collision insurance that compensates for all losses up to the present value of the car.

full endorsement An endorsement that specifies the person or firm to whom the payee wishes to transfer title of a negotiable instrument. Also called *special endorsement.*

full-service broker A broker who does investment research for clients, advises them when to sell or buy, and gives advice at no charge.

full-service wholesaler A wholesaler who takes title to goods and performs a variety of wholesale functions. Also called *regular wholesaler, jobber, service wholesaler.*

functional design The phase of product design that gives a product its operational characteristics. Also called *product development.*

functional rotation A type of internal training that requires an employee to spend some time in different departments so that he or she will know what each department does and how it relates to the organization as a whole.

game A kind of sales promotion that is conducted over a long period of time and does not require skill to win.

garnishment A court order that directs the employer of a defendant to withhold a certain amount of the employee's usual wage each payday until a judgment is satisfied.

general agency An advertising agency that does not specialize but prepares all kinds of advertising for many different clients.

general expense See *administrative expense.*

general partnership A legal relationship between two or more persons who co-own a business for profit and who have unlimited liability for the business's debts.

genuineness of assent The principle that a party cannot be held to a contract if some fact was misrepresented.

geographic rotation A type of internal training that requires an employee to work in several geographic locations as part of his or her development.

GNP See *gross national product.*

good A tangible product.

good will The valuation a company puts on its public acceptance, established brand names, and similar factors.

grapevine The informal organization's communication channel.

grievance procedure The union contract's specification for how complaints (grievances) are to be handled.

gross margin The difference between the price that a retailer charges its customers and the price that it paid for the merchandise.

gross national product (GNP) The total national output of goods and services valued at market prices.

gross profit on sales The cost of goods sold subtracted from the net sales figure.

group policy A life insurance policy that is sold on a group rather than on an individual basis; usually purchased by companies for their employees.

growth stage The second stage in a product's life cycle, which occurs after familiarity is established and customers begin to seek the product out.

hardware The physical components that make up a computer installation.

Hawthorne effect The idea that providing workers with self-esteem, positive co-workers, and status—not simply high pay and good working conditions—is the real key to improving employee productivity.

health insurance Insurance that pays the insured for expenses resulting from sickness and for lost earnings that result from sickness.

health maintenance organization (HMO) An organization of health care personnel and facilities that delivers a comprehensive range of health services to voluntary members.

hierachy-of-needs theory A theory of motivation based on the idea that people are motivated by five basic needs that form a hierarchy (physiological, safety, love, esteem, and self-actualization), and as each need is satisfied the one at the next higher level emerges.

HMO See *health maintenance organization*.

horizontal communication Internal communication in which there is contact with someone in another department.

hospital insurance expense Health insurance that protects against the cost of hospital care resulting from illness or injury of the insured person.

human relations management See *personnel management*.

hygiene factor A job factor that is important but does not motivate, such as fringe benefits, pay, and job security.

imperfect competition A market that exists when a product is considered by the consumer to be clearly different in some way from all competing products. Also called *monopolistic competition*.

implied warranty A warranty that does not state in specific terms, but implies, the characteristics of property being sold.

import broker An intermediary who brings a foreign seller and a U.S. buyer together.

import commission house An intermediary who receives goods on consignment from foreign businesses and sells to U.S. buyers.

import license A control used by a government to limit the volume or value of imports permitted.

import merchant A company that buys from foreign firms on its own account and assumes all risks.

income statement A detailed summary of business operations over a specific period of time. Also called *profit-and-loss statement*.

independent retail store A retail store that is separate from any other store in operation and ownership.

index number A statistical device that is used to compare business activity during one time period with similar activity during another time period.

indirect export channel A marketing channel whereby a U.S. manufacturer sells to foreign markets through a third party.

indirect import channel A marketing channel whereby an intermediary in this country purchases goods from a foreign firm.

individual income tax A federal tax on personal income; the government's largest single source of revenue.

individual objective A goal that a specific person will have to achieve if departmental objectives are to be met.

individual proprietorship See *sole proprietorship*.

Individual Retirement Account (IRA) An individual pension plan under which workers may take a tax deduction of up to $2,000 a year and place the funds in a special account at an approved bank, mutual fund, or insurance company.

industrial advertising Advertising that is directed to manufacturers and other industrial users.

industrial concentration A group of similar companies located in one area because of the area's geographic advantages.

industrial consumer A business that purchases industrial goods.

industrial good A product used to make other products or to operate a business.

industrial park A land area with buildings that have been planned and developed as optimal environments for industrial occupants.

industrial robot A reprogrammable multifunctional manipulator designed to move materials, parts, tools, or specialized devices through variable programmed motions for the performance of a variety of tasks.

industry-wide collective bargaining Collective bargaining in which the negotiations are held for an entire industry.

inelastic demand Demand that is comparatively insensitive to changes in price.

informal evaluation Evaluation that is based solely on observation of an employee's performance.

informal investigation The second step in the research procedure, which should result in a concise definition of the problem and determination of the most logical method of collecting the data needed to solve it.

informal organization Organization that is created by the members of the group and consists of people who usually work together and elect their own leader.

injunction A court order directing a person or persons to refrain from a certain act or acts.

inland marine insurance Insurance that protects against (1) risks while goods are being transported by ship, truck, plane, or railroad or (2) risk of fire, theft, and other hazards to personal property while a person is away from home.

inland transportation insurance A type of inland marine insurance that covers goods being transported not only by water but by truck, plane, and railroad as well.

input Data or instructions fed to a computer.

installment credit Credit for which the customer's obligation is repaid in fractional amounts at stated intervals after the purchase is made.

institutional advertising Advertising that attempts to enhance the image of a business.

insurable interest A clear interest in insured property.

insurable risk A risk for which an insurance company is willing to insure, determined by predictability, possible financial loss, pure risk, insurable interest, and the absence of moral hazard.

insurance A process in which an insurance company agrees, for a sum of money (the premium), which is paid by the buyer (the insured), to pay the buyer a certain sum if he or she should suffer a specified loss.

intangible asset An asset that does not have tangible form but is of value to a business, such as a patent or a copyright.

intelligence test A test that tries to measure mental abilities, such as verbal comprehension, word fluency, memory, facility with numbers, and speed of perception.

interest rate The price that must be paid to borrow money.

interlocking directorate The situation in which a director of one company also serves on the board of a competitor.

international trade The management of business between countries; the application of efficiency and good business judgment to the conduct of business between domestic and foreign organizations.

introductory stage The first stage in a product's life cycle, which requires the greatest promotional effort and is the riskiest segment of the product's life.

inventory A stock of raw materials, supplies, work in progress, and finished goods held for sale.

investment asset A fund invested in the securities of another corporation for income or to control the second company.

investment bank A bank that specializes in helping corporations acquire long-term capital and thus acts as an intermediary between a corporation that wants to sell securities and the investing public.

investment company See *mutual fund.*

involuntary bankruptcy Bankruptcy proceedings initiated by the creditors of a person or a business.

IRA See *Individual Retirement Account.*

issued stock That portion of authorized stock that has been sold.

job analysis A systematic detailed study of the work to be done in a specific position.

jobber See *full-service wholesaler.*

job description A detailed statement explaining the specific tasks to be performed, the reporting relationships of the jobholder, and the results expected.

job enlargement The process of adding more responsibilities and tasks to an employee's present job.

job enrichment The process of designing jobs to make them more interesting, challenging, and meaningful.

job redesign The process of restructuring a job to make the work more appealing to the employee.

job specification A statement of the qualifications a person must have to perform the work involved.

joint venture A group of people or businesses who combine under an agreement to carry out a particular transaction or project. Also called *syndicate.* Also, an arrangement whereby a U.S. firm and a foreign firm combine interests, usually to finance a new, third company in the foreign country.

journal A chronological record of all accounting transactions of a company.

Keogh Plan An individual pension plan for the self-employed, similar to the IRA except the maximum is $15,000 annually or 15 percent of earnings, whichever is less.

keyboard The part of a computer that looks essentially like a modified typewriter, with additional function keys to control the computer. Also called *terminal.*

label A marker that identifies a product; a complete label also identifies the producer, where the product was produced, the ingredients and weight, and instructions for use.

labor Human energy expended to perform the various tasks associated with the production and distribution of goods and services.

labor force All people over 16 years of age who are willing and able to work and who are either employed or seeking employment.

Labor-Management Relations Act See *Taft-Hartley Act*.

Labor Management Reporting and Disclosure Act See *Landrum-Griffin Act*.

labor union An association of nonmanagement employees that is formed to maintain and advance the economic and working conditions of its members.

laissez faire An economic system in which business is conducted with relatively little interference or direction from the government.

Landrum-Griffin Act (1959) A law that is directed mainly at the regulation of the internal affairs of unions. Also called *Labor-Management Reporting and Disclosure Act*.

large-scale integration (LSI) A computer technology that uses chips of silicon the size of a pinhead as electronic circuits.

law of agency A relationship whereby one person is authorized to act for another in transactions with a third party.

law of averages See *law of large numbers*.

law of comparative advantages The principle that a nation has some advantages—technology, wage, climate, resources, land—over other nations in producing certain products and services.

law of employer-employee The principle that the relationship between employer and employee is contractual even when no written agreement is used.

law of large numbers A mathematical law that holds that out of a very large number of similar risks, only a certain number of losses will occur. Also called *law of averages*.

law of supply and demand A principle stating that if supply is greater than demand, the buyer has the advantage and a lower price will result, and that if supply is less than demand, the seller has the advantage and a higher price will be set.

leasing An important business practice designed, among other things, to reduce initial capital requirements, whereby a firm rents rather than buys equipment.

level-premium plan A life insurance policy for which the insured pays the same amount each year.

leveraged buyout (LBO) The situation in which the new owner or owners of a corporation (often the managers themselves) borrow heavily to buy out public stockholders of the corporation.

liability Money a company owes to bankers, employees, suppliers, holders of bonds, and other creditors.

liability insurance Insurance against the chance of loss resulting from injury to another person or damage to that person's property. Also called *third-party insurance*.

licensee See *franchisee*.

licenser See *franchisor*.

licensing agreement An agreement made between a manufacturer in this country and a manufacturer abroad (the licensee) whereby the licensee obtains rights to sell a product in a specified market on a royalty basis.

lie detector test See *polygraph test*.

lien The situation in which a seller passes title to a buyer but retains either possession of the goods or the right to their possession.

life insurance Insurance that provides financial benefits to the beneficiary—or to a company—when death of the insured occurs.

limited-function wholesaler A wholesaler who does not grant credit or make deliveries.

limited liability Liability limited to the amount of capital partners have contributed to the firm unless otherwise stated in the agreement.

limited-line retailer A retailer that carries only part of a broader merchandise line. Also called *specialty store*.

limited order An order to a broker to purchase securities at a specified price on a certain day only, unless a longer time period is specified.

limited partnership An agreement between one or more general partners, whose liability is unlimited, and one or more special, or limited, partners, whose liability is limited to the amount of capital they have contributed to the firm unless otherwise stated in the agreement.

limited-payment policy A life insurance policy for which premiums are paid not for an entire lifetime but for a definite number of years—usually 20.

line-and-staff organization Organization that is similar to the pure line arrangement in that line managers still make all major decisions and issue orders. However, in this case line managers use the services of staff specialists, none of whom have direct authority except in their own departments.

line graph A graphic device that is used primarily to indicate trends. Also called *curve graph*.

line manager A manager whose orders and authority flow in a straight line from the chief executive down to lower levels in the organization; a line manager is usually involved directly in producing or selling the firm's products or services.

line of credit See *credit limit*.

line organization Organization in which all members perform line functions.

line printer A computer printer that prints one line at a time.

listed security A security that has been approved for trading on an organized securities exchange.

list price A manufacturer's suggested price.

load A commission charged by a mutual fund when shares in the fund are sold to investors.

loading Operational costs of business.

lobby A person or a group of people who try to influence legislation at state and federal levels and gain public sympathy for their cause.

local advertising See *retail advertising*.

long-term capital Money needed for extended periods, used to acquire permanent assets.

long-term liability A debt that extends over more than one year. Also called *fixed liability*.

LSI See *large-scale integration*.

magnetic ink and optical scanner An input/output device that consists of printing in magnetic ink characters that can be read by both people and computers.

mail-order operation A retail arrangement by which consumers order merchandise through a catalog and receive it by mail.

mail questionnaire A type of survey in which a set of questions is sent to a selected group of people.

major medical expense insurance Health insurance that finances the expense of a major illness and injury.

make-or-buy decision A firm's decision about whether to make a part itself or purchase it from another firm.

management The process of achieving an organization's goals through the coordinated performance of five specific functions: planning, organizing, staffing, directing, and controlling.

management by objectives (MBO) A system by which managers let their subordinates participate in setting tangible, usually numerical, work objectives, and then periodically discuss with subordinates what progress has been made, revising the goals if necessary.

mandatory law A law that forces a business to do something.

manufacturer's agent An agent intermediary who sells only a part of a producer's output, is limited as to the territory he or she can cover, has limited authority over price and terms of sale, and rarely finances his or her principals.

manufacturer's excise tax An excise tax levied on the manufacturer, who adds it to the cost of the product.

manufacturer's suggested price A price suggested by a manufacturer that sells consumer goods to retailers.

marine insurance Insurance that covers private property (1) being transported by ship, truck, plane, or railroad or (2) while the insured is away from home or while the property is in transit. Also called *transportation insurance*.

market All possible customers for a firm's goods or services.

market description A definition of the total target market for goods and services.

marketing Business activities that involve the movement of goods and services from producers to consumers.

marketing area The territory from which a business draws most of its customers.

marketing concept A marketing approach by which consumer preferences are considered before a product is designed or manufactured.

marketing intermediary A person who performs most marketing functions in the channel of distribution and bridges the gap between producer and consumer. Also called *middleman*.

marketing mix The combination of the four P's (product, place, price, and promotion) to satisfy consumer demands.

marketing research The systematic gathering, recording, and analyzing of data about problems relating to the marketing of goods and services.

marketing strategy The overall plan a business creates to market its product.

market order An order to a broker to purchase securities immediately, at the current market price.

market segment A submarket.

market value The price offered on the market at a given time.

markup The difference between what a retailer pays for goods and their selling price; generally expressed as a percentage of either cost or selling price.

mass production The large-scale production of goods using standard, interchangeable parts.

maturity date The time at which principal is due.

maturity stage The third stage in a product's life cycle, during which marketing management should (1) look for ways to improve the product that will extend its life cycle (or start a new life cycle if the improvements are significant enough) or (2) gradually phase out the item and replace it with another product.

MBO See *management by objectives*.

mechanization The substitution of mechanical effort for human effort and the process by which people and machines work according to systematic procedures.

median A type of average that is the midpoint of a series of items arranged in order from smallest to largest. Also called *position average*.

mediation An attempt to settle labor disputes with the assistance of a disinterested third party.

Medicaid A system of state public health assistance to persons, regardless of age, whose income and resources are insufficient to pay for health care.

Medicare A hospital insurance system and supplementary medical insurance for the aged created by 1965 amendments to the Social Security Act.

member See *franchisee*.

member firm A brokerage firm whose partner or officer is a member of the NYSE or AMEX.

mercantile credit See *open-account credit*.

merchant wholesaler An intermediary who takes title to the products in which he or she deals and assumes the risks of ownership.

microcomputer A small minicomputer than can perform a broad range of memory and control functions. Also called *computer on a chip*.

microprocessor A computer core consisting of one silicon chip.

middleman See *marketing intermediary*.

middle management The second level of management, which is responsible for developing operational plans and procedures to implement the broader ones conceived by top management.

minicomputer A small general-purpose computer that can perform many of the functions of a large computer.

MNC See *multinational*.

modal average See *mode*.

mode A type of average that is the number that occurs most frequently in a series of data. Also called *modal average*.

monopolistic competition See *imperfect competition*.

monopoly A firm that controls such a large part of the total business done in an industry that it can dictate or control the market prices for the output of that industry.

moral hazard A danger that insured property will be deliberately destroyed by the insured to collect the insurance.

mortgage bond A bond that is secured by a mortgage on fixed assets owned by the corporation.

motion-and-time study A study of a specific act to determine whether it can be performed more quickly and efficiently.

multinational (MNC) A company that has major operating facilities in more than five countries.

municipal bond A bond that is issued by a state or local government. Also called *tax-exempt bond*.

mutual A nonprofit corporation similar to a cooperative but without stockholders; the members are the owners.

mutual fund A company that sells shares to individual investors and uses this capital to invest in the securities of other companies. Also called *investment company*.

mutual savings bank A bank that accepts deposits of individuals, pools them, and then channels them into real-estate mortgages and other productive loans and investments.

narrow span of supervision Supervision in which one manager supervises only a few people.

national advertising Advertising that is used to sell nationally distributed, branded merchandise.

national bank A commercial bank that is chartered by the federal government.

National Labor Relations Act See *Wagner Act.*

National Labor Relations Board (NLRB) A board established to certify the appropriate bargaining representatives of employees and to review and make decisions concerning alleged unfair labor practices.

national resources The tangible and intangible wealth of a nation.

negotiable bond A bond that the original purchaser can sell to someone else.

negotiable instrument A written contractual obligation that is used extensively in business transactions as a substitute for money.

Negotiable Order of Withdrawal account See *NOW account.*

negotiated pricing Pricing in which the seller and buyer bargain over price, usually used for products made to buyer specifications.

negotiating The exchanging of viewpoints in an attempt to seek agreement.

net income See *net sales.*

net profit or loss The figure arrived at by subtracting the cost of goods sold, operating expenses, and administrative expenses from net sales.

net sales The amount of money received by a company for goods sold minus returns and allowances and discounts given to purchasers. Also called *net income.*

New Deal A sweeping program of government-directed economic actions designed to lift the country out of the Depression.

NLRB See *National Labor Relations Board.*

no-fault insurance An insurance plan whereby a victim is entitled to receive specified benefits from his or her own insurance company without regard to fault.

no-load fund A mutual fund that does not charge a sales commission.

no-name brand An unbranded product that is priced below branded products. Also called *generic brand.*

nonbank An enterprise whose primary business is to provide a variety of financial services, such as marketing installment consumer loans, business loans, brokerage services, insurance, real estate mortgages, and credit card loans.

nonbusiness marketing See *social marketing.*

nonbusiness organization See *nonprofit organization.*

noncumulative discount A quantity discount used to encourage large single purchases.

noncumulative dividend A means of paying dividends on preferred stock whereby a company has no obligation to pay skipped dividends.

nonprofit corporation A corporation formed to facilitate the operation of a nonprofit organization.

nonprofit organization An enterprise whose primary purpose is something other than to make money. Also called *nonbusiness organization.*

nonpublic corporation See *private corporation.*

no-par-value stock Stock that has no printed value on the certificates.

notes receivable See *accounts receivable.*

NOW (Negotiable Order of Withdrawal) account An interest-bearing checking account.

objective Any goal that an organization or group seeks to achieve.

observation A procedure for collecting data by actually watching certain events take place.

ocean marine insurance Marine insurance that protects shippers while goods are on the sea or temporarily in port.

OECD See *Organization for Economic Cooperation and Development.*

offer A proposal by one party (the offeror) to enter into a contract with a second party (the offeree).

Office of Advocacy Part of the Small Business Administration, established in 1976, which represents small business in policy decisions and serves as an ombudsman for individual small businesses trying to resolve their problems with other federal agencies.

officer An executive appointed by the board of directors who is responsible for carrying out business policies.

off-line device A separate input/output device that is not part of the main computer installation.

on margin A way of buying securities whereby the customer pays for a certain portion of the purchase and secures credit through the broker for the balance.

OPEC See *Organization of Petroleum Exporting Countries.*

open-account credit The sale of goods by one business to another, with payment expected at a later date. Also called *trade credit, mercantile credit.*

open-market operation The sale and purchase of short-term government securities on the open market by Federal Reserve Banks.

open order An order to a broker to purchase securities at a specific price but with no specified time limit.

operating expense An expense that is incurred in the course of specific business activities.

operating income The net sales of a business, used to operate it.

operating management The lowest level of management, which is concerned primarily with putting into action the operational plans devised by middle management.

operating supply Something used to operate a business.

order bill A bill of lading that does not specify the consignee.

ordinary life policy A life insurance policy that requires that premiums be paid from the date of purchase until death of the insured. Also called *whole-life policy, straight-life policy.*

organization chart A diagram that shows how people and the work they do relate to other people and their activities.

Organization for Economic Cooperation and Development (OECD) A group of 24 nations that was formed to guide the economic fortunes of the noncommunist world.

Organization of Petroleum Exporting Countries (OPEC) A cartel whose aim is to coordinate and unify the petroleum policies of member nations, establish the best means for safeguarding their interests, and stabilize world oil prices so that harmful and unnecessary fluctuations will be eliminated.

organizing The management function of deciding how work will be divided and coordinated; the process of logically grouping activities, delineating authority and responsibility, and establishing working relationships that enable the employees, and thus the entire unit, to work with maximum efficiency and effectiveness.

orientation program A type of internal training that introduces new employees to an organization.

OTC market See *over-the-counter market.*

outlet See *franchise.*

output The result of the data-processing operation.

over-the-counter (OTC) market A market dealing in unlisted securities outside the organized securities exchanges.

owners' equity The right to share in the assets of a business.

package A covering or container that protects and identifies the basic product.

panel interview A type of survey in which the people who form the panel are selected carefully to represent a group typical of those to whom a business wants its product to appeal. Also called *consumer-jury interview.*

participative leader A democratic leader; one who invites subordinates to make suggestions in planning what to do and how to do it.

partnership agreement An oral, written, or implied (by actions of the parties) agreement among partners as to the specifics of the business.

par-value stock Stock that has been assigned a fixed dollar value.

patent An exclusive legal right to a product that is granted by the Patent and Trademark Office for 17 years and is not renewable.

patronage motive The reason people buy where they do.

penetration pricing The practice of pricing below competition to introduce a new product or expand the market for an old one.

per capita income Income per person.

performance evaluation See *results evaluation.*

permissive law A law that a business may take advantage of to protect itself.

personal interview A type of survey in which trained interviewers ask questions of selected people.

personality test A test that tries to measure personal characteristics, such as maturity and temperament.

personal selling The process of personally assisting and convincing a prospective customer to buy a product or service.

personnel management The process of providing an organization with qualified employees and maintaining an atmosphere in which they will be productive and loyal and develop their abilities. Also called *human relations management*.

Peter Principle A theory that holds that most people in organizations are promoted until they reach their level of incompetence.

physician's expense insurance Health insurance that provides benefits toward the cost of such services as doctor's fees for nonsurgical care in a hospital, at home, or in a physician's office, and fees for X-rays and laboratory tests performed outside the hospital.

pictogram A graphic device that is a variation of the bar chart and uses symbols to indicate quantities.

piece-rate plan Compensation whereby workers are paid a certain amount for each unit of work done.

pie chart A graphic device in which the pie equals 100 percent and the items being compared are shown as slices of the pie in proportion to their size.

pilfering Employee theft.

place utility Products' being available where consumers want them.

planned shopping center A group of retail stores developed as a unit and usually located in a suburban shopping area. Also called *controlled shopping center*.

planning The management function of deciding what work will be done and how it will be accomplished.

POE pricing See *port-of-entry pricing*.

point-of-purchase display A device that displays a product near where the purchase decision is made, so as to stimulate immediate sales.

policy A broadly stated course of action that individuals are to follow in making decisions.

polygraph test A test that tries to measure honesty by revealing if stress is present when a person answers certain questions. Also called *lie detector test*.

population See *universe*.

port-of-entry (POE) pricing A geographic price policy by which the buyer pays all shipping charges from the point of entry to the point of delivery.

position average See *median*.

possession utility The possibility of ownership of a product.

POS terminal See *point-of-sale terminal*.

power of attorney A legal tool that establishes a principal-agent relationship by granting someone the authority to act on another person's behalf.

preemptive right A privilege usually accorded to current stockholders whereby subsequent stock issues are offered to them first.

preferred stock Stock that has a preference, such as a stated dividend rate or a specified claim on assets in the event the corporation is dissolved.

premium A kind of sales promotion by which a product is offered free or at a lower price than usual to encourage a consumer to buy another product.

price escalator clause A business's hedge against inflation that calls for an increase in the price of a finished product when the seller's costs increase.

price lining A retail policy of selling all merchandise at one of a set number of prices.

pricing The process of setting prices so as to generate sufficient revenues to cover all direct and indirect costs of doing business and to yield a profit so that the business can survive and prosper.

primary boycott A labor boycott in which employees refuse to patronize only their own employer.

primary source A source of information that supplies original data.

prime contractor A manufacturer that employs a subcontractor.

prime rate The lowest rate of interest that Federal Reserve member banks charge borrowers with the highest credit ratings.

principal An amount of money that is borrowed; also, in law of agency, the party that grants authority to act.

printer The part of a computer, often a separate unit, that prints information either by line or by character; it may vary in regard to functions and printing speeds.

private carrier A carrier that is part of a business that does not specialize in transportation.

private corporation A corporation whose stock is not offered for sale to the public. Also called *nonpublic corporation.*

private enterprise system An economic system under which individuals have certain basic rights and one of whose major objectives is profit making. Also called *free enterprise system, capitalism, profit system.*

procedure A detailed plan of action for handling a specific situation.

process-control computer A computer that controls a physical process.

producer cooperative A cooperative organized to enable producers to obtain better prices for their products than they would if they bargained individually.

product Anything that a business sells; all the peripheral factors that contribute to a customer's satisfaction.

product design The combination of functional design and style design.

product development See *functional design.*

production business A firm that manufactures its own goods.

production planning The determination of where and how to manufacture a product.

productivity Output per hour of work.

product life cycle The duration of a product's popularity, during which there are four stages: introduction, growth, maturity, and decline.

product line Any group of products that are closely related.

product mix The mix of all products offered for sale by a business.

product modification A change that most businesses make in their products in hopes of lengthening the products' life cycles.

professional corporation A special form of corporation for licensed professionals (doctors, dentists, accountants, attorneys, and the like) which permits them to gain tax advantages by incorporating their practices but does not relieve them of responsibility for negligent acts.

profit Income in excess of expenditures.

profit-and-loss statement See *income statement.*

profit maximization An attempt to chose a price that strikes the best balance between costs and revenue.

profit principle The idea that no business can operate at a loss indefinitely.

profit sharing A plan for sharing some of the company's profits with employees after the stockholders have received their returns.

profit system See *private enterprise system.*

program A set of instructions for a computer, usually written by a specially trained programmer.

programmer A person who develops the actual instructions (programs) for a computer based on a systems analyst's specifications.

programming specification A fairly detailed description of the tasks a computer will perform and how each task or process will work in conjunction with all other tasks and processes in the new system.

prohibitive law A law that forbids certain practices by business.

promotion An upward move to a position of more responsibility and greater pay; also, the process of making prospective customers desire a product enough to buy it.

property tax A tax levied against privately owned property.

proprietorship See *sole proprietorship.*

prospecting The process of contacting potential customers to see if they are interested in buying.

proxy A legal statement by which stockholders can transfer the right to cast their votes to someone else.

psychographics The study of how a person's life style affects his or her consumption pattern.

psychological pricing The use of price to suggest either that the product is a bargain or that it is of high quality.

public A special-interest group with the power to influence or potentially influence the welfare of an organization.

public accountant An independent organization or an individual that specializes in selling its services to businesses.

public corporation A corporation whose stock is offered for sale to the general public.

publicity News items about a business, its products, and its personnel; an important part of public relations.

public relations The process by which a business attempts to obtain the good will or favorable attitude of the public.

purchase group An arrangement by which an investment bank invites other investment banks to

Glossary

join in the purchase of a large issue of securities. Also called *underwriting syndicate*.

purchasing The process of buying what is needed in the manufacturing process.

purchasing manager A person in business who is in charge of orders for equipment, supplies, raw materials, and other goods.

pure competition A market that exists when no one seller controls enough of the supply of a product to influence its price in the marketplace.

pure risk A risk in which there is a chance only to lose.

qualified endorsement An endorsement made by writing "without recourse" before the holder's name so that he or she is exempt from liability for the default of the party that is primarily responsible for the payment of the instrument.

qualitative standard of living A measure of how "good" life is in terms of crime, education, the environment, and so on.

quality-of-work-life programming (QWL) The process of installing programs to promote job satisfaction and productivity.

quantitative standard of living A measure of how many products and services are consumed and of per capita income.

quantity discount A discount based either on the dollar value of a transaction or on the number of units involved.

questionnaire technique See *survey*.

QWL See *quality-of-work-life programming*.

random sample A sample that is chosen so that the selection of any member of the universe does not affect the selection of any other member; that is, each unit has the same chance of being included in the sample.

ratio analysis The use of ratios (percentages) to compare the operating results of similar companies.

rational buying motive A buying motive that is based on a logical analysis of why a purchase should or should not be made.

raw material A natural and "nurtured" basic used in the manufacturing process.

real income The amount of goods and services a dollar will buy compared with what a dollar would purchase during a previous year.

real-time system A computer that operates so that output is available quickly enough to control real-life activity.

receipt Money that is paid into a company.

receipt transaction See *income transaction*.

recession A period of well-below-average profits, economic activity, and sales, accompanied by well-above-normal unemployment.

regular wholesaler See *full-service wholesaler*.

regulation See *rule*.

Report Program Generator See *RPG*.

research park An industrial park in which the activities are dominated by research.

reserve In banking, the portion of deposits that a bank keeps on hand to meet the withdrawal demands of depositors; generally, a fund set aside to meet future obligations.

restrictive endorsement An endorsement that restricts the negotiability of an instrument to a specific purpose.

results evaluation Evaluation that assesses what an employee actually accomplishes over a period of time; that is, it deals with measurable achievements, such as units produced, volume sold, and costs reduced. Also called *performance evaluation*.

retail advertising Advertising that is much more specific than national advertising in describing price and terms of sale; it informs consumers exactly where and when the product or service can be purchased. Also called *local advertising*.

retailer A business outlet that sells principally to ultimate consumers.

retailer's excise tax An excise tax that is collected by the retailer.

retailing The activities involved in selling directly to the ultimate consumer.

retirement benefits Benefits paid under Social Security to covered workers who have reached the age of 62 (minimum).

revitalization The process of turning the country around economically.

rider A supplement to a standard insurance policy.

right-to-work law A law that prohibits requiring a person to join a union in order to keep his or her job.

risk rating A determination of a bond issuer's ability to meet the promises specified on a bond.

Robinson-Patman Act (1936) An act that regulates marketing activity.

RPG (Report Program Generator) A computer language that is specifically designed for business applications.

rule The most detailed form of a plan. Also called *regulation*.

salary Compensation paid on a weekly, monthly, or annual basis.
sales finance company A company that specializes in financing the sale of automobiles and other durable goods, such as sewing machines and refrigerators.
sales manager The person who directs the activities of a sales force.
sales tax A tax on retail sales.
sample A kind of sales promotion by which a product is given away to consumers in an effort to build consumer demand; also, a relatively small number that would have the same characteristics as the larger group from which it is taken.
savings account An account that earns interest and from which withdrawals are permitted only on presentation of a passbook. Also called *time deposit*.
savings and loan association An organization that accepts deposits from savers and invests this capital in local home mortgages.
SBA See *Small Business Administration*.
S corporation A special form of corporate ownership in which taxable income passes directly to the individual stockholder.
seasonal discount A discount that is offered during an off-season by businesses that market products for which demand is seasonal.
secondary boycott A labor boycott in which employees refuse to handle, process, manufacture, or transport goods of a second employer that is accused of being unfair to its employees.
secondary source A source of information that supplies information already collected from primary sources.
secured obligation A short-term obligation that is backed by the pledge of some asset.
securities exchange An organized market that provides a meeting place for buyers and sellers of stocks and bonds. Also called *stock exchange*.
Securities Exchange Act (1934) An act meant to prevent abuses in stock market transactions.
security A common stock, a preferred stock, or a bond, through which a business obtains long-term capital.
self-actualization Doing what one most wants to do with one's life.
self-insurance The setting aside of a financial reserve that can be drawn on when losses occur. Also called *underwriting one's own insurance*.
seller See *franchisor*.
selling agent An agent intermediary who handles the entire output of the principal he or she represents, has a continuous contractual relationship with the principal, and sells in unlimited territories.
semimanufactured good A processed material that will be further processed.
serial-plan method A method of retiring bonds by which they are retired each year according to the numbers on them.
service business An organization that provides assistance but does not produce or distribute a tangible good.
service wholesaler See *full-service wholesaler*.
shareholder See *stockholder*.
Sherman Antitrust Act (1890) An act of Congress passed to curb the growth of trusts and monopolies, which threatened free competition.
shoplifting Customer theft.
shopping good A good of relatively high unit value, purchased infrequently, and often bought only after a customer has compared several offerings as to price, style, quality, and general suitability.
short-term capital Money that is needed to purchase raw materials and goods that are to be resold, pay wages and salaries, and meet other obligations of debts that fall due in the short term (usually 12 months or less.) Also called *working capital*.
signature loan A loan made with no co-signer.
single-line retailer A retail store that specializes in only one basic product.
single proprietorship See *sole proprietorship*.
sinking-fund plan A method of retiring bonds by which periodic deposits of an amount that will ensure that money is available at maturity are made with the trustee.
small business A business that is independently owned and operated and is not dominant in its field of operation.
Small Business Administration (SBA) A permanent, independent government agency created by Congress to advise and assist small business enterprises.

small loan company See *consumer finance company.*

SMSA See *Standard Metropolitan Statistical Area.*

social auditing Auditing that tends to cover such things as social goals, energy conservation, ethics, safety, minority employment, and community activities.

social costs of unemployment The negative effects of unemployment on society.

social insurance A group of programs established by the Social Security Act of 1935 that provide protection against wage loss resulting from old age, prolonged disability, or death, and protection against the cost of medical care during old age and disability. Also called *Social Security.*

social insurance tax A federal tax earmarked for retirement, disability, and other insurance-related benefits; the second largest source of federal revenue. Also called *Social Security.*

socialism An economic system in which the country's major resources and industries are owned by the government.

social marketing The application of marketing concepts and techniques to promote worthwhile social goals. Also called *nonbusiness marketing.*

social responsibility The duty of business to promote (or at least not damage) the welfare of society.

Social Security See *social insurance, social insurance tax.*

software The programs used to give a computer its instructions.

software package A generalized packaged computer program that is used for tasks that are performed in a similar fashion by many different businesses.

sole proprietorship A business owned by a single person who receives all profits and assumes all risks. Also called *single proprietorship, individual proprietorship, proprietorship.*

span of supervision The number of persons one manager can supervise effectively.

special endorsement See *full endorsement.*

specialty good A good that is found in few retail outlets, commands much customer loyalty, and is relatively high priced.

specialty store See *limited-line retailer.*

speculative risk A risk in which there is a chance to gain or lose.

spread An investment bank's commission for selling securities.

staffing The management function of selecting, training, compensating, and evaluating people so that the work in an organization is performed according to established standards.

staff manager A manager whose orders and authority do not flow in a straight line down from the top of the organization; a staff manager is usually a technically trained specialist and is employed to advise and inform line and other staff executives on specialized problems.

standard A preestablished performance level.

standard cost A figure that indicates what the cost of an activity should be.

Standard Metropolitan Statistical Area (SMSA) An integrated economic and social unit with a large population nucleus.

standard policy A basic contract form for an insurance policy.

state bank A commerical bank that is chartered by a state.

statistics The collection, analysis, interpretation, and presentation of numerical data.

stock A share of ownership in a corporation.

stock company A corporation owned and operated by stockholders for profit.

stock exchange See *securities exchange.*

stockholder An owner of a share of a corporation's stock. Also called *shareholder.*

straight bill A bill of lading stating that the goods are being shipped to a specific person.

straight-life policy See *ordinary life policy.*

strategic control point A measurable activity that can make or break an enterprise, such as income, expenses, and inventory.

strategy A broad-based plan to achieve the objectives of an organization.

strike A deliberate work stoppage or slowdown to force management to grant concessions.

strikebreaker A new employee hired in an effort to cause a regular striking worker to return to work out of fear that his or her job might be lost permanently.

stub In a statistical table, the part that tells what the data in the horizontal rows represent.

style design The phase of product design that adds attractiveness, distinctiveness, and aesthetic value to the product.

Subchapter S See *S corporation.*

subcontracted production service A portion of a job contracted by one firm to another, more specialized firm.

subdivision regulation A community's regulation about such matters as sewage disposal and public facilities to be provided.

suicide clause A statement in a life insurance policy to the effect that in the event the insured commits suicide within two years after purchasing the policy, the company will pay the beneficiary only the amount of the premiums paid, not the face value of the policy.

supermarket Principally a self-service retail food store, although fast-moving nonfood items are sold as well.

supply-side economics The theory that states that stimulating the elements of the productive process—capital investment, savings, productivity, work effort, and initiative—will improve the economy.

surety bond A type of insurance against the failure of a second party to fulfill an obligation.

surgical expense insurance Health insurance that provides benefits toward the physician's or surgeon's operating fees.

survey A procedure for collecting data by asking questions. Also called *questionnaire technique.*

sweepstake A kind of sales promotion by which a participant enters his or her name, which has a chance of being drawn from a "pot" containing all other consumer-entrants' names, and may win a prize.

syndicate See *joint venture.*

systems analyst A person who decides what a computer will do and how it will do it.

Taft-Hartley Act (1947) A law meant to equalize the rights and privileges of management and labor. Also called *Labor-Management Relations Act.*

target market The most likely purchasers of a product.

tariff A tax or customs duty levied on imported goods.

tax-exempt bond See *municipal bond.*

telemarketing A type of non-store retailing whereby a consumer sees a product advertised on television and orders it either by calling a toll-free 800 number or by writing to an address.

terminal See *keyboard.*

term policy A life insurance policy that pays a given sum of money to the insured's beneficiary if death occurs during the term of the policy.

Theory X A style of managing in which the typical worker is viewed negatively.

Theory Y A style of managing in which the typical worker is viewed positively.

third-party insurance See *liability insurance.*

time deposit See *savings account.*

time utility Products' being available when people want them.

top management The highest level of management, which determines the broad objectives and policies of the company.

tort law See *fault law.*

trade advertising Type of advertising that tells retailers and wholesalers what to stock and conveys messages about price, markups, special offers, discounts, point-of-purchase materials, and other information retailers and wholesalers want to know.

trade association A nonprofit organization that represents the common interests of its members, who belong to the same industry.

trade credit See *open-account credit.*

trade discount A discount that is awarded by producers to wholesale and retail merchants for help in performing marketing functions.

trademark A brand name, symbol, or other device that has been officially registered by an owner or a manufacturer and is legally restricted to that person's use.

trait evaluation Evaluation that assesses employees in terms of personal characteristics. Also called *attribute evaluation.*

transportation The movement of raw materials, components, parts, and other items from the point where they are produced to the point where they are processed or assembled and on to the point of ultimate purchase.

transportation insurance See *marine insurance.*

transportation mix A combination of different modes of transportation and specific carriers.

trust department A department in a bank that manages funds of individuals or businesses.

trust indenture See *bond indenture.*

ultimate consumer Anyone who purchases products for personal or family use.

underwriter The insurance company or agent that writes the insurance, or the insurance company employee who determines the acceptability of risks, the premium, and so on.

underwriting one's own insurance See *self-insurance*.

underwriting syndicate See *purchase group*.

unemployment insurance Social insurance that guarantees people income for a period of time after becoming unemployed.

uniform delivered pricing A geographic price policy by which the entire country is regarded as one zone, so that the same charge is made to ship goods anywhere in the country.

union contract A legal document that spells out the terms of and procedures for the relationship between an employer and a union.

union shop A situation in which management may hire any employee it wishes, but he or she must join the union within a certain period of time.

unissued stock Authorized stock that has not yet been offered for sale.

Universal Product Code (UPC) A method of identification by which a product is assigned both a manufacturer and a product number, which are translated into a machine-readable symbol, printed on packages, and read by an optical scanner.

universe The larger group from which a sample is taken; it includes all things or entities that might have been selected. Also called *population*.

unlimited liability Liability wherein creditors may have the owner's personal possessions attached if debts are not paid by the business.

unsecured obligation A short-term obligation that involves no collateral and thus is usually available only if a firm has a high credit rating.

UPC See *Universal Product Code*.

variable cost A cost that varies with volume of business.

vending machine A nonpersonal self-service type of retailing.

video terminal A computer output device that displays images electronically rather than mechanically.

voluntary bankruptcy Bankruptcy proceedings initiated by the person or organization wishing to be declared bankrupt.

voluntary chain See *voluntary group*.

voluntary group A group of independently owned retailing establishments that have banded together to create the impression that they constitute a corporate chain. Also called *voluntary chain*.

wage Compensation based on the number of hours worked.

Wagner Act (1935) A law that assures workers in any plant the right to organize and bargain collectively with their employers. Also called *National Labor Relations Act*.

warehouse receipt A receipt issued by a warehouse that serves as title to the stored merchandise and can be used as collateral by the owner of the merchandise.

warranty A seller's legal promise that property being sold is or will be as represented.

whole-life policy See *ordinary life policy*.

wholesaler A business that sells to customers who buy for resale or for industrial and institutional use.

wide span of supervision Supervision in which one manager supervises many people.

word processing (WP) The transformation of ideas and information into a readable form of communication through the management of procedures, equipment, and personnel.

working capital See *short-term capital*.

workmen's compensation Social insurance that provides insurance protection in the event of work-connected injury or death.

WP See *word processing*.

yield The annual dividend of a stock divided by the current price.

youth differential A proposed special minimum wage for employees under the age of 21 and for students.

zone delivered pricing A geographical price policy by which the nation is divided into two or more zones, so that a flat transportation charge is then made on a per-zone basis.

zoning regulation A community's regulation about how land may be used.

CREDITS

All illustrations are by Greg Lloyd.

Figures

10-8 Copyright 1984 Time, Inc. All rights reserved. Reprinted by permission from Time. **13-2** L. J. Carter, "Research Triangle Park Succeeds Beyond Its Promoters' Expectations," *Science*, Vol. 200, 30 June 1978, pp. 1469–1470. Copyright 1978 by the American Association for the Advancement of Science.

Photos

pp. 2-3 © Ellis Herwig/Stock, Boston. **4** © Alan Carey/The Image Works. **5** © Roger W. Neal. **12** © Griffith/Veronneau. **13** © James L. Shaffer. **19** Wide World Photos. **20** Library of Congress. **26** *top*, © Grant Heilman, Lititz, Pa.; *bottom*, Sovfoto/Eastfoto. **29** Library of Congress. **36** © Bohdan Hrynewych/Stock, Boston. **37** © Alan Carey/The Image Works. **39** and **41** © Griffith/Veronneau. **56** Wide World Photos. **58** © Mark Antman/The Image Works. **64** © Melanie Kaestner/Zephyr Pictures. **65** Sharloh Hall Museum. **72** © Bohdan Hrynewych/Stock, Boston. **78** © Michael Weisbrot/Stock, Boston. **79** © Griffith/Veronneau. **92** Wide World Photos. **93** © Michael D. Sullivan/TexaStock. **96** © George W. Gardner. **98** © Peter Menzel/Stock, Boston. **105** UPI/Bettmann Newsphotos. **107** © Harry Wilks/Stock, Boston. **109** UPI SunRadiophoto/Bettmann Newsphotos. **122-23** © Peter Menzel/Stock, Boston. **124** © Charles Gupton/Stock, Boston. **125** © Hazel Hankin/Stock, Boston. **128** © Mark Antman/The Image Works. **135** Federal Express Corporation. **144** Reprinted from the November, 1980 issue of Venture, The Magazine for Entrepreneurs, by special permission. © 1980 Venture Magazine, Inc., New York, N.Y. **152** © Risque/Irwin. **153** © Janice Fullman/The Picture Cube. **156** © James Holland/Stock, Boston. **163** © Alan Carey/The Image Works. **171** © Stuart Silverstone. **180** © Mark Antman/The Image Works. **189** © Barbara Alper/Stock, Boston. **196** © The Bettmann Archive. **210** Wide World Photos. **211** © Walter S. Silver/The Picture Cube. **218** © Owen Franken/Stock, Boston. **220** Wide World Photos. **221** © Miro Vintoniv/Stock, Boston. **224** © Bob Daemmrich/TexaStock. **233** *top*, *left*, © Mark Antman/The Image Works; *right*, © Michael D. Sullivan/TexaStock; *bottom*, *left*, © Peter Cartsanyi/EKM-Nepenthe; *right*, © Eric Neurath/Stock, Boston. **248-49** © Michael D. Sullivan/TexaStock. **250** © Roger W. Neal. **251** HUD. **260** Four Winds Enterprises, Photo by Edward A. Golich. **262** © Dan McCoy/Rainbow. **269** *left*, © Peter Menzel/Stock, Boston; *right*, © Griffith/Veronneau. **276** Courtesy of Fred Bureau. **282** © Roger W. Neal. **283** © Alan Carey/The Image Works. **290** © Jeffrey Muir Hamilton/Newsweek, May 6, 1985. **295** © Michal Heron/Woodfin Camp & Associates. **301** © Roger W. Neal. **305** © Alan Carey/The Image Works. **314** © HBJ Photo. **315** © Griffith/Veronneau. **317** *left*, © Griffith/Veronneau; *center*, © Carolyn McKeone; *right*, © Richard Wood/The Picture Cube. **323** © Stephen Ferry/Gamma Liaison. **328** © Griffith/Veronneau. **344** and **345** © Roger W. Neal. **348** © Hazel Hankin/Stock, Boston. **354** © James Nachtwey/Black Star. **355** © Roger W. Neal. **370** © Ellis Herwig/The Picture Cube. **371** Courtesy of Chrysler Corporation. **373** Bureau of Reclamation, U.S. Department of the Interior. **382** Courtesy of Chrysler Corporation. **387** © Elizabeth Hamlin/Stock, Boston. **391** © Ellis Herwig/Stock, Boston. **396-97** HBJ Photo. **398** © Gale Zucker/Stock, Boston. **399** © Ken Karp. **405** Photograph courtesy of Genentech, Inc. **410** Courtesy of Peter Drucker. **423** Dana Corp. **424**

I.T.T. **428** © Michal Heron/Woodfin Camp & Associates. **429** © Alan Carey/The Image Works. **435** © Alan Carey/The Image Works. **442** © Peter Southwick/Stock, Boston. **443** © Owen Franken/Stock, Boston. **452** Courtesy of John J. Allen. **464** Wide World Photos. **465** © Robert V. Eckert, Jr./EKM-Nepenthe. **466** © Bob Daemmrich/TexasStock. **471** © Melanie Kaestner/Zephyr Pictures. **478** © Photo by Lewis Hine, International Center of Photography at George Eastman House. **483** © Ellen Shub/The Picture Cube. **484** UPI/Bettmann Newsphotos. **485** © John Manos/The Picture Cube. **496–97** © Christopher S. Johnson/Stock, Boston. **498** © Richard Wood/The Picture Cube. **499** © John Maher/EKM-Nepenthe. **506** © Mark Antman/The Image Works. **509** © Harry W. Rinehart. **519** © Drawing by Mankoff; © 1982 The New Yorker Magazine, Inc. **526** © Peter Legrand/Kay Reese and Associates. **527** © Alan Carey/The Image Works. **530** © David Burnett/Contact. **534** © Charles Gatewood. **535** © Andrew Brilliant/The Picture Cube. **549** © Steven Stone/The Picture Cube. **560** © Laverty/Gamma Liaison. **561** © Thomas McInnes/The Picture Cube. **570** © Bob Daemmrich/TexaStock. **572** MCI Electronic Mail. **573** © Alan Carey/The Image Works. **575** © Eric Neurath/Stock, Boston. **590–91** © Ira Kirschenbaum/Stock, Boston. **592** Peat, Marwick and Mitchell. **593** Four Winds Enterprises, Photo by Edward A. Golich. **613** © Helen Faye; General Foods Corp. **622** © Harry W. Rinehart. **623** Aer Lingus. **624** Wide World Photos. **625** Courtesy of The Coca Cola Company. **632** Wide World Photos. **639** © Ellis Herwig/The Picture Cube. **643** © Helen Faye. **654** Courtesy of The Red Cross. **655** © Paul Vandermark/Stock, Boston. **660** Courtesy of The American Cancer Society. **663** Courtesy of The American Red Cross. **665** Courtesy of The Arthritis Foundation. **667** Courtesy of Nathaniel P. Woods. **676** © Frank Sitemen/The Picture Cube.

Copyrights and Acknowledgments

pp. **7** Reprinted by permission from *The Economist Newspaper.* **42** Reprinted from the June 20, 1983 issue of *Business Week* by special permission, © 1983 by McGraw-Hill, Inc. **87, 99, 116, 364, 595** Reprinted by permission from the *Business & Society Review* 1982, 1983 & 1984 respectively. Published by Warren, Gorham & Lamont, Inc., 210 South St., Boston, MA 02111. Copyright © 1982, 1983, 1984. All rights reserved. **110** Both tables are reprinted from *Public Opinion* (August/September 1980), pp. 15, 16, by permission of the American Enterprise Institute. **115** Reprinted with permission, *INC.* magazine (June, 1980). Copyright © 1980 by INC. Publishing Company, 38 Commercial Wharf, Boston, MA 02110. **193** Reprinted by permission of Barron's, © Dow Jones & Company, Inc. 1984. All rights reserved. **196** Reprinted by permission of *The Wall Street Journal*, Educational Edition only, © Dow Jones & Company, Inc. 1984. All rights reserved. **197** Reprinted by permission of Dow Jones & Company. **198** Reprinted by permission of Dow Jones & Company. **216** Eleanor Johnson Tracy, *Fortune*, © 1984 Time Inc. All rights reserved. **257** Reprinted from the November 26, 1984 issue of *Business Week* by special permission, © 1984 by McGraw-Hill, Inc. **329** From *Marketing Today*, Third Edition, David Schwartz, copyright © 1981 by Harcourt Brace Jovanovich, Inc. Reprinted by permission of the publisher. **337** NCR Corporation © 1981. **356** Reprinted with permission from the April 16, 1984 issue of *Advertising Age*. Copyright 1984 by Crain Communications, Inc. **365** Patricia Sellers, *Fortune*, © 1985 Time Inc. All rights reserved. **366** From *Marketing Today*, Second Edition, by David Schwartz, copyright © 1977 by Harcourt Brace Jovanovich, Inc. Reprinted by permission of the publisher. **403** From *So You Want to Be a Manager?* by Francis J. Bridges, copyright 1984 by ESM Books. Reprinted by permission. **432** From *Creative Supervision* by Karen R. Gillespie, copyright © 1981 by Harcourt Brace Jovanovich, Inc. Reprinted by permission of the publisher. **436** From *Professional Development: The Dynamics of Success* by Mary Wilkes and C. Bruce Crosswait, copyright © 1981 by Harcourt Brace Jovanovich, Inc. Reprinted by permission of the publisher. **445** Reprinted from the May 10, 1982 issue of *Business Week* by special permission, © 1982 by McGraw-Hill, Inc. **472** Reprinted from the December 17, 1984 issue of *Business Week* by special permission, © 1984 by McGraw-Hill, Inc. **480** From *This Is the AFL–CIO*, American Federation of Labor and Congress of Industrial Organizations, Washington, D.C., 1984, no. 20, 6, 7. Reprinted by permission. **517** Questions from *Introduction to Management* by David Schwartz, copyright © 1983 by Harcourt Brace Jovanovich, Inc. Reprinted by permission of the publisher. **551** Excerpt from "The Elephant's Child," from *Rudyard Kipling's Verse, Definitive Edition.* Used by permission of the National Trust, The Macmillan Company of London & Basingstoke, and Doubleday & Company, Inc. **583** Reprinted from the September 1, 1980 issue of *Business Week* by special permission, © 1980 by McGraw-Hill, Inc. **656** From *Marketing Today*, Third Edition, by David Schwartz, copyright © 1981 by Harcourt Brace Jovanovich, Inc. Reprinted by permission of the publisher. **668** From *Introduction to Management* by David Schwartz, copyright © 1983 by Harcourt Brace Jovanovich, Inc. Reprinted by permission of the publisher. **680, 681** Copyright © 1982 *College Placement Annual*. Reproduced with permission of the CPC Foundation. **682** Copyright © 1982 *College Placement Annual*. Reproduced with permission of the College Placement Council.

INDEX

A

Accountants
 certified public (CPAs), 506
 public, 506–507
 role of, in business, 500–502, 504
Accounting, 500–518
 auditing, 514–18
 bookkeeping versus, 501
 defined, 500
 as a profession, 504–506
 ratio analysis and, 513–14
 retail versus manufacturing, 506
 standard costs and cost, 514
 statements and, 509–13
Accounting process, 508–509
Accounts payable, 511
Accounts receivable, 143–44, 509
Achievement tests, 434
Actuary, 214n
Adjustable rate mortgages (ARMs)
 advantages and disadvantages of, 204–205
 defined, 204
Administrative expenses, 513
Advertising
 criticisms of, 358–60
 defined, 346
 personal selling versus, 352–53
 as a promotional tool, 351–60

 public relations versus, 363
 types of, 354–55
Advertising agencies, 357–58
Advertising medium, 355–56
Advocacy, 77
Affirmative action, 101–102
Aftermarket, 195
Age Discrimination Employment Act (1967), 435
Agency for Consumer Advocacy, 97
Agent, in law of agency, 603
Agent intermediaries, 273–74
 manufacturers', 274
 merchandise brokers, 273–74
 selling, 274
Agent wholesalers, 273
Allen, John J., profile of, 452–53
American Cancer Society, 674–76
American Federation of Labor (AFL), 478–80
 goals of, 480–81
 merging of CIO and, 479–80
 origin of, 478–79
American Institute of Certified Public Accountants, 506
American Stock Exchange (AMEX), 49
 future integration with NYSE and OTC, 190

 interpreting stock quotations of, 197–98
 membership of, 183–84
 trading procedures of, 183–87
Analog function, 575–76
Annual report, 516
 defined, 195, 515
Aptitude tests, 134
Arbitration, 487
Area-wide collective bargaining, 486
Arithmetic average, 542
Arithmetic mean, 542
Assessment centers, 442
Assets
 defined, 509
 types of, 509–10
Assignment of contract, 601–602
Attribute evaluation, 450
Auditing, 514–18
 defined, 514
 social, 515–17
Authorized stock, 129
Autocratic leaders, 457
Automated clearinghouse (ACH), 158
Automatic reinvestment of distributions, 192
 defined, 195
Automatic teller machines (ATMs),

716

155, 158–59
Automation, 382
Automobile insurance, 221–25
  collision coverage, 221
  comprehensive coverage, 222
  deductible coverage, 221
  determining premiums of, 222–23
  fire and theft coverage, 222
  full-coverage, 221
  liability coverage, 222
Average, 541–43

B

Balance of payments, 643
Balance of trade, 643–44
Balance sheet, 511
  defined, 509
Bankruptcy, 608–11
  Chapters in, 608–609
  defined, 608
Bankruptcy Amendments and Federal Judgeship Act (1984), 608
Banks, 156–61
  commercial, 156–59
  investment, 159–60
  mutual savings, 160
  response of, to supercompany competition, 172
  savings and loan associations, 160–61
Bar chart, 550
Bear market, 195
Better Business Bureau
  defined, 97–98
  role of, 98
Bill of lading, 145
Bill payment by phone (BPP), 159
Binary code, 582
Biodegradable packaging materials, 325
Blank endorsement, 606
Blue Cross Association (Plan), 235
Blue Shield Association (Plan), 235
Board of directors
  defined, 56
  of nonprofit organizations, 667
  responsibilities of, 56–57
Board of Governors of the Federal Reserve System, 194
Bona fide occupational qualification (BFOQ), 433
Bondholders, 133–34
Bond indenture, 134
Bond quotations, 199–200

Bonds, 127, 133–38
  advantages to corporation, 134
  classification of, 199
  defined, 133
  denominations of, 136
  determining interest on, 137
  fidelity, 226
  financing through, 133–38
  indenture, 134
  interest payments on, 136
  methods of retiring, 136–37
  negotiable, 134
  price fluctuation of, 137–38
  quotations, 199–201
  risk rating of municipal, 200
  surety, 226
  types of, 137
Bond trustee, 136
Bonus, 447
Bookkeepers, role of, 501
Bookkeeping, accounting versus, 501
Boycotts, 483
Branding, 327–29
Brand name, 327–29
Breach of contract, 602
Break-even analysis, 334
Broker
  discount, 186
  full-service, 186
  merchandise, 273–74
  security, 184
Budget, 518–20
Building codes, 375
Bull market, 195
Bureau, Fred, profile of, 276–77
Bureaucracy, 416 n
Bureau of International Commerce (BIC), 644–45
Bureau of Labor Statistics, 544
Business
  accounting for, 500–520
  application of marketing concept to, 258–62
  classification of retailers by, 267–69
  computers and, 562–85
  credit investigation of a, 173–74
  credit management in, 172–75
  crime and, 614–17
  defined, 6
  effects on society, 94
  forms of, 38
  group insurance policies for, 230
  information sources for, 536–39
  international, 624–50

law, 594–618
long-term financing of, 126–47
management of, 400–424
non-store retail, 270–71
partnerships in, 44–47
protecting against risk, 212–16
reasons for listing shares of, 184
relation of labor unions to, 476–83
reports, 550–54
research, 528–56
role played by government in, 102–109, 116–17
short-term financing of, 139–45
social movements affecting, 95–102
social responsibility of, 94
types of, 6
use of demographics in, 284–301
wholesale, 271–73
Business law, 597–618
  bankruptcy and, 608–11
  contracts and, 598–602
  crime and, 614–18
  defined, 597
  law of agency, 602–603
  law of employer-employee, 603–604
  negotiable instruments and, 605–607
  negotiating and, 607–608
  sale of personal property and, 604–605
  trademarks, patents, and copyrights and, 611–14
Business research, 528–56
  defined, 528–33
  forecasting in, 546–48
  presentation of statistical data in, 548–50
  procedures in, 533–36
  reporting, 550–56
  statistics in, 541–46
Business risk
  defined, 212
  preventive measures against, 212–14
Buyers, benefits of cash discounts by, 141
Buyers for export, 639–40
Buying cooperatives, 59
Buying motives, 301–307
  defined, 301
  emotional, 301
  patronage, 306–307
  rational, 302

C

Call option, 136
Canada, capitalism in, 24
Capital
  business failure rate and, 75
  defined, 21
  difficulty in raising, 43
  methods of raising, 43
Capital gain, 195
Capital-investment goods, 380
Capitalism, 10, 17, 19
  capital ownership under, 21
  comparison with socialism and communism, 24–25
  socialism and communism versus, 21
  survival of, 27–31
  in United States versus other countries, 24–25
Capital loss, 195
Carnegie, Andrew, 410–11
Carrier, defined, 391
Carson, Rachel, 100
Cartel, 646
Cash discounts, 141–42
  defined, 141, 334
Cash rebate, 362
Catalog operation, 271
Central American Common Market (CACM), 647
Centralized organization, 413
Central processing unit (CPU), 577–78
Certified check, 158
Certified public accountant (CPA), 506
Chain of command, 412–13
Chain stores, 267
Channel of distribution, 263–65
Chapter 7 bankruptcy, 608
Chapter 11 bankruptcy, 609
Chapter 13 bankruptcy, 609
Character printers, 579
Charge-account credit, 163
Chattel mortgage, 145
Checking account
  corporate, 157
  defined, 156
  individual, 156–57
  partnership, 157
Checkout scanner, 573–74
China, People's Republic of, capitalism in, 27
CIT Financial Corporation, 165
Civil Rights Act of 1964, 101
Civil rights movement, 101–102
  defined, 95

Class action suit, 242 n
Clayton Act of 1914, 105
  defined, 106
Closed shop, 482
Coaching, 441
COBOL (COmmon Business Oriented Language), 582
Co-determination, 491
Coinsurance clause, 218–19
Collateral
  defined, 127
  reasons for requirement of, 142
Collective bargaining, 486–88
  area- and industry-wide, 486
  defined, 486
Collision insurance, 221
Commercial bank credit, 142
Commercial banks
  defined, 156
  engagement of, in interstate banking, 143
  function of, 142
  nonbanks versus, 172
Commercial loans, 157
Commission, 445–46
Commodity contracts, 201
Commodity-market quotations, 201
Common carriers, 391
Common stock, 127
  advantages and disadvantages of, 130–31
  defined, 129
Communication, 458–60
  defined, 458
  types of, 459
Communism, 19, 21, 23–24
  advantages of, 23
  capital ownership under, 21
  comparison with capitalism and socialism, 24–25
  defined, 23
  weaknesses of, 23–24
Company-wide objectives, 403–404
Competition
  defined, 12
  in financial services industry, 154–55
  government promotion of, 105–107
  imperfect, 331–32
  pricing and, 332–33
  pure, 331
Components, 380
Comprehensive coverage (auto), 222
Computer, 562–85
  advantages of, 568–69
  business use of, 570–77

  defined, 562
  development of, 566–67
  future of, 584–85
  hardware, 577–80
  languages, 582
  microprocessor, 567
  software, 580–81
Computer on a chip, 567
Conditional endorsement, 606
Conglomerate, 48–49
Congress of Industrial Organizations (CIO)
  merging of AFL and, 479–80
  origin of, 479
Consideration, in contract, 599–600
Consumer
  Advisory Council, 96
  "bill of rights" for, 96
  cooperative, 59, 673
  direct retailing to, 270
  finance companies, 165–66
  industrial, 263
  loans, 157
  motivation, 301–306
  prices and, 12, 253
  Protection Act, 97
  right to privacy, 175
  service and, 12
  the ultimate, 263
Consumer Advisory Council, 96
Consumer bill of rights, 96
Consumer cooperatives, 59, 673
Consumer credit
  applicants of, 174
  credit bureaus and, 174
  defined, 163
  sources of, 164–68
Consumer finance companies, 165–66
Consumer goods, 316–18
  defined, 316
  marketing of industrial goods versus, 318–19
Consumerism, 95
Consumer-jury interview, 535
Consumer loan, 157
Consumer movement, 95–100
  defined, 95
  during early 1900s, 95
  during the Great Depression, 95
  future of, 98–100
  1960s to present, 95–96
Consumer Price Index (CPI), 202, 544
Consumer products
  defined, 263
  purposes of advertising, 353

Consumer Product Safety Commission (CPSC), 108
Consumer Protection Act (1975), 97
Consumer Reports, 98
Consumers Union, functions of, 98
Consumption
　buying motivation and, 301–307
　education and, 294–95
　household sizes and, 287–90
　income and, 296–301
　population and, 284–96
　psychographics and, 307–10
Containerized shipping, 389–91
Contests, as sales promotions, 361
Contract, 598–607
　assignment of, 601–602
　breach of, 602
　conditions of, 599–601
　defined, 598
　oral versus written, 601
　sale of personal property and, 604–605
Contract carriers, 391
Contracted industrial services, 380
Contract manufacturing, 641
Controlled sample, 546
Controlled shopping center, 269–70
Controlling, defined, 421–24
Convenience food store, 269
Convenience goods, 317
Convertible bonds, 137
Cooperatives, 59
Coordinated shipping, 389
Copyright, 614
Corporate entrepreneur, 86
Corporate income tax, 113
Corporate risk manager, 242
Corporations, 47–59
　advantages and disadvantages of, 49–52
　advantages of bonds to, 134
　advantages of issuing common stock, 130–31
　checking account of, 157
　comparison with sole proprietorship and partnership, 38
　considerations in selection of, 53–57
　defined, 47
　dissolution methods of, 49
　expansion by stock in, 128–30
　federal tax on, 113
　formation of, 48, 53–57
　naming of, 55
　reasons for issue of preferred stock by, 131–32

　rights of, 48
　special kinds of, 58–59
　transfer of ownership of, 49
　types of, 48–49
Corporation charter, 48
　amending of, 51–52
　obtaining a, 55
Corrective action, 424
Cost
　fixed, 334
　variable, 335
Cost accounting, 514
Cost analysis, 514
Cost of goods sold, computing, 512
Cost-plus basis, 641
Coupons, as sales promotions, 361
Craft unions, 478–79
Credit bureaus, 174
Credit card companies, 164–65
Credit life insurance, 231
Credit limit, 175
Credit management, 172–75
Credit terms, 141
Credit unions, 167–68
Crime
　business and, 614–17
　white-collar, 617–18
Criminal loss protection insurance, 225–26
　fidelity bonds for, 226
Cumulative discounts, 333–34
Cumulative preferred dividend, 133
Currency, international trade and, 637–38
Current account, international, 643
Current assets, 509
Current liabilities, 510
Curve graph, 550

D

Data processing, 565–66
Debenture bonds, 137
Debt, secured versus unsecured, 609–10
Debt capital, 127
Decentralized organization, 413
Decline stage, of product, 321
Decision making
　government influences on, 18
　in management, 400
　variables in marketing, 255
Deductible coverage insurance (auto), 221

Deficit, reason for, 111
Delegation of authority, 411
Demand, elastic versus inelastic, 330
Demand deposit, 156
Demand-side economics, 13
Demographics
　business uses of, 284–301
　defined, 284
Dental insurance, 234
Departmentalization, 417
Departmental objectives, 404
Department of Commerce, role of, 109, 285, 537
Department store, 269
Digital function, 575–76
Direct export channel, 640–41
Direct import channel, 643
Directing, managerial function of, 451
Direct Mail Marketing Association, shop-by-mail guidelines of, 271
Direct-to-the-consumer retailers, 270
Disability benefits, 238
Disability income expense insurance, 234
Disbursements, 508
Discharge, of employees, 451
Discount, in pricing, 333–34
Discount brokers, 186–87
Discount rate, 162
Discount store, 268–69
Discrimination
　in employment, 101–102, 108, 435–37
　in price, 106–107
Disposable personal income, 296
Distribution business, 6
Dividends, 131
　cumulative preferred, 133
　defined, 128
　noncumulative preferred, 133
Dollar cost averaging, 195
Double taxation
　advantages and disadvantages of, 51
　policy of, 52
Dow, Charles, profile of, 196–97
Dow Jones average, 196–97
　defined, 195
Drucker, Peter, profile of, 410–11
Dumping, defined, 632
Dun and Bradstreet, 74, 173
　National Business Information Center, 173
Du Pont Corporation, 19

E

Economic organizations, international, 646–47
Economics
 demand-side, 13
 supply-side, 13
Economic systems, division of, 19
Economy
 business profits and United States, 16
 control by Federal Reserve System of, 161
 significance of retailing to, 266
Elastic demand, 330
Electronic funds transfer (EFT), 158–59
Employees
 communication with, 458–60
 compensation of, 444–47
 discontent among, 453
 evaluation methods of, 450–51
 motivation of, 451–57
 organization and, 409–19
 policies and, 406
 procedures and, 407
 rules and, 407–408
 selection of, 430–37
 suggestion systems for, 420
 training, 439–44
Employers' association, 484
Employment agencies, private, 432
Endorsement, 605–607
 defined, 605–606
Entrepreneur, 21
 corporate, 86
 defined, 15
 franchisee as an, 81–83
 women as, 80–81
Entrepreneurship
 big business and, 85–88
 defined, 66
 education for, 86–88
 importance of, 66–67
Environmental movement, 100–101
 defined, 95, 100
Environmental Protection Agency (EPA), 107, 108–109
 powers of, 101
Equal Credit Opportunity Act (1975), 175
Equal Employment Opportunity Commission (EEOC), 101–102, 108, 435
 function of, 101
Equifax, 174

Equity capital, 131
 defined, 127
Evaluation centers, 442
Exchange licenses, 635
Exchange rate, 638
Excise tax, 113
Ex-dividend date, 195
Eximbank, 645
Experiment, in business research, 536
Export, 630
 direct channels of, 640–41
 indirect channels of, 639–40
 subsidized, 635
Export agents, 640
Export-Import Bank, 645
Exporting
 channels of, 639–41
 of U.S. goods, 630–31
Export merchants, 639
Express warranty, 605
External communication, 459
Exxon Corporation, 55

F

Fair Credit Reporting Act (1970), 174
Fair Labor Standards Act (1938), 481
Fair Packaging and Labeling Act (1966), 325
Fault law, 223–24
"Featherbedding," 482
Federal Deposit Insurance Corporation, 156, 161, 162–63, 241
 defined, 162
Federal Express Corporation, 135
Federal Housing Administration, 241
Federal Land Bank, 127
Federal regulatory agencies, 107–109. *See also* Government regulation
 function of, 107
Federal Reserve Bank Act (1913), 103, 161
Federal Reserve Banks, 161
 discount rate of, 162
 prime rate of, 162
Federal Reserve Board, 140
Federal Reserve System, 161–62
Federal Savings and Loan Insurance, 161
Federal Trade Commission (FTC), 96, 97, 108, 271, 359
Federal Trade Commission Act of 1914, 105
 amendment of, 95

 defined, 106
Federal Wage and Hour Law (1938), 481
Federation of Organized Trades and Labor Unions (1881), 478–79
Fidelity bond, 226
Financial Accounting Standards Board (FASB), 515
Financial information
 frequently used terms in, 195
 influences affecting, 201–203
 interpretation of, 194–203
 market quotations in, 195–201
 sources of, 194
Financial institutions, 154–75
 consumer credit and, 163–68
 credit management and, 172–75
 emergence of supercompany, 168–72
 Federal Reserve System, 161–62
 functions of, 154
 major types of, 156–61
Financial management, 145–46
Financial manager, functions of, 145–46
Financial publications, 194
Financial services industry
 advances in, 155–56
 competition in, 154–55
 emergence of supercompanies into, 168–71
 nonbanks in, 168–71
Financial supercompanies, emergence of, 168–72
Financial supermarkets, 168
Financing
 of nonprofit organizations, 661
 of Social Security, 239
 with bonds, 138–39
 with stock, 138
Fire-and-theft coverage (auto), 222
Fire insurance, 218–219
First-line supervisors, 412
Fixed assets, 509
Fixed costs, 334–35
Fixed liabilities, 511
Flextime, 457
Floorbroker, 183
Floor member, 183
Floor planning, 142–43
Flow chart, 582
Food and Drug Administration (FDA), 108
Food, Drug, and Cosmetics Act (1938), 95
Foreign aid, 644–45
Foreign branch, defined, 640

Foreign subsidiary, 640–41
Form utility, 254
France, capitalism in, 25
Franchise
  defined, 79
  importance of system, 80
Franchisee
  advantages for, 81–83
  defined, 79
  role of, 80–81
Franchising, 79–85
  advantages and disadvantages of, 82–85
  defined, 79
  future of, 84–85
  mechanics of, 80–81
Franchisor
  advantages for, 81
  defined, 79
  problems with franchisees, 85
  role of, 80–81
Free enterprise system. *See* Private enterprise system
Free market, 13
Free-on-board (FOB) pricing, 338
Fringe benefit, 447
Full-coverage insurance (auto), 221
Full endorsement, defined, 606
Full function wholesalers, 272
Full-service brokers, 186
Functional design, 383–85
Functional rotation training, 441–42

G

Games, in sales promotions, 361
Garnishment, 602
Garn-St. Germain Depository Institutions Act of 1982, 160
General Accounting Office (GAO), 515, 517–18
General agencies, 357–58
General expenses, 513
General Motors Acceptance Corporation, 155, 165, 166
General partnership, 44–47
  advantages and disadvantages of, 45–46
  defined, 44
Generic brands, 329
Genuineness of assent, of contract, 599
Geographic rotation training, 442
Gompers, Samuel, 476, 479
Goods

classification of, 317–18
defined, 316
purchasing, 380
and services, 13
Goodwill, defined, 510
Government
  agencies, 104
  influence on financial decisions, 202
  insurance sponsored by, 237–41
  as nonprofit organizations, 657–59
  promotion of competition by, 105–107
  regulation of business by, 17–19, 102–109
  taxation, 109–15
Governmental agencies
  list of, 104
  as long-term financers, 127
Government regulation, 18
  agencies, 107–109
  of business, 102–109
  controversy over, 18–19
  history of, 103
  purposes of, 102–103
Grapevine, defined, 419
Great Britain, capitalism in, 25
Grievance procedure, 488
Gross margin, 335
Gross national product (GNP), 6–7, 617
  defined, 6
  national health expenditures and, 232
  of United States (1960 and 1983), 7
Gross profit on sales, 512
Group policies
  defined, 230
  health insurance, 231
  life insurance, 230
Growth stage, of product, 321
Guarantees, government insurance in form of, 241
Gucci family, profile of, 308

H

Hardware, computer, 577–80
Hawthorne effect, 454
Health insurance, 231–37
  benefits provided by, 231
  defined, 231
  plan categories of, 232–34
  private, 231–37
  profit and nonprofit, 231–37
  public, 237–38
Health maintenance organization

(HMO), 235–37
Herzberg, Frederick, 456
Hewlett, Bill, profile of, 378
Hewlett-Packard, 378
Hierarchy-of-needs theory (Maslow), 454–55
Hoadley, Walter E., 116–17
Horizontal communication, 459
Hospital expense insurance, 232
Human resource management, 430
Hungary, capitalistic practices in, 26–27
Hygiene factors, motivation and, 456

I

IBM Corporation, Four Principles of Privacy of, 175
Imperfect competition, 331–32
Implied warranty, 605
Import, 630
  direct channels of, 643
  indirect channels of, 641–43
  licenses, 635
Import broker, 643
Import commission house, 642–43
Importing
  channels of, 641–43
  to the United States, 631–32
Import licenses, 635
Import merchants, 642
Income
  consumption and, 296–301
  disposable personal, 296
  distribution, 297–300
  per capita, 297–99
  real income, 297
Income distribution, 297–300
  of the family, 7–8
  inequality of, 7
  in the United States (1982), 8
Income statement, 512
  defined, 511
Independent retail stores
  advantages and disadvantages of, 71–74
  defined, 266
  voluntary groups (chains) of, 270
Index number, 543–45
  defined, 543–44
Indirect export channel, 639–40
Indirect import channel, 641–43
Individual income tax, 111
Individual objectives, 404
Individual proprietorship, 40

Individual Retirement Account
    (IRA), 240
  defined, 73
Industrial advertising, 354–55
Industrial concentrations, 375
Industrial consumers, 263
Industrial goods
  defined, 263, 318
  marketing of consumer goods versus, 318–19
Industrial parks, 375
Industrial robot, 384
  defined, 572
Industry-wide collective bargaining, 486
Inelastic demand, 330
Informal evaluation, 450
Informal investigation, 534
Informal organization, 419
Injunction, defined, 486
Inland marine insurance, 220
Inland transportation insurance, 221
Input devices, 578
Inquiry into the Nature and Causes of the Wealth of Nations (Smith), 20
Installment credit
  defined, 163–64
  suppliers of, 164
Institute for the Advancement of Small Business, 73
Institutional advertising, 355
Insurable interest, 215
Insurable risk, qualifications for, 215–16
Insurance
  advances in, 242–43
  arson, 219
  automobile, 221–25
  criminal loss, 225
  defined, 213
  fault law, 223–24
  fire, 218–19
  health, 231–37
  liability, 225
  life, 226–31
  marine (or transportation), 220–21
  no-fault plan, 224–25
  property and related, 218–26
  public or social, 237
  self-insurance, 213
  space, 243
  surety bonds, 226
  unemployment, 239–41
  worker's compensation, 241
Insurance companies

  law of large numbers and, 214
  mutual, 216–17
  qualifications of insurable risk, 215–16
  stock, 216
Intangible assets, 510
Intelligence tests, 434
Interest
  determining of bond, 137
  payment on bond, 133, 136
  rate on bond, 137
Interest rate, 138
  of consumer finance companies, 166
  defined, 137
Interlocking directorate, 106
Intermediaries, 264
  agent wholesale, 273–74
  marketing, 263
Internal communication, 459
Internal Revenue Service (IRS), 111, 115, 174, 661
International trade, 626–50
  defined, 626
  effect of United States and foreign laws on, 635–36
  future of, 649–50
  restrictions in, 633–39
  and United States economy, 629–32
Interstate Commerce Commission (ICC), 108
  purpose of, 103
Introductory stage, of product, 321
Inventory, management and storage of, 386–87
Investment assets, 509–10
Investment banks, 159–60
Investor
  advantages and disadvantages of common stock to, 130–31
  advantages of mutual fund to, 190–92
  as capitalist, 21
  performance of mutual funds for, 192
Involuntary bankruptcy, 608
Issued stock, 129
Italy, capitalism in, 25

J

Japan
  capitalism in, 25
  productivity growth in, 31
Job analysis, 430
Job application, 433

Job description, 430
Job enlargement, 457
Job enrichment, 456
Job interviews, 435–38
Job redesign, 457
Job specification, 431
Job training, 439–44
  external, 443
  internal, 439–42
Joint ventures, 60, 641
Jones, Edward, profile of, 196–97
Journals, 508
Jungle, The (Sinclair), 95

K

Kaiser Foundation, 236
Karmel, Robert S., 57
Keogh Plan, 73
Keyboard, computer, 579–80
Krebs, Juanita, 109
Kroc, Ray A., 53. *See also* McDonald's
  profile of, 82

L

Label, 325
Labeling, 325–27
Labor, 466–89
  collective bargaining, 486–88
  defined, 466
  restraint by management, 484–86
  today, 488–89
  unions, 476–83
Labor force
  changes in, 467–69
  defined, 466–67
Labor-Management Relations Act (1947), 482
Labor-Management Reporting and Disclosure Act (1959), 482
Labor unions
  decline of, 489–91
  defined, 476
  origin of, 477–80
  relation to business, 476–83
Laissez faire system, 17
Landrum-Griffin Act, 482
Language, international trade and, 638–39
Large-scale integration (LSI), 567
Latin American Free Trade Association

INDEX 723

(LAFTA), 647
Law
  in business, 594–618
  of packaging and labeling, 325–27
  Small Business Administration and, 76
  of supply and demand, 13, 330
Law Enforcement Assistance Administration, 219
Law of agency, 602–603
Law of averages, 214
Law of comparative advantage, 627–29
Law of employer-employee, 603–604
Law of large numbers
  application to life insurance, 226–27
  defined, 214
Lawyers
  growth in demand for, 594–96
Leases
  advantages and disadvantages of, 144
  defined, 144
Level-premium plan, 229
Leveraged buyout (LBO), 85
Liability
  defined, 510
  types of, 510–11
Liability insurance
  automobile, 222
  personal and property, 225
Licensing agreement, 641
Lie detector tests, 434
Lien, 605
Life insurance, 226–31
  defined, 226
  types of policies, 229–31
  use of Standard Ordinary Mortality Table in, 226–28
Limited function wholesalers, 272
Limited liability, of corporation, 49
Limited-line retailers, 267
Limited order, 186
Limited partnership
  advantage of, 47
  defined, 46
Limited-payment policy, 230
Line-and-staff organization, 414
  defined, 417
Line graph, 550
Line manager
  defined, 416
  personnel management and, 449
Line of credit, 142
Line organization, 414
  defined, 416–17

Line printers, 579
Listed stock, 184
List price, 268
Load, defined, 192
Loading, defined, 228
Loans
  secured and unsecured, 142
  signature, 165
Lobby, 485
  defined, 483
Local advertising, 354
Local taxes, 113–15
Long-term capital
  acquisition from investment banks, 159
  defined, 73–74, 126
  sources of raising for small business, 126–27
Long-term financing
  large businesses and, 127–39
  small businesses and, 126–27
  through bonds, 133–38
Long-term liabilities, 511

M

McDonald's Corporation, 53, 82.
  See also Kroc, Ray A.
  franchisee training for, 83
McGregor, Douglas
  Theory X and Theory Y, 455–56
Magnetic ink and optical scanners, 578
Mail-order retailing, 270
Mail questionnaire, 535
Major medical expense insurance, 234
Make-or-buy decision, 381
Management, 400–424
  control by, 421–24
  defined, 400
  future of, 424
  future of business information, 555
  labor relations and, 466–89
  levels of, 412
  of nonprofit organizations, 667–76
  by objectives (MBO), 404–405
  organizing in, 409–19
  personnel, 430–60
  planning in, 402–409
Management by objectives (MBO), 404–405
Manager
  defined, 401–402
  line, 416

staff, 416
Mandatory laws, 597
Manufacturer, wholesalers' service to, 273
Manufacturer's agent, 274
Manufacturer's excise tax, 113
Manufacturer's suggested price, 334
Marine insurance, 220–21
Market
  defined, 71, 258
  description, 259
  segments, 259–60
  target, 258–59, 284
Market description, 259
Marketing, 252–77
  area, 284
  characteristics of industrial-goods, 263
  communications in, 346–66
  concept, 255–62
  of consumer versus industrial goods, 318–19
  defined, 252
  demand created by, 253–54
  future in service business, 277
  importance of, 253–55
  intermediaries, 263–64
  mix, 255
  in nonprofit organizations, 661–66, 670–72
  research, 260, 284–310
  by service businesses, 274–75
  strategy, 261–62
  of tangible products versus services, 275–77
Marketing area, 284–85
Marketing concept
  application versus nonapplication of, 259
  defined, 255
  steps in application of, 258–62
Marketing intermediaries, 263–64
Marketing mix
  advertising in, 351–60
  defined, 255
  personal selling in, 347–51
  promotion in, 346–65
Marketing orientation, 258
Marketing research, 260
Marketing strategy
  defined, 261
  developing a, 261–62
  role of research and computers in a, 262

Market order, 184
Market segments
  defining, 259–61
  research to define, 260
Market value, 131
Markup, 335
Marshall, John, 47
Maslow, Abraham H., 454–55
  Hierarchy-of-needs theory of, 454–55
Mass production, 381
Maturity date, 134
  defined, 136
Maturity stage, of product, 321
Mayo, G. Elton, 454
Mechanization, 381–82
Median, 542
  defined, 543
Mediation, 487
Medicaid, 237–38
Medicare, 239
  defined, 237
Member firm, 183
Mercantile credit, 141
Merchandise brokers, 273–74
Merchant wholesalers
  defined, 272
  full and limited functions of, 272
Microcomputers, 567
Microprocessor, 567
Middle management, 412
Middlemen, 263
Minicomputers, 567
Modal average, 543
Mode, 542
  defined, 543
Monopolistic competition, 331
Monopoly, 105–107
Moral hazard, defined, 215–16
Mortgage bonds, 137
Motion-and-time study, defined, 382 n
Motivation
  defined, 454
  of employees, 451–57
  Hawthorne effect and, 454
  Hierarchy-of-needs theory and, 454
  Theory X and, 455–56
  Theory Y and, 456
Motivator factors, 456
Multinationals (MNCs), 645
Multi-unit operations, 267
Municipal (tax-exempt) bonds, 137
Mutual fund
  advantages to investor of, 190–92
  defined, 190
  investment objectives of, 192
  performance for investors of, 192
  production of profit of, 192
Mutual funds market, investing in, 190–92
Mutual insurance companies
  defined, 216
  demutualization of, 216–17
Mutuals, 60
Mutual savings bank, 160

N

Nader, Ralph, 95–96
  future of consumer movement and, 98–100
Narrow span of supervision, 415, 416
  defined, 413
National advertising, 354
National Association of Securities Dealers (NASD), 188
National Association of Securities Dealers Automated Quotations (NASDAQ)
  efficiency of, 190
  function of, 188
  reasons for rapid growth of, 188–90
National banks, 156
National Casualty and Surety Underwriters Bureau, 225
National Credit Union Administration, 168
National debt, 111
National Labor Relations Act (1935), origin of, 481
National Labor Relations Board (NLRB), 481, 483, 486, 489
National Quotation Bureau, 188
National resources, 13
National Safety Council, 447–48
Negotiable bond, 134
Negotiable instruments, 605
Negotiated pricing, 333
Negotiating, 607–608
Net income, 511
Net loss, calculation of, 513
Net profit, calculation of, 513
Net sales, 511
New Deal (Roosevelt), 103
New York Stock Exchange (NYSE), 48, 49
  future integration with AMEX and OTC, 190
  interpreting stock quotations of, 197–98
  membership in, 183–84
  requirements for listing securities on, 184
  trading procedures on, 183–87
No-fault insurance, 223–25
  principle of, 224
No-load funds, 192
No-name (generic) brands, 329
Nonbank, 168–71
  commercial banks versus, 172
  defined, 168
Nonbusiness marketing, 670
Noncumulative discounts, 334
Noncumulative preferred dividend, 133
Nongovernmental Protective Agencies, 97–98
Nonprofit corporation, 48
  reasons for incorporation of, 48
Nonprofit organizations, 656–73
  competition and, 669
  cooperatives, 673
  defined, 656
  governments as, 657–59
  government versus other, 659
  health insurance, 235–37
  health maintenance, 235–37
  marketing of, 661–66
  operation of, 660–61
Nonpublic corporation, 48
Non-store retailing, types of, 270–71
No-par-value stock, 129
Notes receivable, 509
NOW (Negotiable Order of Withdrawal) accounts, 156

O

Objectives, in planning, 403–404
Observation, 535–36
Occupational Safety and Health Administration (OSHA), 107, 108, 449
Ocean marine insurance, 220
Odd lot, 195
Offer, on contract, 599
Office of Advocacy, 77–78
Office of Information and Regulatory Affairs (OIRA), 115
Office of Special Assistant to the President for Consumer Affairs, 97
Officers, in corporation, 57

INDEX

Off-line devices, 578–79
Old-Age, Survivors, Disability, and Health Insurance (OASDHI), 237
On margin, buying securities, 187
Open-account credit, 141–42
Open-market operations, 162
Open order, 186
Operating expenses, 513
Operating income, 511
Operating management, 412
Operating supplies, 380
Order bill, 145
Ordinary life policy, 229–30
Organization chart, 412
Organization for Economic Cooperation and Development (OECD), 647
Organization of Petroleum Exporting Countries (OPEC), 646
Organizing, 409–19
  defined, 409
  importance of, 409–11
  informal, 419
  management levels and, 412
  supervision and, 413–19
Orientation program, 439–40
Outplacement counselors, 451
Output devices
  defined, 578
  video terminal, 580
Over-the-counter (OTC) market, 182–83
  defined, 187
  function of, 49
  interpreting stock quotations of, 198–99
  trading in, 187–88
Owners' equity, 511
Ownership, 59–60
  common forms of, 39
  considerations in selection of types of, 53
  transfer of, 604–607

P

Package, 324
Packaging, 324–27
Packard, Dave, profile of, 378
Panel interview, 535
Paperwork, government, 115
Paperwork Reduction Act (1980), 115
Participative leaders, 457
Partnership, 113

checking account of, 157
comparison with corporation and sole proprietorship, 38
compatibility in a, 47
considerations in selection of, 53
as source of capital, 127
Partnership agreement, 44–45
Par-value stock, 129
Patent, 612
Patent and Trademark Office, 612
  Official Gazette of, 614
Patronage motives, 306–307
Penetration pricing, 333
Per capita income, 6, 297–99
Performance evaluation, 450
Permissive laws, 597
Personal assets, as collateral for loans, 127
Personal interviews, 535
Personality tests, 434
Personal savings, as long-term capital, 126
Personal selling
  defined, 346
  distinction between advertising and, 352–53
  as a promotional tool, 347–51
Personnel management, 430–60
  defined, 430
  directing and, 451–60
  employee compensation and, 444–49
  employee evaluation and, 449–51
  selection of employees by, 430–38
  training of employees by, 439–44
Peter Principle, 451
Physicians expense insurance, 234
Pictograms, 550
Piece-rate plan, 445
Pie chart, 550
Pilfering, 338
Place utility, 254
Planned shopping center, 269–70
Planning
  defined, 402
  management, 402–409
  objectives, 403–405
  policies, 406
  procedures, 407–408
  rules, 408–409
  strategies, 405–406
Point-of-purchase displays, 361–62
Point-of-sales (POS) terminals, 159
Policy, as a plan, 406
Political action committees,

contributions to Congress (1981–82), 99
Politics, influence of financial decisions, 202
Polygraph test, 434
Port-of-entry (POE) pricing, 338
Position average, 543
Possession utility, 254
Power of attorney, 603
Preemptive right, 129
Preferred stock, 127
  defined, 131–32
Premiums
  automobile insurance, 222–23
  as sales promotions, 361
Price
  law of supply and demand and, 330
  markup, 335–38
  in service businesses, 338–39
  transportation and, 338
Price escalator clauses, 332
Price lining, 334
Pricing, 329–39
  defined, 329
  discounts used in, 333–34
  inflation and, 332
  methods of, 334–39
  policies of, 332–33
  under pure versus imperfect competition, 331–32
Primary boycott, 483
Primary sources, of information, 536
Prime contractor, 380
Prime rate, defined, 162, 195
Principal
  bond, 133
  broker's, 273
  law of agency and, 603
Principle of diminishing utility, 330
Printer, computer, 579–80
Private carriers, 391
Private corporation, 48
Private enterprise system, 6–31
  characteristics of, 11–19
  in Communist societies, 26–27
  comparison with other countries, 19
  defined, 10
  government influence in, 17–18
  needs of Americans, 6–11
  risks in, 19
  survival of, 27–31
Procedure, 406–407
Process-control computer, 574–75
Producer cooperatives, 59

Product, 12
  concept in marketing, 254–55
  consumer, 263
  defined, 316
  life cycles of, 319–24
Product design, 383–85
Production business
  choice of location, 372–76
  defined, 6
  inventory management and storage for, 386–87
  production management in, 381–86
  purchasing for, 376–81
  transportation for, 387–92
Production management, 381–86
  automation and, 382
  mechanization and, 381
  product design and, 383–86
  production planning and, 386
Production orientation, 258
Production planning, 386
Productivity
  defined, 29
  of marketing efforts, 366
  in the United States, 29–31
Product life cycle, 319–23
  defined, 321
  product modifications during, 322–23
  stages of, 321–22
Product line, 323
Product mix, 323
Product modifications, 322
Professional corporations, 59
Profit
  in American business (1984), 16, 17
  defined, 17
  efficiency and, 17
  as investment incentive, 16–17
  sharing, 447
  taxation of corporate, 113
  tax revenue and, 17
Profit-and-loss statement, 511
Profit maximization, 332
Profit principle, 16
Profit sharing, 447
Profit system, 10
Program, computer, 580
Programmer, 582–84
  role of, 580–81
Programming specifications, 584
Prohibitive laws, 597

Promotion, 255
  in employment, 450–51
  in marketing, 346–65
  Peter Principle and, 451
  sales, 360–62
Property ownership, taxation and, 11
Property tax, 115
Proprietorship, 40
Prospecting, 350
Prospectus, 195
Proxy, 57–58
Psychographics, 307
Psychological pricing, 333
Public, public relations and, 363
Public accountants, 506–507, 515, 517–18
Public corporation, 48
Public insurance, 237
Publicity, 363
Public relations
  advertising versus, 363
  defined, 347
  nonprofit organizations and, 661–66
  as a promotional tool, 362–65
  special interest groups and, 363
Purchase group, 160
Purchasing
  defined, 379
  goods and services, 380
  for production business, 376–81
Purchasing manager, 380–81
Pure competition, 331
Pure Food and Drug Act of 1906, reason for passage of, 95
Pure risk, 215

Q

Qualified endorsement, 607
Qualitative standard of living
  defined, 8
  of selected nations, 9
Quality-of-work-life programming (QWL), 491
Quantitative standard of living, 6
Quantity discounts, 333
Questionnaire technique, 534
Quotations
  bond, 199–200
  commodity-market, 201
  reading market, 195–201
  security, 197–98

R

Random sample, 546
Ratio analysis, 513–14
Rational buying motives, 304–306
  defined, 302
Raw materials, 380
Real income, 297
Real-time system, 576
Receipts, 508
Recession, 471
Reference, defined, 434–35
Regulation, defined, 407
Regulatory Flexibility Act of 1980, 115
Research parks, 375
Reserve
  defined, 161, 217
  regulation of bank, 161
Resources, 13
Restrictive endorsement, 606
Results evaluation, 450
Résumés, 433
Retail advertising, 354
Retailers, 265–71
  classified by ownership, 266–67
  classified by types of business, 267–69
  cooperation of, 269–70
  defined, 265
  markup by, 336–38
  wholesalers' service to, 272–73
Retailer's excise tax, 113
Retailing
  defined, 265
  efficiency of, 573–74
  non-store, 270–71
  significance to economy, 266
Retirement benefits, 238
Revitalization
  defined, 28
  relation of United States and global, 634
Rider, defined, 218
Rights
  choice of occupation, 15
  of competition, 12
  consumer bill of, 96–97
  of entrepreneurship, 15
  under private enterprise system, 11–15
  of property ownership, 11
  in sale of goods and services, 13
Right-to-work law, 482
Risk, 19
  business, 212

individuals and, 19
insurable, 215
management of, 242, 243
protecting against, 212–16
pure, 215
speculative, 215
"Risk capital," 129
Risk ratings
  defined, 137
  for municipal bonds, 200
Robinson-Patman Act of 1936, 105, 106–107
Robot, industrial, 384, 572
Roosevelt, Franklin D., 103
Round lot, 195
RPG (Report Program Generator), 582
Rule, defined, 407–408

S

Salary, 444–45
Sales finance companies, function of, 165
Sales manager, responsibilities of, 350–51
Sales tax, 113
Sample
  research, 546
  sales promotion, 360
Savings accounts, 157–58
Savings and loan associations, 160–61
S corporations, 58–59
Sears, Roebuck & Company, 102, 168, 171, 292
Seasonal discounts, 334
Secondary boycott, 483
Secondary sources, of information, 537
Secured obligations, 141
Securities
  cost of trading, 186–87
  issuing of, 127–28
  listed, 184
  regulation of trading of, 192–94
  tax-exempted securities, 195
  trading methods of, 184–86
  types of, 127
Securities and Exchange Commission (SEC), 57, 190, 194, 515
Securities Exchange Act of 1934, requirements of, 193–94
Security exchange, 131, 182–83
  defined, 182
Security markets, 182–83

future of integration, 190
Security quotations, 197–98
Self-actualization, 455
Self-insurance
  defined, 213
  growth of, 243
Self-service concept, 268
Sellers, cash discounts offered by, 141
Selling
  personal, 346–51
  processes of, 348–49
Selling agents, 274
Semimanufactured goods, 380
Serial-plan method, 137
Service business
  defined, 6
  future of marketing in, 277
  marketing by, 274–75
  pricing in, 338–39
  types of, 275
Shareholders, 128
  defined, 49
Sherman Antitrust Act of 1890, 97
  purpose of, 103, 105–106
Shipping, 392
  containerized, 389–91
  coordinated, 389
Shoplifting, 338
Shopping goods, 317
Short sale, 195
Short-term capital, 126
Short-term financing
  by business, 139–45
  credit instruments used in, 144–45
  necessity for, 139–41
Short-term obligations, types of, 141–42
Showroom operation, 271
Signature loans, 165
Silent Spring (Carson), 100
Sinclair, Upton, 95
Single-line retailers, 267
Single proprietorship, 40
Sinking-fund plan, 137
Small business, 67–79. *See also* Business
  advantages of, 71
  characteristics of, 67–70
  defined, 67
  established versus new, 75–76
  long-term financing for, 126–27
  minority groups and, 78–79
  reasons for failure of, 74–75
  role of, 70
  strengths and weaknesses of, 71–74

women and, 78–79
Small Business Act of 1953, 67
Small Business Administration (SBA), 67
  defined, 76
  functions of, 76–79
  size guidelines for loans, 68
  types of aid offered by, 76, 127
Small Business Innovation Research Program (SBIR), 77–78
Small loan companies, 165–66
Smith, Adam, profile of, 20
Smith, Frederick W., profile of, 135
Social auditing, 515–17
Social costs of unemployment, 474
Social insurance, 237–41
  Social Security, 237
  tax, 113
Socialism, 19, 21–23
  advantages and weaknesses of, 22
  capital ownership under, 21
  comparison with capitalism and communism, 24–25
  defined, 21
Social marketing, 670–72
Social Security, 113, 237–39, 437
  advantages and disadvantages of, 240, 241
  death benefit, 239
  financing of, 239
  payment through automated clearinghouses, 158
Social Security Act of 1935, 239
  provisions of, 237
Social responsibility
  defined, 94
  in public relations, 365
Software, computer, 580–81
Software packages, 580
Sole proprietorship, 40–44, 113
  advantages and disadvantages of, 40–44
  comparison with partnership and corporation, 38
  considerations in selection of, 53
  defined, 40
Space insurance, 243
Span of supervision, 413, 415, 416
Special endorsement, 606
Special-interest groups, 363
Specialty goods, 317
Specialty stores, 267
Speculative risk, 215
Split, defined, 195

Spread, defined, 160
Staffing, 430–51
　compensating employees, 444–49
　defined, 430
　discrimination in, 435–37
　evaluation of employees, 449–51
　methods used in selection of employees, 430–35
　training of employees, 439–44
Staff manager, 416
Standard
　defined, 421
　measurement of performance versus, 421–22
　setting a, 421
Standard & Poor's Stock Guide, 538
Standard costs, 514
Standard Metropolitan Statistical Areas (SMSAs), defined, 291 n
Standard of living, 6
　components of in United States, 10
　qualitative, 8
　quantitative, 6
Standard policy, 218
Standard Rate and Data Service, 356
State banks, 156
State taxes, 113–15
Statistical Abstract of the United States, 285, 537
Statistics, 541–46
　defined, 541
　index numbers and, 543–46
Stock, 21, 128–33
　defined, 128
　financing through, 128–30, 138
　ownership in American business (1970, 1983), 21
　preferred, 131–32
　sale of, 129
　types of, 129–30
Stock exchanges, 49
Stockholders, 134
　defined, 49
　meeting of, 57
　preemptive right of, 129
　rights of, 58
　role in management of corporation, 57
　voting privileges of, 133
Stock insurance company, 216
Straight bill, 145
Straight-life policy, 229
Strategic control points, 422–24
Strategy, defined, 405–406

Strike, 483–84
　breakers, 486
　defined, 483
　wildcat, 453
Stub, in tables, 549
Style design, 385
Subcontracted production services, 380
Subdivision regulations, 375
Subsidized exports, 635
Suicide clause, 216
Supermarkets, 267
Supply and demand, law of, 13, 111
　defined, 330
Supply-side economics, 13
Surety bonds, 226
Surgical expense insurance, 232
Survey, 534–35
Survivors benefits, 238–39
Sweden, capitalism in, 25
Sweepstakes, as sales promotion, 361
Syndicate, 60
Systems analyst, 582–84
　role of, 581

T

Taft-Hartley Act, 482
Target market, 258–59
　defined, 258, 284
　division into market segments, 259–60
Tariff, 635
Tax
　accountants and, 501–503
　federal, 111–13
　local, 113–15
　policy logic, 502–503
　property, 115
　sales, 113
　state, 113–15
　use of, 109–11
Taxation, 109–15
　double, 51–52
　federal, 111–13
　public attitude toward, 110
　state and local, 113–15
Telemarketing, 271
Terminal
　computer, 579
　video, 580
Term policies, 230–31
　credit life insurance, 231

Theory X (McGregor), 455–56
Theory Y (McGregor), 456
Third-party insurance, 225
Time deposits, 157
Time utility, 254
Title transfer, of personal property, 604
Top management, 507–508
　defined, 412
Trade advertising, 355
Trade association, 678
Trade credit, 141
Trade discounts, 334
Trademark, 611–12
　defined, 327, 611
Trait evaluation, 450
Transportation
　advantages and disadvantages of, 390
　defined, 387–88
　in production business, 387–92
Transportation insurance, 220
　inland, 221
Transportation mix, 388
Trust department, 158–59
Trust indenture, 134
Truth-in-Lending Act of 1969, reason for, 97

U

Ultimate consumers, 263
Underwriter, 243
Underwriting one's own insurance, 213
Underwriting syndicate, 160
Unemployment, 470–76
　causes of, 470–72
　social costs of, 474
　solving the problem of, 474–76
Unemployment insurance, 239–41
Unemployment Trust Fund of the United States, 239
Uniform delivered pricing, 338
Union contract, 487–88
Union shop, 482
Unissued stock, 129
United States Bureau of the Census, 285
　wholesale trade and, 272
Universal product code (UPC), 326
Universe, in sampling, 546
Unlimited liability agreement, 43
Unsecured obligations, 141

V

Variable costs, 335
Vending machine retailing, 270
Vertically downward communication, 459
Vertically upward communication, 459
Video terminal, 580
Voluntary acceptance, in contract, 599
Voluntary bankruptcy, 608
Voluntary chain, 270
Voluntary group, 270
Voting privileges
  of credit union members, 167
  of preferred stockholders, 133

W

Wages, 444
Wagner Act, 481
Wall Street Journal, 194, 196–97
  interpreting security quotations from, 197–98
Warehouse operation, 271
Warehouse receipt, 145
Warranty, 605
West Germany, productivity growth in, 31
Whole-life policy, 229
Wholesalers, 271–73
  agent, 273–74
  defined, 271
  merchant, 272
  service to manufacturers, 273
  service to retailers, 272–73
  volume of goods versus retail volume, 272
Wholesaling, importance of function of, 273
Wide span of supervision, 415, 416
  defined, 413
Wolfberg, Alvarez, Taracido & Associates, profile of, 547–48
Woods, Nathaniel R., profile of, 667
Word processor, 570–72
Worker's compensation, 241
Working capital, 126

Y

Yield
  computing of, 191
  defined, 195
Youth differential, 446

Z

Zone delivered pricing, 338
Zoning regulations, 375